# Food
## Marketing

*Joseph J. Belonax, Jr., Ph.D.*

WESTERN MICHIGAN UNIVERSITY

Cover Photos: Top Left: © Dennis MacDonald (NMR)/
The Picture Cube, Inc.
Top Right: © Jeff Greenberg / The Picture Cube, Inc.
Center: © Camerique / The Picture Cube, Inc.
Bottom Left: © Tom McCarthy / The Picture Cube, Inc.
Bottom Right: Photo courtesy of Crown Equipment Corporation,
New Bremen, Ohio, USA.

Copyright © 1999, 1997 by Joseph J. Belonax, Jr.
All rights reserved.

This copyright covers material written expressly for this volume by the editor/s as well as the compilation itself. It does not cover the individual selections herein that first appeared elsewhere. Permission to reprint these has been obtained by Simon & Schuster Custom Publishing for this edition only. Further reproduction by any means, electronic or mechanical, including photocopying and recording, or by any information storage or retrieval system, must be arranged with the individual copyright holders noted.

Printed in the United States of America

10 9 8 7 6 5 4 3

*Please visit our web site at www.pearsoncustom.com*

ISBN 0-536-01754-9

BA 98517

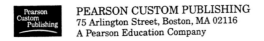

PEARSON CUSTOM PUBLISHING
75 Arlington Street, Boston, MA 02116
A Pearson Education Company

# Contents

*Preface*   v

**PART ONE**   **INTRODUCTION TO THE U.S. FOOD MARKETING SYSTEM**
1. U.S. Food Marketing System   1

**PART TWO**   **STRUCTURAL AND FUNCTIONAL DIMENSIONS OF THE PRODUCER SECTOR**
2. Producers   27
3. Marketing Decisions   71

**PART THREE**   **STRUCTURAL AND FUNCTIONAL DIMENSIONS OF THE MANUFACTURING SECTOR**
4. Processors and Manufacturers   107
5. Marketing Decisions   151

**PART FOUR**   **STRUCTURAL AND FUNCTIONAL DIMENSIONS OF THE WHOLESALE SECTOR**
6. Wholesale Distributors   203
7. Marketing Decisions   243

**PART FIVE**   **STRUCTURAL AND FUNCTIONAL DIMENSIONS OF THE RETAIL FOOD STORE SECTOR**
8. Retail Food Stores   285
9. Marketing Decisions   323

**PART SIX**   **FOOD CONSUMER SECTOR**
10. Consumer Behavior Trilogy   369
11. Market Segmentation   417

**PART SEVEN**   **ADDITIONAL DIMENSIONS OF THE FOOD MARKETING SYSTEM**
12. Food Service Sector and Marketing Decisions   457
13. International Perspective   507
Index   551

# PREFACE

Of all the activities in which we normally engage on a daily basis, nothing is more essential to life than eating. We spend a great deal of time shopping, purchasing, preparing, and consuming food. In fact, if you add the time we spend earning money to buy food, most of our waking lives are centered around food. Ironically, despite the intimate familiarity we all have with food and its significance in daily life, few of us understand the system that has evolved to meet our growing demand for nourishment. One of the main reasons for writing this book was to reduce our collective ignorance regarding the **U.S. food marketing system**. To accomplish this goal, I followed a number of objectives.

First, existing food related books focus ordinarily on a single sector such as agriculture or manufacturing, an approach that provides only a partial perspective of the U.S. food marketing system. Thus, one of my objectives was to write a text that would provide a more complete perspective of the U.S. food marketing system. The domain of this book is bounded on one end by food producers who are responsible for the system's raw material input, and at the other end by food consumers whose satisfaction represents the system's output. Together with the sectors in between these ends, manufacturers, wholesalers, and retailers, this book provides the reader with a comprehensive perspective of the U.S. food marketing system.

Second, based on the observations of many economists, the structure of a system tends to influence the competitive behavior of its organizational participants, which in turn influences how the system functions. Thus, another objective I had was to write a text that would identify not only the structural and functional dimensions of the U.S. food marketing system, but also the changes currently taking place. In this book, each of the sectors, other than the consumer sector, begins with an historical perspective of its structural formation. Census data for the years 1982, 1987, and 1992 are used to identify structural changes in these sectors. The censuses of agriculture, manufacturing, wholesaling, and retailing are conducted only in years ending in two and seven. They are available for analyses usually two to three years later. Therefore, whenever possible, structural changes in the sectors are extended by using more current industry data. By including industry information on each sector, beginning with manufacturers, this book provides the reader with a vivid description of the U.S. food marketing system's **structural organization** from two perspectives: government and industry.

Third, as mentioned previously, the output of the U.S. food marketing system is **customer satisfaction**. Therefore, another of my objectives was to write a book that explained how the U.S. food marketing system functions to create this output. Because customer satisfaction is the consequence of effective marketing, this text explores the marketing decisions made by producers, manufacturers, wholesalers, and retailers to create, price, promote, and distribute food products. This approach provides the reader with a **functional perspective** of the U.S. food marketing system.

Fourth, there is a consensus among members of the business community that "customer satisfaction" extends beyond our national borders. Thus, the last objective I had was to write a text that recognized the internationalization of the U.S. food marketing system. I end this book with an international perspective that recognizes global markets as well as global segments of a market.

*Food Marketing* can serve readers in many ways, depending on their background and interest. This book was designed for a course I developed and now teach. It can be used in an introductory course by undergraduates enrolled in academic programs such as food marketing or agricultural business. Given its emphasis on the U.S. food marketing system, *Food Marketing* is also an appropriate text for an introductory undergraduate course in agricultural economics.

*Food Marketing* contains a vast array of information and numerous tables dealing with the structural organization of the U.S. food marketing system. Thus, it can be used as a valuable reference text for graduate students and industry practioners. This book can also provide newly hired entry-level personnel in food marketing with an understanding of the industry they have chosen as their source of their employment.

Finally, at the core, this is fundamentally an applied marketing textbook. The functional chapter that follows each sector's structural chapter focuses on marketing mix decisions. The chapter on consumer behavior examines the shopping, purchase, and consumption behaviors of food consumers. The chapter on market segmentation defines possible target markets for food. The international chapter extends the market for food beyond our national borders. Throughout this text, it is emphasized that the decisions to create, price, promote, and distribute food products to target markets of consumers represent fundamental decisions in the marketing of food products both in the U.S. and abroad. In short, *Food Marketing* is a suitable textbook for an introductory course in applied marketing.

## PLAN OF THE BOOK

The complexity of the U.S. food marketing system is examined by using a framework that embodies both structural and functional perspectives. Because the structure of a system tends to influence the marketing decisions made by the firms it comprises, using both perspectives provides the reader with a broader and deeper comprehension of the entire system.

*Food Marketing* takes you on a journey through the U.S. food marketing system beginning at the point of production and ending at the point of consumption. Part One, **Introduction**, introduces you to a thorough perspective of the U.S. food marketing system. The structural organization and functional marketing decisions are explored as well as the causes of the system's industrialization.

Part Two, **Structural and Functional Dimensions of the Producer Sector**, focuses on the organization structure of raw foodstuff producers. Chapter 2 examines the firms that provide the raw materials for the system: livestock, crop, and marine animal producers. Chapter 3 explores the decisions producers make to create, price, promote, and distribute raw foodstuffs.

Part Three, **Structural and Functional Dimensions of the Manufacturing Sector,** looks at the organizational structure responsible for creating form utility. Chapter 4 describes the firms involved in transforming raw foodstuffs into ingredients and finished food products. Chapter 5 deals with the marketing decisions of processors and manufacturers.

Part Four, **Structural and Functional Dimensions of the Wholesaler Sector**, examines how the system adjusts the discrepancies between the supply of products from manufacturers and the retailers' demand for these products. Chapter 6 focuses on the organizational structure of wholesalers. Chapter 7 deals with marketing to the retail sector.

Part Five, **Structural and Functional Dimensions of the Retail Food Store Sector**, explores how the form, time, place, and possession utilities created by the system come together at the retail store. Chapter 8 describes the alternative retail store formats that the system comprises. Chapter 9 looks at the decisions made by retailers in the marketing of food products to consumer markets.

Part Six, **Food Consumer Sector**, examines the behavior of food consumers in the market place and potential target markets for food. Chapter 10 explores the shopping, purchasing, and consumption behaviors of food consumers. Chapter 11 uses a lifestyle model to examine the segmentation of food consumers into viable target markets.

Part Seven, **Additional Dimensions of the U.S. Food Marketing System**, recognizes the growing trend toward food consumption away from home and the internationalization of the U.S. food marketing system. Chapter 12 examines the structural and functional dimensions of the retail foodservice sector. Chapter 13 provides an international perspective of the U.S. food marketing system.

# ACKNOWLEDGMENTS

Preparing *Food Marketing* has been a consuming, four year effort. It began with lecture notes designed for an introductory course I developed for our food marketing program. Lacking any suitable text, these notes were later transcribed into topical outlines and distributed to students. Soon after, I began to elaborate on these outlines and formalized them into textbook chapters. Like any text that relies heavily on data and their interpretation, *Food Marketing* has all the makings of a never-ending book.

A textbook is seldom the effort of one person. This book is no exception. In an effort to be as accurate as possible, I have drawn on the expertise of many people from government, industry, and academe. It is impossible to acknowledge all the people who have guided and assisted me, and provided me with information. However, I can identify their respective organizations.

Conclusions regarding the structural organization of the U.S. food marketing system are largely drawn from governmental data on agriculture, manufacturing, wholesaling, and retailing. I am grateful to all those individuals at the **U.S. Bureau of the Census** for their patience with my endless requests for clarification. I am also thankful to the people at the **USDA's Economic Research Service (ERS)**, **National Agriculture Statistical Service (NASS)**, and **Foreign Agricultural Service (FAS)** for their assistance. Anthony E. Gallo of the **Commodity Economic Division (ERS)** has been an invaluable source of information and assistance. The **U.S. Bureau of Labor Statistics** helped me to better understand the Consumer Expenditure Survey. Finally, I appreciate the efforts of all those at the **National Marine Fisheries Service**.

Whenever possible, I have tried to extend the reader's understanding of the U.S. food marketing system by relying on industry expertise and information. I have cited the trade sources of information in the text. However, a special thanks is due to James Gawley at **The Food Institute**, Mark Schesney at **NCH Promotional Service**, Lily Lev-Gilich at **Point of Purchase Advertising Institute** (POPAI), Bethany J. Stantley at **Carol Wright Promotions, Inc.**, Paul Weitzel at **Willard Bishop Consulting, Ltd.**, and Ruby Rogers-Thompson at the **Food Marketing Institute** (FMI).

I have relied heavily on my academic colleagues, some of whom I know personally, others I have met only through their writings. To them, I owe much and hope that their names have been spelled correctly. This book would not be possible without the technical support and reviewers from Simon & Schuster. Finally, to my family, who always knew they could find me in the study working on *Food Marketing*, I owe a great deal. I am grateful to my wife Barbara for her patience, encouragement, and oh yes, nourishment! Her exceptional culinary skills have resulted in meals that constantly remind me of her love. To our son Michael, who kept me on task by frequently checking on my progress, I would like to say, "I have arrived at the end of the tunnel, and yes, there is light!"

# Chapter 1

# U.S. Food Marketing System

**Chapter Outline**

U.S. Food Marketing System
- A. Structural Approach (Who)
- B. Functional Approach (What)

Competitive Differential Advantage
- A. Product Decisions
- B. Price Decisions
- C. Promotion Decisions
- D. Place Decisions

Industrialization of the U.S. Food Marketing System
- A. Specialization
- B. Diversification
- C. Decentralization
- D. Integration
- E. Internationalization
- F. Globalization

Summary

"Oh Barbara, they are going to love these! Just look at that beautiful red color. I still can't believe we were able to find them."

Barbara and her friend, Rachel, were preparing a special dinner for four. The main course was lobster, fresh from the waters off the coast of Maine. Just yesterday morning, over one thousand miles to the east, these scrumptious creatures had been hauled up onto a small, family boat owned by Mike Bello and his brother Don. The Bellos have been setting lobster traps in that area for three generations and are typical of many similar operators up and down the coast. The boat reached shore about 9:00 a.m., and the men carried their catch to Gordon's, the seafood distributor, just across the road from the dock.

About 4:00 p.m., a Gordon's truck pulled up to a small cargo plane at the county airport. Two other distributors had already been there and left. The plane was owned by Paul Finley (the pilot) and was leased to Consolidated Seafood of New England, a brokerage outfit that handled both fresh and frozen seafood. Soon after, the plane was on its way, this time to Cleveland; other days it was to Philadelphia, Richmond, or Knoxville. Once in Cleveland, the cargo was transferred to a bonded warehouse with cold-storage facilities for the frozen items. The four live lobsters Barbara and Rachel were to buy were still under seawater, held in one of the twenty-six metal drums with the Gordon's name on them.

A regional salesman for Consolidated Seafood, James Hunter, showed up at the bonded warehouse in Cleveland just after sunrise the next morning. He pasted Consolidated labels on each of the live containers, but left the frozen packages alone. A commercial airliner carried the lobsters to Detroit, where the local wholesaler's truck was waiting. Everything was counted, and the truck was on its way by 10:45 a.m. The lobsters were on display when Barbara and Rachel walked into the local supermarket at noon. They walked right over to the Seafood Deli. The Maine lobsters were under water in the glass display tub. "We'll take those four big ones" they said. In addition to the lobsters, they needed to pick up a few other things for their special dinner.

Nearby, they spotted some tender asparagus shoots that, at one time, had been lined up in neat rows in the sandy soil of California. A few aisles over, Barbara and Rachel stopped to buy some muffins, baked locally from processed flour that once grew as golden-hued wheat in the open fields of North Dakota. Next stop was the dairy section for some butter and sour cream. What's lobster without drawn butter—manufactured from the milk taken from Jersey cows grazing the pastures of Wisconsin, or potatoes without Wisconsin sour cream? The large baking potatoes grown in the fertile soil of Idaho displayed in bulk form in the produce section looked especially appealing.

Next came the dessert challenge. Barbara said, "I saw some very succulent-looking cherries back in the produce, we could make Cherries Jubilee." The cherries had been picked from rows of trees in southwest Michigan. Finally, to top it all off, they bought some coffee—not just any coffee, but coffee made from ground Arabica beans, grown on bushes high in the mountains of Colombia, then shipped to New Orleans and roasted there to concentrate their flavor.

Later that night, after dinner, while enjoying their coffee, the conversation turned to how much they depended upon others to provide them with the foods they had just eaten. Like others, they recognized that food and beverages that end up on consumers' forks and spoons and in their glasses and cups originate on numerous farms, ranches, orchards, fields, and vineyards, and in the waters of oceans, lakes, and rivers. However, many consumers don't fully understand how the present day **U.S. food marketing system** operates to take both perishable and relatively non-perishable food products from their point of production to their point of consumption. A system that is capable of turning the rather humble soybean into ingredients for literally hundreds of food products certainly deserves some attention! Further, the system that provides the source of satisfaction for our most basic needs, and indeed enables our very survival, deserves our deepest concern.

# U.S. FOOD MARKETING SYSTEM

The U.S. food marketing system consists of a variety of firms employing millions of people, making a myriad of decisions, and performing countless specialized activities that all contribute to the marketing of food. To fully grasp the complexity of the U.S. food marketing system, a dual approach is necessary. The first approach, the **structural approach** considers the nature and character of the various firms making up the system. The second approach, the **functional approach** focuses on the nature and specialization of the activities performed and decisions made by food marketing companies. This dual approach enables us to answer two primary questions about the U.S. food marketing system: 1) **who does** 2) **what in the marketing of food?**

## The Structural Approach (Who)

**Figure 1** provides a framework for a structural analysis. It begins with the point of food production (its origin or source), then flows through intermediate, transitional, or transfer locations, to the final point of food consumption (its ultimate destination).

### Food Producers

Historically, the production of food has been a way of existence. Those who produced the food consumed most of what they produced. Today, although the sources of food have changed little, the production of food has become very commercialized. There are literally millions of firms involved in the production of food, to be used either as ingredients for other products, edible consumer products or both. In many cases, producers (mostly farmers) have formed cooperatives to do collectively what they couldn't do operating as individual firms.

One way of focusing our perspective on the myriad number of producers operating in the food system is to consider them in terms of the contribution they make to the everyday meals of consumers. There are producers who contribute to the so-called **main dish**, such as livestock ranchers, wild-catch fishers, fish farmers, and poultry and egg farmers. There are numerous producers who contribute by supplementing the main dish. These **side dish** producers are largely fruit orchards and vegetable farms. Finally, there are producers who contribute by complementing the meal with drink. These **beverage** producers dairy farms, coffee plantations, tea estates, and vineyards.

Even though classifying producers according to their contribution to our everyday meals is useful, it doesn't recognize producers whose major output is mainly used as ingredients for finished food products. These producers are largely grain farmers. Grains are used to feed livestock that, in turn, become the main dish. Such ingredients are also used to create side dishes and to produce the beverages that complement the meal. Thus, it must be recognized that the output of producers is used to make both intermediate food ingredients and finished food products.

The perspective provided by the above description of food producers is not meant to be all inclusive, but rather an introduction to the diversity of food sources. The U.S. food marketing system begins with decisions made by firms that produce food and thus, represents input into the system.

### *Processors and Manufacturers*

Primary processors transform raw material provided by producers into basic ingredients for other, downstream products. In turn, these ingredients are used by finished processors to produce the final product for the consumer. Often, processors will sell their entire product to a single finished-goods processor. To distinguish between the two types of processors and to identify their sequence of operation in the throughput of the U.S. food marketing system, primary processors are referred to throughout this book as simply **processors**, and finished goods processors are referred to as **manufacturers**.

Processors and manufactures change or alter foodstuffs, in some manner, to create form utility. Processors include such operations as flour mills, livestock slaughterhouses, egg breaking operations, and dairy plants. In turn, these ingredients are then used by cereal manufacturers, meat packing plants, poultry and milk plants, and fruit and vegetable manufacturers. An illustration of the sequential processing of raw foodstuffs is found in the vegetable oil industry. Processors extract oil from soybeans, sunflower seeds, corn, and other oil-bearing seeds and plants. These are then refined into finished products such as cooking oil and shortening by manufacturers further along in the U.S. food marketing system.

Although the differentiation between a processor and a manufacturer on the basis of their sequence of operation may appear to be slight, this distinction identifies a major difference. Processors and manufacturers differ in the amount of form utility they create. In general, a processor creates less form utility than a manufacturer. Further, because the basic ingredients lose their identities in the finished product, manufacturers often put brand names on their products, while most processors do not.

### *Wholesalers (Distributors)*

Wholesalers represent the first phase in the distribution of food products. In the course of moving food products to consumers, manufacturers have the option of undertaking all of the activities necessary to sell their products, or rely on others to perform them. One useful way of viewing wholesalers is to note **who** performs these activities. The manufacturer may employ its own salesforce at different offices and branches throughout its market area. Such a salesforce, in general, would function to distribute the manufacturer's product to the next phase in the U.S. food marketing system—retailers. A second option is to use agents or brokers. Like the manufacturer's salesforce, agents and brokers act as the salesforce for the firms they represent (principals). A third option is to rely on independent firms in the market area to do this selling. It is this latter group that has traditionally been labeled a wholesaler and now is called, more conventionally, a distributor. Despite the differences among wholesalers (distributors), their activities focus on adjusting the product, spatial, and temporal discrepancies between the quantity and assortment of a manufacturer's output and the retail customer's need for that output.

Wholesaling operations consist mainly of breaking down larger quantities of product into smaller sizes. Wholesalers are said to take the **whole sale**, or the entire sale from suppliers, thus reducing the supplier's marketing costs. The whole sale usually consists of a very large quantity, too much for any single retailer to handle. To resolve the **product discrepancy** the wholesaler then creates smaller quantities that retailers can handle. Usually, by handling bulk transactions, the wholesaler also saves on inbound traffic costs.

After the product is received, the wholesaling functions are essentially storage and transportation. To resolve the **temporal discrepancy** between the time the manufacturer's output is produced and the time it is demanded, food products are stored. In the case of fresh fruits and vegetables, storage doesn't last very long. With packaged goods, items can remain in the wholesaler's warehouse for weeks or even longer. To resolve the **spatial discrepancy** between the location of the manufacturer's output and the location of demand, food products must be transported. In the U.S. food marketing system products are hauled primarily by trucks. The cost of storage, along with such considerations as inbound traffic costs, outbound transportation costs, and product costs, is then passed on to retailers. Wholesalers often profit from buying when product is cheap, and then from storing it until the price goes up. But the process works both ways, and prices can decline further and stay there. Such mistakes can be costly because of the volumes of product involved in a **whole sale**.

### Food Store/Foodservice Retailers

Retailing represents the final phase in the distribution of the U.S. food marketing system's products. There are really two separate food retailing segments, each of which includes both "independent" and "chain store" operations. Food stores provide food to consumers for consumption at home, and foodservice firms cater to the consumption of food away from home.

Both segments have experienced considerable change over the years because of fundamental changes in merchandise philosophies. Although not obvious, these changes represent different answers to the recurring philosophical question that all retailers must ask: "What do we want to be to our customers?"

In the food store segment, varying responses to this question have resulted in a proliferation of retail firms with highly distinguishable merchandise strategies. Specialty stores such as bakeries, fish markets, and butcher shops, which offer a limited, or narrow variety and assortment of merchandise, represent a more constrained response to the question; whereas, grocery stores such as supermarkets, wholesale clubs, and super combos, which offer a broad variety and assortment of merchandise, represent a more robust response to the question.

The foodservice segment, on the other hand, is made up of both commercial and noncommercial firms. Like the foodstore segment, the **commercial foodservice industry** is made up of numerous retail firms with highly distinguishable merchandise strategies. These activities focus on the preparation, service, and sale of food to the general public. It is also useful to classify the many diverse firms in commercial foodservice by their response to the philosophical question mentioned earlier: "What do we really want to be to our customers?"

Limited menu format firms, largely made up of fast-food establishments, represent a more restrained response to the question, while full menu format firms, such as restaurants, cafeterias, hotel and retail-host restaurants represent a more robust response to the question. Finally, the **noncommercial foodservice industry** is made up of institutions that prepare, service, and sell food as a support service. Generally, these have a full menu format, and include hospitals, universities, nursing homes, and military bases.

The distinction between food stores and foodservice retailers continues to dissipate as a result of competitive efforts to gain an increased share of the customer's food dollar. Foodservice firms, focusing on the **food-at-home** consumers, have greatly expanded their **take-out-to-eat** operations, while food stores, aiming at the **food-away-from-home** consumer, have added another dimension to their merchandise offering: ready to eat hot/cold entrees.

In many respects, food retailers play a pivotal role in the U.S. food marketing system. To many consumers, if not all, the most visible aspects of the system are the food retailers. It is at this juncture that form, time, place, and possession utilities come together and are offered to consumers. All that the U.S. food marketing system plans to accomplish is contained in the market offerings presented by the food retailers. Thus, as a consequence of their position, they carry the entire burden of the U.S. food marketing system.

In a very real sense, retail firms serve as purchasing agents for consumers. Despite the differences among food retailers, all of their activities focus on creating and securing a variety and assortment of merchandise, providing a time and a place to promote merchandise, and offering that merchandise to consumers at a reasonable price. The performance of the entire U.S. food marketing system rests on how consumers evaluate food retailers' abilities to meet their needs.

### *Consumer Markets*

The U.S. food marketing system is driven by the tastes and preferences of consumers. Consequently, **consumer satisfaction** represents the U.S. food marketing system's output. What is produced, transformed, moved, and/or stored is destined to be bought and consumed by the public. A consumer purchase, then, is a vote of confidence in the entire U.S. food marketing system. Getting this vote is a never-ending, and increasingly difficult, task. The reason is a simple one: The perceived homogeneity of the consumer market is a myth. Today, consumers are fragmented into increasingly smaller segments that are themselves in a constant state of change.

In the past, the consumer food market was more homogeneous than it is now. A number of factors contributed to such homogeneity. Historically, ethnicity, customs, and regionality combined to bring about an American diet that consisted largely of meat and potatoes and bread. These basic foods were washed down with milk, coffee, tea, and soft drinks. Today, these same factors and new factors (such as technology, scarcity of time, concern for the environment, increased wealth, and the desire to pursue differing lifestyles) have contributed to much diversity in food tastes and preferences.

This diversity in tastes, preferences, and lifestyles is described by the term **micromarkets**. It is important to realize that, although the food market today is composed largely of micromarkets, a mass market for meat, potatoes, and other such goods still exists.

What implications do these small, rapidly changing micromarkets have for the U.S. food marketing system? Eternal vigilance to the changing demands of micromarkets can be the only answer. For example, today's consumers—many of whom believe **"they are what they eat,"** will continue to exercise their sovereignty, demand healthier products, and drive the U.S. food marketing system to supply them. Targeting food products at the vast array of micromarkets that exist in the market will challenge the marketing ingenuity of producers, processors, manufacturers, wholesalers and retailers alike.

### The Functional Approach (What)

The **ultimate goal** of the U.S. food marketing system, and its only real output, is to satisfy the needs of consumers—consumers who belong to an increasing array of micromarkets. What must each of the firms do to achieve this goal of consumer satisfaction? The answer may be found by examining the philosophical basis of competition in general—individual differences. Each firm must create and maintain a competitive differential advantage (individual difference). To meet the challenge posed by today's consumer, the firm must create a market offering that is substantively different from that offered by competitors. These differences must be large enough for consumers to perceive. In addition, consumers must perceive these differences as better than the existing market offering of competitors. To create and maintain a competitive, differential advantage, each firm must excel at food marketing. We define **food marketing** as the performance of business activities that reflect decisions to create, price, promote, and distribute food products for the purpose of satisfying consumer needs. These decisions and how they are implemented represent the domain of functional analysis. Decisions to create, price, promote, and distribute food products, and the functions that must be carried out to implement these decisions, are known as the firm's **marketing mix**. Even though they are functionally separate, marketing mix-decisions must be carefully coordinated so as to have a synergistic impact on consumers.

## COMPETITIVE DIFFERENTIAL ADVANTAGE

To create and maintain a **competitive differential advantage**, each of the participating firms in the U.S. food marketing system must make product, price, place, and promotion decisions. These decisions reflect **what** they do. Although the manner in which these decisions are made varies among the participating firms, they are the fundamental basis for each firm's market offering. If the consumer perceives this market offering as different from, and better than, competitive offerings, then it can be said that the firm has created a competitive differential advantage.

Despite the apparent operating independence of the participating firms, their marketing decisions are actually coordinated by the U.S. food marketing system's goal of consumer satisfaction. It is this goal that creates the interdependence among the participating firms. Working together to achieve consumer satisfaction is, in the final analysis, what makes the whole system function as well as it does. Thus, the firms make major marketing decisions about their product, price, place, and promotion within the context of their respective markets,and are ever-mindful of the system's goal of consumer satisfaction.

## Product Decisions

The product decisions made by food marketing firms focus on providing what consumers want, and that has several dimensions. The first, and most obvious dimension, is physical. Food products have size, shape, weight, color, and aroma. A second, aesthetic, dimension appeals to consumers' senses. Food products must meet consumers' standards for smell, feel, sound, look, and, most importantly, taste. The essential and expected services that are provided in addition to the physical and aesthetic product make up the third, service dimension. Consumers also expect to benefit as a result of the purchase and consumption of a product. This final "bundle of benefits" dimension, in conjunction with the physical, aesthetic, and service dimensions, define what consumers want. Each of the firms in the U.S. food marketing system contributes to the multidimensional meaning of product in the minds of consumers by focusing on one or more of these dimensions.

### *Producer Product Decisions*

The first, and most obvious, decision that firms must make in the U.S. food marketing system concerns the production or output of product. Such decisions generally concern what and how much to produce. If we focus for a moment on the decisions of farmers to produce agricultural products, we observe an interesting phenomenon. The U.S., like many other parts of the world, is regionally specialized in terms of food production. Just ten states produce the vast majority of the soybeans each year. Six produce the majority of cattle and calves. One produces the majority of domestically raised catfish. And, while five produce the majority of tomatoes, another five produce all of the oranges. Each group of states is located in a specific region to handle the specific products in question.

If a producer chose to specialize in something out of the ordinary, there might not be facilities, expertise, or readily available markets to handle this new product. On the other hand, if the producer chose to specialize in the products his region is suited for, facilities, markets, and expertise would be readily available. Thus, the key decision for many producers is often not what to produce, but how much.

### *Processor/Manufacturer Product Decisions*

The modification of raw foodstuffs is the primary decision for processors and/or manufacturers. Raw foodstuffs are purchased from producers in large quantities. Processors must decide the extent to which they wish to process foodstuffs prior to selling the processed product to manufacturers. Manufacturers must decide the point at which they wish to begin the manufacturing process.

Both processors and manufacturers make decisions on product quality and can significantly alter or change the product to yield essentially new and different products. Technology is an important factor here, but the decision to make the change in the product is a marketing decision. Processors and manufacturers also make market-oriented decisions to delete specific products from their list of product offerings. Decisions on packaging are generally much more important for manufacturers (because of their closeness to consumers), but both processors and manufacturers are concerned with creating form utility for their buyers. Generally speaking, the higher the form utility, the higher the price that purchasers will pay.

### *Wholesaler/Retailer Product Decisions*

Wholesalers and retailers do not *create* products in the true sense of the word. These middlemen make **product mix** decisions. The mix is made up of different product lines and product items within each line. The product mix decisions these middlemen make are the consequences of answering two questions: "What does the firm need to carry in inventory?" and "How much product inventory must the firm carry?" The answers to these questions are based on the middlemen's target market.

The target market for the wholesaler is the retailer. Thus, the product mix decisions for distributors, agents, and brokers is based on satisfying retail demand. For the manufacturer's separate salesforce (another type of wholesaler) the product decisions are answered by the manufacturer's output of the firm.

The target market for the retailer is the consumer. However, retailers answer product questions within the context of the type of retail format operated. For example, a supermarket retailer will respond differently to product questions than will a convenience store operator. Retail firms make a number of decisions to develop the product (merchandise) mix. First, retailers make a merchandise variety to determine which product categories to carry. Perishables, dry grocery food, general merchandise, and health and beauty aids represent the retail firm's merchandise categories. Second, retailers make merchandise assortment decisions to determine how many brands to carry in each category. Third, retailers make brand variation decisions to determine how to express the variations in terms of size, flavor, container, and consistency on some other dimension. These three decisions address the "what to carry" and "how much to carry" questions. Further, these decisions must be consistent with the level of quality demanded by the retailers' customers.

Answers to the questions "what to carry" and "how much to carry" are defined by the needs of the consumer target market. However, the amount of space that the food store retailer can use to display the food products is finite. Therefore, merchandise mix decisions regarding variety, assortment, and brand variation must reflect the ability of the retail firm to satisfy the needs of the marketplace within the context of finite retail space.

### *Foodservice Product Decisions*

The product mix decisions of foodservice retailers involve menu planning. Like food stores, the decisions are made within the context of the type of foodservice format being decided: limited or full-menu firms. Essentially, foodservice retail firms' menu planning involves three major decisions. First, a cuisine must be selected. Limited-menu firms are more likely to offer only one cuisine. The layering of one cuisine on another is not an uncommon menu offered by full-service firms. Second, a food quality standard must be established. Quality is largely a function of the ability of a firm to purchase, store, prepare, and present the food products. Without the professional culinary skills to prepare and present menu items, the firm is forced to rely on many pre-prepared food products. This generally has an unfavorable effect on the consumers' perception of food quality. Third, a standard of service must be established. This includes wait service and customer service. Once again, the type of format plays a crucial role in service. Generally, limited-menu firms offer self-service, whereas full-menu offer table service.

## Price Decisions

The price decisions made by food marketing firms focus on providing what is wanted by consumers at a price which reflects the perceived value of the product to consumers. Each of the firms in the U.S. food marketing system contribute to the value perceived by consumers by establishing a price that reflects the perceived value of the product to their own customers. Thus, price as a statement of value exists throughout the U.S. food marketing system.

### *Producer Price Decisions*

At the producer level, products being offered for sale are undifferentiated commodities such as grain, livestock, poultry, fruit, vegetables, and milk. Because of this, there is a tendency for commodity prices within a market to remain uniform according to the **law of one price**. This law states that under competitive market conditions, all prices within the market are uniform, and price differences in the market reflect only the cost of storing (**time utility**), transporting (**place utility**), and processing (**form utility**) the product.

If this were always the case, the pricing strategies previously mentioned would, when applied, lead to the same price for the commodity. However, buying and selling are conducted by people who have incomplete information, different amounts of bargaining power, and who make errors. Under these conditions, the application of the various pricing strategies does not lead to the same price.

Pricing by competitive bidding at auction sales in terminal markets is best illustrated by the livestock auction. Egg and slaughter cattle are examples of commodities priced on a formula basis. Grain elevators post a nonnegotiable price (administered) at which they will purchase grain from farmers. Milk prices are largely administered. Contracts are used to establish prices for citrus growers and chicken brokers. Finally, private-treaty pricing is the dominant practice in the direct market for livestock, and fresh fruits and vegetables.

### Processors/Manufacturers Price Decisions

Processors typically perform an initial transformation process on commodities. In other words, the processor's output is a processed commodity. The prices for some processed products, such as cheese and butter, are typically formula prices based on the **National Cheese Exchange** prices or the **Chicago Mercantile Exchange** butter prices. Broilers are processed and priced under contract, as are potatoes. Flour is priced using administered and private-treaty pricing.

The manufacturer's output, unlike the processor's, is a branded product in most cases. As such, the dominant pricing method is administered. Manufacturers of national brands have different price lists for different parts of the country, depending on varying costs and competitive conditions. In addition, these manufacturers use extensive monetary inducement aimed at distributors. Pricing of private label and unbranded products is subject to private-treaty negotiations.

### Wholesaler/Retailer Price Decisions

Because wholesaling is essentially a pass-through industry, the prices wholesalers charge to retailers are largely administered with allowances and discounts. Most wholesale-supplied retailers rely heavily on wholesalers for a broad array of financial services, business planning services, information management services, and merchandise services. The costs of these services are passed along to retailers in the prices they change and/or as separate service management fees.

Prices offered by retailers are generally an attempt to meet a particular profit objective. Fundamentally, there are two approaches to reach a profit goal: **everyday low price (EDLP)** and **high-low price**. The former relies on lower prices to generate sufficient volume to offset lower gross margin on the products. The latter relies on the frequent use of price specials (reductions). Products are priced at varying rates of markup or margins. These margins vary among product classes and categories, and consider the rate at which the product is sold over a period of time. The typical food retailer follows a one-price policy, wherein all customers are charged the same price for the same product. Multiple unit price policy is also used to give the customer a discount for making quantity purchases. Another common practice is to use price specials (temporary price reductions) to attract customers to a specific store chain.

### Foodservice Price Decisions

Price decisions in the retail foodservice industry are essentially administered. Menu price-setting represents a response to four questions: What is the competitor's price on a similar menu item? How important is this menu product to the total menu of products? Is the menu product's price consistent with the perceived value of the menu product to the customer? Is the menu product's price compatible with the menu prices for other products on the menu?

Given these considerations, menu pricing is based on four price formats in which menu can be presented. First, all menu products can be priced separately (á la carte). Second, menu products can be priced separately in most areas of the menu and grouped together in other areas (semi á la carte). Third, all menu products included in the meal can be offered in one price (table d'hôte). Finally, menu products can be grouped under one price in some areas of the menu, and priced separately in others (semi table d'hôte).

## Promotion Decisions

The promotion decisions made by food marketing firms focus on communicating the availability of what consumers want at a price that reflects the perceived value of the product to consumers. Each of the firms in the U.S. food marketing system contribute to this availability by making a conscious attempt to influence the purchasing behaviors of their respective customers.

### Producer Promotion Decisions

Promotion at the producer level is usually sponsored by groups of producers and/or commodity organizations. This type of promotion tends not to focus on specific brands of products, but on the commodity class as a whole, and is called **generic promotion** or **generic advertising**. Examples include: "Milk, It does a body good," "Beef, Real food for real people," "Idaho Potatoes," and "Florida Oranges," etc. This type of promotion is usually funded by large producer organizations and is intended to develop consumer awareness and preference for the entire product class or region of production. Individual brand names (such as **Sunkist**) can then build upon the initial levels of awareness and preference generated by this generic advertising.

### Processor/Manufacturer Promotion Decisions

At the processing/manufacturing level, firms direct their promotion at distributors (**push**) and at consumers (**pull**). In both cases, firms integrate their advertising, personal selling, sales promotion, and publicity in order to have a cumulative effect. Processors tend not to advertise as much as manufacturers, but rely more on personal selling and business-to-business communications. Processors often initiate sales promotions intended to increase the flow of product through the U.S. food marketing system. These are often seasonal, reflecting the ebb and flow of agricultural harvests.

Brand advertising is the most visible form of promotion in the U.S. today. Brands are usually promoted by their manufacturers. Brand names and brand equities can be valuable assets to their owners. Manufacturers seek to create brand loyalty by positioning their products in the minds of consumers. In terms of media usage, there is a heavy use of television in an attempt to create and maintain brand imagery. In newspapers, manufacturers make heavy use of **free-standing inserts** (e.g., booklets of ads and coupons), that are simply inserted into newspapers, loosely and otherwise unattached.

Manufacturers also set aside money to share with retailers in cooperative promotion programs. Much of this money goes unused because retailers can't possibly participate in all of the programs available to them. Further, retailers and manufacturers disagree on how the money should be used. Manufacturers wish to use these monies to promote brand images to the marketplace. Imagery is best managed through advertising (typically national, network television). On the other hand, retailers wish to use these monies to create store traffic and generate higher immediate sales. Store traffic and sales are best generated not by advertising, but rather by sales promotion (e.g., coupons in newspapers and direct mail). Thus the fundamental objectives of the two parties differ somewhat, which reduces the use of cooperative monies. Also, many smaller retailers do not fully understand how to participate in cooperative programs; still others see the paperwork required for reimbursement by manufacturers as burdensome.

### Wholesaler/Retailer Promotion Decisions

At the wholesale level, firms rely heavily on advertising in trade publications and sales promotions offered by manufacturers. Wholesalers tend to spend heavily themselves on providing merchandising services to retailers. Generally, these involve the use of personal selling and providing point-of-purchase assistance to retailers. Sales people involved in this kind of retail assistance are usually highly trained experts and have the experience and knowledge derived from visiting many retail establishments.

Retailers are primarily concerned with generating consumer traffic and sales in their stores. Large retail chains can spend heavily on advertising and sales promotions to accomplish these objectives. Smaller retailers are more limited in this regard and tend, therefore, to be dependent on wholesalers and manufacturers for assistance with promotion. In general, retailers make heavy use of sales promotion, primarily through local newspapers. Sales in papers are commonly reviewed by many consumers prior to shopping. Local television stations and other media often offer lower rates to local advertisers than to national companies. This rate differential can be substantial. Cable stations can also offer reasonable (lower) rates to local retailers, as the cable stations seek, competitively, to increase their own revenues.

Other promotional avenues open to retailers include in-store coupons, sampling, and continuity programs. Retailers often offer their own coupons, independent of manufacturer coupons. Coupons are legal certificates, offered by both manufacturers and retailers, that grant specified savings on selected products when presented for redemption at the point-of-purchase. A common sight in retail outlets is a station giving out free samples of selected products to consumers. Consumer sampling is a very effective strategy for introducing a new or modified product, or for dislodging an entrenched market leader. Sampling is generally most effective when reinforced on the spot with product coupons. The purpose of any type of continuity program is to tie the consumer to the organization by rewarding them for their loyalty.

### *Foodservice Promotion Decisions*

In the realm of foodservice retailing, firms like **McDonald's** and **Pizza Hut** spend heavily on network television advertising. The larger chains are as concerned with image-oriented advertising as food manufacturers. The so-called **burger wars** demonstrate the extent to which foodservice chains have viewed the value of television advertising. Radio is also a common medium for foodservice advertising. Typically, firms try to broadcast their ads during the noon hour and other meal times. Sales promotion is also very popular in foodservice. Often, newspapers contain coupons for discounts at foodservice establishments. Direct mail is also frequently used for this purpose.

## Place Decisions

No matter how superior the product, how appropriate the price, or how effective the promotion, the U.S. food marketing system cannot be successful unless it can place the product into the hands of consumers. There are three basic problems of exchange inherent in the U.S. food marketing system. First, there is a discrepancy between the quantity and assortment of food products produced and the quantity and assortment demanded by consumers. Second, there is a discrepancy between where food products are produced and where they are demanded. Third, there is a discrepancy between when food products are produced and when they are demanded. Each of the firms in the U.S. food marketing system adapts its distribution activities to resolve these discrepancies. Thus, the place decisions made by food marketing firms focus on distributing what consumers want, where and when they want it, at a price that reflects the perceived value of the product to consumers.

### *Producer Distribution Decisions*

At the producer level, distribution decisions are driven by the need to assemble small lots of products from a myriad of producers into larger lots for sale to buyers. The initial assembly or concentration of food products is usually performed by firms that are located in the producing areas. The concentration of supply makes it easier, more convenient, and less expensive for buyers to frequent these locations and to ship what they buy, than it does for them to travel to many producers and arrange for shipment independently. Producers, therefore, tend to ship their product to these initial concentrators. Depending upon the product, these concentrators may sell to terminal markets or directly to processors, manufacturers, wholesalers, and retailers.

In general, **terminal markets** are large central markets where even greater concentration of food products take, place. In some cases, concentrators may sell to processors such as livestock slaughter plants, millers, who in turn distribute to manufacturers who create finished consumer goods. Products may also be distributed directly to the retail level. This is not necessarily the individual store level. In the case of large, self-distributing chain stores, there is usually a central warehouse located near every district of stores, and in the case of smaller independent stores, there is usually a wholesaler nearby. Fresh products such as produce and seafood are delivered directly to these warehouses or wholesalers who, in turn, distribute to retailers in regularly scheduled deliveries (sometimes daily).

### *Processor/Manufacturer Distribution Decisions*

At the processor/manufacturer level, distribution decisions focus on the efficient movement of goods to wholesalers or retailers. This movement is accomplished in a number of ways. Firms (typically the larger ones) may own their transportation facilities. For other firms, the capital investment, labor contract negotiations, and the day-to-day problems associated with operating transportation facilities make leasing a better option. Another option is to engage the transportation services of common and/or contract carriers to distribute the firm's products. The final option available to the firm is to contract with wholesalers or self-distributing retailers for backhaul delivery services. Basically, when the wholesaler finishes its retail deliveries it is left with an empty truck. Rather than return empty, the wholesaler picks up merchandise from a manufacturer and "hauls it back" to the wholesale facility.

Many manufacturers also provide what is called **direct to store door (DSD)** delivery. This is direct to the retail store delivery and transfer onto the retailer's shelves or into the retailer's display cases by the delivery sales person. Originally, store door delivery was largely restricted to products such as milk and bread. Now, however, companies such as **Coca-Cola** and **Frito Lay** provide store-door delivery services. This allows the processor or manufacturer to have some control over retail space and general appearance of the product on display within the store. Obviously, store-door delivery is a more expensive proposition than distribution through a wholesaler's warehousing operations because sales-route delivery people must be paid and trucks, etc., must be owned or leased by the processor/manufacturer.

### *Wholesaler Distribution Decisions*

Wholesalers grew to be the primary intermediaries between manufacturers and retailers because they procured food in large quantities at low prices, consolidated their purchases in warehouses, and resold these products and delivered them to retailers at lower costs than any other procurement and delivery options. Basically, then, the distribution decisions of wholesalers are aimed at minimizing the cost of assembling from many manufacturers large quantities of finished food products, and then dispersing these products to retailers. The traditional operating system used by wholesalers to minimize the delivered cost of products to the retailer consists of four parts: (1) receiving, (2) storage and replenishment, (3) order selection, and (4) shipping.

The physical movement of products into a distribution center begins with the receiving function. Products are delivered to the wholesaler direct from manufacturers or backhaul truck shipments, or in some cases, by rail. The objective is to receive merchandise when inventory is low so that enough is on hand to fill retail orders. The second function is merchandise storage and replenishment. The objective of storage and replenishment is to have the right product at the right location in the facility, so that store orders can be filled efficiently and effectively. Order selection is the third function. Its objective is to provide a flow of accurate and complete retail orders. The fourth operational function is shipping. The objective, obviously, is to ensure that the correct merchandise is delivered to stores in the most cost-effective manner.

### Retailer Distribution Decisions

Rather than rely on wholesalers to distribute food items to them, many large retail chain stores perform their own distribution functions. The order processing, warehousing, inventory, and transporting functions are undertaken by the chain stores for a number of reasons. For instance, self-distribution allows the chains to control the receipt, storage, and shipment of food items to their retail outlets. In addition, the procurement advantage associated with volume purchasing is passed directly and wholly to the retailer instead of being shared with a wholesaler. The revenues generated from backhauling merchandise from manufacturers represent another reason for self-distribution. Other revenues generated from operations add still another motivation to engage in self-distribution.

### Foodservice Retailer Distribution Decisions

Unlike retail food stores, the foodservice chains don't engage in self-distribution. Generally, foodservice retailers are supplied by distributors defined as "broadliners" (who carry wide assortments of food and nonfood products) and specialists in specific product categories or market segments.

## INDUSTRIALIZATION OF THE U.S. FOOD MARKETING SYSTEM

Industrialization is a term that reflects the restructuring of the U.S. food marketing system. We have referred to the U.S. food marketing system as a "system" because it operates so harmoniously, as one well-oiled machine. This harmonious operation is critical in the food industry because of the length of the marketing channels involved (from producer to consumer), the large number of specialized companies that operate within the system, the inherent uncertainties of prices, supplies, and qualities of farm products, and the urgency involved with the marketing of perishable products. Over the years, a number of developments have contributed to the industrialization of the U.S. food marketing system. The purpose of this section is to review briefly several of the more important developments: specialization, diversification, decentralization, integration, internalization, and globalization.

## Specialization

The operating opportunities and subsequent improved profits associated with specialization have long acted as inducements to firms in the U.S. food marketing system. Specialization is pervasive throughout the U.S. food marketing system. Farmers produce one or two crops; feedlots specialize in feeding cattle to market weight; fish farms focus on raising one species of fish; food processors operate a plant that breaks eggs; food manufacturers transform raw foodstuffs to produce cereal; wholesalers specialize in distribution of food products to one type of retailer—convenience stores; retailers like wholesale clubs are created to secure the specialized customer needs of large sizes and bulk sales.

## Diversification

Diversification in the U.S. food marketing system is the result of the tremendous number of mergers that have taken place. Mergers allow processors and manufacturers to broaden their product lines. Wholesalers and retailers are able to enter new geographical areas. Diversification allows the food marketing firm to compound the growth that usually accompanies specialization.

## Decentralization

Historically, the U.S. food marketing system has relied on specialized firms to assemble or *concentrate* farm crops and animals from the myriad number of producers. These central terminal markets, as they are called, provide a public arena for buyers and sellers. To avoid these terminal markets, processors, wholesalers, and retail buyers have gone straight to smaller country dealers for livestock, and to shipping-point firms for crops. These decentralizing sales have resulted in the relocation of food processing facilities from the terminal market areas to the producing areas.

## Integration

There are two basic types of integration: horizontal and vertical. In horizontal integration, a firm acquires an additional firm engaged in its own type of activity—for example, a poultry farm acquires another poultry farm; a produce wholesaler acquires additional produce wholesaling interests; a convenience store chain acquires another chain of convenience stores. Horizontal integration satisfies a firm's need to grow externally through specialization.

Rather than behave as independent firms in the U.S. food marketing system, the individual companies in a **vertical marketing system** (VMS) behave as a unified organization, with each firm acting in harmony with its food partners. Such coordination of activities can substantially reduce the risks and uncertainties inherent in other forms of distribution and marketing. There are three major types of vertical marketing systems in existence today: 1) corporate, 2) contractual, and 3) administered.

### *Corporate*

The **corporate VMS** combines successive stages of production, distribution, and marketing under a single ownership. A corporate system can occur, for example, when a manufacturer purchases its own wholesaler or retailer (forward integration) or when a retailer or wholesaler purchases a manufacturer (backward integration).

### *Contractual*

A **contractual VMS** integrates the efforts of production, distribution, and the marketing of food products by using a contractual agreement. These systems fall into three categories: wholesaler-sponsored voluntary chains, retailer sponsored cooperatives, and franchises.

In **wholesaler-sponsored** chains a wholesaler contracts with retailers in order to standardize and coordinate buying practices, merchandising programs, and inventory management. The voluntary chain is able to take advantage of distribution economies of scale and volume purchases discounts. The major wholesalers in the U.S. food marketing system are of this type.

Basically, the purpose of the **retailer-sponsored** cooperative is to operate a low-cost central buying and warehousing facility. This type of VMS is organized as a corporation whose stock is owned by the retailers themselves. Like the voluntary group, the retailer cooperative enjoys the distribution economies of scale and volume purchase discounts that accompany integration. A declining number of the food wholesalers are of this type.

The **franchise**, as a contractual VMS, represents an agreement between a parent company (franchisor) and an individual firm (franchisee). The agreement spells out the duties and responsibilities of the franchisor and the franchisee. This type of system is not often used in the U.S. food marketing system.

Contractual integration also exists at the producer level. In this case, producers contract with their input suppliers or buyers of farm products. These contracts may involve product specifications, production resources supplied, payment guarantees, and other terms. Contractual integration at the producer level is more evident for animal products, and less so for crops, fruits, and vegetables.

### Administered

The administered VMS is not an integrated system in the true sense. Under this arrangement, production, distribution, and marketing are coordinated by a food marketing firm that is perceived to be powerful by other firms in the U.S. food marketing system.

**Power** is the ability to influence market demand, supply, and prices. It is particularly critical in the U.S. food marketing system because it is often used to coordinate the activities of many members in an administrative channel. There are many potential sources of power. However, they tend to fall into just seven categories. The first has to do with company size, number of competing firms, and level of competition in the industry. Power tends to be stronger for a given size of company in a concentrated industry than in an unconcentrated industry. The second source is based on supply control. The most important source of power is vested in the firm that can control the amount of product produced and distributed to a market. Third is information. Firms with the greatest amount of information have superior power. Fourth is diversification. Firms that are diversified by products and geography have more power than specialized firms. Fifth, firms with strategic resources (e.g., brands, consumer loyalty, and retail shelf space) have superior power. Sixth, product differentiation leads to a better management of demand and, thus, more power for the firm. Finally, firms with more financial resources can compete more effectively and, thus, have more market power.

Generally speaking, who has power in the U.S. food marketing system and who doesn't? Producers, in general, tend to have little or no power because the large number of small firms composing this level tend to produce undifferentiated, homogeneous products. Manufacturers tend to have power mainly because of the strong brand loyalties they build for their products. Because of their size, the voluntary groups and retail cooperatives enjoy power resulting from large scale distribution economies and volume purchase discounts. Finally, food retailers tend to possess market power because they control shelf space.

## Internationalization

The borders of the United States do not confine firms in the U.S. food marketing system. Indeed, today U.S. food products are increasingly being marketed worldwide. Excess capacity and production in the agricultural sector, and the desire for new markets, are just two of the factors that appear to influence a firm's involvement in exporting, joint venturing, licensing, and direct investment in foreign based manufacturing, wholesaling, and retailing operations.

### Globalization

The international operations of many firms have evolved to the point where they see themselves not as marketers to other countries, but rather as global marketers. These U.S. based multinational corporations operate throughout the U.S. food marketing system with the philosophy that the world represents a single market without boundaries. As the trend toward globalization continues, the competitive environment for U.S. food marketing firms will be characterized by rivalry, interdependence, and cooperation. The accelerated merger activity in the U.S. food marketing system may, in part, reflect the belief that only large-scale companies can effectively compete in the global marketplace.

## SUMMARY

The chapter provided an overview of the U.S. food marketing system and developments leading to a changing system. Using a structural approach, the primary system participants were identified.

The U.S. food marketing system begins with decisions made by firms who produce food. The farmers, ranchers, and fishers provide the system's input. The input is transformed either into basic ingredients by processors, or into finished food products by manufacturers. In both cases, form utility is created.

Wholesalers represent the first phase in the distribution of the system's output created by manufacturers. Merchant wholesalers, agent wholesalers, and manufacturer's sales branches represent three forms of wholesaling. Wholesalers contribute to the creation of time and place utilities.

Retailing represents the final phase in the distribution of the system's output. Food stores provide food to consumers for consumption **at home**, while foodservice firms cater to the consumption of food **away from home**. It is at this point in the system that form, time, place, and possession utilities come together and are offered to the consumer.

The U.S. food marketing system is driven by the tastes and preferences of the consumer. Thus, customer satisfaction represents the output of the U.S. food marketing system. What is produced, transformed, stored, and/or moved is destined to be bought and consumed by the public. Today, consumers are fragmented into increasingly smaller segments or micromarkets. To meet the challenge posed by these micromarkets the participating firms in the system seek to create a competitive differential advantage. Using a functional approach, the marketing decisions needed to create this advantage were identified.

The product decisions made by food marketing firms focus on providing what consumer want. Consumers' expectations that they will benefit from the purchase and consumption of food products direct the transformation of agricultural commodities into products that have physical, aesthetic, and service dimensions.

Price decisions made by firms focus on providing products at a price that reflects the perceived value of the products to consumers. In this way, price as a statement of value (rather than a statement of costs) exists throughout the U.S. food marketing system.

Promotion decisions focus on communicating the availability of value priced products. At each stage in the system, firms make a conscious attempt to influence the purchase behaviors of their customers.

Place decisions focus on distributing value priced products. In the process of moving products closer to the hands of consumers, each of the firms resolves product, spatial, and temporal discrepancies.

Over the years, a number of developments have contributed to the efficiency of the U.S. food marketing system. Specialization is pervasive throughout the system because it can improve operating efficiency and increase profits. Diversification allows food marketing firms to grow beyond the limits set by specialization economies and antitrust regulations. Decentralization provides firms with an opportunity to exercise greater quality control by defining agricultural production specifications. Integration enhances the movement of goods from producers to consumers. Internationalization provides new markets for U.S. products. Globalization, in turn, reflects an attempt to compete in the increasingly global marketplace.

## SELECTED REFERENCES

*Farm Facts.* American Farm Bureau Federation, Park Ridge, Ill. 1994.

Kotler, P. and G. Armstrong. *Marketing an Introduction.* 3rd edition. Englewood Cliffs, N.J.: Prentice Hall, 1993.

Marion, B. W. and The NC-117 Committee. *The Organization and Performance of the U.S. Food System.* Lexington, Mass: Lexington Books, D. C. Heath and Company, 1986.

Scanlon, N. *Restaurant Management.* New York, N.Y.: Van Nostrand Reinhold, 1993.

Schertz, L. P. and L. M. Daft. *Food and Agricultural Markets—The Quiet Revolution.* Economic Research Service, U.S. Department of Agriculture, National Planning Association, 1993.

Senaur, B., E. Asp, and J. Kinsey. *Food Trends and The Changing Consumer.* St. Paul, Minn.: Eagan Press, 1991.

## REVIEW QUESTIONS

1. Discuss the difference between food processors and food manufacturers.

2. Using a functional and structural approach, how would you define the U.S. food marketing system?

3. Input, throughput, and output are all system's components. Discuss them within the context of the U.S. food marketing system.

4. Explain the difference between the structural and functional perspectives of the U.S. food marketing system.

5. What is meant by the phrase, "adjusting the discrepancies between the quantity and assortment of output and the needs of the marketplace?"

6. Contrast two local retailers with regard to how they answer the question, "What do we want to be to our customers?"

7. Discuss: "The marketplace for food products is made up of numerous micromarkets."

8. Explain how food marketing firms can satisfy the needs of consumers by creating and maintaining a competitive differential advantage.

9. Do you agree that the real power in the U.S. food marketing system is held by the retailer? Why or why not?

10. Discuss and provide examples of specialization, diversification, decentralization, integration, and globalization in the U.S. food marketing system.

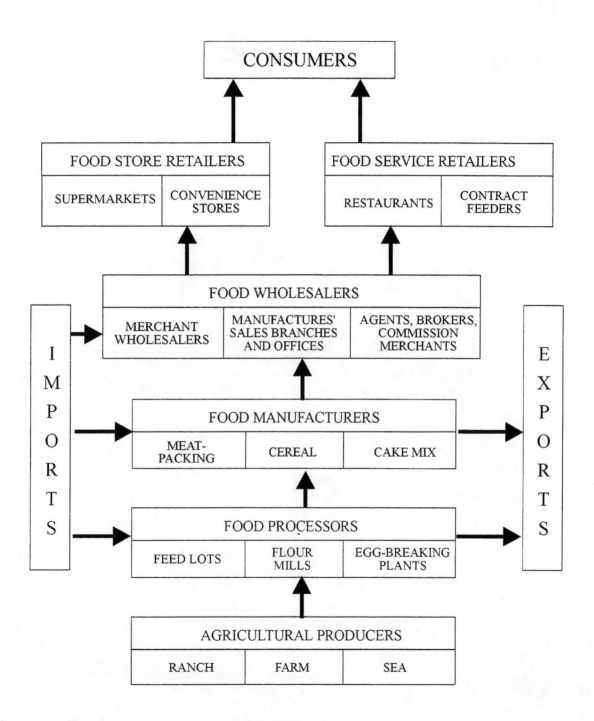

**FIGURE 1-1.** U.S. FOOD MARKETING SYSTEM

# Chapter 2

# Producers

**Chapter Outline**

Agricultural Sector
    A. Commodity Subsectors

Livestock Subsectors (021)
    A. Beef Cows
    B. Hogs/Pigs
    C. Sheep/Lambs

Poultry Subsectors (025)
    A. Chickens (Broilers)
    B. Layers (Eggs)
    C. Turkeys

Aquatic Subsectors
    A. Wild Harvest (091)
    B. Aquaculture (027)

Fruit and Vegetable Subsectors
    A. Fruits, Berries, Tree Nuts (017)
    B. Vegetables (016)

Dairy Subsector (024)
    A. Milk Cows

Grain Subsectors (011)
    A. Food and Feed Grains

Agricultural Cooperatives
    A. Marketing, Supply, and Service Cooperatives

Structural Characteristics
    A. Number and Relative Size of Producers
    B. Product Offerings
    C. Ease of Entry

Summary

Using both a structural and functional approach. Chapter 1 examined the **U.S. food marketing system**. The primary participants were identified as producers, processors/manufacturers, wholesalers, retailers, and consumers. The U.S. food marketing system is driven by the tastes and preferences of the consumers. Thus, it was shown that each of the participating firms engages in business activities that reflect decisions to create, price, promote, and distribute food products for the purpose of satisfying consumers.

This chapter begins with a structural examination of the participants in the agricultural sector of the U.S. food marketing system: food producers. To facilitate the analysis, attention is focused on subsectors that reflect the output from the primary methods of food production: farming, ranching, and fishing. These subsectors are classified as three-digit industry groups in the Census of Agriculture's Major Standard Industrial Classification: groups 01 (crops), 02 (livestock), and 09 (fishing). As mentioned earlier;the perspective taken throughout the text is that the structure of a system has a fundamental influence on the marketing decisions made by the firms composing it. Because the U.S. food marketing system is made up of many sectors, the text also maintains that the structure of a sector has a fundamental influence on the marketing decisions made by the firms composing the sector. The purpose of this chapter is to identify the structural characteristics of the agricultural sector.

# AGRICULTURAL SECTOR

Now, as before, the structure of the agricultural sector continues to change in ways that will have a profound effect on the U.S. food marketing system. **Table 2-1** looks at the situation in U.S. agriculture over the census years 1982, 1987, 1992, and reveals several major trends.

In the first place, the number of people engaged in farming has decreased. During the ten-year census period, farm/ranch population has decreased from 5.6 to 4.7 million. Farm/ranch population as a percent of U.S. population also declined from 2.5 to 1.9 percent over this period. There seems to be a major trend for young people who grow up on farm/ranches to leave when they come of age. It is becoming increasingly difficult to earn a good living on the traditional family farm or ranch. Furthermore, acquiring or beginning a farm or ranch has become enormously expensive, so fewer people are moving into farming and ranching from other occupations.

**Table 2-1** shows two other trends. The number of farms has declined from 2.2 million to 1.9 million in this ten-year period, while the average size has increased from 440 to 491 acres. Taken together, these trends reinforce the popular notion that the small-family farm operation is in trouble. Plagued with problems of survival, the only apparent solutions are either, a sell-out or a buy-out. In either case, farm operations continue to increase in size.

As shown in **Table 2-1** between 1982 and 1992 the amount of cropland declined by ten million acres while pastureland/ranchland has increased by thirty-six million. The efficiency of the farm operation has also increased. The farm worker can now feed approximately 131 people for the entire year. The mechanization of farms, combined with new farming technologies and chemical usage, have replaced the need for labor on the farm. Unfortunately, not all farm operations have been able to take advantage of these newer technologies.

The sharp contrast between highly capitalized farm operations and smaller less capitalized farms is shown in **Table 2-2**. Between 1982 and 1992 farms with sales less than fifty thousand dollars (approximately seventy-six percent of all farms), on average, accounted for twelve percent of all farm sales. In contrast, farms with sales of five hudred thousand or more (approximately two percent of all farms) on average, accounted for thirty-six percent of all farm sales. The two trends clearly show that crop and livestock producers are separated into two distinct groups. A few very large and heavily capitalized farms generate most of the farm sales. In contrast, a large number of small farms generate an increasingly smaller percent of sales.

An examination of farm sales by type of ownership provides further evidence of two separate farm groups. As shown in **Table 2-3**, the vast majority of farms (eighty-seven percent) are organized as individual proprietorships. These farms are typically small, family operations. On the other hand, corporations, although a small percentage of farms (three percent), generate an increasingly larger percentage of all sales. However, most of the farm corporations are family-owned farms that have incorporated because of the benefits associated with doing so.

Another dimension that characterizes the structure of the agricultural sector is specialization. Farms specialized by commodity are shown in **Table 2-4**. Between 1982 and 1992, the proportion of farms that have more than half of their sales in a single commodity has remained constant at ninety-six percent. The share of production for which such farms accounted increased from 96.6 percent to 97.2 percent over the same period. Fueled by the twin goals of greater productivity of output and efficiency of input, and aided by new technology, food producers continue to find it profitable to specialize.

Although agricultural commodities are produced in every state, farm production is also geographically specialized. Commodities produced in an area are generally determined by climate, technology, costs, transportation networks, and, in many cases, by the availability of land. The geographical specialization of farm production is specified in the various commodity subsections.

## Commodity Subsectors

Structurally, the U.S. agricultural sector is made up of numerous commodity subsectors. Thus, the previously identified changes in the U.S. agricultural sector represent the culmination of structural changes at the commodity subsector level. The subsectors examined here are classified by the Census of Agriculture into industry groups and designated by three digit **Standard Industrial Classification (SIC) codes**. These subsectors were chosen because they represent major agricultural commodity groups, and as such they make a significant contribution to the everyday meals of consumers. The "main dish" producers are examined initially: livestock ranchers (021), poultry/egg farmers (025), wild-catch fishing fleets (091), and farmers of domestically raised fish (027). Next "side dish" producers, such as fruit and vegetable growers (016), are examined, followed by an analysis of producers who complement the meal with drink: milk and dairy farmers (024). Finally, producers whose major output is mainly used as ingredients for finished food products are examined: grain farmers food (011) and feed (013). An examination of these subsectors will show that the unique characteristics of each commodity have, a strong effect, on the way the subsector is structured.

# LIVESTOCK SUBSECTORS (021)

During the years 1982 to 1992, beef cow, hog, and sheep subsectors made up approximately forty-two percent of all U.S. farms. Beef cows, hogs, and sheep are commodities that have relatively long biological production periods. Years pass between livestock births and the time when these animals are ready to be processed into food products. In addition, because livestock must be bred, raised, and fed to market weight, these commodity subsectors exhibit a complex structural arrangement. Taken together, the length of the biological production period and the time it takes to expand the breeding stock results in a slow response in supply to changes in demand or prices.

## Beef Cows

Prior to the slaughter/processing stage, the beef cow subsector involves three stages: producing, growing, and feeding. The number of beef cow operations has declined about five percent between the years 1991 to 1995. At the same time the beef cow inventory has increased by approximately six percent (**Table 2-5**). The composition of these beef cow operations by size groups is shown in **Table 2-6**. Most beef cow producers are small. The number of operations that have fewer than fifty head has declined between 1991 and 1995. However, these producers make up approximately eighty percent of all beef cow farms. Further, over the same time period, the number of operations having fifty to ninety-nine head has grown four percent, while the number having one hundred head or more has grown by one percent. The apparent conclusion is that while the total number of beef cow operations has decreased, the subsector now has a higher percent of larger beef cow farms.

**Table 2-7** indicates how the beef cow inventory is allocated across various size groups. The trends in the inventory show that smaller operations, with one to ninety-nine head, represent a declining share of inventory, while the larger operations, with one hundred head or more, account for an increasing share. When the data in both tables are combined, a clear picture of beef cow operations emerges. Approximately eighty percent of the operations have about thirty percent of the inventory, and the other twenty percent have the remaining seventy percent of the beef cow inventory.

The cow-calf farms that produce young, weaned animals for subsequent feeding and finishing exist in all states. In 1995, Texas, Montana, Tennessee, Oklahoma, and Kentucky had thirty-eight percent of all cow-calf farms. Adding five more states results in ten states having fifty-five percent of all such operations. Because most of the cow-calf operations have fewer than fifty head, five of the leading ten states are not the leading states in beef cow inventory. Texas alone has about as much beef cow inventory as the next four leading states of Montana, Oklahoma, Nebraska, and South Dakota combined.

Calves are weaned at about four hundred pounds, and then enter the second stage of the growing operation. In this stage, they will gain another three hundred to four hundred pounds while grazing on pastureland. The growing operation takes place either where the calves are produced or where they are fed to slaughter weight. It is estimated that approximately sixty percent of the growing operation is performed by cow-calf producers, thirty percent by feedlots, and ten percent by farms that integrate the breeding, raising, and feeding of calves.

When beef cows have reached seven hundred to eight hundred pounds, they are sent to feedlots, where they are fed to slaughter weight of nine hundred to one thousand pounds. The numbers of feedlots, and beef cows shipped out of feedlots to the slaughter market (marketings) are shown in **Table 2-8**. Between 1991 and 1995, the number of feedlots has declined by approximately twelve percent, while the number of head sold for slaughter has increased, about four percent. The composition of these feedlots by size group is shown in **Table 2-9**. Like the beef cow producers, most feedlot operations are small. Feedlots having fewer than one thousand head represented about ninety-six percent of all the feedlots between 1991 and 1995. During the same period, the number of these feedlots has declined, while feedlots having more than one thousand head have increased. Thus, the decline in total feedlots is due to the decline in smaller feedlot operations. The number of cattle shipped out of feedlots to the slaughter market (marketings) is shown in **Table 2-10**. Between 1991 and 1995, feedlot marketings increased for feedlots with four thousand head or more. Approximately ninety-six percent of the feedlots ship about ten percent of the cattle to be slaughtered, while the remaining four percent of the feedlots account for ninety percent of the marketings.

Cattle feeding is far more concentrated geographically than is cattle breeding. Approximately eighty-five percent of all feedlots are located in thirteen states. Iowa, the leading state, has almost twice as many feedlots as the second leading state, Minnesota. Illinois, Nebraska, and South Dakota are ranked third, fourth, and fifth respectively. However, because the vast majority of feedlots have fewer than one thousand head, the states that have the greatest marketings have only a fraction of the number of feedlots. Texas, the leading state for cattle marketed, has only four percent of the number of Iowa feedlots, but four times the number of marketings. The state's dominance is reflected in the fact that five of the top ten beef cow feeding corporations are headquartered in Texas. Nebraska, Kansas, Colorado, and Iowa make up the remaining top five states in marketings.

Finally, because the states with significant beef cow inventory are not necessarily the states with significant beef cow feedlot marketings, there are large-scale movements of animals from cow-calf production to feedlot operations throughout the U.S.

## Hogs/Pigs

The hog/pig subsector involves three stages: breeding, growing, and feeding. Some firms specialize in the initial breeding stage and are referred to as *farrow only* operations. Firms that specialize in the final feeding stage are referred to as *finish only* operations. Still other firms integrate all the stages in one *farrow to finish* operation. These integrated firms represent thirty-five percent of all hog operations, but seventy-two percent of all hog inventory.

Hog producers generally produce their own female breeding stock (sows) and rely on commercial breeders for boars. Sow litters, or farrowing, are raised in feeder pig operations and then fed to market weight or shipped to market hog firms who specialize in finishing hogs to market weight.

The number of hog and pig operations has declined by about twenty-eight percent between 1991 and 1995. At the same time, the hog/pig inventory has increased approximately four percent (**Table 2-11**). Most of the decline in the number of operations has occurred in the "farrow only" and "finish only" operations.

The composition of the hog/pig operations is shown in **Table 2-12**. Most hog/pig firms are small. Firms with fewer than one hundred head have declined between 1991 and 1995, and make up about sixty percent of all hog/pig farms. However, over the same time period, the percentage of operations with one thousand or more head has increased from 4.3 to 6.8 percent. Once again, like the beef cow subsector, while the total number of hog/pig operations has decreased, the subsector now has a higher percentage of larger hog/pig operations.

**Table 2-13** indicates how the hog/pig inventory is allocated across various size groups. The trends in the inventory show that operations with fewer than one thousand head have declined between 1991 and 1995. When the data in both tables are combined, approximately ninety-three percent of all hog/pig operations have forty percent of the inventory; the other seven percent have the remaining sixty percent of the inventory. As mentioned previously, most of the hog inventory is held by firms that integrate the farrowing and finishing stages.

Although hog/pig firms exist in all states, the sector is geographically concentrated in the Grain Belt states. In 1995, five states—Iowa, Minnesota, Ohio, Nebraska, and Indiana—had thirty-eight percent of all hog/pig operations and forty-nine percent of all inventory. Iowa dominates this sector. It has fourteen percent of all the operations and twenty-four percent of all the inventory. It surpasses the combined inventory of the next three leading states: Illinois, Minnesota, and North Carolina.

## Sheep/Lambs

The sheep/lamb subsector is similar to the beef cow and hog subsectors. Lambs are bred, grown, and mature before being placed on feed for slaughter. Sheep/lamb producers, like hog producers, generally produce their own female and male breeding stock: ewes and rams. New crop lambs grow and mature to between fifty and ninety pounds before being placed on feed. Approximately seventy percent of all lambs are placed in feedlots for eventual slaughter.

The number of sheep/lamb operations has declined by about twenty-two percent between 1991 and 1995. At the same time, the sheep/lamb inventory has declined by about twenty-one percent, as shown in **Table 2-14**.

The composition of the sheep/lamb operations is shown in **Table 2-15**. Like the other livestock producers, most sheep/lamb operations are small. Between 1991 and 1995, firms with fewer than one hundred head have increased to ninety percent, while the larger operations have declined to ten percent.

Table 2-16 indicates how sheep/lamb inventory is allocated across various size groups. The trends in the inventory show that operations with fewer than five thousand head have declined between 1991 and 1995. When the data in both tables are combined just two percent of all sheep/lamb operations have fifty-six percent of all the inventory, the other ninety-eight percent have the remaining forty-four percent.

Sheep/lamb operations are of two types. *Farm flock* operations are found in the states east of the Rocky Mountains and in Alaska and Hawaii. *Range type* operations are found in the states containing the Rocky Mountains and the western United States. In 1995, five states—Iowa, Texas, Ohio, California, and Minnesota—had seven percent of all sheep/lamb operations. However, because Iowa, Ohio, and Minnesota have many small operations, these states only have seven percent of the inventory. The range type operations in the Western states of Wyoming, California, Montana, Colorado, Utah, and South Dakota, combined with Texas, account for sixty-three percent of all the sheep/lamb inventory.

# POULTRY SUBSECTORS (025)

Chickens, turkeys, and eggs make up the poultry subsectors. The subsectors are dominated by firms that have integrated the breeding, growing, feeding, and processing stages. Chickens and turkeys are commodities that have relatively short biological periods. Chickens raised for their meat (broilers) are ready for the market at nine to twelve weeks of age; layers must be raised for eighteen to twenty weeks before they begin to lay eggs; and turkeys are ready for the market at eighteen weeks for toms and fourteen weeks for hens. Because of the relatively short time it takes to increase the breeding stock, and short biological production period, producers can increase supply rapidly in response to changes in demand or prices.

## Chickens (Broilers)

Broiler companies purchase their breeding stock from commercial genetic companies. Each genetic company intermixes breeding-stock lines to produce birds for either a high yield of breast meat or overall size. The day-old male and female breeder chicks are raised to maturity in grandparent growing farms, where fertile eggs are produced. The fertile eggs are incubated at the company's grandparent hatchery, and produce male and female broiler breeder chicks (broilers). The chicks are the commercial broilers that are sent on to broiler growers. Broiler growers are contracted to care for and raise these chicks. Most broiler companies operate their own feed production facility in order to supply the broiler growers with the scientifically designed feed used by the birds.

Integration in the broiler subsector has progressed to the point where broiler companies typically own the hatching facility, chicks, and broiler growing. These integrated companies are the dominant force in the broiler subsector.

**Table 2-17** shows the number of broiler hatcheries, inventory capacity, and average capacity for three selected census years. The number of hatcheries has declined by seven percent over these years, while the average capacity has increased by forty-one percent. Although fewer, but larger, hatcheries now exist, the unavailability of inventory capacity by size of hatcheries data precludes any conclusion regarding the allocating of inventory capacity across the different hatchery sizes.

**Table 2-18** shows the number of broiler farm operations, broiler inventory, and average flock size for these selected census years. The number of broiler operations has declined by four percent while the average flock size has increased by sixty-one percent. However, the unavailability of inventory by size of farm data precludes any conclusion about how the broiler inventory is allocated across different farm sizes.

More than 80 percent of U.S. broiler inventory is generated by the "Broiler Belt" states. In 1993, three of these states—Arkansas, Georgia, and Alabama—produced forty-four percent of the broiler inventory. North Carolina, Mississippi, Texas, Maryland, Delaware, Virginia, and California make up the other "Broiler Belt" states and account for thirty-six percent of the broiler inventory.

## Layers (Eggs)

Although the egg subsector is less integrated than the broiler subsector, there are a number of similarities between the largest egg production firms and the broiler integraters. Egg producers buy parent-level breeding stock from genetic companies. In hatcheries, these breeders produce and multiply the day-old chicks that will be used to produce eggs. At sixteen weeks of age, these pullets are moved to laying facilities and begin to lay eggs at between eighteen and twenty weeks of age. Once the first cycle of egg production is completed (usually twelve months), the hens are either sent to the market as spent hens or rested through a molting period and brought back into production. Hens are not usually molted more than twice.

The largest integrated companies have a million or more layers in several buildings that are environmentally controlled and utilize computer technology to control egg flow, quality control, and packaging. Eggs are typically collected on egg collector belts so that they can be transported from the laying house to an on-farm grading and packing station without being touched by human hands. Even the smaller, less integrated, firms usually have 100,000 or more layers on their farms.

**Table 2-19** indicates the number of layer farms, inventory, eggs produced, and eggs per layer for three selected census years.

The number of farms and inventory have declined by forty and three percent respectively. However, the average flock size has increased by sixty percent. The number of eggs produced, and eggs per layer have also increased over this time period.

In general, fewer, but larger, farms—based on average flock size—produce more eggs with fewer birds. The unavailability of inventory by size of farm data precludes any conclusion with regard to how the layer inventory is allocated across different sizes of farms.

About sixty percent of the eggs are produced in ten states. In 1993, three of these states—California, Pennsylvania, and Indiana—produced 25 percent of the egg inventory. Ohio, Georgia, Arkansas, Texas, Iowa, North Carolina, and Minnesota accounted for thirty-five percent of the eggs.

## Turkeys

As in the broiler and larger subsectors, turkey companies purchase their breeding stock from commercial genetic companies. The day-old male and female poults are raised to maturity in parent growing farms where fertilized eggs are produced. The fertile eggs are incubated at the company parent hatchery and produce male and female commercial poults. These newly hatched turkey poults are transported to grow-out farms, where independent or contract growers raise them. Most turkey companies operate their own feed production facility in order to supply the turkey growers with the scientifically designed feed needed to produce specific size and quality turkeys. Integrated turkey companies typically own the hatching facility, feed mill, and processing plant, and contract for day-old breeder poults and turkey growing.

**Table 2-20** identifies the number of turkey hatcheries, inventory capacity, and average capacity for three selected census years. The number of hatcheries has declined by twenty-four percent over these years, while the average flock size has increased by sixty-nine percent. In general, fewer but larger farms now characterize this subsector. The unavailability of inventory capacity by size of hatchery data precludes any conclusion with regard to how the inventory is allocated across different size hatcheries.

In **Table 2-21**, turkey farms, inventory, and average flock size are shown for three selected census years. The turkey inventory has increased faster than the number of farms, thus the average flock size has increased by forty-two percent. Data on inventory by size of farms is not available, so no conclusion can be drawn regarding the allocation of inventory across different sizes of farms.

In 1993, ninety-eight percent of all turkeys were produced in seven states. Two of these states—North Carolina and Minnesota—had as much inventory (forty-nine percent) as the next five largest states of Arkansas, California, Missouri, Virginia, and Indiana.

# AQUATIC SUBSECTORS

The aquatic subsector is made up of the wild harvest of fish from lakes, coastal waters, and oceans, and the production of fish in controlled environments: aquaculture. Currently aquaculture is viewed as a competitor to the wild harvest of fish. However, with the continued depletion of wild seafood stocks, the wild harvest fishing industry is expected to include aquacultural production in their plans to manage resources for long-term growth. The diversity of fish species does not permit any general statement regarding the length of the biological production periods.

## Wild Harvest (091)

The waters of the United States contain a vast renewable natural resource. The U.S. has approximately ninety thousand miles of shoreline, which support marine resources that are among the largest, most varied, and valuable in the world. Commercial landings by U.S. fishermen also occur at ports outside the fifty states. These waters are fished using the centuries-old methods of hook and line, traps and pots, dredges, scoops, and the newer method of synthetic fiber in stationary or towed fishing nets.

Commercial landings by U.S. fishermen of edible and industrial (non-edible) fish at ports in the fifty states are shown in **Table 2-22**. The amount of fish landings in the U.S. has increased by about four percent. However, when landings outside the U.S. are considered, the increase in total landings is only two percent. Despite the generally increasing volume of U.S. commercial landings over the years, the U.S. imports more fishing products than it exports. Between 1991 and 1995, imports decreased by two percent (**Table 2-23**). When imports are added to domestic landings, total U.S. supply of fishing products increased by two percent over this same period. Finally, imports have averaged forty-three percent of total U.S. supply.

Over three hundred species of fish are taken commercially. Seven species alone account for approximately eighty percent of the commercial landings inside the U.S. (**Table 2-24**) Six of the seven species are edible fish. The other, the Menhaden species, is an oily fish used in the production of meal, oil, and solubles. Small quantities are used for bait and animal food. Approximately eighty percent of commercial landings in the U.S. are used for human food. When imports are added in, the percentage of total supply used for human food remains at eighty percent.

In the conventional sense, there are no producers of the wild catch. There are, however, harvesters that prowl the waters in search of fish: the U.S. fishing fleet (**Table 2-25**). Between 1990 and 1994, the only increases in the number of craft were found in the South Atlantic, Gulf, and Great Lakes regions. The other regions show a declining number of vessels and boats. Within each of these regions, two states account for more than fifty percent of all craft in the region: Maine and Massachusetts in the Northeast; Florida and Louisiana in the South Atlantic and Gulf; Alaska and California on the West Coast; and Michigan and Wisconsin in the Great Lakes.

**Table 2-26** indicates the geographical landings by regions. Because Alaska pollock represents the largest share of domestic landings, it should be no surprise that Alaska/Pacific Coast is the leading region. Further, shrimp and Menhaden are the principal species in the second largest region—the Gulf. Combined, these two regions account for approximately eighty percent of all domestic landings.

## Aquaculture (027)

U.S. aquaculture is supplying more and more of the fish that consumers eat. Aquaculture, or fish farming, is the rearing of fish under controlled or semi-controlled conditions. The diversity of aquacultural production ranges from only slight modifications of the natural environment to highly technical systems. These systems manipulate environmental parameters such as the temperature and current of the water, and oxygen and ammonia levels, and use sophisticated technology to recirculate and purify the water. Because of this production diversity, aquaculture is conducted in fresh waters, seawater, earth ponds, concrete ponds, flooded fields, and even rice paddies. Perhaps the newest advancement in aquaculture is the production of fish in tanks housed in environmentally controlled buildings.

The entire aquaculture industry is driven by the fact that fish will grow more quickly under controlled conditions than they will in the wild. In addition, they will withstand disease better and provide consistent texture, color, and fat distribution under controlled conditions.

U.S. aquaculture production involves a number of species. However, despite the diversity of species, aquaculture is concentrated in catfish, trout, oysters, and crawfish (**Table 2-27**). It has been estimated that these four species alone amount for approximately eighty-five percent of the edible U.S. aquaculture production.

Although aquaculture is identified as an industry (SIC 0273) in the Census of Agriculture, data regarding the structural characteristics of this industry are incomplete for the census years of 1982, 1987, and 1992. Some appreciation for the dimensions of this industry can be gained from an analysis of catfish and trout operations.

**Table 2-28** shows the change in number of catfish and trout farm operations. The number of catfish operations declined by 27.4 percent. But the number of pounds produced increased by thirteen percent from 1991 to 1994. The number of trout farm operations declined by only four percent. But the number of pounds produced decreased by twelve percent from 1991 to 1994.

For each aquaculture species grown in the U.S., a single state or region dominates. In most cases, the species being grown are native to the area. Mississippi is the largest catfish-producing state, accounting for seventy percent of U.S. catfish production. Alabama—which has as many farms as Mississippi, but not the water surface—and

Arkansas are expanding their catfish operation. Trout is grown in many states. North Carolina has more trout farms than any other state, but Idaho accounts for eighty percent of all trout production. The second largest aquaculture species, crawfish, are produced mainly in Louisiana. Maine and Washington produce about eighty-five percent of all the salmon. North and South Carolina are the leading hybrid striped bass producers. Tilapia—a fish native to Africa—is grown in Florida, Louisiana, Idaho, and Arizona.

Mollusk (clam, oyster, and mussel) operations are scattered along the East Coast from Maine to Florida, and some are found in the Gulf. The majority of aquacultural production of mollusks—chiefly oysters—comes from the West Coast. Oysters, which account for over ninety percent of total mollusk production are centered in the state of Washington. Shrimp are produced mainly in Texas and South Carolina. Almost all of the alligators are grown in Louisiana and Florida.

Two segments of the aquacultural industry do not impact on food production. The bait-fish industry is centered in Arkansas. Larger fish are used for ocean-fishing, and smaller ones as live food for tropical fish. The second segment, tropical fish, is located mainly in Florida. The tropical fish industry tends to overlap with the bait fish industry, with goldfish grown both as ornamental and bait fish.

## FRUIT AND VEGETABLE SUBSECTORS

The fruit subsector is made up of citrus and non-citrus fruits, berries, and tree nuts. In terms of the number of acres planted, non-citrus fruit, are the largest, followed in descending order by citrus, tree nuts, and berries.

The vegetable subsector is made up of a wide array of unique crops. Unlike the fruit subsector, there are no major divisions within the vegetable subsector.

Taken together, fruits and vegetables are highly perishable, seasonally produced, bulky, and low-value per-unit commodities because they contain mostly water. In addition, their production is regional by specialized, and they appear at the retail store in either fresh or processed form. The biological production period, or the time it takes to expand or contract production and the time when the market supply of the commodity actually changes, is short with annual vegetable and fruit crops. Further, with annual vegetable crops, substantial shifts in acres planted can occur from one year to the next. In contrast, fruits, berries, and tree nuts producers commit their land to a particular crop for many years and with few ways of expanding the supply from one year to the next.

### Fruits, Berries, and Tree Nuts (017)

Although there are a myriad of fruits, each of the divisions is dominated by only a couple of varieties. Apples and grapes account for the majority of non-citrus production. Citrus production is dominated by oranges and grapefruit. Almonds and walnuts represent the majority of tree nuts produced. Berry production is dominated by blueberries and strawberries.

The size of farms engaged in the production of fruits, berries, and nuts, and their share of total sales for the three census years are shown in **Table 2-29**. The majority of the farms (eighty-one percent) have fewer than one hundred acres and account for about twenty-two percent of sales. Over these same years, the farms with two thousand acres or more (0.6 percent) have accounted for approximately the same percentage of sales—twenty-two percent. If we consider farms of five hundred acres or more, we are left with the conclusion that approximately 3.5 percent of the farms account for about forty-six percent of all sales.

Although fruits, berries, and tree nuts are grown in all the states, five states account for eighty-four percent of their cash receipts. California alone accounts for fifty-seven percent of all cash receipts followed by Florida, Washington, Oregon, and Michigan.

### Vegetables (016)

Like the fruit subsector, the vegetable subsector is made up of a large number of vegetables. However, the sale of vegetables is concentrated in only three varieties. Approximately forty-five percent of all cash receipts were received by producers of potatoes, tomatoes, and lettuce. When onions are added, these four vegetables make up fifty percent of all vegetable cash receipts.

The size of the farms engaged in vegetable production and their share of total sales are shown in **Table 2-30**. Over the census years 1982, 1987, and 1992, the majority of the farms (sixty-seven percent) had fewer than one hundred acres and accounted for about eight percent of the total sales. In contrast, over these same years, farms with one thousand acres or more (three percent) accounted for more than fifty percent of all vegetable sales. Both the fruit and vegetable subsectors are dominated by a small percentage of farms that account for most of the sales.

Vegetables are grown in all states, but five states account for sixty-two percent of all vegetable cash receipts. California is the largest producer, accounting for thirty-five percent of all cash receipts. Florida, Washington, Idaho, and Arizona account for the remaining twenty-seven percent of vegetable cash receipts.

## DAIRY SUBSECTOR (024)

During the years 1982 to 1992, milk cow farms declined from 12.4 percent of all farms to 8.1 percent. Milk cows have relatively long biological production periods. It takes two years from the birth of a heifer calf to raise a milk-producing cow. Thus the length of the biological period, and the time it takes to adjust the number of offspring from breeding stock, result in a slow response in supply to change in demand or prices.

Although cull cows and bulls are used for beef consumption, the primary focus in this subsector is on milk production. Almost all of the milk produced enters the commercial market as whole milk. Fluid milk and processed dairy products are the main milk products. Fluid Grade A milk includes all the variety of regular and flavored milks. The processed dairy products include soft manufactured products such as yogurt and ice cream and hard manufactured products such as butter and cheese. Grade B milk meets lower sanitary standards, but because it undergoes processing at higher temperatures than pasteurized fluid milk, it is used in making processed dairy products. It has been estimated that more than one-half of all Grade A milk is also used to make processed dairy products.

## Milk Cows

The structure of the dairy farm in the U.S. has changed significantly as a result of technological innovations such as computerized systems for testing, monitoring, feeding, waste and forage handling, and pipeline systems where milk flows directly from the cow to refrigerated bulk tanks. The net result of these many capital-intensive technologies has been to raise the minimum economically feasible size of the dairy farm.

**Table 2-31** indicates the number of milk cow operations, inventory, and milk production per cow. The number of milk cow operations and milk cow inventory have declined by twenty-three and five percent, respectively. However, at the same time, milk production measured in million pounds has increased by 4.8 percent. The average milk per cow has increased by 10.4, percent from 14,860 pounds to 16,406 pounds. In fact, since 1955, the milk per cow has increased from 5,810 pounds, or by 183 percent! This phenomenal rate of change is largely attributed to genetic improvements, higher rates of concentrated feeding, higher-quality forage, better feeding management, health care, and other miscellaneous changes.

The distribution of milk cow operations by size is shown in **Table 2-32**. Between 1991 and 1995, the number of farms with fewer than forty-nine head declined, operations having fifty to ninety-nine head increased slightly, and farms with one hundred or more head increased by sixteen percent of all milk cow farms.

**Table 2-33** shows the allocation of cow inventory by size of farm. Operations with one hundred or more milk cows increased the percentage of milk cow inventory from 45.4 percent in 1991 to fifty-five percent in 1995. Farms with fewer than one hundred head have all experienced a decline in their milk cow inventory. When the data in both tables are combined, a clear picture of the milk cow operations emerges. Approximately eighty-five percent of the milk cow operations have forty-five percent of the inventory; the other fifteen percent have the remaining fifty-five percent of the milk cow inventory.

Wisconsin, California, New York, Pennsylvania, and Minnesota account for slightly more than fifty percent of the milk production. With the exception of California, their share of total U.S. milk output has declined or remained stagnant. Milk production has grown faster in the Pacific, Mountain, and Southern regions when compared to the traditional milk-producing areas of the Northeast and Great Lakes states. Rapid population growth, middle climate, lower rainfall and humidity, and large-scale operations are factors contributing to the shifting of milk production to the West and Southwest regions.

# GRAIN SUBSECTORS (011), (013)

The grain subsector is made up of cash grains that are divided into food grains and feed grains. The major food grains in the U.S. are wheat, rice, rye, and soybeans. The principal feed grains are corn, oats, barley, and sorghum. Unlike the other commodities reviewed in this chapter, the food grains lose their identity at the processing level. Essentially, they are used as ingredients in making higher-valued consumer products. Small amounts of corn, oats, and barley are also used in consumer food products.

## Food and Feed Grains

Many intermediate stages are involved in the assembly, handling, storing, grading, and inspecting of grain as it moves from farms to the processing stage. Generally, farms sell most of their grain to local county elevators that are scattered throughout the grain-producing areas. In turn, most county elevators send their grain to terminal elevators that are located along railroads in major grain centers such as Chicago, Kansas City, and Minneapolis, and major seaports such as New Orleans and Baltimore. Needless to say, rail and barge are the dominant modes of grain movement. Unlike other commodities whose primary focus is domestic, grain subsectors engage in the exportation of grains to international markets. A few large, privately held multinational grain leading companies do nearly all of the exporting of the U.S. grain. These same companies also have significant holdings in county, terminal, and port elevators.

Complete data on food grains and feed grains are not available. However, combined data for food and feed grains are provided and appear in **Table 2-34**. Over the census years 1982 through 1992, the number of farms with more than one thousand acres increased from eleven to seventeen percent of all grain farms. In addition, their share of total sales over these years increased from forty to fifty percent of all sales. Clearly, the trend suggests that grain production continues to be concentrated into fewer, but larger, operations.

Grains are grown in all states. However, within the food and feed grain divisions a few states dominate the production. In 1993, North Dakota, Kansas, Montana,

Washington, and Oklahoma accounted for forty-eight percent of all food grain cash receipts. North Dakota was the leading producer of wheat, and Arkansas produced most of the rice. Most of the soybeans came from Illinois, and Georgia harvested most of the rye.

For this same year, five states accounted for approximately fifty-two percent of all feed grain cash receipts: Illinois, Iowa, Nebraska, Indiana, and Minnesota. Illinois led in the production of corn. Oats were produced mainly in North Dakota. Barley came mostly form North Dakota, and Texas harvested most of the sorghum for feed.

# AGRICULTURAL COOPERATIVES

An analysis of the structural characteristics of the agricultural sector would be incomplete without an examination of agricultural cooperatives. Cooperatives add another dimension to the structure of the agricultural sector because they allow producers to operate as a single large firm for the purpose of purchasing input supplies and selling their output. These cooperative organizations were made legal by the enactment of the **Capper-Volstead Act of 1922**. This act permits farmers to organize collectively on a cooperative basis without violating antitrust laws.

## Marketing, Supply, and Service Cooperatives

Cooperatives can be classified according to their primary purpose. Marketing cooperatives assist members with the grading, sale, and packaging of their products. Farm supply cooperatives help members purchase production inputs, such as feed, fertilizer, fuel, seed, and chemicals. Service cooperatives provide producers with services such as insurance, credit, utilities, banking, water, and telephone.

**Table 2-35** examines cooperatives between 1990 and 1994. The total number of cooperatives has declined by twelve percent. This decline is made up of a thirteen percent decline in marketing cooperatives, a fourteen percent decline in supply cooperatives, and a nine percent increase in service cooperatives. The reduction was largely due to the merger activity of the individual cooperatives. Despite the decline in marketing cooperatives, the market share for all farm sales increased by seven percent. For 1994, cooperative sales represented thirty-one percent of all farm sales. This significant market share can be analyzed further by examining the distribution of sales across various size groups.

**Table 2-36** shows that about eighty percent of cooperatives are small dollar volume organizations. These cooperatives accounted for approximately eighteen percent of total sales between 1990 and 1994. Over the same time, about three percent of the cooperatives produced sixty-seven percent of total sales. From 1990 to 1994, these large cooperative have increased their market share of total cooperatives sales.

The impact that cooperatives have on different commodity groups is illustrated in **Table 2-37**. Cooperatives' share of milk purchased at the farm gate, or first handler, level for 1994 was a record-setting eighty-five percent for milk. Other shares were forty-two percent for grains, twenty-one percent for fruits and vegetables, and ten percent for livestock. The largest number of cooperatives are in grain commodities, and the smallest number are in poultry.

The geographical dispersion of agricultural commodities closely parallels their impact on their respective commodity groups. Most of the cooperatives are found in the Corn Belt states of Iowa, Minnesota, Illinois, and Nebraska. Milk cooperatives are found largely in the states of Wisconsin, New York, California, Pennsylvania, and Minnesota. California has the second largest number of cooperatives, many of which are fruit and vegetable cooperatives. The state of Texas is home to most of the livestock cooperatives. Poultry cooperatives are found in the top producing states of Arkansas, Georgia, North Carolina, Minnesota, and Alabama.

## STRUCTURAL CHARACTERISTICS

As stated earlier in this chapter, the structure of a system has a fundamental influence on the marketing decisions made by the firms it comprises. Economists typically define the structure of any system on three dimensions: the number and relative size of sellers, the nature of product offerings, and the ease with which new firms can enter the system.

### Number and Relative Size of Producers

The analysis of the agricultural sector reveals that there are a large number of producers who can be categorized into one of two distinct groups. One group is made up of a small number of large firms that, in many commodity sectors, produce a disproportionately large share of agricultural products. Agricultural cooperatives play a major role in some of the commodity subsectors because they allow many producers to operate collectively as large firms. In other subsectors, they play more of a minor role, as evidenced by their minimal share of total farm sales for the commodity.

Another group consists of a very large number of small firms that account for a small share of volume. Despite this apparent dichotomy of size, no single producer is large enough to influence the price of a commodity by acting independently. The market price of a commodity is determined by the actions of all sellers and buyers.

## Product Offerings

The output of the agricultural sector is essentially homogeneous. Products such as beef, corn, apples, milk, chicken, eggs, and salmon are examples of homogeneous commodities. Although there may be quality differences within a commodity, products with the same quality are not differentiated. Thus USDA Prime beef is of a higher quality than USDA Choice or USDA Good, but all USDA Prime beef is of the same quality. This lack of differentiation within the same quality results in buyers having no preference for one seller's USDA Prime beef over another producer's USDA Prime beef. Ultimately, the lack of a buyer preference for undifferentiated commodities means that no single seller can affect the price of the commodity.

## Ease of Entry

To determine how easy it is for potential producers to enter the agricultural sector requires an examination of the factors that prevent entry: barriers to entry. Although anything that provides the existing producers with an advantage over potential entrants is a barrier, there are four commonly recognized entry barriers.

Absolute cost advantage barriers exist if the existing producers have lower unit costs at all levels of output than can be achieved by new firms. Scale barriers exist if, in order to operate efficiently, the new firm must enter at a size that is large enough to capture the required market share. Capital cost barriers exist if the size of the initial investment required to operate an efficient firm is large. Product differentiation barriers exist if existing producers have highly differentiated products.

Even though the situation is changing, an analysis of the agricultural sector reveals that it approximates the conditions of a purely competitive market. First, there are many sellers, many of which are cooperatives, engaged in the marketing of commodities. No single producer is large enough to influence the price of the commodity. Second, buyers have no preference for undifferentiated commodities. Finally, the relatively small investment in assets required, compared to other sectors, supports "relatively easy entry" into the agricultural sector.

# SUMMARY

The average consumer today knows very little about the agricultural sector of the U.S. food marketing system. This chapter was an attempt to reduce our ignorance of the structural characteristics of the nation's largest economic sector—agriculture. This sector continues to change in ways that will affect the entire U.S. food marketing system.

Both the number of people involved in agriculture—and their percent of the population—have declined, as have, the number of farms. However, farms are now larger and, because of technology, more efficient than they have been in the past. Unfortunately, not all farm operations have been able to take advantage of these new technologies. As a consequence, the agricultural sector consists of two distinct groups. One group consists of a small number of very large, heavily capitalized farms that generate most of the agricultural product sales. The other group consists of a very large number of small farm operations generating an increasingly smaller amount of farm sales. In both groups, the family-owned farm is still the dominant type, even though cooperations have increased their share of all farm sales slightly. Finally, farms continue to be more specialized by commodity and geography. Geographical specialization is largely determined by climate, technology, costs, transportation networks, and in many cases, the availability of land.

A deeper understanding of the changing agricultural sector was gained by a structural examination of its major commodity groups or subsectors. The unique characteristics of each commodity have a strong influence on the way each subsector is organized. In general, because livestock must be bred, raised, and fed to market weight, these commodity subsectors exhibit a more complex structural arrangement than do the crop subsectors. Further, although the poultry subsector is dominated by farms that have integrated the breeding, growing, feeding, and producing stages, all of the subsectors have experienced an increase in the vertical coordination of their various markets—from input suppliers to distributors.

The conclusion that a small group of very large, heavily capitalized farms generate the majority of the farm sales is reinforced in each of the commodity subsectors. Despite the diversity of the subsectors, they all share one dominant characteristic—agricultural production is becoming concentrated in fewer, but larger, farms.

An examination of the impact of agricultural cooperatives revealed a structure that parallels the structure found in the agricultural sector. A few very large cooperatives account for the majority of cooperative sales. When analyzed by share of commodity group sales, cooperatives vary from a minor role in some to a major role in others.

Although the situation is rapidly changing, the structural organization of the agricultural sector approximates a purely competitive market. There are a large number of sellers, and a market price that cannot be influenced by the output of any single firm. These producers are engaged in the production and sale of undifferentiated commodities. The barriers to entry into the agricultural sector have not been so high as to prevent the entry of new firms.

It is within the context of an agricultural sector that approximates a purely competitive market that producers must make marketing decisions.

# SELECTED REFERENCES

Ackefors, H. A., J. V. Huner, and M. Konikoff. *Introduction to the General Principles of Aquaculture.* Binghamton, N.Y.: Food Product Press, an imprint of the Haworth Press, Inc., 1994.

*Annual Crop Summary.* National Agricultural Statistics Service. U.S. Department of Agriculture, January 1994.

*Aquaculture Situation and Outlook.* Economic Research Service. U.S. Department of Agriculture, October 1994.

*Cattle.* National Agricultural Statistic Service. U.S. Department of Agriculture, February 1994.

*Cattle Buyers Weekly.* August 30, 1993.

*Cattle on Feed.* National Agricultural Statistic Service. U.S. Department of Agriculture, February 1994.

*Fisheries of the U.S.* National Marine Fisheries Service. U.S. Department of Commerce, 1994.

*Fruit and Tree Nuts.* Yearbook Issue, Economic Research Service. U.S. Department of Agriculture, September 1994.

Harvey, D. J. *Aquaculture: Meeting Fish and Seafood Demand.* National Food Review, Economic Research Service. U.S. Department of Agriculture, October–December 1988.

Harvey, D. J. *Aquaculture: A Diverse Industry Poised for Growth.* Food Review, Economic Research Service. U.S. Department of Agriculture, October–December 1991.

Herring, H. B. "900,000 Striped Bass, and Not a Fishing Pole in Sight." *The New York Times,* 1994.

*Hogs and Pigs,* National Agricultural Statistical Service. U.S. Department of Agriculture, December 1993.

Jolly, C. M. and H. A. Clonts. *Economics of Agriculture.* Binghamton, N.Y.: Food Products Press, an imprint of the Haworth Press, 1993.

Lesser, W. H. *Marketing Livestock and Meat.* Binghamton, N.Y.: Food Products Press, an imprint of the Haworth Press, Inc., 1993.

Marion, B. W. and The NC-117 Committee. *The Organization and Performance of the U.S. Food System.* Lexington, Mass.: Lexington Books, D.C. Heath and Company, 1986.

Martin, R. E. and G. J. Flick. *The Seafood Industry.* New York, N.Y.: Van Nostrand Reinhold, 1990.

Perez, A. M. *Changing Structure of U.S. Dairy Farms.* Economic Research Service. U.S. Department of Agriculture. Agricultural Economic Report No. 690, July 1994.

*Poultry Outlook.* Economic Research Service. U.S. Department of Agriculture, May 1994.

*Sheep and Goats.* National Agricultural Statistics Service. U.S. Department of Agriculture, January 1994.

Strickland, R. P., C. Johnson, and R. P. Williams. *Ranking of States and Commodities by Cash Receipts.* Economic Research Service. U.S. Department of Agriculture, Statistical Bulletin No. 848, 1994.

*Vegetable Yearbook.* Economic Research Service. U.S. Department of Agriculture, CD-ROM # 93050, 1994.

*Watt Poultry Yearbook*, USA Edition. Mt. Morris. Ill.: Watt Publishing Co., 1994–95.

# REVIEW QUESTIONS

1. Do you think that the number of producers, farms, and ranches will continue to decline? Why or why not?

2. The agricultural sector is made up of two distinct groups of producers. Explain.

3. The major commodity groups have all experienced a decline in the number of producers. What implications does this have for the agricultural sector?

4. What is aquaculture? Does it have a future in the American diet?

5. What three factors are typically used to identify a sector's organizational structure?

6. How would you characterize the structural organization of the agricultural sector?

7. The market price of the commodity is determined by the actions of all the sellers and buyers. Explain

8. Agricultural output consists of undifferentiated commodities. How does this affect producers?

9. What impact do "barriers to entry" have on existing producers?

10. What do you think the agricultural sector will look like in the future?

**TABLE 2-1.** SELECTED TRENDS IN U.S. AGRICULTURE

|  | **1982** | **1987** | **1992** |
|---|---|---|---|
| FARM POPULATION (THOUSANDS) | 5,628 | 4,986 | 4,665 |
| PERCENT OF U.S. POPULATION ON FARMS | 2.5 | 2.1 | 1.9 |
| NUMBER OF FARMS | 2,240,976 | 2,087,759 | 1,925,300 |
| AVERAGE FARM SIZE (ACRES) | 440 | 462 | 491 |
| CROPLAND (THOUSANDS OF ACRES) | 445,362 | 443,318 | 435,366 |
| PASTURELAND AND RANCHLAND (THOUSANDS OF ACRES) | 374,514 | 410,329 | 411,306 |
| FARM EFFICIENCY (PERSONS FED PER FARM WORKER)* | 118 | 123 | 131 |

*USDA ESTIMATE.

*SOURCE:* CENSUS OF AGRICULTURE 1982, 1987, 1992, AND 1993 STATISTIC ABSTRACT OF U.S. RESIDENCE OF FARM AND RURAL POPULATION 1992 FORTHCOMING.

**TABLE 2-2.** PERCENT OF FARMS AND VALUE OF PRODUCTS SOLD

| VALUE OF SALES | 1982 | | 1987 | | 1992 | |
| --- | --- | --- | --- | --- | --- | --- |
| | % OF FARMS | % of SALES | % OF FARMS | % OF SALES | % OF FARMS | % OF SALES |
| LESS THAN $10,000 | 48.2 | 3.2 | 49.2 | 2.5 | 47.1 | 1.9 |
| $10,000 - $49,999 | 26.3 | 11.0 | 26.1 | 9.6 | 25.8 | 7.3 |
| $50,000 - 99,999 | 11.2 | 13.7 | 10.4 | 11.5 | 9.8 | 8.3 |
| $100,000 - $249,999 | 9.6 | 30.3 | 9.7 | 22.9 | 10.8 | 20.1 |
| $250,000 - $499,999 | 2.6 | 15.1 | 2.9 | 15.2 | 4.1 | 16.5 |
| $500,000 - OR MORE | 1.2 | 32.4 | 1.5 | 38.2 | 2.4 | 45.9 |

*SOURCE:* CENSUS OF AGRICULTURE 1982, 1987, AND 1992.

**TABLE 2-3.** FARM SALES BY TYPE OF ORGANIZATION

| DESCRIPTION | 1982 | | 1987 | | 1992 | |
| --- | --- | --- | --- | --- | --- | --- |
| | % OF FARMS | % OF SALES | % OF FARMS | % OF SALES | % OF FARMS | % OF SALES |
| INDIVIDUAL OR FAMILY | 87 | 59 | 87 | 57 | 86 | 54 |
| PARTNERSHIP | 10 | 17 | 10 | 17 | 10 | 18 |
| CORPORATION | 3 | 24 | 3 | 26 | 4 | 28 |
| ALL FARMS | 100 | 100 | 100 | 100 | 100 | 100 |

*SOURCE:* CENSUS OF AGRICULTURE 1982, 1987, 1992

**TABLE 2-4.** FARM SPECIALIZATION BY COMMODITY

| TYPE OF FARMS | 1982 | | 1987 | | 1992 | |
|---|---|---|---|---|---|---|
| | % OF FARMS | SHARE OF SALES* | % OF FARMS | SHARE OF SALES* | % OF FARMS | SHARE OF SALES* |
| CASH GRAIN | 25.7 | 85.8 | 22.0 | 86 | 21.0 | 86.7 |
| FIELD CROPS | 11.3 | 95.6 | 11.7 | 96.1 | 13.0 | 96.2 |
| VEGETABLES AND MELONS | 1.4 | 86.1 | 1.4 | 87.3 | 1.5 | 88.0 |
| FRUIT AND TREE NUTS | 3.8 | 95.1 | 4.2 | 96.2 | 4.6 | 96.7 |
| HORTICULTURAL SPECIALITY | 1.3 | 98.1 | 1.5 | 98.5 | 2.1 | 98.5 |
| LIVESTOCK | 40.5 | 88.0 | 42.7 | 89.2 | 42.0 | 90.3 |
| DAIRY | 7.3 | 84.0 | 6.6 | 84.2 | 5.9 | 84.3 |
| POULTRY AND EGGS | 1.9 | 95.1 | 1.8 | 96.3 | 1.8 | 96.3 |
| ANIMAL SPECIALITY | 2.9 | 95.2 | 4.2 | 96.6 | 4.2 | 96.3 |
| TOTAL | 96.1 | 96.6 | 96.1 | 97.1 | 96.2 | 97.2 |
| OTHER FARMS | 3.9 | 2% | 3.9 | 2% | 3.8 | 2% |

*SALES FROM PRIMARY COMMODITY.

*SOURCE:* CENSUS OF AGRICULTURE 1982, 1987, AND 1992.

**TABLE 2-5.** U.S. BEEF COW OPERATIONS AND INVENTORY

| YEAR | BEEF COW OPERATIONS (thousands) | BEEF COW INVENTORY (thousands) |
|---|---|---|
| 1991 | 913,620 | 33,271 |
| 1992 | 907,230 | 33,775 |
| 1993 | 910,080 | 33,888 |
| 1994 | 906,810 | 34,650 |
| 1995 | 909,130 | 35,156 |

*SOURCE:* CATTLE JULY 1991, 1992, AND 1993; FEB 1996, AGRICULTURAL BOARD, NASS, USDA.

**TABLE 2-6.** U.S. BEEF COW OPERATIONS (PERCENT BY SIZE GROUP)

| HEAD | 1991 | 1992 | 1993 | 1994 | 1995 |
|---|---|---|---|---|---|
| 1-49 | 81.2 | 81.0 | 80.7 | 80.5 | 80.0 |
| 50-99 | 11.2 | 11.2 | 11.3 | 11.4 | 11.6 |
| 100-499 | 7.6 | 7.8 | 7.3 | 7.5 | 7.7 |
| 500+ | N/A | N/A | .7 | .6 | .6 |
| TOTAL | 100.0 | 100.0 | 100.0 | 100.0 | 100.0 |

*DATA FOR OPERATIONS WITH 500+ HEAD AVAILABLE ONLY FROM 1993.

*SOURCE:* CATTLE, FEB. 1992, 1993, 1994, AND 1996 AGRICULTURAL STATISTICS BOARD, NASS, USDA.

**TABLE 2-7.** U.S. BEEF COW INVENTORY (PERCENT BY SIZE GROUP)

| HEAD | 1991 | 1992 | 1993 | 1994 | 1995 |
|---|---|---|---|---|---|
| 1-49 | 33.1 | 32.6 | 32.6 | 31.6 | 31.0 |
| 50-99 | 19.9 | 19.6 | 19.5 | 19.4 | 19.2 |
| 100-499 | 47.0 | 47.8 | 35.0 | 34.7 | 35.6 |
| 500+ | N/A | N/A | 12.9 | 14.3 | 14.2 |
| TOTAL | 100.0 | 100.0 | 100.0 | 100.0 | 100.0 |

*DATA FOR OPERATIONS WITH 500+ HEAD AVAILABLE ONLY FOR 1993.

SOURCE: CATTLE, FEB. 1992, 1993, 1994, AND 1996, AGRICULTURAL STATISTICAL BOARD, NASS, USDA.


**TABLE 2-8.** U.S. FEEDLOTS AND MARKETINGS

| YEAR | FEEDLOTS | MARKETINGS (thousands of head) |
|---|---|---|
| 1991 | 46,851 | 22,388 |
| 1992 | 46,446 | 22,059 |
| 1993 | 44,270 | 22,316 |
| 1994 | 43,332 | 22,979 |
| 1995 | 41,365 | 23,365 |

SOURCE: CATTLE ON FEED, FEB. 1993, 1994, AND 1996, AGRICULTURAL STATISTICS BOARD, NASS, USDA.

**TABLE 2-9.** U.S. FEEDLOT OPERATIONS (PERCENT BY SIZE GROUP)

| HEAD | 1991 | 1992 | 1993 | 1994 | 1995 |
|---|---|---|---|---|---|
| 1-999 | 96.37 | 96.14 | 96.00 | 95.18 | 95.32 |
| 1000-3999 | 2.34 | 2.49 | 2.60 | 2.87 | 3.13 |
| 4000-23999 | .98 | 1.06 | 1.07 | 1.16 | 1.20 |
| 24000+ | .31 | .31 | .33 | .32 | .35 |
| TOTAL | 100.00 | 100.00 | 100.00 | 100.00 | 100.00 |

*SOURCE:* COMPUTED FROM CATTLE ON FEED, FEB. 1993, 1994, AND 1996, AGRICULTURAL STATISTICS BOARD, NASS, USDA.

**TABLE 2-10.** U.S. FEEDLOT MARKETINGS (PERCENT BY SIZE GROUP)

| HEAD | 1991 | 1992 | 1993 | 1994 | 1995 |
|---|---|---|---|---|---|
| 1-999 | 15.13 | 12.83 | 12.73 | 11.23 | 9.71 |
| 1000-3999 | 9.82 | 10.37 | 9.65 | 9.64 | 9.43 |
| 4000-23999 | 31.13 | 30.20 | 30.32 | 30.49 | 31.67 |
| 24000+ | 43.92 | 46.60 | 47.39 | 48.64 | 49.19 |
| TOTAL | 100.00 | 100.00 | 100.00 | 100.00 | 100.00 |

*SOURCE:* COMPUTED FROM CATTLE ON FEED, FEB. 1993, 1994, AND 1996, AGRICULTURAL STATISTICS BOARD, NASS, USDA.

**TABLE 2-11.** U.S. HOG/PIG OPERATIONS AND INVENTORY

| YEAR | HOG/PIG OPERATIONS | HOG/PIG INVENTORY (THOUSANDS) |
|---|---|---|
| 1991 | 253,890 | 57,684 |
| 1992 | 248,700 | 58,116 |
| 1993 | 235,840 | 56,768 |
| 1994 | 207,980 | 59,992 |
| 1995 | 182,700 | 60,190 |

*SOURCE:* HOGS AND PIGS, DEC. 1992, 1993, AND 1995, AGRICULTURAL STATISTICS BOARD, NASS, USDA.


**TABLE 2-12.** U.S. HOG/PIG OPERATIONS (PERCENT BY SIZE GROUP)

| HEAD | 1991 | 1992 | 1993 | 1994 | 1995 |
|---|---|---|---|---|---|
| 1-99 | 62.0 | 60.6 | 62.1 | 60.0 | 59.6 |
| 100-499 | 26.0 | 26.5 | 24.8 | 25.5 | 25.1 |
| 500-999 | 7.7 | 7.9 | 8.0 | 8.5 | 8.6 |
| 1000+ | 4.3 | 3.5 | 3.4 | 3.9 | 4.2 |
| 2000+ | N/A | 1.5 | 1.7 | 2.2 | 2.6 |
| TOTAL | 100.0 | 100.0 | 100.0 | 100.0 | 100.0 |

*DATA FOR OPERATIONS WITH 2000+ HEAD NOT AVAILABLE FOR 1991.

*SOURCE:* HOGS AND PIGS, DECEMBER 1992, 1993, 1995, AND 1996, AGRICULTURAL STATISTICAL BOARD, NASS, USDA.

**TABLE 2-13.** U.S. HOG/PIG INVENTORY (PERCENT BY SIZE GROUP)

| HEAD | 1991 | 1992 | 1993 | 1994 | 1995 |
|---|---|---|---|---|---|
| 1-99 | 5.5 | 5.5 | 5.5 | 4.5 | 4.00 |
| 100-499 | 26.5 | 25.5 | 23.0 | 20.5 | 18.0 |
| 500-999 | 24.0 | 22.0 | 21.5 | 20.0 | 18.0 |
| 1000-1999 | 44.0 | 19.0 | 17.0 | 18.0 | 17.0 |
| 2000+ | N/A | 28.0 | 33.0 | 37.0 | 43.3 |
| TOTAL | 100.0 | 100.0 | 100.0 | 100.0 | 100.0 |

*DATA FOR OPERATIONS WITH 2000+ HEAD, NOT AVAILABLE FOR 1991.

SOURCE: HOGS AND PIGS, DECEMBER 1992, 1993, 1995, AND 1996, AGRICULTURAL STATISTICAL BOARD, NASS, USDA.


**TABLE 2-14.** U.S. SHEEP/LAMB OPERATIONS AND INVENTORY

| YEAR | SHEEP/LAMB OPERATIONS | SHEEP/LAMB INVENTORY (thousands) |
|---|---|---|
| 1991 | 105,090 | 11,200 |
| 1992 | 97,890 | 10,750 |
| 1993 | 93,280 | 10,013 |
| 1994 | 87,150 | 9,714 |
| 1995 | 82,120 | 8,885 |

SOURCE: SHEEP AND GOATS, JAN. 1992-1996, AGRICULTURAL STATISTICS BOARD, NASS, USDA.

**TABLE 2-15.** U.S. SHEEP/LAMB OPERATIONS (PERCENT BY SIZE GROUP)

| HEAD | 1991 | 1992 | 1993 | 1994 | 1995 |
|---|---|---|---|---|---|
| 1-99 | 88.0 | 89.3 | 90.3 | 89.7 | 91.3 |
| 100-499 | 9.5 | 8.2 | 7.7 | 8.2 | 6.7 |
| 500-4999 | 2.3 | 2.3 | 1.9 | 2.1 | 2.0 |
| 5000+ | .2 | .2 | .1 | .1 | .1 |
| TOTAL | 100.0 | 100.0 | 100.0 | 100.0 | 100.0 |

*SOURCE:* SHEEP AND GOATS, JANUARY 1992-1996, AGRICULTURAL STATISTICAL BOARD, NASS, USDA.


**TABLE 2-16.** U.S. SHEEP/LAMB INVENTORY (PERCENT BY SIZE GROUP)

| HEAD | 1991 | 1992 | 1993 | 1994 | 1995 |
|---|---|---|---|---|---|
| 1-99 | 23.3 | 20.7 | 21.9 | 22.3 | 24.1 |
| 100-499 | 21.9 | 20.4 | 21.1 | 22.9 | 19.9 |
| 500-4999 | 37.3 | 38.9 | 35.8 | 38.4 | 41.4 |
| 5000+ | 17.5 | 20.0 | 21.2 | 16.4 | 14.6 |
| TOTAL | 100.0 | 100.0 | 100.0 | 100.0 | 100.0 |

*SOURCE:* SHEEP AND GOATS, JANUARY 1992, 1993, 1994, AND 1996, AGRICULTURAL STATISTICAL BOARD, NASS, USDA.

**TABLE 2-17.** U.S. BROILER HATCHERIES AND INVENTORY CAPACITY BY STANDARD INDUSTRIAL CLASSIFICATIONS*

| Census Year | Broiler Hatcheries | Inventory Capacity (millions) | Average Capacity (thousands) |
|---|---|---|---|
| 1982 | 460 | 456.0 | 991.3 |
| 1987 | 385 | 486.7 | 1,263.3 |
| 1992 | 427 | 598.4 | 1,401.4 |

*ESTABLISHMENTS WITH FIFTY PERCENT OR MORE OF TOTAL SALES FROM SINGLE (FOUR-DIGIT) AGRICULTURAL COMMODITY.

SOURCE: CENSUS OF AGRICULTURE 1982, 1987, AND 1992; POULTRY PRODUCTION AND VALUE, MAY 1982, 1987, AND 1992.

**TABLE 2-18.** U.S. BROILER FARM OPERATIONS AND INVENTORY BY STANDARD INDUSTRIAL CLASSIFICATIONS*

| Census Year | Broiler Farm Operations | Broiler Inventory (billions) | Average Flock Size |
|---|---|---|---|
| 1982 | 19,100 | 4.149 | 217,224 |
| 1987 | 19,264 | 5.004 | 259,736 |
| 1992 | 18,284 | 6.403 | 350,196 |

*ESTABLISHMENTS WITH FIFTY PERCENT OR MORE OF TOTAL SALES FROM SINGLE (FOUR-DIGIT) AGRICULTURAL COMMODITY.

SOURCE: CENSUS OF AGRICULTURE 1982, 1987, AND 1992; POULTRY PRODUCTION AND VALUE MAY 1982, 1987, AND 1992.

**TABLE 2-19.** U.S. LAYER FARM OPERATIONS AND INVENTORY AND EGGS PRODUCED BY STANDARD INDUSTRIAL CLASSIFICATIONS*

| Census Year | Layer Farm Operations | Layer Inventory (millions) | Average Layer Inventory | Number of Eggs Produced (billions) | Eggs Per Layer |
|---|---|---|---|---|---|
| 1982 | 17,570 | 286.4 | 16,299 | 69.6 | 243 |
| 1987 | 13,343 | 280.6 | 21,027 | 70.3 | 251 |
| 1992 | 10,636 | 277.9 | 26,128 | 70.5 | 254 |

* ESTABLISHMENTS WITH FIFTY PERCENT OR MORE OF TOTAL SALES FROM SINGLE (FOUR-DIGIT) AGRICULTURAL COMMODITY.

SOURCE: CENSUS OF AGRICULTURE 1982, 1987, AND 1992; POULTRY PRODUCTION AND VALUE, MAY 1982, 1987, AND 1992.

**TABLE 2-20.** U.S. TURKEY HATCHERIES AND INVENTORY CAPACITY

| Census Year | Turkey Hatcheries | Inventory Capacity (millions) | Average Capacity |
|---|---|---|---|
| 1982 | 101 | 37.9 | 375,248 |
| 1987 | 81 | 41.5 | 512,346 |
| 1992 | 77 | 48.9 | 635,065 |

SOURCE: WATT POULTRY YEARBOOK USA EDITION 1994-95.

**TABLE 2-21.** U.S. TURKEY FARM OPERATIONS AND INVENTORY BY STANDARD INDUSTRIAL CLASSIFICATION*

| Census Year | Turkey Farm Operations | Turkey Inventory (millions) | Average Flock Size (thousands) |
|---|---|---|---|
| 1982 | 2,728 | 165.5 | 60,654 |
| 1987 | 3,239 | 240.4 | 74,232 |
| 1992 | 3,361 | 289.0 | 85,986 |

*ESTABLISHMENTS WITH FIFTY PERCENT OR MORE OF TOTAL SALES FROM SINGLE (FOUR-DIGIT) AGRICULTURAL COMMODITY.

SOURCE: CENSUS OF AGRICULTURE 1982, 1987, AND 1992; POULTRY PRODUCTION AND VALUE, MAY 1982, 1987, AND 1992.


**TABLE 2-22.** COMMERCIAL LANDINGS INSIDE/OUTSIDE U.S. AND TOTAL SUPPLY

| YEAR | INSIDE U.S. Edible (billion lbs.) | Industrial* (billion lbs.) | TOTAL | OUTSIDE Edible/Industrial (billion lbs.) | TOTAL Inside/Outside |
|---|---|---|---|---|---|
| 1991 | 7.0 | 2.5 | 9.5 | 0.7 | 10.2 |
| 1992 | 7.6 | 2.0 | 9.6 | 0.6 | 10.2 |
| 1993 | 8.2 | 2.3 | 10.5 | 0.5 | 11.0 |
| 1994 | 7.9 | 2.5 | 10.5 | 0.5 | 11.0 |
| 1995 | 7.8 | 2.1 | 9.9 | 0.5 | 10.4 |

*PRIMARILY MENHADEN SPECIES.

SOURCE: FISHERIES OF THE UNITED STATES, MAY 1991-1994, AUGUST 1995, MAY 1996; U.S. DEPARTMENT OF COMMERCE, NATIONAL MARINE FISHERIES SERVICE (NMFS).

**TABLE 2-23.** U.S. SUPPLY (DOMESTIC LANDINGS PLUS IMPORTS IN BILLIONS OF POUNDS)

| YEAR | Total Supply | Total Imports | Imports % of Total Supply |
|---|---|---|---|
| 1991 | 16.3 | 6.8 | 42.0 |
| 1992 | 16.1 | 6.5 | 40.0 |
| 1993 | 20.3 | 9.8 | 48.3 |
| 1994 | 19.3 | 8.8 | 45.8 |
| 1995 | 16.6 | 6.7 | 40.3 |

*SOURCE:* FISHERIES OF THE UNITED STATES MAY 1991-1995; U.S. DEPARTMENT OF COMMERCE (NMFS).


**TABLE 2-24.** COMMERCIAL LANDINGS INSIDE AND OUTSIDE THE U.S.

| SPECIES | 1991 % | 1992 % | 1993 % | 1994 % | 1995 % |
|---|---|---|---|---|---|
| Alaska Pollock | 30.1 | 30.6 | 31.3 | 29.9 | 28.9 |
| Menhaden | 20.8 | 17.1 | 18.9 | 22.2 | 18.6 |
| Salmon | 8.3 | 7.4 | 8.5 | 8.6 | 11.5 |
| Crabs | 6.8 | 6.5 | 5.8 | 4.3 | 3.7 |
| Cod | 6.8 | 8.4 | 5.2 | 4.8 | 6.3 |
| Flounder | 4.3 | 6.7 | 5.7 | 4.1 | 4.3 |
| Shrimp | 3.4 | 3.5 | 2.8 | 2.7 | 3.1 |
| Other | 19.5 | 21.8 | 22.0 | 23.4 | 23.6 |
| TOTAL | 100.0 | 100.0 | 100.0 | 100.0 | 100.0 |

*SOURCE:* FISHERIES OF THE UNITED STATES 1991-1995; U.S. DEPARTMENT OF COMMERCE (NMFS).

**TABLE 2-25.** COMMERCIAL FISHING VESSELS AND BOATS BY REGIONS*

| REGIONS | 1990 | 1991 | 1992 | 1993 | 1994 |
|---|---|---|---|---|---|
| Northeast | 24,471 | 20,141 | 23,233 | 23,071 | 22,922 |
| South Atlantic And Gulf | 37,259 | 38,896 | 39,784 | 48,496 | 46,010 |
| West Coast | 34,025 | 32,467 | 31,075 | 32,937 | 32,088 |
| Great Lakes | 371 | 373 | 367 | 394 | 382 |
| TOTAL | 96,126 | 91,877 | 94,459 | 104,898 | 101,402 |

*VESSELS ARE CRAFT GREATER THAN FIVE NET REGISTERED TONS

*BOATS ARE CRAFT LESS THAN FIVE NET REGISTERED TONS

SOURCE: FISHERIES OF THE UNITED STATES 1992, 1995, AND 1996; U.S. DEPT OF COMMERCE (NMFS).


**TABLE 2-26.** U.S. DOMESTIC LANDINGS BY REGIONS

| REGION | 1991 | 1992 | 1993 | 1994 | 1995 |
|---|---|---|---|---|---|
| New England | 6.8 | 6.7 | 5.8 | 5.3 | 6.0 |
| Mid Atlantic | 2.5 | 2.7 | 2.5 | 2.4 | 2.4 |
| Chesapeake | 8.1 | 7.1 | 7.8 | 6.2 | 8.5 |
| South Atlantic | 3.1 | 2.5 | 2.4 | 2.7 | 2.8 |
| Gulf | 17.7 | 14.8 | 16.4 | 20.6 | 14.8 |
| Pacific Coast and Alaska | 61.1 | 65.6 | 64.6 | 62.2 | 64.9 |
| Great Lakes | .4 | .3 | .3 | .3 | .3 |
| Hawaii | .3 | .3 | .3 | .3. | .3 |
| TOTAL | 100.0 | 100.0 | 100.0 | 100.0 | 100.0 |

SOURCE: FISHERIES OF THE UNITED STATES 1992-1996; U.S. DEPARTMENT OF COMMERCE (NMFS).

**TABLE 2-27.** U.S. AQUACULTURE PRODUCTION (MILLION POUNDS)

| SPECIES | 1990 | 1991 | 1992 | 1993 | 1994 |
|---|---|---|---|---|---|
| FIN FISH: | | | | | |
| Bait Fish | 21.6 | 21.2 | 20.6 | 20.6 | 21.7 |
| Cat Fish | 360.4 | 390.9 | 457.4 | 459.0 | 439.3 |
| Salmon | 9.1 | 16.8 | 23.9 | 25.3 | 24.7 |
| Trout | 56.8 | 59.4 | 56.3 | 54.6 | 52.1 |
| SHELL FISH: | | | | | |
| Clams | 3.7 | 3.8 | 4.3 | 6.1 | 4.8 |
| Crawfish | 71.0 | 60.6 | 63.0 | 56.8 | 49.1 |
| Mussels | .6 | .2 | .2 | .3 | .4 |
| Oysters | 22.2 | 20.6 | 24.0 | 24.4 | 28.0 |
| Shrimp (fw) | .4 | .4 | .3 | .4 | .3 |
| Shrimp (sw) | 1.9 | 3.5 | 4.4 | 6.6 | 4.4 |
| Miscellaneous | 24.7 | 26.7 | 36.7 | 24.7 | 40.7 |
| TOTALS | 572.5 | 604.1 | 691.2 | 678.2 | 665.6 |

NOTE: FW (FRESH WATER), SW (SALT WATER), AMD MISCELLANEOUS. INCLUDES ORNAMENTAL FISH, HYBRID STRIPED BASS, TILAPIA, ALLIGATORS, AND OTHERS

*SOURCE:* FISHERIES OF THE UNITED STATES, 1995, U.S. DEPARTMENT OF COMMERCE, (NMFS), JULY 1996.

**TABLE 2-28.** U.S. AQUACULTURE (CATFISH AND TROUT)

| YEAR | CATFISH OPERATIONS | TROUT OPERATIONS |
|---|---|---|
| 1991 | 1,818 | 450 |
| 1992 | 1,886 | 461 |
| 1993 | 1,527 | 452 |
| 1994 | 1,404 | 466 |
| 1995 | 1,267 | 434 |
| 1996 | 1,320 | 423 |

SOURCE: TROUT PRODUCTION, SEPTEMBER 1996; CATFISH PRODUCTION, APRIL 1996; AGRICULTURAL STATISTICAL BOARD, NASS, USDA.


**TABLE 2-29.** U.S. FRUIT BERRIES AND TREE NUTS BY SIZE OF FARM AND SALES*

| | CENSUS YEARS | | | | | |
|---|---|---|---|---|---|---|
| | 1982 | | 1987 | | 1992 | |
| Farm Acres | % of Farms | % of Sales | % of Farms | % of Sales | % of Farms | % of Sales |
|---|---|---|---|---|---|---|
| 1-99 | 80.9 | 22.3 | 80.7 | 22.7 | 80.7 | 20.5 |
| 100-199 | 10.8 | 15.6 | 11.0 | 16.3 | 10.8 | 15.6 |
| 200-499 | 5.1 | 15.9 | 5.0 | 15.8 | 5.1 | 16.6 |
| 500-999 | 1.8 | 12.2 | 2.0 | 12.8 | 2.0 | 13.2 |
| 1,000-1,999 | 0.8 | 10.4 | 0.8 | 9.9 | 0.8 | 10.9 |
| 2,000+ | 0.6 | 22.4 | 0.5 | 22.4 | 0.6 | 23.1 |
| TOTAL | 100.0 | 100.0 | 100.0 | 100.0 | 100.0 | 100.0 |

*FARMS THAT DERIVE FIFTY PERCENT OR MORE OF SALES FROM SINGLE COMMODITY GROUP (INDUSTRY CODE 017).

SOURCE: CENSUS OF AGRICULTURE 1982, 1987, AND 1992.

**TABLE 2-30.** U.S. VEGETABLES BY SIZE OF FARM AND SALES*

|  | CENSUS YEARS | | | | | |
|---|---|---|---|---|---|---|
|  | 1982 | | 1987 | | 1992 | |
| Farm Acres | % of Farms | % of Sales | % of Farms | % of Sales | % of Farms | % of Sales |
|---|---|---|---|---|---|---|
| 1-99 | 70.5 | 8.5 | 66.1 | 8.0 | 66.0 | 6.8 |
| 100-199 | 14.9 | 8.1 | 15.9 | 7.9 | 15.7 | 7.0 |
| 200-499 | 7.8 | 14.5 | 9.6 | 14.8 | 9.3 | 12.4 |
| 500-999 | 3.9 | 18.2 | 4.9 | 18.9 | 5.0 | 17.0 |
| 1,000-1,999 | 1.9 | 18.9 | 2.3 | 19.7 | 2.4 | 19.2 |
| 2,000+ | 1.1 | 31.8 | 1.3 | 30.7 | 1.6 | 17.6 |
| TOTAL | 100.0 | 100.0 | 100.0 | 100.0 | 100.0 | 100.0 |

*FARMS THAT DERIVE FIFTY PERCENT OR MORE OF SALES FROM SINGLE COMMODITY GROUP (INDUSTRY CODE 016).

*SOURCE:* CENSUS OF AGRICULTURE 1982, 1987, AND 1992.


**TABLE 2-31.** U.S. MILK-COW OPERATIONS AND INVENTORY

| YEAR | Milk-Cow Operation | Milk-Cow Inventory (thousands) | Milk-Cow Production (millions of lbs.) | Average Milk per Cow (lbs.) |
|---|---|---|---|---|
| 1991 | 181,270 | 9,992 | 148,477 | 14,860 |
| 1992 | 171,560 | 9,839 | 151,647 | 15,413 |
| 1993 | 162,450 | 9,705 | 150,954 | 15,554 |
| 1994 | 148,690 | 9,528 | 153,664 | 16,128 |
| 1995 | 140,090 | 9,487 | 155,644 | 16,406 |

*SOURCE:* CATTLE, JULY 1991 AND 1992, FEB. 1994 AND 1996, AGRICULTURAL STATISTICAL BOARD, NASS., CHANGING STRUCTURE OF U.S. DAIRY FARMS (NO. 690) ERS, USDA.

**TABLE 2-32.** U.S. MILK-COW OPERATIONS (PERCENT BY SIZE GROUP)

| HEAD | 1991 | 1992 | 1993 | 1994 | 1995 |
|---|---|---|---|---|---|
| 1-29 | 39.8 | 38.9 | 37.6 | 35.8 | 34.3 |
| 30-49 | 22.8 | 22.1 | 21.9 | 22.0 | 22.2 |
| 50-99 | 25.9 | 26.0 | 26.9 | 27.7 | 27.9 |
| 100+ | 11.5 | 13.0 | 13.6 | 14.5 | 15.5 |
| TOTAL | 100.0 | 100.0 | 100.0 | 100.0 | 100.0 |

*SOURCE:* CATTLE, JULY 1992 AND 1993, FEB. 1994 AND 1996, AGRICULTURAL STATISTICAL BOARD, NASS. USDA.


**TABLE 2-33.** U.S. MILK-COW INVENTORY (PERCENT BY SIZE GROUP)

| HEAD | 1991 | 1992 | 1993 | 1994 | 1995 |
|---|---|---|---|---|---|
| 1-29 | 6.3 | 5.5 | 5.1 | 4.6 | 4.0 |
| 30-49 | 16.6 | 15.2 | 14.8 | 14.0 | 13.0 |
| 50-99 | 31.7 | 30.0 | 29.6 | 28.7 | 28.0 |
| 100+ | 45.4 | 49.2 | 50.5 | 52.7 | 55.0 |
| TOTALQ | 100.0 | 100.0 | 100.0 | 100.0 | 100.0 |

*SOURCE:* CATTLE, JULY 1992 AND 1993, FEB. 1994 AND 1996, AGRICULTURAL STATISTICAL BOARD, NASS, USDA.

**TABLE 2-34.** U.S. GRAINS BY SIZE OF FARMS AND SALES*

| | CENSUS YEARS | | | | | |
|---|---|---|---|---|---|---|
| | 1982 | | 1987 | | 1992 | |
| Farm Acres | % of Farms | % of Sales | % of Farms | % of Sales | % of Farms | % of Sales |
| 1-99 | 25.4 | 2.8 | 22.5 | 2.3 | 20.6 | 1.8 |
| 100-199 | 21.5 | 7.7 | 21.1 | 6.7 | 20.1 | 5.6 |
| 200-499 | 24.7 | 22.3 | 24.5 | 19.9 | 23.4 | 16.4 |
| 500-999 | 16.2 | 27.2 | 17.8 | 28.7 | 18.8 | 27.1 |
| 1,000-1,999 | 8.3 | 21.6 | 9.8 | 24.5 | 11.5 | 27.1 |
| 2,000+ | 3.9 | 18.4 | 4.3 | 17.9 | 5.6 | 22.0 |
| TOTAL | 100.0 | 100.0 | 100.0 | 100.0 | 100.0 | 100.0 |

*FARMS WHICH DERIVE FIFTY PERCENT OR MORE OF SALES FROM SINGLE COMMODITY GROUP (INDUSTRY CODE 011).

*SOURCE:* CENSUS OF AGRICULTURE 1982, 1987, AND 1992.

**TABLE 2-35.** AGRICULTURAL COOPERATIVES AND SHARE OF FARM PRODUCT MARKETINGS

| YEAR | TOTAL COOPS | MARKETING COOP | FARM SUPPLIES | SERVICE COOPS | % OF TOTAL FARM PRODUCT MARKETINGS |
|---|---|---|---|---|---|
| 1990 | 4,663 | 2,519 | 1,717 | 427 | 26 |
| 1991 | 4,494 | 2,384 | 1,689 | 421 | 27 |
| 1992 | 4,315 | 2,218 | 1,618 | 479 | 27 |
| 1993 | 4,244 | 2,214 | 1,547 | 483 | 30 |
| 1994 | 4,174 | 2,173 | 1,496 | 505 | 31 |

*SOURCE:* FARMERS COOPERATIVE STATISTICS 1990 - 93; FARMER COOPERATIVE, MAY 1992, FEBRUARY 1995.

**TABLE 2-36.** AGRICULTURAL COOPERATIVES BY SIZE AND DOLLAR VOLUME

| VOL. ($ thousands) | 1990 NO. % | 1990 VOL. % | 1991 NO. % | 1991 VOL. % | 1992 NO. % | 1992 VOL. % | 1993 NO. % | 1993 VOL. % | 1994 NO. % | 1994 VOL. % |
|---|---|---|---|---|---|---|---|---|---|---|
| 5 | 59 | 6 | 60 | 5 | 56 | 5 | 55 | 5 | 52 | 4 |
| 5 - 9.9 | 18 | 7 | 18 | 6 | 20 | 7 | 19 | 6 | 20 | 6 |
| 10 - 14.9 | 7 | 4 | 7 | 4 | 8 | 4 | 9 | 5 | 8 | 4 |
| 15 - 99.9 | 13 | 19 | 13 | 19 | 14 | 20 | 15 | 20 | 17 | 21 |
| 100 - 249.9 | 1 | 9 | 1 | 9 | 1 | 10 | 1 | 10 | 1 | 9 |
| 250 - 999.9 | 1 | 30 | 1 | 30 | 1 | 26 | 1 | 26 | 1 | 25 |
| 1000 | .2 | 26 | .2 | 26 | .3 | 28 | .3 | 29 | .3 | 31 |
| TOTAL | 100 | 100 | 100 | 100 | 100 | 100 | 100 | 100 | 100 | 100 |

*MAJORITY OF NUMBERS ROUNDED TO THE NEAREST WHOLE NUMBER.

*SOURCE:* FARMERS COOPERATIVE STATISTICS 1990,–1994.


**TABLE 2-37.** AGRICULTURE COMMODITY GROUP AND SHARE OF FARM-PRODUCT MARKETINGS

| YEAR | LIVE STOCK NO. | LIVE STOCK % | POULTRY NO. | POULTRY % | FRUITS & VEGETABLES NO. | FRUITS & VEGETABLES % | MILK NO. | MILK % | GRAINS NO. | GRAINS % |
|---|---|---|---|---|---|---|---|---|---|---|
| 1990 | 235 | 9 | 12 | * | 297 | 18 | 264 | 82 | 1,400 | 38 |
| 1991 | 194 | 8 | 13 | * | 299 | 18 | 264 | 81 | 1,287 | 38 |
| 1992 | 108 | 9 | 13 | * | 290 | 18 | 265 | 82 | 1,243 | 38 |
| 1993 | 106 | 10 | 13 | * | 282 | 21 | 258 | 85 | 1,193 | 42 |
| 1994 | 100 | 13 | 17 | * | 247 | 20 | 288 | 86 | 1,159 | 40 |

*DATA NOT REPORTED

*SOURCE:* FARMERS COOPERATIVE STATISTICS 1990–1993; FARMER COOPERATIVES MAY 1992, FEBRUARY 1995.

# Chapter 3

# Marketing Decisions

**Chapter Outline**

Agricultural Sector
    A. Historical Perspective
    B. Structural Influence on Marketing Decisions

Product Decisions
    A. What to Produce
    B. How Much to Produce
    C. When to Produce
    D. Where to Produce

Price Decisions
    A. Price Discovery Systems
    B. Price Patterns
    C. Law of One Price

Promotion Decisions
    A. Generic Promotion
    B. Generic Advertising
    C. Advertising Decisions

　　　　D. Generic Advertisers
Distribution Decisions
　　　　A. Product Discrepancy
　　　　B. Spatial Discrepancy
　　　　C. Temporal Discrepancy
Summary

The changing nature of the agricultural sector's structural characteristics was examined in Chapter 2. Over the years, the number of people engaged in farming—and the number of farms—have declined while farm size, efficiency, and specialization have increased. Together these changes have produced an agricultural sector comprising two distinct producer groups. A few large scale operations generate most of the farm sales and a large number of small farms account for an increasingly smaller percentage of agricultural product sales. An examination of particular commodity subsectors reinforced the coexistence of these two distinct producer groups.

The structural organization of the agricultural sector was characterized as having a large number of producers—many of which are cooperatives—involved in the production of undifferentiated commodities in an environment that has not erected significant barriers to entry by new firms. It is within the context that approximates a purely competitive agricultural sector that producers must make marketing decisions.

The purpose of this chapter is to examine the marketing decisions that producers make and the factors that influence their decisions. To establish the modern-day environment within which producers' marketing decisions are made, the chapter begins with a historical perspective of the major developments in the agricultural sector. Subsequent sections represent a functional analysis of producers' marketing decisions to create, price, promote, and distribute agriculture products.

## AGRICULTURAL SECTOR

The promise of unlimited freedom, and stories of abundant resources and rich soil, represented a new opportunity to those who were willing to travel to the new land we now know as America. These early Americans brought with them an agricultural tradition that served as a basis upon which they would create what is today the most technologically efficient agricultural market system in the world.

## Historical Perspective*

The U.S. agricultural sector in 1776 was made up of small, self-sufficient, pioneer, farms. To influence the movement of people to the vast lands in the public domain located in the west, the federal government passed the first of its many land acts—**Land Act of 1796**. Settlers soon discovered that with the new land came new problems and opportunities. To meet these new demands farmers formed societies in order to advance methods of farming. The first of these societies, the **Philadelphia Society for Promoting Agriculture**, provided farmers with information about agricultural experiments, and the best agricultural practices.

As the West became more populated and newer technologies more used, it began to compete with the East in both crop and animal products. In part, to meet the competition from the West, farmers in the East began to specialize in perishables that could not be transported over long distances. Their proximity to major urban population centers gave them a distinct advantage. This trend toward specialization was not limited to the East; farmers all over the U.S. were concentrating on the products for which their soil, climate, and geographical location were best suited.

Beginning in 1850 and lasting to 1940, the agricultural sector began to transform itself from family-owned, self-sufficient pioneer operations into modern-day commercial enterprises. A number of forces, evident in the first half of the nineteenth century, were responsible for this transformation.

In 1850, Congress began granting federal land to the states to help build railroads. In addition it proposed that Eastern rail lines be extended all the way westward across the U.S. Two companies were granted large tracts of land and millions of dollars in government loans. On May 10, 1869 the **Union Pacific** and **Central Pacific** met in Promontory, Utah and established the first **Transcontinental Railroad**. Not only did the railroads put farming on a year-round basis, but they also enabled the government to move the pioneers farther west to California. The **Homestead Acts of 1862, 1904, and 1909** were passed to provide, once again, relatively cheap land to anyone who would settle them.

As the farms were being homesteaded, they became more mechanized. The seed drill combined the operations of sowing, fertilizing, and covering the soil. **McCormick's mechanical reaper** cut the cost of harvesting. The **Pitt thresher** threshed, separated, and winnowed the grain. By 1880, the **combine**, which combined all harvesting and threshing operations, was being used extensively. The invention of the **gasoline tractor** led to the development of smaller combines that all farmers could use, regardless of the size of their farms.

Coincident with these developments, transportation in America went through major changes. Because food was transported largely by boats, the natural location of rivers, lakes, and canals, along with cold weather, limited the movement of food

---

\* This section is based on E. C. Hampe and M., Writtenberg *The Food Industry—Lifeline of America,* N.Y.: Cornell University Press, 1980.

products. The expansion of the railroad system allowed for the transportation of agricultural products throughout the entire year and vastly reduced the delivery time between the producing area and the consuming markets. The motor truck allowed the farmer to live farther away from the railroad depot and thus expanded the boundaries of farm marketing.

To meet the needs of a growing domestic and foreign population, many farmers transformed their farms into large scale, highly specialized commercial enterprises. The increased flow of agricultural products from geographically dispersed farm operations resulted in a system of local and central markets designed to accumulate these products for domestic and export markets. Commission agents, auction houses, and exchanges (to facilitate buying and selling of agriculture products) began to play a central role in the food industry.

As a result of the growing competition among farmers and other sectors of the economy, farmers now began to organize in order to have a bigger voice in the politics and economy of the country. The **Grange Movement of 1867** was formed to foster economic cooperation among farmers. The **Grange** established stores, banks, insurance companies, food processing plants, farm employment factories, and many other enterprises. Unfortunately, most of their cooperatives failed by the 1880s. By 1931, cooperatives reached the peak of their numerical expansion, and a trend toward consolidation began. Some of these federated cooperatives still exist today. In addition to the **Grange**, a number of private farmer associations were formed. The largest, the **American Farm Bureau Federation,** operates today in the interest of the farmers.

Much of the advancement of the agricultural sector was due to the increased educational opportunities that were made available. The **Land Grant College Bill of 1862** is said to have been the single most important piece of legislation for agricultural education. The **Hatch Bill of 1887** authorized a system of experimental stations. Each station specialized in research on crops and livestock in its area—including scientific research on soil, plant life, animals, and growing conditions.

As science and technology continued to contribute to the efficiency of farming, it created a problem of abundance. Production in excess of demand caused the federal government to enact much legislation to protect the income of farmers. Although the suppliers' problem was chronic, it did not affect all crops or animal products. However, the surplus problem brought forth legislation that continues today. Soil conservation, allotments, parity prices, crop insurance, marketing quotas, and price-support loans make up just a few of the basic mechanisms of **U.S Farm Policy**.

Today, these forces and some newer ones continue to transform the U.S. agricultural sector. Increasingly sophisticated computers, genetic engineering, and biotechnology breakthroughs in crops and animals, are changing the supply side of agricultural products. Rapid changes in consumer tastes and dietary habits (both in the U.S. and abroad), concern for food quality and safety, and a growing emphasis on the ecological impact of farming are changing the demand side for agricultural products.

## Structural Influence on Marketing Decisions

As previously stated, the structural characteristics of a sector have a fundamental influence on the marketing decisions made by the firms it comprises. The agricultural sector was characterized as an approximation of purely competitive markets. This structure has profound implications for producers. In fact, this structure places the most severe restrictions on marketing because it limits the marketing options available to producers.

In pure competition, there are so many producers that no individual firm—by its decisions or actions—can influence the price of a commodity. The amount that each firm produces is such a small share of the total market supply that the price of a commodity is determined by the interaction of market demand and supply. The individual firm can sell all of its output at the going market price so that there is no reason to offer a lower price. At prices above the market price, the firm can sell nothing because its product is exactly the same as that of every other firm selling the commodity. The inability of a firm to influence price because of its insignificant output relative to the total market supply, and the lack of any preferential demand (because the output is essentially an undifferentiated commodity), means that a firm operating in the agricultural sector is a **price taker**. Price is taken as dictated by market demand and supply. Under these conditions, we would expect the marketing of agricultural products to be very different from that practiced by other sectors of the **U.S. food marketing system**.

Although this is true in general, there are differences among the major commodity subsectors identified earlier. These differences explain why we observe variability in the way these subsectors market their products. As we examine the nature of agricultural marketing under conditions that approximate pure competition, we will identify how some of these differences influence the marketing decisions made in these subsectors.

# PRODUCT DECISIONS

Producer product decisions are multidimensional and interdependent. Not only must producers decide what to produce, but they must also decide how much to produce, when to produce, and where to produce.

## What to Produce

The key to determining what to produce is in finding out what the consumer demands. Two factors make this difficult to accomplish. First, the consumers are far removed from producers; they are at the opposite end of the U.S. food marketing system. This lack of contact makes it difficult for producers to translate consumer demand back into raw commodities. Second, many, if not most, commodities lose their identities as they move toward the consumer. They become ingredients in the final processed product, which may be made up of several commodities. This lack of identity, once again, makes it difficult for producers to translate consumer demand back into raw commodities.

Despite these difficulties, producers product decisions are generally guided by demand and supply under conditions that approximate purely competitive markets.

### Consumer Demand

The demand for a product is not represented by a single figure but rather as a series or schedule of different quantities that consumers are willing to purchase at different prices. The law of demand states that more of a product will be purchased at lower prices and conversely less of a product will be purchased at higher prices. The demand curve slopes downward to the right as shown in **Figure 3-1**.

How much are consumers willing to purchase at different prices? The answer can be expressed in terms of price elasticity or the percent change in quantity demanded to a percent change in price. Demand curves are classified, according to their elasticities, into two groups: elastic or inelastic. If a change in price generates a proportionately larger change in quantity demanded, then demand is elastic. A change in price that produces a proportionately smaller change in quantity demanded is seen as inelastic. When a change in price produces a proportionate change in quantity demanded, then demand has reached unitary elasticity. Elasticity can be computed as follows:

$$\frac{\text{PERCENT CHANGE IN QUANTITY DEMANDED}}{\text{PERCENT CHANGE IN PRICE}} \begin{cases} > 1 \text{ ELASTIC} \\ = 1 \text{ UNITARY} \\ < 1 \text{ INELASTIC} \end{cases}$$

Three other important dimensions of demand need to be identified. First, the demand for agricultural commodities is said to be inelastic, and derived from the level of demand for the final product made from it. Second, elasticity changes throughout the demand curve for the same product. Demand is less sensitive to price changes at higher quantities than it is at smaller volumes. Third, food products generally increase in price elasticity as they move toward the consumer. **Figure 3-2** shows how the increased number of substitutes impacts on price elasticity.

Demand schedule A represents the inelasticity of all food. Schedule B represents the demand for all poultry products. C represents the demand for all chicken. Line D could be the demand for boneless/skinless chicken breasts. Line E, the most elastic, could be the demand for **Holly Farms** boneless/skinless chicken breasts.

## Agricultural Supply

The supply of a product is represented by a schedule of different quantities that producers are willing to supply at different prices. The law of supply states that more of a product will be supplied at higher prices and, conversely, less of a product will be supplied at lower prices. The supply curve slopes upward to the right as shown in **Figure 3-3**.

The elasticity concept used in demand can be applied to supply as well. If a change in the price of a commodity generates a proportionately greater change in quantity supplied, then supply is elastic. If a change in price generates a proportionately smaller change in supply, it is inelastic. When a change in price produces a proportionate change in supply, then supply is unitary. Elasticity can be computed as follows:

$$\frac{\text{PERCENT CHANGE IN QUANTITY SUPPLIED}}{\text{PERCENT CHANGE IN PRICE}} \quad \begin{array}{l} > 1 \text{ ELASTIC} \\ = 1 \text{ UNITARY} \\ < 1 \text{ INELASTIC} \end{array}$$

**Figure 3-4** illustrates the impact of time on the elasticity of supply. In the short run, producers are unable to respond with greater supply regardless of the movement in price. The supply curve becomes more elastic in the intermediate long run because producers are able to make adjustments to changing prices. Supply elasticities are highest for those commodities where adjustments are relatively easy to make, and lowest for those commodities where adjustments are difficult to make. For most agricultural commodities, supply is inelastic.

## Equilibrium Prices

In a purely competitive market, the intersection of market demand and supply determines what products sellers are willing to supply, and buyers are willing to spend. There is a tendency for this equilibrium price to exist unless demand shifters or supply shifters cause price to change.

Several factors are capable of shifting the desire of the consumers. A change in the number of buyers, purchasing power, preference, or expectations of future prices, as well as a change in the prices of substitute products, can shift the demand curve. The motivations of producers can change as a result of change in the weather, expectations of future price levels, resource prices, production costs, and technology. If such changes occur, a new equilibrium price will be found.

Because the demand and supply for agricultural commodities are inelastic, even small shifts in supply and demand of a commodity bring about large changes in price, and as such create great income instability for producers.

### Product Characteristics

Regardless of what is produced, the outputs of the agricultural sector are raw materials that share some common characteristics. First, commodities have a low value in relation to their volume or weight. This bulkiness influences the costs of transportation. In turn, transportation influences the form in which these products are transported to the market. Second, food commodities are perishable. Being parts of living organisms from the land or sea, they are subject to deterioration over time. Third, they are subject to varying conditions of nature, and as a consequence vary in quality from season to season and year to year. Finally, they are essentially undifferentiated either by uniformity in all physical characteristics as they leave the farm, ranch, or sea, or by the classification of the product into distinct groups based on grades and standards.

### Grades and Standards

Homogeneity by grade standardization is evident in many agricultural commodity markets. It is a means of sorting diversity into homogeneous bundles. This sorting is done according to a set of standards, and the resulting groups are called grades. As grading is ordinarily voluntary, grades are useless unless they represent differences in demand. However, grades are used more by firms in the U.S. food marketing system than by consumers. This is true for several reasons. First, grade standards are so precise that buyers may purchase without personally inspecting the commodity. Second, grades represent an assurance of quality demanded by firms. Third, many commodities reach the consumer only after they have been processed into manufactured products. Thus, even though commodities loses their identity in the final product, buyers can be assured of their original quality. Fourth, grades exist because they save time in the negotiation process and allow price discrimination on the basis of discernable product quality differences. Because the market is indifferent as to producers, firms all receive the market-determined price for a particular grade of product.

Ironically, commodity grades allow producers to differentiate themselves from other producers of the same commodity. The various grades of a commodity compete among themselves in the marketplace. Thus, a producer may compete by producing higher grades of a commodity. Producers watch the price relationships among grades and act accordingly. Grades then communicate changing demands to producers who respond by altering the commodities they produce. Because grades carry with them price discrimination, they contain an incentive to meet changing demand. In the long run, grades impact on the relative proportions of what is produced, and greatly aid in the development of new commodities for the future.

## How Much to Produce

Under conditions that approximate pure competition, the individual firm can sell all of its output at the existing market price. Thus, the producer sees the demand curve for its output as perfectly horizontal (elastic) at the market price. However, determining how much to produce depends not only on the demand for the output but also on the availability and prices of four basic resources: land, labor, capital, and management. Different quantities and combinations of these resources will produce different amounts of a product. The relationship between various levels of resources input and product output is referred to as a production function and is shown in **Figure 3-5**.

The shape of the total product curve tells us that as the amount of a variable resource input is changed while all the other resources are held constant, total product will increase at an increasing rate, then increase at a decreasing rate, reach a maximum, and eventually decline. This is the **law of diminishing returns**.

Given the law of diminishing returns, the producer must now decide how to adjust its output so that the firm can achieve its primary objective of profit maximization. We need to go back to **Figure 3-5** and establish a rational range of production outputs. The answer to the economic questions of how much resource input to use and how much product to produce are found within the rational range of production. Any input that produces less than point **A** or greater than point **B** does not maximize the firm's profits. To establish where in this range to produce, the firm is guided by economic theory. If the cost of producing the last unit of output (**marginal cost**) is less than the revenue received from selling the last unit of output (**marginal revenue**), the firm will expand its output. If, however, marginal cost is greater than marginal revenue, then the firm will reduce output. By operating at the point on the production function where one more unit of variable input adds to revenue just what it adds to costs (that is, where marginal revenue equals marginal costs), the firm maximizes its total profits. It is at that point that the firm answers the question of how much to produce.

## When to Produce

The major coordinating problem facing producers is regulation of the market supply during different time periods so that it is consistent with consumer demand. In order to understand how firms make the decision of when to produce, it is essential to understand how biological lags affect agricultural production. A biological lag is the time period between producers' decision to expand (or contract) production and when the output on the market actually increases (or decreases). For example, planting decisions for major annual crops must be made well in advance of harvest time. For corn that is harvested from October through December and soybeans that are harvested during early fall, these decisions are made in the spring as much as seven months before harvest. For hard, winter wheat used largely in making bread, the lag is closer to ten months.

Not all food comes from annual crops. Fruit trees may not bear fruit for three or four years, and may not reach peak production for another six to ten years. The lag for beef cattle is seldom less than thirty months. For pork it is almost a year. A new batch of broiler chicken can be produced every seven weeks. With turkeys it is about six months. Thus, the length of the biological lag of the various commodities limits any short-run adjustment producers can make regarding the decision of when to produce.

There is another factor that also influences the producer's decision of when to produce: whether a commodity is a stock or flow commodity. Livestock and poultry production are consummated throughout the year and are described as **flow** commodities. Commodities in continuous production, such as these, with little storage and little capacity for storage, result in producers having little control over the level of market supply within a market period once the production process is initiated.

By contrast, crops such as corn, wheat, fruit, and vegetables are harvested once per year and are **stock** commodities. These commodities must be stored so that the supply will be available at other times during the market period. Stock commodities, such as these, permit a rapid adjustment of market supply in the short run. Whether a commodity is a stock or flow commodity, and the length of its biological lag, are two factors that influence the ability of producers to regulate the market supply during different time periods.

## Where to Produce

To a large degree the decision of where to produce a commodity is determined by the availability and costs of key natural production resources. The major commodities are produced in almost every state, but there are regional concentrations of production. Each region specializes in the production of commodities for which its resource base is best suited.

The subtropical climate of the **Pacific Coast** states enable them to supply the majority of all fruits and vegetables. Livestock and garden production are centered in the fertile soils of the **Corn Belt** states. Milk production is centered in the **Great Lakes** states. Poultry is heaviest in the **Southeastern** states. Finally, the infant, but growing, aquaculture subsector is centered in selected **Southeastern** and **Northwestern** states.

In addition to having a natural comparative advantage due to climate and soil, the location where a commodity is produced is also influenced by manmade factors. Technology, irrigation, farm labor, transportation economies, and managerial skills are manmade factors that contribute to geographical specialization.

Despite the facts that producers are far removed from consumers, and that most of their output becomes part of a processed product, they must make four product related decisions. *What* to produce is determined, in part, by their ability to determine correctly the demand and supply for a commodity. *How much* to produce is defined by the level of output that allows producers to maximize their profit in markets approaching pure competition. Decisions regarding *when* to produce must consider the nature and the biological lag of a commodity. Finally, *where* to produce is influenced both by the natural endowment of an area and by manmade factors.

# PRICE DECISIONS

Under conditions that approximate pure competition, the price of a commodity is determined by the interaction of market demand and supply. The market-clearing equilibrium price established is a compromise between the seller's demand for a higher price and the buyer's demand for a lower price. This compromise between seller and buyer takes place within the process called **price determination** and is of immense value to producers who need to understand the long-run impact of changes in the market place.

Although actual price tends to move toward the equilibrium price, producers on a day-to-day basis often lack complete information about such things as market supply and demand, and input prices. Thus, producers and buyers must engage in a process to discover a mutually acceptable price. Through the **price discovery process**, a commodity is priced for a specific time, at a specific place, and in a specific form. Price discovery is not an exact science, but rather a process involving human negotiation. The mutually acceptable price agreed upon depends on the quantity, quality, and timeliness of information available to the seller and buyer and their relative bargaining power.

## Price Discovery Systems

Price discovery systems continually rediscover price. At times, consecutive price discoveries find the same price. Mostly, consecutive price discoveries result in different prices. Five price discovery systems have been identified: (1) organized markets, (2) decentralized, individual negotiation, (3) group negotiation, (4) formula pricing, and (5) governmental pricing.

### *Organized Markets*

Historically, commodities were priced in "public markets" structured to give all potential sellers and buyers access to each other. In essence, sellers and buyers engage in competitive bidding for commodities that are physically assembled in the market facility at the time of sale. Although each market participant is free to sell high or buy low, competition from other participants results in a price that is close to or equal to the equilibrium price of the commodity.

Electronic markets are a form of organized markets. Commodities, through the use of telecommunication, may be auctioned without the presence of the market participants or the commodities themselves. This results in significant savings in travel time for buyers and sellers, and savings in commodity transportation time and costs. Together with the increased likelihood of greater participation by buyers and sellers, these advantages explain much of the interest in electronic markets. There are a number of electronic markets in operation today. The **National Electronic Marketing Association (NEMA)** is a computerized livestock system. **Computer Aided Marketing Program (CAMP)** serves the fruit and vegetable market. **Cattlex** is an electronic market for feeder cattle.

Another type of price discovery that takes place within the organized markets is **forward contracting** in either the cash or futures market. In both cases, the price of a commodity is established before the physical transfer of the commodity to the buyer. Forward contracting reduces the amount of market risk caused by price fluctuations resulting from changing supply and/or consumer demand.

In the cash market, price is negotiated and delivery is expected. However, in the futures market, the seller does not intend to deliver, nor does the buyer intend to accept delivery of, a commodity. The seller wants to shift the risk of a price decrease so the owner will sell a futures contract to protect a cash market position. The buyer wants to shift the risk of a price increase, and so buys a future contract to protect a cash market position. By taking equal and opposite positions in the cash and futures markets the seller offsets any loss from a price decline, and a buyer offsets any loss from a price increase.

Trading in futures contracts takes place in federally licensed exchanges found in cities through which a significant portion of the commodity moves. The **Chicago Board of Trade** and the **Chicago Mercantile Exchange** account for about seventy-five percent of all commodity futures trading.

### *Decentralized, Individual Negotiation (DIM)*

This method, also known as direct marketing, includes any discovery system in which a buyer and seller privately negotiate a price. In addition to transportation costs savings, much of the interest in **DIM** is due to the convenience of having to move the commodity only once to a processor instead of to an organized market first. However, the information on commodity transaction prices that is normally available in organized markets is lacking in direct marketing and is a major concern to both parties. Nonetheless, this form of pricing is increasingly used because sellers enjoy their level of involvement in the exchange process and buyers are better able to control the quality of their commodity purchases. **DIM** pricing is the dominant pricing system in the major commodity markets.

### *Group Negotiation*

This method enables a group of producers to bargain price and non-price terms of trade, but not the assembly, processing, or distribution of the commodity. These groups, known as bargaining associations, have been very active in a number of specialty groups such as dairy, fruits, vegetables, and sugar beets. Examples of bargaining associations operating today are **Dairymen, Inc., California Canning Peach Association, American Farm Bureau Federation, American Agricultural Marketing Association**, and the **National Farmers Organization**.

### *Formula Pricing*

The price of a commodity using this method is based on a mathematical formula that reflects a relationship between a price an indicators of value. The formula is generally negotiated prior to a transaction. Formula pricing is used extensively in markets for some farm commodities. Egg prices, for example, are formulated relative to the **Urner-Barry price quotes. Yellow Street** prices are prices reported by a private news service as representative of bona fide transactions on beef carcasses. Prices for Grade A milk sold under federal market orders are based on a formula that uses **USDA's** public report of market prices for manufacturing-grade milk (M-W price series).

### *Government Pricing*

Price floors, price ceilings, marketing orders, and supply control are all forms of governmental pricing. **Price floors** are used to "support" commodity prices such as feed grains, honey, sugar, rice, and soybeans. It is a legally set price above the equilibrium price. In contrast, a **price ceiling** is legally set below the equilibrium price. Its purpose is usually to prevent inflation.

**Federal marketing orders** are used in milk, fresh fruits and vegetables, tree nuts, and specialty crops. However, only the **49** non-overlapping milk marketing orders contain provisions that set the minimum prices for producer milk according to the average use of milk in that market. About eighty percent of all the Grade A fluid milk consumed is covered by federal orders, and most of the remainder is covered by state orders.

**Non-recource storage loans** and **government purchase and storage programs** influence price by altering the supply of the commodity. A producer attains a non-recource loan on the crop at harvest when it is stored. Because the loan price is equal to the support price, the producer is assured of a minimum price for the crop. If the price rises above the loan price later in the season, the producer will sell at the market price, repay the loan, and make a profit.

The government also supports a commodity price by purchasing the quantity that will make the price rise to the support level. The government inventory can be later sold, given away in food programs, or destroyed. Finally, the government can make a deficiency payment to producers when prices fall below the support level.

## Price Patterns

Many agricultural commodities exhibit recurring price patterns over time. Seasonal price patterns occur within a crop or marketing year, while price cycles last beyond a crop or marketing year.

### *Seasonal Price Patterns*

The prices of most farm commodities follow some regular seasonal pattern caused by the seasonality of supply and demand. Stock commodities are harvested primarily once a year and must be stored in order to be available at other times during the year. The inconsistency between a once-a-year supply and continuous demand results in the commodity being at its lowest price at harvest and increasing each month as the supply is depleted. The extent of the seasonal price increase is largely a function of the cost of storage and seasonal demand. Durable commodities (such as wheat) that can be stored for extended periods of time at comparatively low cost have small seasonal fluctuations in prices. In contrast, strawberries, which cannot be stored for months, exhibit more extreme price seasonality.

Flow commodities such as livestock, poultry, and other perishable products are produced throughout the year. Nonetheless, prices vary seasonally because of weather patterns, seasonal differences in production costs, and the amount of supply. Livestock producers, for example, reduce their stock during the winter months when production costs are highest, thus causing a price increase during these months. Likewise, slaughter-hog price seasonality mainly reflects seasonal supply fluctuations.

### *Price Cycles*

The fluctuation in prices due to periodic expansion or contraction in the supply of agricultural commodities beyond a marketing year are referred to as **price cycles**. These variations are the result of decisions made by producers. The length of a price cycle is composed of two time periods or lags. The first, a biological lag, represents the elapsed time between the decision to expand or contract supply and the actual change in the market supply. A full cycle of expansion and contraction for cattle runs eleven to twelve years; for hogs the cycle runs three to four years, and for poultry it is only about seven weeks!

The second, a psychological lag, represents the length of time prices are low or high to convince producers to alter their production plans. Thus high prices lead eventually to higher output, which reduces prices and leads eventually to lower output, which raises prices. Given the rather steep inelasticities of supply and demand, small output shifts usually lead to much larger price changes. Thus extreme price variations over time are not unusual in the agricultural sector. However, crops (unlike livestock) do not exhibit well-identified price cycles because crop sizes are only partially influenced by producer decisions. They are chiefly determined by the weather, which is itself not cyclical in its changes.

As with seasonal price movements, knowledge of price cycles can be of enormous value to producers. However, price cycles do not follow perfectly predictable patterns. Nor are seasonal price variations perfectly predictable.

## Law of One Price

When markets are competitive there should be only one price for each commodity after adjusting for the costs of adding form, time, and place utility. The law of one price helps keep in equilibrium markets that are separated by form, time, and place.

In markets separated by differences in product form, the costs of processing must be equal to the difference between input prices and output prices. If the costs of processing are greater, no output will be produced; if processing costs are less, output will be increased.

In markets separated by distance, the cost of transportation must be equal to the difference in price between the two locations. If transportation costs are greater, nothing will be shipped between these two locations; if transportation costs are less, too much will be shipped from the lower to the higher priced location.

In markets separated by time, the cost of storage must be equal to the difference between the current price and the future price. If the cost of storage is greater, products will be sold now, and not enough will be stored; if the storage costs are less, products will be stored, and not enough will be available now.

When price differs by more than the cost of adding a particular utility, there is an economic incentive to shift resources so as to take advantage of the disequilibrium. However, as other producers follow, these higher priced commodities eventually decline to normal price levels and thus bring the price back in line with the costs of adding the utility. In this way, markets are kept in equilibrium.

As we have seen, sellers and buyers engage in a process to discover a mutually acceptable price for a commodity in a specific form, for a specific time, and at a specific place. Even though there are five identifiable price discovery systems, **decentralized, individual negotiation (DIM)** is the dominant system in major commodity groups.

To make more informed decisions regarding the "mutually acceptable price" requires the producer as well as the buyer to be knowledgeable about seasonal price variations caused by the seasonality of supply and demand. Prices frequently fluctuate rather sharply because of significant changes in demand or in quantities supplied. Of course, the other significant cause of seasonal price variations is weather. In addition, the participants in the transaction must be knowledgeable about underlying price cycles due to biological and psychological lags.

Finally, the law of one price identifies the relationship between prices in form, time, and place markets. This law allows producers to consider how price is influenced by the form in which a commodity will be produced, the time at which it will be sold, and the place at which it will be sold. Predicting price changes in form, time, and place markets is made easier because the price of a commodity will be uniform after adjusting for the costs of adding form, time, and place utility to the commodity.

# PROMOTION DECISIONS

The unique characteristics of agricultural commodities present particular challenges that must be overcome if producers are to be able to influence economic demand through promotional activities. First, commodities are undifferentiated in physical characteristics as they leave the farm, ranch, or sea, or by their classification into quality grades. Second, many, if not most, commodities end up as ingredients in processed food products, thereby losing their identity. Third, the demand for commodities is derived from the level of demand for the final product made from it, and is relatively price inelastic.

As a consequence of these characteristics, any promotional expenditures by one producer of a particular commodity will benefit another producer of the same commodity even if this producer does not expend any funds to promote the commodity. Further, with the exception of commodities that reach the consumer market in fresh form, much of the influence on demand will be due to the increased demand for processed products in which the raw commodity is an input. Adding to producer difficulties, the relative price inelasticity of commodities means that demand is insensitive to price changes. If competition can't be influenced even by price reductions, it is difficult to see how promotional activities will have any sustainable long-run impact on consumer demand.

Given the existing situation, producers don't find it feasible to engage in individual promotional activities, but rather prefer to engage in cooperative promotional arrangements with other producers of like commodities.

## Generic Promotion

Generic promotion, undertaken by a group of producers, focuses on a single commodity. Its purpose is to increase total demand for a commodity so that a buyer will purchase more of the product at the same or higher price, or pay a higher price for the same volume. Thus the task is to move the demand curve rightward. This shift in demand can be brought about directly by increasing the demand for the commodity, or indirectly by increasing demand for processed products in which the raw commodity is an input.

Producer-funded generic commodity promotion has largely relied on advertising to carry out its overall goal of demand stimulation.

## Generic Advertising

Because generic advertising assumes the primary role of producer promotion, its purpose is that of generic promotion—that is, to increase overall demand for a commodity that will result in a higher price, increased sales volume, or both. Whether the increase in demand is for the raw commodity or the processed product in which it is an input is of secondary importance. What is of primary importance is that the increase in sale revenue exceeds the costs of advertising by a margin that returns a profit to the producers.

### Sales and Advertising Expenditures

One of several functional relationships between sales and advertising expenditures is seen in **Figure 3-6**. According to this relationship, a certain amount of dollars must be spent before any change in sales will occur. Expenditures from $a_0$ to $a_1$ produce no effect on sales volume. Beyond the threshold point ($a_1$), advertising has a positive effect up to the point of diminishing returns ($a_3$), where additional advertising efforts result in sales losses. Although there are other functional forms feasible, this traditional S-shaped curve is the one most frequently used to depict the theoretical response of sales to advertising. Its preferred use is largely due to empirical evidence that shows positive advertising elasticities at the commodity level. These positive elasticities mean that the percent change in sales is greater than the one percent change in advertising expenditures.

## Advertising Decisions

Despite the unique situation faced by producers of relatively homogeneous commodities, generic advertising must, like brand advertising, influence consumer perceptions about the raw commodity or the processed product in which the commodity is an input. As such, the promotional activities and decisions parallel the decisions made by brand advertisers. The basic considerations involved in the preparation of a generic advertising program are market, message, media, momentum, money and measures. These six "M's" of advertising will be examined briefly within the context of the planning process for producer-promoted generic advertising.

### Market

Knowing the audience is the first major stage in any promotional attempt to influence consumer demand. For the producer, the market may consist of those who consume the commodity in fresh form, or those who consume the commodity as part of a processed food, or both. By and large, generic advertising appears to be more successful for commodities that are consumed in fresh form because they don't change their identity. For commodities that end up as part of a processed product, most of the advertising task is performed by manufacturers with little or no cooperative effort by producers. The basic task, here, is to target a specific market for the commodity. In turn, these markets must be profiled on demographic, economic, geographic, and psycho-social factors in order to answer the question, **"Who makes up the market for the commodity?"**

### Message

The task at this stage is to determine what to say, and how to say it. When determining creative strategy the advertiser is guided by the criteria that make for effective message appeals. These appeals should be meaningful, distinctive, and believable so as to create a **unique selling position (USP)**.

The impact of the message on the consumer also depends on how it is said—its message execution. The challenge is to translate the USP in such a way as to capture the attention and interest of the target market. Because advertising messages speak both to the head and the heart, message execution involves the manipulation of all those elements of the advertisement that can have an impact on the persuasive success of the message.

### Media

Unless the advertiser can communicate with the target market, any attempt at influence will fail. It follows, then, that the task at this stage is to identify the various opportunities to communicate with the market. These opportunities are defined along three dimensions. First, the type of medium must be chosen. This choice is generally determined by the type of creative strategy used. In the case of food products that are sold on the basis of appeals to sight and taste, TV and magazines carrying colorful ads are logical choices. Second, a decision must be made regarding when to advertise. Consideration must be given to the seasonality of consumption as well as other fluctuations. Third, when we acknowledge the influence of a market, we must acknowledge that this market exists somewhere. Thus, the geographical area in which the product is sold must be identified.

### Momentum

The task at this stage is answer two questions. What percentage of the people in the target market will be exposed to the ad message during a given time period (**reach**)? How many times should the average person in the target market see the advertising message in a given time period (**frequency**)? Because there is seldom enough money to satisfy both, most media plans emphasize either one or the other. Food producers can maximize reach by using a variety of media. To maximize frequency on a national level, one medium is designated for increased repetition. On a local level, radio-with its loyal listeners-is one of the better frequency-building media.

### Money

One of the most difficult decisions for a producer to make is how much to spend on advertising. There is, in addition, another problem unique to agricultural products. Because all producers of a like commodity benefit from advertising, those who don't voluntarily contribute to the promotional expenditures are given a **free ride**. This free-rider problem motivated producers to secure various state and federal laws authorizing compulsory **check-offs**, or mandatory assessments, to cover the cost of generic advertising. For example, in 1985, special legislation began a fifteen-cent per hundredweight mandatory check-off on milk. In the following year, a mandatory one-fourth of one percent of the value of all hogs, pigs, and breeding stock at the point of sale took effect. In some of these cases, mandatory program procedures allow producers to apply for a refund at the time of assessment.

Because so many of these compulsory check-off assessments are related to the volume of the product sold, it should be no surprise that most generic advertising budgets are based on current or forecasted sales. However, this approach views sales as a cause of promotion rather than as a result, and thus prevents increased spending when sales are decreasing. Fortunately, more and more producer groups are determining their budgets based on how much it will cost to perform the tasks necessary to achieve specific objectives.

### Measure

The final stage in planning a generic advertising program is to evaluate the effectiveness of the expenditures. A growing body of research has been conducted on the generic promotion of agricultural commodities. Most of these studies have included advertising expenditures as an explanatory variable to provide an estimate of the extent to which generic advertising shifts aggregate commodity demand. The advertising elasticities reported in these studies have all been positive—that is, the percent change in sales associated with a one-percent change in advertising expenditures is greater than one. Thus, they support the general hypothesis that generic advertising efforts by a commodity group can have a positive impact on demand.

On a more scientific level, generic advertising for commodities that reach the consumer in fresh form tend to be quite successful. Because they do not lose their identity, they can be promoted as a brand.

## Generic Advertisers

Generic advertising is generally sponsored by commodity organizations. For example, the **National Livestock and Meat Board** sponsors promotions with slogans such as **"Pork—the Other White Meat,"** and **"Beef, Real Meat for Real People."** The **Generic Egg Board** has used **"The Incredible, Edible Egg,"** and **"Eggs, a Naturally Smart Food,"** as recent promotional slogans. The **National Dairy Promotion and**

**Research Board** and the **American Dairy Association** have sponsored a number of promotional campaigns with the following slogans: **"Milk—You're Not a Kid Anymore!"** **"Milk—It's Good for You,"** and **"Just Say 'Cheese'."** Recently, dairy cooperatives have developed their own promotion campaigns. **"Quality Checked"** is an attempt to differentiate the milk of a specific cooperative.

Generic advertisers also use a specific geographical basis for their promotional campaigns. Examples of some regional promotions include **Florida Oranges**, **Georgia Peaches**, **Idaho Potatoes**, **California Raisins**, **Vidalia Onions**, **Maine Lobsters**, **Michigan Cherries**, **Nebraska Corn-Fed Beef**, **Washington Apples**, and **Wisconsin Cheese**.

It appears likely that generic advertising will increase in the future because in general there has been a net benefit to producers. Yet there are many unanswered questions concerning the impact of generic advertising. Chief among them is, *how do the advertising activities of one commodity group affect the activities of other commodity groups?* Opponents point out that as more and more commodity groups engage in advertising, cannibalization occurs. Recognizing that the capacity of the human stomach is finite, the consumption of one commodity happens at the expense of a competitive product. The pork promotion impacts on the beef, turkey, or chicken promotion. The **Idaho** potato campaign probably impacts on the sale of **Michigan White** potatoes. This leads to an interesting dilemma. When consumers are eating more of one commodity, they are eating less of another commodity. Thus, generic advertising may lead to little or no long-term increase in price or producer's profits.

Because agricultural commodities are undifferentiated, lose their identity when processed, and exhibit a derived demand, producers are faced with unique promotional challenges. Given these challenges, producers find it in their best interest to cooperate with other producers of like commodities in their promotional activities. This cooperative effort results in promotion and advertising that is intended to increase the demand for the commodity rather than the demand for the output of only one producer. To increase commodity demand, producers make fundamental decisions regarding the nature of the market, message, media, momentum, money, and the measured effectiveness of their promotional efforts.

## DISTRIBUTION DECISIONS

As previously mentioned in Chapter 1, there are three basic problems of exchange inherent in the U.S. food marketing system. First, there is a discrepancy between the quantity and assortment of the food products that are economical to produce, and the quantity and assortment that consumers want. Second, there is a discrepancy between where food products are produced and where they are demanded. Third, there is a discrepancy between when food products are produced and when they are demanded. The specific characteristics of the various agricultural commodities greatly influence how these problems will be solved. However, as with other firms in the U.S. food marketing system, distribution decisions made by producers must contribute to solving the three basic problems of exchange.

## Product Discrepancy

From coast to coast, a wide variety of commodities of varying qualities and sizes are produced either annually or throughout the year. The task of the U.S. food marketing system is to match the specialized production with specific demand. To accomplish this task, commodities must be assembled into large quantities of commodities standardized by quality grades. These accumulations are primarily built up for shipment in economically feasible quantities—truckload, carload, trainload, or shipload.

Producers contribute to the task of matching production with demand by making the fundamental decision of where to sell their output. The specific characteristics of the commodities such as their bulkiness, perishability, seasonality, product forms (fresh versus processed), and geographical specialization of production influence, in part, where the output of producers will be sold. For example, **shipping point firms**, which assemble large quantities of fruits and vegetables, prepare them (sort, grade, clean, and package), and ship them to different markets, are typically located in the fruit and vegetable producing areas, The same is true for livestock and poultry. Buyers of livestock can bypass the few remaining central terminal markets and purchase directly from feedlots or from the producers themselves. Milk, which on many farms flows directly from cows to refrigerated bulk tanks, is picked up by large, specialized, and usually cooperatively owned, trucks on a regular basis. Grain is generally sold to a country grain elevator located along the rail lines. Finally, much of the wild harvested fish is sold at dockside.

### *Price Surface*

Where producers decide to sell their output is also influenced, in part, by the price they can receive. When commodities are produced in a competitive economic environment, products bring different prices at different geographical markets. To illustrate this point, consider the geographic price surface in **Figure 3-7**. Suppose the figure represents the local market for soybeans at two dollars per bushel in the central market. The producer's price at any location is equal to the central market price, less the appropriate transfer costs—transportation and handling costs incurred when a commodity is moved from one market to another. The concentric circles indicate that net producer prices are equal at equal distances from the central market for a given quality and quantity of the commodity. In general, producers will sell in the market where they can receive the highest market price less transfer costs.

The price that producers can receive from their output, together with the specific characteristics of the commodity under consideration, will influence where the output will be sold. Further, because the commodity's price is a reflection of demand in that market, specialized production is matched with specific demand when the commodity is sold.

## Spatial Discrepancy

Spatial discrepancy refers to the fact that there is a difference between where commodities are produced and where they are demanded. Since agricultural commodities are most often not produced where they are demanded, transportation is necessary to resolve this discrepancy. The resolution of this discrepancy creates **place utility.**

The physical transportation of commodities has a tremendous impact, not only on producers, but also at every level in the U.S. food marketing system. Transportation influences both the size of the producer's market and the nature of competition from other producers in that market. Transportation also influences commodity prices because it represents a share of total marketing costs. Finally, the availability and speed of transportation influence how many storage facilities will be needed, as well as the amount of storage space needed to maintain consistent supplies.

At the producer level, commodities present a number of special transportation needs. The demand for transportation services is not consistent throughout the year because of the seasonality of production. The perishability and bulkiness of commodities require special considerations such as refrigeration. Low unit value commodities such as grains require high capacity equipment. Lastly, the primary concern of producers is to distribute and sell their output to what is referred to as the **first handler**. This firm may be only a few miles from the point of production, or a few hundred or even thousands of miles from the seller. Thus, the distance the commodity must travel to reach the first handler can impose another special transportation need.

### Transportation Decisions

To understand how producers resolve the spatial discrepancy by using transportation, let's examine the fundamental questions they must answer. How should the commodity be shipped? Who should ship the commodity? To answer these questions, the producer must first define what level of service is required, and then determine the least costly mode of transportation that will meet the required service level.

Producers, like other participants in the U.S. food marketing system, define their service levels using the following criteria. **Speed** refers to the elapsed time between pickup and delivery. **Availability** focuses on the ability to reach the site for pickup or delivery. **Dependability** refers to the difference between the published delivery time and the actual delivery time. **Capability** is the ability to handle the special transportation needs imposed on the nature of the commodity. The final criterion, **frequency**, relates to the number of deliveries.

The second factor that producers consider is costs of the various modes of transportation. **Table 3-1** summarizes the cost structure of the various modes. There are two economies of scale principles, not included in this figure, that are typically considered when evaluating transportation modes on the basis of costs. First, the larger the size of the shipment, the lower the cost per unit of distance. Second, the longer the length of shipment, the lower the cost per unit of distance.

### *Transportation Modes*

Let's review the various modes as a producer might consider them. Of course, the mode chosen will depend on the producer's service level requirement and cost. Four types of water carriers handle agricultural commodities. Internal water carriers that operate on the internal navigable waterways such as the Mississippi, Ohio, and Missouri rivers. Great Lakes carriers operate on the Great Lakes. Coastal carriers operate between ports on the same coast while intercoastal carriers operate between ports on the Atlantic and Pacific oceans via the Panama Canal. Water carriers are the lowest cost mode and are capable of handling most agricultural commodities, however, they have some major limitations: they are the slowest mode, and ice and water levels have a strong, negative impact on their dependability and frequency of delivery. In addition, this mode can only be used by those producers who are adjacent to a waterway. Thus, this mode is not available to most producers. Water carriers are basically long-distance haulers of low-value-to-weight, high-density commodities that can be easily loaded and unloaded. For this reason, grains are the major commodities moved by water carriers.

Rail service is the next lowest cost mode of transportation. It has a distinct advantage in being able to transport the widest variety of commodities. Railroads run on dependable schedules and can reach many sites along their tracks. For the most part, their speed and frequency of delivery are hampered only by the consolidation of boxcars and transfer to train units going in the same direction that takes place in the railway consolidation yards at major terminals. Like water carriers, railroads are basically long-distance, large-volume movers of low-value-to-weight, high-density commodities. For these goods, transportation costs account for a significant percentage of their selling price.

Truck service is the third lowest cost mode of transport. The U.S. highway system allows motor carriers to reach any point in the country. Although weather can be a factor, trucks are more dependable, and make a greater number of deliveries, than all other modes. Their speed of delivery is second only to air transport. As a consequence, virtually all producer-to-first-handler hauling is done by truck.

Shipment by air is the fourth mode of transportation. Air carriers make frequent deliveries and are the fastest mode of transport. Air transportation dependability is negatively impacted by weather conditions. Further, deliveries and pickups can only be made at airports, so their availability is hampered. Lastly, air transport is limited to specific cargo. For these reasons, commodities with high value to weight are the commodities most likely to be shipped by air.

The final alternative is intermodal shipment, which refers to the use of two or more carriers of different modes. Intermodal services maximize the advantages inherent in the combined modes, and minimize their disadvantages. Birdyback, fishyback, and piggyback are examples in which a truck trailer is loaded onto an airplane, ship, or railroad, respectively.

Despite the availability of alternative modes of transportation, most agricultural commodities are hauled by truck. However, as previously indicated, agricultural products are transported by virtually every mode of transportation. A summary of the ratings of transportation modes based on customer-service and cost criteria is shown in **Table 3-2**.

## Temporal Discrepancy

Temporal discrepancy refers to the difference between when a commodity is produced and when it is demanded. Since commodities are most often not produced at the time they are demanded, storage is required in order to resolve the discrepancy. The resolution of this discrepancy creates **time utility**.

There are two reasons why the imbalance between supply and demand exists. First, many commodities are harvested primarily once a year, but consumed throughout the year. If supply is to be available throughout the year, some portion of the harvest must be stored. Second, even though other **flow** commodities are produced year round, it is unrealistic to think that these commodities will move smoothly through the **food pipeline** uninterrupted. In fact, every participant in the U.S. food marketing system—producer, manufacturer, wholesaler, retailer, and consumer—engages in storage to prevent an interruption. What might cause these participants to hold larger than usual inventories and thus precipitate an interruption in the food pipeline? The primary cause is an anticipated price increase. Commodities are purchased now to avoid purchasing later at higher prices. Likewise, a price decrease will motivate these participants to **stock up** because of the savings involved in the purchase. The distinction between a **stock** and **flow** commodity is an important one. Storage plays a major role in an annually produced commodity, but only a minor role in a flow commodity produced year-round.

### Storage Decisions

How can producers resolve the temporal discrepancy by using storage? Let's examine the fundamental questions regarding storage. How much of the commodity, if any, should be stored? Where should the commodity be stored? How should the commodity be stored?

Because the demand for most commodities is inelastic, the producer's perception of future prices will influence how much is stored. An anticipated price increase will increase the total revenue to the producer and thus provide the motivation to store more of the commodity. An anticipated price decrease will decrease total revenue to the producer and thus motivate the producer to store less of the commodity.

Another factor that is considered is how much of the commodity is produced by all producers of like commodities (yield). An anticipated decrease in a commodity's yield will shift the supply curve to the left and result in an increase in total revenue to the producer because of the inelastic demand for that commodity. On the other hand, an anticipated increase in a commodity's yield will shift the supply curve to the right and result in a total decrease to the producer. These relationships are shown in **Figures 3-8** and **3-9**. The astute producer will store contrary to the anticipated yield. If an increase is anticipated, less of the commodity is stored because a higher price can be received now. If a decrease is anticipated, more of the commodity is stored because a higher price can be received later when the supply is reduced.

In general, the location where commodities are stored depends upon the commodity. Highly perishable commodities (e.g., milk and strawberries) are stored only en route to the consumer and/or near the point of consumption. Commodities low in value per weight (e.g., grains) are ordinarily stored in the vicinity of their production for longer time periods. In the case of livestock, some storage takes place **on the hoof**. Animals are kept on the production premises rather than sold.

The alternatives for the producers are to store the commodity on the premises, rent commercial storage, or let some other participant in the U.S. food marketing system undertake the storage operation. The alternative chosen is largely a function of the costs and risks of storage. Three costs are associated with storage: storage rates, interest on capital invested in the stored commodity, and the deterioration in value due to shrinkage, insect and rodent damage, and quality deterioration.

The two primary risks involved in storage are price changes and quality deterioration. If a commodity's price declines or does not increase enough to cover storage costs, the producer will suffer a loss. For many commodities, this risk can be offset by relying on the **Commodity Credit Corporation (CCC)**. This agency buys, stores, and sells commodities in conjunction with the federal price and income support programs. Another way the producer can offset a loss due to a price decrease is to store the commodity and sell a futures contract on one of the commodity exchanges such as the **Chicago Board of Trade** or the **Chicago Mercantile Exchange**. Later the producer can sell the commodity and buy a futures contract, or deliver the commodity on the futures contract at a guaranteed price.

The risk of the deterioration in quality due to storage focuses the producer's attention on the third major question: How should the commodity be stored? The improvement in quality due to storage occurs for only a few products like cheese, wine, and meat for special markets (e.g., restaurants). Most commodities will deteriorate in quality while in storage. Because different commodities have different temperature and humidity requirements for optimum maintenance of quality, the manner in which commodities are stored is handled on a case by case basis. Public cold storage warehouses are frequently used to store commodities, as are private cold-storage firms.

**Biotechnology** continues to play a significant role in reducing product deterioration. Crops that are resistant to insects and disease are being developed. New biological pest controls are being developed as well. The organic compositions of many commodities are being altered to extend storage life. Finally, new animal health technologies are leading to a decrease in animal diseases.

As we have seen, the distribution decisions made by producers help resolve three exchange problems inherent in the U.S. food marketing system. First, producers resolve product discrepancies by selling their products in designated markets. Exactly where the output is sold is influenced by both the characteristics of the commodity and the price producers anticipate receiving for their products. Second, producers resolve spatial discrepancies by transporting their output to where it is demanded. Product characteristics, service levels, and costs combine to influence the way commodities will be transported. Trucks transport most commodities to first handlers. Finally, producers resolve the temporal discrepancy by storing their output. Product characteristics, costs, and risks are examined before a storage decision is made.

# SUMMARY

This chapter has examined the marketing decisions that producers make and the factors that influence their decisions. The structural characteristics of a sector have a fundamental influence on the marketing decisions made by firms composing the sector. Thus, the marketing decisions were examined within the context that approximates a purely competitive agricultural sector. To establish the modern-day environment within which producer marketing decisions are made, the chapter began with a historical perspective of the major developments in the agricultural sector.

Product decisions must be made regarding what to produce, how much to produce, when to produce, and where to produce. The key to determining what to produce is in identifying consumer demand. How much to produce depends not only on demand but also on the availability and prices of land, labor, capital, and managerial expertise. When to produce is influenced by the length of a commodity's biological lag and whether the commodity is produced annually (stock) or throughout the year (flow). In addition to climate and soil, where a commodity is produced will depend upon technology, irrigation, labor, transportation, and managerial skills.

Buyers and sellers have a number of price discovery methods whereby they arrive at a mutually acceptable price for a commodity in a specific form, for a specific time, and at a specific place. Individual negotiation is the dominant pricing method of discovery in the major commodity markets. To make informed decisions regarding the mutually acceptable price, the producer must be knowledgeable about recurring price patterns due to seasonality and the expansion or contraction in the commodity's supply. The law of one price allows the producer to consider how price is influenced by the form in which the commodity is produced (fresh versus processed), the time at which it will be sold (current versus future), and the place at which it will be sold (on premises versus off premises).

Commodities are undifferentiated in physical characteristics as they leave the farm, ranch, or sea, or by their classification into quality grades. Most commodities lose their identity when they become ingredients in processed food products. Further, the demand for commodities is derived from the demand for the final products made from them and is relatively price inelastic. As a consequence of these characteristics, producers don't find it profitable to promote on an individual basis, but rather to engage in cooperative promotional activities with other producers of like commodities. To promote homogeneous commodities, producers must first identify their market for the commodity. Then the message is prepared and the medium is selected. Decisions are made as to the momentum of their promotional effort or the reach and frequency of their promotional message. How much to spend to accomplish the promotional objectives, and how to measure the effectiveness of the promotional effort, are the final considerations.

Distribution decisions are made by producers in order to solve three basic problems inherent in exchange. Producers resolve product discrepancies when they make the decision to sell their output in designated markets. Spatial discrepancies are resolved by making transportation decisions regarding how commodities are to be shipped and by whom. Finally, the difference between the time a commodity is produced and when it is demanded is brought into balance by making storage decisions. In so doing, temporal decisions are resolved.

## SELECTED REFERENCES

Beierlein, J. G. and M. W. Woolverton. *Agribusiness Marketing: The Management Perspective.* Englewood Cliffs, N.J.: Prentice Hall, 1991.

Bowersox, D. J., D. J. Choss, and O. K. Helferich. *Logistical Management.* 3rd ed. New York: Macmillan Publishing Co., 1986.

Bowersox, D. J. and M. B. Cooper. *Strategic Marketing Channel Management.* New York: McGraw-Hill, 1992.

Coyle J. J., E. J. Bardi, and C. J. Langley, Jr.. *The Management of Business Logistics.* 5th ed. New York: West Publishing Company, 1992, p. 285

Cramer, G. L. and C. W. Jensen. *Agricultural Economics and Agribusiness. 5th ed.* New York: John Wiley and Sons, 1991.

Darrah, L. B. *Food Marketing.* New York: The Ronald Regan, 1967.

Hampe, E. C. and M. Wittenberg. *The Food Industry—Lifeline of America.* Ithaca, N.Y.: Cornell University, 1980.

Jolly, C. M. and H. A. Clonts. *Economics of Aquaculture.* Binghamton, N.Y.: Food Products Press, Inc., 1993.

Kohls, R. L. and J. N. Uhl. *Marketing of Agricultural Products. 7th ed.* New York: Macmillan Publishing Co., 1990.

Lenz, J. E. and O. D. Forker. "Generic Advertising as a Nonprice Marketing Strategy" in *Competitive Strategy Analysis in the Food System.* R.W. Cotterill, ed. San Francisco: Westview Press, 1993.

Lesser, W. H. *Marketing Livestock and Meat.* Binghamton, N.Y.: Food Products Press, Inc., 1993.

Marion, B. W. and The NC-117 Committee. *The Organization and Performance of the U.S. Food System.* Lexington, Mass.: Lexington Books, D. C. Heath and Company, 1986.

Rhodes, V. J. The Agricultural Marketing System. 3rd ed., New York: John Wiley and Sons, Inc., 1983.

## REVIEW QUESTIONS

1. Explain: The structural characteristics of the agricultural sector have a fundamental influence on the marketing decisions made by producers.

2. How would you characterize the environment within which producers must make marketing decisions?

3. Which factors make it difficult for producers to translate consumer demand back into the demand for raw commodities?

4. In terms of elasticity, how would you characterize the supply and demand for agricultural commodities?

5. What are the characteristics common to agricultural commodities?

6. What is meant by the concept: rational range of production?

7. Price is determined by supply and demand, but is discovered by buyers and sellers. Explain.

8. Which factors make it difficult for producers to promote agricultural commodities?

9. Give an example of a product discrepancy, a spatial discrepancy, and a temporal discrepancy.

10. Select any two commodities and describe how their marketing decisions are similar and different.

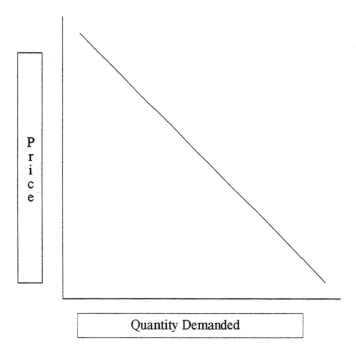

**FIGURE 3-1.** DEMAND

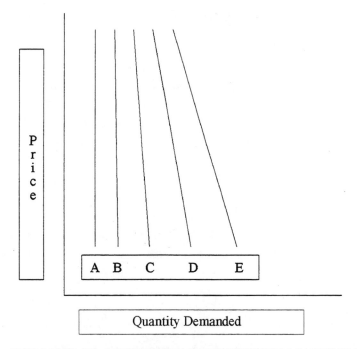

**FIGURE 3-2.** DEMAND ELASTICITY AT DIFFERENT MARKET LEVELS

Marketing Decisions ■ 101

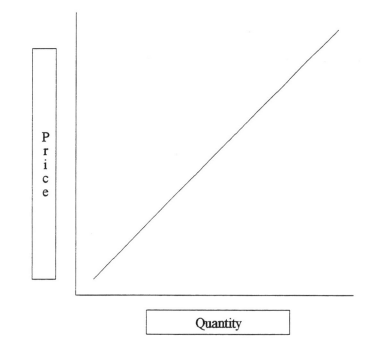

**FIGURE 3-3.** SUPPLY

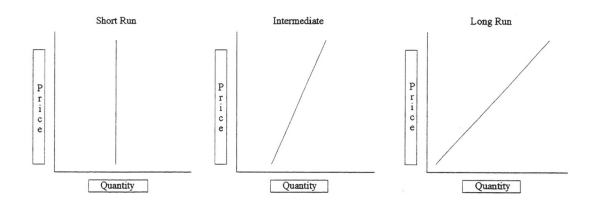

**FIGURE 3-4.** EFFECT OF TIME ON SUPPLY ELASTICITY

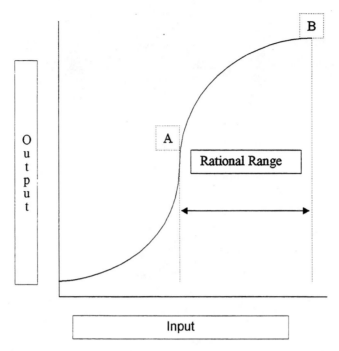

**FIGURE 3-5.** RATIONAL RANGE OF PRODUCTION

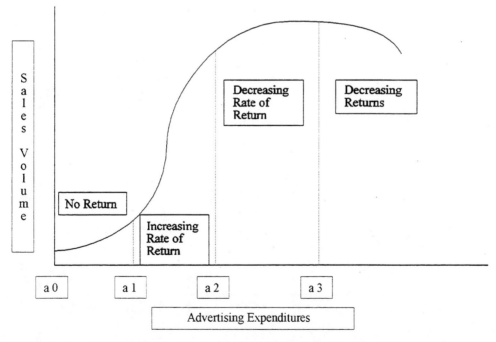

**FIGURE 3-6.** THEORETICAL ADVERTISING RESPONSE FUNCTION

Marketing Decisions ■ 103

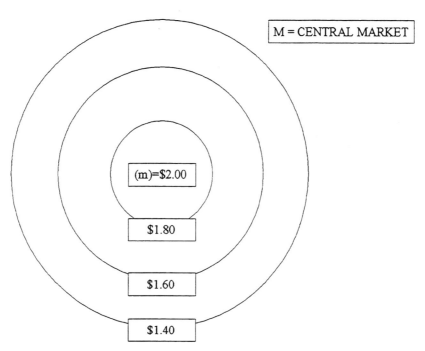

**FIGURE 3-7.** GEOGRAPHIC PRICE SURFACE

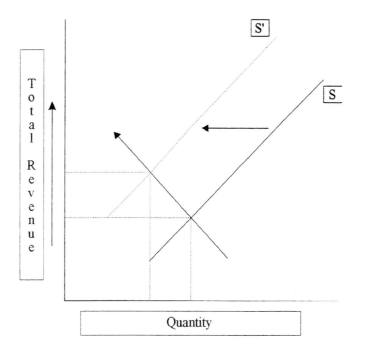

**FIGURE 3-8.** INCREASE IN TOTAL REVENUE DUE TO SUPPLY RESTRICTION

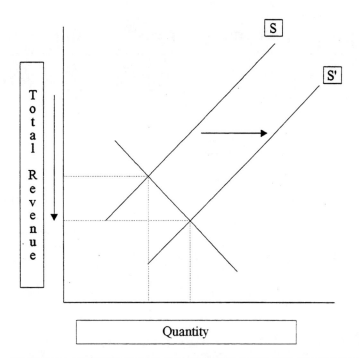

**FIGURE 3-9.** DECREASE IN TOTAL REVENUE DUE TO SUPPLY EXPANSION

**TABLE 3-1.** COST STRUCTURE OF TRANSPORTATION MODES

| MODE | FIXED | VARIABLE |
|---|---|---|
| Rail | HIGH–Terminals, Track, Engines | LOW |
| Truck | LOW–Public Highways, Cab, and Trailer | Medium–Fuel, Labor |
| Water | MEDIUM–Ships, Dock, Facilities | LOW |
| Air | MEDIUM–Aircraft, Handling and Cargo Systems | HIGH–Fuel, Maintenance, Labor |

SOURCE: BOWERSOX, D.J., D.J. CLOSS, AND O.K. HELFERICH, *LOGISTICAL MANAGEMENT*, 3rd ed., MACMILLAN PUBLISHING CO., NEW YORK, 1986.


**TABLE 3-2.** RATINGS OF TRANSPORTATION MODES ON CUSTOMER SERVICE CRITERIA* AND COST

| SERVICE CRITERIA | TRANSPORTATION MODE | | | |
|---|---|---|---|---|
| | RAIL | TRUCK | WATER | AIR |
| Speed | 3 | 2 | 4 | 1 |
| Availability | 2 | 1 | 4 | 3 |
| Dependability | 2 | 1 | 3 | 4 |
| Capability | 1 | 3 | 2 | 4 |
| Frequency | 3 | 1 | 4 | 2 |
| Cost | 2 | 3 | 1 | 4 |

*RATINGS: 1-BEST, LOWEST 5=WORST, HIGHEST

SOURCE: COYLE, J.J, E.J. BARDI, AND C.J. LANGLEY, JR., *THE MANAGEMENT OF BUSINESS LOGISTICS 5TH ed.*, WEST PUBLISHING COMPANY, NEW YORK, 1992. p. 285.

# Chapter 4

# Processors and Manufacturers

**Chapter Outline**

Manufacturing Sector
- A. Company and Establishment Trends
- B. Shipments (Sales)
- C. Value Added

Location of Manufacturing Sector
- A. Employment
- B. Value Added
- C. Value of Shipments

Industry Groups
- A. Meat (201)
- B. Dairy (202)
- C. Preserved Fruits and Vegetables (203)
- D. Grain Mill (204)
- E. Bakery (205)
- F. Sugar and Confectionery (206)
- G. Fats and Oils (207)

H. Beverages (208)

I. Miscellaneous Food (209)

Industries

    A. Value Added

    B. Value Added Intensities

Companies

    A. Number of Companies

    B. Share of Shipments (Sales)

    C. Leading Companies

Summary

The agricultural sector of the **U.S. food marketing system** was examined in the two previous chapters. In chapter 2 the structural organization of the sector was characterized as one that approximates a purely competitive market. This sector has a large number of small producers and a small number of large-scale operations. These producers are involved in the production of undifferentiated commodities. Chapter 3 examined the marketing decisions made by producers in an agricultural sector that approximates a purely competitive market. The inability of a firm to influence price because of its insignificant output relative to the total market supply, and the lack of any preferential demand because the output is essentially an undifferentiated commodity, mean that a producer in a purely competitive market is a "price taker." Price is taken as dictated by the market demand and supply. Under this market structure, the marketing of agricultural products is severely limited.

This chapter begins with a structural analysis of the manufacturing sector in the U.S. food marketing system. Attention is focused on the industries and industry groups that reflect food manufacturing output. The food manufacturing sector is made up of forty-nine four digit industries organized into nine three-digit industry groups. These industries and industry groups are classified in the **Census of Manufacturing Standard Industrial Classification Major Group 20—Food & Kindred Products**. The food products made by these industry groups and industries represent over ninety-five percent of all processed foods consumed. Three categories of food are not considered as output from food manufacturers. First, unprocessed foods such as fresh produce and never-frozen, unpackaged fish are not reflected in these industry groups. Second, some foods are processed in retail stores—e.g., ice cream, candy, cookies— and are considered as retail operations. Third, food from home gardens or from household hunting and fishing are also excluded from these industry groups.

# MANUFACTURING SECTOR

In the first chapter, a distinction was made between primary and finished food processors. The former process relatively homogenous commodities into basic ingredients and were referred to as "processors." The latter use ingredients to manufacture final consumer products and were referred to as "manufacturers." Even though most of the firms in the forty-nine food industries sell some of their output for further processing by manufacturers, there are some industries that sell most, if not all, of their output to manufacturers in the same or different industry groups. Flour, for example, is the major ingredient purchased for the pastry and pasta industries. Grain mill products are used by the cereal and pet food industries. Sugar is used by many industries, as are refined and unrefined oils. Dried fruits and vegetables are sold primarily to the canning and dried soup industries. The meat packing industry sell its output to firms that salt, smoke, and cure meats. Confectionery firms sell their output to the baking and dairy industries. The poultry industry sell its output to makers of franks and luncheon meats. As we see in most cases, the forty-nine food industries are some of their own best customers. Because most of the forty-nine food industries sell some part of their output for further processing by manufacturers in the same or other industries, the structural characterizations of the manufacturing section will be examined mainly without regard to the processor-manufacturer distinction. The implications of this distinction will be examined more fully in terms of its impact on the manufacturer's marketing decisions in the next chapter.

# COMPANY AND ESTABLISHMENT TRENDS

Considering the situation in U.S. food manufacturing over the census years 1982, 1987, and 1992, several major trends are revealed in **Table 4-1**. The number of food manufacturing companies (legal entities that own one or more establishments) increased by 160 between 1982 and 1992. **Table 4-2** shows the change in companies over these selected census years. The number of companies increased in industry groups preserved fruits and vegetables (203), bakery (205), sugar and confectionery (206), and miscellaneous food (209). The other five industry groups all show a decrease over these years. Overall, the number of companies decreased by about four percent.

Another trend revealed in **Table 4-1** is a six percent decline in the number of establishments (single places of business with one or more employees, engaged in a single line of commerce). **Table 4-3** shows the nature of this decline over the selected census years. The number of establishments increased in industry groups 205, 206, and 209 and decreased in the other six groups. The decline in the numbers of companies and establishments reflect the increasing consolidation of sales and assets in the manufacturing sector.

## Shipments (Sales)

A third trend revealed in **Table 4-1** is the forty-four percent increase in shipments or sales. **Table 4-4** shows the change over the selected census years. Because these sales are unadjusted for inflation all of its industry groups show an increase. These increases range from a low of fifteen percent in fats and oils (207) to a high of fifty-seven percent in grain mills (204). Three industry groups—meat products (201), dairy (202), and beverages (208)—alone make up about fifty-one percent of the total shipments in the food manufacturing sector.

## Value Added

Despite the decline in companies and establishments, **Table 4-1** shows a seventy-seven percent increase in value added. **Value added is a measure of the economic contribution the food processing sector makes to the U.S. food marketing system.** It is used because it avoids the problem of double counting inherent in sales measures (shipments). It is the difference between the value of shipment sales and most costs of production inputs (i.e., materials and energy).

The change in value added by industry groups over the census years is shown by **Table 4-5**. Although all industry groups show an increase in value added because of price inflation, the increases range from 101 percent in grain mills (204) to thirty-five percent in fats and oils (207). Three industry groups—preserved fruits and vegetables (203), grain mills (204), and beverages (209)—make up forty-eight percent of the total value added by the food processing sector.

The last trend revealed by **Table 4-1** is a seventy-five percent increase in the value added per employee. The number of employees increased over this time period, however, labor productivity, as measured by value added per employee, was due primarily to the use of more capital equipment and technological change. **Table 4-6** shows the change in value added per employee by industry groups over the census years. Beverages (208) experienced a 136 percent increase in value added per employee, and grain mills (204) a 101 percent increase. Further examination of this table suggests virtually no change in the industry group rank order of value added from 1982 to 1992.

**Table 4-7** summarizes the change in food manufacturing establishments and value added over the selected census years. When the industry groups distinctions are removed, the percent of small establishments (one to nineteen employees) increased by six percent, the percent of medium establishments (twenty to ninety-nine employees) decreased by thirteen percent, and the percentage of large establishment (100 to 499 employees) increase was two percent. The most significant change was the twenty-three percent increase in very large establishments (more than 500 employees).

With regard to value added, the trend revealed by **Table 4-7** is clear. The percent of value added by small, medium, and large establishments declined from 1982 to 1992, while the percent of value added by very large establishments increased by twenty-three percent.

When establishments and value added are related to employment size, the conclusion is inescapable. Roughly, eighty-three percent of the establishments (small and medium) generate only eighteen percent of the value added, while seventeen percent of the establishments (large and very large) contribute eighty-two percent of the value added to the food processing sector.

## LOCATION OF MANUFACTURING SECTOR

Food manufacturing activity takes place in all of the 50 states. At the same time, some of these states have higher levels of manufacturing activity than others. A problem arises when trying to rank the states by level of food manufacturing activity. Because there are three factors that have been used in the past to measure manufacturing activity, a state may rank high in one factor but not in the other two factors. For example, states with a large number of employees in the low-value-added poultry industry (e.g., Arkansas, Georgia, and Alabama) will rank higher in employment than in value added or shipments. States (like Maryland and Ohio) with high-value-added industries (bread, cakes, cookies, and crackers) rank lower in employment. States (like Nebraska and Kansas) that are heavily dependent on meat packing plants typically rank much higher on shipments than on employment. Finally, states that have high shipment values (like Nebraska, Kansas, and Iowa) rank lower on value added. Because there isn't a perfect correspondence regarding the rank order of each state on these three factors, the location of the food manufacturing sector will be examined using all three bases: employment, value added, and value of shipments (sales).

Although the number of food establishments can be used as a measure of activity within a state, it does not measure the contribution the state makes to the food manufacturing sector. A state may have a large number of small establishments that manufacture little, or a few large firms that manufacture much. Thus, where food is manufactured is better illustrated as a productivity measure rather than as a numerical count of establishments. Value added and shipments are clearly productivity measures. Further, the number of employees is more closely associated with productivity than is the number of establishments.

## Employment

One basis for identifying the location of food manufacturing is to focus on the number of people in each state who are employed in food manufacturing. It is reasonable to believe that the number of people employed in food manufacturing in each state corresponds to the level of manufacturing activity. Thus, a large number of food employees in a state indicates a higher level of manufacturing activity, and vice versa.

**Table 4-8** shows the nature of employment in food manufacturing over the last three census years. With the exceptions of Alabama and New Jersey, there has been virtually no change in the leading twenty states in food employment. Most of the changes have been in the rank order by the states. In 1992, the twenty leading states accounted for about seventy-five percent of all food employees. The top ten states accounted for over sixty-five percent of all food employment. The five leading states represented about forty-two percent of all food employees, and California alone contributed more than fifteen percent of all employees in food manufacturing.

Over these census years, the percent of total food employment—accounted for by the twenty leading states—declined. However, the percentages of total food employment accounted for by the ten and five leading states both increased. This suggests that the location of food manufacturing has become more concentrated, as measured by employment. The three Mid-Atlantic states (New York, New Jersey, and Pennsylvania) were all leading states. In 1992, these states accounted for 136,000 jobs or twelve percent of the U.S. total. Each of the states in the East North Central division (Ohio, Indiana, Illinois, Wisconsin, and Michigan) were in the top twenty leading states. In 1992, food manufacturing provided 265,000 jobs for these states, or twenty-four percent of the U.S. total. Only three of the seven West North Central division states (Missouri, Minnesota, and Iowa) were leading states. These states accounted for 127,000 jobs or eleven percent of the U.S. total. Four of the eight South Atlantic division states (Virginia, Georgia, North Carolina, and Florida) were leading states in food employment. These states had 185,000 food processing jobs or sixteen percent of the U.S. total in 1992.

Only Tennessee and Alabama in the four state East South Central division were leading states in employment. These states had 72,000 jobs or six percent of the U.S. total employment in manufacturing in 1992. Arkansas and Texas, two of the four states that make up the West South Central division were leading states. Together, they had 134,000 jobs or twelve percent of the U.S. total food employment in 1992. Of the five states in the Pacific division, only California and Washington were leading states in food employment. In 1992, those two states had 207,000 jobs or eighteen percent of the U.S. total food employment. Finally, none of the six states that make up the New England division, and none of the twelve states that make up the Mountain division, were leading states in food employment for 1992.

## Value Added

The location of food manufacturing can also be identified by focusing on how much each state contributes to the food manufacturing sector. It was determined earlier in this chapter that value added is essentially a "margin" concept. Because this margin is used to cover expenses and contribute to operating profits, value added as a margin indicates how much each state spends to manufacture and market its output.

**Table 4-9** shows the ranking of states in terms of value added over three census years. Once again, we see virtually no change in the leading states. In 1982 and 1992, Indiana was ranked sixteenth and seventeenth respectively. In 1987, Maryland replaced Indiana as a leading state. Most of the changes over these census years have been in the rank ordering of states. In 1992, the twenty leading states accounted for eighty-one percent of total value added by all food manufacturers. The top ten states accounted for fifty-five percent. The five leading states represented thirty-six percent of the total value added and California alone contributed twelve percent of the value added in food manufacturing. Over the three census years, the percent of value added by the twenty leading states increased. This reinforces the earlier observation that food manufacturing has become more concentrated, as measured by value added.

The three Mid-Atlantic states (New York, Pennsylvania, and New Jersey) were all leading states. In 1992, they accounted for thirteen percent of the total U.S. value added. Each of the five states in the East North Central division (Ohio, Illinois, Wisconsin, Michigan, and Indiana) were leading value added states. In 1992, they accounted for twenty-three percent of total U.S. value added. Four of the seven West North Central states, (Missouri, Minnesota, Iowa, and Nebraska) were leading states. In 1992, they accounted for twelve percent of total U.S. value added. Five of the eight states in the South Atlantic division (Virginia, Georgia, North Carolina, Florida, and Maryland) were leading states. They accounted for eleven percent of the U.S. total value added. Only Texas in the West South Central division and Tennessee in the East South Central division were leading states. They contributed six percent and three percent to the U.S. total value added, respectively. California and Washington in the Pacific states division were the only leading states. Together, they accounted for fourteen percent of the U.S. total value added in 1992. Finally, none of the six states that make up the New England division, and none of the twelve states that make up the Mountain division, were leading states in value added for 1992.

## Value of Shipments

Another basis for identifying the location of food manufacturing is to use the value of shipments. Shipments represent food manufacturing sales and indicate how much a state generates in sales, regardless of how many people are in manufacturing or what margin results from these sales. Because of this, sales are probably the better indicator of the volume of manufacturing activity.

**Table 4-10** indicates shipments over the last three census years. With the exceptions of Arkansas and Virginia, there has been little change in the leading twenty states in food shipments. Most of the changes have been in the rank ordering of the states. The twenty leading states accounted for seventy-eight percent of all food shipments in 1992. The top ten states contributed over fifty-two percent, while the top five states accounted for about thirty-three of all food shipments. California alone accounted for eleven percent of all food shipments in sales. Over the census years the percentage of total shipments has declined slightly. Food manufacturing, as measured by shipments, has become slightly more geographically dispersed.

The three Mid-Atlantic states (New York, Pennsylvania, and New Jersey) accounted for eleven percent of U.S. shipments in 1992. The Mid-Atlantic states were also leading states in terms of value added. The five states in the East North Central division (Ohio, Illinois, Wisconsin, Michigan, and Indiana) were all leading states. In 1992, they accounted for twenty-one percent of total U.S. shipments. These states were also leading states in terms of employment and value added. Five of the seven West North Central states (Missouri, Minnesota, Iowa, Kansas, and Nebraska) were leading states. They accounted for seventeen percent of total U.S. shipments.

Three of the eight South Atlantic division states (Florida, Georgia, and North Carolina) were leading states in shipments. They accounted for nine percent of the total U.S. shipments. These same three states were leading states in employment and value added. Only Texas, in the West South Central division, and Tennessee, in the East South Central division, were leading states in shipments. They contributed six percent and two percent to U.S. shipments in 1992, respectively. These same two states were leading states in value added. The only leading state in shipments in the Pacific division was California. In 1992, it accounted for eleven percent of all U.S. shipments. In fact, California is the number one state on all three bases: employment, value added, and shipments.

In summary, a number of observations can be made regarding the location of food manufacturing. First, even though there isn't a perfect correspondence regarding the rank order of each state on these three bases, there is a high degree of correspondence. Eighteen of the states are in the top twenty states on all three bases. Eight of these states make up the entire Mid-Atlantic and East North Central divisions. Second, California is clearly the number one state on all three bases. Finally, most of the changes over the census years are basically changes in the rank ordering of the states when measured in terms of employment, value added, and shipments.

## INDUSTRY GROUPS

Up to this point, the food manufacturing sector has been analyzed primarily at the industry group level. Further, the geographical distribution of food manufacturing focused on the contribution made by states. This section extends the preliminary analysis of industry groups. Now, each of the nine industry groups will be examined to provide us with a description of the industries that make up these nine industry groups. The Census of Manufacturing classifies these industries into four-digit codes.

## Meat (201)

This industry group is made up of three industries: Meat Packing Plants (2011) are establishments that engage primarily in the slaughtering of cattle, hogs, sheep, lambs, and calves for meat. The leading state in employment in 1992 was Iowa, but Nebraska had the highest value added and shipments.

Sausages and Other Prepared Meats (2013) establishments primarily manufacture sausages, and cured, smoked, canned, and frozen meats. In 1992, Wisconsin was the leading state in employment, value added, and shipments.

Poultry Slaughtering and Processing (2015) establishments primarily slaughter, dress, pack, freeze, and can poultry, rabbits, and other small game. This industry also includes the drying, freezing, and breaking of eggs. Arkansas was the leading state in employment, value added, and shipments in 1992.

**Table 4-11** presents the changing structure of this industry's group value added by establishment size. In 1992, small establishments (one to nineteen employees) made up fifty-four percent of all establishments, but only two percent of the value added. Very large establishments made up only seven percent of all establishments, but fifty-six percent of the value added. Over the census years, the number of establishments declined by eleven percent (from 3,623 to 3,237).

## Dairy (202)

This industry group is made up of four industries. Creamy Butter (2021) establishments primarily manufacture creamy butter. The leading state in employment in 1992 was Minnesota, but Wisconsin was the leading state in value added and shipments.

Cheese, Natural and Processed (2022) establishments manufacture natural, processed cheese, cheese foods, spreads, and imitation substitutes. Wisconsin was the leading state in employment, value added, and shipments in 1992.

Establishments in industry 2023 make dry, condensed, and evaporated food products. In addition, they make mixes for frozen ice cream, ice milk, and dairy and nondairy cream substitutes, and dietary supplements. Indiana was the leading state in employment, but Michigan led in value added and shipments in 1992.

Ice cream and frozen desserts are manufactured by establishments in industry 2024. California led all states in employment, value added, and shipments in 1992.

Fluid milk (2026) establishments primarily process (pasteurize, homogenize, vitaminize, and bottle) fluid milk and cream, cottage cheese, yogurt, and other fermented milk. Once again, California led all states in employment, value added, and shipments in 1992.

**Table 4-12** presents the changing structure of this industry group. In 1992, small establishments made up forty-three percent of all establishments but only two percent of the value added. Very large establishments made up one percent of the establishments but seventy-six percent of the value added. The number of establishments declined by twenty-six percent (from 2,724 to 2,024) over the census years.

## Preserved Fruits and Vegetables (203)

Six industries make up this industry group. Canned Specialties (2032) establishments can specialty products such as baby foods and soups. The leading state in employment, value added, and shipments in 1992 was Pennsylvania.

Fruits and vegetables and vegetable juices are canned by establishments in industry 2033. In 1992, California led all states in employment, value added, and shipments.

Establishments involved in sun-drying and artificially dehydrating fruits and vegetables make up industry 2034. In 1992, California led all states in employment, value added, and shipments.

Establishments engaged in pickling, brining fruits and vegetables, and manufacturing salad dressings, vegetable relishes, sauces, and seasonings make up industry 2035. In 1992, California led all states in employment, value added, and shipments.

The freezing and cold packing of fruits, fruit juice, and vegetables make up the establishments in industry 2037. In 1992, California led in employment, Washington in value added, and Florida led in shipments.

Frozen specialties such as dinners, nationality foods, and pizzas are made by firms in industry 2038. In 1992, California led the states in employment, value added, and shipments.

**Table 4-13** shows the changing structure of this industry group. In 1992, small establishments made up forty-six percent of all establishments and two percent of the value added. Very large establishments made five percent of all establishments and thirty-five percent of the value added. The number of establishments declined by two percent (from 2,093 to 2,046) over the census years.

## Grain Mill (204)

Seven industries make up this industry group. The milling of flour or meal from grain is conducted by establishments in industry 2041. In 1992, Texas led all states in employment, Missouri in value added, and New York in shipments.

The manufacturing of cereal breakfast foods is carried on by establishments in industry 2043. In 1992, Michigan led all states in employment, value added, and shipments.

The cleaning and polishing of rice, and the manufacturing of rice flour and mill are carried on by establishments in industry 2044. In 1992, Arkansas led all states in employment, value added, and shipments.

Establishments engaged primarily in preparing flour mixes or doughs make up industry 2045. In 1992, Missouri led the states in employment, but Illinois led in value added and shipments.

Establishments that mill corn or sorghum grain (milo) by the wet process and produce starch, syrup, oil, sugar, and by-products, such as gluten feed and meal, make up industry 2046. In 1992, Iowa led all the states in employment, value added, and shipments.

The manufacturing of dog and cat food is carried on by establishments in industry 2047. In 1992, Pennsylvania led in employment, California in value added, and New York in shipments.

The manufacturing of prepared feeds and feed ingredients is the primary task of establishments in industry 2048. In 1992, Iowa led in employment, and California in value added and shipments.

**Table 4-14** shows the changing structure of this industry group. In 1992, small establishments made up fifty-nine percent of all establishments and four percent of the value added. Very large establishments made up one percent of the establishments and 33 percent of the value added. The number of establishments declined by five percent (from 2,745 to 2,619) over the census years.

## Bakery (205)

Three industries make up this industry group. Establishments that make fresh or frozen bread, rolls, and fresh cakes, pies, pastries, and other similar perishable bakery products make up industry 2051. In 1992, California led all the states in employment, value added, and shipments.

Establishments that make fresh cookies, crackers, pretzels, and similar "dry" bakery products make up industry 2052. In 1992, Illinois led all states in employment and shipments, but Pennsylvania led in value added.

The manufacturing of frozen baby products is carried on by establishments in industry 2053. In 1992, Pennsylvania led in employment, value added, and shipments.

**Table 4-15** indicates the changing structure of this industry group. In 1992, small establishments accounted for sixty percent of all establishments and three percent of value added. Very large establishments made up two percent of the establishments and thirty-seven percent of the value added. The number of establishments increased by eighteen percent (from 2,663 to 3,151) over the census years.

## Sugar and Confectionery (206)

Six industries make up this industry group. Establishments that manufacture raw sugar, syrup, molasses, and finished (granulated or clarified) cane sugar make up industry 2061. In 1992, Florida led all states in employment, value added, and shipments.

The refining of raw cane sugar and sugar syrup is carried on by establishments in industry 2062. In 1992, California led in employment. Due to the small number of establishments, data was not disclosed on value added and shipments.

Establishments that manufacture sugar from sugar beets make up industry 2063. In 1992, Minnesota led all states in employment. Once again, due to the small number of firms, no data was disclosed on value added and shipments.

Establishments that manufacture candy, including chocolate candy and other confections, make up industry 2064. In addition, establishments that manufacture chewing gum or chewing gum base make up industry 2067. For 1992, are combined in the totals. In 1992, Illinois led in employment, value added, and shipments.

Establishments in industry 2066 shell, roast, and grind cocoa beans to make chocolate liquor and manufacture solid chocolate bars, chocolate coatings, and other chocolate and cocoa products. In 1992, New York led the states in employment. Value added and shipments were not disclosed due to small number of establishments.

Establishments that manufacture salted, roasted, dried, cooked, or canned nuts, or process grains or seeds for snack purposes, make up industry 2068. In 1992, California led all states in employment, value added, and shipments. **Table 4-16** shows the changing structure of this industry. In 1992, small establishments made up fifty-six percent of all establishments and three percent of the value added. Very large establishments made up three percent of the establishments and thirty-seven percent of the value added. The number of establishments increased by nine percent (from 1,033 to 1,130) over the census years.

## Fats and Oils (207)

Five industries make up this industry group. Establishments that manufacture cottonseed oil, cake, meal, and linters, or process cottonseed oils, make up industry 2074. In 1992, Texas led all states in employment, value added, and shipments.

Establishments that manufacture soybean oil, cake, and meal, or that process soybean oils, make up industry 2075. In 1992, Illinois led all states in employment, value added, and shipments.

Establishments that make vegetable oils, cake, and meal, or that process vegetable oils, make up industry 2076. In 1992, North Dakota led in employment. No data was disclosed for value added or shipments due to small number of establishments.

Establishments that make animal oil, fish and other marine oils, fish and animal meal, and render inedible stearin, grease, and tallow from animal fat, bones, and meat scraps make up industry 2077. In 1992, California led in employment, value added, and shipments.

Establishments that manufacture shortening, table oils, margarine, and other edible fats and oils not elsewhere classified make up industry 2079. In 1992, Illinois led the states in employment and shipments but California led in value added.

**Table 4-17** presents the changing structure of this industry group. In 1992, forty percent of all establishments were small and accounted for four percent of the value added. Large establishments made up thirteen percent of the establishments and fifty-two percent of the value added. The number of establishments declined by twenty-five percent (from 724 to 543) over the census years.

## Beverages (208)

Six industries make up this industry group. Establishments that manufacture malt beverages make up industry 2082. In 1992, California led all the states in employment, value added, and shipments.

Establishments that manufacture malt or malt byproducts from barley and other grains make up industry 2083. In 1992, Wisconsin led the states in employment, value added, and shipments.

Establishments engaged in manufacturing wines, brandy, and brandy spirits make up industry 2084. In 1992, California led the states in employment, value added, and shipments.

Industry 2085 is made up of establishments that manufacture alcoholic liquors, cordials, and alcoholic cocktails. In 1992, Kentucky led all the states in employment, value added, and shipments.

Establishments that manufacture soft drinks and carbonated waters make up industry 2086. In 1992, Texas led the states in employment, but California led in value added and shipments.

The manufacturing of flavoring extracts, syrups, powders, and related products not elsewhere classified is conducted by establishments in industry 2087. In 1992, Illinois led all the states in employment, value added, and shipments.

**Table 4-18** shows the changing structure of this industry group. In 1992, small establishments made up fifty-three percent of all establishments and three percent of the value added. Very large establishments made up two percent of the establishments and thirty-three percent of the value added. The number of establishments declined by twenty percent (from 2,584 to 2,066) over the census years.

## Miscellaneous Food (209)

There are seven industries that make up this industry group. Establishments that cook and can fish, shrimp, crabs, and other seafood, and those that smoke, salt, dry, or cure fish and other seafood make up industry 2091. In 1992, California led the states in employment, value added, and shipments.

Establishments that prepare fresh or frozen fish make up industry 2092. In 1992, California led the states in employment, but Washington led in value added and shipments.

Establishments that primarily roast coffee and make coffee concentrates and extracts in powdered, liquid, or frozen form, including freeze-dried, make up industry 2095. In 1992, Texas led the states in employment and shipments, but California led in value added.

Establishments that manufacture potato chips, corn chips, and similar snacks made up industry 2096. Pennsylvania led the states in employment, but Texas led in value added and shipments in 1992.

Establishments that manufacture ice make up industry 2097. In 1992, California led in employment, value added, and shipments.

Establishments that make dry macaroni, spaghetti, vermicelli, and noodles make up industry 2098. In 1992, New York led the states in employment, value added, and shipments.

Foods that are not elsewhere classified, such as baking powder, yeast, peanut butter, tea, vinegar, and cider, are made by establishments in industry 2099. In 1992, California, led all the states in employment, value added, and shipments.

**Table 4-19** presents the changing structure of this industry group. In 1992, small establishments made up sixty-three percent of all establishments, and six percent of the value added. Very large establishments made up less than one percent and accounted for fifteen percent of the value added. The number of establishments increased by one percent (from 3,941 to 3,976) over the census years.

# INDUSTRIES

Having described the food manufacturing sector by industry groups, the focus will now turn to the industries that make up these industry groups. The nine industry groups comprise of forty-nine industries. These forty-nine industries are analyzed in terms of their value added contributions and value added intensities for the year 1992 only. This was done because there has been virtually no change in the rank order of the industry groups from 1982 to 1992. The relative stability in the rank order of the industry groups emanates from the stability in the industries that make up the industry groups.

## Value Added

**Table 4-20** represents the rank order of the forty-nine industries by value added. For 1992, the **Census of Manufacturing** reported only a combined total for industries

2064 and 2067, ostensibly to prevent disclosure of the few companies that make up industry 2067 (chewing gum). In general, industries that manufacture highly processed, differentiated, and convenient consumer products are ranked higher than those industries that are considered processors of raw materials. Bread (first), malt beverages (second), soft drinks (third), and cereal (fourth) are examples of finished goods manufacturers that top the list. Industries that process ingredients to be used by manufacturers in the production of finished consumer products are typically lower value added industries. Cane sugar (fortieth), rice milling (forty-second), cottonseed oil (forty-fifth), and vegetable oil (last) are examples of lower value added industries. In the aggregate, the ten industries that mainly sell ingredients to manufacturers account for only 6.7 percent of the total value added by the food processing sector, whereas, the top ten food manufacturers of consumer goods account for about fifty percent of the value added by this sector.

## Value Added Intensities

Another method of analyzing the value added differences among industries is to determine the percentage of value added per dollar of shipments (sales). Using this perspective, value added is essentially a margin concept, that is, when production inputs are subtracted (similar to cost of goods sold) from shipments (sales) what remains is a margin (similar to a gross margin) that is used to cover expenses and contribute to operating profits.

**Table 4-21** is derived from **Table 4-20** and represents the food processing industries ranked by intensity or the percentage of value added to total shipments. Once again, the resulting quotient represents how much of each sales dollar the industry can spend to produce and market its output. Industries that have a high value added margin or intensity provide greater flexibility in the marketing of their output than do industries with low intensities.

A number of factors explain the variations in industry value added intensities. First, industries that produce highly differentiated, convenient, and processed consumer products have high value added intensities. Breakfast cereals, malt beverages, cookies, breads, candy, and snacks are intensities that contain highly differentiated brands. To market these foods, a higher margin is needed.

The costs of raw materials also impacts on value added intensity. In general, industries that purchase relatively expensive farm commodities or semiprocessed ingredients have low value added intensities. Sugar and oilseed are examples of products that have very low value added, whereas poultry processing and prepared meats and sausages use relatively costly processed ingredients.

The perceived amount of value that the consumer must add to the food item purchased also influences the variation in intensity of value. When consumers anticipate having to contribute a significant amount of their own labor in order to produce food ready to eat, less value added by the industry is demanded. Thus, the convenience foods have more value added by the processor than basic ingredients because little has to be done by the consumer before the convenience food is consumed. Breakfast cereals, cookies, cakes, and salad dressings, are examples of highly processed and convenient foods requiring minimal preparation before serving.

The intensity of value added is also influenced by the level of new product development. In general, industries that introduce many new products have higher value added intensities. The higher margin is needed in order to cover the product development and marketing costs. The industries at the top of the intensity list generally introduce many more new products than those at the bottom of the list.

# COMPANIES

As previously mentioned, the number of companies increased by one percent between 1982 and 1992. The analysis that follows will focus on the changes in companies and their share of total shipments (sales) for three selected census years. Because a company is defined as a legal entity that owns one or more establishments, the number of companies will be less than the number of establishments in each industry. However, the same company may appear in several industries, if it has diversified activities. The result of this double counting for some companies is to produce a larger number of companies than was specified earlier in this chapter.

## Number of Companies

**Table 4-22** indicates the change in the number of companies that make up the forty-nine industries. From 1982 to 1992, thirty-three industries showed a decrease in the number of companies, while thirteen industries indicated an increase in companies. The change in companies for three industries could not be determined because data was not available. Industry 2051—bread, cakes, and related products—experienced the largest increase (311) in number of companies. Major increases in companies also occurred in wine, brandy, and spirits (190), and malt beverages (93). The largest decrease (599) in the number of companies occurred in industry 2086—bottled and canned soft drinks. Major decreases in companies also occurred in meat packing plants (361) and fluid milk (328).

The number of companies in each industry varies widely. In 1992, there were 2,180 companies in bread and related products (2051), but only twelve cane sugar refining companies (2062). Fourteen of the industries had fewer than one hundred companies, twenty-three had between 101 and 500 companies, seven had between 501 and 1,000, and five had 1,000 or more companies. This distribution parallels that of industry establishments.

## Share of Shipments (Sales)

To complete the structural analysis of the food manufacturing sector, emphasis will now be placed on determining the market share of the leading firms in the forty-nine industries. Market share is generally computed by dividing the sales of the leading firms by the total sales for the respective industry. The market share, sometimes referred to as a concentration ratio, can then be determined for any number of leading companies. By convention, economists have generally defined industries as strongly oligopolistic if the four-company concentration is greater than fifty percent.

An examination of **Table 4-22** indicates that between 1982 and 1992, the concentration ratios have increased in thirty-one industries, declined in nine industries, and remained virtually unchanged in seven industries. The most concentrated industries were malt beverages, vegetable oil, cane sugar refining, and cereal breakfast foods (all above eighty percent). The least concentrated were fresh, frozen packaged fish, fluid milk, food preparation, prepared feeds, ice cream, and manufactured ice (all below thirty percent).

For the most recent 1992 census, **Table 4-22** identifies the number of industries that may be characterized as having a particularly competitive structure. Using the previously mentioned convention, twenty-one industries may be defined as strong oligopolies. The other twenty-eight industries may be characterized as being more or less monopolistically competitive.

Because the structure of the manufacturing sector has an influence on the marketing decisions made by the firms it comprises, a brief description of the relevant competitive structures will be presented.

Under conditions that approximate an oligopoly, a few sellers dominate the sales of a product and the entry of new firms is difficult or impossible. Although the largest firms can influence price by virtue of their large market shares, they realize that a change in their price or output will cause a reaction by competing firms. The expected reactions by competitors become a crucial determinant of its marketing decisions. Thus, the way a firm competes will depend on how it thinks its competitors will react to changes in products, distribution, promotions, and prices.

Under conditions that approximate monopolistic competition, many sellers compete to sell a differentiated product. Entry into the market by new firms is possible. Because the product of each firm is a close, but not perfect, substitute for competitive products, firms make marketing decisions to cause consumers to prefer one product over another. Further, the market share of monopolistic competitors is small. Thus, marketing decisions made by these firms are presumed not to bring about reactions from competitors.

Although the market structures of oligopolies and monopolistic competitors is different, the approach they use to compete is essentially the same. Marketing decisions focus on new product introduction, better packaging, increased services, expanded retail availability and credit, reasonable prices, and other merchandising efforts.

## Leading Companies

The structural analysis of the manufacturing sector would be incomplete if it didn't identify the leading firms. Although merger activity makes it difficult to determine ownership, there is a degree of stability in the leading firms.

**Table 4-23** identifies the top fifty food processing companies. According to the **U.S. Bureau of the Census**, in 1982 the top fifty firms had forty-three percent of all food manufacturing sales, and in 1987 it increased to forty-seven percent. Concentration ratios were not computed for the top fifty firms in 1992. However, because thirty-one of the forty-nine industries increased their level of concentration, it is reasonable to assume that the level of concentration for the top fifty firms also increased. Although there are changes in the rank order of these firms from time to time, almost all of them remain leading firms from year to year. These firms are all multi-product, multi-plant, and, for the most part, multi-national enterprises. However, their output is not restricted solely to food processing. In fact, only twenty-one of the top fifty firms have one hundred percent food sales. **Phillip Morris**, the top ranked firm, has significant holdings in the food processing sector and is an excellent example of a firm that doesn't generate one hundred percent of its sales from food sales.

In general, these fifty leading firms play a significant, if not dominant, role in their industry groups. For example, **ConAgra, Inc.** and **IBP, Inc.** are the two largest livestock processors. **Tyson Foods** is the largest broiler company. **ConAgra, Inc. (Butterball Turkey Co.)** is the largest turkey manufacturer. **Kellogg Co., General Mills, Inc., Ralston Purina Co.,** and **Quaker Oats Co**. dominate the cereal industry. **Pepsi Cola, Inc.** and **Coca-Cola Co.** are the top two firms in the soft drink industry. **Campbell Soup Co.** dominates the canned soup industry. **Dole Food Co.** and **Del Monte Foods** are the major companies in canned fruits and vegetables. **Sara Lee Corp., RJR Nabisco, Inc., Keebler Co.,** and **Interstate Bakeries Corp.** are all major firms in bakery products. **Cargill, Inc., Archer Daniels Midland Co.** and **CPC International** are the top firms in grain mill products. **Dean Foods Co., Mid-America Dairymen, Inc., Borden, Inc., Associated Milk Producers, Inc.,** and **Land O' Lakes, Inc.** are major firms in dairy products. **Continental Grain Co., Pet Incorporated**, and **H. J. Heinz Co.** are all top firms in fats and oils. Finally, **Hershey Foods, Wm. Wrigley Jr. Co.,** and **Nestle USA, Inc.** are all major producers of sugar and confectionery products.

Although these leading firms have substantial sales, the dominance of large firms in the food manufacturing sector is even more apparent when you consider that the combined sales of the next fifty largest firms barely equal the total sales of the leading firm—**Phillip Morris Co., Inc.**

## SUMMARY

This chapter examined the food manufacturing sector. This highly diverse sector is made up of nine industry groups classified in the **Census of Manufacturing Food and Kindred Products (SIC 20)** as three-digit **Standard Industrial Classification (SIC) groups 201 to 209**. These industry groups are further classified into forty-nine industries, each of which is designated by a four-digit SIC code number.

At the sector level, a number of trends were evident across the three most recent census years—1982, 1987, and 1992. First, both the number of companies and establishments have declined. This continues the trend that began in 1947 when there were over 31,430 companies and 39,933 establishments. Second, shipments (sales), value added, number of employees, and value added per employee have all increased. These data suggest an increasingly efficient sector. Third, the twenty leading states in food processing employment, shipments, and value added were virtually the same in each of the census years. At the sector level, the regional specialization of manufacturing has resulted in a good deal of stability in these states. Finally, when examined by employment size, it is apparent that the food manufacturing sector, like the agricultural sector, consists of two distinct groups. One group consists of a few very large establishments that manufacture well-known brands and account for about eighty percent of sales. The other group consists of a very large number of small establishments that account for a declining share of sales.

A deeper understanding of the ever-changing manufacturing sector was gained by a structural examination of its industry groups. Six of the nine groups experienced a decline in the number of establishments, while five of the nine experienced a decrease in the number of companies. In each of the nine industry groups, the combined percentage of large and very large firms increased over the census years, as did their share of value added. Again, we find the industry groups to be made up of a few large establishments with a dominant share of the value added, and a large number of small establishments with an ever-decreasing share.

An examination of the manufacturing sector by its forty-nine industries identified the diversity of their market structures. Fewer than forty percent of all the industries can be characterized as oligopolistic in nature, while the rest are better described as monopolistic competitors. Even though the market structures of oligopolies and monopolistic competitors are different, they rely on essentially the same approach to marketing. It is within the context of these market structures that food manufacturers must make marketing decisions.

## SELECTED REFERENCES

Connor, J. M. *Food Processing—An Industrial Powerhouse in Transition.* Lexington, Mass. Lexington Books, D.C. Health and Company: 1988.

Connor, J. M., R. T. Rogers, B. W. Marion, and W. F. Mueller. *The Food Manufacturing Industries—Structure, Strategies, Performance, and Policies,* Lexington, Mass. Lexington Books, D.C. Health and Company: 1985.

Kohls, R. L. and J. N. Uhl. *Marketing of Agricultural Products.* 7th ed. New York. Macmillan Publishing Co.: 1990.

Marion, B. W. and the NC-117 Committee. *The Organization and Performance of the U.S. Food System.* Lexington Books, D.C. Health and Company, Lexington, Mass.: 1986.

*Food Marketing Review, 1992–93.* Commodity Economics Division, ERS, U.S.D.A. Agricultural Economic Report No: 678.

*Food Processing—The Magazine of Strategy and Technology.* A Putnam Publication, December, 1994.

## REVIEW QUESTIONS

1. Explain how the structure of the food manufacturing sector is defined by the Census Manufacturing.

2. Distinguish between food processors and food manufacturers.

3. What implications do the decline in food companies and establishments have for the future of the food manufacturing sector?

4. How would you summarize the structure of the food manufacturing sector?

5. How would you answer the question, Where is food processed or manufactured?

6. What is meant by the term "high-value added industry"?

7. How is value added intensity defined?

8. Identify the factors that explain the variations in industry value added intensities.

9. Given the market share of the four leading firms in the forty-nine industries, how would you characterize the structure of the food manufacturing sector?

10. Give some examples of the leading firms in the nine industry groups.

**TABLE 4-1.** SELECTED TRENDS IN U.S. FOOD MANUFACTURING

| YEAR | ALL CO. | ALL EST. | SHIPMENTS (millions) | VALUE ADDED (millions) | NUMBER OF EMPLOY. (thousands) | VALUE ADDED PER EMPLOY. |
|---|---|---|---|---|---|---|
| 1982 | 16,813 | 22,130 | 280,529 | 88,419 | 1,488 | $59,733 |
| 1987 | 15,692 | 20,583 | 329,725 | 121,603 | 1,489 | 81,682 |
| 1992 | 16,075 | 20,798 | 403,836 | 156,843 | 1,504 | 104,229 |

*SOURCE:* CENSUS OF MANUFACTURERS 1982, 1987, AND 1992


**TABLE 4-2.** U.S. FOOD MANUFACTURING COMPANIES BY INDUSTRY GROUPS

| **INDUSTRY GROUPS, SIC** | **1982** | **1987** | **1992** |
|---|---|---|---|
| MEAT, 201 | 3,218 | 2,767 | 2,797 |
| DAIRY, 202 | 2,103 | 1,700 | 1,538 |
| PRESERVED FRUITS AND VEGETABLES, 203 | 1,642 | 1,438 | 1,648 |
| GRAIN MILL, 204 | 1,915 | 1,722 | 1,763 |
| BAKERY, 205 | 2,165 (1) | 2,349 | 2,714 |
| SUGAR AND CONFECTIONERY, 206 | 880 (2) | 918 | 1,016 |
| FATS AND OILS, 207 | 474 | 340 | 313 |
| BEVERAGES, 208 | 2,019 | 1,697 | 1,634 |
| MISC. FOOD, 209 | 3,469 (3) | 3,271 | 3,550 |

(1) DOES NOT INCLUDE INDUSTRY 2053
(2) DOES NOT INCLUDE INDUSTRY 2068
(3) DOES NOT INCLUDE INDUSTRY 2096

*SOURCE:* MANUFACTURING CENSUS OF 1982, 1987, AND 1992.

**TABLE 4-3.** U.S. FOOD MANUFACTURING ESTABLISHMENTS BY INDUSTRY GROUPS

| INDUSTRY GROUPS, SIC | 1982 | 1987 | 1992 |
|---|---|---|---|
| MEAT, 201 | 3,623 | 3,240 | 3,237 |
| DAIRY, 202 | 2,724 | 2,366 | 2,024 |
| PRESERVED FRUITS AND VEGETABLES, 203 | 2,093 | 1,918 | 2,046 |
| GRAIN MILL, 204 | 2,745 | 2,607 | 2,619 |
| BAKERY, 205 | 2,663 | 2,850 | 3,151 |
| SUGAR AND CONFECTIONERY, 206 | 1,033 | 1,075 | 1,130 |
| FATS AND OILS, 207 | 724 | 586 | 543 |
| BEVERAGES, 208 | 2,584 | 2,211 | 2,066 |
| MISC. FOOD, 209 | 3,941 | 3,730 | 3,976 |
| TOTAL ESTABLISHMENTS | 22,130 | 20,583 | 20,792 |

*SOURCE:* CENSUS OF MANUFACTURING INDUSTRY SERIES 1982, 1987, AND 1992.

**TABLE 4-4.** SHIPMENTS BY FOOD MANUFACTURING INDUSTRY GROUPS ($MILLIONS)

| INDUSTRY GROUP, SIC | 1982 | 1987 | 1992 |
|---|---|---|---|
| MEAT PRODUCTS, 201 | 67,602 | 77,002 | 93,466 |
| DAIRY PRODUCTS, 202 | 38,771 | 44,755 | 54,096 |
| PRESERVED FRUITS AND VEGETABLES, 203 | 29,874 | 36,343 | 45,192 |
| GRAIN MILL, 204 | 31,386 | 36,737 | 49,169 |
| BAKERY, 205 | 17,808 | 23,677 | 28,629 |
| SUGAR AND CONFECTIONERY, 206 | 15,576 | 18,887 | 22,718 |
| FATS AND OILS, 207 | 16,752 | 15,881 | 19,340 |
| BEVERAGES, 208 | 38,801 | 47,327 | 56,983 |
| MISC. FOOD, 209 | 23,959 | 29,116 | 34,244 |
| TOTAL SHIPMENTS | 280,529 | 329,725 | 403,836 |

*SOURCE:* CENSUS OF MANUFACTURERS 1982, 1987, AND 1992.

**TABLE 4-5.** VALUE ADDED BY U.S. FOOD MANUFACTURING INDUSTRY GROUPS ($MILLIONS)

| INDUSTRY GROUPS, | SIC | 1982 | 1987 | 1992 |
|---|---|---|---|---|
| MEAT PRODUCTS | 201 | 11,002 | 13,842 | 19,076 |
| DAIRY PRODUCTS | 202 | 8,360 | 11,847 | 16,062 |
| PRESERVED FRUITS AND VEGETABLES | 203 | 12,353 | 17,364 | 22,434 |
| GRAIN MILL | 204 | 10,333 | 15,409 | 20,739 |
| BAKERY | 205 | 10,650 | 15,213 | 17,905 |
| SUGAR AND CONFECTIONERY | 206 | 6,234 | 8,466 | 10,951 |
| FATS AND OILS | 207 | 2,785 | 3,210 | 3,759 |
| BEVERAGES | 208 | 16,684 | 22,585 | 29,256 |
| MISC. FOOD | 209 | 10,017 | 3,672 | 16,322 |
| TOTAL VALUE ADDED | | 88,419 | 121,609 | 156,504 |

*SOURCE:* CENSUS OF MANUFACTURERS 1982, 1987, AND 1992.

**TABLE 4-6.** VALUE ADDED PER EMPLOYEE BY U.S. FOOD MANUFACTURING INDUSTRY GROUPS

| INDUSTRY GROUP | SIC | 1982 | 1987 | 1992 |
|---|---|---|---|---|
| MEAT PRODUCTS | 201 | 34,631 | 40,653 | 47,488 |
| DAIRY PRODUCTS | 202 | 59,756 | 83,722 | 116,988 |
| PRESERVED FRUITS AND VEGETABLES | 203 | 56,252 | 83,322 | 104,783 |
| GRAIN MILL | 204 | 96,122 | 150,475 | 193,101 |
| BAKERY | 205 | 49,192 | 70,075 | 83,277 |
| SUGAR AND CONFECTIONERY | 206 | 65,141 | 93,654 | 120,077 |
| FATS AND OILS | 207 | 71,974 | 108,456 | 134,735 |
| BEVERAGES | 208 | 85,954 | 140,365 | 202,742 |
| MISC. FOOD | 209 | 63,400 | 86,533 | 98,443 |
| TOTAL ALL INDUSTRY GROUPS | | 59,433 | 81,682 | 103,990 |

*SOURCE:* CENSUS OF MANUFACTURERS 1982, 1987, AND 1992.

**TABLE 4-7.** PERCENT OF U.S. FOOD MANUFACTURING ESTABLISHMENTS AND VALUE ADDED BY EMPLOYMENT SIZE

| Number of Employees | 1982 % Est. | 1982 Value Added | 1987 % Est. | 1987 Value Added | 1992 % Est. | 1992 Value Added |
|---|---|---|---|---|---|---|
| 1-19 (small) | 51.7 | 3.6 | 52.9 | 3.5 | 55.1 | 3.1 |
| 20-99 (medium) | 31.6 | 19.6 | 29.5 | 17.5 | 27.5 | 15.0 |
| 100-499 (large) | 14.4 | 49.8 | 15.2 | 45.9 | 14.7 | 48.9 |
| 500+ (very large) | 2.2 | 27.0 | 2.4 | 33.1 | 2.7 | 33.0 |
| Total | 100.0 | 100.0 | 100.0 | 100.0 | 100.0 | 100.0 |

SOURCE: COMPUTED FROM THE CENSUS OF MANUFACTURING INDUSTRY SERIES 1982, 1987, AND 1992.

**TABLE 4-8.** TWENTY LEADING U.S. STATES IN FOOD MANUFACTURING EMPLOYMENT

| State, Ranked by Employment (1992) | 1992 Employment (Rank)(thousands) | 1987 Employment (Rank)(thousands) | 1982 Employment (Rank)(thousands) |
|---|---|---|---|
| 1. California | 170.4 | 162.2 (1) | 173.5 (1) |
| 2. Texas | 87.5 | 85.4 (2) | 89.9 (2) |
| 3. Pennsylvania | 81.1 | 83.1 (3) | 85.1 (4) |
| 4. Illinois | 81.8 | 81.0 (4) | 88.0 (3) |
| 5. Wisconsin | 55.6 | 53.5 (7) | 56.3 (7) |
| 6. Georgia | 55.5 | 52.8 (8) | 50.6 (8) |
| 7. New York | 54.9 | 63.0 (5) | 66.2 (5) |
| 8. Ohio | 53.2 | 65.5 (6) | 62.8 (6) |
| 9. North Carolina | 53.2 | 49.7 (9) | 43.9 (11) |
| 10. Iowa | 47.1 | 40.0 (12) | 44.8 (10) |
| 11. Arkansas | 46.3 | 37.2 (14) | 30.4 (19) |
| 12. Minnesota | 41.8 | 40.8 (11) | 41.0 (13) |
| 13. Florida | 41.5 | 44.7 (10) | 45.3 (9) |
| 14. Michigan | 40.0 | 39.2 (13) | 42.2 (12) |
| 15. Missouri | 38.3 | 35.8 (17) | 3808 (15) |
| 16. Alabama | 36.4 | | |
| 17. Washington | 36.3 | 29.9 (20) | 38.8 (15) |
| 18. Tennessee | 35.4 | 36.7 (15) | 36.3 (17) |
| 19. Virginia | 34.8 | 34.8 (18) | 36.8 (16) |
| 20. Indiana | 34.7 | 34.5 (19) | 32.9 (18) |
| 21. New Jersey | | 36.1 (16) | 39.1 (14) |
| Total Employees | 1,502.7 | 1,448.8 | 1,787.7 |
| Percent of Total Food Employment: | | | |
| Top 20 States | 74.9 | 75.6 | 76.2 |
| Top 10 States | 65.8 | 50.4 | 51.2 |
| Top 5 States | 42.3 | 32.8 | 33.8 |

SOURCE: CENSUS OF MANUFACTURING 1982, 1987, AND 1992.

**TABLE 4-9.** TWENTY LEADING U.S. STATES IN FOOD MANUFACTURING VALUE ADDED

| State, Ranked by Value Added (1992) | 1992 Value Added (Rank) (millions) | 1987 Value Added (Rank) (millions) | 1982 Value Added (Rank) (millions) |
|---|---|---|---|
| 1. California | 19,585 | 15,542 (1) | 10,937 (1) |
| 2. Illinois | 11,746 | 9,031 (2) | 6,810 (2) |
| 3. Texas | 9,563 | 7,039 (4) | 5,329 (3) |
| 4. Pennsylvania | 8,589 | 7,040 (3) | 4,951 (4) |
| 5. Ohio | 7,468 | 5,871 (5) | 4,260 (6) |
| 6. New York | 6,660 | 5,833 (6) | 4,702 (5) |
| 7. Michigan | 6,293 | 4,077 (10) | 2,974 (10) |
| 8. Wisconsin | 6,108 | 4,698 (7) | 3,324 (7) |
| 9. Iowa | 5,632 | 3,728 (11) | 3,131 (9) |
| 10. Missouri | 5,539 | 3,219 (14) | 2,501 (12) |
| 11. Georgia | 5,076 | 3,577 (12) | 2,457 (13) |
| 12. New Jersey | 4,515 | 4,192 (9) | 3,266 (8) |
| 13. Florida | 4,432 | 4,209 (8) | 2,915 (11) |
| 14. Tennessee | 4,349 | 3,342 (13) | 2,161 (15) |
| 15. Minnesota | 4,222 | 3,124 (15) | 2,392 (14) |
| 16. North Carolina | 3,888 | 2,840 (16) | 1,930 (18) |
| 17. Indiana | 3,799 | | 2,064 (16) |
| 18. Virginia | 3,787 | 2,534 (17) | 2,059 (17) |
| 19. Washington | 3,059 | 2,146 (18) | 1,499 (20) |
| 20. Nebraska | 2,786 | 1,858 (20) | 1,557 (19) |
| Maryland | | 1,977 (19) | |
| Total | 157,260 | 121,603 | 88,419 |
| Percent of Total Value Added: | | | |
| Top 20 States | 80.8 | 78.8 | 80.5 |
| Top 10 States | 55.4 | 55.5 | 56.2 |
| Top 5 States | 36.2 | 36.6 | 37.0 |

SOURCE: CENSUS OF MANUFACTURING 1982, 1987, AND 1992.

**TABLE 4-10.** TWENTY LEADING U.S. STATES IN FOOD MANUFACTURING SHIPMENTS

| State, Ranked by Shipments | 1992 Shipments (Rank) (millions) | 1987 Shipments (Rank) (millions) | 1982 Shipments (Rank) (millions) |
|---|---|---|---|
| 1. California | 44,297 | 35,451 (1) | 31,263 (1) |
| 2. Illnois | 27,263 | 22,426 (2) | 19,248 (2) |
| 3. Texas | 25,852 | 20,110 (3) | 17,303 (3) |
| 4. Pennsylvania | 19,456 | 16,588 (4) | 13,240 (5) |
| 5. Wisconsin | 18,825 | 15,469 (5) | 13,044 (6) |
| 6. Iowa | 18,610 | 14,412 (6) | 13,747 (4) |
| 7. Ohio | 16,539 | 13,588 (8) | 11,513 (8) |
| 8. New York | 15,254 | 13,932 (7) | 12,237 (7) |
| 9. Georgia | 12,877 | 9,380 (11) | 7,386 (15) |
| 10. Minnesota | 12,770 | 10,383 (10) | 9,307 (10) |
| 11. Missouri | 12,485 | 9,302 (12) | 8,549 (12) |
| 12. Nebraska | 12,365 | 8,886 (16) | 9,423 (9) |
| 13. Michigan | 12,314 | 9,067 (13) | 7,908 (14) |
| 14. Florida | 11,719 | 10,776 (9) | 8,717 (11) |
| 15. Kansas | 10,757 | 9,039 (14) | 6,891 (16) |
| 16. North Carolina | 10,302 | 7,935 (18) | 6,319 (18) |
| 17. New Jersey | 9,644 | 9,030 (15) | 8,041 (13) |
| 18. Tennessee | 9,302 | 8,493 (17) | 6,557 (17) |
| 19. Indiana | 9,236 | 7,775 (19) | 6,188 (19) |
| 20. Arkansas | 9,113 | | |
| Virginia | | 6,770 (20) | 5,903 (20) |
| Total Shipments | 406,836 | 329,725 | 280,529 |
| Percent of Total Shipments: | | | |
| Top 20 States | 78.4 | 78.5 | 79.4 |
| Top 10 States | 52.0 | 52.5 | 53.6 |
| Top 5 States | 33.3 | 33.4 | 33.8 |

*SOURCE:* CENSUS OF MANUFACTURING 1982, 1987, AND 1992.

**TABLE 4-11.** MEAT PRODUCTS—PERCENT OF INDUSTRY GROUP ESTABLISHMENTS AND VALUE ADDED BY EMPLOYMENT SIZE

| Number of Employees (size) | 1982 Est. | 1982 Value Added | 1987 Est. | 1987 Value Added | 1992 Est. | 1992 Value Added |
|---|---|---|---|---|---|---|
| 1-19 (small) | 53.6 | 3.1 | 52.7 | 3.3 | 54.2 | 2.0 |
| 20-99 (medium) | 26.9 | 14.0 | 25.1 | 12.5 | 23.5 | 9.7 |
| 100-499 (large) | 15.8 | 41.5 | 16.7 | 39.2 | 15.2 | 32.3 |
| 500+ (very large) | 3.8 | 41.4 | 5.6 | 44.8 | 7.2 | 56.4 |
| Total | 100.0 | 100.0 | 100.0 | 100.0 | 100.0 | 100.0 |

SOURCE: COMPUTED FROM THE CENSUS OF MANUFACTURING INDUSTRY SERIES MEAT PRODUCTS (201), 1982, 1987, AND 1992.

**TABLE 4-12.** DAIRY PRODUCTS—PERCENT OF INDUSTRY GROUP ESTABLISHMENTS AND VALUE ADDED BY EMPLOYMENT SIZE

| Number of Employees (size) | 1982 Est. | 1982 Value Added | 1987 Est. | 1987 Value Added | 1992 Est. | 1992 Value Added |
|---|---|---|---|---|---|---|
| 1-19 (small) | 46.8 | 3.8 | 45.5 | 3.4 | 43.3 | 2.2 |
| 20-99 (medium) | 37.8 | 34.7 | 37.8 | 30.5 | 34.9 | 21.8 |
| 100-499 (large) | 15.9 | 56.9 | 18.0 | 57.5 | 20.7 | 53.2 |
| 500+ (very large) | .4 | 4.6 | .6 | 8.5 | 1.1 | 22.8 |
| Total | 100.0 | 100.0 | 100.0 | 100.0 | 100.0 | 100.0 |

SOURCE: COMPUTED FROM THE CENSUS OF MANUFACTURING INDUSTRY SERIES DAIRY PRODUCTS (202), 1982, 1987, AND 1992.

**TABLE 4-13.** PRESERVED FRUITS AND VEGETABLES—PERCENT OF INDUSTRY GROUPS ESTABLISHMENTS AND VALUE ADDED BY EMPLOYMENT SIZE

| Number of Employees (size) | 1982 Est. | 1982 Value Added | 1987 Est. | 1987 Value Added | 1992 Est. | 1992 Value Added |
|---|---|---|---|---|---|---|
| 1-19 (small) | 41.2 | 2.0 | 42.1 | 2.1 | 45.9 | 2.0 |
| 20-99 (medium) | 30.3 | 11.09 | 29.3 | 11.4 | 27.5 | 10.5 |
| 100-499 (large) | 24.4 | 54.3 | 23.5 | 48.5 | 22.3 | 52.3 |
| 500+ (very large) | 4.0 | 31.5 | 4.9 | 38.0 | 4.6 | 45.1 |
| Total | 100.0 | 100.0 | 100.0 | 100.0 | 100.0 | 100.0 |

*SOURCE:* COMPUTED FROM THE CENSUS OF MANUFACTURING INDUSTRY SERIES PRESERVED FRUITS AND VEGETABLES (203), 1982, 1987, AND 1992.

**TABLE 4-14.** GRAIN MILL PRODUCTS—PERCENT OF INDUSTRY GROUPS ESTABLISHMENTS AND VALUE ADDED BY EMPLOYMENT SIZE

| Number of Employees (size) | 1982 Est. | 1982 Value Added | 1987 Est. | 1987 Value Added | 1992 Est. | 1992 Value Added |
|---|---|---|---|---|---|---|
| 1-19 (small) | 61.3 | 7.0 | 61.2 | 6.1 | 58.8 | 4.2 |
| 20-99 (medium) | 31.3 | 22.1 | 30.5 | 18.7 | 32.6 | 17.6 |
| 100-499 (large) | 6.5 | 43.1 | 7.3 | 45.7 | 7.5 | 44.4 |
| 500+ (very large) | .9 | 27.9 | 1.0 | 29.5 | 1.1 | 33.3 |
| Total | 100.0 | 100.0 | 100.0 | 100.0 | 100.0 | 100.0 |

*SOURCE:* COMPUTED FROM THE CENSUS OF MANUFACTURING INDUSTRY SERIES GRAIN MILL PRODUCTS (204), 1982, 1987, AND 1992.

**TABLE 4-15.** BAKERY PRODUCTS—PERCENT OF INDUSTRY GROUP ESTABLISHMENTS AND VALUE ADDED BY EMPLOYMENT SIZE

| Number of Employees (size) | 1982 | | 1987 | | 1992 | |
|---|---|---|---|---|---|---|
| | Est. | Value Added | Est. | Value Added | Est. | Value Added |
| 1-19 (small) | 38.3 | 2.0 | 54.8 | 2.1 | 60.1 | 2.5 |
| 20-99 (medium) | 18.5 | 10.0 | 26.2 | 10.3 | 22.3 | 8.8 |
| 100-499 (large) | 13.8 | 51.9 | 16.2 | 51.7 | 15.3 | 51.6 |
| 500+ (very large) | 2.1 | 36.0 | 2.7 | 36.1 | 2.3 | 37.0 |
| Total | 100.0 | 100.0 | 100.0 | 100.0 | 100.0 | 100.0 |

*SOURCE:* COMPUTED FROM THE CENSUS OF MANUFACTURING INDUSTRY SERIES BAKERY PRODUCTS (205), 1982, 1987, AND 1992.


**TABLE 4-16.** SUGAR AND CONFECTIONERY PRODUCTS—PERCENT OF INDUSTRY GROUP ESTABLISHMENTS AND VALUE ADDED BY EMPLOYMENT SIZE

| Number of Employees (size) | 1982 | | 1987 | | 1992 | |
|---|---|---|---|---|---|---|
| | Est. | Value Added | Est. | Value Added | Est. | Value Added |
| 1-19 (small) | 51.2 | 2.1 | 51.7 | 3.8 | 56.4 | 3.1 |
| 20-99 (medium) | 29.8 | 8.8 | 27.6 | 11.7 | 23.5 | 7.2 |
| 100-499 (large) | 17.7 | 41.7 | 18.2 | 38.1 | 17.0 | 52.1 |
| 500+ (very large) | 3.7 | 47.4 | 2.4 | 46.3 | 3.0 | 37.6 |
| Total | 100.0 | 100.0 | 100.0 | 100.0 | 100.0 | 100.0 |

*SOURCE:* COMPUTED FROM THE CENSUS OF MANUFACTURING INDUSTRY SERIES SUGAR AND CONFECTIONERY PRODUCTS (206), 1982, 1987, AND 1992.

**TABLE 4-17.** FATS AND OILS—PERCENT OF INDUSTRY GROUP ESTABLISHMENTS AND VALUE ADDED BY EMPLOYMENT SIZE

| Number of Employees (size) | 1982 Est. | 1982 Value Added | 1987 Est. | 1987 Value Added | 1992 Est. | 1992 Value Added |
|---|---|---|---|---|---|---|
| 1-19 (small) | 40.3 | 3.5 | 39.2 | 5.0 | 40.3 | 4.2 |
| 20-99 (medium) | 45.3 | 37.5 | 47.3 | 43.4 | 46.8 | 44.1 |
| 100-499 (large) | 14.0 | 59.0 | 13.3 | 51.6 | 12.5 | 51.7 |
| 500+ (very large) | .4 | (0) | .1 | (0) | .0 | 0 |
| Total | 100.0 | 100.0 | 100.0 | 100.0 | 100.0 | 100.0 |

NOTE: DATA SHOWN AS (0) ARE INCLUDED IN FIGURES IMMEDIATELY ABOVE.

*SOURCE:* COMPUTED FROM THE CENSUS OF MANUFACTURING INDUSTRY SERIES FASTS AND OILS (207), 1982, 1987, AND 1992.

**TABLE 4-18.** BEVERAGES—PERCENT OF INDUSTRY GROUP ESTABLISHMENTS AND VALUE ADDED BY EMPLOYMENT SIZE

| Number of Employees (size) | 1982 Est. | 1982 Value Added | 1987 Est. | 1987 Value Added | 1992 Est. | 1992 Value Added |
|---|---|---|---|---|---|---|
| 1-19 (small) | 41.9 | 3.3 | 48.7 | 2.8 | 52.9 | 3.1 |
| 20-99 (medium) | 39.5 | 25.6 | 30.9 | 20.1 | 28.6 | 15.8 |
| 100-499 (large) | 16.8 | 44.7 | 18.5 | 46.6 | 16.7 | 48.4 |
| 500+ (very large) | 1.9 | 12.6 | 1.7 | 28.6 | 1.8 | 33.3 |
| Total | 100.0 | 100.0 | 100.0 | 100.0 | 100.0 | 100.0 |

*SOURCE:* COMPUTED FROM THE CENSUS OF MANUFACTURING INDUSTRY SERIES BEVERAGES (208), 1982, 1987, AND 1992.

**TABLE 4-19.** MISC. FOOD AND KINDRED PRODUCTS—PERCENT OF INDUSTRY GROUP ESTABLISHMENTS AND VALUE ADDED BY EMPLOYMENT SIZE

| Number of Employees (size) | 1982 Est. | 1982 Value Added | 1987 Est. | 1987 Value Added | 1992 Est. | 1992 Value Added |
|---|---|---|---|---|---|---|
| 1-19 (Small) | 60.5 | 6.0 | 61.3 | 5.9 | 63.2 | 5.7 |
| 20-99 (medium) | 30.1 | 21.8 | 28.0 | 20.0 | 25.6 | 19.5 |
| 100-499 (large) | 8.7 | 63.0 | 10.0 | 66.6 | 10.4 | 56.1 |
| 500+ (very large) | .7 | 9.2 | .8 | 7.5 | .8 | 15.7 |
| Total | 100.0 | 100.0 | 100.0 | 100.0 | 100.0 | 100.0 |

SOURCE: COMPUTED FROM THE CENSUS OF MANUFACTURING INDUSTRY SERIES MISC. FOOD AND KINDRED PRODUCTS (206), 1992, 1987, AND 1992.


**TABLE 4-20.** RANKING OF FOOD PROCESSING INDUSTRIES BY VALUE ADDED—1992

| (TABLE 4-20. cont.) SIC Code | Industry | Value Added ($millions) | Shipments ($millions) |
|---|---|---|---|
| 1. 2051 | Bread, Cakes | 11,431 | 18,121 |
| 2. 2082 | Malt Beverages | 10,600 | 17,328 |
| 3. 2086 | Soft Drinks | 10,017 | 25,485 |
| 4. 2043 | Breakfast Cereal | 7,338 | 9,799 |
| 5. 2033 | Canned Fruits and Vegetables | 6,970 | 14,876 |
| 6. 2011 | Meat Packing Plants | 6,852 | 49,679 |
| 7. 2015 | Poultry Slaughtering and Processing | 6,547 | 23,741 |
| 8. *2064-67 | Candy, Chewing Gum | 6,350 | 10,219 |
| 9. 2099 | Food Preparations, N.E.C. | 6,245 | 12,247 |
| 10. 2026 | Fluid Milk | 5,983 | 21,920 |
| 11. 2013 | Sausages and Other Prepared Meats | 5,551 | 20,043 |
| 12. 2052 | Cookies and Crackers | 5,542 | 8,755 |
| 13. 2087 | Flavorings, Syrups | 4,470 | 6,197 |
| 14. 2022 | Cheese, Natural and Processed | 4,467 | 18,319 |

| (TABLE 4-20. cont.) SIC Code | Industry | Value Added ($millions) | Shipments ($millions) |
|---|---|---|---|
| 15. 2096 | Potato Chips and Other Snacks | 4,230 | 7,161 |
| 16. 2038 | Frozen Specialties, N.E.C. | 4,100 | 7,838 |
| 17. 2047 | Dog and Cat Food | 3,685 | 7,057 |
| 18. 2035 | Salad Dressings, Sauces | 3,641 | 6,244 |
| 19. 2023 | Dry, Condensed, Evaporated Dairy | 3,370 | 7,530 |
| 20. 2046 | Wet Corn Milling | 3,271 | 7,064 |
| 21. 2032 | Canned Specialties | 3,224 | 6,300 |
| 22. 2048 | Prepared Feeds, N.E.C. | 2,987 | 13,457 |
| 23. 2037 | Frozen Fruits and Vegetables | 2,936 | 7,598 |
| 24. 2095 | Roasted Coffee | 2,695 | 5,259 |
| 25. 2092 | Fresh, Frozen Prepared Fish | 2,335 | 6,875 |
| 26. 2024 | Ice Cream and Frozen Desserts | 2,097 | 5,291 |
| 27. 2085 | Liquors, Distilled and Blended | 2,055 | 3,499 |
| 28. 2084 | Wines, Brandy, and Spirits | 1,820 | 3,917 |
| 29. 2045 | Prepared Flour Mixes and Doughs | 1,800 | 3,946 |
| 30. 2041 | Flour, Grain Mill Products | 1,599 | 6,212 |
| 31. 2066 | Chocolate and Cocoa Products | 1,475 | 3,106 |
| 32. 2079 | Edible Fats, N.E.C. | 1,334 | 4,829 |
| 33. 2075 | Soy Bean Oil | 1,275 | 10,659 |
| 34. 2034 | Dehydrated Fruits and Vegetables, Soups | 1,133 | 2,335 |
| 35. 2068 | Salted, Roasted Nuts and Seeds | 1,026 | 2,828 |
| 36. 2053 | Frozen Bakery, Except Bread | 959 | 1,753 |
| 37. 2077 | Animal and Marine Fats and Oils | 882 | 2,489 |
| 38. 2063 | Beet Sugar | 800 | 2,282 |
| 39. 2096 | Potato Chips and Snacks | 764 | 7,161 |
| 40. 2062 | Cane Sugar Refining | 737 | 2,123 |
| 41. 2061 | Raw Cane Sugar | 562 | 1,460 |
| 42. 2044 | Rice Milling | 501 | 1,634 |
| 43. 2091 | Canned, Cured Fish and Seafood | 365 | 957 |
| 44. 2097 | Manufactured Ice | 253 | 359 |
| 45. 2074 | Cottonseed Ohio | 192 | 737 |
| 46. 2083 | Malt | 153 | 559 |
| 47. 2021 | Creamery Butter | 150 | 1,036 |
| 48. 2076 | Vegetable Oil | 123 | 666 |

*NOTE: THE 1992 CENSUS OF MANUFACTURING REPORTED ONLY A COMBINED TOTAL FOR INDUSTRIES 2064 AND 2067.

*SOURCE:* CENSUS OF MANUFACTURING, 1992.

**TABLE 4-21.** RANKING OF FOOD PROCESSING INDUSTRIES BY VALUE ADDED INTENSITIES—1992a.

**(TABLE 4-21. cont.)**

| SIC Code | Industry | Intensity |
|---|---|---|
| 1. 2043 | Breakfast Cereals | 74.9 |
| 2. 2087 | Flavorings | 72.1 |
| 3. 2097 | Manufactured Ice | 70.5 |
| 4. 2052 | Cookies and Crackers | 63.3 |
| 5. 2051 | Bread, Cakes | 63.1 |
| 6. *2064-67 | Candy and Chewing Gum | 62.1 |
| 7. 2082 | Malt Beverages | 61.2 |
| 8. 2096 | Potato Chips, Snacks | 59.1 |
| 9. 2035 | Salad Dressings, Sauces | 58.3 |
| 10. 2085 | Liquors, Distilled and Blended | 57.3 |
| 11. 2053 | Frozen Bakery, Except Bread | 54.7 |
| 12. 2038 | Frozen Specialties, N.E.C. | 52.3 |
| 13. 2047 | Dog and Cat Food | 52.2 |
| 14. 2032 | Canned Specialties | 51.2 |
| 15. 2095 | Roasted Coffee | 51.5 |
| 16. 2099 | Food Preparation, N.E.C. | 51.0 |
| 17. 2034 | Dehydrated Fruits, Vegetables and Soups | 48.5 |
| 18. 2066 | Chocolate and Cocoa Products | 47.5 |
| 19. 2033 | Canned Fruits and Vegetables | 46.9 |
| 20. 2084 | Wines, Brandy, Spirits | 46.5 |
| 21. 2046 | Wet Corn Milling | 46.3 |
| 22. 2045 | Prepared Flour Mixes and Doughs | 45.6 |
| 23. 2023 | Dry, Condensed, Evaporated Dairy | 44.8 |
| 24. 2024 | Ice Cream and Frozen Desserts | 39.3 |
| 25. 2086 | Soft Drinks | 39.3 |
| 26. 2037 | Frozen Fruits and Vegetables | 38.6 |
| 27. 2061 | Raw Cane Sugar | 38.5 |

(TABLE 4-21. cont.)

| SIC Code | Industry | Intensity |
|---|---|---|
| 28. 2091 | Canned, Cured Fish and Seafood | 38.2 |
| 29. 2068 | Salted, Roasted Nuts and Seeds | 36.3 |
| 30. 2077 | Animal, Marine Fats and Oils | 35.4 |
| 31. 2063 | Beet Sugar | 35.1 |
| 32. 2092 | Fresh and Frozen Prepared Foods | 34.0 |
| 33. 2044 | Rice Milling | 30.7 |
| 34. 2013 | Sausages, Prepared Meats | 27.7 |
| 35. 2015 | Poultry Slaughtering and Processing | 27.6 |
| 36. 2079 | Edible Fats and Oils, N.E.C. | 27.5 |
| 37. 2026 | Fluid Milk | 27.4 |
| 38. 2083 | Malt | 27.3 |
| 39. 2062 | Cane Sugar Refining | 26.2 |
| 40. 2074 | Cotton Seed Oil | 26.1 |
| 41. 2041 | Flour and Grain Mill Products | 25.7 |
| 42. 2022 | Cheese, Natural and Processed | 24.4 |
| 43. 2048 | Prepared Feeds, N.E.C. | 22.2 |
| 44. 2076 | Vegetable Oil N.E.C. | 18.5 |
| 45. 2021 | Creamery Butter | 14.5 |
| 46. 2011 | Meat Packing Plants | 13.8 |
| 47. 2075 | Soybean Oil | 12.0 |
| 48. 2063 | Beet Sugar | 10.7 |

a. INTENSITY IS COMPUTED BY DIVIDING THE VALUE ADDED FOR All INDUSTRY BY ITS SHIPMENTS OR SALES.

*NOTE: INTENSITY REPRESENTS A COMBINATION OF INDUSTRIES 2064 AND 2067.

SOURCE: CENSUS OF MANUFACTURING, 1992.

**TABLE 4-22.** SHARE OF SHIPMENT VALUE (SALES) FOR FOUR LARGEST FOOD MANUFACTURERS a.

| (TABLE 4-22. cont.) | 1982 | | 1987 | | 1992 | |
|---|---|---|---|---|---|---|
| SIC, Industry | Total Firms | Top 4 Firms Share of Sales | Total Firms | Top 4 Firms Share of Sales | Total Firms | Top 4 Firms Share of Sales |
| 2011, Meat Packing | 1,658 | 29 | 1,328 | 32 | 1,296 | 50 |
| 13, Sausage/Other | 1,193 | 19 | 1,207 | 26 | 1,128 | 25 |
| 15, Poultry | 367 | 44 | 284 | 28 | 373 | 34 |
| 2021, Cream Butter | 61 | 41 | 44 | 40 | 31 | 49 |
| 22, Cheese | 575 | 34 | 508 | 43 | 418 | 42 |
| 23, Dairy | 132 | 35 | 124 | 45 | 153 | 43 |
| 24, Ice Cream/Frozen Dessert | 482 | 22 | 469 | 25 | 411 | 24 |
| 26, Fluid Milk | 853 | 16 | 652 | 21 | 525 | 22 |
| 2032, Canned Specialties | 171 | 62 | 183 | 59 | 200 | 69 |
| 33, Canned Fruits/Vegetables | 514 | 21 | 462 | 29 | 502 | 27 |
| 34, Dehydrated Fruit/Vegetables and Soup | 119 | 42 | 107 | 39 | 124 | 39 |
| 35, Pickles, Sauces and Salad Dressing | 325 | 56 | 344 | 43 | 332 | 41 |
| 37, Frozen Fruits and Vegetables | 195 | 27 | 194 | 31 | 182 | 28 |
| 38, Frozen Special N.E.C. | 318 | 38 | 244 | 43 | 308 | 40 |
| 2041, Flour/Other Grain Milling | 251 | 40 | 237 | 44 | 230 | 56 |
| 43, Cereal Breakfast | 32 | 86 | 33 | 87 | 42 | 85 |
| 44, Rice Milling | 49 | 47 | 48 | 56 | 44 | 50 |
| 45, Flour Mixes and Doughs | 91 | 58 | 120 | 43 | 156 | 39 |
| 46, Wet Corn Milling | 25 | 74 | 31 | 74 | 28 | 73 |

(TABLE 4-22. cont.)

| SIC, Industry | 1982 Total Firms | 1982 Top 4 Firms Share of Sales | 1987 Total Firms | 1987 Top 4 Firms Share of Sales | 1992 Total Firms | 1992 Top 4 Firms Share of Sales |
|---|---|---|---|---|---|---|
| 47, Dog and Cat Food | 222 | 52 | 130 | 61 | 102 | 58 |
| 48, Prepared Feeds | 1,245 | 20 | 1,182 | 20 | 1,160 | 23 |
| 2051, Bread and Cake | 1,869 | 34 | 1,948 | 34 | 2,180 | 34 |
| 52, Cookies and Crackers | 296 | 59 | 316 | 58 | 374 | 56 |
| 53, Frozen Bakery | N/A | N/A | 103 | 59 | 160 | 45 |
| 2061, Raw Cane Sugar | 43 | 41 | 31 | 48 | 37 | 52 |
| 62, Cane Sugar Refining | 19 | 65 | 14 | 87 | 12 | 85 |
| 63, Beet Sugar | 14 | 67 | 14 | 72 | 13 | 71 |
| 64, Candy, Other Confection | 718 | 40 | 623 | 45 | b 705 | 45 |
| 66, Chocolate/Cocoa | 77 | 75 | 173 | 69 | 146 | 75 |
| 67, Gum | 9 | 95 | 8 | 96 | N/A | N/A |
| 68, Nuts and Seeds | N/A | N/A | 79 | 43 | 102 | 42 |
| 2074, Cotton Seed | 47 | 51 | 31 | 43 | 22 | 62 |
| 75, Soy Oil Mill | 52 | 61 | 47 | 71 | 42 | 71 |
| 76, Vegetable Oil Mill | 26 | 52 | 20 | 74 | 18 | 89 |
| 77, Animal and Marine Fats and Oils | 270 | 34 | 194 | 35 | 159 | 37 |
| 79, Edible Fats and Oils N.E.C | 79 | 43 | 67 | 45 | 72 | 35 |
| 2082, Malt Beverage | 67 | 77 | 101 | 87 | 160 | 90 |
| 83, Malt | 24 | 60 | 15 | 64 | 16 | 65 |
| 84, Wines, Brandy and Spirits | 324 | 51 | 469 | 37 | 514 | 54 |
| 85, Distilled and Blended Liquors | 71 | 46 | 48 | 53 | 43 | 62 |
| 86, Bottled and Canned Soft Drinks | 1,236 | 14 | 846 | 30 | 637 | 37 |

(TABLE 4-22. cont.)

| SIC, Industry | 1982 Total Firms | 1982 Top 4 Firms Share of Sales | 1987 Total Firms | 1987 Top 4 Firms Share of Sales | 1992 Total Firms | 1992 Top 4 Firms Share of Sales |
|---|---|---|---|---|---|---|
| 87, Flavored Extract Syrups, N.E.C. | 297 | 65 | 245 | 65 | 264 | 69 |
| 2091, Canned, Cured, Fish and Seafood | 170 | 62 | 153 | 26 | 144 | 29 |
| 92, Fresh, Frozen Prepared Fish | 697 | 14 | 579 | 18 | 600 | 19 |
| 95, Roast Coffee | 118 | 65 | 110 | 66 | 134 | 66 |
| 96, Potato Chips | N/A | N/A | 277 | N/A | 333 | 70 |
| 97, Manufactured Ice | 530 | 18 | 503 | 19 | 513 | 24 |
| 98, Macaroni Spaghetti | 208 | 42 | 196 | 73 | 182 | 78 |
| 99, Food Preparations, N.E.C. | 1,746 | 32 | 1,510 | 261 | 1,644 | 22 |

NA: N/A DATA UNAVAILABLE

B: INCLUDES CHEWING GUM (2067)

A: COMPANY MAY APPEAR IN MORE THAN ONE INDUSTRY.

*SOURCE:* CENSUS OF MANUFACTURING, SUBJECT SERIES CONCENTRATION RATIOS IN MANUFACTURING 1982, 1987, AND 1992.

**TABLE 4-23.** FIFTY LEADING FOOD MANUFACTURERS

| 1995 Rank | 1994 Rank | Company | 1995 Food Sales ($millions) | 1995 Total Sales ($millions) | Food % to Total |
|---|---|---|---|---|---|
| 1 | 1 | Phillip Morris Co., Inc. | 35,966 | 65,125 | 55.2 |
| 2 | 2 | ConAgra, Inc. | 20,600 | 24,108 | 85.4 |
| 3 | 3 | Cargill, Inc. | 18,673 | 50,991 | 36.6 |
| 4 | 4 | PepsiCo., Inc. | 17,951 | 28,500 | 63.0 |
| 5 | 5 | Coca Cola Co. | 16,172 | 16,172 | 100.0 |
| 6 | 7 | Archer Daniels Midland Co. | 12,672 | 12,672 | 100.0 |
| 7 | 8 | IBP | 11,592 | 12,075 | 100.0 |
| 8 | 6 | Anheuser-Busch Cos, Inc. | 11,364 | 13,733 | 82.7 |
| 9 | 9 | Sara Lee Corp. | 8,887 | 17,719 | 50.2 |
| 10 | 12 | H.J. Heinz Co. | 7,791 | 8,086 | 96.3 |
| 11 | 17 | Pillsbury Co. | 7,776 | 13,500 | 57.6 |
| 12 | 11 | RJR Nabisco Inc. | 7,700 | 15,336 | 50.2 |
| 13 | 18 | CPC International Inc. | 7,425 | 7,425 | 100.0 |
| 14 | 10 | Nestle USA Inc. | 7,300 | 7,300 | 100.0 |
| 15 | 13 | Campbell Soup Co. | 7,278 | 7,278 | 100.0 |
| 16 | 14 | Kellogg Co. | 6,830 | 6,830 | 100.0 |
| 17 | 20 | Ralston Purina | 6,439 | 6,439 | 100.0 |
| 18 | 16 | Quaker Oats Co. | 6,395 | 6,395 | 100.0 |
| 19 | 15 | Seagram's Beverage Group | 5,563 | 5,563 | 100.0 |
| 20 | 21 | Tyson Foods Inc. | 5,300 | 5,300 | 100.0 |
| 21 | 19 | General Mills Inc. | 5,026 | 5,026 | 100.0 |
| 22 | 29 | Chiquita Brands International Inc. | 3,900 | 3,962 | 100.0 |
| 23 | 23 | Hershey Foods Corp. | 3,606 | 3,606 | 100.0 |
| 24 | 22 | Borden Inc. | 3,534 | 5,626 | 62.8 |
| 25 | 24 | Proctor & Ganble Co. | 3,510 | 33,434 | 10.5 |
| 26 | 25 | Dole Food Co., Inc. | 3,498 | 3,841 | 91.1 |
| 27 | 27 | Hormel Foods Corp. | 3,064 | 3,064 | 100.0 |

| (TABLE 4-23. cont.) 1995 Rank | 1994 Rank | Company | 1995 Food Sales ($millions) | 1995 Total Sales ($millions) | Food % to Total |
|---|---|---|---|---|---|
| 28 | 30 | Dean Foods Co. | 2,625 | 2,630 | 99.8 |
| 29 | 28 | Associated Milk Producers Inc. | 2,563 | 2,628 | 97.5 |
| 30 | 26 | Mid-America Dairymen Inc. | 2,500 | 2,500 | 100.0 |
| 31 | 32 | Adolph Coors Co. | 2,040 | 2,040 | 100.0 |
| 32 | 31 | Specialty Foods Corp. | 1,979 | 1,979 | 100.0 |
| 33 | 77 | W.R. Grace & Co. | 1,743 | 5,093 | 34.2 |
| 34 | 37 | Perdue Farms Inc. | 1,700 | 1,700 | 100.0 |
| 35 | 33 | Keebler Co. | 1,673 | 1,673 | 100.0 |
| 36 | 41 | McCormick & Co., Inc. | 1,603 | 1,801 | 89.0 |
| 37 | 35 | Continental Grain Co. | 1,600 | 14,000 | 11.4 |
| 38 | 40 | Wm. Wrigley Jr. Co. | 1,597 | 1,597 | 100.0 |
| 39 | 39 | Smithfield Foods, Inc. | 1,550 | 1,550 | 100.0 |
| 40 | 42 | Ag Processing Inc. | 1,535 | 2,151 | 71.4 |
| 41 | 36 | Del Monte Foods | 1,500 | 1,500 | 100.0 |
| 42 | 91 | Burns Philip Foods Inc. | 1,500 | 1,500 | 100.0 |
| 43 | 38 | Land O Lakes Inc. | 1,468 | 2,859 | 51.3 |
| 44 | 45 | Central Soya Co., Inc. | 1,447 | 1,520 | 95.2 |
| 45 | 84 | Cadbury Beverages Inc. | 1,41 | 1,441 | 100.0 |
| 46 | 47 | Gold Kist Inc. | 1,438 | 1,747 | 82.3 |
| 47 | 61 | American Home Products Corp. | 1,396 | 11,634 | 12.0 |
| 48 | 43 | Warner-Lambert Co. | 1,368 | 6,417 | 21.3 |
| 49 | 49 | Ocean Spray Cranberries Inc. | 1,361 | 1,361 | 100.0 |
| 50 | - | Tate & Lyle Inc. | 1,280 | 1,280 | 100.0 |

SOURCE: FOOD PROCESSING—THE MAGAZINE FOR STRATEGY AND TECHNOLOGY, A PUTMAN PUBLICATION, DECEMBER, 1995.

# Chapter 5

# Marketing Decisions

**Chapter Outline**

Manufacturing Sector
- A. Historical Perspective
- B. Structural Influence on Marketing Decisions
- C. Processors Versus Manufacturers

Product Decisions
- A. Food Product Classification
- B. Food Product Development Phases
- C. Product Development Organizations
- D. Branding
- E. Packaging
- F. The Product Life Cycle
- G. Managing the Product Mix

Price Decisions
- A. Consumer Influence
- B. Cost Influence
- C. Competitive Influence
- D. Governmental Influence

E. Marketing Mix Influence

   F. Price-setting Process

Promotion Decisions

   A. Promotional Objectives

   B. Promotional Budget

   C. Promotional Mix

   D. Promotional Dollar Allocation

   E. Trade Promotions

   F. Personal Selling

   G. Advertising

   H. Consumer Promotions

   I. Public Relations

Place Decisions

   A. Channel Design

   B. Logistical Design

   C. Integrated Channel/Logistics Structure

Efficient Consumer Response

   A. Efficient Store Assortments

   B. Efficient Product Introductions

   C. Efficient Replenishment

   D. Efficient Promotion

   E. ECR Benefits

Summary

The changing nature of the manufacturing sector's structural characteristics was examined in Chapter 4. The number of companies and establishments continued to decline. At the same time, shipment sales and value added continued to increase. Although the number of employees increased slightly, the value added per employee increased dramatically. The direct result of these changes has been the creation of a sector comprising two distinct manufacturing groups. A few large- and very-large-scale operations generate the vast majority of value added and shipments. The other group consists of small and medium size operations that generate an ever-declining output.

An examination of the manufacturing sector at the industry level reinforced the coexistence of these two distinct groups. In addition, market share data at the industry level suggests a range of competitive conditions from oligopolistic to monopolistic competition. It is within this diversity of competitive conditions that manufacturers make marketing decisions.

The purpose of this chapter is to examine the marketing decisions of food manufacturers. A historical perspective of the manufacturing sector's quest to prepare and process food is presented to establish the modern day environment within which manufacturer marketing decisions are made. Subsequent sections represent a functional analysis of manufacturer marketing decision to create, price, promote, and distribute food products.

# MANUFACTURING SECTOR

The capacity of the human stomach to consume most agricultural products in their raw forms is limited. As a consequence, people throughout time have sought ways in which these raw food stuffs could be prepared and preserved for consumption at some future time—hours, days, weeks, and even years later. The contemporary food manufacturing sector is the culmination of the myriad of successful transformations of raw animal, grain, fruit, vegetable, dairy, and marine commodities into intermediate food ingredients or finished, edible consumer products.

## Historical Perspective [*]

Since the beginning of time, man has processed food. As it is today, the goal then was to prepare raw agricultural products to make them digestible (grains converted to flour), palatable (flour made into bread), portable (transport bread from the oven to the consumer's table), and storable (maintain freshness for later consumption).

---

[*] This section is based, in part, on E.C. Hampe and M. Wittenberg, *"The Food Industry—Lifeline of America"* Ithaca, N.Y.: Connell University, 1980.

We may never know when man learned to use nature to process foods. What we do know is that many of our modern day food processing techniques are adaptations of, and great improvements on, nature's ways of processing food. For example, the rays of the sun were used to dry and preserve nuts, grains, fruits, and meat. The cold climates in the northern parts of the world were ideal for freezing meat, as were ice-cold waters for freezing fish.

Over the ages, salt rubbed on meat was found to preserve its taste. Vegetables and fruits soaked in a salt brine solution (later called pickling) could be preserved for use during the winter months. Fermentation of milk, a natural process of chemical change, produced cheese while fruit juices left to stand brought about wine.

Early settlers to this country used what others had learned before them to process food for their own needs. They salted and smoked their meats, pickled their home-grown fruits and vegetables, fermented their cow's milk, and processed any other foods available to them.

Over time, these methods gave way to more modern techniques of canning, mechanical refrigeration, quick freezing, dehydration, and irradiation. In 1809, in response to a contest sponsored by Napoleon, Nicolas Appert showed that to preserve foods they had to be heated in sealed glass containers. Appert won the prize, and went on to bottle over fifty different food items. The glass container gave way to tin-coated cans, and then to aluminum.

Before the invention of the can, all forms of food processing were adaptations of nature's methods. Thus, it has been said that canning is probably the single most significant advance in food processing in the history of the **U.S. food marketing system**. Equally important is the realization that canning led the revolution in food packaging that has continued to this day in the form of vacuum sealed, shelf stable food products.

Mechanical refrigeration and freezing are processing methods that preserve food by focusing on the opposite end of the thermometer. William Davis's development of the refrigerated railroad car around 1869 preceded the introduction of mechanical refrigeration found throughout the U.S. food marketing system. Before refrigeration, the perishability of fruits, vegetables, dairy products and meats prevented the development of anything but a local market. Refrigeration as a means of preservation meant that processors could now reach more distant markets.

Mechanical freezing as a method of preservation can be traced to the insight and foresight of Clarence Birdseye. His experiments showed that slow freezing of foods was inadequate. Only fast **(quick) freezing would preserve quality.** Although fish were the food items frozen initially, by 1930 poultry, meat, and sixteen fruits and vegetables were introduced to food consumers. Wartime led to a rapid expansion of frozen food consumption. Up to the time of World War II, only about ten percent of all frozen food was sold to consumers. With the outbreak of World War II, foods in cans were needed to feed the soldiers fighting abroad. With canned foods scarce and frozen foods packaged in unrationed paper, consumers were more than willing to buy frozen foods.

The rigidity and weight of canned foods made carrying them an unpleasant and sometimes painful experience to the individual soldier. Scientists sought ways to reduce the weight and bulkiness of food, as to well as provide the soldiers with fresh foods. This urgency accelerated the technical progress of **dehydration**. Using heat to remove the water content of foods resulted in foods that weighed only ten percent of their original weight. The process of removing moisture by first freezing a product and then removing the water content as a vapor (freeze-drying) improved the process of dehydration further.

A more recent approach to the preservation of food, **irradiation**, is still in limited commercial use. This process uses ionized radiation (gamma rays from radioactive cobalt-60) to destroy harmful microorganisms that cause foodborne illnesses, and to delay spoilage and prolong shelf life by retarding mold growth. Because irradiation replaces chemical fumigants, it is seen as a major step toward food safety.

Today, many experts feel that the food manufacturing sector is on the eve of another era—biotechnology. Simply stated, **biotechnology** uses living organisms (e.g., cells, viruses, and bacteria) to make food products. Biotechnology developments such as animal somatotropin can boost milk output per cow, yield leaner meat and produce genetically improved breeds. Biopesticides genetically alter microorganisms that protect crops from diseases, insects, and fungi. Biotechnological processing, which consists of controlled biological processes that transform these agricultural raw materials into intermediate foodstuffs, will play a major role in the future of the manufacturing sector and in the kind of food Americans will find on their table.

## Structural Influence on Marketing Decisions

As previously stated, the structural characteristics of a sector have a fundamental influence on the marketing decisions made by firms composing the sector. The manufacturing sector was characterized as having a diverse market structure. The market structure of the forty-nine industries that the sector comprises vary from oligopolistic to monopolistically competitive. Both of these market structures represent examples of imperfect competition.

Imperfect competition exists when sellers must compete with other sellers of similar products, each of which has some control over price. Firms can control price either by gaining large market share, as in the case of oligopolists, or by differentiating their products by quality and/or brand, as in the case of monopolistic competitors. Because the manufactured product of the oligopolist can be standardized (e.g., vegetable oil) or differentiated (e.g., **Wesson** vegetable oil) their marketing decisions are, for the most part, indistinguishable from those of the monopolistic competitor.

There is one important difference to remember between oligopolists and monopolistic competitors. In oligopolistic industries, a hierarchy of leaders and followers is likely to exist. Because of this interdependency, industry leaders must consider how their followers will react to their marketing decisions. In monopolistically competitive industries, this interdependency does not exist. Thus, the anticipated reactions to each firm's marketing decisions are of less importance. Of course, how important competitive reactions are to any firm depends on whether or not a firm has established a competitive differential advantage.

Regardless of the market structure, firms in the manufacturing sector must make decisions to create, price, promote, and distribute their products. To better understand the realities of the marketing decisions made by firms in the manufacturing sector, the distinction between processors and manufacturers made in earlier chapters must be re-examined.

## Processors Versus Manufacturers

**Processors** are firms that purchase raw agricultural products and transform them into intermediate food ingredients to be used by manufacturers in the creation of finished consumer products. These ingredients are virtually homogeneous commodities that lose their identity in the finished product. Thus, processors operate in a market structure that limits the flexibility they have to market their products. In fact, these firms make marketing decisions under the same constraints found in the agricultural sector.

**Manufacturers** are firms that transform raw materials and ingredients into finished food products. In turn, these food products are sold as either unbranded or branded products to foodservice firms and food stores. Manufacturers who sell unbranded food products to the foodservice segment face the same constraint to their marketing decisions as those faced by producers and processors. However, the unbranded products sold to food stores may or may not be purchased by the consumer in unbranded form. Certainly, there are some products that remain unbranded, such as fish, meat, seafood, and generic grocery products. At the same time, there are products that are sold initially as unbranded, but later are branded by a store or a distributor. Manufacturers who sell unbranded products to food stores, even though they are labeled later by stores or distributors, face the same constraints to their marketing decisions as those faced by producers and processors.

Manufacturers who sell branded food products to the foodservice and/or food store markets face a market structure that is best characterized as monopolistically competitive. A differentiated product makes the manufacturer's demand curve more inelastic. Said another way, purchasers, whether distributors or consumers, are less sensitive to price changes. This insensitivity to price allows the firm more discretion in pricing their products, and consequently more flexibility in their decisions to create, promote, and distribute these products.

Although the desire to utilize excess production capacity is a powerful motivating factor, most firms don't produce both advertised brands and private, store, or distributor labels. While there may be some exceptions, manufacturers that produce dual brands probably hold an insignificant market share in their respective industries.

An examination of the forty-nine manufacturing industries reflects a manufacturing sector that is made up of essentially two groups: brand manufacturers and private label (or generic) manufacturers. Processors and manufacturers of unbranded products face the same constraints to their marketing decisions as producers. Because producers' marketing decisions were explained in Chapter 3, the focus of this chapter will be on the marketing decisions of manufacturers of branded products.

# PRODUCT DECISIONS

It has been suggested by many observers of the U.S. food marketing system that manufacturing is the most significant sector in the entire system. The significance is due primarily to the manufacturer's role in the process of transforming consumer needs into tangible, digestible, palatable, portable, and storable food products (Connor, 1988). This section will focus on the product decisions that manufacturers make to transform these consumer needs into food products. The transformation process involves both the development of new differentiated food products to meet the existing needs of the marketplace and the management of these food products over their life cycle as the needs of the marketplace change.

A number of dynamic forces continually redefine the scope of new food product development. Consumers' needs are constantly changing and redefining how they shop, purchase, and consume food products. The competitive marketplace is continually redefining what contributions existing differential advantages are making to long-run success. Technological advances in the processing and preservation of food are continually redefining the bundle of benefits consumers seek. Evolving government mandates in food safety, nutrition, and labeling are continually redefining the operational constraints in processing and preservation techniques.

Given the environment within which food product development takes place this section will discuss food product classifications, phases in food product development, product development organizations, branding, packaging, product life cycle, and managing the food manufacturer's product mix.

## Food Product Classification

Before proceeding, recall from an earlier chapter that food products have a multidimensional meaning to consumers. The first dimension is physical. Food products have size, shape, weight, color, and aroma. Food must also be aesthetically appealing to the consumers' smell, feel, look, sound, and taste. To manufacturers, the third dimension, service, is a matter of convenience in preparation and/or preservation. The final **bundle of benefits** dimension defines what the product, in its totality, means to the consumer. A new product, then, represents a modification of one or more of these dimensions to an existing product, or the development of a product not previously manufactured by a firm.

### Line Extensions

Food product modifications that focus on the physical, aesthetic, or service dimension are referred to as line extensions. These new products extend a brand by adding new flavors, forms, ingredients, or packaging. Thus, General Food's new **Jell-O** flavors, CPC's new **Mazola Corn Oil** spray, **Breyer's** non-fat ice cream, and **French's** mustard in the squeezable bottle represent modifications in flavors, form, ingredients, and packaging under the same brand name. Unfortunately, line extensions often receive some of their sales from existing brands in the same product category. When this happens, a brand is said to **cannibalize** another. For example, the sales of a new flavor of **Jell-O** will most likely cannibalize the sales of an existing **Jell-O** flavor. **Campbell's Healthy Request** line of soups will switch some of its customers from its **Home Cooking** line of soups.

### New Brands

Food product development may also focus on the "bundle of benefits" dimension by creating a new product that has not been previously manufactured by a firm. When a new product is introduced under an established brand name, it is referred to as a **brand extension**. The launching of **Heinz Bar-B-Que** sauce under the Heinz brand name extends the brand into a new category of sauces. A product may also be introduced under a new brand name. **Mars, Inc.'s** new **Skittles** is a separate brand, and distinguishable from **Mars's** existing brands.

Table 7-1 represents the number of new food products introduced over the last five years. Although not specifically identified, the overwhelming majority of new food products on a year-to-year basis are basically line extensions. Further, just three categories—condiments, beverages, and candy/gum/snacks—make up over fifty percent of all new food introductions.

## Food Product Development Phases

The introduction of line extensions, brand extensions, and new brands is basically the result of a process that contains nonsequential phases. The process begins with an idea that may end in a new food product. However, an intermediate phase may not end before another begins. Further, information generated by this process may require that certain phases run concurrently or that previously completed phases be examined. In short, the development process is constantly adapting to information generated during the various phases of the process.

### Idea Generation

The process begins with a search for new product ideas that are consistent with company objectives and satisfy the perceived needs of consumers. Ideas for new food products can come from inside or outside a firm.

A firm's sales force, research and development function, and special organizational arrangements are essential sources of new product ideas. The eyes and ears of the company are its sales force. When they make sales calls, they have the opportunity to talk with retailers, observe the competition, and suggest new ideas for review. A company's product and process research is expected to identify new ideas that focus on the physical and aesthetic dimensions of products. Many companies have developed organization arrangements that foster new product development. These arrangements will be examined later in this chapter.

New product ideas also come from outside a company. Trade shows sponsored by such national organizations as the **Food Marketing Institute (FMI)**, the **National Grocers Association (NGA)**, the **Grocery Manufacturers of America (GMA)**, and the **Private Label Manufacturing Association (PLMA)** exhibit wide arrays of products and manufacturing technologies. Exposure to domestic and foreign competitors at these shows provides a wealth of information. Trade publications such as **Food Processing, Prepared Foods**, and **Frozen Foods** are filled with information that can be used in new product development. Government publications such as **Food Review** and the voluminous reports and monograms generated by the **USDA Economic Research Service** are representative samples of the information available to firms. Finally, an analysis of the shopping, purchasing, consumption habits, and motives of consumers, available from public and private sources, will help a company to generate new product ideas.

### Screening

The purpose of screening is to reject ideas that are inappropriate, so as to increase the likelihood of success of a new product. There are a number of criteria that are used to decide which ideas will move forward by the process.

First, a firm must determine if it has the marketing skills and personnel to introduce the new food product. (Can the company develop an effective marketing strategy?) Second, a firm must assess its ability to manufacture the product. (Does the company have the technical expertise to develop the product?) Third, a firm must estimate the size and nature of the market. (Is the market large enough?) Fourth, existing and potential competition must be identified. (Does the product have a competitive advantage?) Fifth, a firm must determine the extent to which the product meets its financial criteria. (What is the potential profit from the new product?)

The application of these criteria at this phase does not mean that any of the criteria can't be used later to abandon development at any of the phases. In fact, the remaining phases represent a more specific and focused application of these same criteria.

### Concept Development and Testing

The task of a firm, at this stage, is to translate the product idea into meaningful consumer language called a **product concept**. This concept consists of verbal statements and often pictorial illustrations of the idea in terms of its product features and benefits. The objective is to determine whether consumers would buy this product.

### Business Analysis

The new product concepts that have survived are subjected to a review of their sales, costs, and profit potential. Although a preliminary business analysis is undertaken in the screening phase, at this stage more detailed forecasts of sales costs and profits are performed.

### Product Development

During this phase, a new product concept is transformed into a prototype food product by food technologists, and a preliminary marketing strategy is designed. Food technologists focus on the physical, aesthetic (sensory), and service aspects when developing the prototype. This development is guided by a number of concerns.

One of the major concerns is food safety in use and storage. Another issue is how to stabilize the product to prevent spoilage and thus increase shelf life. A third concern is the list of ingredients used in the formulation of the food product.

Once the prototype has been developed, **sensory analysis** is conducted in order to help the food technologist refine the prototype. Basically, the analysis seeks to identify whether trained panelists, (1) can detect a difference between prototypes with respect to some sensory quality, and (2) prefer one particular prototype over other prototypes. In the end, food technologists must determine whether the formulated product is as good as (or better than) competition, or the best formulation of a product concept.

The preliminary marketing strategy consists of packaging, branding, and product positioning. Since branding and packaging will be discussed later in this chapter, the focus here is on positioning the product in the minds of consumers. A **product position** refers to how consumers perceive one brand relative to competitive brands on criteria they use to evaluate and make brand choices. The goal is to create a product that consumers perceive as providing unique benefits desired by the marketplace.

### Test Marketing

Test marketing involves the placement of a new product into regions selected for geographical, marketing, and company reasons. After a predetermined time period, the results are analyzed, and a decision is made to go forward with the product or withdraw it for reevaluation.

*Commercialization*

A decision to move forward with the product means that it will be introduced to the entire target market. Within the context of finalizing its market strategy, a company must make three decisions. The first decision is when to introduce the new food product. The answer to this question depends as much on the promotional opportunities as it does on the seasonality of the product. Where to introduce the product is another consideration. A company will develop a roll-out plan for the product into selected regions over time. A third decision to make is how to launch the new product. Here, a firm specifies its market strategy for each of the intended target markets. The commercialization of the new food product corresponds to the introductory stage of the product life cycle, which will be discussed later.

## Product Development Organizations

There are several organizational structures for developing new products. Under a new **product (brand)** manager arrangement, a single executive has the responsibility of bringing new ideas to the point of commercialization. New **product committees** usually involve executives from the major operating departments. Their task is to review and approve new products. New **product departments** typically have the responsibility for the entire food development process from idea generation to commercialization. New product **venture teams** consist of specialists from the various operating departments. They are given the responsibility of developing a specific product. In many cases, these individuals remain as a team long after the product has been introduced. Any one (or any continuation) of these organizational arrangements are used to coordinate the new food development process.

## Branding

As part of the new product development process, a firm must be able to help consumers identify its new product and perceive it as different from, and better than, the competition. In short, a firm must create a **brand image** in the consumer's mind. While the brand's position indicates how consumers perceive a brand relative to competitive brands, a brand's image summarizes what a brand is perceived to mean to consumers. To create a brand image a firm must make a variety of key branding decisions.

A **brand name** must first be selected by the food manufacturer. This name may identify the firm, a brand, or both, such as **Kellogg's Corn Flakes**. A firm may decide to use its established and successful brand name to introduce new products under the same name. This **brand extension** approach has been applied by **Sunkist** to oranges, vitamins, and soft drinks. A firm may also decide to pursue a **multibrand** approach to create distinctive brand names to appeal to different market segments. The brands

**Michelob, Budweiser,** and **Busch** are examples of the multibrand approach used by **Anheuser-Busch Co.**

In addition to brand names, firms must decide whether to use trade characters—mostly created—to imbue the brand with a human personality. Food manufacturers have used trade characteristics extensively. The **Pillsbury Doughboy, Kellogg's Tony the Tiger,** the **Jolly Green Giant, Charlie the Tuna,** and the **Keebler Elves,** are examples of cartoon characters created to personify the brand. Firms have also created fictional humans to create a distinctive brand personality. **Betty Crocker, Ronald McDonald, Aunt Jemima,** and **Pepperidge Farm's Charlie Welch** are classic examples of trade characters who reinforce consumer perceptions of brand images.

Finally, a firm must decide whether to apply for trademark protection for their brand names and trade characters. Without the legal protection afforded by trademarks, it is virtually impossible to maintain a unique brand image.

## Packaging

Like branding, packaging is part of the new product development process that focuses on creating a container that will serve five functions: (1) store the contents, (2) transport the contents, (3) identify the contents, (4) promote the contents, and (5) protect the contents against damage, spoilage, and pilferage. The package may include the product's immediate container (the bottle storing **Mrs. Butter-Worth's Syrup**); a secondary package that is discarded when the product is about to be used (the cardboard wrapper surrounding the **Land O' Lakes Sweet Cream Spread**), and the package necessary to store and identify the contents that are shipped (usually a corrugated box).

Developing a package requires a firm to make a variety of decisions. The first decision is to develop the package concept. This concept defines the relative importance of the five functions. Because food purchasing at the retail level is essentially self-service, the promotional function has become increasingly important. The package is the silent salesperson in the competitive retail environment. Decisions must also be made concerning the physical aspect of the package. Packaging engineers and psychologists collaborate to specify the size, shape, material, and color of the packages.

Labeling decisions are, for the most part, governed by the **Nutritional Labeling and Education Act of 1991.** Figure 5-1 illustrates a label that conforms to the provisions of this legislation. In brief, the act, among other things, requires food manufacturers and processors to provide detailed nutritional information on the label of most foods. Food manufacturers' labeling decisions, in most cases, also include the use of **date codes**. These codes indicate the dates by which the product should be sold and used.

Another essential aspect of the label is the **Universal Product Code (UPC)**. In 1973, the Universal Product Committee adopted a ten-digit numerical code. The first five digits identify the manufacturer and the second five, the product. In 1987, the **National Retail Federation** endorsed the **UPC** as a voluntary manufacturer marking standard. The role of the **UPC** in the U.S. food marketing system has increased dramatically because of its critical significance to the **Efficient Consumer Response (ECR)** movement. This movement will be discussed later in the chapter.

## The Product Life Cycle

The life cycle concept can be applied to a product category (e.g., soft drinks), a product form (e.g., caffeine free), or a brand (e.g., **Caffeine Free Pepsi**). Product categories have the longest life cycles. Soft drinks have been in the marketplace for over one hundred years. Product forms, on the other hand, tend to pass through the entire life cycle in far less time. Frozen egg rolls and dry beer are examples of product forms that never gained consumer acceptance. Brand life cycles tend to be the shortest of all cycles. **New Coke**, and **Campbell's Fresh Chef** soups had unusually short life cycles.

Once a new product—now a brand—is launched, the goal of a firm is to manage the brand over its life cycle. The life cycle a brand lives out over time is the result of decisions made by a firm and the consumer marketplace. These decisions are made within an environment consisting of competitors and other forces not under the control of a firm, such as technology, political climate, the legal system, and the economy. It follows, then, that the shape and length of the introduction, growth, maturity, and decline life-cycle stages should vary as a response to these factors. **Figure 5-2** depicts the stages of the life cycle.

As you read the following descriptions of each life-cycle stage, keep in mind that it is not unusual for a product category, form, and brand to be at different stages of the life cycle at the same time. Thus, while the soft drink category is in its maturity stage, the product form caffeine free is in its growth stage, and **Coca-Cola Caffeine Free Sprite** is in its introductory stage.

### Introductory Stage

The life cycle begins when the brand is commercialized in the last stage of the new product development process. The objective of a firm is to gain consumer acceptance for the new brand. Advertising and promotional spending is aimed at gaining awareness and trial by consumers. The wholesalers and retailers distributing the product are likely to be limited in number. Price may be set high to quickly recapture development costs, or low to discourage competition. Because costs are high and sales are only beginning to rise during this stage, profits are low, if they exist at all.

### Growth

As consumers begin to respond to introductory advertising and promotion, sales increase more rapidly than in any other stage. The objective at this stage is to develop a preference for the brand among its competitors, who have entered the market because of its attractiveness. Emphasis is placed on expanding the number of distributors handling the brand. Price may be set high in order to meet demand, and firms may experiment with introducing variations (line extensions) of the brand. Profits increase during this stage as marketing and manufacturing costs are spread over a larger volume.

### Maturity

As more and more consumers purchase the many brands offered by competitors, the sales growth of any one brand may begin to slow. To remain a viable competitor, the objective of a firm at this stage is to modify its market offering. A firm may look for ways to increase usage among present customers or seek new markets. The use of **Arm and Hammer** baking soda as a refrigerator deodorant is an attempt to reposition the brand to current and new users. The promotion of oatmeal fiber as a dietary factor in reducing cholesterol is an attempt to reposition the **Quaker Oats** brand to a larger market.

A firm may also focus on altering the flavors, colors, and ingredients of the brand. Procter & Gamble introduced new flavors of its **Hawaiian Punch** to appeal to children. **General Foods'** new blue **Jell-O** and **M&M Mars'** new blue **M&Ms** are color modifications. **General Mills'** new **Betty Crocker** raspberry dessert bar now includes **Kraft** raspberry filling. This practice, called **co-branding**, seeks to differentiate the brand from competitors by altering the ingredients of the brand.

Finally, a firm may improve sales by lowering its price, increasing incentives to distributors to carry and sell more of the brand, or increasing incentives to consumers, such as higher coupon values, to induce them to buy more or to switch brands.

### Decline

In the final stage of the cycle, sufficient numbers of consumers have stopped buying a brand, and the sales have begun to decline. This decline may be due to a shift in tastes. The decline in ground decaffeinated coffee—and increase in decaffeinated gourmet coffee—represent shifting tastes. The sales decline of a brand may also be the result of increased competition in the product category. As described earlier, a firm may decide to **rejuvenate** the brand by modifying the physical aspects of the product, focus on new markets or uses, or alter its primary promotion.

## Managing the Product Mix

Most firms are multi-product organizations. A **product line** consists of a group of products that share common characteristics, customers, and/or uses. **PepsiCo** has two product lines: soft drinks (e.g., **Pepsi Cola, Diet Pepsi, Mountain Dew**) and snacks (e.g., **Tostitos Tortilla Chips, Fritos Corn Chips**).

A **product mix** consists of all the product lines sold by a firm. **Phillip Morris Co.** markets numerous product lines under such brand names as **Kraft, Oscar Meyer, Miller,** and **Tombstone. Campbell's Soup Co.** markets numerous lines under such brand names as **Vlasic Foods, Pepperidge Farms**, and **Mrs. Paul's Kitchens**. In addition to making decisions about individual brands, a company must make decisions to manage its product mix.

A company's product mix has four dimensions. The **width** of a product mix is based on the number of product lines a company offers. The **length** of a product mix refers to the number of brands in each product line. The number of flavors, colors, forms, or other variables of a brand are referred to as the **depth** of a product mix. **Campbell's Soup Co.** has a very deep assortment of **Chunky, Home Cooking**, and **Healthy Request** soups. The **consistency** of a product mix refers to how closely related a company's product lines are in end use (**Heinz** markets a number of food lines, such as **Ore-Ida Fries, Starkist Tuna**, and **Heinz Ketchup** and **Bar-B-Q sauce**).

**Product planning** is systematic decision making related to all aspects of the product mix. To aid in this decision making, multi-product organizations have developed a new form of product manager called the **category manager**. Each category manager is responsible for all of the brands in an assigned product category or line. Brand managers report to category managers, who have complete profit and loss responsibility for their respective categories (product lines). Managing the product mix through the use of category managers is more closely related to how consumers define their needs and make purchases. Shoppers come to a food store to purchase cereal, soft drinks, condiments, and more. It makes perfect sense to marketers that the product mix of the firm should be managed in the way consumers think of satisfying their needs—by categories.

The essence of category management is **strategic category planning**. Strategic category plans parallel the four dimensions of a company product mix. The product mix can be widened by adding a new category (product line). A firm can lengthen the category by adding a new brand. Or it can deepen the category by creating a new variation in flavor, color, ingredients, form, or packaging. Finally, a company can alter the consistency by adding or deleting a food or non-food category.

In summary, food manufacturers occupy a critical sector in the U.S. food marketing system. It is at this sector that consumer needs are transformed into tangible food products. The transformation process begins with an idea and ends with a commercialized new brand. This process may be managed by several different organizational arrangements, from the new product (brand) manager to venture teams. Once a new brand is launched, it must be managed over the course of its life cycle. In addition to managing new brands, manufacturers must manage their entire product mix. A new form of management, category managers, has entered the scene. The have been given the responsibility of managing their categories. Their strategic planning determines the length, width, depth, and consistency of the food manufacturer's product mix.

# PRICE DECISIONS

How a manufacturer determines the price of a food product is crucial because of its impact on demand and profits. Demand is discouraged if price is too high; profits are lowered if price is too low. A manufacturer's price-setting process, shaped by many factors, determines the optimum price between these two extremes.

This section will discuss the influence of consumers, costs, competition, government, and other marketing mix variables on the price-setting decision process. Lastly, the manufacturer's price-setting process will be discussed in more detail.

## Consumer Influence

The consumer's interest in value is what drives demand for food products. This value represents the perceived benefits received versus the perceived price:

$$\text{Consumer Perceived Value} = \frac{\text{Perceived Benefits}}{\text{Perceived Price}}$$

Although the types of benefits are endless, quality is one of the most significant benefits sought by consumers. Thus, increases in perceived quality generally lead to increases in perceived value, and vice versa. But benefits represent only one component of value; the other is a consumer's perception of the product's price.

The perceived price of a food product is made up of both a monetary cost and the time costs to make the food consumable. At one extreme, you have food that costs little but requires significant preparation time. Home grown products or food prepared from scratch ingredients are examples of low monetary, high time cost products. At the other extreme, you have food that is very costly but requires little to no investment in preparation time. Convenience foods, such as frozen pizzas and hot or cold entrees are high monetary, low time cost foods.

Even where customers agree on the perceived benefits (quality) of a particular food item, they may disagree on the perceived value. This is due to differences in how consumers perceive the monetary and time costs associated with price. The dollar-rich, time-poor consumer perceives price differently from the dollar-poor, time-rich consumer because she has a different **reference price**. The **reference price** represents what the customer regards as fair or reasonable monetary and time costs for the value received. Of course, even where consumers agree on the perceived price of a food item, they may disagree on its perceived benefits. The dollar-rich, time-poor consumer perceived the combined benefits of the product differently from the dollar-poor, time-rich consumer because she has different **price thresholds**. These upper and lower thresholds represent, respectively, a price that is too high relative to its perceived quality, and a quality (benefit) that is too low relative to its perceived price.

What does this all mean to the food manufacturers? They will experience difficulty when trying to assess the consumer's perception of value for their food products. However, these difficulties are manageable and should not detract from charging a price that reflects the amount of value the customer perceives in the manufacturer's product.

## Cost Influence

The most obvious influences on a product's price are its costs. A firm must be able to identify how the costs of producing and marketing a product change at different levels of production and sales. The manufacturer's costs consist of those that don't vary with volume (**fixed**) and those that do vary with volume (**variable**). However, to understand the influence of costs, a firm must consider how these costs decrease with increases in volume.

As volume increases, total fixed costs are affected by economies of scale. With more and more units produced, total fixed costs are spread over a greater number of units. The efficiency due to such factors as longer production run and better equipment results in a decrease in average fixed costs as volume increases. Likewise, as volume increases, variable costs are affected by production experience. People learn to perform an activity more efficiently, the more times they have to repeat the activity. As people develop experience, their efficiency results in a decrease in average variable costs as volume increases. Taken together, average total costs tend to fall with increases in volume. Although costs set a price floor (minimum price), there are a number of problems associated with establishing price solely on costs. The primary problem is deciding how to allocate fixed costs to units of a product. The price charged will vary depending on how fixed costs are allocated. In addition, the profitability of a product can be distorted, depending on the allocation approach used. To deal with this allocation problem, food manufacturers are using an **Activity Based Costing (ABC)** approach. The underlying logic of **ABC** is that all of the firm's **activities** are performed in order to support the production and marketing of a product. Thus, the first step in **ABC** analysis is to identify all activities performed by a firm when a new product is added. Next, the underlying costs that drive each of the activities are identified. These activity costs are then assigned to the individual products that consume these activities. Because these costs represent the actual amount of variability and costs associated with a product, the effect of **ABC** is a truer picture of profitability.

## Competitive Influence

Probably the most significant supply-related factor influencing product prices is the competitive environment within which the product will be marketed. In the previous chapter it was stated that the forty-nine food manufacturing industries were characterized as either oligopolistic or monopolistically competitive.

In oligopolistic markets, a firm must consider the competitive costs, prices, and most importantly, how they believe competitors will react to their price. In many oligopolistic industries there is a dominant firm called the **price leader**. This price leader is usually the one who has the dominant market share, lowest cost, superior distribution, greatest technological provenness, superior information, or some other competitive differential advantage. The price leader sets its price to maximize its own profits; other firms follow its lead by setting exactly the same price.

In monopolistically competitive markets, a firm prices its product to reflect its own differentiated product offering. The differentiation may be based on its product image, promotion, distribution, or other factors considered relevant to a buyer's perception of value in the product category. As long as the manufacturer can maintain its differential advantage in the marketplace, the product's price is free from competitive actions. In this case, price is set at a level that will establish a loyal customer base.

The influence that competition has on a product's price depends on the structure of the market. In oligopolistic markets, unless the firm is a price leader, the freedom to set a product's price is severely limited. In this case, competition has a significant impact. In monopolistically competitive markets, the firm's price-setting is affected by competition only when its differential advantage is neutralized and the prices are likely to change as conditions change.

## Governmental Influence

The price a firm plans to charge for its product can also be influenced by legislative antitrust law. The principal pieces of such legislation include the **Sherman Act** (1890) and the **Federal Trade Commission Act** (1914), which made price-setting agreements among manufacturers illegal. The **Miller-Tyding Act** (1937) and the **McGuire Act** (1952), which allowed manufacturers to set and control prices at the retail level, were declared illegal by the **Consumers' Goods Pricing Act** (1975). By far the most significant influence on pricing is the **Robinson-Patman Act** (1936). This act prohibits **price discrimination**—charging different customers different prices for the same product of like quality. The act is very broad and covers not only prices, but also discounts, rebates, coupons, guarantees, and advertising allowances. Despite its many restrictions, the law allows price discrimination if a firm can demonstrate (1) cost difference in selling to different customers, (2) that its price meets a competitor's lower and lawful price, and (3) that a lower price is charged because of unique circumstances of the products—obsolescence, perishability or seasonality. This act is a major legal restriction on manufacturer price because it affects the ability of a firm to set price regardless of the market's ability to pay.

## Marketing Mix Influence

In order to market a manufacturer's product effectively, the price of a product must be consistent with the other elements of the marketing mix. The price the consumer pays reflects the price charged by the firms involved in distributing the product. These prices are likely to be influenced by the profit margins that distributors believe are sufficient to warrant their participation. Although it is legally difficult to control prices through the distribution channel, it is possible to motivate distributors to participate in the product's distribution. This motivation may take the forms of trade, quantity, seasonal, and cash discounts. In addition, manufacturers encourage participation by offering promotional incentives to supplement their basic prices. These will be discussed in more depth later in this chapter.

Promotional decisions also influence price to the extent that they help define how consumers perceive the benefits associated with the product. The decision to position a product as a high quality one usually requires a higher price. To cover the cost of maintaining the product's position, costs associated with advertising, personal selling, and sales promotion must be considered.

The product influences prices by determining the production cost, product quality, and the associated benefits it conveys to consumers. Price is also influenced by the product's life cycle because consumer sensitivity to price will change over the course of a product's life cycle. Finally, price is influenced by the product's position in the manufacturer's product mix. In multiproduct firms, products are positioned at different quality levels and thus at different prices. This positioning is referred to as **price lining** and involves defining a price range (lowest to highest) and establishing specific prices within the range.

**Figure 5-3** provides an illustration of the influences on a firm's price-setting decision process. It is extremely difficult to state the relative importance of all these influences. However, a few things can be said about the factors that are likely to be most and least influential.

No matter how much competition charges for its products, or what the firm's costs, consumers will not purchase a product unless they perceive value in its purchase and consumption. Therefore, consumer perceptions of the product's value, reflected in their demand, is more important than the other factors. Further, because consumers are seldom concerned about, or even aware of, what it costs to offer a product, costs are probably the least influential of all the factors. At most, costs typically define the lowest price (floor) a manufacturer may charge for its product.

## Price-Setting Process

The price-setting process has three interrelated components: objectives, strategies, and structure. Each component is expected to provide direction to the one that follows it, and must be consistent with the one that precedes it.

### Objectives

The price-setting process for new and existing products is designed to achieve objectives that are consistent with a firm's marketing strategy. Price objectives define what the process is to achieve with its strategy and structure. These objectives are generally categorized as sales, competitive, and profit or customer based.

**Sales based objectives** are oriented toward achieving a stated level of dollar or unit sales, achieving a specific market share, and balancing seasonal demand. **Competitive based objectives** are oriented toward matching competitive prices, pricing below competition to take advantage of lower costs, and pricing above competition to take advantage of superior quality. **Profit based objectives** are oriented toward realizing a return on investment, maximizing current profits, and maintaining specific profit margins. **Customer based objectives** are oriented toward equating price with the customer perception of value. Once the price process is initiated by defining the price objectives, pricing strategies must be specified to obtain the objectives.

### Strategies

Setting prices to achieve the firm's pricing objectives reflects the selection of a specific strategy or a combination of strategies. Pricing strategies may be oriented internally (toward the firm), or externally (toward the competition or customers). In addition, firms must establish strategies for pricing new products, by-products, and product lines.

A firm's need to cover costs or seek a desirable profit may cause it to adopt an **internally oriented strategy**. With this strategy, a firm can set prices by either computing the direct product costs and then adding a desired profit, or by specifying a target profit that is to be added to costs.

A firm using a **competitive oriented strategy** bases its price largely on competitive prices rather than costs or consumer demand. The degree of flexibility a firm has in establishing strategy depends on whether it is a price leader or follower in the industry. Price leaders have the ability to redefine the price range. Price followers develop strategies that result in prices between the upper and lower limits of the price range.

A firm using a **customer oriented strategy** bases its prices on the product's perceived value to consumers and distributors of the product. Because the perceived value of a product is defined by the relationship between perceived benefits and perceived price, **value pricing** involves setting a price that is below the perceived benefits associated with the product. This price would, of course, take into consideration the markups needed to motivate distributors to carry the product.

A firm must also establish a strategy to price new products. A **skimming strategy** sets relatively high prices initially to take advantage of the price **insensitivity** of the marketplace. A **penetration strategy** sets relatively low prices initially because of the **sensitivity** of the marketplace. The initial strategy places constraints on any subsequent pricing decisions over the new product's life cycle. However, a firm can be expected to react to changes in the price sensitivity of its customer's. How the customers price sensitivity changes depends on the initial price, changes in the product's price over time, and the perceived value of the product relative to competitive products.

As a consequence of producing a finished food product, many manufacturers are left with **by-products**. A firm must establish a strategy to identify how the by-products will affect the finished product's price. When by-products are of no value, then costs are typically reflected in the finished product's price. Fortunately, most by-products produced by manufacturers have a market willing to buy them. To the extent the sale of by-products is possible, a firm must establish how the price of the finished product will be affected.

Since few manufacturers offer single products, a strategy must be devised to price **product lines**. Because these products are interrelated in costs as well as demand, a firm must establish the lowest and highest prices in the line and the differentials among the different products in the line. The expected variation in customer threshold prices must be considered when establishing these strategies because buyers are unlikely to purchase products outside of their acceptable price range.

### Structures

Once a price strategy is established, a firm must determine how prices will be set and adjusted to accommodate the market. Rarely is the list price the actual price paid by a buyer. Adjustments must take into account sales made to different customers in different geographic locations, in different quantities, at different times of the year.

The most widely used adjustment is the discount. A **discount**, or reduction in price, may be offered for purchasing a particular quantity (**quality**), during a certain time of the year (**seasonal**), and paying within a specific time period (**cash**). In addition, the manufacturer may offer a reduced price to distributors (**trade**) for performing certain marketing functions and/or reward the firm for promoting the manufacturer's product (**promotional allowance**). Finally, a discount may be offered to the consumer (**promotional**) to induce him or her to try a new or existing product.

A firm also must decide how it wishes to account for transportation cost in its price structure. There are two general methods they can use: F.O.B. (Free On Board) origin pricing and **uniform delivered pricing**. **F.O.B. origin** pricing means that the buyer pays all his product costs. In **uniform delivered pricing**, the price quoted by a manufacturer includes both the list price and an average freight cost regardless of the buyer's location.

In summary, to achieve their marketing objectives, food manufacturers engage in a price-setting decision process. This process begins when price objectives are established by a marketer for new and existing products. Once objectives are defined, a marketer must define strategies to achieve these objectives. These strategies are based either inwardly—toward the firm—or outwardly—toward competition and customers. The final step in the process is to design a price structure to reflect how actual prices paid by distributors and consumers will vary depending upon who they are, where they live, how much they buy, and when they buy.

Finally, the price-setting decision process does not take place in a vacuum. A number of factors influence this process. Thus, the price finally arrived at for a manufacturer's food product will reflect the consumer's perceived value, product costs, competition, governmental restrictions, and the influence of the marketing decisions made in product, promotion, and distribution.

## PROMOTION DECISIONS

The ultimate goal of promotion is to influence the behaviors of its many audiences. Given this goal, a food manufacturer's promotional planning must identify objectives, establish a budget, determine its promotional mix, and measure its effectiveness. This section will discuss the promotional planning process, with a particular emphasis on the promotional mix.

### Promotional Objectives

To begin the planning process manufacturers must establish objectives for both distributors and consumers. Because wholesale and retail distributors are intermediate customers, promotional objectives aimed at distributors focus on **pushing** products from manufacturers, through distributors, to consumers. To push products, distributors must be motivated to include them in their merchandise offerings and promote them to consumers. Thus, promotional objectives aimed at distributors are mostly defined within the context of **trade promotion** and **personal selling**.

Promotional objectives aimed at consumers focus on **pulling** products from manufacturers, through distributors, to consumers. To pull products, consumers must be motivated to purchase the products offered by manufacturers. Thus, promotional objectives aimed at consumers are defined mostly within the context of **advertising** and **consumer promotion**.

The final set of promotional objectives deals with maintaining and improving a manufacturer's relationship with all of its interested audiences. These audiences include not only distributors and consumers, but also employees, stockholders, legislators, and the general public. Promotional objectives aimed at these audiences are defined mostly within the context of **public relations**.

## Promotional Budget

Once promotional objectives have been identified, manufacturers must determine how much to spend on their promotional activities. Three budget-setting methods do not take into consideration the previously mentioned promotional objectives. The **affordable method** defines a budget based on what the firm believes they can afford to spend. The **percent of sales method** defines a budget based on a percentage of current or forecasted sales. The **competitive parity method** defines a budget based on what competitors spend.

The **objective-task method** is the only budgeting technique that defines a budget based on the promotional objectives of manufacturers. Essentially, this method determines what tasks must be performed to accomplish these objectives, and then estimates the costs of performing these tasks.

## Promotional Mix

Once promotional objectives have been defined and a promotional budget established to accomplish these objectives, manufacturers must allocate the budget among the major promotional elements to achieve their respective objectives. These elements, as previously mentioned, include sales promotion, personal selling, advertising, and public relations. They are defined in the following manner:

**Sales Promotion:** Any short term incentive designed to encourage distributor and consumer purchases. These incentives are referred to as trade and consumer promotions, respectively.

**Personal Selling:** Oral personal communication between one or more potential buyers and one or more sales representatives for the purpose of making sales.

**Advertising:** Any paid form of nonpersonal communication of products, organizations, or ideas through various mass media by an identifiable sponsor.

**Public Relations:** Any communication (paid or nonpaid; personal or nonpersonal) undertaken by an organization to maintain or improve its relationship with all of its interested audiences.

To properly allocate the promotional budget, manufacturers must consider the major components of promotion strategy: (1) what is to be communicated (**message**), (2) where should the communications appear (**media**), (3) how frequently and when should the firm communicate (**momentum**), and (4) how can the effectiveness of the communications be determined (**measure**).

## Promotional Dollar Allocation

To understand how manufacturers allocate their promotional expenditures among these elements, an annual survey is conducted by **Carol Wright Promotions, Inc**. Even though personal selling and public relations are not explicitly considered, the survey reports the share of promotional dollars allocated to three main categories of promotional expenditures for the current and preceding years. **Table 5-2** illustrates a five-year trend in the allocation of promotional dollars. Overall, the trend suggests that trade promotion continues to receive the largest share. The media-advertising trend has been notably stable, while consumer promotions share has declined. However, the most recent data show an increase in media advertising and a decrease in consumer promotion.

When asked what they would do next year, sixty percent of the manufacturers predicted they would spend more on media advertising, and thirty percent predicted they would spend more on consumer promotions, while one-half predicted they would spend less on trade promotion (**Table 5-3**). The predicted decline in share for trade promotion may be the result of the U.S. food marketing system's **Efficient Consumer Response** initiative.

## Trade Promotion

Sales promotion that is aimed at **pushing** products from manufacturers, through distributors, to consumers is referred to as **trade promotion**. The products that consumers may or may not purchase are determined by what the distributors make available to them. Thus, trade promotion objectives are defined to create and maintain product availability throughout the distribution channel.

Basically, there are two trade promotion objectives. The most fundamental one is to motivate distributors to include a product in their merchandise offerings. In some cases, this involves carrying a new product, and in others it means carrying more of a product. The second major objective is to influence distributors to participate in the promotion of a product to consumers. To gain product distribution and promotional support by distributors, food manufacturers rely on a number of trade promotional techniques: trade allowances, market development funds, and merchandise materials.

There are two types of trade allowances. Trade allowances given for purchasing specific quantities over a stated promotional time period are called **purchase allowances**. These purchase allowances can take several forms. A **cash discount** is paid to a distributor for paying an invoice within a certain time period. A **quantity discount** is paid to a distributor for purchasing a certain amount of inventory. A **functional discount** is paid to a distributor for performing certain functions. These discounts appear as **off-invoice** deductions on distributor invoices. Purchase allowances may also take the form of **free goods** (e.g., a free case for every **X** number of cases ordered). Purchase allowances paid to distributors to obtain space for new products in wholesalers' distribution centers and on retailers store shelves are called **slotting**

**allowances** (also known as stocking allowances, introductory allowances, or street money). Another type of purchase allowance is the **forward buy**. A distributor is allowed to buy more of a product than it can sell during a promotional time period at a "deal" price. This practice allows distributors to have on hand enough inventory to carry them from one deal period to another.

**Performance allowances** are trade allowances given to encourage distributors to perform a specific activity. **Display allowances** are provided to a retailer for featuring a manufacturer's brand in an "in-store" display. **Advertising allowances** are given to a retailer when the manufacturer's brand is included in the store's TV, radio, and newspaper advertising. **Roto participation allowances** are given to a retailer when the manufacturer's brand ad is printed by a rotogravure process. The ad then is sent to newspapers for inclusion in their Sunday supplements and/or used in a retailer's in-store advertising inserts. If the manufacturer's brand is featured in the retailer's advertising, the store is given a **cooperative advertising allowance**. Because these allowances are based on performance, distributors are required to keep accurate records on the eligible merchandise in order to receive the allowance. An invoice or bill is sent to the manufacturer along with performance verification records. This **bill back** approach is not favored by distributors because of the time and effort involved in record keeping.

Another form of purchase allowance given to a retailer to develop a special display is called a **dealer loader**. Dealer loaders may be either gifts or premiums. A gift may be in the form of cash, merchandise, or a free vacation trip. The premium is usually the display that the retailer is allowed to keep after the promotion ends.

A **market development fund (MDF)** is a lump sum of money that a distributor can use to offset any expenses incurred in the promotion and sale of the manufacturer's brand. This sum is generally determined on a per-case volume. The growing emphasis on **MDF** activities reflects a shift in emphasis toward micro-managing retail accounts.

Manufacturers also offer many kinds of **merchandise materials** to help promote their brands in the stores, such as point-of-purchase displays, mobiles, banners, price cards, shopping cart ads, seasonal display cartons and racks, checkout signs, shelf extenders/talkers, and the new instant coupon machine (**ICM**) that dispenses coupons at-shelf.

How important these promotional techniques are to distributors is reflected in an annual survey conducted by *Grocery Marketing*. **Table 5-4** lists the promotional techniques rated extremely or very important by distributors from 1991 to 1995. Regardless of the nature of the promotional allowance, distributors prefer to have the payment deducted from their invoices rather than maintain records and bill back the manufacturers. **Failure fees** paid because product sales don't reach stated levels are of little importance to distributors. Finally, some factors not normally considered essential elements of a manufacturer's trade promotion nonetheless impact on distributor buying decisions: **vendor damage** policies, **pick-up** of out-of-season, discontinued, or damage products, and **extended payment terms**.

## Personal Selling

Pushing a product from a manufacturer through distributors to the final consumers also involves personal selling. Distributors are made aware of the various trade promotions offered, and buy products through the efforts of a manufacturer's salesforce or another salesforce called **food brokers**. Food brokers, like a manufacturer's salesforce, engage in wholesale activities and will be discussed in a later chapter on wholesaling.

A manufacturer's salesforce, in general, has two opportunities to promote and sell product. The first opportunity is through personal contact with distributors. The second opportunity is through trade shows. Regardless of which opportunity is taken, the emphasis is on **relationship selling**. The sales objective is focused on establishing mutually beneficial long-run relationships. To reach this objective, the salesforce must assume the role of consultant to distributors. In this role, the salesforce engages in a process that results in solving distributor problems. Once solved, the solutions provide the salesforce with an opportunity to enhance their relationship through follow-up activities.

Manufacturers also rely on **trade shows** to push products to consumers. Manufacturers set up exhibit booths to demonstrate their products, identify potential buyers, provide information on new and existing products, write sales orders, and strengthen their existing relationships with distributors. In general, the participants at these shows are distributors who are members of the various trade associations that sponsor these shows. Trade shows that have national appeal are sponsored by a number of trade associations including the **Food Marketing Institute (FMI)**, the **National Grocers Association (NGA)**, the **Grocer Manufacturers of America (GMA)**, the **National Food Distributors Association (NFDA)**, the **Food Distributors International (FDI)**, and the **Private Label Manufacturers Association (PLMA)**. To reinforce the contact made, manufacturers frequently distribute specialty advertising items that carry a firm's **logo**. The nature of these specialties is limited only by the imaginations of advertisers, but they share a common purpose: to create long-run reminders of manufacturers and their brands.

## Advertising

By purpose, advertising can be classified as brand or corporate advertising. **Brand advertising** is one of the promotional elements used to **pull** a product (brand) from a manufacturer, through distributors, to consumers. Brand advertising pulls a brand by creating consumer awareness of the brand, interest in its perceived benefits, desire to own the brand, and action to purchase and consume the brand. Brand advertising is also used to position a new brand or reposition an old brand in the minds of consumers.

A **brand's position** reflects how consumers perceive it, relative to competitive brands on important criteria. These criteria are assumed to be those used when consumers make brand purchase decisions. The brand's position is subsequently used to create a unique selling proposition (**USP**)—the specific benefit(s) a consumer will receive when the brand is purchased and consumed.

Brand advertising is also undertaken to establish, maintain, and reinforce brand image. A **brand image** reflects the thoughts, feelings, and expectations of satisfaction evoked by the brand name. The most advertised food and beverage brands are shown in **Table 5-5**.

In addition to pulling a brand from a manufacturer, advertising is used to create and reinforce positive attitudes toward a brand's manufacturer. This form of corporate advertising is used in two ways. First, advertising is designed to establish the image and reputation of a manufacturer among its many audiences. These audiences include employees, stockholders, suppliers, consumers, governmental agencies, special interest groups, and the general public. Second, advertising is used to establish the manufacturer's concern with environmental, social, or some other issue of interest to the firm's well-being. This advertising is designed to identify, to its many audiences, a firm's position on particular issues.

Although brand and corporate advertising are not stated separately, *Advertising Age* publishes the top two hundred advertisers on an annual basis. **Table 5-6** identifies advertising spending, U.S. sales, and the advertising-to-sales ratios for the food manufacturers identified in the top two hundred advertisers. Twenty-three of the top fifty food manufacturers are among the top two hundred national advertisers.

One way of standardizing the amount of money spent on advertising by manufacturers is to relate the money spent in advertising to the sales generated by an industry, firm, or product category. The **advertising-to-sales ratio** represents the annual advertising expenditures divided by the sales of an industry, firm, or product category. The advertising-to-sales ratios in **Table 5-6** represent advertising spending by food manufacturing firms. The average advertising-to-sales ratio for these twenty-three manufacturers is nine percent, versus 6.5 percent for all food manufacturers. Further, of the two hundred largest advertising spending industries reported in *Advertising Age* (July 1, 1996), fourteen of them are food manufacturers. The range of advertising-to-sales ratios is from a low of 1.3 percent (SIC 2033, Canned Fruits and Vegetables) to a high of 9.2 percent (SIC 2041, Grain Mill Products).

## Consumer Promotions

Sales promotion that is aimed at **pulling** products from manufacturers, through distributors, to consumers is referred to as **consumer promotion**. These promotions are designed to encourage consumers to ask for and purchase products offered by manufacturers. The demand created by these promotions pulls the products from the manufacturers. **Table 5-7** represents Carol Wright Promotions, Inc.'s five year comparison of the most frequently used consumer promotions by food manufacturers. The *Magazine of Promotion Marketing*, in its 1996 annual report of the promotion industry, estimates that manufacturers spent 70.1 billion dollars on consumer promotions. Food manufactures employ a number of consumer promotions to create demand: coupons, cents-off promotions, tie-ins, money-back offers, sampling, sweepstakes, premium offers, pre-pricing, and contests.

### *Coupons*

By far the most frequently used consumer promotion is couponing. This should be of no surprise, for the simple reason that coupons benefit the consumer, retailer, and manufacturer. According to coupon trends and consumer usage patterns, the number of food coupons distributed has grown from 33 billion in 1984 to 205 billion in 1995. Over these same years, the redemption of manufacturer coupons has ranged from 3.5 percent to 2.0 percent. Today, the average face value and expiration date is sixty cents and 3.3 months, respectively. The five leading food product categories in coupon distribution are cereals and breakfast foods, packaged meats, condiments, gravies/sauces, bread/baked goods, and ice cream novelties (**NCH Promotional Services**, 1996).

There are two methods of coupon distribution: out-of-store (direct) and in-store. Today, almost ninety percent of manufacturer coupons are distributed directly through **Free Standing Inserts (FSI)** in the nation's Sunday newspapers (82.1 percent), **handouts** (6.3 percent), **direct mail** to consumer homes (3.0 percent), magazine (3.0 percent).

In-store coupons are distributed in a number of ways. A retailer **in-ad coupon** is a manufacturer's or retailer's coupon that appears in a retailer's own newspaper or in-store flyer. The coupon is redeemable only at the store. The **Instant Coupon dispenser**, by **Act Media**, is a coupon dispenser mounted on the shelf in front of the products being promoted. **Electronically dispensed coupons** are distributed at the point of sale when a specific product is scanned at the checkout. Coupons are also distributed as part of an in-store **sampling/demonstration**.

Coupons are also enclosed in, or printed on, a product's package. **Regular in/on pack** coupons may be redeemed later for the same product. **Cross ruff in/on pack** may be redeemed later for a different product. The **instant on-pack** may be immediately redeemed for the same or, in some cases, different product.

Redemption rates, reported by **NCH Promotional Services**, vary tremendously among these distribution methods and are, in general, higher for in-store coupons than for out-of-store coupons. The top ten redemption rates include only two direct methods: direct mail (3.8 percent) and free standing insert (1.7 percent). The in-store redemption rates include instant-on-pack (31.3 percent), on shelf dispensed (12.2 percent), regular on-pack (9.7 percent), electronically dispensed (8.0 percent), regular in-pack (8.8 percent), in-store handout sampling/demonstration (4.6 percent), in-pack cross ruff (3.8 percent), and on-pack cross-ruff (3.5 percent). **Cents-off deals** offer a manufacturer's brand at less than the regular price. The reduced price is typically printed on the package. **Price-pack** deals may involve buying a larger than usual size package (twenty percent or more) for the price of the normal size. Sometimes two related products are co-branded together, or included in one or the other's package and offered at the normal price of one of them (e.g., **M&Ms** in **Betty Crocker Brownie Mix**). **Tie-ins** promote two products together and are sometimes called cross-promotion. The consumer must buy both in order to receive the price reduction. Any reduction in the normal price of a product is called a **markdown**.

### Money Back Offers/Other Refunds

Cash refunds are given to consumers after the purchase of a product has been made. Typically, the consumer sends a "proof of purchase" (mostly the universal product code) to the manufacturer within the stated rebate time. The refund represents a certain percentage of the purchase price.

### Sampling

Samples represent a free trial size product. The primary reason that sampling works so well is that it involves no risk to the consumer. The "try it, if I like it, I'll buy it" approach is very appealing to consumers.

### Sweepstakes

A sweepstakes allows consumers to compete for prizes by filling out forms. No product purchase is required, and winners are determined by random drawings.

### Premium Offers

An offer of merchandise—free or at a reduced price—for responding in a certain way is called a premium. Premiums may appear attached to the product's package, in the package, or be the package itself (containers). In addition, premiums may be sent for in the mail.

### Pre-pricing

Pre-pricing takes place when a manufacturer prints a reduced price on a product's package that already contains a printed price. The purpose is to offer a temporary price reduction without changing a product's permanent price printed on the package.

### Contests

An offer of cash or merchandise as a prize for demonstrating some skill is called a contest. These skills may include writing a jingle or poem, submitting a recipe, or other skills.

### Public Relations

Public relations (PR) is intended to maintain and/or improve a manufacturer's relationship with all of its interested audiences. The audiences include customers, distributors, employees, special interest groups, stockholders, legislators, and the general public. Most frequently, **PR** activities are carried on so that they reflect positively on a firm and its products. A firm has many opportunities to build on its relationship with its audiences.

A firm may make new product release announcements, sponsor sports and charitable fund raising events, link product purchases with fund raising for a worthwhile ecological or social cause, lobby legislators to promote or defeat legislation and regulations, advertise to support a firm's position on critical issues before the general public, undertake some form of public service, support local community activities, and defend the firm against negative information and events.

Public relations is intended to increase the effectiveness of pushing and pulling products through the distribution channel. However, because it plays a supportive role in a firm's promotional mix, the precise impact that public relations has on sales and profits is difficult to evaluate.

## PLACE DECISIONS

No matter how superior the product, how appropriate the price, and how effective the promotion, to create customer value manufacturers must also get their product into the hands of consumers. Thus distribution decisions, like the other marketing mix decisions, are driven by manufacturers' understanding of their consumer markets.

Prior to making distribution decisions, manufacturers must understand two macro dimensions of their markets. First, how many consumers are in their relevant target market? Second, how are the consumers geographically dispersed?

In addition to understanding consumer markets on a macro level, manufacturers must also understand their markets on a micro level. In particular, they need to know the answers to several questions. Where do consumers want to buy food products? How much of a food product do they buy? When are they likely to buy a food product? How often do they buy food products? How do consumers purchase food products?

Once manufacturers understand their consumer markets on both macro and micro levels, their distribution decisions will focus on creating both a channel design and a logistics design. This section will examine more closely the nature of these distribution design decisions. Following this examination, the U.S. food marketing system **Efficient Consumer Response** initiative will be discussed.

## Channel Design

Even though channel design is presented before logistics design, it is done only for purposes of discussion. In actuality, these decisions are made concurrently to properly reflect their interdependence. The process by which a channel is designed involves establishing objectives, identifying channel alternatives, and determining the channel structure.

### *Channel Objectives*

The basis for stating channel objectives is the desired service level of the consumer market. The desired service level should be defined to reflect the purchase behavior for food products at the retail level. Food products are purchased frequently, and involve substantial search costs (time, effort, money) relative to the price of a product. To reflect consumer purchase behavior, the desired level of service must ultimately be defined in terms of availability at the retail store.

For consumers, availability means simply having food items available at particular times and locations to meet their demand. Thus, the most acceptable approach to defining channel objectives is to specify them in terms of the consumer **in stock percentage**. This percentage reflects the number of times a consumer can actually purchase a food item relative to his or her purchase intentions.

### *Channel Alternatives*

Once the manufacturer has defined the consumer in-stock objectives, to place food products into the hands of consumers, certain functions must be performed. The nature of these functions determines whether the manufacturer will perform them (self-distribution) and/or the functions will be carried out by distributors. If these functions are to be carried out by distributors, then the manufacturer will select distributors (both wholesalers and retailers) based on the functions they perform. However, the manufacturer must still decide on how many distributors to use at both the wholesale and retail levels.

For food manufacturers, consumer purchase behavior dictates that food products be conveniently available. This means that most manufacturers will strive for maximum product exposure. This **intensive** distribution involves placing their food products in as many retail outlets as possible. The goal of maximum product exposure usually means that a manufacturer will use wholesalers who distribute to all the different types of retailers. A manufacturer may use any or all of seven different wholesale formats (firms), and any or all of fourteen different retail formats (stores).

By contrast, some manufacturers may purposely limit the number of retail outlets offering their food products. Usually these manufacturers market "gourmet" food items and/or seek to maintain an image of exclusivity. To accomplish this the food item is distributed either on a **selective basis** (a few different retail formats, and a few stores within each format) or an **exclusive basis** (stores within one retail format).

A manufacturer's decision either to engage in self-distribution or to use distributors must be evaluated based on how efficiently the channel objective can be reached. To evaluate the efficiency of the channel alternatives, a manufacturer must determine how each differs with regard to the costs of transporting, warehousing, order processing, and handling food products.

### *Channel Structure*

The last step in channel design is to determine a channel structure. Ordinarily, manufacturers would make decisions whether to use direct or indirect channels, single or multiple channels, or one or more of the three vertical marketing systems. However, food manufacturers mostly seek maximum product exposure in order to ensure availability at any and all possible retail formats and their stores. As a consequence, for most food manufacturers, channel structure decisions are seldom "either one or the other," but rather "one and the other." To illustrate, the three major decisions will be examined.

A **direct** channel moves a food product from the manufacturer to the consumer without the services of distributors. Food manufacturers sell directly to consumers when they establish their retail outlet stores on their own premises (e.g., **Butternut Bakeries**). An **indirect** channel uses the service of distributors.

In general, the most practical way to achieve the objective of maximum product exposure is to use distributors. These indirect channels take many forms. Food manufacturers may deliver directly to the retailer's door. This **direct store delivery (DSD)** is common for manufacturers of soft drinks, bread, snacks, milk, and other food items supported by driver-route salespeople. Food manufacturers may use both wholesale and retail distributors. Most food products are distributed in this manner. Food manufacturers may also use food brokers along with other wholesalers and retailers. Food brokers represent mostly the small manufacturers' sales force, who in turn call on other wholesalers or retailers.

The second channel structure decision focuses on how many channels to use. A **single** channel uses only one retail format to reach consumers. A **multiple** channel uses more than one retail format to reach consumers. Manufacturers who produce a "gourmet" food item and/or wish to maintain a brand image of exclusivity are most likely to use a single retail format (e.g., **supermarket**). Most manufacturers will use multiple channels. Thus, **Kellogg's Co.** sells its breakfast cereals to consumers through convenience stores, supermarkets, supercenters, wholesale clubs, restaurants, schools, universities, and other institutions.

The decision to use one or more vertical marketing systems (VMS) is the last channel structure decision. As previously identified in Chapter 1, there are three types of vertical marketing systems. A **corporate VMS** achieves a coordination of the manufacturing and distribution of food products through ownership. **Starbucks Coffee Company** sells its coffee through its own retail stores. A **contractual VMS** achieves a coordination of the manufacturing and distribution of food products by using formal contracts. A contractual **VMS** such as a **wholesaler-sponsored chain** (e.g., **Flemings Cos.**), and a **retailer sponsored cooperative** (e.g., **Wakefern Food Corp**.), account for a significant amount of food distribution sales. Because both of these arrangements are basically wholesale operations, they will be discussed in the next chapter. A **franchise system** is the third type of contractual VMS. In this arrangement, the franchiser (manufacturer) grants another party (franchisee) the right to distribute a food product. Although limited in use, soft drink manufacturers like **Coca-Cola** and **Pepsi** license bottlers at the wholesale level who buy syrup and carbonate and contain the finished product and sell it to retailers.

The last type of VMS is an **administered** channel system. The coordination of manufacturing and distribution is brought about by the exercise of power by one of the members of the channel—manufacturer, wholesaler, or retailer. Manufacturers such as **Phillip Morris, Nestlé, RJR Nabisco**, and **Quaker Oats** are able to administer the VMS for the benefit of all the channel members. **Quaker Oats**; "Total Customer Development" program is designed to make the distribution and marketing of its products more efficient and profitable to the channel member stores.

## Logistical Design

A logistics design is created concurrently with a channel design and enables a manufacturer to have food products available when and where target market consumers want them. The process by which the logistics aspect of a channel is designed involves establishing objectives, and identifying the key logistics activities. Although the following discussion assumes a manufacturer is using an **indirect** channel comprising distributors, the discussion is also relevant to a manufacturer who engages in **self-distribution**.

### Logistical Objectives

Unlike channel objectives that focus on target market consumers, logistical objectives focus on a manufacture's intermediate customers—distributors. Thus, logistical objectives must be defined in terms that are consistent with the in stock channel objective. To achieve this consistency, logistical objectives are defined and measured in three ways: (1) inventory availability, (2) service capability, and (3) service quality.

**Inventory availability** may be defined and measured in three ways. First, it is defined in terms of the percentage of **SKUs** (Stock Keeping Units) at a storage facility (warehouse) available for shipment to distributors. Second, it is defined in terms of the number of **SKUs** filled relative to those ordered. Third, it is defined as a percentage of orders shipped complete. Inventory availability defined in these three ways meet the inventory needs of distributors.

**Service capability** focuses on a manufacturer's order cycle and may also be defined and measured in three ways. The speed at which a distributor's order is received, approved, processed, invoiced, and delivered is one measure of capability. The consistency at which the actual time of performance for any of the order cycle activities meets the expected performance time over a number of order cycles is a second measure of capability. A third measure of capability involves the ability of a manufacturer to accommodate a distributor's special request. Taken together, these objectives and their measurement meet the service needs of distributors.

**Service quality** may be defined and measured in terms of a manufacturer's ability to perform all the order cycle activities to the satisfaction of its distributors. This means that shipments arrive free of damage, when and where they are needed, and with invoices that reflect exactly what the distributor ordered. It also means that a manufacturer is committed to resolving any and all logistical problems within a reasonable time.

### Logistical Functions

The functions that must be performed to reach the logistical objectives are storage, inventory management, order processing, and transportation. These functions are carried out within the context of a manufacturer's order cycle.

A manufacturer can choose to **store** its food products in its own warehouse (private) or in a for-hire (public) warehouse. Another option a manufacturer has is to store its products in a **distribution center**. In addition to storage, the typical distribution center receives, processes, and ships orders.

**Inventory management** activities are carried out to control inventory levels. A manufacturer defines the level of inventory that balances the risks and associated costs of being unable to fill distributors' orders against the costs of carrying inventory. A wide array of "bar codes" are used to monitor and control inventory levels. In addition to the **Universal Product Code (UPC)**, a new bar code—the **UCC/EAN128**--has been created to contain a much broader range of information. The **UCC/EAN128** can identify production dates, sell-by dates, weight, and quantity, as well as the manufacturer and product identification. Tied in with advanced ship notices, or **ASNs** (an electronic transmission by which the supplier advises the customer of an impending shipment), the bar code, when placed on a case or pallet load, will contribute significantly to crossdocking and efficient replenishment—key components of **Efficient Consumer Response**.

**Order processing** involves three phases. **Order entry** is initiated by an order. The simultaneous transmission of the order to a warehouse/distribution center and the credit department begins the **order handling** phase. The warehouse checks for product availability while the credit department checks the customer's credit. If the product is available and the customer credit is worthy, the order is filled and scheduled for **delivery**.

The backbone of the **transportation** infrastructure in the U.S. food marketing system is the truck. The manufacturer has a number of ways it can move products to distributors. First, a manufacturer may provide its own transportation as a **private motor carrier**. Second, a manufacturer may lease the tractors and trailers to haul their food items. Third, a manufacturer may employ the for-hire common or contract carriers. **Common** carriers are available to the general public while **contract** carriers engage in transportation under a contract with one manufacturer (exclusive use) or a limited number of firms (multiple use). Both common and contract carriers are regulated by the **Interstate Commerce Commission (ICC)**. Another option to a manufacturer is to **outsource**, or use a third-party **dedicated contract carrier**. These firms offer services such as specifying and supplying vehicles on a lease basis, designing routes, and arranging backhauls, providing drivers, truck loaders, and administrative support personnel.

Instead of returning empty after delivery to a retail store, a distributor's truck may pick up food items at a manufacturer and **backhaul**, or deliver them to a designated distribution center. According to *Progressive Grocer* (September, 1990), the number of backhauls has tripled since 1984. Today, it is estimated that dry grocery backhauls represent thirty percent of all cases received at food distribution centers. The growth is due to the **Motor Carrier Act of 1980**. This act specified how manufacturers can give backhaul allowances to distributors without violating the **Robinson-Patman Act**.

## Integrated Channel/Logistics Structure

The design of a manufacturer channel and logistic designs require the creation of an integrated structure. The goal is to make products available when and where target market consumers want them, at the **least possible cost**. The task is made difficult because transportation, storage, order processing, and inventory-carrying costs interact, often in ways that prevent these costs from being minimized separately. For example, reduced expenditures in inventory (smaller inventories) can mean increased expenditures for faster transportation services. Reduced order processing expenditures (fewer orders) can mean increased expenditures in inventory carrying charges (larger inventories maintained). Reduced expenditures for storage (fewer warehouses) can mean increased expenditures for transportation services (products moved longer distances).

In summary, the major place decisions manufacturers face are: Should they self distribute or use distributors? How many of which types of distributors should they use to reach their target market consumers? How much inventory should be maintained? Where should inventory be located? How should inventory be delivered? And how should orders be handled? Given the channel and logistics objectives, a manufacturer must make these decisions in such a way that the costs of achieving these objectives are minimized.

# EFFICIENT CONSUMER RESPONSE*

**Efficient Consumer Response (ECR)** is a process by which manufacturers, wholesalers, and retailers cooperate to remove **costs** that do not add **value** for consumers. **ECR** is basically a reaction to the realization that many of the business practices engaged in by distributors and suppliers have added costs but not value to the product.

The ultimate goal of **ECR** is to make the U.S. food marketing system more responsive to consumer demand and in a more efficient manner—thus the name **Efficient Consumer Response**. To accomplish this goal, **ECR** strategies are predicated on both a timely, accurate, and paperless information flow that reflects precisely consumer demand and a smooth, continuous product flow supply to match this demand. Each of four strategies focuses on creating value by satisfying consumers' needs. These four strategies are efficient store assortments, efficient product introductions, efficient replenishment, and efficient promotion. These strategies will be examined based on how they create customer value.

## Efficient Store Assortments

To create customer value, the goal of a firm is to provide an assortment of products wide enough to satisfy consumers while optimizing the use of store and shelf space. This is achieved through three practices. First, a firm must create an organizational structure based on **category management** profitability. These categories are managed as strategic business units (**SBUs**) so as to maximize sales with minimal cost and use of space.

Second, a firm must allocate its space based on accurate data. There are four types of data essential to successful **space management**: (1) scan data from every store, (2) store-level sales history adjusted for promotion and seasons, (3) point of sale identification of the consumer purchaser, and (4) item information regarding the product characteristics, price, and costs. To reflect costs accurately, a firm needs to determine activity based cost for each product. **Activity based costing (ABC)** is an accounting system that focuses on activities that consume direct and indirect costs. It allocates these costs based on what drives the costs (e.g., cost drivers may be products, manufacturers, or transactions). Because it allocates all costs, **ABC** is intended to

---

\* This section is based on Kurt Salmon Associates, Inc., *Efficient Consumer Response—Enhancing Customer Value in the Grocery Industry,* Food Marketing Institute, Washington, D.C., 1993.

give the firm a better measure of the actual costs, and thus the profitability of different categories.

Third, a firm must frequently monitor the category and space allocation. By doing so, the category manager can make more informed decisions regarding new product introduction and deletions.

## Efficient Product Introductions

To create customer value, the goal of a firm is to meet, in a more timely manner, the ever-changing needs of consumers through new product introductions. Regardless of where the changes take place—tastes, nutrition, or lifestyle—a firm must meet these changing needs with a minimum amount of delay.

To achieve efficient product introductions, a firm relies on two practices. First, **Electronic Data Interchange (EDI)** is the electronic exchange of business information. **EDI** transmits information using the current language for communications in the grocery industry—**Uniform Communication Standard (UCS)**. **EDI** allows manufacturers, brokers, and distributors to order and invoice electronically, and then track the movement of orders and the status of invoices through the distribution channel.

**EDI** enables a firm to practice a **Quick Response (QR)** strategy. **QR** represents a partnership between distributors and suppliers that seeks to respond more quickly to consumer needs by sharing information. **QR** begins with point of sale (**POS**) activity. In response to scanner-generated product movement data, an electronic purchase order is created and transmitted to a supplier. The supplier confirms the order and ships the item to a warehouse or directly to a store and transmits an invoice to the distributor. The distributor matches the invoice against the receiving data and transfers payment via **Electronic Funds Transfer (EFT)** to the supplier's bank account. With the aid of **EDI** and **QR** a paperless system from beginning (**POS**) date to end (**EFT**) payment is created.

## Efficient Replenishment

To create customer value the goal of a firm is to minimize the time, inventory and physical assets in the replenishment system while maintaining a high level of in-stock performance. To achieve efficient replenishment a firm may use several practices.

**Computer Assisted Ordering (CAO)** uses store-**SKU** perpetual inventories with an order point level to automatically trigger the replenishment orders for items with a store. In turn, **CAO** requires that the operations of distributors and suppliers be integrated to replenish the distributor on the basis of actual and forecasted sales at the store item level rather than on an economic order quantity. Information is transmitted via **EDI** and deliveries are made on a **continuous replenishment (CR)** basis. Under a **CR** program distributors would carry substantially less inventory because of their ability to receive orders on a **just-in-time (JIT)** basis.

Shipments received on a just-in-time basis are aided by the distribution channel ability to **cross dock** inventory. In cross docking facilities, supplier shipments are unloaded at the receiving dock and loaded onto store-bound trucks at the shipping dock without ever going into storage.

## Efficient Promotion

To create customer value, the goal of a firm is to use trade and consumer promotions in a more efficient manner. To achieve efficient promotions a firm must create consumer purchase incentives without causing inventory surges by buying more than they plan to sell during the deal period (**forward buying**), or buying product on a price deal in one region and reselling it at a profit in another region (**diverting**).

Several practices may be used in order to achieve efficient trade promotions. First, a supplier may offer a **continuous deal** price arrangement as an alternative to current trade-promotion practices. This price arrangement would reflect an average weighted value of promotional spending and supplier savings realized from smoothing the inventory flow. Second, a supplier may offer to simplify the administrative burden associated with delivering the value of various promotional deals. Third, a supplier may use **UCS** transactions to communicate accurate up-to-date information on promotional deals.

To achieve efficient consumer promotions, a firm may use two practices. First, a supplier may reimburse retailers directly based on **POS** scan-validated coupon redemption. This eliminates much of the costly redemption processing and validation expense. Second, a supplier may eliminate paper coupons entirely and reimburse the distributor electronically based on **POS** scan data.

## ECR Benefits

**Table 5-8** illustrates the **ECR** strategies and their potential savings. Total savings in the dry grocery segment is estimated to be ten billion dollars. When estimated savings from other segments (e.g., frozen, HBC, or dairy) and, to a lesser extent, perishables are considered, total potential savings are in excess of thirty billion dollars. The estimated reduction in dry grocery inventories is forty-one percent, from 104 days' supply to sixty-one days' supply.

The consumer will be the primary beneficiary of **ECR**. Ultimately, the cost savings and financial savings will be passed through to the consumer in the form of an eleven percent decrease in price for dry groceries. **Cost savings** include the direct cost reductions resulting from the elimination of activities or expenses such as the automation or ordering activities and labor savings from cross docking. Cost savings also result from the reduction of fixed costs from more efficient utilization of store space or manufacturing capacity.

**Financial savings** result when less inventory or fewer physical assets are required to generate each consumer sales dollar. The improved productivity of assets will result in a nineteen percent reduction in the amount of invested capital required to generate each dollar of consumer sales.

Overall, suppliers will realize approximately fifty-four percent of the total system savings (forty-seven percent from cost savings and seven percent from financial savings). Distributors will realize forty-six percent of the total system savings (thirty-two percent from cost savings and fourteen percent from financial savings). Although the cost savings for the supplier are greater than for the distributors, suppliers incur a much higher proportion of total supply chain costs (approximately seventy percent) than do the distributors (approximately thirty percent). Taking this into account, the percentages of reduction in operating costs are similar.

## SUMMARY

This chapter examined the marketing decisions that manufacturers make and the factors that influence their decisions. The forty-nine industries the manufacturing sector comprises were characterized as having structures that vary from oligopolistic to monopolistically competitive. Because the product of oligopolists can be either standardized commodities or differentiated brands, their marketing decisions are, for the most part, indistinguishable from those of the monopolistic competitor. The chapter began with a historical perspective of the major developments in the manufacturing sector.

Product decisions made by manufacturers involve new product introduction, product modification, and product deletions. Product development decisions focus on the process needed in order to bring an idea to the marketplace as a tangible food item. Once developed, the product must be managed through its life cycle. A number of internal product development organizations, from the brand manager to the venture team, have enabled firms to manage new products. Because most manufacturers are multi-product firms, decisions must be made regarding the width, length, depth, and consistency of their respective product mixes.

The manufacturers' price-setting processes consider the influence of consumers, costs, competition, government, and other marketing-mix variables. To create consumer value, manufacturers develop a price structure that is consistent with a product's perceived benefits. Product benefits that outweigh costs represent value to consumers.

The ultimate goal of promotion is to influence the behaviors of consumers. To do this, manufacturers identify objectives that push and pull products to consumers. Once objectives are determined, a budget is established to attain these objectives. Trade promotions and personal selling are two promotional mix elements that push products from manufacturers, through distributors, to consumers. Consumer promotion and advertising are two promotional mix elements that pull a product from manufacturers, through distributors, to consumers. Public relations plays a supportive role in a manufacturer's promotional planning. Its main purpose is to maintain and/or improve a manufacturer's relationship with its many interested audiences.

Manufacturers must not only create products, price them realistically, and promote them aggressively, but they must also place their products into the hands of consumers. Distribution decisions do this by designing channel and logistic structures. The former defines its purpose in terms of the desired service level of consumers. The latter defines its purpose in terms of its intermediate customers—distributors. These structures are integrated in such a way that products are made available to consumers at the least possible costs.

The chapter ended with a brief examination of Efficient Consumer Response. **ECR** is basically an attempt to remove the costs that don't add value to the consumer. To do so, manufacturers use four strategies. Efficient Store Assortments are designed to provide product assortment while optimizing store and shelf space. Efficient Product Introductions are developed to meet the changing needs of the marketplace in a more timely fashion. Efficient Replenishment focuses on maintaining a high level of in-stock performance while minimizing the time, inventory, and physical assets involved in replenishment. Efficient Promotions seek to create consumer incentives without causing inventory surges due to forward buying and diverting.

**ECR** will benefit consumers because of reduced out-of-stock items, fresher products, and increased product choice. Distributors will benefit through increased consumer loyalty and improved supplier relationships. Finally, suppliers will benefit because of increased brand integrity, reduced, out-of-stock, and improved distributor relationships.

## SELECTED REFERENCES

Bearden, W. O., T. N. Ingram, and R. W. Laforge. *Marketing Principles and Perspectives*. Chicago, Ill. Irwin Publ., 1995.

Blattberg, R. C. and S. A. Neslin. *Sales Promotion Concepts, Methods and Strategies*. Englewood Cliffs, N.J. Prentice-Hall, Inc., 1990.

Bowersox, D. J. and M. B. Cooper. *Strategic Marketing Channel Management*. New York, McGraw-Hill, Inc., 1992.

Connor, J. M., R. T. Rogers, B. W. Marion, and W. F. Mueller. *The Food Manufacturing Industries—Structure, Strategies, Performance, and Policies*, Lexington, Mass.: Lexington Books, D.C. Heath and Company., 1986.

Connor, J. M. *Food Processing—An Industrial Powerhouse in Transition*. Lexington, Mass.: Lexington Books, D.C. Heath and Company, 1988.

Coyle, J. J., E. J. Bardi, and C. J. Langley, Jr., *The Management of Business Logistics*. New York: West Publishing Co., 1992.

Fuller, G. W. *New Food Product Development*. Boca Raton, Fl. CRC Press., 1994.

Hampe, E. C. and M. Wittenberg. *The Food Industry—Lifeline of America*, Ithaca, N.Y.: Connell University, 1980.

Keegan, W., S. Moriarty, and T. Duncan. *Marketing*. Prentice-Hall, N.J.: Englewood Cliffs, 1992.

Kurt Salmon Associates, Inc.. *Efficient Consumer Response—Enhancing Customer Value in the Grocery Industry*. Food Marketing Institute., Washington D.C. 1993.

Monroe, K. B., *Pricing Making Profitable Decisions,* 2nd ed. McGraw-Hill Publishing Co., New York 1990.

Morris, M. H. and G. Morris. *Market Oriented Pricing*. Lincolnwood, Ill.: NTC Publishing Group., 1990.

Wells, W., J. Bunnett, and S. Moriarty. *Advertising, 2nd ed.* Englewood Cliffs, N.J.: Prentice-Hall, Inc., 1992.

*The 18th Annual Survey of Promotional Practices*. Naperville, Ill.: Carol Wright Promotions, Inc., A Subsidiary of Cox Target Media, Inc. 1996.

The 1995 Annual Report of the U.S. Promotion Industry. *Promo: The Magazine of Promotion Marketing*. Smith Communications, Inc., Vol VIII, No. 8, July 1995.

*The 1996 Coupon Trends and Consumer Usage Patterns*. Lincolnshire, Ill.: NCH Promotional Services., 1996.

Agriculture 2001. *The Kiplinger Agriculture Letter*. Washington, D.C.: The Kiplinger Washington Editors, 1992.

Top 100 Food Companies. *Food Processing*. A Putnam Publication, December 1995.

The 100 Leading National Advertisers. *Advertising Age*. September 27, 1996.

## REVIEW QUESTIONS

1. What role does the food manufacturer play in the U.S. food marketing system?

2. Distinguish between a processor and a manufacturer of food.

3. Why do many observers of the new U.S. food marketing system believe that the manufacturing sector is the most significant sector in the entire system?

4. Explain the phases of the new food product development process.

5. What is meant by the statement, "Once a new product—now a brand—is introduced, the goal of the firm is to manage the brand over its life cycle"?

6. What role does a product's price play in defining customer perceived value?

7. Promotion objectives aimed at distributors push products to consumers, while those aimed at consumers pull products. Explain.

8. How does a manufacturer's channel design differ from its logistics design?

9. Briefly explain "Efficient Consumer Response" (ECR).

10. How will the U.S. food marketing system benefit from implementation of the ECR initiative?

**TABLE 5-1.** NEW FOOD PRODUCT INTRODUCTIONS

| Food Categories | 1991 | 1992 | 1993 | 1994 | 1995 |
|---|---:|---:|---:|---:|---:|
| Baby Foods | 95 | 53 | 7 | 45 | 61 |
| Bakery Foods | 1,631 | 1,508 | 1,420 | 1,636 | 1,855 |
| Bakery Ingredients | 335 | 346 | 383 | 544 | 577 |
| Beverages | 1,367 | 1,538 | 1,845 | 2,250 | 2,854 |
| Breakfast Cereals | 104 | 122 | 99 | 110 | 128 |
| Candy/Gum/Snacks | 1,885 | 2,068 | 2,042 | 2,461 | 2,462 |
| Condiments | 2,787 | 2,555 | 3,148 | 3,271 | 3,698 |
| Dairy | 1,111 | 1,320 | 1,099 | 1,323 | 1,614 |
| Desserts | 124 | 93 | 158 | 215 | 125 |
| Entrees | 808 | 698 | 631 | 694 | 748 |
| Fruit and Vegetables | 356 | 276 | 407 | 487 | 545 |
| Pet Food | 202 | 179 | 276 | 161 | 174 |
| Processed Meat | 798 | 785 | 454 | 565 | 790 |
| Side Dishes | 530 | 560 | 680 | 980 | 940 |
| Soups | 265 | 211 | 248 | 264 | 292 |
| Total Food | 12,398 | 12,312 | 12,897 | 15,006 | 16,868 |

*SOURCE:* NEW PRODUCT NEWS REPRINTED IN *THE FOOD INSTITUTE REPORT*, FEB. 19, 1996, p. 3.

**TABLE 5-2.** ALLOCATION OF PROMOTIONAL DOLLARS BY MANUFACTURERS 1991–95

|  | 1991 | 1992 | 1993 | 1994 | 1995 |
|---|---|---|---|---|---|
| Media Advertising | 25 | 25 | 24 | 23 | 25 |
| Trade Promotions | 48 | 48 | 49 | 51 | 51 |
| Consumer Promotions | 27 | 27 | 27 | 26 | 24 |

SOURCE: ADAPTED FROM WRIGHT PROMOTIONS, INC.'S, A SUBSIDIARY OF COX TARGET MEDIA, INC., 14TH–18TH ANNUAL SURVEY OF PROMOTIONAL PRACTICES.

**TABLE 5-3.** PREDICTIONS FOR PROMOTIONAL ALLOCATIONS–1995

|  | Increase | Decrease | Same |
|---|---|---|---|
| Media Advertising | 60 | 18 | 20 |
| Trade Promotion | 24 | 50 | 26 |
| Consumer Promotion | 30 | 32 | 38 |

SOURCE: ADAPTED FROM CAROL WRIGHT PROMOTIONS, INC., A SUBSIDIARY OF COX TARGET MEDIA, INC., 18TH ANNUAL SURVEY OF PROMOTIONAL PRACTICES.

**TABLE 5-4.** RELATIVE IMPORTANCE OF TRADE PROMOTIONS*

| Sales Promotion | 1991 | 1992 | 1993 | 1994 | 1995 |
|---|---|---|---|---|---|
| Off-invoice Allowance | 88 | 91 | 89 | 87 | 86 |
| Marketing Funds | 85 | 86 | 87 | 86 | 85 |
| Slotting Allowance | 69 | 66 | 66 | 73 | 66 |
| Co-op Advertising | 70 | 66 | 68 | 71 | 63 |
| Extended Payment Terms | 65 | 65 | 58 | 64 | 55 |
| Vendor Damage Policy | 71 | 67 | 60 | 64 | 58 |
| Bill Backs | 61 | 62 | 57 | 62 | 54 |
| Retail Display Allowance | 61 | 61 | 62 | 62 | 58 |
| Forward Buy Availability | 62 | 59 | 48 | 57 | 50 |
| Roto Participation | 59 | 54 | 54 | 54 | 48 |
| Pick-up Allowance | 49 | 43 | 38 | 49 | 42 |
| Free Goods | 56 | 52 | 47 | 46 | 39 |
| Failure Fees | 28 | 25 | 25 | 28 | 25 |

*PERCENT OF DISTRIBUTORS WHO INDICATED EXTREMELY OR VERY IMPORTANT

*SOURCE: GROCERY MARKETING* DECEMBER 1991, 1992, 1993, 1994, AND 1995, BUYERS STUDY.

**TABLE 5-5.** MOST ADVERTISED FOOD AND BEVERAGES BRANDS

| Rank | Brand | Measured ad spending ($millions)* |
|---|---|---|
| 1 | Kellogg breakfast foods | 488.2 |
| 2 | General Mills cereals | 253.0 |
| 3 | Budweiser beers | 201.0 |
| 4 | Kraft foods | 192.1 |
| 5 | Post cereals | 173.0 |
| 6 | Miller beers | 161.5 |
| 7 | Coke and Diet Coke | 125.7 |
| 8 | Pepsi and Diet Pepsi | 122.9 |
| 9 | Wrigley's gum | 121.4 |
| 10 | Nabisco foods | 98.0 |
| 11 | Coors beers | 83.0 |
| 12 | Folqers coffees | 80.1 |
| 13 | Maxwell House coffees | 76.3 |
| 14 | Campbell's soup and foods | 72.4 |
| 15 | Betty Crocker foods | 64.4 |
| 16 | Quaker foods | 62.5 |
| '7 | Dr. Pepper and Diet Dr. Pepper | 62.1 |
| 18 | Nabisco cereals | 58.7 |
| 19 | Jell-O desserts | 57.9 |
| 20 | Red Dog beer | 57.7 |
| 21 | Hershey foods | 51.1 |
| 22 | Pillsbury foods | 51.8 |
| 23 | Sprite and Diet Sprite | 51.7 |
| 24 | Nestle food products | 50.8 |
| 25 | Lipton tea and food products | 47.5 |
| 26 | M&Ms candies | 46.9 |

*INCLUDES CONSUMER MAGAZINES; SUNDAY MAGAZINES; LOCAL AND NATIONAL NEWSPAPERS; OUTDOORS; NETWORK, SPOT, SYNDICATED AND CABLE TV; NATIONAL SPOT RADIO AND NETWORK RADIO SOURCE: COMPETITIVE MEDIA REPORTING.

*SOURCE:* TOP 200 MEGABRANDS BY 1995 AD SPENDING ADVERTISING AGE, MAY 6, 1996, pp. 36

**TABLE 5-6.** FOOD MANUFACTURERS IDENTIFIED IN TOP 200 ADVERTISERS (MILLIONS)

| 1994 Rank | Company | U.S. Ad Spending | U.S. Sales | Advertisement to sales ratio (a) |
|---|---|---|---|---|
| 1 | Procter & Gamble Co. | 2,777 | 33,434 | 8.3 |
| 2 | Phillip Morris Co., Inc. | 2,577 | 65,125 | 4.0 |
| 8 | PepsiCo, Inc. | 1,197 | 28,500 | 4.2 |
| 16 | Kellogg Co. | 740 | 6,830 | 10.8 |
| 23 | Anheuser-Busch Cos., Inc. | 534 | 13,734 | 3.9 |
| 25 | General Mills | 490 | 5,027 | 9.7 |
| 26 | Seagrams Co. | 490 | 5,563 | 8.8 |
| 27 | Nestle Sa | 487 | 7,300 | 6.7 |
| 32 | Coca-Cola Co. | 433 | 16,172 | 2.7 |
| 33 | Hershey Foods Corp. | 430 | 3,606 | 11.9 |
| 35 | Sara Lee Corp. | 420 | 17,719 | 2.4 |
| 36 | Cadbury-Schweppes | 418 | 13,767 | 3.0 |
| 37 | Ralston Purina Co. | 417 | 6,439 | 6.5 |
| 38 | Mars | 416 | 13,000 | 3.2 |
| 41 | RJR Nabisco | 405 | 15,336 | 2.6 |
| 55 | Quaker Oats Co. | 283 | 6,395 | 4.4 |
| 62 | Campbell Soup Co. | 253 | 7,278 | 2.5 |
| 65 | H.J. Heinz Co. | 247 | 8,086 | 3.1 |
| 69 | ConAgra | 222 | 24,109 | .9 |
| 85 | CPC International | 164 | 7,425 | 2.2 |
| 88 | Wm. Wrigley Jr. Co. | 160 | 1,597 | 10.0 |
| 147 | Geo A. Hormel Co. | 85 | 3,065 | 2.8 |

a. AD SALES RATIO COMPUTED

SALES FIGURES FROM FOOD PROCESSING DEC. 1995

SOURCE: ADVERTISING AGE 40TH ANNUAL LEADING ADVERTISERS, SEPT. 27, 1996.

**TABLE 5-7.** TYPE OF CONSUMER PROMOTIONS USED BY MANUFACTURERS

|  | Percent of Respondents in Each Year | | | | |
| --- | --- | --- | --- | --- | --- |
|  | **1991** | **1992** | **1993** | **1994** | **1995** |
| Couponing Consumer Direct | 100 | 100 | 100 | 100 | 97 |
| Couponing in Retailers' Ads | 66 | 65 | 88 | 90 | 84 |
| Cents-off Promotions | 87 | 77 | 90 | 90 | 84 |
| Money Back Offers/Other Refunds | 77 | 88 | 80 | 85 | 66 |
| Sampling Established Products | 43 | 66 | 78 | 78 | 72 |
| Sampling New Products | 64 | 73 | 84 | 75 | 72 |
| Sweepstakes | 64 | 61 | 63 | 70 | 63 |
| Premium Offers | 70 | 69 | 78 | 70 | 56 |
| Pre-Pricing | 45 | 41 | 51 | 55 | 44 |
| Contests | 40 | 47 | 51 | 48 | 44 |

SOURCE: CAROL WRIGHT PROMOTIONS INC., A SUBSIDIARY OF COX TARGET MEDIA, INC., 18TH ANNUAL SURVEY OF PROMOTIONAL PRACTICES.

**TABLE 5-8.** ECR STRATEGIES AND SAVINGS

| STRATEGY | % COST SAVINGS | SAVINGS* FINANCIAL SAVINGS | % TOTAL SAVINGS |
| --- | --- | --- | --- |
| Efficient Store Assortments | 1.3 | .2 | 1.5 |
| Efficient Replenishment | 2.8 | 1.3 | 4.1 |
| Efficient Promotion | 3.5 | .8 | 4.3 |
| Efficient Product Development | .9 | 0 | .9 |
| Total | 8.5 | 2.3 | 10.8 |

*AS PERCENTAGE OF AVERAGE CONSUMER PRICES

SOURCE: KURT SALMON ASSOCIATES, INC. EFFICIENT CONSUMER RESPONSE-ENHANCING CUSTOMER VALUE IN THE GROCERY INDUSTRY FOOD MARKETING INSTITUTE, WASHINGTON, D.C. 1993.

## Nutrition Facts

Serving Size 1/3 cup flakes (22g)
(about 1/2 cup prepared)
Servings Per Container about 34

| Amount Per Serving | Flakes | Prepared with 2% Milk, Margarine, Salt & Water |
|---|---|---|
| **Calories** | 80 | 160 |
| Calories from Fat | 0 | 60 |

| | % Daily Value** | |
|---|---|---|
| **Total Fat** 0g* | **0%** | **11%** |
| Saturated Fat 0g | 0% | 8% |
| **Cholesterol** 0mg | **0%** | **1%** |
| **Sodium** 45mg | **2%** | **10%** |
| **Total Carbohydrate** 18g | **6%** | **7%** |
| Dietary Fiber 1g | 4% | 4% |
| Sugars 0g | | |
| **Protein** 2g | | |
| Vitamin A | 0% | 6% |
| Vitamin C | 0% | 0% |
| Calcium | 0% | 6% |
| Iron | 0% | 2% |

*Amount in Flakes

**Percent Daily Values are based on a 2,000 calorie diet. Your daily values may be higher or lower depending on your calorie needs:

| | Calories: | 2,000 | 2,500 |
|---|---|---|---|
| Total Fat | Less than | 65g | 80g |
| Sat Fat | Less than | 20g | 25g |
| Cholesterol | Less than | 300mg | 300mg |
| Sodium | Less than | 2,400mg | 2,400mg |
| Total Carbohydrate | | 300g | 375g |
| Dietary Fiber | | 25g | 30g |

Calories per gram:
Fat 9 • Carbohydrate 4 • Protein 4

**FIGURE 5-1.** NUTRITIONAL LABEL

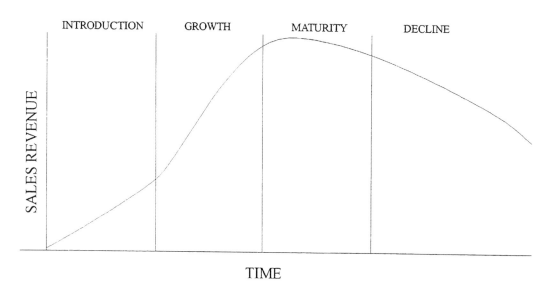

**FIGURE 5-2.** HYPOTHETICAL LIFE CYCLE FOR FOOD BRAND

*SOURCE:* Fuller, G. W., New Food Product Development, CRC Press, Boca Raton, FL, 1994.

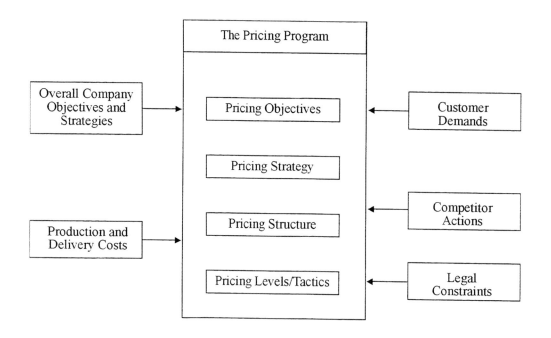

**FIGURE 5-3.** MANUFACTURER'S PRICE SETTING PROCESS AND ITS DETERMINANTS

# Chapter 6
# Wholesale Distributors

**Chapter Outline**

Wholesaling Sector
- A. Merchant Wholesalers
- B. Manufacturers' Sales Branches and Offices
- C. Agents, Brokers, and Commission Merchants
- D. General Line and Specialty Wholesalers
- E. Wholesalers by Type of Operation
- F. Sales Size
- G. Single Unit and Multiunit Wholesalers
- H. Wholesalers by Kind of Business
- I. Cross Classification of Wholesalers
- J. Affiliated and Unaffiliated Wholesalers
- K. Sales by Class of Customer
- L. Employment

Location of Wholesaling Sector
- A. Establishments and Sales

> Industries
>> A. Establishments, Sales, and Employment
>
> Companies (Firms)
>> A. Single Unit and Multiunit Firms
>> B. Sales Size of Firms
>> C. Share of Sales by Largest Firms
>> D. Leading Companies—General
>> E. Leading Companies—Specialized Convenience Stores Wholesalers
>
> Summary

The manufacturing sector of the **U.S. food marketing system** was examined in the two previous chapters. In Chapter 4, the structural organization of the forty-nine industries that make up the sector was characterized as diverse. Fewer than forty percent of these industries can be characterized as oligopolistic in nature, while the remainder are essentially monopolistic competitors.

Chapter 5 examined the marketing decisions made by manufacturers in this sector. In oligopolistic industries, a hierarchy of leaders and followers results in an interdependency of firms. As a consequence, industry leaders must consider how their followers will react to their marketing decisions. Because followers can react immediately to price changes made by leaders, the nature of competition is likely to take the form of nonprice marketing activities. In monopolistically competitive industries, no interdependence exists among firms. As in the oligopolistic industries, competitive efforts focus on nonprice marketing factors. In both market structures firms attempt to create and maintain their competitive differential advantages.

This chapter begins with a structural analysis of the wholesaling sector of the U.S. food marketing system. **Wholesalers are defined as businesses that engage primarily in the sale of merchandise to retailers, organizational users, governments**, and other wholesalers. This definition excludes wholesale sales made by manufacturers, retailers, and other businesses whose primary activity is **other than** wholesale trade. This exclusion means, for example, that the wholesale sales made by many of the large retail store chain operations, to supply their own stores, are not considered wholesale. These **self distributing** wholesale sales are considered **intrafirm transfers**.

Another important clarification should be made concerning manufacturers: Sales generated by manufacturers' sales branches and offices that are maintained **apart** from their production locations are reported as wholesale sales. Thus total sales reported by food manufacturers reflect both manufacturing and wholesale sales.

## WHOLESALING SECTOR

Wholesalers are classified in the **Census of Wholesale Trade**. Their **Standard Industrial Classification** major group, is **51—Nondurable Goods**. The food wholesaling sector is made up of one industry group, **514—Grocery and Related Products**. This industry group is further divided into nine industries with **SIC** codes **5141** through **5149**. Census data are reported on the basis of firms and establishments by **type of operations** and **kind of business**. A **firm** is a legal entity that owns one or more establishments. An **establishment** is a single, physical location at which wholesale business is conducted.

Wholesalers are classified, by **type of operation**, into three categories: (1) merchant wholesalers, (2) manufacturers' sales branches and offices, and (3) agents, brokers, and commission merchants.

### Merchant Wholesalers

Merchant wholesalers take title and possession of the merchandise they sell. They are the largest type of wholesale operation in number. They may be either full service or limited service wholesalers.

**Full service** wholesalers perform a wide range of services for their retail customers and the manufacturers from which they purchase merchandise. These services include storage, delivery, merchandise and promotion assistance, credit extension, and other essential business services. There are two types of full service merchant wholesalers that are especially important to the U.S. food marketing system: voluntary groups and retailer cooperatives.

A **voluntary group** wholesaler is affiliated with a group of retailers who voluntarily adhere to its supply and service program in order to benefit from its integrated food merchandising program. The group of retailers known as the **Independent Grocers Alliance (IGA)** is an example of a voluntary group. **Fleming Cos.** and **Super Value**, the two largest wholesalers in the U.S., are also voluntary groups.

A **retailer cooperative** wholesaler is affiliated with the group of retailers who own its wholesale facilities. They are organized as corporations, and major decisions are made by a board of directors made up of the member retailers. **Wakefern Food Corp.** and **Associated Wholesale Grocers, Inc.** are examples of retailer cooperatives.

A **limited service** wholesaler doesn't offer the comprehensive services of full service wholesalers. Two types of limited service wholesalers play an important role in the U.S. food marketing system: truck jobbers and cash-and-carry wholesalers.

**Truck jobbers** are used by manufacturers whose products require quick and frequent delivery to maintain their freshness on retail store shelves. Snacks, meat, dairy, baked goods, and candy are examples of merchandise delivered by truck jobbers.

**Cash-and-carry** wholesalers do not extend credit, nor do they deliver the products they sell to retailers. These wholesalers are most often used by retailers too small to be profitable for larger wholesalers.

The census data reported for merchant wholesalers doesn't make a distinction between the full service and limited service wholesaler. In addition, the census doesn't provide separate information on truck jobbers, and cash-and-carry wholesalers.

## Manufacturers' Sales Branches and Offices

Manufacturer-owned wholesalers are the field sales forces of manufacturers. The **manufacturers' sales branches and offices**, located apart from their production facilities for the purposes of marketing their products, report their sales as wholesale and not manufacturing sales. The census data reported for sales branches and offices are combined for both.

The essential difference between a sales branch and an office is that the former maintains an inventory on site, while the latter does not. Both the sales branch and office perform wholesale activities, but sales branches usually handle a wider range of functions than do sales offices. Manufacturers' sales branches and offices are the smallest type of wholesale operations in number. Many of the largest food manufacturers maintain sales branches and offices. Examples of firms engaged in manufacturer wholesaling are **Hormel, Procter and Gamble, Sara Lee Corp., Kellogg Co.,** and **PepsiCo., Inc.**

## Agents, Brokers, and Commission Merchants

Agents, brokers, and commission merchants sell the products of others on a commission or agency basis. Essentially, they provide a food manufacturer with a trained sales force.

**Brokers** are more common in the U.S. food marketing system than agents and commission merchants. They provide local and regional sales representation to non-competing manufacturers of food products and arrange for sale and distribution of these products. In addition, they provide buyers with merchandise and promotion assistance. The **Association of Sales and Marketing Companies** is the major trade organization for independent brokers. Food brokers are used often by smaller manufacturers who don't have the financial resources to maintain their own sales forces. They are also used by larger food manufacturers on a contingency basis.

**Commission merchants** provide a wider range of services than do food brokers. It is not uncommon for them to carry inventory, offer credit, and distribute or promote the products of manufacturers. Although of limited use in the U.S. food marketing system, they play a vital role in the marketing of certain types of seafood.

In summary, the Census Bureau reports only the combined data for each type of wholesale operation: merchant wholesalers, manufacturers' sales branches and offices, and agents, brokers, and commission merchants.

### General Line and Specialty Wholesalers

Wholesalers are classified also by **kind of business** as general line and specialty wholesalers. **General line** wholesalers carry a wide variety and assortment of merchandise and provide extensive services to their customers and the manufacturers from which they purchase merchandise.

**Specialty wholesalers**, as the name implies, specialize in the distribution of a narrow variety but an extensive assortment within that variety. The eight specialty wholesale industries are classified by the products they carry: packaged frozen foods, dairy products, poultry, confectionery, fish and seafood, meats, fresh fruits and vegetables, and grocery and related products not elsewhere classified (n.e.c.).

The U.S. Bureau of the Census reports data separately for general line and specialty wholesalers. In addition, data is reported for each of the eight different kinds of specialty wholesalers. Finally, data are cross classified by type of operations and kind of business.

The following sections will use wholesale **establishments** as the basis for the structural analysis because the census represents a summary of reports for establishments rather than companies (firms). The analysis will use data from three census periods, 1982, 1987, and 1992. Each census report summarizes what has happened over the previous five-year period. Thus, using three census periods reveals a fifteen-year trend.

It should be mentioned that food wholesalers distribute only fifty-six percent of the food sold at retail. The other forty-four percent represents retail sales generated by retail store chains that engage in **self-distribution** (NAWGA, 1995). As previously mentioned, the primary activities of these retailers are other than the wholesale trade. Thus, their wholesale sales are considered intrafirm transfers and not included in the census of wholesale trade. It is for this reason that there is general agreement that the census **understates** the sales of general line merchant wholesalers.

### Wholesalers by Type of Operation

The change in the number of wholesale firms and establishments is presented in **Table 6-1**. Firms increased by twelve percent and establishments by eleven percent. There are more establishments than firms because a firm may own one or more establishments. Most of the increase in establishments was among merchant wholesalers. Their fourteen percent increase surpassed the 3.5 percent increase in manufacturers' sales branches and offices and the slight one-percent increase in agents, brokers, and commission merchants.

The sales reported in **Table 6-2** have not been adjusted for inflation. Thus, it is not surprising that total wholesale sales and sales for each type of wholesaler increased over the ten-year period. Manufacturers' sales branches and offices had a ninety-nine percent increase; agents, brokers, and commission merchants had a ninety-six percent increase; merchant wholesalers had a sixty percent increase.

To understand the relative contribution made by the three types of operations, **Table 6-3** reflects their shares of establishments and sales. Clearly, merchant wholesalers were the dominant type of operation and generated the majority of sales. Even though they increased their share of firms, they lost five percent of their sales share to the other two types of operations. The dominance of the merchant wholesaler was significantly reduced when the types of operations were examined on the basis of average sales per establishments. The small number of manufacturers' sales branches and offices generated average sales of twenty-six million dollars, while agents, brokers, and commission merchants averaged twenty-two million dollars. Merchant wholesalers, though large in number, averaged only seven million dollars in sales.

## Sales Size

To continue the examination of dominance, **Table 6-4** reveals the share of wholesale establishments and sales by size. Although establishments with less than twenty-five million dollars in sales declined, as did their sales, they made up about seventy-seven percent of all establishments and generated only nineteen percent of all sales.

Establishments with one hundred million dollars or more in sales dominate the wholesale trade. While only fifteen percent of all wholesalers, they generated sixty-five percent of all sales nonetheless. In fact, these establishments were the only ones that increased their sales over the census periods. They gained roughly thirteen percent over this time frame.

## Single Unit and Multiunit Wholesalers

Earlier, it was mentioned that a firm may own one or more establishments. **Table 6-5** presents the share of single and multiunit establishments and sales. The share of single unit establishments has increased, but their sales share has declined. Multiunit establishments increased their sales share by six percent while losing a one percent share of establishments. The fifteen year trend in multiunit sales share gain and establishment share loss lead to one single conclusion: Multiunit establishments are fewer in number, but larger in size—brought about most likely by merger and acquisition activity.

**Table 6-6** examines single unit and multiunit establishments and sales by the three types of wholesale operations. Single unit establishments are still the dominant types of merchant wholesalers, agents, brokers, and commission merchants. They produced the majority of sales, but their sales share declined by six and nine percent, respectively. Their multiunit counterparts remained somewhat constant in share of establishments and gained six and nine percent sales share, respectively. Interestingly, multiunit—not single unit—manufacturers' sales branches and offices dominate this type in establishments and sales. However, they lost about five percent of sales share over the ten year period. Still, they generated about eighty-five percent of all manufacturing wholesaling sales.

## Wholesalers by Kind of Business

The census bureau also reports wholesale data by kind of business: general line and specialty. The change in establishments and sales is shown in **Table 6-7**. Both general line and specialty establishments increased by eleven percent and their sales increased by eighty-eight and seventy-one percent, respectively. There were almost nine times more specialty wholesalers than there were general line wholesalers. But the average sales of the general line wholesalers was twenty-nine billion dollars while for the specialty wholesaler the average sales was only ten billion dollars. Although smaller in number, the general line wholesaler had, on the average, three times more sales than did the specialty wholesaler. Nonetheless, specialty wholesalers generated roughly ninety percent of all sales.

When examined by share of establishments, **Table 6-8** shows virtually no change. General line wholesalers experienced a slight increase in sales share. The major share of sales was generated by specialty wholesalers.

## Cross Classification of Wholesalers

Wholesale firms can be classified simultaneously by kind of business and type of operation. **Table 6-9** presents this cross classification for sales and establishments. Because manufacturers specialize their production, there are no reported general line manufacturer sales branches and offices.

The specialty wholesaler was previously identified as the dominant kind of wholesaler. Their dominance is clearly seen in **Table 6-9**. Their share of establishments has remained relatively constant over the ten year period. Only agents, brokers, and commission merchants experienced a decline in sales share. Their share of sales declined significantly, from eighty to sixty-two percent of sales.

## Affiliated and Unaffiliated Wholesalers

Earlier in the chapter, a distinction was made between two types of general line merchant wholesalers: voluntary groups and retail cooperatives. Both types are affiliated with retailers. The former is a voluntary affiliation, while the latter is an ownership affiliation.

**Table 6-10** reveals the small number of voluntary group and retail cooperative establishments. While voluntary groups experienced a twenty-five percent increase in the number of establishments, retail cooperatives declined fifty-eight percent to only 184 establishments. Although small in number, the average sales for a voluntary group are eighty-four million dollars and ninety-four million dollars for retail cooperatives. Most general line merchant wholesalers are unaffiliated. However, their average sales are only sixteen million dollars, or less than twenty percent of the average sales of affiliated wholesalers.

An examination of the shares of establishments and sales in **Table 6-11** reveals an increase in both for unaffiliated wholesalers. The affiliated wholesalers, although significant in average sales, experienced a significant loss of sixteen percent sales share.

Even though it appears that the unaffiliated general line merchant generated the major share of sales, sales by affiliated wholesalers are considered "intrafirm transfers" and not wholesale sales. There is considerable agreement that this results in an under-reporting of their sales and thus their true contribution to the wholesale trade.

## Sales by Class of Customer

Wholesalers don't sell only to retailers. In fact, the census defines the wholesaler as a firm that primarily engages in the sale of merchandise to retailers, organizational users, and other wholesalers.

**Table 6-12** presents the sales made to retailers and other wholesalers. Merchant wholesalers sell mainly to retailers, as do manufacturers' sales branches and offices. On the other hand, agents, brokers, and commission merchants generated less than one-half of their sales from retailers. In fact, it was only in 1992 that their retail sales surpassed sales to wholesalers. It should be clear that wholesalers sell in significant amounts to businesses other than retailers.

## Employment

The number of individuals working in food wholesaling increased from 673,765 in 1982 to 811,902 in 1992. By type of operation, **Table 6-13** indicates that most are employed by merchant wholesalers. Their share of employment has declined, while the other two types gained in employment share. Of the two, manufacturers' sales branches and offices experienced the largest gain in employment share. For 1992, merchant wholesalers employed on average seventeen people; manufacturers' sales branches and offices employed on average thirty-six people, and agents, brokers, and commission merchants employed on average twelve people.

The share of employment by kind of business is shown in **Table 6-14**. Specialty wholesaler employment has declined somewhat but still employs most of those in the wholesaling sector. On average, the general line merchant employed thirty-eight people in 1992, while the specialty merchant employed on average about seventeen people in that same year.

General line merchant wholesaler employment can be examined on the basis of affiliated establishments. On average, in 1992, voluntary groups employed 105 people versus an average employment of ninety-two people for retail cooperatives.

## LOCATION OF WHOLESALING SECTOR

Food wholesaling activity takes place in all fifty states. At the same time, some of these states have higher levels of wholesaling activity than others. The location of wholesaling activities will be reviewed in terms of sales and number of establishments. It should be remembered that an analysis by establishments doesn't consider the number of firms in a state, but rather the number of different locations at which wholesale sales are made in a state.

The top ten states were chosen as a basis of comparison for two reasons. First, these states contain the majority of all establishments. Second, they produce the majority of wholesaler sales. Because of the need for wholesalers to be near their retail customers, the number of wholesale establishments and sales follow the population of the respective states. In general, densely populated states have larger numbers of establishments and sales than do sparsely populated states.

### Establishments and Sales

The changes in the shares of establishments and sales by states are revealed in **Table 6-15**. The ten leading states increased their share of establishment by roughly four percent but experienced a one percent decline in sales share. These ten states contain the majority of establishments and generated the majority of the sales.

The share of establishments and sales of the top ten states is shown for each individual state in **Table 6-16**. Over the ten years, the states have changed little in their ranking. California, New York, Florida, and Texas have remained the top four states in share of establishments, while Pennsylvania, Ohio, Michigan, and Massachusetts have remained at the lower end of the ranking. With two exceptions, Florida and New Jersey in 1982, there has been no change in the sales ranking of these leading states. Four states—California, New York, Texas, and Illinois—generated over one-half of the sales in the ten leading states and one-third of all wholesale sales.

# INDUSTRIES

Recall that food wholesalers are classified by kind of business into general line and specialty wholesalers. These wholesalers are further defined in terms of industries. Each industry is identified with a four-digit **Standard Industrial Classification Code**. This section will examine the one general line industry and eight specialty industries over the ten year period covered by the 1982, 1987, and 1992 Census of Wholesale Trade.

## Establishments, Sales, and Employment

The number of wholesale establishments increased by eleven percent or 4,358 establishments. **Table 6-17** shows that of the five industries that increased in number, **Groceries and Related Products, n.e.c. (5149)** experienced the largest increase. This industry is a miscellaneous one that includes wholesalers of soft drinks, canned foods, bread and baked goods, coffee, tea, spices, food and beverage basic material, and other grocery specialties. The diversity of included products suggests that this industry will always be the largest wholesale industry.

Of the four industries that lost establishments, the largest decrease occurred in **Meats (5147)**. This industry includes establishments engaged in the wholesale distribution of fresh, cured, and processed meats. Much of this decline was caused by the increased concentration in this industry.

The share of establishments and sales for the industries is revealed in **Table 6-18**. Of the six industries that increased in number of establishments, only three of them increased significantly enough to capture a larger share of establishments. **Packaged Frozen Foods Industry (5142)** includes establishments engaged in the wholesale distribution of packaged quick-frozen vegetables, juices, meats, fish, poultry, pastries, and other "deep freeze" products. This industry gained 1.4 percent. **Fish and Seafood Industry (5146)** includes establishments engaged in the wholesale distribution of fresh, cured, or frozen fish and seafoods. This industry gained 1.8 percent. Finally, **Groceries and Related Products, n.e.c. (5149)** gained 3.5 percent—the largest gain.

Because the census doesn't report sales adjusted for price inflation, all the industries gained in sales over the census periods, as expected. However, only four industries increased sales significantly enough to gain sales share. The **Confectionery Industry (5145)** includes establishments engaged in the wholesale distribution of confectionery and related products, such as candy, chewing gum, fountain fruits, salted or roasted nuts, popcorn, fountain syrups, and potato, corn, and similar chips. This industry gained only .5 percent in sales share. The other three industries have been previously defined. **Packaged Frozen Foods (5142)** gained 2.8 percent, **General Line (5141)** gained 1.9 percent, and **Fish and Seafood (5146)** gained only .3 percent. Lastly, in terms of sales shares, two industries, **General Line (5141)**, and

**Groceries and Related Products, n.e.c., (5149)** generated over one-half (fifty-five percent) of all wholesale sales by industry.

Further understanding regarding the size of the establishments can be gained by dividing an industry's sales by the number of establishments in that industry. **Table 6-19** shows how the average sales of establishments has changed. The largest increase in average sales was experienced by the **General Line Industry (5141)**. The roughly twelve billion dollar increase represents a seventy percent increase over 1982 average sales. The other leading industries in average sales were **Packaged Frozen Foods (5142)** and **Meats (5147)**. These three industries have consistently had average sales higher than the average sales for all food industries.

Finally, the number of people employed in these industries increased by 138,137 over the census periods. Only **Poultry (5144)** and **Meats (5147)** lost employees during this time period. The largest increase occurred in **Groceries and Related Products, n.e.c. (5149)**, which had the largest share of employment, followed by **General Line (5141)** and **Fresh Fruits and Vegetables (5148)**. This ranking has not changed during the ten year time period.

# COMPANIES (FIRMS)

Even though the census of wholesale trade represents an analysis of establishments rather than companies (firms), some analysis can be conducted on a company basis. A company (firm) may have only one establishment engaged in wholesale activities (single unit). A multiunit firm has two or more establishments engaged in wholesale activities.

### Single Unit and Multiunit Firms

Over the census periods 1982, 1987, and 1992 the percentage of single unit firm, remained constant at ninety-six percent of all firms. However, roughly four percent of multiunit firms increased their share of total wholesale sales from fifty-two percent in 1982 to fifty-six percent in 1992. Thus, although small in number, these multiunit firms accounted for a disproportionate share of sales.

### Sales Size of Firms

When firms are examined by sales size, the dominance of large firms (100 million dollars or more in sales) is again revealed. In 1982, 360 firms (1.2 percent of all firms) had sales of 100 million dollars or more. These same firms generated 51.4 percent of all wholesale sales. By 1992, the number of firms with 100 million dollars or more in sales rose to 587 (two percent of all firms). These firms generated 64.3 percent of all wholesale sales.

Clearly, when sales are examined on the basis of firms, rather than establishments, we are better able to identify two segments within the wholesale sector. The first consists of a few large firms that generate a majority of the sales. The second consists of a large number of small firms that generate an increasingly smaller share of all wholesale sales.

## Share of Sales by Largest Firms

The share of sales, sometimes referred to as a **concentration ratio**, is computed by dividing the sales of leading firms by the total wholesale sales. By convention, economists have generally defined **industries** as strongly oligopolistic if the **four-firm** concentration ratio is greater than fifty percent. A concentration ratio between thirty-three and fifty constitutes a weak oligopoly. When the ratio is less than thirty-three percent, the industries are defined as unconcentrated.

**Table 6-20** shows the concentration of sales for the entire wholesale sector. The share of sales for the four, eight, twenty, and fifty largest firms has increased over the census periods. In 1992 alone, the fifty largest firms (or one-tenth of one percent of all firms) generated thirty-five percent of all wholesale sales. Although significant, at the sector level there is no evidence of concentration as earlier defined.

The concentration of firms by type of operations presents another perspective. **Table 6-21** shows that the four, eight, twenty, and fifty largest firms for all three types have increased their share of sales over the census periods. Although not concentrated by definition, the share of sales for manufacturers' sales branches and offices is significantly greater than those of the other types. Of the 529 firms that operated in 1992, the four largest had thirty-one percent of all sales for manufacturers' sales branches and offices. In that same year, the fifty largest firms, or roughly ten percent of all manufacturers' sales branches and offices, generated eighty percent of all sales. Once again, although significant, by type of operations there is no evidence of concentration as conventionally defined by economists.

**Table 6-22** indicates the change in concentration ratios by industry or kind of business. The **Fish and Seafood Industry (5146)** is the only industry that experienced a decrease in concentration for four, eight, twenty, and fifty largest firms over the census periods. **Dairy Products (5143)** experienced a decrease in concentration for the four, eight, and 20 largest firms. **Poultry (5144)** also experienced a decrease in concentration, but only for the four largest firms.

When examined in terms of the conventional definition of concentrated industries, none of the industries can be defined as an oligopolistic market structure. **Confectionery (5145)**, at least, would be considered a "weak" oligopolistic industry. It is, of course, more concentrated than any other industry. Finally, if the industries are analyzed by type of operations, manufacturers' sales branches and offices reflect concentrated market structures. Seven of the nine industries contain manufacturers' sales branches and offices. Six of them had four firm concentration ratios greater than fifty percent, and only one was less than fifty percent concentration. Three industries had concentration ratios greater than seventy percent for manufacturers' sales branches and offices: **Fish and Seafood (5146), Meats (5147),** and **Confectionery (5145).**

In summary, wholesalers by type of operations, and wholesalers by industry are unconcentrated. Only when manufacturers' sales branches and offices are examined within industries do we find concentration ratios for the four largest firms over fifty percent. Thus, there is a degree of concentration **within** those industries that contain manufacturers' sales branches and offices, but there are no conventionally defined concentrated industries.

## Leading Companies—General

The structural analysis of the wholesaling sector would be incomplete if it didn't identify the leading firms. A number of trade publications report the leading wholesale firms on an annual basis. In particular, *U.S. Distribution Journal (USDJ)* publishes two annual reports. One report identifies the fifty leading wholesalers, and the other identifies the fifty leading convenience store wholesalers.

The fifty leading wholesalers are all general line merchant wholesalers and comprise affiliated (voluntary group and retail cooperatives) and unaffiliated wholesalers. Although not reported in the Census of Wholesale Trade, in 1987 there were 164 voluntary and 219 cooperative wholesale firms. In 1992, voluntaries increased to 262 firms, while cooperatives declined to 168 firms. Unfortunately, the number of voluntaries and cooperatives for 1996 is unavailable. The change in the rankings of the wholesalers from year to year shows continued consolidation. Because of this, only the 1995 reports of leading merchant and convenience store wholesalers will be examined.

For the first time in the eight year history of the *USDJ* report, more retail cooperatives made the top fifty list than did voluntary group wholesalers. The rankings for 1996, shown in **Table 6-23**, include twenty-four cooperatives, twenty-two voluntaries, and three unaffiliated wholesalers. One wholesaler was not classified because it operates as a cooperative in one state and as a voluntary in the other states in its trading area (**Roundy's, Inc.**).

Based on industry-estimated sales of 210 billion dollars, excluding convenience store and foodservice distributors, the fifty leading firms' share of 81.8 billion dollars was roughly thirty-nine percent of all merchant wholesale sales. **Fleming Cos.** and **Supervalu, Inc.**, the top two firms, had combined sales equal to forty-two percent of the fifty leading firms' sales. To illustrate their relative sizes, their combined sales equaled the combined sales of the next twenty-one leading wholesalers. Both of these firms recently consolidated with other leading firms. **Fleming Cos.** merged with **Scrivner, Inc.**, the third leading firm in 1993. **Supervalu, Inc.** merged with **Wetterau,** the fourth leading firm in 1991. Currently, it is the only wholesaler that operates in the entire continental U.S. Interestingly, the 1995 sales for the number one ranked **Fleming Cos**. was eighty-three times larger than the sales of the 50th ranked **Associated Grocers of Florida**.

The top forty-eight leading firms serviced roughly sixty-eight thousand retail stores (two firms didn't report retail locations served). Seventeen firms derived the majority of their sales from independent retailers. Another twenty-one firms derived their sales from chain store retailers (firms having eleven or more stores are considered chain stores). Two firms reported sales equally obtained from chains and independents. Finally, six firms reported one hundred percent of sales made to independent retailers, while no firm reports one hundred percent of sales to chain store retailers.

## Leading Companies—Specialized Convenience Stores Wholesalers

The *USDJ* annual report of convenience store (**C-store**) wholesalers does not identify the leading wholesalers by type of operations or kind of business. In general, because they carry a wide variety of merchandise, they are probably classified as general line merchant wholesalers for census purposes.

C-store wholesalers are different from the previously mentioned leading wholesalers in two ways. First, nearly all of the fifty leading C-store wholesalers are privately held firms. Second, a number of these C-store wholesalers are owned by the leading wholesalers identified previously. For example, **Fleming Cos.**, the largest wholesaler, owns two C-store wholesalers that, if combined, would be ranked eighth in the top fifty. **Spartan** and **Nash-Finch Co**. also own C-store wholesalers. Third, in terms of sales size, they are typically smaller than their non C-store counterparts.

**Table 6-24** shows the fifty leading convenience wholesalers for 1996. Based on industry estimated sales of sixty-six billion dollars, the fifty leading firms' share of 20.7 billion dollars was roughly thirty-one percent of all convenience store wholesale sales. The **Wal-Mart**-owned, number-one C-store wholesaler, **McLane Co., Inc.**, had sales equal to thirty-four percent of the fifty leading C-store distributors. Its sales were 143 times larger than the sales of the fiftieth ranked **Quality Foods Cooperative, Inc**. The influence of large C-store distributors is also reflected in the sales dominance of the top four firms. Combined, these four firms had sixty percent of the top fifty C-store wholesale sales.

Of the forty-six reporting C-store wholesalers, the combined number of retail convenience stores serviced was 254,000. This number is nearly four times the number of stores serviced by the leading general wholesalers. Twenty-three firms derived the majority of their sales from independent C-store retailers. Another twenty-one firms generated the majority of their sales from chain C-store retailers. Finally, five firms reported sales equally obtained from chains and independents.

# SUMMARY

This chapter examined the food wholesale sector. Wholesalers are defined as businesses that engage primarily in the sale of merchandise to retailers, organizational users, governments, and other wholesalers. Wholesalers are classified in the **Census of Wholesale Trade** under the **Standard Industrial Classification** major group **51—Nondurable Goods**. The food wholesaling sector is made up of one industry group **514—Grocery and Related Products**. This industry group is further divided into nine industries with four-digit SIC codes 5141 to 5149. At the industry level, wholesalers are classified by type of operation and kind of business.

Merchant wholesalers, manufacturers' sales branches and offices, and agents, brokers, and commission merchants make up the three types of operations. When viewed this way, merchant wholesalers had the largest number of establishments and the majority of sales. However, the average sale of the merchant wholesale establishments was only one-third the average sale of the smaller number of manufacturers' sales branches and offices.

General line and specialty wholesalers make up the two kinds of wholesale businesses. There were nine times more specialty wholesalers than there were general line wholesalers, and they accounted for roughly three-fourths of all sales. However, the general line wholesaler had three times the average sales as that of the specialty wholesaler.

When wholesale establishments were examined by sales size, census data revealed two distinct groups. Those with one hundred million dollars or more in sales made up a small percentage of all wholesalers but generated a disproportionately large share of sales. Establishments with twenty-five million dollars or less in sales made up a very large percentage of wholesalers, but generated a very small percentage of wholesale sales.

Most wholesale establishments are single unit establishments. In this case there is no difference between a wholesale firm and a wholesale establishment. A firm may own more than one establishment. These multiunit establishments made up less than one-fourth of all establishments but generated more than one-half of all wholesale sales.

General line merchant wholesalers were also classified as either affiliated with retailers or unaffiliated with retailers. The affiliated voluntary group and retail cooperative wholesalers were small in number and had roughly six times the average sales as that of the unaffiliated wholesalers.

The census definition of a wholesaler clearly identifies customers other than retailers. Wholesalers of all types sell to other wholesalers, organizational users, governments, and retail stores and foodservice firms. Most of the people involved in the wholesaling sector were employed by merchant wholesalers. Voluntary group and retail cooperatives employed, on average, more employees than unaffiliated wholesalers. When employment was analyzed by kind of business, specialty wholesalers employed most of the people. But, on average, general line wholesalers employed twice as many as did specialty wholesalers.

Food wholesaling activities take place in all fifty states. Wholesalers need to be near their retail customers. Thus, densely populated states tended to have larger numbers of establishments and sales than did sparsely populated states. In terms of establishments and sales, the top four states were **California, New York, Texas**, and **Florida**.

An examination of the wholesale sector by its nine industries revealed that over the three census periods, five industries increased in number of establishments and four decreased. The increase was large enough in three industries to result in a larger share of all establishments. **Groceries and Related Products** captured the largest gain in share, followed by **Fish/Seafoods** and **Packaged Frozen Foods**. The most significant loss of share occurred in **Meats**.

Over one-half of all industry sales were generated by two industries: **General Line, and Groceries** and **Related Products**. Four industries gained in sales share. **Packaged Frozen Foods** gained the most, and **Fish/Seafood** gained the least. Only three industries had average sales larger than the average sales for all industries: **General Line, Packaged Frozen Foods**, and **Meats**. Finally, the largest share of employees worked in the **General Line, Fish/Seafood**, and **Vegetables** industries.

Even though the Census of Wholesale Trade reports data by establishments rather than by firms, some analyses by firms were performed. Single unit firms made up ninety-six percent of all wholesalers, but less than one-half of wholesale sales. A small four percent of multiunit firms made up over one-half of all sales.

When examined by sales size, two percent of all firms made up over sixty percent of all sales. The analysis done by firms reinforced the earlier conclusion derived from the establishment analysis: There are two distinct segments in the food wholesaling sector—a small group of large firms that generate a majority of the sales, and a large group of small firms that generate an increasingly smaller share of wholesale sales.

Despite the dominance of large firms, wholesaling was not shown to be concentrated at the sector level by type of operations or by industry. It was only when industries were examined in terms of manufacturers' sales branches and offices that concentration ratios of fifty percent or more were found. Of the seven industries that contain manufacturers' sales branches and offices, six had four-firm concentration ratios of fifty percent or more. However, taken as a whole, there are no concentrated wholesale industries.

Whether the market structure of the wholesaling sector is defined by type of operations or kind of business (industries) is immaterial. Food wholesalers, regardless of how they are classified, must make marketing decisions. They make these decisions within an environment that is defined as competitive.

## SELECTED REFERENCES

Arthur Andersen and Co., S. C. *Wholesale Food Distribution—Today and Tomorrow.* Falls Church, Va.: National-American Wholesale Grocers' Association, 1995.

Marion, B. W. and the NC-117 Committee. *The Organization and Performance of the U.S. Food System.* Lexington, Mass.: Lexington Books, D.C. Heath and Company, 1986.

*U.S. Distribution Journal.* "50 Grocery Giants." New York, N.Y.: Trade Publishing LLC, an affiliate of Macfadden Publishing, Inc., September 15, 1995.

*U.S. Distribution Journal.* "50 Grocery Giants." New York, N.Y.: Trade Publishing LLC, an affiliate of Macfadden Publishing, Inc., August 15, 1995.

## REVIEW QUESTIONS

1. How are wholesalers defined by the Census of Wholesale Trade?

2. Distinguish between a wholesale firm and a wholesale establishment.

3. How are wholesalers defined by type of operation?

4. How are wholesalers defined by kind of business?

5. How does a voluntary group wholesaler differ from a retail cooperative wholesaler?

6. What conclusions can be drawn from the analysis of wholesalers by type of operation?

7. What conclusions can be drawn from the analysis of wholesalers by kind of business?

8. What generalization can be made regarding the location of wholesalers and the population of states?

9. What conclusions can be drawn from the analysis of food wholesaling industries?

10. How can the leading general and specialized wholesalers be characterized?

**TABLE 6.1.** SELECTED TRENDS IN U.S. WHOLESALING FIRMS AND ESTABLISHMENTS BY TYPE OF OPERATIONS

| YEAR | TOTAL FIRMS | TOTAL ESTABL. | MERCHANT WHOLESALER | MANUF. SALES BR./ OFF. | AGENTS, BROKERS COMM. MERC. |
|---|---|---|---|---|---|
| 1982 | 31,290 | 38,516 | 29,085 | 4,666 | 4,765 |
| 1987 | 34,155 | 42,075 | 32,466 | 4,746 | 4,863 |
| 1992 | 35,177 | 42,874 | 33,227 | 4,829 | 4,821 |

SOURCE: CENSUS OF WHOLESALE TRADE 1982, 1987, AND 1992.


**TABLE 6-2.** WHOLESALE ESTABLISHMENT SALES BY TYPE OF OPERATIONS ($MILLIONS)

| YEAR | ALL SALES | MERCHANT WHOLESALERS | MANUFACTURERS SALES BRANCH OFFICES | AGENTS, BROKERS, COMM. MERC. |
|---|---|---|---|---|
| 1982 | 288,659 | 174,687 | 63,926 | 50,045 |
| 1987 | 380,945 | 223,020 | 89,219 | 68,705 |
| 1992 | 504,567 | 279,217 | 127,257 | 98,093 |

SOURCE: CENSUS OF WHOLESALE TRADE 1982, 1987, AND 1992.

**TABLE 6-3.** SHARE OF WHOLESALE ESTABLISHMENTS AND SALES BY TYPE OF OPERATION

| YEAR | MERCHANT WHOLESALES | | MANUFACTURERS/ SALES BRANCH OFFICES | | AGENTS, BROKERS, COMM. MERC. | |
|---|---|---|---|---|---|---|
| | % EST. | % SALES | % EST. | % SALES | % EST. | % SALES |
| 1982 | 75.5 | 60.5 | 12.1 | 22.2 | 12.4 | 17.3 |
| 1987 | 77.2 | 58.5 | 11.3 | 23.4 | 11.6 | 18.1 |
| 1992 | 77.5 | 55.3 | 11.3 | 25.2 | 11.2 | 19.4 |

*SOURCE:* COMPUTED FROM CENSUS OF WHOLESALE TRADE 1982, 1987, AND 1992.

**TABLE 6-4.** SHARE OF WHOLESALE ESTABLISHMENTS AND SALES BY SIZE OF ESTABLISHMENTS

| EST. ANNUAL SALES | 1982 | | 1987 | | 1992 | |
|---|---|---|---|---|---|---|
| | % OF EST. | % OF SALES | % OF EST. | % OF SALES | % OF EST. | % OF SALES |
| ≥100 MILLION | 12.9 | 52.5 | 15.0 | 59.4 | 15.0 | 65.0 |
| 50-99.9 | 2.8 | 9.4 | 2.8 | 8.6 | 3.5 | 8.2 |
| 25-49.9 | 4.1 | 10.0 | 4.1 | 8.3 | 4.6 | 7.8 |
| 1-24.9 | 43.2 | 26.3 | 45.0 | 22.4 | 45.8 | 18.1 |
| ≤1 MILLION | 37.2 | 1.8 | 33.1 | 1.3 | 31.1 | .9 |
| TOTAL | 100.0 | 100.0 | 100.0 | 100.0 | 100.0 | 100.0 |

*SOURCE:* COMPUTED FROM CENSUS OF WHOLESALE TRADE 1982, 1987, AND 1992.

**TABLE 6-5.** SHARE OF SINGLE UNIT AND MULTIUNIT ESTABLISHMENTS AND SALES

| EST. (UNITS) | 1982 % OF EST. | 1982 % OF SALES | 1987 % OF EST. | 1987 % OF SALES | 1992 % OF EST. | 1992 % OF SALES |
|---|---|---|---|---|---|---|
| SINGLE | 77.4 | 50.3 | 77.7 | 47.2 | 78.6 | 44.8 |
| MULTI | 22.6 | 49.7 | 22.3 | 52.8 | 21.4 | 55.2 |
| TOTAL | 100.0 | 100.0 | 100.0 | 100.0 | 100.0 | 100.0 |

NOTE: MULTIUNIT FIRMS THAT OPERATE ONLY A SINGLE WHOLESALE ESTABLISHMENT WERE CONSIDERED SINGLE UNIT WHOLESALE ESTABLISHMENTS.

*SOURCE:* COMPUTED FROM CENSUS OF WHOLESALE TRADE 1982, 1987, AND 1992.


**TABLE 6-6.** SHARE OF SINGLE UNIT AND MULTIUNIT ESTABLISHMENT AND SALES BY TYPE OF OPERATION

| TYPE OF OPERATION | 1982 % OF EST. | 1982 % OF SALES | 1987 % OF EST. | 1987 % OF SALES | 1992 % OF EST. | 1992 % OF SALES |
|---|---|---|---|---|---|---|
| MERCHANT WHOLESALERS | | | | | | |
| SINGLE UNIT | 88.5 | 57.3 | 87.6 | 53.5 | 88.7 | 51.5 |
| MULTIUNIT | 11.5 | 42.7 | 12.4 | 46.5 | 11.3 | 48.5 |
| MANU. SALES BRANCH OFFICES | | | | | | |
| SINGLE UNIT | 5.9 | 11.0 | 5.0 | 12.3 | 4.9 | 15.2 |
| MULTIUNIT | 94.1 | 89.0 | 95.0 | 87.7 | 95.1 | 84.8 |
| AGENT, BROKER, COMM, MERC. | | | | | | |
| SINGLE UNIT | 85.5 | 72.9 | 86.9 | 72.2 | 87.0 | 63.9 |
| MULTIUNIT | 14.5 | 27.1 | 13.1 | 27.8 | 13.0 | 36.1 |

*SOURCE:* COMPUTED FROM CENSUS OF WHOLESALE TRADE 1982, 1987, AND 1992.

**TABLE 6-7.** NUMBER OF WHOLESALE ESTABLISHMENTS AND SALES BY KIND OF BUSINESS (MILLIONS)

| YEAR | GENERAL LINE | | SPECIALTY LINE | |
|---|---|---|---|---|
| | EST. | SALES | EST. | SALES |
| 1982 | 4,084 | 70,574 | 34,432 | 218,085 |
| 1987 | 4,368 | 93,215 | 37,707 | 287,730 |
| 1992 | 4,528 | 132,603 | 38,346 | 371,964 |

SOURCE: CENSUS OF WHOLESALE TRADE 1982, 1987, AND 1992.

**TABLE 6-8.** PERCENT OF WHOLESALE ESTABLISHMENTS AND SALES BY KIND OF BUSINESS

| YEAR | GENERAL LINE | | SPECIALTY LINE | |
|---|---|---|---|---|
| | % OF EST. | % OF SALES | % OF EST. | % OF SALES |
| 1982 | 10.6 | 24.4 | 89.4 | 75.6 |
| 1987 | 10.4 | 24.5 | 89.6 | 75.5 |
| 1992 | 10.6 | 26.2 | 89.4 | 73.8 |

SOURCE: COMPUTED FROM CENSUS OF WHOLESALE TRADE 1982, 1987, AND 1992.

**TABLE 6-9.** PERCENT OF ESTABLISHMENTS AND SALES BY TYPE OF OPERATIONS AND KIND OF BUSINESS

| TYPE OF OPERATION/KIND OF BUSINESS | 1982 % OF EST. | 1982 % OF SALES | 1987 % OF EST. | 1987 % OF SALES | 1992 % OF EST. | 1992 % OF SALES |
|---|---|---|---|---|---|---|
| **MERCHANT WHOLESALER** | | | | | | |
| General line | 11.4 | 34.8 | 11.2 | 33.4 | 11.3 | 34.3 |
| Specialty line | 88.6 | 65.2 | 88.8 | 66.6 | 88.7 | 65.7 |
| **MANU. SALES BRANCH OFFICES** | | | | | | |
| General line | 0 | 0 | 0 | 0 | 0 | 0 |
| Specialty line | 100.0 | 100.0 | 100.0 | 100.0 | 100.0 | 100.0 |
| **AGENT, BROKER, COMM, MERC.** | | | | | | |
| General line | 16.1 | 19.7 | 15.3 | 27.3 | 16.3 | 37.5 |
| Specialty line | 83.9 | 80.3 | 84.7 | 72.7 | 83.7 | 62.5 |

NOTE: THERE ARE NO GENERAL LINE MANUFACTURERS' SALES BRANCH OFFICES.

*SOURCE:* COMPUTED FROM CENSUS OF WHOLESALE TRADE 1982, 1987, AND 1992.

**TABLE 6-10.** NUMBER OF ESTABLISHMENTS AND SALES FOR VOLUNTARY GROUPS, RETAIL COOPERATIVES, AND UNAFFILIATED GENERAL LINE WHOLESALERS (MILLIONS)

|  | 1982 | | 1987 | | 1992 | |
|---|---|---|---|---|---|---|
| EST. KIND | EST. | SALES | EST. | SALES | EST. | SALES |
| VOL. GROUP | 270 | 19,518 | 293 | 26,303 | 338 | 28,531 |
| RETAIL COOP | 433 | 19,047 | 237 | 15,221 | 184 | 17,332 |
| UNAFFILIATED | 2,613 | 22,141 | 3,094 | 32,929 | 3,218 | 49,944 |
| TOTAL | 3,316 | 60,706 | 3,624 | 74,454 | 3,740 | 95,807 |

SOURCE: CENSUS OF WHOLESALE TRADE 1982, 1987, AND 1992.

**TABLE 6-11.** PERCENT OF ESTABLISHMENTS AND SALES FOR VOLUNTARY GROUPS, RETAIL COOPERATIVES, AND UNAFFILIATED GENERAL LINE WHOLESALERS

|  | 1982 | | 1987 | | 1992 | |
|---|---|---|---|---|---|---|
| ESTABLISHMENT | % OF EST. | % OF SALES | % OF EST. | % OF SALES | % OF EST. | % OF SALES |
| VOL. GROUP | 8.1 | 32.2 | 8.1 | 35.3 | 9.0 | 29.8 |
| RETAIL CO-OP | 13.1 | 31.4 | 6.5 | 20.4 | 4.9 | 18.1 |
| UNAFFILIATED | 78.8 | 36.4 | 85.4 | 44.3 | 86.1 | 52.1 |
| TOTAL | 100.0 | 100.0 | 100.0 | 100.0 | 100.0 | 100.0 |

SOURCE: CENSUS OF WHOLESALE TRADE 1982, 1987, AND 1992.

**TABLE 6-12.** SALES TO CLASS OF CUSTOMER BY TYPE OF OPERATION

| TYPE OF OPERATION | 1982 | | 1987 | | 1992 | |
|---|---|---|---|---|---|---|
| | WHOLE-SALERS | RETAIL-ERS | WHOLE-SALERS | RETAIL-ERS | WHOLE-SALERS | RETAIL-ERS |
| MERCHANT WHOLESALERS | 21.9 | 56.6 | 22.0 | 60.2 | 19.7 | 68.2 |
| MANU. SALES BRANCH OFFICES | 34.9 | 52.9 | 40.9 | 60.8 | 26.3 | 67.1 |
| AGENT, BROKER, COMM. MERC. | 53.9 | 30.6 | 58.7 | 27.7 | 40.7 | 48.7 |
| TOTAL | 30.7 | 51.1 | 31.4 | 51.3 | 25.4 | 63.3 |

SOURCE: COMPUTED FROM CENSUS OF WHOLESALE TRADE-SUBJECT SERIES 1982, 1987, AND 1992.

**TABLE 6-13.** EMPLOYMENT SHARE BY TYPE OF OPERATION

| TYPE OF OPERATION | 1982 | 1987 | 1992 |
|---|---|---|---|
| MERCHANT WHOLESALER | 74.7 | 74.0 | 71.3 |
| MANU. SALES BRANCH OFFICES | 18.3 | 18.7 | 21.4 |
| AGENT, BROKER, COMM. MERC | 7.0 | 7.3 | 7.3 |
| TOTAL | 100.0 | 100.0 | 100.0 |

SOURCE: COMPUTED FROM CENSUS OF WHOLESALE TRADE-GEOGRAPHIC AREA SERIES 1982, 1987, AND 1992.

**TABLE 6-14.** EMPLOYMENT SHARE BY KIND OF BUSINESS

| KIND OF BUSINESS | 1982 | 1987 | 1992 |
|---|---|---|---|
| General line | 20.4 | 20.6 | 21.3 |
| Speciality line | 79.6 | 79.4 | 78.7 |
| TOTAL | 100.0 | 100.0 | 100.0 |

SOURCE: COMPUTED FROM CENSUS OF WHOLESALE TRADE-GEOGRAPHIC AREA SERIES 1982, 1987, AND 1992.


**TABLE 6-15.** SHARE OF ESTABLISHMENTS AND SALES BY STATES

| STATES | 1982 | | 1987 | | 1992 | |
| | % OF EST. | % OF SALES | % OF EST. | % OF SALES | % OF EST. | % OF SALES |
|---|---|---|---|---|---|---|
| 10 LEADING STATES | 55.8 | 60.6 | 59.3 | 59.4 | 59.6 | 59.9 |
| 40 REMAINING STATES | 44.2 | 39.4 | 40.7 | 40.6 | 40.4 | 40.1 |
| TOTAL | 100.0 | 100.0 | 100.0 | 100.0 | 100.0 | 100.0 |

SOURCE: COMPUTED FROM CENSUS OF WHOLESALE TRADE-GEOGRAPHIC AREA SERIES 1982, 1987, AND 1992.

**TABLE 6-16.** RANKING OF TOP TEN STATES BY SHARE OF ESTABLISHMENTS AND SALES

| STATES | 1982 RANKING | | 1987 RANKING | | 1992 RANKING | |
| --- | --- | --- | --- | --- | --- | --- |
| | EST. | SALES | EST. | SALES | EST. | SALES |
| California | 12.4 | 13.0 | 13.5 | 13.1 | 13.9 | 13.1 |
| New York | 11.9 | 9.7 | 11.6 | 8.7 | 11.2 | 8.3 |
| Florida | 5.5 | 4.7 | 6.3 | 5.3 | 6.9 | 5.3 |
| Texas | 5.4 | 6.7 | 6.0 | 6.3 | 5.5 | 6.2 |
| New Jersey | 4.3 | 4.8 | 4.5 | 5.0 | 4.5 | 5.2 |
| Illnois | 2.3 | 6.6 | 4.6 | 5.5 | 4.5 | 5.6 |
| Pennsylvania | 4.5 | 4.5 | 4.4 | 4.9 | 4.2 | 4.8 |
| Ohio | 3.4 | 4.2 | 3.1 | 4.0 | 3.0 | 3.9 |
| Michigan | 3.1 | 3.2 | 3.0 | 3.3 | 3.0 | 3.4 |
| Massachusetts | 3.0 | 3.2 | 2.9 | 3.3 | 2.8 | 3.1 |
| TOTAL | 55.8 | 60.6 | 59.3 | 59.4 | 59.6 | 59.9 |

*SOURCE:* CENSUS OF WHOLESALE TRADE-GEOGRAPHIC AREA SERIES 1982, 1987, AND 1992.

**TABLE 6-17.** NUMBER OF ESTABLISHMENTS BY INDUSTRY

| INDUSTRY | 1982 | 1987 | 1992 |
|---|---|---|---|
| General line (5141) | 4,084 | 4,368 | 4,528 |
| Packaged Frozen Foods (5142) | 2,570 | 2,835 | 3,468 |
| Dairy Products (5143) | 3,701 | 3,743 | 3,378 |
| Poultry (5144) | 1,544 | 1,372 | 1,224 |
| Confectionery (5145) | 2,506 | 2,818 | 2,693 |
| Fish and Seafoods (5146) | 2,062 | 2,745 | 3,100 |
| Meats (5147) | 4,789 | 4,779 | 4,123 |
| Fresh Fruits and Vegetables (5148) | 5,664 | 5,838 | 6,003 |
| Groceries (5149) | 11,596 | 13,577 | 14,357 |
| TOTAL | 38,516 | 42,075 | 42,874 |

SOURCE: CENSUS OF WHOLESALE TRADE 1982, 1987, AND 1992.

**TABLE 6-18.** SHARE OF ESTABLISHMENTS AND SALES BY INDUSTRY

| INDUSTRY and NO. | 1982 % OF EST. | 1982 % OF SALES | 1987 % OF EST. | 1987 % OF SALES | 1992 % OF EST. | 1992 % OF SALES |
|---|---|---|---|---|---|---|
| General line (5141) | 10.6 | 24.4 | 10.4 | 24.5 | 10.6 | 26.3 |
| Package Frozen Foods (5142) | 6.7 | 7.8 | 6.7 | 8.7 | 8.1 | 10.6 |
| Dairy Products (5143) | 9.6 | 7.9 | 8.9 | 7.1 | 7.9 | 7.6 |
| Poultry (5144) | 4.0 | 3.0 | 3.3 | 2.2 | 2.9 | 2.0 |
| Confectionery (5145) | 6.5 | 3.8 | 6.7 | 3.7 | 6.3 | 4.3 |
| Fish and Seafoods (5146) | 5.4 | 2.0 | 6.5 | 2.5 | 7.2 | 2.3 |
| Meats (5147) | 12.4 | 13.4 | 11.4 | 12.4 | 9.6 | 10.9 |
| Fresh Fruits and Vegetable (5148) | 14.7 | 8.4 | 13.9 | 8.0 | 14.0 | 7.6 |
| Groceries, N.E.C. (5149) | 30.1 | 29.3 | 32.3 | 30.9 | 33.5 | 29.1 |
| TOTAL | 100.0 | 100.0 | 100.0 | 100.0 | 100.0 | 100.0 |

*SOURCE:* COMPUTED FROM CENSUS OF WHOLESALE TRADE 1982, 1987, AND 1992.

**TABLE 6-19.** AVERAGE ESTABLISHMENT SALES BY INDUSTRIES ($BILLIONS)

| INDUSTRY and NO. | 1982 | 1987 | 1992 |
|---|---|---|---|
| General line (5141) | 17.28 | 21.34 | 29.28 |
| Packaged Frozen Foods (5142) | 8.81 | 11.73 | 15.36 |
| Dairy Products (5143) | 6.20 | 7.19 | 10.46 |
| Poultry (5144) | 5.67 | 6.23 | 8.27 |
| Confectionery (5145) | 4.34 | 4.95 | 8.10 |
| Fish and Seafood (5146) | 2.77 | 3.42 | 3.70 |
| Meats (5147) | 8.06 | 9.92 | 13.31 |
| Fresh Fruits and Vegetables (5148) | 4.26 | 5.22 | 6.42 |
| Groceries N.E.C. (5149) | 7.28 | 8.68 | 10.21 |
| Average All Industries | 7.49 | 9.05 | 11.77 |

SOURCE: COMPUTED FROM CENSUS OF WHOLESALE TRADE 1982, 1987, AND 1992.


**TABLE 6-20.** CONCENTRATION OF LARGEST WHOLESALE FIRMS

| | PERCENT OF TOTAL SALES | | |
|---|---|---|---|
| | 1982 | 1987 | 1992 |
| 4 LARGEST FIRMS | 6.5 | 7.9 | 11.2 |
| 8 LARGEST FIRMS | 10.1 | 12.2 | 16.9 |
| 20 LARGEST FIRMS | 16.9 | 20.9 | 25.2 |
| 50 LARGEST FIRMS | 27.0 | 32.5 | 35.2 |

SOURCE: CENSUS OF WHOLESALE TRADE 1982, 1987, AND 1992.

**TABLE 6-21.** CONCENTRATION OF LARGEST FIRMS BY TYPE OF OPERATION

| TYPE OF OPERATION | 1982 | 1987 | 1992 |
|---|---|---|---|
| MERCHANT WHOLESALER | | | |
| 4 LARGEST FIRMS | 6.7 | 10.1 | 13.8 |
| 8 LARGEST FIRMS | 10.4 | 14.3 | 17.9 |
| 20 LARGEST FIRMS | 17.4 | 23.1 | 25.2 |
| 50 LARGEST FIRMS | 27.4 | 32.4 | 34.5 |
| MANUFACTURER'S SALES BRANCH OFFICES | | | |
| 4 LARGEST FIRMS | 23.9 | 23.6 | 30.5 |
| 8 LARGEST FIRMS | 36.2 | 36.7 | 44.0 |
| 20 LARGEST FIRMS | 56.3 | 62.9 | 67.9 |
| 50 LARGEST FIRMS | 78.3 | 81.4 | 81.8 |
| AGENTS, BROKERS, COMM. MERC. | | | |
| 4 LARGEST FIRMS | 4.8 | 4.9 | 7.3 |
| 8 LARGEST FIRMS | 8.5 | 8.8 | 12.6 |
| 20 LARGEST FIRMS | 15.8 | 16.1 | 21.0 |
| 50 LARGEST FIRMS | 25.3 | 26.5 | 33.4 |

*SOURCE:* CENSUS OF WHOLESALE TRADE 1982, 1987, AND 1992.

**TABLE 6-22.** CONCENTRATION OF LARGEST FIRMS BY INDUSTRY

|  | 1982 % of Sales | 1987 % of Sales | 1992 % of Sales |
|---|---|---|---|
| GENERAL LINE (5141) | | | |
| 4 LARGEST FIRMS | 15.0 | 20.8 | 25.6 |
| 8 LARGEST FIRMS | 22.8 | 29.4 | 32.2 |
| 20 LARGEST FIRMS | 36.8 | 43.0 | 44.8 |
| 50 LARGEST FIRMS | 55.3 | 58.9 | 61.3 |
| PACKAGED FROZEN FOODS (5142) | | | |
| 4 LARGEST FIRMS | 11.5 | 12.7 | 15.0 |
| 8 LARGEST FIRMS | 17.6 | 19.8 | 21.2 |
| 20 LARGEST FIRMS | 27.1 | 30.6 | 32.4 |
| 50 LARGEST FIRMS | 40.4 | (D) | 44.3 |
| DAIRY PRODUCTS (5143) | | | |
| 4 LARGEST FIRMS | 25.1* | 22.7 | 25.0 |
| 8 LARGEST FIRMS | 33.3* | 30.3 | 32.4 |
| 20 LARGEST FIRMS | 45.4* | 43.8 | 44.6 |
| 50 LARGEST FIRMS | 58.7 | 60.3 | 61.9 |
| POULTRY PRODUCTS (5144) | | | |
| 4 LARGEST FIRMS | 11.3* | 7.4 | 9.6 |
| 8 LARGEST FIRMS | 16.4 | 12.7 | (D) |
| 20 LARGEST FIRMS | 25.0 | 22.5 | 25.2 |
| 50 LARGEST FIRMS | 38.0 | 38.4 | 41.9 |
| CONFECTIONERY (5145) | | | |
| 4 LARGEST FIRMS | 37.2 | 29.9 | 42.1 |
| 8 LARGEST FIRMS | 48.9 | 42.7 | 54.2 |
| 20 LARGEST FIRMS | 57.6 | 54.1 | (D) |
| 50 LARGEST FIRMS | 66.2 | 64.2 | 71.6 |
| FISH and SEAFOODS (5146) | | | |
| 4 LARGEST FIRMS | 11.1* | (D) | 8.3 |

| (TABLE 6-22. cont.) | 1982 % of Sales | 1987 % of Sales | 1992 % of Sales |
|---|---|---|---|
| 8 LARGEST FIRMS | 14.5* | 8.7 | 12.6 |
| 20 LARGEST FIRMS | 22.2* | 16.5 | 20.0 |
| 50 LARGEST FIRMS | 35.1* | 28.0 | 30.9 |
| MEATS (5147) | | | |
| 4 LARGEST FIRMS | 14.9 | 18.8 | 33.6 |
| 8 LARGEST FIRMS | 21.5 | 24.4 | 38.7 |
| 20 LARGEST FIRMS | 29.2 | 33.7 | 45.1 |
| 50 LARGEST FIRMS | 38.9 | 44.3 | 54.2 |
| FRESH FRUITS and VEGETABLES (5148) | | | |
| 4 LARGEST FIRMS | 5.8 | 8.4 | 7.2 |
| 8 LARGEST FIRMS | 9.8 | 10.5 | 11.3 |
| 20 LARGEST FIRMS | 14.2 | 14.8 | 15.7 |
| 50 LARGEST FIRMS | 20.9 | 21.6 | 23.0 |
| GROCERIES N.E.C. (5149) | | | |
| 4 LARGEST FIRMS | 12.7 | 12.7 | 15.3 |
| 8 LARGEST FIRMS | 19.0 | 21.0 | 23.6 |
| 20 LARGEST FIRMS | 31.1 | 36.2 | 38.5 |
| 50 LARGEST FIRMS | 44.3 | 50.2 | 52.0 |

*INDICATES DECREASE IN CONCENTRATION OVER CENSUS PERIODS.
D: WITHHELD TO AVOID DISCLOSING DATA FOR INDIVIDUAL COMPANIES.

*SOURCE:* CENSUS OF WHOLESALE TRADE 1982, 1987, AND 1992.

**TABLE 6-23.** 50 LEADING FOOD (MERCHANT) WHOLESALERS

| 1995 RANK | COMPANY NAME | TYPE V=VOL. C=COOP. N=UNAFF. | SALES (MILLIONS) | PERCENT OF SALES C=CHAIN I=INDEP. C | I |
|---|---|---|---|---|---|
| 1 | FLEMING COS. | V | 17,502 | 35 | 65 |
| 2 | SUPERVALU INC. | V | 16,500 | 55 | 45 |
| 3 | WAKEFERN FOOD CO. | C | 3,740 | 81 | 19 |
| 4 | PENN TRAFFIC CO. | V | 3,536 | 40 | 60 |
| 5 | C&S WHOLESALE GROCERS INC. | V | 3,348 | 97 | 3 |
| 6 | RICHFOOD INC. | V | 3,097 | 62 | 38 |
| 7 | ASSOCIATED WHOLESALE GROCERS INC. | C | 2,975 | 50 | 50 |
| 8 | SPARTAN STORES INC. | C | 2,537 | 60 | 40 |
| 9 | ROUNDY'S INC. | C/V | 2,488 | 0 | 100 |
| 10 | GIANT EAGLE CO. | V | 2,075 | 70 | 30 |
| 11 | NASH FINCH CO. | V | 1,969 | 33 | 67 |
| 12 | CERTIFIED GROCERS OF CALIFORNIA LTD. |  | 1,823 | 51 | 49 |
| 13 | TWIN COUNTY GROCERS | C | 1,200 | 75 | 25 |
| 13 | GROCERS SUPPLY CO. | N | 1,200e | 60 | 40 |
| 13 | UNITED GROCERS CO. | C | 1,200e | N/A | N/A |
| 16 | SUPER FOOD SERVICES INC. | V | 1,155 | 38 | 62 |
| 17 | ASSOCIATED GROCERS INC. | C | 1,055 | 46 | 54 |
| 18 | DIGIORGIO CORP./WHITE ROSE FOODS | V | 1,018 | 55 | 45 |

(TABLE 6-23. cont.)

| 1995 RANK | COMPANY NAME | TYPE V=VOL. C=COOP. N=UNAFF. | SALES (MILLIONS) | PERCENT OF SALES C=CHAIN I=INDEP. C | I |
|---|---|---|---|---|---|
| 19 | AMERICAN SEAWAY FOODS INC. | V | 1,010 | 70 | 30 |
| 20 | FOODLAND DISTRIBUTORS | V | 980 | 80 | 20 |
| 21 | MERCHANTS DISTRIBUTORS INC. | V | 955 | 90 | 10 |
| 22 | ASSOCIATED FOOD STORES INC. | C | 937 | 30 | 70 |
| 23 | CERTIFIED | C | 714 | 1 | 99 |
| 24 | HALE HALSELL CO. | V | 697 | 72 | 28 |
| 25 | PROFESSIONAL FOOD SYSTEMS | N | 644e | 10 | 90 |
| 26 | FAIRWAY FOODS INC. | V | 630e | 20 | 80 |
| 27 | ASSOCIATED WHOLESALERS INC | C | 612 | 10 | 90 |
| 28 | PIGGLY WIGGLY CAROLINA CO. | C | 575e | 50 | 50 |
| 29 | AFFILIATED FOODS INC. | C | 514 | 76 | 24 |
| 30 | AFFILIATED FOODS INC. | C | 530 | 56 | 44 |
| 31 | KEY FOOD STORES COOPERATIVE INC. | C | 514 | 76 | 24 |
| 32 | AFFILIATED FOODS SOUTHWEST | C | 485 | 20 | 80 |
| 33 | U.R.M. STORES INC. | C | 430e | N/A | N/A |
| 34 | KRASDALE FOODS | V | 450 | 0 | 100 |
| 35 | CENTRAL GROCERS COOPERATIVE INC. | C | 443 | 0 | 100 |
| 36 | MID-MOUNTAIN FOODS INC. | C | 442 | 98 | 2 |

(TABLE 6-23. cont.)

| 1995 RANK | COMPANY NAME | TYPE V=VOL. C=COOP. N=UNAFF. | SALES (MILLIONS) | PERCENT OF SALES C=CHAIN I=INDEP. C | I |
|---|---|---|---|---|---|
| 36 | PIGGLY WIGGLY ALABAMA DISTRIB. CO. INC. | C | 442e | 40 | 60 |
| 38 | H.T. HACKNEY CO. | V | 430e | N/A | N/A |
| 39 | DEARBORN WHOLESALE GROCERS L.P. | V | 388 | 30 | 70 |
| 40 | MITCHELL GROCERY CORP. | V | 382 | 26 | 74 |
| 41 | ASSOCIATED GROCERS INC. | C | 380 | N/A | 100 |
| 42 | BOZZUTO'S INC. | V | 372 | 0 | 100 |
| 43 | SCHULTZ SAV-O STORES INC. | V | 365 | 28 | 72 |
| 44 | JAMES FERRERA AND SONS INC. | N | 298 | 57 | 43 |
| 45 | J.B. GOTTSTEIN CO. | V | 293 | 85 | 15 |
| 47 | AFFILIATED FOOD STORES INC. | C | 256 | 34 | 66 |
| 48 | TRI-STATE WHOLESALE ASSO. GROCERS INC. | C | 210 | N/A | N/A |
| 49 | AFFILIATED OF FLORIDA INC. | C | 223 | 20 | 30 |
| 50 | ASSOCIATED GROCERS OF FLORIDA | C | 210 | N/A | N/A |

e=ESTIMATE

V=VOL. (VOLUNTARY)

C=COOP. (COOPERATIVE)

N=UNAFF. (UNAFFILIATED

*SOURCE:* U.S. DISTRIBUTION JOURNAL, SEPTEMBER 15, 1996

**TABLE 6-24.** FIFTY LEADING CONVENIENCE STORE WHOLESALERS

| 1995 RANK | COMPANY NAME | SALES ($millions) | PERCENT OF SALES C=CHAIN C | I=INDEP I |
|---|---|---|---|---|
| 1 | MCLANE CO. INC. | 7,985 | 90 | 10 |
| 2 | CORE-MARK INTERNATIONAL INC. | 2,100 | 40 | 60 |
| 3 | EBY-BROWN CO. L.P. | 1,550 | 65 | 35 |
| 4 | ELI WITT CO. | 1,507 | 65 | 40 |
| 5 | GSC ENTERPRISES INC. | 1,066 | 58 | 42 |
| 6 | S. ABRAHAM and SONS INC. | 644 | 65 | 40 |
| 7 | FLEMING CONVENIENCE MARKETING AND DISTRIBUTION | 476 | 90 | 10 |
| 8 | JOE. H. STOMEL AND SONS | 450 | 50 | 50 |
| 9 | MINTER-WEISMAN CO. | 401 | 75 | 25 |
| 10 | F.A. DAVIS and SONS INC. | 390 | 40 | 60 |
| 11 | J.F. WALKER CO. INC. | 335 | 47 | 53 |
| 13 | MILLER and HARTMAN CO. INC. | 291 | 75 | 25 |
| 14 | CONVENIENCE STORE DISTRIBUTION CO. | 286 | 65 | 35 |
| 15 | SOSNICK COS. | 284 | 70 | 30 |
| 16 | L&L/JIROCH DISTRIBUTION CO. | 252 | 35 | 65 |
| 17 | JAMES BRUDNICK CO. INC. | 252 | 35 | 65 |
| 18 | FARNER BOCKEN CO. | 250 | 35 | 65 |
| 19 | J.T. DAVENPORT AND SONS INC. | 235 | 65 | 35 |
| 20 | GARBER BROS. INC. | 225 | 45 | 35 |
| 22 | ATLANTIC DOMINION DISTRIBUTORS | 197 | 75 | 25 |
| 23 | IMERIAL TRADING CO. INC. | 190 | 50 | 50 |
| 24 | TRIPIFOODS INC. | 181 | 71 | 29 |
| 25 | AMCON DISTRIBUTION CO. | 170 | 36 | 64 |
| 25 | HEAD DISTRIBUTING CO. | 170 | 55 | 45 |
| 27 | HERKIMER WHOLESALE CO. INC. | 149 | 55 | 35 |

(TABLE 6-24. cont.)

| 1995 RANK | COMPANY NAME | SALES ($millions) | PERCENT OF SALES C=CHAIN C | PERCENT OF SALES I=INDEP I |
|---|---|---|---|---|
| 28 | M.O. CARROLL-NEWTON CO. | 145 | 50 | 50 |
| 29 | PINE STATE TOBACCO AND CANDY CO. | 142 | 50 | 50 |
| 29 | HARRISON CO. INC. | 142 | 50 | 50 |
| 31 | J. POLEP DISTRIBUTION SERVICES | 141 | 35 | 65 |
| 32 | MTC DISTRIBUTING | 124 | 10 | 90 |
| 33 | AUBURN MERCHANDISE DISTRIBUTORS | 123 | 22 | 78 |
| 34 | A.H. NOTINI AND SONS INC. | 120 | 35 | 65 |
| 35 | BURKLUND DISTRIBUTORS INC. | 110e | 78 | 22 |
| 36 | MARCUS DISTRIBUTORS INC. | 98 | 60 | 40 |
| 37 | HAGMAN-EDWARDS COS. | 96e | 35 | 65 |
| 37 | GEORGE MELHADO AND CO. | 96 | 55 | 45 |
| 39 | SOUTHCO DISTRIBUTING CO. | 95 | 60 | 40 |
| 40 | FRITZ COS. | 94 | 50 | 50 |
| 41 | HARBOR WHOLESALE GROCERY INC. | 80 | 20 | 80 |
| 42 | CITY SALES INC. | 72 | 12.5 | 87.5 |
| 43 | J.L. LESTER AND SON | 76 | 13 | 87 |
| 44 | AMSTER-KIRTZ CO. | 60 | 25 | 75 |
| 45 | MCCARTY-HALL INC. | 58 | 25 | 75 |
| 45 | MERCHANTS GROCERY CO. INC. | 58 | 47 | 53 |
| 45 | GOLDSMIT-BLACK INC. | 58 | 35 | 65 |
| 48 | DUSA DISTRIBUTION CENTER INC. | 54 | 2 | 98 |
| 49 | T.B.I. CORP. | 50e | N/A | N/A |
| 50 | QUALITY FOODS COOPERATIVE | 50 | 7 | 93 |

e = ESTIMATE

*SOURCE: U.S. DISTRIBUTION JOURNAL, AUGUST 15, 1996.*

# Chapter 7

# Marketing Decisions

**Chapter Outline**

Wholesaling Sector
    A. Historical Perspective
    B. Structural Influence on Marketing Decisions
    C. Wholesalers' Role

Product Decisions
    A. Product Discrepancy
    B. Category Management

Retailer Services Decisions
    A. Store Development
    B. Store Operations
    C. Merchandise

Price Decisions
    A. Price-setting
    B. System Generated Revenue
    C. Inside Margin

Promotion Decisions
    A. Historical Perspective
    B. Trade Promotion

Distribution Decisions
- A. Spatial Discrepancy
- B. External Logistics: Goals and Alternatives
- C. External Logistic Decisions
- D. Temporal Discrepancy
- E. Internal Logistics: Goals
- F. Internal Logistics: Distribution Center Operations
- G. Cross Docking
- H. Continuous Replenishment

Benefits of Using Wholesalers
- A. Manufacturers
- B. Retailers
- C. Consumers

Future Role of Wholesalers
- A. Network Optimizers
- B. Market Maximizers

Summary

The changing nature of the wholesaling sector's structural characteristics was examined in Chapter 6. The number of firms and establishments continued to increase. When analyzed by type of operation (e.g., merchants, manufacturers' sales branches/offices, agents, brokers, and commission merchants), the share of each type remained relatively constant. Most wholesalers are merchant wholesalers and they account for the majority of sales and employment. When examined by kind of business (general vs. specialty), the share of each kind remained relatively constant. Most wholesalers are specialty wholesalers and account for the majority of sales and employment.

The examination further revealed the continued sales dominance of multiunit firms and firms with unit sales of one hundred million dollars or more. Taken together, these trends produced a wholesale sector comprising two distinct groups. A few large-scale, multiunit wholesalers generate the vast majority of sales, while a much larger group of small, single unit wholesalers generate an increasingly smaller share of sales.

An examination by industry revealed that no industry met the conventional definition of an oligopolistic market structure (i.e., four largest firms account for greater than fifty percent of industry sales). However, in five of the nine industries, the top fifty firms had over fifty percent of their industry's sales. Despite the fact that a small percentage of firms account for the majority of wholesale sales, the sector contains industries that are essentially monopolistic competitors. It is within this market structure that wholesalers make marketing decisions.

The purpose of this chapter is to examine the marketing decisions of food wholesalers. A historical perspective of the wholesaling sector's quest to receive, store, and ship food is presented to establish the modern-day environment within which wholesaler marketing decisions are made. Subsequent sections represent a functional analysis of wholesaler marketing decisions to create, price, promote, and distribute food products.

# WHOLESALING SECTOR

The history of food distribution parallels the history of mankind. Whenever people group together in gatherings of substantial size, a specialization of labor invariably develops. As a consequence of this specialization, many people no longer engage in food production and thus must rely on others to meet their food requirements. Because food production becomes concentrated in the hands of a few, the growth of mankind depends upon its ability to get food into the hands of those who will consume it. The contemporary food wholesaling sector reflects the **U.S. food marketing system's** initial attempt to disperse food products so they can be consumed when and where they are demanded, at a price consumers are willing to pay.

## Historical Perspective[*]

The distinction between wholesale distribution and retail distribution was made by the Greeks sometime during the eigth century B.C. They used the word **emporous** (wholesaler) to mean a trader who sold goods to a **hapeloi** (retailer).

Despite this distinction, in the U.S. the separation of the wholesaling function from the retailing was a gradual process. Commerce in early America followed the British tradition. Located in the eastern seaboard cities, the functions of importing, wholesaling, and retailing were carried on by the same merchant. This seemed only

---

[*] This section is based on *The Food Industry—Lifeline of America,* by E.C. Hampe and M. Wittenberg, 2nd ed. New York: McGraw-Hill, Inc., 1990.

natural because the colonies had no manufacturing capabilities and thus relied on importing goods from Europe.

As the pioneers moved into new western territories, European-operated trading posts became the centers of commerce. Later, colonial grocers, who had operated in the eastern seaboard cities, followed the migration to the west. They set up their own trading posts on main waterways and did a brisk business with store boats that sold merchandise along the waterways. Continued population growth and the development of the railroad led to the decline of the store boat's role in distribution. At the same time, the character of the trading post began to change. Barter as the medium of exchange was replaced by money, and the assortment of merchandise carried was greatly expanded. Gradually, the trading posts began to evolve into what was to become a unique American invention: the general store.

As cities grew, the character of the general store changed. The city general store served as a retailer to city dwellers, but as a wholesaler to rural general stores. The rural store keepers traveled to the larger general stores in the city to purchase merchandise. In anticipation of their arrival, the city operators would purchase large quantities and store them to be resold later to the country store keepers. This cooperation between city and country general store keepers lasted to near the end of the nineteenth century.

The growth of cities also brought about an increase in the number of food brokers. Brokers probably have the longest history in the wholesale trade. They were well known in commerce, and mentioned in English common law as far back as 1629. The first reference to brokers in the U.S. dates back to 1811. Essentially sales people, they represented food manufacturers to retailers.

By 1850, the growth in urban populations and the consumer demand for a broader selection of items accelerated the separation of wholesale and retail operations. These two trends encouraged the growth of specialized retail stores for produce, groceries, meats, and baked goods. The buying habits of retailers changed to accommodate this specialization and in turn brought about the need for specialized wholesalers. Wholesaling became such a specialized function that by 1869 roughly ninety percent of all manufactured food products and fifty-two percent of all non-manufactured goods (i.e., milk, meat, produce, and other perishable foods) were distributed by wholesalers to retailers.

Between 1850 and 1900, a number of events took place that helped to expand and redefine the role of the wholesaler in the U.S. food marketing system. In 1865, the first cold-storage warehouse was built in New York City. In 1868, the first refrigerated railroad car was patented and in 1869 the first transcontinental railroad was completed. Taken together, the role of the wholesaler was expanded to include the distribution of produce and cattle from the west to the urban populations of the east.

The emergence of the **service wholesaler** helped to redefine the role of the wholesaler. Unlike wholesalers specialized by product line, these firms carried a complete line of dry grocery products. As service wholesalers began to capture a larger percentage of the wholesale business, in 1888 there emerged a new form of wholesaler operation: the **retailer-owned cooperative wholesaler**. These cooperatives were made up of retailers who jointly owned their wholesale distributor. By doing so, these retailers circumvented the service wholesalers and thus secured lower prices. Although other cooperatives were formed, they were unsuccessful in slowing the growth of service wholesalers. In fact, by 1900, service wholesalers supplied about seventy percent of the items carried by independent retailers, and almost twenty percent of the items carried by chain-store retail firms.

In the years following World War I, the entire U.S. food marketing system of independent wholesalers and retailers was challenged by chain-store retailers. From their modest beginning in 1859, when **A&P** began to sell tea at wholesale prices, chains multiplied to three hundred companies in 1900 and were doing twenty percent of all retail sales. Although these chains sold dry groceries mostly, as they grew in number they were able to deal directly with food manufacturers and assume the key functions of volume buying, warehouse storage, and redistribution to their retail chain stores. Chains began to expand because consumers preferred the low retail prices resulting from faster turnover and lower margin.

To counter the rapid expansion of chains, independent retailers again organized into affiliated groups. This time, retailers did not affiliate with wholesalers by ownership, as in cooperatives, but rather by voluntary agreement to purchase merchandise and adopt a common name and logo for advertising purposes. Like the retail cooperatives of earlier years, these **voluntary group wholesalers** sought to match or exceed the cooperative chains in buying power, operating efficiency, management skill, and other critical merchandising techniques. Despite the success of retailer-owned cooperatives and voluntary groups, by 1930 they were surpassed in number by chains, and gave up thirty-two percent of the nation's retail sales.

In 1930 an event took place that was, once again, to redefine the role of the wholesaler. A new idea in food retailing, the supermarket, was introduced in Jamaica, New York. This **King Kullen** supermarket was, in one way, a return to the general store concept. It carried not only food but also general merchandise. The affiliated wholesalers quickly recognized the potential of this supermarket format and encouraged their retailers to change over to this format. By 1936, the affiliated wholesalers were handling thirty-seven percent of the independent wholesale volume. Of equal importance was the fact that these affiliated wholesalers entered the supermarket business themselves as part owners or, in many cases, as full owners of supermarkets.

The impact of World War II marks another new beginning for the wholesale sector. The challenge of feeding the nation and its armies created the climate for finding more sophisticated methods of distribution. Wholesalers changed physically in structure, administratively in merchandising, and philosophically in operations. The move away from multistory to one-story warehouses made it possible to use labor and machinery more effectively. The change from profit margins based on what the traffic would pay, to profit margins based on expense-to-sales ratios, made it possible to operate more profitably. Finally, the change to viewing the wholesaler as a distribution center, instead of a storage facility, brought about new methods and machines for handling merchandise. In total, these changes produced a new streamlined wholesaler capable of handling the demands of the postwar population explosion.

As wholesalers moved into the mid 1960s, affiliated wholesalers saw many of their independent retailers become successful chain stores that continued to be their customers. In addition, the growth of chains outstripped their ability to distribute to these new stores. Wholesalers then became suppliers to these chains, much as they had in 1920.

The 70s, 80s, and 90s witnessed further improvements in the distribution center functions of receiving, storage, replenishment, selection, and shipping that are still in use today. But probably no innovation has had the effect that information technology has had on these distribution center functions. The **Electronic Data Interchange (EDI)** system has enabled companies to communicate electronically using **Uniform Communications Standards (UCS)**. Together with advances in competitive software, the need for paperwork has been vastly reduced and, in some cases, eliminated.

Perhaps the most popular technology topic in warehousing today is the potential of the **UCC/EAN 128** bar code. The new bar code is capable of identifying information such as production dates, sell-by dates, weights and quantity, as well as the manufacturers and product identification. Everyone who handles a case or pallet with the bar code—from the supplier to the distributor to the retailer—can access the information and use it to handle the case or pallet more effectively. When barcoding technology is combined with **Radio Frequency (RF)** systems and integrated with a warehouse management software system, wholesalers can update and access data in real time. This ensures that inventory is visible, available, accessible, and accurate. These baseline technologies create a speedier and more efficient flow of product through the distribution center. As the use of these technologies matures and understanding of their powerful capabilities grows, the use of information technology in distribution centers will become standard operating procedure.

This brief review of history reinforces a conclusion reached by many in the U.S. food marketing system: no other sector has sought to redefine itself as the wholesale sector. More than a conclusion, it is a testament to the sector's willingness and capacity to change as conditions warrant.

## Structural Influence on Marketing Decisions

As previously mentioned, the structural characteristics of a sector have a fundamental influence on the marketing decisions made by firms composing the sector. The wholesaling sector was characterized as a monopolistically competitive market structure. Although the sector has a small group of large wholesalers that generate the vast majority of sales, at the industry level, all nine industries are fairly competitive.

Each firm seeks to make its market offering different from that of its competitors. However, wholesalers distribute merchandise that is very much like, if not the same as, its competitors. Because manufacturers seek maximum distribution of their products, wholesalers are in many cases marketing the same merchandise mix. As expected, prices under these conditions will be nearly alike among wholesalers. Therefore, to gain a competitive advantage, wholesalers primarily focus their marketing efforts on making their retail customers competitive in the marketplace.

### Wholesaler's Role

Today, the wholesale sector is made up of firms that have slowly evolved to become what many consider themselves to be: **distribution specialists**. These firms have the specialized knowledge and expertise to make the marketing decisions necessary to carry out their fundamental role in the U.S. food marketing system. Their role is to resolve the product, spatial, and temporal discrepancies that exist between the manufacturers' supply and the retailers' demand **(Figure 7-1)**.

Although introduced in Chapter 1, a brief review of these discrepancies is provided here. **Product discrepancies** exist because there is a difference between the quantity and assortment or products produced by manufacturers and the quantity and assortment demanded by retailers. **Spatial discrepancies** exist because there is a difference between where food manufacturers produce their products and where retailers demand them. **Temporal discrepancies** exist because there is a difference between when food manufacturers' products are produced and when they are demanded by retailers. To resolve these discrepancies, wholesalers make product, price, promotion, and place decisions. Merchant wholesalers, manufacturers' sales branches and offices, and food brokers all play a vital role in the wholesaling sector. The marketing decisions made by wholesalers will be examined from the viewpoint of the retailer cooperative and voluntary group. Because they operate distribution centers and are affiliated by ownership or agreement with their retail customers, this perspective provides an expanded opportunity to examine wholesaler marketing decisions. This perspective is not meant to suggest that food brokers and manufacturers' sales branches and offices do not engage in the same activities. In fact, it has been reported that food brokers appear to be far ahead of other wholesalers in adjusting to the new realities brought about by the **ECR** movement.

# PRODUCT DECISIONS

Wholesalers do not create products in the true sense of the word. Rather, they make **merchandise mix** decisions. The mix is made up of different merchandise categories, and the branded and unbranded products that make up the categories. How do wholesalers create a merchandise mix? To begin, wholesalers must anticipate or forecast the product preferences of their retail customers. Many wholesalers rely on their ability to manage merchandise categories to help them determine these forecasts. By managing categories as business units and customizing them on a store-by-store basis, the wholesaler is able to create a merchandise mix that effectively resolves the product discrepancy problem.

## Product Discrepancy

To resolve the product discrepancies of assortment and quantity the wholesalers must address two questions: "What products should the firm purchase and carry in its inventory?" and "How much of each product should be carried in inventory?" The answers to these questions are, of course, determined by the mix of merchandise offered by the wholesaler's retail customers. From an operational standpoint, all wholesalers engage in specific **regrouping** activities to resolve the discrepancies of quantity and assortment (**Figure 7-2**). These discrepancies are interdependent because products are purchased simultaneously by description and quantity. However, they will be examined separately to illustrate more clearly the regrouping activities.

### *Quantity discrepancy*

To adjust the quantity discrepancy, products must first be **accumulated** from many food manufacturers. In other words, products such as bakery, dairy, produce, and dry groceries must be purchased or procured by the wholesaler. The most recent survey of procurement practices shows that approximately one-half of all wholesalers use buying committees, while the other half depend upon individual buyers (*Grocery Marketing,* May 1995). Once products are accumulated, wholesalers will, at some time in the future, **break bulk** to provide the smaller quantities needed by their retail customers.

### *Assortment discrepancy*

The wholesaler does not just buy any product, but rather those that are demanded by its retail customers. The process of purchasing only certain grades or qualities of product is referred to as **sorting**. For example, **U.S. Fancy** cantaloupes (top grade) may be purchased for the wholesaler's upscale retail customers and **U.S. No. 1** (second grade) for its other retail clientele. Once the appropriate quantity and assortment have been purchased, wholesalers, at some time in the future, will **assort** the different products for shipment to retailers. For example, dairy, dry grocery, produce, and bakery items will be combined into one shipment for delivery to retail customers.

The four regrouping activities of accumulating, bulk breaking, sorting, and assorting reveal how wholesalers answer the questions "What to buy?" and "How much to buy?" In turn, these answers are transformed into the wholesaler's merchandise mix.

As we have seen, the effective resolution of the product discrepancy is based on the premise of buying large quantities of specific products in bulk, storing in anticipation of local needs, and ultimately selling in small quantities to retailers. However, buying for resale must be accomplished in a way that will permit subsequent resale at prices that retail customers are willing to pay, while returning a reasonable profit on the wholesaler's investment.

Because the purchasing function is a major activity that must contribute to the overall profitability, there are other considerations that enter into the process of resolving the product discrepancy problem. First, buyers must maintain inventory levels that balance the cost of acquisition with that of possession in quantities that limit overstock and yet minimize the incidence of out-of-stock conditions. Second, buyers must have assurance that the product will be consistently available in the qualities, quantities, and at the times demanded by retail customers. Finally, buyers must analyze product costs in terms of unit prices, trade, quantity, cash and seasonal discounts, freight allowances, and special promotional allowances.

This last consideration has led to two widespread practices by wholesale buyers: forward buying and diverted product buying. **Forward buying** is the practice of buying quantities of products that exceed the wholesaler's normal demand in order to take advantage of a manufacturer's special "deal" price. This investment buy is made when the manufacturer's offered allowance is greater than the additional holding costs such as capital, storage, and inventory handling. When the promotional period is over, the wholesaler can sell the forward-bought products at the normal price and generate an above-average profit on their sale. The wholesaler also has the option of passing some or all of the savings on to its retail customers in the form of lower prices.

Manufacturers attempt to sell greater volumes of product by periodically offering special promotional prices on selected products. This practice is promoted on a regional, not national, basis. As a consequence, the same product is available by a manufacturer at different prices in different regions. Wholesalers take advantage of this situation by buying the product in the region that has the special promotional price and selling, or diverting, it to regions that are not part of the promotional program. **Diverting**, then, is the practice of going outside normal supply arrangements to buy a manufacturer's product at a special deal price. The product is then resold in a region that isn't involved in the manufacturer's promotional program. Once again, the investment buy is made when the manufacturer's offered allowance is greater than the additional costs of capital, storage, and inventory handling. The wholesaler may use the savings in the same manner the savings from forward buying are used.

Forward buying and diverting represent two forms of investment buying. Each practice is an attempt to make money on the "buy" in addition to the more traditional way wholesalers make money: on the "sell" to retailers. The most recent survey of procurement practices shows that eighty-one percent of all wholesalers engage in forward buying and seventy-three percent buy diverted product. (Dori Hickey and Associates, 1995). The average wholesaler now buys between seventy and eighty

Marketing Decisions

percent of its inventory on some type of deal terms. The current **Efficient Consumer Response (ECR)** in the U.S. food marketing system is, in part, designed to eliminate these practices.

## Category Management

Category management is based on the notion that the proliferation of new products has made strategic management by product too impractical, and strategic management by department too unfocused. Category management represents a middle ground, or a way of emphasizing product categories as key strategic focal points.

Wholesalers have been slow to utilize a category management approach to their retail customers' merchandise activities. In part, this may be explained by how category management was originally defined. As a **philosophy**, it involves strategically managing a retailer's or a manufacturer's business that recognizes categories as strategic units for the purpose of planning and achieving sales and profit goals. As a **process**, through joint planning and execution, retailers and manufacturers develop strategically driven, financially based category plans. As an **organizational concept**, it dictates the manufacturers' and retailers' integrated responsibility for merchandise-buying decisions. Whether category management is viewed as a philosophy, process, or concept, the emphasis is on the relationship between manufacturers and retailers, with no mention of the wholesaler's role in the relationship. Of course, this has not prevented many retail cooperatives and voluntary groups—wholesalers, as well as brokers—from providing category management services to their affiliated retail customers (Sansolo, 1993).

There are seven major activities of category management (**Figure 7-3**). Categories are defined first to determine which products make them up. A purpose or objective for each category is then assigned. Next, category strategies and tactics are developed. The business plan is then implemented to achieve category objectives, strategies, and tactics. Later, category performance is assessed. Finally, categories are reviewed and modified as needed.

Wholesalers must then define an organizational structure to enable category managers to function as asset managers. These managers are empowered to make both buying and selling decisions regarding the categories.

To further implement category management, information must be generated in a form and mode of delivery in order to analyze and evaluate category performance. Because neither the retailer nor the manufacturer has all the information, the wholesaler acts to synthesize this information.

Finally, the nature of the relationship between the manufacturer and the wholesaler and what roles each will play are clearly stated. This relationship is, of course, based on the expectations of mutual benefit.

By assuming the role of a category manager, a wholesaler truly becomes the purchasing agent for its retail customers. Further, because wholesalers have no allegiance to particular manufacturers or brands, their category recommendations are likely to be perceived as more unbiased than those of manufactures. It also allows the wholesalers' retail customers to develop their merchandise mix more closely in terms of their customer preferences. Finally, category management allows the wholesaler to resolve the product discrepancy problem and answer many more fundamental merchandising questions for its retail customers.

## RETAILER SERVICES DECISIONS

The survival and growth of wholesalers depends upon the ability of their retail customers to remain competitive in the marketplace. As a consequence, wholesalers provide a number of services to retailers to enhance their competitiveness. An examination of the different services offered by wholesalers suggests that they can be categorized as services to support retail store development, store operations, and merchandising.

### Store Development

One of the store development services offered by wholesalers involves locating the retail store. Given the long-term commitment, substantial financial investment, and the effect on other retail decisions, location assistance is perhaps the single most important service offered. Demand, supply, and competitive factors are examined at each dimension and used as a basis for selection. The wholesaler's location service must address a three-dimensional problem.

First, the service must identify which regional area presents an opportunity to establish a store. Second, the service must further designate a trade area. This is the area from which a majority of the customers will be drawn to the store. Third, the service must ultimately identify a particular site within the trade area that will allow a retailer to maintain a competitive advantage through spatial monopoly.

The second store development service offered by wholesalers involves designing the store environment. Again, the wholesalers' environment service addresses a three-dimensional problem. First, the service must design the environment within which the store will be placed. At this level the emphasis is on the contribution the immediate surroundings and the store exterior will make to the overall image of the retail firm. Second, the service must design the environment within the store. The primary concern here is to design the store's layout, aisles, fixtures, and equipment to encourage consumers to "shop the store." Third, the service must design the environment within which merchandise is presented.

The presentation of merchandise involves the creation of retail displays that motivate the shopper to buy the displayed items. Taken together, these services are designed to create a buying atmosphere by appealing to the consumer's senses.

## Store Operations

There are literally hundreds of services that wholesalers can offer to help their retail customers operate their stores. Only the more important ones will be discussed here. One of the important services offered is that of training retail personnel. This service is designed (1) to increase employee productivity, (2) to reduce the level of supervision needed, (3) to promote greater conformity and standardization of operations, and (4) to provide a higher level of customer service. This training is available not only for new employees, but also for existing employees to update their knowledge and skills.

A second operational service offered involves the use of information and technology. This often means that wholesalers will provide their retailers with hardware, software, and information management services. Basic services that involve the use of hand-held ordering and inventory devices, point-of-sale system support, and other technologies needed to support information systems are provided. This information is vital to category management.

The last operational service to be discussed are support services. Wholesalers extend credit, finance retail inventories, and offer business planning services. In addition, transportation, storage, and handling services are provided. These and other services are performed for retailers so that they can maintain their competitiveness in the marketplace.

## Merchandise

Retailers buy merchandise in anticipation of reselling it at a reasonable profit. It follows, then, that the category management service provided to retailers is of paramount importance.

Advanced scanner-based data allows manufacturers and distributors to derive a more competitive analysis of category performance. However, when wholesalers offer this service to retailers, they—and not the manufacturers—participate with retailers in a three-step analysis of category performance.

First, category performance is reviewed to answer questions such as: What is a category's market share? How did the variety/assortment of products, pricing, and advertising, help attain the market share goal? What products should be dropped from, or added to, the category? How did subcategories within each category influence overall performance? How did consumers and trade promotions affect specific products and the whole category? How did the location within the store, and the space allocated to the product and category, affect profitability?

Second, customers in the trade area are characterized demographically, economically, psychologically, physically, and culturally. Their purchase, shopping, consumption, and media behavior are then examined to determine what they purchased, where, how often, and how they responded to promotions.

Third, the category analysis is communicated to store managers and employees responsible for carrying out the plans. In addition, this communication includes any adjustments such as new planograms, advertising and promotion plans, price changes, shelf labels, stocking instructions, and products to discontinue and their removal dates.

Offering retail customers a category management service allows the wholesaler to act as both a purchasing and sales agent. The integration of the buying and selling responsibilities ensures that someone will be held accountable for a category's performance results.

# PRICE DECISIONS

As stated previously, to gain a competitive advantage, wholesalers focus their marketing efforts on enhancing their retail customers' competitiveness in the marketplace. To accomplish this, they must effectively and efficiently resolve the product, spatial, and temporal discrepancies that exist between the manufacturers' supply and the retailers' demand. It follows that the wholesalers' pricing objective is to generate a reasonable return for resolving these discrepancies. The pricing objective is ultimately specified in pricing strategies. These strategies specify how cost, demand, and competitive factors will determine basic prices and adjustments to accommodate the variations in the wholesalers' retail customers.

## Price-Setting

Once these strategies have been defined, in a practical sense, wholesalers must price the **merchandise** they purchase for resale and price the **services** (fees) they provide to their retail customers. Unfortunately, setting prices for merchandise and services becomes more complicated at the wholesale level. This complexity is due to the fact that there are other, **non-traditional**, sources of operating revenue that wholesalers consider when setting merchandise and service prices. A review of various components of the wholesalers' operating revenue shows that revenue is generated from two separate streams: system generated and what's known as inside margin (**Figure 7-4**).

## System Generated Revenue

System generated revenue is derived from three sources: markups and net fees, cash discounts, and backhaul revenue. Conceptually, the markups on merchandise and services must cover costs and contribute profit. Operationally, wholesalers have found it difficult to determine what it costs to serve different retail customers. As a consequence, more and more wholesalers are using **Activity Based Costing (ABC)**. Activity based costing focuses on attaching costs to products and services based on the activities performed to produce, perform, distribute, or support those products and services.

The underlying logic of **ABC** is that all wholesale activities exist to support the distribution of a product: acquisition, handling, storage, and delivery. All costs associated with these activities are allocated to **cost drivers** (i.e., those factors that have a cause-effect relationship to a cost). **Cost objects** are then specified. These cost objects may be products, categories, or, in this case, retail customers. Once these activity based costs are allocated, they can be reflected as markups on merchandise and added to the net acquisition cost of the product. Conceptually, with some modification, **ABC** costing can also be applied to markups on services provided to retail customers. Here, the focus would be on identifying all the activities performed to deliver a service to a retail customer. Once identified, these activity costs can be reflected as markups on services performed for retail customers.

Another source of revenue, and thus adjustment to cost, is the cash discount. The discount represents a reduction in merchandise prices because the wholesaler has purchased merchandise and paid for it within a stated period of time.

The third source of system generated revenue is the revenue earned from **backhauling** merchandise. Instead of returning empty after delivery to a retail store, a wholesaler truck will pick up merchandise at a manufacturer and deliver, (or backhaul), it to the wholesaler's distribution center. The compensation paid to distributors is permitted under the **Motor Carrier Act of 1980**. Industry sources report that for every one dollar of wholesaler operating revenue approximately sixty-six cents comes from system generated revenue: forty-five cents comes from net fees and markups, eighteen cents comes from cash discounts, and three cents comes from backhaul revenue (Mathews, 1993).

## Inside Margin

Inside margin, the second stream of revenue, is that portion of a wholesalers' operating revenue generated by some activity other than the distribution of products. When forward bought and diverted inventory is purchased, the savings that are obtained when the merchandise is resold at normal prices represent two sources of inside margin. The promotional money that manufacturers attach to their merchandise on special deals, (not passed on to retailers) represents another source of inside margin. The fourth source of inside margin is the revenue from **slotting allowances**. These fees were developed in response to the proliferation of new products introduced into the U.S. food marketing system. These fees are usually a fixed sum charged directly to the manufacturer to compensate for the time and effort needed to place a new product into the distribution center inventory. The last source of inside margin is the revenue from salvage (damaged items). Industry sources report that for every dollar of wholesaler operating income approximately thirty-four cents comes from inside margin: fifteen cents from forward buy, twelve cents from program income revenue sharing, four cents from slotting fees, three cents from diverting, and less than one cent from salvage (Mathews, 1993).

In the past, wholesalers have used their inside margins to determine merchandise and service prices. Today, many of these wholesalers have moved away from reliance on inside margin. The new thrust is to sell products at cost, passing through all cash discounts, allowances, deals, and diverting and forward buy monies to retail customers. In turn, wholesalers will charge for all services performed for retailers. Computed via **ABC** analysis, this new approach will reposition most wholesalers as service businesses that specialize in distribution. Regardless of what merchandise they handle, what wholesalers are actually selling and what manufacturers and retail customers are actually buying, is a value-added service.

# PROMOTIONAL DECISIONS

There are three major promotional activities in the U.S. food marketing system: consumer advertising, consumer promotion, and trade promotion. In a practical sense, these activities are initiated by manufacturers, not wholesalers. While it is true that many large wholesalers initiate promotional programs for their retail customers, most retail promotions are passed from the manufacturers, through the wholesaler, to the retailer. Industry sources estimate that retail chain stores may have seven thousand to eight thousand deals on file at any time. The net effect is numerous misunderstandings over deal terms, the cause of seventy-eight percent of invoice deductions. (Kurt Salmon Associates, Inc., 1993).

## Historical Perspective

As part of the **ECR** movement in the U.S. food marketing system, promotional practices have received considerable scrutiny. It is not consumer advertising that is seen as inefficient. Rather, the major areas of inefficiency are consumer promotions and trade promotions. Although these inefficiencies affect the entire U.S. food marketing system, it is only trade promotion inefficiencies that directly impact on wholesalers.

These inefficiencies can be traced back to price controls imposed in 1971 during the Nixon administration. Many food manufacturers found themselves unable to raise prices in an inflationary environment. Not wanting to let it happen again, after the price controls were lifted in 1974, they adopted a system of high list prices from which they would offer temporary price reductions or allowances. These temporary price reductions were referred to as **trade promotions**. Initially, these trade promotions were simple off-invoice allowances for shipments made in a given time period. Distributors soon realized that they could make an additional profit if they bought more than they sold during the deal period. Once the deal period ended, any remaining inventory could be sold at their regular prices. In addition, distributors realized that they could purchase merchandise selling on deal in one region and resell it in another region where no deal was running. These forward buying and diverting activities created production and shipping surges in inventory, and motivated manufacturers to reassess their trade promotions.

## Trade Promotion

Manufacturers realized that their trade promotion spending was not being passed through to the consumer. The trade promotion dollars were being used to subsidize the wholesalers' operations. These dollars became part of the wholesalers' **inside margin** and were used to offset other wholesaler costs. To ensure that more of their trade promotion funds would get to consumers, manufacturers created more complex trade promotions. To supplement the off-invoice allowance, manufacturers devised bill-back arrangements, market development funds and pay for performance agreements.

A **bill back** is an alternative to the off-invoice allowance. This approach requires that records of amount of merchandise sold be kept; a statement is then sent to the manufacturer for the cash allowance. **Market Development Funds (MDF)** are allocated toward merchandising, features, displays, and retailer TV advertising programs. **Pay for performance** programs are sometimes referred to as **Scan-Downs** or **Scan-Backs**. Under this arrangement, an incentive is paid to retailers based on the amount of product that actually moves through, or is scanned through, the check-out during the promotional period.

Clearly, trade promotion practices are designed to provide an incentive for the consumer to purchase the manufacturer's merchandise. Because this can only happen at the retail store, manufacturers have begun to offer wholesalers a **fixed net price** arrangement, sometimes referred to as a **continuous deal**. This price reflects the average weighted value of promotional spending and the manufacturer's savings realized from smoothing the inventory shipping pattern.

In recent years, wholesalers have come to rely on forward buying on deal and diverting for a portion of their profits. In an ECR environment, with its focus on removing excess inventory, these practices will become distinct. Once wholesalers are no longer able to subsidize retail customer services through these **buy-side** practices, they will begin to charge the true costs to service their retail customers. When this is possible, promotional revenues will be passed through to retailers.

# DISTRIBUTION DECISIONS

Product discrepancy is resolved partially by merchandising, pricing, and promotional activities. To resolve spatial and temporal discrepancy, wholesalers focus on their distribution activities. Spatial discrepancies exist because there is a difference between **where** food manufacturers produce their products, and **where** retailers demand them. Temporal discrepancies exist because there is a difference between **when** food manufacturers produce their products, and **when** retailers demand them.

## Spatial Discrepancy

To resolve spatial discrepancies, wholesalers focus on their **external** (**inbound, outbound**) **logistical activities.** That is, they must move goods from where they are produced to where they are demanded. **(Figure 7-5)** External logistical decisions made by wholesalers are especially important for two reasons: (1) their expenses typically represent the second largest operating expense, and (2) the image of the wholesaler is projected by its fleet of trucks and drivers.

In the U.S. food marketing system, products are moved to retail customers either **indirectly** through wholesalers, or **directly** from manufacturers to retail customers. When products are distributed indirectly, there are two distinct movements. First, there is the movement of products from the manufacturers to the wholesalers. This movement is referred to as **traffic**, or **inbound logistics**. Products that arrive at wholesalers are generally carried by more than one mode of carrier. For instance, products may be shipped initially by rail, air, or water. Invariably, these products will be placed aboard trucks for delivery to the wholesalers' receiving docks.

The second movement of products is from wholesalers to retail customers. This movement is referred to as **transportation** or **outbound logistics**. Products that are shipped from wholesalers to retail customers arrive typically aboard trucks. According to industry estimates, approximately seventy percent of all products delivered to retailers are shipped indirectly from wholesalers. The other thirty percent delivered to retailers comes directly from manufacturers. This practice is known as Direct Store Delivery (Kochersperger, 1990). Manufacturers may own, lease, or hire a fleet of trucks to move their products. Wholesalers may also move manufacturers' products to retailers under a common carrier or contract carrier designation. Common carriers offer transportation services to the general public, whereas the contract carrier offers contracted services to one customer (exclusive use) or many customers (multiple use). There are no industry estimates available regarding the percent of DSD performed by wholesalers.

The *Motor Carrier Act of 1980* redefined the role of traffic and transportation in wholesaler operations. Prior to this act, the federal government regulated the ownership, operation, and rates charged by trucking firms. Deregulation opened up competition in the trucking industry and created new opportunities for wholesalers. Under this act, manufacturers were allowed to compensate wholesalers, under a uniform zone-determined pricing system, for backhauling products. In addition, wholesalers could generate additional income by operating their private fleets as common or contract carriers. Despite an era of deregulation, most states still administer **intra-**

**state** regulations. Further, several federal agencies enforce **interstate** regulations: the **Department of Transportation**, the **Interstate Commerce Commission**, the **Environmental Protection Agency**, the **Department of Labor**, the **Department of Justice**, and the **Department of Commerce**. It is within this environment that wholesalers make inbound and outbound logistic decisions.

## External Logistics: Goals and Alternatives

Generally, the goal of inbound and outbound logistics management is to achieve the lowest delivered cost of product from the manufacturers to the retailer. Thus, the most fundamental decision that wholesalers make regarding external logistics is whether to manage their inbound/outbound logistics or turn the management over to a third party logistics management specialist. The decision is made usually after an evaluation of the following six factors.

### Human Resources

Administrative, supervisory, and operational personnel must be recruited, tested, hired, and trained. Although everyone plays a crucial role in the operation of a truck fleet, the operationally defined drivers and mechanics are of particular concern. The **Department of Transportation** has defined specific, minimum standards and policies for employing truck drivers. Drivers must be at least twenty-one years old, pass background, physical, and drug tests, have a commercial license from the state in which they reside, and be able to read and write English. Additionally, skilled mechanics who are knowledgeable in computerized diagnostics must, by law, be employed in order to maintain the operation of the fleet or trucks.

### Equipment

To operate a fleet of trucks properly requires the purchase, use, and replacement of tractors, trailers, refrigeration units, and all other equipment that supports the movement and delivery of merchandise. The purchase, operating, maintenance, and residual value of equipment are major concerns.

### Information Systems

Computer-based mobile information systems constitute the third factor. These systems must be designed to facilitate the scheduling, dispatching, and routing of the truck fleet. Onboard computer systems must be able to track pickups and deliveries, record driver habits and truck performance such as speed, brake use, idling time, fuel consumption and mileage, locate the fleet, create a number of reports such as fuel tax, billing, pallets, maintenance and backhauls, and transmit all the data from the truck to the wholesaler's distribution center.

### Fuel supplies

Fuel must be measured for quality, stored for subsequent use, dispensed upon demand, and conserved. The **EPA** regulates underground fuel storage tanks.

### Security

Anti-hijacking measures must be developed to protect the tractor trailers and their contents. On-site security must be established to monitor incoming and outgoing vehicles.

### Fleet Maintenance

Its purpose is to provide the firm with safe, well maintained, and fully operational vehicles and equipment. Shop operators, maintenance and replacement part procedures, and waste disposal are the major concerns in fleet maintenance.

These six factors are evaluated based on their overall costs and the impact they have on the overall goal of servicing the customer. The basic question the wholesaler must answer is "Can the firm achieve a ninety-five to ninety-eight percent on-time delivery performance by managing its own inbound and outbound logistics, or should they use a third-party logistical specialist?"

The theory behind turning over the logistics management to third-party logistics firms, also called **outsourcing**, is that they can operate a fleet of delivery vehicles more cost-efficiently and service-effectively than can wholesalers. Third party-logistics services offered by these firms vary from specifying and supplying equipment on a lease basis to a dedicated contract carriage agreement. Under this agreement the third-party logistics specialist has total management responsibilities over manpower, equipment, fuel suppliers, security, and maintenance facilities for a particular wholesaler.

Although outsourcing is an alternative, most wholesalers operate as **private carriers**, that is, they own their equipment, employ their drivers, and manage all of the resources and assets necessary to achieve a desired customer service level. However, wholesalers do use, for at least some of their transportation needs, **for-hire** common and contract carriers. **Common carriers** offer transportation services to the general public. The rates charged are regulated by the **Interstate Commerce Commission (ICC)**. **Contract carriers** offer transportation services either for the exclusive use of a particular customer or multiple use of more than one customer. The rates are negotiated by the wholesaler and the carrier.

Because most wholesalers operate their own fleet of trucks, the current deregulated environment has allowed them to use their fleets to generate additional income. For example, some wholesalers operate their private fleet as common and contract carriers and solicit business from other companies. Wholesalers have also created **transportation subsidiaries** to backhaul for manufacturers. Finally, wholesalers have acted as transportation brokers, that is, they hire an independent trucking firm to make a delivery at a rate paid by a manufacturer. The wholesaler keeps, as profit, the difference between the manufacturer's backhaul rate and the rate paid to the independent trucking firm.

## External Logistics Decisions

Technically, it would be correct to state that inbound logistics **ends** when merchandise arrives at the wholesalers' distribution center. In the same way, it would be technically correct to state that outbound logistics **begin** when merchandise leaves the wholesalers' distribution center. In reality, some of the loading and unloading activities overlap with the receiving and shipping functions in a distribution center. These functions are more appropriately discussed later within the context of distribution center operations. Here, we will focus only on the functions common to both inbound and outbound logistics (deliveries).

Both inbound and outbound deliveries must be **scheduled**. Decisions are made regarding what is to be received or shipped, how much is to be received or shipped, when the merchandise is to be received or shipped, where in the distribution center the merchandise is to be received or shipped, how the merchandise is to be unloaded or loaded, and how the merchandise is to be checked for accuracy.

What to order, how much, and when are decisions made by the wholesaler's buyer or buying committee. Retail customer orders specify what to order or ship. Buying or selling the amount that minimizes the lowest total cost of operation (i.e., purchasing, receiving, handling, storing, selling, shipping) determines how much is to be received or shipped. When to order or ship is determined by the lead time, sales forecast, safety stock, and level of service sought by manufacturers and retailers.

Inbound and outbound deliveries must also be **dispatched**. Decisions are made regarding which drivers and equipment are to be assigned to specific trips or deliveries. Drivers may be assigned by seniority, labor contract, or by management policy. Regardless of the method of assignment used, it must meet the **DOT** regulations limiting to sixty the number of hours a driver can log during a seven-day work week. In addition, **DOT** regulations govern how long drivers can drive per day (ten hours), how much time they may spend on related activities such as loading, unloading, and paperwork per day (five hours), and how much time drivers must rest after a fifteen hour work day (eight hours).

Equipment is assigned to deliveries based on what is ordered for manufacturers and what is shipped to retailers. The type of equipment assigned depends, in part, on the temperature requirements for the merchandise during delivery. Decisions to use single-temperature or multi-temperature trailers are required. Related decisions are also made based on the type of load to be received or shipped. **Mixed loads** (different merchandise categories such as grocery, meat, and dairy for one or more customers) and **combination loads** (different merchandise categories for the same customer) require multi-temperature (dry, chilled, frozen) trailers. A **straight load** (one merchandise category for one customer) may or may not require a temperature-controlled trailer.

Finally, inbound and outbound deliveries must also be **routed**. Decisions are made regarding pickup or delivery time, the number of vehicles to use, and the distance traveled by the vehicles. Pickup and delivery times may be stated at specific times plus or minus thirty minutes (pinpoint), at some time during the morning, afternoon, or night (a.m./p.m.) or when pickups and deliveries are not to be made during the day, week, or month.

In summary, wholesalers focus on transportation activities to resolve spatial discrepancies. Today, wholesalers are actively involved in moving merchandise from manufacturers to their distribution centers (inbound logistics) as well as moving merchandise from their distribution centers to retailers (outbound logistics). In general, inbound and outbound deliveries are scheduled, dispatched, and routed to meet a ninety-five to ninety-eight percent on-time delivery performance in a cost efficient manner.

## Temporal Discrepancy

To resolve temporal discrepancies, or the difference between when food manufacturers produce their products and when retailers demand them, wholesalers focus on their **internal logistical** activities. These activities are planned in order to achieve customer service goals at the lowest delivered cost of product from the manufacturers to the retailers.

## Internal Logistics: Goals

Like manufacturers, wholesalers establish their customer service goals in terms of inventory availability, service capability, and service specialty. **Inventory availability** is defined in terms of percentage of stock-keeping units (SKUs) available for shipment, **SKUs** shipped as a percentage of all **SKUs** ordered, and the percentage of orders shipped complete. **Service capability** is defined in terms of the speed at which retail orders are received, approved, processed, invoiced, and delivered. The consistency of performance over a number of order cycles, and the ability to meet retail customers' special requests are also considered. **Service quality** means that shipments arrive damage-free, when and where they are needed, and with error-free invoices. The willingness of the wholesaler to resolve any and all problems within a reasonable time is another component of service quality.

It is difficult to state, with any degree of accuracy, the current level that wholesalers have achieved in each of three multifaceted customer-service goals. What is known is that each level of service has a different minimum delivered cost of product. It follows that wholesalers establish their customer-service goals based on a level of performance—less than one hundred percent—but one the retail customer is willing to pay.

## Internal Logistics: Distribution Center Operations

To achieve customer service goals, at a minimum delivered cost of product, four basic operating functions must be performed (**Figure 7-6**). The operations are carried out in distribution centers categorized on the basis of the materials handling equipment they use to move merchandise short distances. These distribution centers are referred to as conventional, mechanized, or automated.

**Conventional distribution** centers, the simplest type, operate using pallets, pallet racks, and fork lifts. **Pallets** are wooden or plastic, movable platforms used for stacking cases so that they can be moved as a unit load. Although seemingly insignificant, industry sources estimate that there are more than 120 million pallets circulating throughout the U.S. food marketing system. Further, pallets cost the U.S. food marketing system nearly two billion dollars a year in product damage, productivity losses, trucking inefficiencies, and pallet replacement costs.

To store unit loads, one, two, and three level metal pallet racks were created. Several types of racks, such as conventional, gravity flow, drive in or drive through, have been developed to handle unit loads of merchandise in various sizes.

The workhorse of the distribution center is the battery-operated, counterbalanced forklift truck. The weight of the truck, plus the weight at the back of the truck, counterbalances the weight of the pallets being picked up. In summary, pallets, pallet racks, and forklifts make up the materials-handling equipment in conventional distribution centers.

**Mechanized distribution** centers retain the materials handling equipment of the conventional center. They add to this mechanized systems such as conveyors, electric hand-operated pallet trucks, carts, and tractors to tow carts.

**Automated distribution** centers use computer-driven, high-rise systems such as the automated storage and retrieval systems (**AS/RS**) and automated guided vehicles (**AGVs**). The AS/RS uses computerized, unmanned materials-handling equipment to unload, move, and load merchandise. The system is made up of high-rise shelving, multi-level conveyors, and high-rise industrial truck equipment. AGVs are computer guided machines that can move unitized pallets of merchandise into and from storage.

Regardless of the type of distribution center, they all attempt to achieve a number of objectives. The first objective is to maximize the use of the center's useable cubic (length, width, height) capacity. The second objective is to reduce the number of times pallets/cases are handled. The third objective is to provide a safe working environment. The fourth objective is to facilitate inbound and outbound logistics. The final objective is to minimize the cost of performing basic operating functions.

From a system's perspective, all distribution centers have three components: **input**, **throughput**, and **output**. These components correspond to a distribution center's four basic operating functions: receiving, storage and replenishment, order selection, and shipping.

### *Receiving (Input)*

Shipments arrive at the receiving docks of distribution centers. These loads are checked for conformity to the bill of lading and invoice to verify that the correct merchandise has been received in the right amount and undamaged. Shipments arriving at the loading docks are either truck load (**TL**) or less than truck load (**LTL**). The former comes directly from the manufacturers, while the latter comes from a terminal that combines other **LTL** going to the same distribution center.

Inbound shipments are unloaded by truck drivers, in-house personnel, a combination of truck drivers and in-house personnel, or mechanized equipment. The method used depends on union contracts or distribution center policy. The method used to unload the shipments depends upon how they were loaded onto the carrier. Shipments may come in on pallets, ship sheets (fiberboard), or in individual cases (dead piled). The merchandise is moved to a temporary staging area on the receiving dock. Labels are attached to the pallets to indicate where the merchandise is to be stored. In some operations, bar-coded labels on pallets are scanned to update company records.

Because one of the main objectives of a distribution center is to balance inbound deliveries with outbound shipments, more and more wholesalers are involved in controlling inbound logistics. Decisions are made regarding the trucks that will arrive, at what time, and how long it will take to unload them. These decisions are reflected in an inbound delivery log referred to as the **Record of Trucks in Transit**.

### *Storage and Replenishment (Throughput)*

Once merchandise is received, it must be placed in the facility so as to minimize handling costs associated with meeting existing and future retail customer orders. To meet existing orders, merchandise is stored in a temporary holding area so that orders can be filled or "picked" efficiently. This is typically referred to as **active inventory**. Merchandise received to meet future orders is stored in a more permanent area and is typically referred to as **passive inventory**. When active inventory falls to a certain level, personnel replenish it with merchandise from the passive inventory.

There are three basic ways to lay out the active inventory area. One is to lay out the merchandise based on **commodity** groupings. This approach is a reflection of layouts formed in retail stores. Personnel who pick the orders literally "shop" the distribution center. The second basic layout is based on the case movement of merchandise, or **turnover**. The faster the case movement, the closer to the shipping dock the merchandise is placed. Merchandise layout by the **case cube** is the third method, in which merchandise that is packed in the same size cases is grouped together.

Each of these layouts may be chosen for its own reasons. The layout by commodity means that merchandise will arrive at the retailer in a way that facilitates their shelf stocking. Layout by case movement is perhaps the least costly and most efficient method from the wholesaler's perspective. Layout by case cube enables selection to build more solid, well-built pallet loads. Whichever layout is chosen, it must use the vertical and horizontal space in the facility to its maximum capacity, minimize aisle space, and reduce the number of times merchandise is handled.

To further increase the efficiency of the distribution center, the exact location of the merchandise in active and passive inventory must be identified. This is usually accomplished by using a numbering system which indicates the aisle, bay, and slot where the merchandise can be found.

Finally, efficiency is enhanced by the specialization and division of labor. Personnel are assigned specific tasks to perform. For example, the day-shift personnel move the incoming merchandise to its active and passive inventory locations. The second- and third- shift personnel select the merchandise for shipment in the morning.

### *Order Selection (Throughput)*

The next step in distribution-center operations is order selection. The objective here is to ensure that every order can be completed. This step is the most labor intensive of all the steps, but it can be performed efficiently as long as retail customer orders conform to certain guidelines. Whenever possible, retail orders should be in full pallet quantities and in full case quantities. Further, orders should be placed at a time that is consistent with the distribution center's order cycle time.

Once the order has been received, in most instances via data transmission to the distribution center's central computer, the order must be selected and moved to the staging area for shipment. At the time the order is processed, a computer will print out a series of case labels until a predetermined number (of cubes) is reached—sixty-six to seventy-two—cubes for each pallet. The computer prints a total label and goes on to the next items until the pallet cube is again reached. These pressure-sensitive labels are then distributed to the selectors who are given the responsibility of affixing them on each case as it is selected. Out-of-stocks are also noted and usually back-ordered for shipment on the next delivery to the customer. Using the **case cube** method ensures that the capacity of the transportation vehicles is used to the fullest capacity.

To select orders, most distribution centers use a **selector-to-case** system. The order selector must travel to the slot location within the aisle. As previously mentioned, the equipment used to select the merchandise can be one or more of three types. **Flexible path** equipment allows the equipment to operate without any instructions. Electric pallet jacks, forklift trucks, tow tractors, and carts are examples of flexible path equipment. **Continuous-flow fixed path** equipment consists of roller and towline conveyors. The former uses the gravity principle. Cases move down the conveyor by force of their own weight. Towline conveyors require power equipment to move cases either on a level surface or up inclines. **Intermittent-flow fixed path** equipment includes overhead bridge cranes and monorails. This equipment can lift, move, and load heavy items quickly and efficiently.

In addition to specifying equipment, the method of selection must be identified. The selector will be given either the entire retail order to pick, or only a portion of the order. If the former, the selector must travel the entire facility, while if the latter, the selector travels within one zone of a designated multizone facility. In this case, the merchandise must be moved to a staging area and combined with other merchandise to fill the order.

After each order is selected, the completed cube is moved to a staging area to be unitized, secured with stretch plastic film, or shrink wrap, and readied for delivery.

### *Shipping (Output)*

The last step in distribution-center operations is shipping. At this step, the unitized load is ready for delivery. Because outbound logistics begin when the merchandise leaves the distribution center, five major shipping decisions must be made.

First, a decision must be made regarding when the shipment will be made. Typically, merchandise is scheduled to be shipped in the morning hours.

Second, a decision must be made that identifies where in the distribution center the merchandise will be shipped. Here, the shipping dock area or door is specified.

Third, a decision must be made to ensure shipment accuracy. The goal is to provide the right product, in the right quantity and the right condition, at the right price, to the right customer. Unfortunately, by this time the orders have been loaded on pallets, and secured with stretch or shrink wrap. To check for accuracy would mean that the loads would have had to be broken down to individual cases. Thus, most distribution centers perform daily audits of loads and check for shortages, overages, and mispicks (incorrect products) and damage on a random basis.

Fourth, a decision must be made regarding the type of truck or trailer to haul the shipment. The primary concern is to ensure that products are being transported at the right temperatures. Most wholesalers are using multitemperature trailers to accommodate retail orders.

Finally, a decision must be made that specifies how the trailer is to be loaded. Although ninety percent of all merchandise is shipped on pallets, carts and hand stacked cases on the floor (dead pile) can also be used.

Once the shipment has been loaded, outbound logistical personnel make decisions to dispatch and route the transportation trucks and trailers.

## Cross Docking

For some types of merchandise, the distribution center's throughput component can be modified substantially to virtually eliminate the steps of storage, replenishment, and order selection. The activity that eliminates these steps is referred to as **cross docking**. **Figure 7-7** illustrates the layout of a distribution center that is designed to allow the traditional steps of storage and replenishment and order selection to be carried out. The layout also allows merchandise to be cross docked.

In its truest form, cross docking is referred to as **unitized** or **palletized continuous movement**. It involves taking a pallet load of merchandise from the receiving truck and moving it directly onto a shipping vehicle, without any intermediate storage or handling inside the facility.

A second form of cross docking is called **consolidated movement**. Merchandise is received in palletized form and moved to a staging area. Here, it is consolidated with other palletized loads and then moved to the shipping vehicle. **Distributed movement** is cross docking at the case level. Merchandise is received, placed on a conveyor, sorted, scanned, and directed down the appropriate lane for outbound shipment (Casper, 1994).

It is estimated that by eliminating the put-away and picking factors through cross docking, the wholesaler's variable labor costs can be reduced by fifty to sixty-six percent. Further, the average number of times a case is handled can be reduced from 4.3 times to only two—once when received, and once when shipped. The most significant barrier to cross docking is the relatively low proportion of products (twenty percent) with sufficient velocity of movement (turnover) to enable any appreciable number of stores to take delivery of full pallet loads. In addition, to operate efficiently, advanced shipping notices (**ASNs**) must be sent by the manufacturer to the wholesaler to indicate what is being delivered for cross docking. These notices are more of a requirement than an impediment (Kurt Salmon Associates, Inc., 1993).

## Continuous Replenishment

Cross docking often takes place within a broader movement referred to as **continuous replenishment**. This system is designed to reduce inventories at the manufacturing, wholesaling, and retailing levels, shorten the time it takes a customer to receive an order once it has been placed (order cycle time), and deliver frequent replenishment quantities error-free. Its goal is to integrate the information of product flows, from manufacturer to wholesaler, and wholesaler to retailer, into one single replenishment loop—from manufacturer to retail point-of-sale.

There are four key elements to continuous replenishment: point-of-sale (**POS**) scan data, electronic store receiving, perpetual store inventory, and computer assisted ordering (**CAO**).

Continuous replenishment is driven by using **POS** data to forecast consumer sales at the store-item level. Basically, the scan data pulls the merchandise from manufacturers, who replenish wholesalers. They, in turn, replenish their retail customers.

All receiving documents must be electronic in order to eliminate redundant and error-prone re-keying of items and receipt quantities and captures data accurately. The receipt documents are electronically transmitted using **UCS (Uniform Communications Standard)** or **SIL (Standard Interchange Language)**.

Integration of the **POS** scanning and electronic receiving systems provides the inputs for maintaining accurate store-level perpetual inventory systems. These systems combine inputs to maintain, on an on-going basis, the quantities of each item in each store.

**CAO** systems use store perpetual inventories coupled with the reorder point level to automatically trigger the replenishment orders for items within the store. CAO systems result in a more balanced flow of product out of and into the retail store. Of course, the success or failure of a CAO system depends on the accuracy of the store-level SKU levels of perpetual inventories, which in turn depend upon the accuracy of the POS scan data and the electronic receiving systems.

# BENEFITS OF USING WHOLESALERS

The discussion on wholesaling would be incomplete if no mention were made of how manufacturers, retailers, and consumers benefit from the services performed by wholesalers. Because of the interdependence of the manufacturing, wholesaling, and retailing sector activities, benefits to manufacturers have implications for retailers and vice versa.

## Manufacturers

The most obvious benefit to manufacturers is the effect that wholesalers have on product inventory. Manufacturers move their inventory to wholesalers so that their warehouse facilities and inventory investment are minimized. Coordinated backhaul programs reduce traffic costs. Further, shipments to wholesalers are larger and less frequent, and thus less costly than they would be if manufacturers had to deal with retailers directly.

The feedback on item movement improves the efficiency of manufacturers' production schedules. Feedback is used also to evaluate the marketing decisions made by category managers, including new product development.

Wholesalers further benefit manufacturers by helping them to disperse their products. This allows manufacturers to control the size, travel, and expenses of their salesforce and still receive the product exposure at the retail level. At the same time, wholesalers promote new product introductions, thus increasing their awareness and building market share.

### Retailers

The benefits wholesalers provide to retailers derive, in part, from some simple observations: There are fewer wholesalers to deal with than manufacturers; they purchase in large quantities and carry extensive inventory; and they are closer to their retail customers than manufacturers.

Wholesalers, because of their location, can deliver merchandise to retailers faster, more frequently, and at a lower cost. This enables retailers to use less space, carry smaller safety stocks, offer a wider variety of product categories, and provide a higher level of service to their customers. All of these advantages reduce the operating costs and investment retailers have in their merchandise. In addition, the more productive use of square-footage selling space, ensured by lower inventory requirements, accelerates product turnover and the consequent profits.

Wholesalers offer many services to retailers in order to maintain their competitiveness in the marketplace. Retail sales training, merchandising, display, and layout are just a few of these services.

Finally, retailers only need to deal with one or two wholesalers, and thus procurement costs and personnel are minimized. Dealing with fewer sources enables retailers to build strong relationships with wholesalers.

### Consumers

Retailers offer products to consumers in the sizes suitable and convenient for household consumption. Consumers are able to buy more frequently and thus reduce the storage space and funds needed to maintain their household inventories.

Retailers also provide a wide assortment of product categories in one location. This reduces the time, expense, and travel necessary to meet household needs. It contributes also to a more varied diet than would be possible otherwise.

The prices of merchandise to consumers are much lower at retailers than they would be if products were purchased directly from manufacturers.

Finally, retailers provide an environment that consumers find conducive to shopping the store. At the same time, the atmosphere of the retail store adds another dimension to the products and services that customers demand.

## FUTURE ROLE OF WHOLESALERS

Historically, wholesalers have always responded to change in the U.S. food marketing system. Today is no exception. The changes being brought about by the **Efficient Consumer Response** movement requires wholesalers to reexamine their role in the U.S. food marketing system. A study sponsored by the **National American Wholesale Grocers' Association** explored the future role of wholesalers. It suggested that the wholesaler must evolve to become a *network optimizer* and eventually a *market maximizer* for the entire (food and non-food) supply chain.

## Network Optimizers

The goal of the network optimizer is to **minimize the delivered cost of product** from the manufacturer to the retail shelf. To achieve this goal, the wholesalers will coordinate the entire logistics process for their retailers. Regardless of whether the product moves through the wholesaler's own distribution center, in order to function as a network optimizer, a distribution network and information network must be created to support cost-effective product replenishment and payment transactions. Doing so will enable the wholesaler to reposition itself in the entire supply chain.

To ensure the lowest net delivered cost, the **distribution network system** must be able to specify how merchandise is to be shipped (e.g., full pallet, mixed pallet, or case) and the appropriate delivery method to use: cross docking, direct store delivery, or traditional receive, store, replenish, pick, and ship (**Figure 7-8**).

The **information network system** must be able to link all the participants in the U.S. food marketing system. The network must capture and manage **POS** data for forecasting and perpetual inventory management. In addition, it must support all **EDI** transactions, electronic funds transfer, and **POS** auditing to support trade promotion activities.

Finally, the role of a network optimizer calls for the wholesaler to reposition itself. This new position will allow the wholesalers to offer services to any retailer or manufacturer.

## Market Maximizers

By using the information network built to support the *network optimizer* role, wholesalers can provide more sophisticated services to their retail customers.

In the role of market maximizer, wholesalers must help retail customers develop **store-level market strategies**. Product assortments, space management, in-store merchandising, pricing, and customer service are just a few of the major areas that can be used to develop a differential advantage.

The market maximizer must also provide retailers with a better understanding of consumer behavior by linking **POS** data with the demographic profile of their customers. More effective promotions, price strategies and state-of-the-art target marketing programs should result from this linkage.

Market maximizers must customize category management. By providing activity based costing (**ABC**) and direct product profit (**DPP**) services to their retail customers, retailers and wholesalers can jointly make better category decisions.

Finally, the market maximizer must support basic communication of promotion/pricing information and **POS** audits of promotional performance. In addition, it must offer promotion coordination and promotion management services.

## SUMMARY

This chapter examined the marketing decisions that wholesalers make in order to maintain and enhance their role in the U.S. food marketing system. The nine industries that the wholesaling sector comprises were characterized as having market structures that are monopolistically competitive.

The chapter began with a historical perspective of the wholesale sector and the current role of the wholesaler. The wholesaler's role is to resolve the product, spatial, and temporal discrepancies that exist between the manufacturers' supply and the retailers' demand. To resolve these discrepancies, wholesalers make product, price, place, and promotion decisions.

Wholesalers don't create products—they create a mix of products. This mix is made up of a number of categories. To resolve **product discrepancies** (what and how much is supplied by manufacturers and demanded by retailers), wholesalers must determine the categories and quantities to purchase. From an operational viewpoint, wholesalers engage in four regrouping activities to resolve the product discrepancies of quantity and assortment: accumulating, bulk-breaking, sorting, and assorting. In the process of carrying out these regrouping activities wholesalers engage in the controversial practices of forward buying and diverting. From a strategic perspective, product decisions require that they be made within the context of category management. This management process requires that categories be defined, objectives be assigned, strategies and tactics be developed and implemented, and performance be assessed and reviewed.

To maintain the competitiveness of their retail customers, wholesalers make decisions regarding the services to offer them. Store development, store operations, and merchandising are three categories that contain several services offered to retailers.

Wholesalers make price decisions so that they generate a reasonable return for resolving product, spatial, and temporal discrepancies. The price decisions are heavily influenced by alternative revenue-generating activities that constitute the wholesaler's inside margin: forward buying, diverting, promotional deals, slotting allowances, and salvage.

While it is true that major wholesalers initiate promotional programs for their retail customers, most retail promotions are passed from manufacturers, through wholesalers, to retailers. It was estimated that at any time, retailers have between seven thousand and eight thousand deals in their files. Many of the manufacturers' promotional deals were not being passed through to retailers, so manufacturers created more complex deal terms, especially pay-for-performance programs or continuous deals.

To resolve spatial and temporal discrepancies, wholesalers make distribution decisions. To resolve **spatial discrepancies** (where merchandise is produced and where it is demanded) wholesalers focus on **external logistical** activities. These activities are referred to as inbound logistics when goods move from manufacturer to wholesaler and outbound logistics when goods move from wholesaler to retailer. The goal of external logistics is to achieve the lowest pickup and delivered cost of product from the manufacturer to the retailer. To manage external logistics, wholesalers must consider human resources, equipment, information systems, fuel supplies, security, and fleet maintenance. Further, external logistics must be scheduled, dispatched, and routed.

To resolve **temporal discrepancies** (when merchandise is produced and when it is demanded), wholesalers focus on **internal logistical** activities. The goal of internal logistics, like external logistics, is to achieve the lowest pickup and delivered cost of product from the manufacturer to the retailer. To accomplish this goal, wholesalers further specify their customer service goals in terms of inventory availability, service capability, and service quality.

Regardless of the type of distribution center operated (conventional, mechanized, or automated), from a system's perspective they all have three components: input, throughput, and output. These components correspond to a distribution center's operating functions. Shipments must first be received (input). Merchandise is then stored in active and passive inventory locations and periodically replenished (throughput). Merchandise is selected to fill retail customer orders (throughput). Lastly, merchandise is shipped to retail customers (output). To increase the efficiency of distribution centers, some merchandise comes in the receiving door and is loaded on to a trailer to be shipped without going into storage. The activity called cross docking is often carried out within a larger movement referred to as continuous replenishment. Its goal is to integrate information and product flows into a single replenishment loop from manufacturer to retail point of sale. To accomplish this goal, **POS** scan data must be used to forecast sales based on actual demand, electronically receive all receiving documents, maintain a perpetual inventory system, and utilize computer assisted ordering (**CAO**).

Wholesalers occupy a unique position in the U.S. food marketing system and are able to provide numerous benefits to manufacturers, retailers, and consumers. In general, it is less costly to use wholesalers, and products can be moved more efficiently because of the services provided by wholesalers.

Finally, the future role of the wholesaler was explored. **Network optimization** will be a core competency of the wholesaler in the future. To minimize delivered cost of product, the wholesaler must coordinate the entire logistics process by creating and operating information and distribution networks. Doing so will enable wholesalers to reposition themselves in the entire supply chain and allow them to offer their services to any retailer or manufacturer.

Eventually, the role of the network optimizer will be expanded to include market maximization. As a **market maximizer** a wholesaler must develop more sophisticated value-added services that retailers can use to expand their sales.

## SELECTED REFERENCES

Bearden, W. O., T. N. Ingram, and R. W. Laforge. *Marketing Principles and Perspectives.* Chicago: Richard D. Irwin, Inc., 1995.

Blattberg, R. C. and S. A. Neslin. *Sales Promotion Concepts, Methods, and Strategies.* Englewood Cliffs, N.J.: Prentice Hall, 1990.

Block, J. "Brave New World: The Evolving Role of Wholesalers," *Grocery Marketing*, September 1994, 14–18.

Bowersox, D. J. and M. B. Cooper. *Strategic Marketing Channel Management.* New York: McGraw-Hill, Inc., 1992.

Casper, C. "Efficient Promotion—Conquering The Maze," *U.S. Distribution Journal,* September 15, 1995, 31–43.

———. "Crossdocking at a Crossroads," *U.S. Distribution Journal,* July 15, 1995, 34–40.

———. "From Here to There," *U.S. Distribution Journal,* January 15, 1994, 25–28.

Coyle, J. J., E. J. Bardi, and C. J. Langley, Jr. *The Management of Business Logistics.* 5th ed. New York: West Publishing Co., 1992.

Dannenburg, W. P., R. L. Moncrief, and W. E. Taylor. *Introduction to Wholesale Distribution.* Englewood Cliffs, N.J.: Prentice-Hall, Inc., 1980.

Doherty, K. "SIL to the Rescue," *U.S. Distribution Journal,* October 15, 1994, 35–37.

Dori Kickey and Associates. *Grocery Marketing's* Fifth Annual National Retail and Wholesale Buyers Survey, October 18, 1995.

"Distribution Revolution," *U.S. Distribution Journal,* March 15, 1993, 22–28.

"Form = Function, The Grocery Warehouse of the Future," *U.S. Distribution Journal,* November 15, 1995, 27–29.

Fucini, S., "The Outsourcing Option," *U.S. Distribution Journal,* November 15, 1993, 25–28.

Hampe, E. C. and M. Wittenberg. *The Food Industry—Lifeline of America.* 2nd Ed. New York: McGraw-Hill, Inc., 1980.

Kaplan, A., "The 21st Century Supply Chain," *U.S. Distribution Journal,* December 15, 1995, 18–20.

Kochersperger, R. H. *Traffic and Transportation: Servicing the Grocery Industry.* Cornell/NAWGA Distribution Management Series, Cornell University Home Study Program, 1990.

———. *Grocery Distribution Center Management: Warehouse Operations.* Cornell/NAWGA Distribution Management Series, Cornell University Home Study Program, 1990.

Kurt Salmon Associates, Inc. *Efficient Consumer Response—Enhancing Customer Value in the Grocery Industry.* Washington, D.C.: Food Marketing Institute., 1993.

Lowe, K. "Brokers Key in on Technology," *Grocery Marketing*, February 1996, 10–18.

Marion, B. W. and the NC-117 Committee. *The Organization and Performance of the U.S. Food System.* Lexington, Mass: Lexington Books, D.C. Heath and Company, 1986.

Mathews, R. "Redesigning for Success . . . Wholesaling," *Grocery Marketing*, May 1993, 22–31.

Nielsen Marketing Research and the American Marketing Association, *Category Management—Positioning Your Organization to Win,* Lincolnwood, Ill: NTC Business Books, 1992.

Olson, P. R., "How Market Forces Will Drive Wholesaling," *U.S. Distribution Journal*, February 15, 1996, 12, 4.

Partch, K. "EDI and the Market-Driven Distribution System," *Supermarket Business*, January 1993, 30–40.

———. "Are You Ready for Flow-Through Logistics?" *Supermarket Business*, January 1995, 21–32.

Petreycik, R. M. "The (Second) Coming of EDI," *U.S. Distribution Journal*, October 15, 1993, 30–32.

Rosenbloom, B. *Marketing Functions and the Wholesale-Distributor: Achieving Excellence in Distribution.* Washington, D.C.: Distribution Research and Education Foundation, 1987.

Sansolo, M. "Partners vs. Profits," in *The Dynamics of Category Management, A Supplement to Promo and Progressive Grocer Magazines,* December 1993.

*Wholesale Food Distribution Today and Tomorrow.* National American Wholesale Grocers' Association. Anderson Consulting, Arthur Andersen and Co., S.C., 1994.

Wright, M. W. "The Redefining of Distribution," *U.S. Distribution Journal,* February 15, 1995 14–15, 42.

## REVIEW QUESTIONS

1. Explain the fundamental role of the wholesaler.

2. How do wholesalers resolve product, spatial, and temporal discrepancies?

3. Explain category management from philosophical, process, and organizational perspectives.

4. What services do wholesalers provide retailers to enable them to maintain their competitiveness?

5. Explain the wholesaler's two streams of revenue.

6. What is meant by a manufacturer's "continuous deal" promotion?

7. How do external logistical activities resolve spatial discrepancies?

8. How do internal logistical activities resolve temporal discrepancies?

9. What benefits do wholesalers provide to manufacturers, retailers, and consumers?

10. What is the future role of the wholesaler in the U.S. food marketing system?

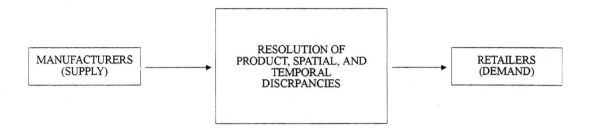

**FIGURE 7-1.** FUNDAMENTAL ROLE OF WHOLESALERS

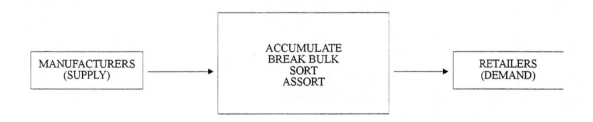

**FIGURE 7-2.** PRODUCT DISCREPANCY RESOLUTION: REGROUPING ACTIVITIES

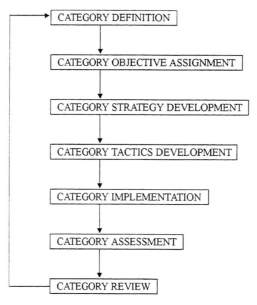

**FIGURE 7-3.** MAJOR ACTIVITIES OF CATEGORY MANAGEMENT

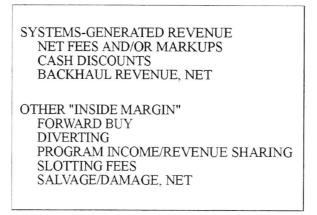

**FIGURE 7-4.** WHOLESALER OPERATING REVENUE

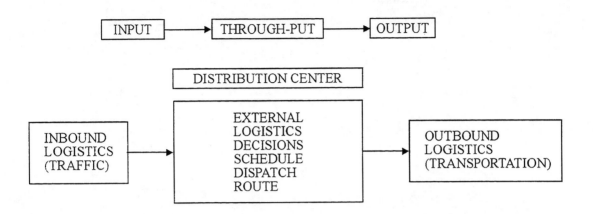

**FIGURE 7-5.** SPATIAL DISCREPANCY RESOLUTION: EXTERNAL LOGISTICS

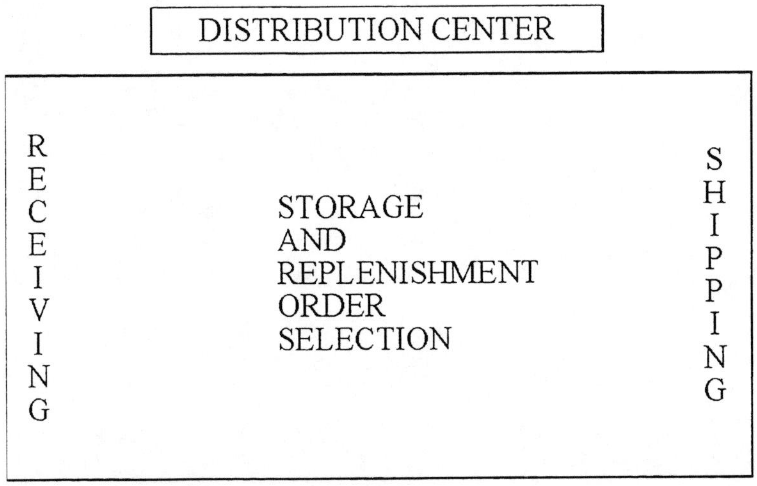

**FIGURE 7-6.** TEMPORAL DISCREPANCY RESOLUTION: INTERNAL LOGISTICS

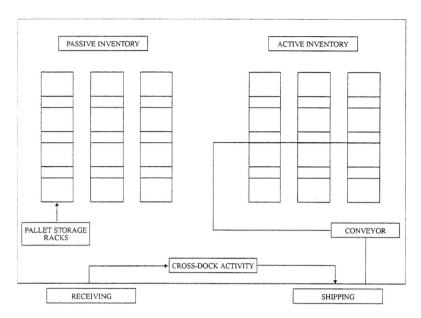

**FIGURE 7-7.** DISTRIBUTION CENTER LAYOUT

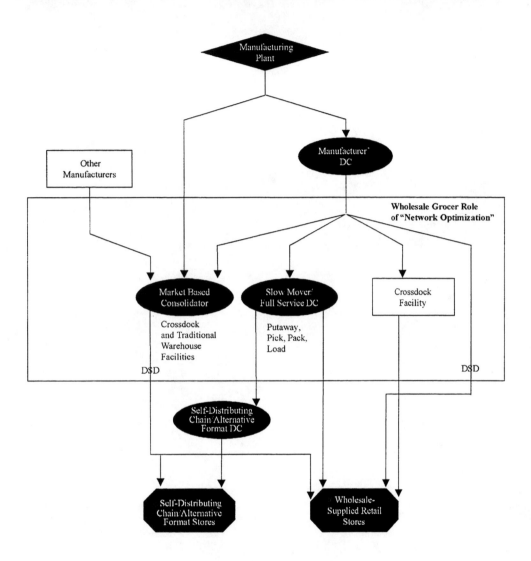

**FIGURE 7-8.** FUTURE ROLE OF WHOLESALERS

*SOURCE: Grocery Marketing*, Brave New World: The Evolving Role of Wholesalers, September 1994.

Marketing Decisions ■ 283

# Chapter 8

# Retail Food Stores

**Chapter Outline**

Foodstore Retailing Sector
- A. Industry Groups
- B. Establishments and Sales
- C. Employment
- D. Location

Retail Firms
- A. Single Unit and Multiunit Firms
- B. Sales Size of Firms
- C. Share of Sales by Largest Firms

Retail Trade Perspective
- A. Annual Report of the Grocery Industry
- B. Annual Consumer Expenditure Survey
- C. Annual Update of Store Formats and All Commodity Volume (ACV)

Leading Companies
- A. Supermarkets
- B. Wholesale Clubs

C. Supercenters

D. Limited Assortment Stores

E. Convenience Stores

Summary

The wholesaling sector of the **U.S. food marketing system** was examined in the two previous chapters. In Chapter 6 the structural organization of the nine industries that make up the sector was characterized as monopolistically competitive. When examined by sales size, most of the sales are generated by a small group of multiunit firms classified as merchant wholesalers. These merchant wholesalers are, in most cases, affiliated with retailers either by ownership (retail cooperative) or by agreement (voluntary group).

Chapter 7 examined the marketing decisions made by merchant wholesalers in this monopolistically competitive sector. The role of the wholesaler is to resolve the product, spatial, and temporal discrepancies that exist between the manufacturers' supply and the retailers' demand. Wholesalers resolve product discrepancies by their merchandising, pricing, and promotional activities. Spatial and temporal discrepancies are resolved by their distribution activities.

This chapter begins with a structural analysis of the retailing sector of the U.S. food marketing system. **Retailers are generally defined as businesses that engage primarily in the sales of merchandise to final consumers for personal or household consumption,** and the rendering of services that facilitate the sale of merchandise.

From a U.S. food marketing system's perspective, these businesses are retail stores. The merchandise they sell is food for home preparation and consumption. The services they offer are, in some cases, *essential* to operate the retail store. In other cases, these services may be *expected* by customers. Finally, in still other cases, retailers may offer services that are neither essential nor expected *(optional)*.

Because of the significant amount of data available on retailing, the structural analysis uses data from two sources. Census of Retail Trade data for the years 1982, 1987, and 1992 is used to establish earlier trends. This data is supplemented with data from industry sources. Although the use of both sources of data enhances the structural analysis, there is an absence of consistency in the retail classifications used by government and industry. Thus, any conclusions regarding the structure of the retailing sector are based essentially on the perspective chosen to analyze the data: government or industry.

# FOODSTORE RETAILING SECTOR

Foodstore retailers are classified in the **Census of Retail Trade**. Their **Standard Industrial Classification** major group is **54—Food Stores**. The foodstore retailing sector is made up of seven (three-digit) industry groups classified on the basis of firms and establishments by kind of business. A **firm** is a legal entity that owns one or more establishments. An **establishment** is a single physical location at which retail business is conducted.

The industry groups are Grocery Stores (541), Meat and Fish (Seafood) Markets (542), Fruit and Vegetable Markets (543), Candy, Nut, and Confectionery Stores (544), Dairy Products Stores (545), Retail Bakeries (546), and Miscellaneous Food Stores (549).

The 1987 and 1992 Census of Retail Trade data reflect changes not found in the 1982 Census of Retail Trade. Beginning in 1987, **Retail Bakeries (546)** were subdivided into retail bakeries that bake and sell and those that only sell bakery products. In 1992, **Grocery Stores (541)** were subdivided into supermarkets and other general-line grocery stores, convenience food stores, convenience food/gasoline stores, and delicatessens. None of these subdivisions has a four-digit industry code designation.

## Industry Groups

The structural analysis of major group **54—Food Stores** is based on the seven industry groups. Grocery stores, the first group, is essentially a general line retail store. The other six industry groups are classified based on the products they offer to the consuming public. To understand their differences a brief definition of each industry group is provided.

### Grocery Stores (541)

This industry group consists of four subdivisions. **Supermarkets and other general-line stores** includes all establishments (supermarkets, food stores, grocery stores, food warehouses) primarily engaged in the retail sale of a wide variety of merchandise. **Convenience food stores** engage in the retail sale of a medium variety of grocery items in limited amounts. **Convenience Food/Gasoline Stores** sell, in addition to a medium variety of grocery items, gasoline. Gasoline sales may not exceed forty-nine percent of total sales. **Delicatessens** primarily engage in the retail sale of prepared sandwiches, carry-out, party, and gourmet platters for take-home consumption.

### Meat and Fish Markets (542)

This industry group is primarily engaged in the retail sale of fresh, frozen, or cured meats, fish, shellfish, and other seafoods. They may also sell poultry, dairy products, eggs, or other commodities.

### Fruit and Vegetable Markets (543)

These establishments primarily sell fresh fruits and fresh vegetables. They may also sell a limited variety of grocery items.

### Candy, Nut, and Confectionery Stores (544)

This group of stores sell nuts, popcorn, boxed or bulk candy, and other confections. Candied fruits, chewing gum, ice cream, frozen yogurt, and soft drinks are often sold in these stores.

### Dairy Products Stores (545)

These establishments primarily engage in the retail sale of packaged dairy products such as milk, cream, butter, cheese, and related products to over-the-counter customers.

### Retail Bakeries (546)

This industry group consists of stores that sell, at retail, bakery products. These products may be purchased from others or made on the premises.

### Misc. Food Stores (549)

Establishments not classified elsewhere are included in this industry group. Eggs, poultry, health foods, vitamins, spices, herbs, coffee, and tea are examples of specialized foods sold in this industry group's retail establishments.

## Establishments and Sales

The changes in the number of firms, establishments, sales, and employees is shown in **Table 8-1**. Firms increased by seven percent, and establishments by 2.5 percent. There are more establishments than firms because a firm may own one or more establishments. Unadjusted for inflation, sales increased fifty-four percent over the ten-year period.

**Table 8-2** examines establishments and sales by industry groups. The number of establishments increased in four industry groups: grocery, fruits and vegetables, bakeries, and miscellaneous food stores. Three industry groups experienced decreases in sales over the census years: meat and fish, confections, and dairy products stores. Dairy products stores declined from 4,777 to 880, or by eighty-two percent.

The share of establishments and sales by industry groups is shown in **Table 8-3**. The share of retail stores increased for grocery, bakeries, and miscellaneous food stores. However, only grocery stores increased their share of retail sales. Clearly, grocery stores had the largest share of stores and sales.

The census bureau provided a more detailed breakdown of grocery stores in the 1992 census. **Table 8-4** presents this grocery store breakdown. Supermarkets and other general-line grocery stores had fifty-five percent of the stores, eighty-nine percent of all grocery store sales, and eighty-five percent of all U.S. retail food store sales (not shown in table). The dominance of supermarkets and other general-line stores is apparent throughout the food retailing sector.

## Employment

The employment trends in food retailing are revealed in **Table 8-5**. The number of employees increased by twenty-six percent. Grocery, candy, nut, and confectionery, and miscellaneous food stores accounted for this increase. The largest share of employees are in grocery and retail bakeries. Although not shown, supermarkets and other general-line stores employ over eighty-seven percent of grocery employees and seventy-nine percent of all retail employees.

## Location

Food retailing activity is reported by all fifty states. However, as expected, some of the states had higher levels of retail activity than others. The location of retailing will be reviewed in terms of food store sales and number of establishments. Because the Census Bureau doesn't geographically analyze sales by firms, the analysis by establishments identifies the number of different locations at which retail sales are made in a state.

The top ten states were chosen as a basis of comparisons for the same two reasons that the top ten wholesalers were chosen for comparison. First, these states contain the majority of all retail establishments. Second, they produce the majority of retail sales. Because retailers need to be near their consumer customers, the numbers of retail establishments and sales are closely related to the population sizes of the respective states. In general, densely populated states have larger numbers of retail establishments and sales than do sparsely populated states.

The change in the share of establishments and sales is revealed in **Table 8-6**. The ten leading states increased their share of establishments from 53.5 to 54.6 percent, but lost about one percent of their sales share.

The share of establishments and sales of the leading ten states is shown in **Table 8-7**. Over the ten years, the states have changed very little. The top nine states remained in the same order over the census periods. Only North Carolina and Virginia changed places in 1992. Three states—California, New York, and Texas—generated over one-half of the sales in the ten leading states, and over one-quarter of all retail sales.

# RETAIL FIRMS

The Census of Retail Trade provides an analysis of firms as well as establishments. A firm (company) may have only one establishment engaged in retail food activities (single unit) or two or more establishments engaged in retail food activities (multiunit).

## Single Unit and Multiunit Firms

As shown in **Table 8-8**, over the census periods, the number of single unit and multiunit firms increased seven and four percent respectively. Unadjusted for price inflation, single unit sales increased forty-two percent and multiunit sales increased sixty percent.

**Table 8-9** presents the trend in the share of firms and sales for single unit and multiunit firms. Single unit firms remained relatively constant at ninety-four percent of all firms, but their share of sales declined by two percent. The roughly six percent of multiunit firms increased their share of sales two percent to seventy-six percent of all retail sales. Thus, although small in number, these multiunit firms accounted for a disproportionate share of sales.

## Sales Size of Firms

When firms are examined by sales size, the dominance of large firms (250 million dollars in sales or more) is clearly revealed. **Table 8-10** presents a breakdown of firms by sales size. With the exception of firms whose sales are less than one million dollars, all other retail firms increased in number. Unadjusted for price inflation, all firms increased their sales.

**Table 8-11** shows the share of firms and sales by the sales size of firms. Approximately one-tenth of all stores (250 million dollars or more) accounted for fifty-eight percent of all sales. Stores with ten million or more in sales, while representing only two percent of all stores, accounted for about seventy-three percent of all sales. It is apparent that the retail sector has two distinct groups: a small group of firms that account for a disproportionately large share of all retail sales, and a large group of firms that account for an increasingly smaller share of sales. Although not shown in **Table 8-11**, ninety percent of the firms in the small group are supermarkets and other general-line stores.

## Share of Sales by Largest Firms

The share of sales, or **concentration ratio**, is computed by dividing the sales of leading firms by the total retail sales. As previously noted, a four-firm ratio greater than fifty percent is considered an oligopolistic industry; between thirty-three and fifty percent a industry is classified as a weak oligopoly; below thirty-three percent, an industry is considered competitive.

**Table 8-12** presents the concentration of sales for the entire retail sector. The share of sales for the four largest firms stayed unchanged from 1982 to 1992. However, the share of sales for the eight, twenty, and fifty largest firms increased. In 1992, the fifty largest retail firms (or three-tenths of all 127,575 retail firms) generated forty-eight percent of all retail sales. Although significant, at the sector level there is no evidence of concentration.

**Table 8-13** indicates the change in concentration ratios by industry groups. Meat and Fish Stores (542) and Candy, Nut, and Confectionery (544) are the only industry groups that experienced an increase in concentration for the four, eight, twenty, and fifty largest firms over the census periods. Dairy Products Stores (545) is the only industry group that experienced a decrease in concentration for all of its largest firms over the census periods.

When examined in terms of the four-firm concentration ratio, none of the industry groups can be defined as even a weak, let alone strong, oligopoly. However, unlike manufacturers and wholesalers who sell in national geographic markets, the relevant geographic market for the retailer is much smaller. In fact, there is considerable agreement that retailers sell in geographic markets that are inherently local. Typically, consumers do not travel great distances to purchase food. As a consequence, the Federal Trade Commission (FTC) has accepted the **Metropolitan Statistical Areas (MSA)** as more relevant geographic markets for the purpose of concentration ratio analysis. An **MSA** is an integrated economic and social unit consisting of one or more counties with a population nucleus of at least fifty thousand inhabitants. Unfortunately, the Census of Retail Trade does not, as a matter of policy, analyze and publish, in their Census of Retail Trade, four-firm concentration ratios for the 268 metropolitan statistical areas. However, concentration ratios can be computed from *Progressive Grocer's* annual **Market Scope.**

**Table 8-14** identifies the sales share of the four largest supermarkets in the one hundred largest MSAs. The MSAs contain sixty-two percent of the U.S. population. *Progressive Grocer* defines a supermarket as a retail firm that generates two million dollars or more in annual sales. Thus, conventional supermarkets, combination stores, superstores, limited assortment stores, warehouse stores, super warehouse stores, and supercenters are included in the general umbrella of "supermarkets."

The median share of sales in the MSAs was seventy percent in census years 1992 and 1995. The **average** level of sales concentration increased from 66.4 percent in 1992 to 68.6 percent in 1995. Using the economic convention for market structure definition, in 1992, only two of the top one hundred **MSAs** had competitive market structures, ten MSAs had weak oligopolistic market structures, and the remaining eighty-eight **MSAs** were oligopolistic in structure. In 1995, only one **MSA** remained a competitive structure; eight had weak oligopolistic market structures, and the remaining ninety-one MSAs were defined as oligopolistic market structures. The most significant change in sales concentration occurred in those **MSAs** whose concentration was sixty-six percent or greater. Although the number of **MSAs** in these categories remained the same, the number of **MSAs** with concentrations of eighty-one percent or greater increased by seventy percent (from ten to seventeen).

It is clear, from the analysis of Table 8-14, that the retail sector is highly concentrated in the one hundred largest MSAs. Even though there isn't any information available on the remaining 168 MSAs, there is no reason to believe that they are any less concentrated.

# RETAIL TRADE PERSPECTIVE

The previous structural analyses used U.S. Bureau of the Census retail classification as a basis for conclusions. Food stores are classified into either one of four subdivisions in the industry group **Grocery Stores** or one of six specialty industry groups defined by the products they carry.

Information provided by the retail trade does not exactly correspond to U.S. Bureau of the Census classifications. What's more, the classifications used in the annual trade industry reports are not in exact agreement with each other. The inconsistencies in retail classification definitions make it difficult to compare their conclusions. However, because these reports are published in respected trade journals, there is much face validity in their analyses.

The purpose of the following is to extend the analysis of the retail sector. The three major annual trade industry reports will be examined, and conclusions drawn accordingly.

## Annual Report of the Grocery Industry

The annual report of the grocery industry is produced and published by *Progressive Grocer Associates*. One section of the report tracks industry sales volume by store format or classification. This report classifies food stores into four groups: supermarkets, convenience, wholesale clubs, and other.

**Table 8-15** shows a three-year trend in store formats and sales volume. Supermarkets have increased from 21.9 to 23.2, percent and their sales share has increased from 74.9 to 75.6 percent. Clearly, supermarkets generated the vast majority of sales. Even though they make up fewer than one percent of all firms, wholesale clubs produced five percent of all grocery sales. The trend in convenience and other stores continued to decline both in share of stores and sales.

Three **supermarket** formats are shown in **Table 8-16**. Over the three-year period, **conventional** supermarkets have declined in share of stores (sixty-four percent to sixty-two percent) and sales (forty-eight percent to forty-five percent). **Extended** supermarkets increased their share of stores (twenty-four percent to twenty-six percent) and sales (thirty-eight percent to forty-two percent), while **economy** supermarkets declined in share of stores (12.3 percent to twelve percent) and share of sales (fifteen percent to thirteen percent).

**Table 8-17** tracks the performance of chains and independents from 1993 to 1995. Independents declined in share of stores (forty percent to thirty-eight percent) and sales (twenty-seven percent to twenty-three percent). A substantial portion of the decline is attributable to the year to year graduation of independents into the chain category. However, although not shown in the table, a number of independent supermarkets are no longer in operation.

## ANNUAL CONSUMER EXPENDITURE SURVEY

The annual consumer expenditure survey appears in *Supermarket Business* and is published by **Howfrey Communications, Inc**. One section of the report tracks industry sales volume by store format. This report classifies stores into grocery and specialty stores. Although similar to census classifications, grocery stores are subdivided on the basis of annual sales volume.

**Table 8-18** reveals a three-year trend in store formats and sales volume. Supermarkets increased their share of stores (twenty-two percent to 22.8 percent) and sales (74.1 percent to 74.9 percent) and other grocery stores declined in share (68.5 percent to 66.6 percent) and sales (14.6 percent to 13.6 percent). Both of these findings are consistent with the findings from the previous analysis of *Progressive Grocer* data.

The shares of chain and independent stores and sales are shown in **Table 8-19**. Unlike the *Progressive Grocer,* the chain designation is not restricted to supermarkets only. Thus, the share of chain stores to all food stores, except specialty food stores, is roughly twenty percent. Chains increased their share of sales (85.1 percent to 86 percent) as well as store share (19.2 percent to 24 percent). These findings are not only consistent with those reported for *Progressive Grocer,* but also with the findings from the Census of Retail Trade analysis.

### Annual Update of Store Formats and All Commodity Volume (ACV)

The annual update of store formats and all commodity volume appears in *Competitive Edge* published by **Willard Bishop Consulting, LTD. All Commodity Volume (ACV)** represents the share of total grocery sales achieved by a particular store

**format.** The constantly changing store sizes, product mixes, and merchandising philosophies have produced fourteen distinct store formats. The format definitions, along with examples provided by *Competitive Edge,* are reproduced in **Figure 8-1**.

**Table 8-20** tracks the three-year trend in share of store formats and **ACV**. The share of stores has declined for traditional channels and increased for non-traditional channels. Although not shown, the number of stores in traditional channels has declined from 163,110 in 1993 to 154,680 in 1995. The largest decrease occurred in the small corner-grocery format referred to as **other**. The 6,800 decrease in these stores continues the decline that began in 1980. It is this **mom and pop** store format that's been most impacted by the **ECR** movement. Over this same period, the number of stores in **non-traditional** channels increased from 1,709 to 1,892. Most of the increase in stores occurred in the supercenter format and clearly reflects the aggressive growth strategies of these firms. The increase in stores for all non-traditional formats was offset by the 213-store decline in the deep discounter format.

Despite the decline in share of stores, **traditional** channels experienced an increase in **ACV** share. Superstores, food-and-drug combos, super-warehouse stores, and petro-based convenience stores all increased their share of **ACV**. Even though the **ACV** of other **mom and pop** stores increased, it is significantly less than the 22.5 **ACV** share they had in 1980. The **ACV** share of traditional convenience stores declined. In addition, the decline in **ACV** share of conventional stores continued the decline from 1980, when the format's **ACV** was 55.2 percent. Over this same period, the share of **ACV** for **non-traditional** channels decreased. With the exception of supercenters, all **non-traditional** formats lost **ACV** share.

Despite the inconsistencies in format descriptions, a few general conclusions can be drawn from the trade reports and census data. First, conventional supermarkets continue to decline in number of stores and sales volume. Second, chain store firms continue to increase in number of stores and sales volume. Third, smaller formats, such as convenience stores, dominate the industry in number of stores, but generate a disproportionately small share of total grocery sales. Fourth, specialty retail stores account for a small share of total grocery sales. Finally, the retail sector consists of two segments. The first segment is small in number of stores, but generates the majority of sales. The second is large in number of stores, but generates an increasingly smaller share of sales.

## LEADING COMPANIES

To complete the retail sector's structural analysis, leading retail firms will be identified. While a number of trade publications report leading firms on an annual basis, none of them reports the leading firms separately in each of the fourteen store formats previously identified. What follows are trade publications of leading firms for five store formats.

## Supermarkets

Supermarkets are very broadly defined by trade industry services. Thus, any listing of leading supermarket retailers typically includes firms that operate different store formats under the same name. When this is the case, these firms do not normally report sales for each format separately. Rather, sales for all formats are combined and reported as a total.

The leading supermarkets formed in **Table 8-21** contain examples of these multi-format firms. **Kroger Co.** operates supermarkets, but also superstores and convenience stores under different names (e.g., **Dillions, Sav-Mor,** and **King Soopers**). **American Stores** operates supermarkets, superstores, and warehouse stores under names such as **Jewel Food Stores, Lucky Store, Jewel Osco,** and **Super Savor. A&P** operates supermarkets, superstores, convenience stores, and other formats under **A&P, Walbaum's, Farmer Jack, Super Fresh,** and **Kohl's. Ahold USA** operates numerous formats under names such as **Bi-Lo, Giant, Finast, Tops, Edwards Super Foods,** and **Stop and Shop**. The ten leading supermarket firms operate one-third of all supermarket chain stores and one-half of all sales reported by supermarket chains.

## Wholesale Clubs

Three firms dominate the wholesale club format: **Sam's Wholesale Club, Price Costco,** and **BJ's. Table 8-22** shows total sales for these firms. Because wholesale clubs devote a majority of their retail space to general merchandise/health and beauty aids, these sales figures exaggerate actual food sales. Together, these firms make up eighty percent of all wholesale club stores and ninety-three percent of all club sales.

## Supercenters

Although not a new store format, supercenters have grown faster than any other format in the last five years. **Wal-Mart, Meijer's, Fred Meyer,** and **Super K-mart** dominate this format. **Table 8-23** shows total sales for these firms. Together, these firms account for over ninety percent of all supercenter stores and over ninety percent of all sales.

## Limited Assortment Stores

A number of stores have introduced limited (**box**) assortment stores recently, (e.g., **Marsh Supermarkets, Certified Grocers of California,** and **Overwaitea, B.C.**). However, the format is clearly dominated by only two firms, **Aldi,** and **Save-A-Lot. Table 8-24** shows the number of stores and sales for these firms. Together, these two firms make up ninety-five percent of all box stores, and over ninety percent of all limited assortment store sales.

### Convenience Stores

The convenience store format is divided into those firms that began as convenience stores and may have added gasoline later (traditional), and gasoline stations that later added food (petroleum). Of the twenty leading firms, only eight of them are traditional, the other twelve are operated by oil companies. **Table 8-25** identifies the five leading convenience store firms, three of which are petroleum based: **Mobil, Chevron,** and **Texaco**. Together, these stores account for forty percent of all stores and roughly twenty percent of all **C-store** sales. The **Southland Corp.** alone accounts for fifteen percent of all stores and ten percent of all **C-store** sales.

# SUMMARY

This chapter examined the food retailing sector. Retailers are defined as businesses that engage primarily in the sale of merchandise to final consumers for personal or household consumption, and in the rendering of services that facilitate the sale of merchandise.

Retailers are classified in the **U.S. Census of Retail Trade** under **Standard Industrial Classification** major group **54—Food Stores**. The food retailing sector is further classified into seven industry groups with three-digit SIC codes, 541 to 549 (excluding 547 and 548). At the industry-group level, retailers are defined by kind of business.

**Grocery stores (541)** is essentially a general-line retailer that is further subdivided into supermarkets, convenience stores, and delicatessens. Supermarkets had over one-half of all grocery establishments and roughly ninety percent of all grocery sales. The other six industry groups are classified based on products they offer to the consumer public: **Meat and Fish Markets (542), Fruit and Vegetable Markets (543), Candy, Nut, and Confectionery Stores (544), Dairy Products Stores (545), Retail Bakeries (546),** and **Miscellaneous Food Stores (549)**. When examined by industry groups, grocery stores were seen to have increased their already dominant shares of stores and sales to seventy-four and ninety-six percent respectively.

The number of retail employees increased over the census periods. More than ninety percent of all retail employees work in the **Grocery (541)** industry group.

The ten leading states contain the majority of all retail food establishments and sales. Because the number of establishments and sales are closely related to population, in general, the larger the population, the larger the number of establishments and sales. Three states alone, **California**, **New York**, and **Texas**, accounted for over one-quarter of all retail sales.

When the retail sector was examined using firms instead of establishments, a number of conclusions were drawn. Both single unit firms (operating one establishment) and multiunit firms (operating two or more establishments) increased in number and sales. Single unit firms increased their share of stores to ninety-four percent, but decreased their share of sales to twenty-four percent.

A further examination revealed two distinct segments in the retail sector. A small group of very large retailers accounted for over seventy percent of all sales. The remaining large group of small retailers accounted for an increasingly smaller share of all sales. When examined in terms of four-firm concentration ratios, none of the industry groups could be classified as oligopolistic in market structure. However, at the local level a significant number of metropolitan statistical areas (MSAs) could be classified as strongly oligopolistic.

A second analysis of the retail sector was undertaken from the perspective of the retail industry itself. Despite the inconsistencies in store format descriptions, a few general conclusions could be drawn from trade industry reports and census data. First, conventional supermarkets, along with **mom and pop** (other) store formats, continued to decline in number and share of stores and sales volume. Second, **convenience** stores, although dominant in number, generated a disproportionately small share of total grocery sales. Third, **specialty** stores accounted for a small share of stores and sales. Fourth, **chain** store firms continued to increase their shares of sales and stores. Finally, the analysis of industry data reinforced the conclusion drawn from the census data analysis. The retail sector consists of two distinct segments. The first segment is small in number of stores, but generates the majority of sales. The remaining segment is larger in number of stores, but generates an increasingly smaller share of sales. An examination of the leading companies in five store formats lends support to this conclusion.

## SELECTED REFERENCES

*U.S. Census of Retail Trade*, U.S. Department of Commerce, Bureau of the Census 1982, 1987, and 1992.

*Competitive Edge*, Willard Bishop Consulting, LTD. Barrington, Ill. May 1994, 1995, and 1996.

Marion, B. W. and the NC-117 Committee. *The Organization and Performance of the U.S. Food System*. Lexington, Mass.: Lexington Books, D. C. Heath and Company, 1986.

*Private Label*, E. W. Williams Publications Co. Fort Lee, N.J. March–April 1996.

*Progressive Grocer*, Progressive Grocer Associates, Stamford, Conn. April 1994, 1995, and 1996.

*Supermarket Business*, Howfrey Communications. Teaneck, N.J. September 1993, 1994, and 1995.

# REVIEW QUESTIONS

1. How are retailers defined by the Census of Retail Trade?

2. How are retailers defined by kind of business?

3. Distinguish between a retail firm and a retail establishment?

4. In terms of establishments, what conclusions could you draw regarding the share of stores and sales?

5. What is the relationship between population size and retail store location?

6. In terms of sales size, what can you conclude regarding the share of stores and sales?

7. How would you characterize the impact of chain store firms on retail sales?

8. Comment on the fourteen store formats. Are the distinctions too small to be meaningful?

9. Do you believe consumers recognize fourteen different store formats? If not, how do you think consumers classify stores in their minds?

10. How would you characterize the retail food sector?

**TABLE 8-1.** SELECTED TRENDS IN U.S. RETAILING FIRMS AND ESTABLISHMENTS

| YEAR | TOTAL FIRMS | TOTAL ESTABLISHMENTS | SALES ($millions) |
|---|---|---|---|
| 1982 | 119,090 | 176,219 | 240,520 |
| 1987 | 132,050 | 190,706 | 301,847 |
| 1992 | 127,575 | 180,568 | 369,199 |

*SOURCE:* CENSUS OF RETAIL TRADE 1982, 1987, AND 1992.

**TABLE 8-2.** NUMBER OF U.S. RETAIL ESTABLISHMENTS AND SALES BY INDUSTRY GROUPS

| INDUSTRY GROUP, SIC | 1982 EST. | 1982 SALES ($millions) | 1987 EST. | 1987 SALES ($millions) | 1992 EST. | 1992 SALES ($millions) |
|---|---|---|---|---|---|---|
| GROCERY, 541 | 128,494 | 226,609 | 137,584 | 285,481 | 133,263 | 352,558 |
| MEAT AND FISH, 542 | 10,995 | 5,274 | 11,364 | 5,616 | 8,941 | 5,041 |
| FRUITS AND VEGETABLES, 543 | 2,943 | 1,330 | 3,271 | 1,802 | 2,971 | 1,809 |
| CANDY, NUT, CONFECTION, 544 | 5,113 | 800 | 6,124 | 1,182 | 5,029 | 1,224 |
| DAIRY PRODUCTS, 545 | 4,777 | 1,375 | 3,302 | 880 | 2,340 | 515 |
| RETAIL BAKERY, 546 | 17,580 | 3,543 | 21,790 | 4,871 | 20,418 | 5,387 |
| MISC. FOOD STORES, 549 | 6,317 | 1,589 | 7,271 | 2,014 | 7,606 | 2,665 |

*SOURCE:* COMPUTED FROM CENSUS OF RETAIL TRADE 1982, 1987, AND 1992.

**TABLE 8-3.** SHARE OF U.S. RETAIL ESTABLISHMENTS AND SALES BY INDUSTRY GROUPS

| INDUSTRY GROUP, SIC | 1982 % OF EST. | 1982 % OF SALES | 1987 % OF EST. | 1987 % OF SALES | 1992 % OF EST. | 1992 % OF SALES |
|---|---|---|---|---|---|---|
| GROCERY, 541 | 72.9 | 94.2 | 72.1 | 94.6 | 73.8 | 95.5 |
| MEAT AND FISH, 542 | 6.2 | 2.2 | 6.0 | 1.9 | 5.0 | 1.4 |
| FRUIT AND VEGETABLE, 543 | 1.7 | .5 | 1.7 | .6 | 1.6 | .5 |
| CANDY, NUT, CONFECTION, 544 | 2.9 | .3 | 3.2 | .4 | 2.9 | .3 |
| DAIRY PRODUCTS, 545 | 2.7 | .6 | 1.7 | .3 | 1.3 | .1 |
| RETAIL BAKERIES, 546 | 10.0 | 1.5 | 11.4 | 1.6 | 11.3 | 1.5 |
| MISC. FOOD STORES, 549 | 3.6 | .7 | 3.8 | .7 | 4.2 | .7 |
| TOTAL | 100.0 | 100.0 | 100.0 | 100.0 | 100.0 | 100.0 |

SOURCE: COMPUTED FROM CENSUS OF RETAIL TRADE 1982, 1987, AND 1992.

**TABLE 8-4.** SHARE OF U.S. RETAIL ESTABLISHMENTS AND SALES FOR INDUSTRY GROUP, 541-GROCERY STORES

| GROCERY STORES (541) | % ESTABLISHMENTS | % SALES |
| --- | --- | --- |
| Supermarkets and Other General Line Grocery Stores | 55.0 | 89.1 |
| Convenience | 23.1 | 4.9 |
| Convenience/Gasoline | 17.3 | 5.5 |
| Delicatessens | 4.6 | .5 |
| Total | 100.0 | 100.0 |

*SOURCE:* COMPUTED FROM CENSUS OF RETAIL TRADE 1992.

**TABLE 8-5.** NUMBER AND SHARE OF EMPLOYMENT BY INDUSTRY GROUPS

| INDUSTRY GROUP, SIC | 1982 (thousands) | (%) | 1987 (thousands) | (%) | 1992 (thousands) | (%) |
|---|---|---|---|---|---|---|
| GROCERY, 541 | 2,031 | 86.5 | 2,502 | 87.6 | 2,682 | 90.3 |
| MEAT AND FISH, 542 | 62 | 2.6 | 59 | 2.1 | 45 | 1.5 |
| FRUITS AND VEGETABLES, 543 | 17 | .7 | 20 | .7 | 16 | .5 |
| CANDY, NUT, CONFECTION, 544 | 23 | 1.0 | 31 | 1.1 | 26 | .9 |
| DAIRY PRODUCTS, 545 | 27 | 1.1 | 17 | .6 | 8 | .3 |
| RETAIL BAKERY, 546 | 159 | 6.8 | 186 | 6.5 | 157 | 5.3 |
| MISC. FOOD STORES, 549 | 29 | 1.2 | 40 | 1.4 | 35 | 1.2 |
| TOTAL | 2,348 | 100.0 | 2,855 | 100.0 | 2,969 | 100.0 |

*SOURCE:* COMPUTED FROM CENSUS OF RETAIL TRADE 1982, 1987, AND 1992.

**TABLE 8-6.** SHARE OF ESTABLISHMENTS AND SALES BY STATES

| States | 1982 | | 1987 | | 1992 | |
|---|---|---|---|---|---|---|
| | % of Est. | % of Sales | % of Est. | % of Sales | % of Est. | % of Sales |
| 10 Leading States | 53.5 | 54.8 | 54.1 | 54.6 | 54.6 | 54.1 |
| 40 Remaining States | 46.5 | 45.2 | 45.9 | 45.4 | 45.4 | 45.9 |
| Total | 100.0 | 100.0 | 100.0 | 100.0 | 100.0 | 100.0 |

SOURCE: COMPUTED FROM CENSUS OF RETAIL TRADE, GEOGRAPHIC AREA SERIES 1982, 1987, AND 1992.

**TABLE 8-7.** LEADING TEN STATES BY SHARE OF ESTABLISHMENTS AND SALES

| STATE | 1982 EST. | 1982 SALES | 1987 EST. | 1987 SALES | 1992 EST. | 1992 SALES |
|---|---|---|---|---|---|---|
| California | 9.5 | 11.5 | 10.1 | 12.1 | 10.2 | 12.3 |
| New York | 8.4 | 7.1 | 8.6 | 7.1 | 9.2 | 7.0 |
| Texas | 7.4 | 7.7 | 7.2 | 7.1 | 7.0 | 7.1 |
| Florida | 5.3 | 5.2 | 5.5 | 5.6 | 5.4 | 5.7 |
| Pennsylvania | 4.9 | 4.9 | 4.7 | 4.8 | 4.6 | 4.7 |
| Ohio | 4.4 | 4.6 | 4.3 | 4.3 | 4.1 | 4.1 |
| Michigan | 3.7 | 3.5 | 3.9 | 3.3 | 4.0 | 3.0 |
| Illinois | 3.6 | 4.3 | 3.6 | 4.1 | 3.9 | 4.0 |
| New Jersey | 3.3 | 3.5 | 3.3 | 3.7 | 3.5 | 3.5 |
| North Carolina | 3.0 | 2.5 | 2.9 | 2.6 | - | - |
| Virginia | - | - | - | - | 2.7 | 2.7 |
| Total | 53.5 | 54.8 | 54.1 | 54.6 | 54.6 | 54.1 |

SOURCE: COMPUTED FROM CENSUS OF RETAIL TRADE, GEOGRAPHIC AREA SERIES 1982, 1987, AND 1992.

**TABLE 8-8.** SINGLE UNIT AND MULTIUNIT FIRMS AND SALES* (MILLIONS)

| Year | Single Unit Firms | Single Unit Sales | Multiunit firms | Multiunit Sales |
|---|---|---|---|---|
| 1982 | 111,336 | 61,665 | 7,754 | 176,297 |
| 1987 | 123,644 | 74,956 | 8,406 | 226,891 |
| 1992 | 119,514 | 87,375 | 8,061 | 281,824 |

*INCLUDES ONLY FIRMS IN BUSINESS AT END OF YEAR.

SOURCE: CENSUS OF RETAIL TRADE 1982, 1987, AND 1992.

**TABLE 8-9.** SHARE OF SINGLE UNIT AND MULTIUNIT FIRMS AND SALES

|  | 1982 | | 1987 | | 1992 | |
|---|---|---|---|---|---|---|
|  | % of Firms | % of Sales | % of Firms | % of Sales | % of Firms | % of Sales |
| Single Unit | 93.5 | 25.9 | 93.6 | 24.7 | 93.7 | 23.7 |
| Multiunit | 6.5 | 74.1 | 6.4 | 75.3 | 6.3 | 76.3 |
| Total | 100.0 | 100.0 | 100.0 | 100.0 | 100.0 | 100.0 |

SOURCE: COMPUTED FROM CENSUS OF RETAIL TRADE 1982, 1987, AND 1992.

**TABLE 8-10.** SALES SIZE OF RETAIL FIRMS*

| Annual Sales ($millions) | 1982 | | 1987 | | 1992 | |
|---|---|---|---|---|---|---|
|  | No. of Firms | Sales (millions) | No. of Firms | Sales (millions) | No. of Firms | Sales (millions) |
| ≥$250 | 102 | 120,255 | 112 | 161,892 | 125 | 211,216 |
| $100-249 | 91 | 13,987 | 118 | 17,655 | 125 | 19,744 |
| $10-99 | 1,323 | 32,616 | 1,599 | 39,021 | 1,881 | 46,988 |
| $1-9 | 16,761 | 44,300 | 19,233 | 51,087 | 21,114 | 55,250 |
| < $1 | 91,291 | 24,476 | 87,377 | 27,337 | 82,125 | 29,640 |
| Total | 109,567 | 235,634 | 108,439 | 296,994 | 105,370 | 362,838 |

*INCLUDES FIRMS OPERATED DURING THE ENTIRE YEAR.

SOURCE: CENSUS OF RETAIL TRADE 1982, 1987, AND 1992.

**TABLE 8-11.** SHARE OF FIRMS AND SALES BY SIZE OF FIRMS

| Annual Sales ($millions) | 1982 | | 1987 | | 1992 | |
|---|---|---|---|---|---|---|
| | % of Firms | % of Sales | % of Firms | % of Sales | % of Firms | % of Sales |
| ≥$250 | .09 | 51.30 | .10 | 54.50 | .12 | 58.20 |
| $100-249 | .08 | 5.90 | .11 | 5.90 | .12 | 5.40 |
| $10-99 | 1.20 | 13.80 | 1.47 | 13.10 | 1.79 | 13.00 |
| $1-9 | 15.30 | 18.80 | 17.74 | 17.20 | 20.04 | 15.20 |
| < $1 | 83.32 | 10.40 | 80.57 | 9.20 | 77.94 | 8.20 |
| Total | 100.00 | 100.00 | 100.00 | 100.00 | 100.00 | 100.00 |

SOURCE: COMPUTED FROM CENSUS OF RETAIL TRADE 1982, 1987, AND 1992.


**TABLE 8-12.** SALES CONCENTRATION OF LARGEST RETAIL FIRMS

| NO. OF FIRMS | PERCENTAGE OF TOTAL SALES | | |
|---|---|---|---|
| | 1982 | 1987 | 1992 |
| 4 LARGEST FIRMS | 15.4 | 16.5 | 15.4 |
| 8 LARGEST FIRMS | 22.7 | 25.1 | 24.2 |
| 20 LARGEST FIRMS | 35.5 | 35.2 | 35.9 |
| 50 LARGEST FIRMS | 42.1 | 45.1 | 47.6 |

SOURCE: CENSUS OF RETAIL TRADE 1982, 1987, AND 1992.

**TABLE 8-13.** SALES CONCENTRATION OF LARGEST RETAIL FIRMS BY INDUSTRY GROUPS

| (TABLE 8-13. cont.) Industry Group, SIC | 1982 % of Sales | 1987 % of Sales | 1992 % of Sales |
|---|---|---|---|
| Grocery Stores, 541 | | | |
| 4 Largest Firms | 16.4 | 17.4 | 16.1 |
| 8 Largest Firms | 24.1 | 26.5 | 25.3 |
| 20 Largest Firms | 35.6 | 37.2 | 37.6 |
| 50 Largest Firms | 44.7 | 47.7 | 49.9 |
| Meat and Fish Stores, 542 | | | |
| 4 Largest Firms | 2.4 | 3.3 | 4.7 |
| 8 Largest Firms | 3.6 | 4.3 | 5.8 |
| 20 Largest Firms | 5.9 | 6.7 | 7.9 |
| 50 Largest Firms | 9.3 | 10.5 | 11.5 |
| Fruit and Vegetable Stores, 543 | | | |
| 4 Largest Firms | 4.5 | 4.1 | 4.1 |
| 8 Largest Firms | 7.3 | 6.6 | 6.7 |
| 20 Largest Firms | 12.7 | 12.4 | 12.7 |
| 50 Largest Firms | 21.3 | 21.5 | 21.9 |
| Candy, Nut, Confection Stores, 544 | | | |
| 4 Largest Firms | 23.8 | 21.6 | 25.1 |
| 8 Largest Firms | 29.0 | 27.1 | 29.7 |
| 20 Largest Firms | 36.1 | 34.3 | 36.5 |
| 50 Largest Firms | 44.0 | 42.5 | 44.5 |
| Dairy Products Stores, 545 | | | |
| 4 Largest Firms | 28.0 | 20.7 | 27.4 |
| 8 Largest Firms | 38.7 | 28.3 | 33.0 |
| 20 Largest Firms | 47.1 | 36.4 | 39.7 |
| 50 Largest Firms | 53.9 | 44.5 | 48.6 |
| Retail Bakeries, 546 | | | |

| (TABLE 8-13. cont.)<br>Industry Group, SIC | 1982 % of<br>Sales | 1987 % of<br>Sales | 1992 % of<br>Sales |
|---|---|---|---|
| 4 Largest Firms | 7.6 | 8.8 | 7.4 |
| 8 Largest Firms | 10.0 | 11.8 | 10.6 |
| 20 Largest Firms | 12.7 | 15.6 | 14.2 |
| 50 Largest Firms | 16.1 | 19.1 | 17.3 |
| Misc. Food Stores, 549 | | | |
| 4 Largest Firms | 23.7 | 21.0 | (D)* |
| 8 Largest Firms | 26.6 | 23.3 | (D)* |
| 20 Largest Firms | 32.4 | 27.7 | 24.7 |
| 50 Largest Firms | 38.7 | 34.3 | 29.8 |

(D)* DATA NOT DISCLOSED.

*SOURCE:* CENSUS OF RETAIL TRADE 1982, 1987, AND 1992.

**TABLE 8-14.** LARGEST FOUR FIRM'S SHARE OF SALES IN TOP 100 METROPOLITAN STATISTICAL AREAS (MSAs)

| Largest Four Firm's Share of Sales | 1992 Number of MSAs | 1995 Number of MSAs |
|---|---|---|
| 0-30 | 1 | 0 |
| 31-35 | 1 | 1 |
| 36-40 | 2 | 1 |
| 41-45 | 4 | 1 |
| 46-50 | 4 | 5 |
| 51-55 | 13 | 9 |
| 56-60 | 15 | 17 |
| 61-65 | 9 | 16 |
| 66-70 | 17 | 13 |
| 71-75 | 14 | 12 |
| 76-80 | 10 | 8 |
| 81-85 | 5 | 10 |
| 86-90 | 5 | 7 |

SOURCE: COMPUTED FROM *PROGESSIVE GROCER'S* MARKET SCOPE, 1993 AND 1996.

**TABLE 8-15.** GROCERY INDUSTRY STORE FORMAT AND SALES VOLUME TRENDS

|  | 1993 | | 1994 | | 1995 | |
| --- | --- | --- | --- | --- | --- | --- |
| Format | % of Firms | % of Sales | % of Firms | % of Sales | % of Firms | % of Sales |
| Supermarket (1) | 21.9 | 74.9 | 22.6 | 74.9 | 23.2 | 75.6 |
| Convenience | 42.7 | 6.9 | 44.3 | 6.9 | 43.8 | 6.6 |
| Wholesale Club | .5 | 4.9 | .6 | 5.1 | .6 | 4.8 |
| Other Store (2) | 34.9 | 13.3 | 32.5 | 13.1 | 32.4 | 13.0 |
| Total | 100.0 | 100.0 | 100.0 | 100.0 | 100.0 | 100.0 |

(1) SUPERMARKETS ($2 MILLION OR MORE IN SALES) INCLUDES COMBINATION, SUPERSTORES, LIMITED ASSORTMENT, WAREHOUSES, SUPER WAREHOUSES, AND HYPERMARKET/SUPERCENTERS.

(2) OTHER-NOT ELSEWHERE CLASSIFIED.

*SOURCE:* ANNUAL REPORT OF THE GROCERY INDUSTRY, *PROGESSIVE GROCER*, APRIL 1994, 1995, AND 1996.

**TABLE 8-16.** TRENDS IN SALES VOLUME AND SUPERMARKET FORMATS

| Supermarket Format | 1993 | | 1994 | | 1995 | |
|---|---|---|---|---|---|---|
| | % of Firms | % of Sales | % of Firms | % of Sales | % of Firms | % of Sales |
| Conventional | 64.3 | 47.6 | 63.2 | 45.8 | 61.8 | 45.4 |
| Extended * | 23.5 | 37.7 | 24.7 | 39.2 | 26.2 | 41.7 |
| Economy ** | 12.3 | 14.5 | 12.1 | 15.0 | 12.0 | 12.9 |
| Total | 100.0 | 100.0 | 100.0 | 100.0 | 100.0 | 100.0 |

*INCLUDES COMBINATION AND SUPERSTORES.

**INCLUDES LIMITED ASSORTMENT, WAREHOUSES, SUPER WAREHOUSES, HYPERMARKET/SUPERCENTERS.

SOURCE: ANNUAL REPORT OF THE GROCERY INDUSTRY, PROGRESSIVE GROCER, APRIL 1994, 1995, AND 1996.

**TABLE 8-17.** SHARE OF SUPERMARKET CHAIN AND INDEPENDENT STORES AND SALES VOLUME

| Supermarket Format | 1993 | | 1994 | | 1995 | |
|---|---|---|---|---|---|---|
| | % of Firms | % of Sales | % of Firms | % of Sales | % of Firms | % of Sales |
| Chain* | 59.7 | 72.7 | 60.7 | 74.4 | 62.1 | 77.1 |
| Independent | 40.3 | 27.3 | 39.3 | 25.6 | 37.9 | 22.9 |
| Total | 100.0 | 100.0 | 100.0 | 100.0 | 100.0 | 100.0 |

*CHAIN=11 OR MORE STORES

SOURCE: ANNUAL REPORT OF THE GROCERY INDUSTRY, PROGRESSIVE GROCER, APRIL 1994, 1995, AND 1996.

**TABLE 8-18.** FOOD STORE SALES AND FORMAT TRENDS

|  | 1993 | | 1994 | | 1995 | |
| --- | --- | --- | --- | --- | --- | --- |
| Format | % of Firms | % of Sales | % of Firms | % of Sales | % of Firms | % of Sales |
| Supermarkets (1) | *22.0 | 74.1 | 22.3 | 75.0 | 22.8 | 74.9 |
| Superettes (2) | 9.6 | 5.8 | 9.6 | 5.8 | 10.6 | 6.0 |
| Other Grocery (3) | 68.5 | 14.6 | 68.1 | 13.8 | 66.6 | 13.6 |
| Specialty (4) | - | 5.5 | - | 5.4 | - | 5.4 |
| Total | 100.0 | 100.0 | 100.0 | 100.0 | 100.0 | 100.0 |

(1) OVER $2 MILLION IN SALES, COMPLETE FULL-LINE SELF AND PARTIAL SERVICE.

(2) $1 MILLION TO $2 MILLION SELF SERVICE, OR SERVICE FOOD STORE.

(3) UNDER $1 MILLION, GENERAL FOOD STORE NOT CLASSIFIED ABOVE.

(4) SINGLE LINE INCLUDES MEAT, SEAFOOD, BAKERY, PRODUCE. (NUMBER OF FIRMS NOT DISCLOSED.

* SPECIALTY STORES NOT CONSIDERED IN COMPUTATION.

*SOURCE:* ANNUAL CONSUMER EXPENDITURE SURVEY, *SUPERMARKET BUSINESS*, SEPTEMBER, 1994, 1995, AND 1996.

**TABLE 8-19.** SHARE OF CHAIN AND INDEPENDENT STORES AND SALES VOLUME*

| Format | 1993 | | 1994 | | 1995 | |
|---|---|---|---|---|---|---|
| | % of Firms | % of Sales | % of Firms | % of Sales | % of Firms | % of Sales |
| Chain (1) | 19.2 | 85.1 | 21.1 | 85.8 | 24.0 | 86.0 |
| Independent | 80.8 | 14.9 | 78.9 | 14.2 | 76.0 | 14.0 |
| Total | 100.0 | 100.0 | 100.0 | 100.0 | 100.0 | 100.0 |

(1) CHAIN=11 OR MORE STORES.

* DOES NOT INCLUDE SPECIALTY STORES.

SOURCE: ANNUAL CONSUMER EXPENDITURE SURVEY, *SUPERMARKET BUSINESS*, SEPTEMBER 1994, 1995, AND 1996.

**TABLE 8-20.** STORE FORMAT AND ACV SHARE TRENDS

|  | 1993 | | 1994 | | 1995 | |
| --- | --- | --- | --- | --- | --- | --- |
|  | % of Stores | % of ACV | % of Stores | % of ACV | % of Stores | % of ACV |
| Traditional Channel* | | | | | | |
| Conventional | 9.3 | 26.1 | 9.5 | 25.6 | 9.5 | 24.3 |
| Superstore | 3.8 | 22.4 | 4.1 | 23.3 | 4.3 | 24.2 |
| Food Drug Combo | 1.3 | 10.2 | 1.5 | 11.2 | 1.7 | 12.3 |
| Warehouse Store | 1.5 | 6.5 | 1.3 | 5.4 | 1.1 | 4.8 |
| Super-Warehouse | .3 | 3.4 | .3 | 3.5 | .3 | 3.7 |
| Limited Assortment | .4 | .6 | .6 | .6 | .6 | .6 |
| Convenience (Trad)* | 30.2 | 6.6 | 30.3 | 6.4 | 29.6 | 5.9 |
| Convenience (Petro)* | 20.8 | 3.6 | 22.2 | 3.7 | 22.9 | 3.8 |
| Other | 31.3 | 11.8 | 29.1 | 11.4 | 28.6 | 12.1 |
| Sub-total | 98.9 | 91.2 | 98.8 | 91.1 | 98.8 | 91.6 |
| Non-Traditional Channel** | | | | | | |
| Hypermarket | .0 | .2 | .0 | .1 | .0 | .1 |
| Wholesale Club | .4 | 5.6 | .4 | 4.8 | .4 | 4.7 |
| Mini Club | .1 | .3 | .1 | .3 | .1 | .3 |
| Supercenter | .2 | 1.5 | .2 | 2.0 | .3 | 2.5 |
| Deep Discounter | .4 | 1.2 | .4 | 1.7 | .3 | .8 |
| Sub-total | 1.1 | 8.8 | 1.2 | 8.9 | 1.2 | 8.4 |
| Total | 100.0 | 100.0 | 100.0 | 100.0 | 100.0 | 100.0 |

*MERCHANDISE SALES ONLY (NON-GAS).

**REFLECTS SHARE ADJUSTMENTS FOR ITEMS NOT COMMONLY FOUND IN TRADITIONAL GROCERY CHANNEL.

*SOURCE:* COMPUTED FROM *COMPETITIVE EDGE*, MAY 1994, 1995, AND 1996.

**TABLE 8-21.** TEN LEADING SUPERMARKET COMPANIES BY SALES VOLUME, 1996

| Company | Stores | Sales ($millions) | Number of States |
|---|---|---|---|
| Kroger Co. | 2,147 | 23,938 | 27 |
| Safeway | 1,058 | 16,398 | 18 |
| American Stores | 817 | 12,877 | 11 |
| Albertson's Inc. (1) | 720 | 12,537 | 19 |
| Winn-Dixie Stores | 1,175 | 11,788 | 14 |
| A & P (2) | 1,108 | 10,084 | 24 |
| Publix Super Markets, Inc. | 573 | 9,690 | 3 |
| Ahold USA (3) | 630 | 8,300 | 14 |
| Food Lion, Inc. (4) | 1,073 | 8,200 | 14 |
| Ralph's Grocery Co. | 373 | 5,600 | 1 |
| Total | 9,674 | $119,412 | |

(1) FOREIGN OWNERSHIP: MAJORITY OWNED BY THEO ALBRECHT, GERMANY

(2) FOREIGN OWNERSHIP: MAJORITY OWNED BY TENGLEMANN GROUP, GERMANY.

(3) FOREIGN OWNERSHIP: U.S. SUBSIDIARY OF ROYAL AHOLD, ZAANDAM, NETHERLANDS.

(4) FOREIGN OWNERSHIP: U.S. SUBSIDIARY OF DELHAIZE FRÉRES ET CIE LE LION, FRANCE.

*SOURCE:* PRIVATE LABEL, DIVISION OF E.W. WILLIAMS PUBLISHING CO., FORT LEE, N.J., MARCH–APRIL 1996, p. 22.

**TABLE 8-22.** LEADING WHOLESALE CLUB COMPANIES BY SALES VOLUME

| COMPANY | STORES | SALES ($billions) |
|---|---|---|
| Sam's Wholesale Club | 461 | 20.3 |
| Price Costco | 267 | 17.9 |
| BJ's | 71 | 2.5 |
| Total | 799 | 40.7 |

*SOURCE:* SUPERMERCHANTS: MEMBERSHIP WAREHOUSE CLUB AND SUPERCENTER INDUSTRIES, OVERVIEW 1995, JAMES M. DEGEN AND CO., CAYUCOS, CA.

**TABLE 8-23.** LEADING SUPERCENTERS BY SALES VOLUME

| COMPANY | STORES | SALES ($billions) |
|---|---|---|
| Wal-Mart, Supercenters | 247 | 11.5 |
| Meijer, Inc. | 98 | 6.6 |
| Super K-mart Centers | 93 | 3.7 |
| Fred Meyer, Inc. | 93 | 2.9 |
| Total | 537 | 24.7 |

*SOURCE:* SUPERMERCHANTS: MEMBERSHIP WAREHOUSE CLUB AND SUPERCENTER INDUSTRIES, OVERVIEW 1995, JAMES M. DEGEN AND CO., CAYUCOS, CA.

**TABLE 8-24.** LIMITED ASSORTMENT (BOX) STORES BY SALES VOLUME

| COMPANY | STORES | SALES ($millions) |
|---|---|---|
| Aldi, Inc. (1) | 445 | 1,760 |
| Save-A-Lot (2) | 140 | 554 |
| Total | 585 | 2,314 |

(1) FOREIGN OWNERSHIP: U.S. SUBSIDIARY OF ALDI, GERMANY.

(2) OWNED BY SUPERVALU INC.

SOURCE: *PRIVATE LABEL* DIVISION OF E.W. WILLIAMS PUBLISHING CO., FORT LEE, N.J., MARCH-APRIL 1996, p. 22.


**TABLE 8-25.** CONVENIENCE STORES BY SALES VOLUME

| COMPANY | STORES | SALES ($millions) |
|---|---|---|
| The Southland Corp. | 6,283 | 6,746 |
| Mobil Corp. | 4,000 | 1,756 |
| Tosco Corp. | 3,057 | 3,600 |
| Chevron Corp. | 2,100 | 1,962 |
| Texaco Corp. | 1,984 | 1,698 |
| Total | 17,424 | 15,762 |

SOURCE: CONVENIENCE STORE NEWS, AUGUST 5, 1996, pp. 18-22.

1. **Conventional Supermarket**—The original supermarket format offering a full line of groceries, meat, and produce with at least two million dollars in annual sales. Conventional stores will realize six to eight percent of their sales in GM/HBC. These stores typically carry at least nine thousand items and offer a service deli, and frequently a service bakery, e.g., most smaller chain stores.

2. **Superstore**—A larger version of the conventional supermarket with at least thirty thousand square feet in total selling area and fourteen thousand or more items. Superstores offer an expanded selection of non-foods (at least ten percent GM/HBC), e.g., Kroger, American Stores, and Safeway.

3. **Food-Drug Combo**—A combination of a superstore and a drug store under a single roof with common checkouts. GM/HBC represents at least one-third of the selling area and a minimum of fifteen percent of store sales. These stores also have a pharmacy, e.g., Jewel/Osco.

4. **Warehouse Store**—A low-margin grocery store offering reduced variety, lower service levels, minimal decor, and a streamlined merchandising presentation along with aggressive pricing. Generally, warehouse stores don't offer specialty departments, e.g., Xtra.

5. **Super Warehouse**—A high-volume, hybrid format of a superstore and a warehouse store. Super warehouse stores typically offer a full range of service departments, quality perishables, and reduced prices, e.g., Cub and Omni.

6. **Limited-Assortment Store**—A "bare-bones," low-priced grocery store that provides very limited services and carries fewer than 1,500 items with limited (if any) perishables, e.g., Aldi and Save-A-Lot.

7. **Other**—The small, corner grocery store that carries a limited selection of staples and other convenience goods. These stores generate approximately one million dollars in business annually.

8. **Convenience Store (Traditional)**—A small, higher-margin grocery store that offers an edited selection of staple groceries, non-foods, and other convenience food items, i.e., ready-to-heat and ready-to eat foods. The traditional format includes those stores that started out as strictly convenience stores but might also sell gasoline, e.g., 7-Eleven, Dairy Mart, and White Hen Pantry.

9. **Convenience Store (Petroleum-Based)**—The petroleum stores are primarily gas stations with a small convenience store, e.g., Mobil Mart, Amoco Food Shops, and Shell Food Mart.

FIGURE 8-1. STORE-FORMAT DEFINITIONS

*Source: Competitive Edge*, Williard Bishop Consulting, LTD. May 1996.

10. **Hypermarket**—A very large food and general-merchandise store with at least one hundred thousand square feet of selling space. While these stores typically devote as much as seventy-five percent of their selling area to general merchandise, their sales ratio is typically 60/40, e.g., Bigg's, Twin Value, and Auchan.

11. **Wholesale Club**—A membership retail/wholesale hybrid with a varied selection and limited variety of products presented in a warehouse-type atmosphere. These ninety-thousand plus square-foot stores have sixty to seventy percent of their sales in GM/HBC and a grocery line dedicated to large sizes and bulk sales. Memberships include both business accounts and consumer groups, e.g., Sam's Club, Price Costco, BJ's, and Warehouse Club.

12. **Mini-Club**—A scaled-down version of the wholesale club. The mini-club is approximately one-fourth the size of a typical wholesale club and carries about sixty percent of the SKUs, e.g., including all of the major food and sundry departments and a limited line of merchandise (e.g., soft goods, office supplies, and opportunistic, one-time buys), e.g., Smart & Final and Mega Warehouse. Some of these stores do not have membership fees and often operate as "cash and carries."

13. **Supercenters**—A large food and drug combination store and mass merchandiser under a single roof. The supercenters offer a wide variety of food as well as non-food merchandise. These stores average more than 150,000 square feet and typically devote as much as forty percent of the space to grocery items, e.g., WalMart, K-mart, Meijer, and Fred Meyer.

14. **Deep-Discount Drug Store**—A low-margin, GM/HBC store with approximately thirty thousand square feet of selling space and 25,000 SKUs. These stores typically carry fewer sized but more GM/HBC brands than a supermarket. Food accounts for twenty percent of store sales, e.g., Drug Emporium.

**FIGURE 8-1.** (Continued)

# Chapter 9

# Marketing Decisions

**Chapter Outline**

Retailing Sector
- A. Historical Perspective
- B. Store Formats as Strategic Groups
- C. Structural Influence on Marketing Decisions
- D. Competitive Differential Advantage

Location
- A. Market Area
- B. Trade Area
- C. Store Site
- D. Location Stalemate

Store Atmosphere
- A. Interior Design
- B. Store Layout
- C. Merchandise Presentation
- D. Stalemate

Merchandise
- A. Variety—What Categories?

    B. Assortment—How Many Brands?
    C. Variation—How Much of Each Brand?
    D. Quality—The Right SKU
    E. Stalemate

Services
    A. Variety—What to Offer
    B. Assortment—How Many Services
    C. Quality
    D. Stalemate

Price
    A. Philosophies
    B. Costs
    C. Demand
    D. Competition
    E. Policies
    F. Stalemate

Promotion
    A. Advertising
    B. Sales Promotion
    C. Publicity
    D. Personal Selling
    E. Stalemate

Distribution
    A. Self-Distribution
    B. Home Delivery
    C. Home Shopping
    D. Stalemate

Summary

The changing nature of the retailing sector's structural characteristics were examined in Chapter 8. Retailers were defined as businesses that engage primarily in the sale of merchandise to final consumers for personal or household consumption and the rendering of services that facilitate the sale of merchandise.

The retail sector is made up mostly of single unit general line grocery stores. However, the majority of sales are produced by multiunit firms with sales of 250 million dollars or more. This shared dominance results in a retail sector made up of two distinct groups. A few, large multiunit retailers generate the vast majority of sales, while a much larger group of single unit retailers generate an increasingly smaller share of sales. As expected, the location of retail stores and population are highly related. The ten leading states in population contain most of the retailers and represent a majority of sales.

When examined by industries, no industry met the conventional definition of an oligopolistic market structure. The retail sector can be characterized as essentially monopolistically competitive in structure. Still, just fifty retail firms generated nearly one-half of all retail sales.

Despite the inconsistencies in retail store classifications, an examination of the retail sector from an industry perspective reinforced the conclusions drawn from census data. The examination also revealed a retail sector that is currently made up of fourteen distinct store formats. This greatly expanded perspective of competitive store formats portrays most vividly the environment within which retailers make marketing decisions.

The purpose of this chapter is to examine the marketing decisions of food retailers. Major developments that have occurred in food retailing are presented first. To establish the current competitive environment within which retailers make marketing decisions, a discussion of existing retail store formats as strategic groups is presented. Subsequent sections represent a functional analysis of retail marketing decision to create, price, promote, and distribute food products to final consumers.

# RETAILING SECTOR[*]

Although demand for manufacturers' products is ultimately determined by consumers, demand is essentially recorded at the retail level. It is the retailer that markets food to final consumers and, as such, is the first to experience the changing needs and wants of the marketplace. But these are not the only changes that retailers experience. Changes in the competitive, economic, technological, political, and legal environments also impact on retailers. Thus, the contemporary food retailing sector is the

---

[*] This section is based, in part on E.C. Hampe and M. Wittenberg, *The Food Industry—Lifeline of America,* Ithaca. N.Y.: Cornell University Press, 1990.

culmination of the countless numbers of successful attempts to (1) anticipate changes in the marketplace and environments, (2) interpret these changes within the context of the firm, (3) adapt long-run strategies to these changes, and (4) react to these changes on a tactical, day-to-day basis.

## Historical Perspective

The origin of retailing can be traced back to the pioneer trading posts. Early settlers depended on them for items they couldn't produce themselves. Most transactions at the trading post involved the exchange of commodities grown by farmers, animals killed by hunters, and fur pelts brought in by trappers for commodities imported from Europe, such as spices, tea, salt, and clothing.

As the pioneers moved into new western territories they relied on trading posts operated by the **Hudson's Bay Company** as well as store boats. These boats traveled the coasts, lakes, rivers, and canals, and like the trading posts, bartered their goods for those of the settlers. Continued population growth and the development of the railroad led to the decline of the store boat's role in retail distribution. Gradually, as trading posts expanded their merchandise offering and money became the medium of exchange, a unique American invention evolved—**the general store**.

The general store carried about one hundred items of food, mostly in bulk form. Clerks served their customers, negotiated prices, and granted credit. Although the general store remained in existence beyond the Civil War, it was to be replaced by stores specializing in a narrow range of merchandise.

The transition from an agricultural society to an industrial society, as well as the increased growth of cities, brought about the slow demise of the general store. Stores could no longer meet the entire needs of their communities. As a consequence, stores began to specialize their merchandise offerings. The grocery store, butcher shops, bakeries, and dairy stores began to replace the general store. In 1859, the **Great Atlantic and Pacific Tea Company (A&P)**, a specialty store selling tea, coffee, and spices was formed. By 1860, the specialty store replaced the general store as the dominant retail establishment.

The success of **A&P** spawned other stores. **Grand Union (1872), Kroger Company (1882), Acme Markets (1887), First National Stores (1897), and Jewel Foods (1899)** began to imitate the success of **A&P**, who by this time had two hundred stores in operation. As these stores grew in number they changed in character. The **Trade Mark Law of 1905** allowed manufacturers to brand their goods. **John Wanamaker** is credited with establishing the "all customers pay the same price" policy. Customers no longer negotiated price, but rather paid the price marked on the merchandise. The stores offered credit and delivery service and carried a limited line of groceries.

During the expansion of these early "chain" stores, the independent retail stores organized themselves into **cooperatives**. In 1888, the **Frankford Grocery Company** was established as the first retailer-owned cooperative. The basic objective of cooperatives was to secure lower prices by circumventing what was by now the dominant form of wholesaler—the **service wholesaler**. By forming their own wholesale operation, cooperatives could buy in large quantities and pass along the savings in the form of dividends. These retailer-owned cooperatives were in an excellent position to deal with what was to take place in the early 1900s.

In 1912, **A&P** opened a group of experimental **economy** stores. The objective was to reduce the cost of operating a store, and pass these savings on to consumers in the form of lower prices. These stores needed only one person to run them. Rent was low, fixtures were minimal, and no credit or delivery was offered. These stores were so successful that **A&P** decided to build all they could as quickly as possible. Other chains soon followed.

In 1916, **Clarence Saunders**, operator of **Piggly Wiggly** Food stores, had an idea to reduce costs in his stores. By reducing the number of clerks, moving the cash register to the front of the store, and having shoppers select their own merchandise, the cost savings could be passed on to customers. The idea of **self-service** was born.

The growth and expansion of large chains led independent retailers to organize once again, this time into **voluntary** groups. Red & White (1921), and **Clover Farm (1926)** were the first voluntary groups. Retailers who joined these groups agreed to work as a team to match the power of chains in buying power, operating efficiency, management shifts, and merchandising techniques. By this time most of the stores were **combinations stores**. They carried groceries, meat, and dairy products.

All the changes that had taken place up to this point in time (cash and carry, one price to all, expanded merchandise, and self-service) laid the foundation for the next phase in the evolution of retail food establishments—the **supermarket**. In August 1930, the first supermarket (**King Kullen**) opened in a huge converted garage in Jamaica, New York. In 1932, it was followed by a store called **Big Bear** in Elizabeth, New Jersey. It occupied fifty thousand square feet, fifteen thousand of which was devoted to food alone. The name *supermarket* was first used by **Albers Super Markets**, located in Cincinnati, Ohio, in 1933. In 1936, **Sylan Goldman**, the owner of two Oklahoma supermarkets, had an idea to increase sales. He reasoned that customers would buy more if they didn't have to carry the groceries around while they were shopping. His idea produced the first grocery (shopping) cart. The combination of expanded merchandise, low prices, and shopping ease led to a proliferation of supermarkets. By 1936, there were twelve hundred of them, and more being built.

The success of the supermarket was due to a number of factors. First, the supermarket adopted the concept that the consumer was paramount. Everything was done to satisfy their needs and wants. Second, it believed that customers would buy more if they could see more on display. This meant that the store had to be designed to maximize product exposure. Third, mechanical refrigerators provided dependable home storage for perishables. This meant that customers would buy more (and store it) if it was made available in open, self-service refrigerator cases. Fourth, the automobile would draw customers from miles around. This meant that the supermarket could draw customers beyond its local market if it offered them an incentive to travel the distance. Consumer promotions were designed to meet the challenge. Finally, consumers could be offered lower prices and still generate more than adequate profits. This meant that the store had to base its profits on volume (turnover) rather than markup.

Today, the supermarket, despite all its consumer-oriented policies and technological advances, is being challenged by other retail formats. In fact, the conventional supermarket's share of grocery store sales peaked at seventy percent in 1965, and is now at twenty-two percent.

## Store Formats as Strategic Groups

Fourteen distinct store formats operating in the food industry were identified in Chapter 8. Each store format can be viewed as a strategic group. A **strategic group** is a group of firms following the same, or a similar, strategy along strategic dimensions (Porter, 1980). In food retailing, these dimensions are, in almost all cases, products, services, and prices. **Figure 9-1** classifies the fourteen formats in two-dimensional space. The vertical dimension represents the extensiveness of a format's merchandising offering. These offerings range from extensive variety (many categories) to intensive variety (few categories). The horizontal axis represents a format's pricing policy as measured by its gross margin. Because of the close relationship between price levels and service offerings, the horizontal dimension includes service levels (Marion, 1986). The intersection of the horizontal and vertical dimensions represents the position occupied by the conventional supermarket.

Firms in strategic groups compete directly with other firms in the same group, and indirectly with firms in other strategic groups. At the same time, these strategic groups, or formats, compete with each other when they are in close physical or temporal proximity to one another. The degree of strategic group rivalry is determined by four factors (Porter, 1980).

The first factor is the **market interdependence** among groups, or the extent to which their target markets overlap. The most intense rivalry occurs when strategic groups are competing for the same customer. The second factor is the **degree of differentiation** in merchandise, service offerings, and price appeal. The more similar the consumer's perception of sameness in price appeal and merchandise offerings, the greater the strategic group rivalry. A third factor is the **number and size** of strategic groups. The more numerous and more equal in size the greater the competitive rivalry. The final factor is the **strategic distance** among groups, or the extent to which strategies differ. Surprisingly, the greater the distance among groups, the more rigorous the competition. Firms using widely different strategies find it difficult to understand behaviors of other groups and often react mistakenly to actions initiated by other strategic groups.

Considering the interrelationship of these four factors, a strategic group will experience the most intense rivalry when there are several equally sized groups, each competing for the same target market, using widely different strategies.

When applied to **Figure 9-1**, intense rivalry exists indirectly between and among the four quadrants because they pursue widely different strategies. Further, intense rivalry exists directly among formats in the same quadrant because several formats are competing for the same customer. On the other hand, competition is reduced because formats are unequal in size within each quadrant.

On a macro level, the direction and intensity of competition in the food retailing sector can be reviewed in terms of strategic groups that are in close physical or temporal proximity to each other. However, for this competition to exist at the micro (consumer) level, consumers must perceive the formats as close competitors or substitutes for each other. Consumers can buy canned soup at supercenters, hypermarkets, or a super-warehouse store. But do consumers see these stores as competitors? If the answer is yes, then these formats are competing for the same consumer dollars. If the answer is no, then any competition for the same consumer dollar exist among firms in the same format, and not among different formats or strategic groups. Regardless of the answer, competition has a tendency to create a **stalemate**. This concept will be explored later in the chapter.

## Structural Influence on Marketing Decisions

As stated in Chapter 1, the structural characteristics of a sector have a fundamental influence on the marketing decisions made by firms composing the sector. The retailing sector was characterized as a monopolistically competitive market structure. Even though the sector has a small group of multiunit retailers that generate the majority of sales, at the industry group level all seven industry groups have four-firm concentration ratios reflective of monopolistic competition.

Although these concentration ratios are of some value, they provide no indication of the level of concentration in local markets. Competition among retail store formats occurs at the local level. Consumers no longer travel great distances to purchase food. Fortunately, empirical data exists on sales concentration at the local level—in **MSAs**. This data reveals that the market structures in a significant number of MSAs are strongly oligopolistic.

## Competitive Differential Advantage

To create and maintain a competitive differential advantage, each of the participating firms in the **U.S. food marketing system** makes product, price, place, and promotion decisions. Taken together, these discussions create the firm's market offering. If the market offering is perceived by the consumer as different and better than competitive offerings, the firm has created a **competitive differential advantage (CDA)**. There are two important aspects of the **CDA** process that must be made clear. Both of them deal with consumer perceptions. In order for consumers to recognize differences among competitive market offerings, differences must be large enough to be perceived. Consumers are notoriously poor at recognizing small differences. Trivial differences, no matter how well intentioned, have no value to consumers. The perceived value of any market offering is determined by the relationship of its perceived benefits to perceived price.

Marketing decisions made by producers, manufacturers, and wholesalers have already been examined. Now, marketing decisions made by retailers, to create their **CDA**, need to be identified. But, before doing so, the concept of the stalemate created by competition will be explored. The **stalemate** concept is taken from the game of chess. It means that neither opponent wins. Within the context of retailing, it means that a firm can't maintain a **long run** competitive differential advantage. The dynamic nature of competition neutralizes any and all efforts to differentiate the firm's market offering. Exactly how retailers are able to neutralize a **CDA** will be introduced after the discussion on each marketing decision.

The goal of the retailer is to use the **right** promotion to persuade the **right** consumers, that the **right** product, in the **right** quantities, at the **right** price, is available at the **right** place, at this, the **right** time. To realize this goal the retailer must first identify the target of its marketing efforts: the consumer. Once identified, the retailer then engages in **micromarketing**. This means that the retailer must tailor its **"rights"** to the intended target market of consumers. The following discussion will examine the marketing decisions made by retailers to ensure that what is **right** for the consumer is **right** for retailer profits. The decisions make up what is commonly referred to as the **retailer marketing mix:** location, atmosphere, merchandise, price, promotion, and place.

## LOCATION

It is a truism that food retailers sell in local geographical markets. Consumers don't travel great distances, either spatially or temporally, to purchase groceries. Surveys do show that how far and how long people will travel to a store varies by the merchandise offering of the store. However, these surveys don't alter the fact that food retailing is inherently a local business activity.

Perhaps the intuitiveness of this truism is responsible for what has now become a cliché: The three most important considerations in retailing are location, location, and location. However trivial it may seem, it implicitly suggests that the retailer's location decision will impact on virtually all other retail marketing decisions. Equally important, this cliché identifies the three-dimensional nature of the retailer's location decision.

The following discussion will examine these dimensions: market area, trade area, and store site. In each of these decisions, demand, supply, and competitive factors are analyzed to determine if an area is understored or overstored. An **understored** condition exists when there are too few stores and/or too little selling space (shelf and other) devoted to a product category. Conversely, an **overstored** condition exists when there are too many stores and/or too much selling space devoted to a product category. It is, of course, the understore condition that represents the best opportunity to retail.

## Market Area

While it is possible to define market areas in terms of four census regions, nine U.S. census divisions, or fifty U.S. states, the U.S. food marketing system defines market areas in one of at least five ways.

*Progressive Grocer's Marketing Guidebook* delineates the entire U.S. population into fifty-two market areas. These areas are drawn to represent, as well as possible, actual distribution patterns. The data are drawn from the census of supermarkets maintained by the **Trade Dimensions Data Center** and updated daily to reflect store openings and closings.

**Scantrack** market areas are defined by **Nielsen**. Each of the fifty market areas covers a number of counties, from one to sixty-eight with an average of thirty counties. These areas contain seventy-seven percent of the U.S. population and are created by considering retailer warehousing patterns, manufacturers' sales districts, and television market coverage.

**Metropolitan Statistical Areas (MSA)** is a term used by the U.S. Office of Management and Budget to designate market areas. There are 268 MSAs in the U.S that contain the entire population. However, the top one hundred **MSAs** contain sixty-two percent of the entire population.

**Designated Market Areas (DMA)** are created by **A. C. Nielsen, Inc**. Each **DMA** defines a television market, exclusive of all others, based on measurable reviewing patterns. The top one hundred **DMAs** contain eighty-five percent of the U.S. population. Each of 3,111 counties (excluding Hawaii and Alaska) is allocated exclusively to a **DMA**. There is no overlay.

**Infoscan** market areas are defined by **Information Resources, Inc**. Each of the sixty-four markets encompass a central city plus surrounding counties. Together, these markets contain seventy-two percent of the U.S. population.

All of the organizations that publish market area data provide retailers with information related to the capacity of the market area to purchase groceries, and the capacity of retailers to supply groceries. Retailers compare demand to supply in order to determine whether an area is overstored or understored.

## Trade Area

Once the market area has been selected and evaluated, the area must be segmented into trade areas. A **trade area** is a geographically designated area from which a retailer draws its potential customers. To determine the potential of any trade area, the retailer first selects a single site or focal point. Once selected, the trade area is defined in terms of size, shape, structure, and stability.

### *Size*

The size of a trade area is influenced by several factors. The number of merchandise groups (food and non-food) carried, amount of retail space, and transportation networks are important factors. All other things being equal, retailers that carry food and non-food merchandise in larger stores located on major thoroughfares have larger trade areas than smaller stores that carry only food and are located on secondary streets.

The number, location, and size of competitors are other important influence on size. Retailers that carry competing merchandise (food and non-food) and are located near one another have larger trading areas than two similar retail stores located far apart from each other.

Finally, the number and type of adjacent stores influence the trade area size. Motivated by the consumer's need for **one stop** shopping, the more varied the adjacent stores, all other things being equal, the larger the trade area.

### *Shape*

The shape of a trade area is determined by the location of competitors, transportation networks, and barriers. The trade areas of all retailers in a market area overlap to some degree. In cases where competitors are next to or across the street from each other, they literally share the trade area.

Transportation networks define the ease with which shoppers can travel a trade area. In general, trade areas are elongated in the direction of uninterrupted thoroughfares.

The shape of a trade area is also influenced by barriers. These may be physical barriers such as water (e.g., lakes or rivers), psychological barriers such as store image (i.e., favorable vs. unfavorable), store reputation in community (i.e., involved vs. uninvolved), social barriers such as community reputation (i.e., high vs. low crime rate), and community spirit (e.g., many cooperatively sponsored events vs. few to no events).

### *Structure*

**Figure 9-2** identifies three different perspectives of trade area structure. The **general trade area** defines the outermost geographical limit from which potential customers will be drawn. A **composite trade area** specifies the outermost limits from which potential customers will be drawn to purchase a particular merchandise group. A **proportional trade area** specifies the outermost limits from which most, some, and few potential customers will be drawn to the store. These limits define "zones": primary, secondary, and tertiary. Most of the potential customers come from the primary zone. Some come from the secondary zone, and few customers come from the tertiary zone. The size of these zones, and thus their limits, are specific in terms of the physical and/or temporal distance from the store. Generally, the greater the physical or temporal distance from the retail site, the lower the probability that the consumer will travel the distance.

### Stability

The final dimension of a trade area is its stability. How do the size, shape, and structure of a trade area change during the course of a day, week, month, or season? This is easily the most difficult dimension to assess. Why? It is presumed that the trade area's capacity to consume is determined by the number of households or people who reside in the trade area. In other words, the **point of origin**, for the purpose of designating a trade area, is the household, or person's residence. However, the time-poor, two-income family may initiate the typical **"grocery shopping"** trip from work. These nonresidents may cause instability in all the trade area dimensions.

People who are residents and engage in significant shopping outside this trade area also impact on trade area dimensions. Consumers who travel to the trade area for entertainment, recreational, or professional reasons are also capable of influencing the stability of a trade area.

When the size, shape, structure, and stability of a trade area have been assessed, the retailer must determine whether the trade area is understored or overstored. If an understored condition is identified, the retailer must then determine if the share of the total sales in a trade area that the firm can achieve represents an opportunity to retail.

## Store Site

Once the decisions on which market area and which trade area have been made, the retailer must choose a specific physical location or site. There are numerous checklists of criteria used to determine a site's desireabilty. What follows are the most significant questions that retailers use to evaluate alternate sites.

- Is the site *available*? This question must always be asked first. If the site can't be leased or purchased, there is no need to consider it any further.
- Is the site *affordable*? This is the next question that should be asked. Regardless of all its advantages, a site that doesn't allow the retailer to reach its financial goals, now or in the near future, is worthless.

- Is the site *sufficient*? in size and quality? Sites that are too small or of poor environmental quality are impediments to profit making.
- Is the site *visible*? to pedestrian and/or vehicular traffic? Hidden stores make it difficult and expensive to uncover them promotionally to the consuming public.
- Is the site *accessible*? When consumers find it hard to approach, enter, travel through, and exit a site, they don't go there to shop.
- Is the site *compatible* with neighboring stores? The opportunity for consumers to engage in one-stop shopping means that the merchandise offered by non-competing stores should be considered.

Although there are many research organizations actively involved in trade area evaluation, one particularly useful approach used in the food retailing sector is conducted by **Market Metrics**. Their **"Supermarket Solutions Site Locator Report"** lists all 50,400 census tracts located in the 268 metropolitan statistical areas. For each census tract, it computes a saturation (**SI**) and retail development index (**RDI**). The **saturation index** measures the intensity of competition by considering the number, size, and location of competitors from the proposed site. This index can be interpreted as a capacity to supply groceries. The **RDI** represents total weekly grocery dollars spent by customers in the census tract. This index can be interpreted as a capacity to purchase. Thus, the retailer can use these indices to determine whether there is an opportunity to retail at a particular site.

### Location Stalemate

Stalemate means nobody wins! The retailer can't sustain a **long run** competitive advantage based on location. Despite the notion that a site confers a **spatial monopoly** to the retailer, reality indicates otherwise. Why is the location advantage neutralized in the long run? Because firms use much the same data to analyze trade areas, they arrive at the same conclusions about the alternative sites. With the data in hand, retailers locate in close proximity to each other, and consequently, saturate the trade areas. This saturation leads to overlapping trade areas and stores **fighting** for the same customer. In cases like this, the consumer, who doesn't travel far or long to purchase food, perceives competitors as all being convenient and thus doesn't attribute very much importance to the location criterion when choosing stores. In effect, the location advantage is lost to all competitors—stalemate!

## STORE ATMOSPHERE

Having examined the environment within which a store is located, the next environment the retailer must evaluate is the store atmosphere. The atmosphere must be designed to influence both the shopping and buying behavior of customers. The store's atmosphere is created by both the exterior and the interior of the store.

The first impression that consumers develop about a store is based on its exterior: front, sign, and architecture. The front is made up of its window displays and entrances. Windows have long been used by food retailers to hang or otherwise affix promotional flyers. To many in the industry, this is a distraction; to some, it "cheapens" the impression. Entrances are constructed so that they are convenient to the customer and facilitate the flow into and out of the store.

The store's sign not only serves to identify the store, but also to attract the attention of the consumer. The size, shape, color, and lighting all contribute to the sign's ability to attract attention.

The architecture has the greatest impact on the initial impression created in the minds of consumers. Most of the architecture found in food retailing resembles what most industry sources refer to as "rectangular boxes." Built from an efficiency perspective rather than an aesthetic one, the structure's form follows its function. Energy efficiency, security systems, and operational efficiency for truck deliveries serve to define the form of the retail food store.

Despite its significance, the retailer considers the store's interior to be far more important than the exterior when creating an atmosphere. This seems reasonable; after all, the consumer spends more time shopping *in* the store than on the outside. Further, while in the store, the retailer has an opportunity to influence consumer shopping and buying behavior.

To influence consumers' **in-store shopping** behavior, the retailer will focus on the two dimensions that make up the atmosphere of the general interior space: interior design and store layout. To influence **in-store buying** behavior, the retailer will focus on the atmosphere that immediately surrounds the merchandise: merchandise presentation.

The task of the retailer is to use interior design, store layout, and merchandise presentation in such a way as to have an impact on the consumer's senses. The retailer uses size, shape, and color to create **sight** appeal. Because sight provides the consumer with more information than other senses do, it can be used effectively to create a harmonious or inharmonious atmosphere. **Sound** can be used to create a mood that is conducive to browsing, or one that calls special attention to a theme or event. Unlike other retailers, the food retailer has the opportunity to influence the consumer by creating **scent** appeal. The bakery, delicatessen, and floral departments are opportunities to capitalize on the influence of aromas. To appeal to the sense of **touch**, the retailer needs to provide the opportunity, within sanitary guidelines, for tactile experiences. Prepacking of fruits, vegetables, and meats maintain sanitation and product quality at the cost of lost tactile experiences. Finally, the retailer can use "sampling" to appeal to the sense of **taste**. So important is taste that consumer surveys consistently show that consumers' buying is most influenced by sampling—coupons are a close second.

In the following sections interior design, store layout, and merchandise presentation will be discussed. Emphasis will be focused on their objectives and operational strategies for attaining these objectives.

## Interior Design

The objective of interior design is to induce the customer to shop the entire, or more of the store. Operationally, the retail food store relies on flooring, color, lighting, climate control, and music to create a mood and thus increase the time spent shopping.

Most flooring in retail stores are hard surfaced. This promotes efficiency and accelerates the speed at which consumers can travel through the store. Some stores, such as supercenters, have installed soft carpeting in their apparel departments. Carpeting is more conducive to browsing. It slows down traffic.

Most of the color provided in the typical retail store originates from the merchandise. In fact, the supermarket is a cacophony of color. Under these circumstances, color is used to highlight some of the departments. In other departments, grocery and pharmacy, for example, color is purposely neutral.

Lighting has received special attention lately. As more and more retailers move toward the "boutique" layout, lighting takes on a new role. In addition to producing illumination, lighting is used to highlight or spotlight selected merchandise.

Climate control in the retail food store is necessary to maintain the quality of its merchandise. Additionally, climate control is used to maintain a temperature that doesn't distract (too hot or too cold) the shoppers.

Background music is primarily a mood setter in retail food stores. Most shoppers are annoyed by "fast tempo" music. It distracts them and increases the speed at which they shop. In turn, the amount of time spent in the store is reduced, as is probably the percentage of the store shopped. One interesting development that is closely related to music as a mood setter, is the playing of customized ads and promotional messages during gaps in the store's background music formats. Its success is largely attributed to the ability of a store to personalize messages based on specific customer needs.

## Store Layout

The objective of store layout is to expose as much of the merchandise as possible to shoppers within their perception of **in-store** convenience. Consumers typically determine convenience based on the (1) time required to complete a shopping trip, (2) ease with which the store can be shopped, and (3) ease with which merchandise can be located. Store layout has taken on an increased role in food stores because of the emphasis on self-service. The retailer must allocate store space to non-selling and selling space. The **non-selling** area is space devoted to customer services (e.g., merchandise and bottle returns), merchandise processing (e.g., bakery, deli, meat, and backroom general merchandise inventory), and management and staff activities (e.g., offices, changing rooms). The **selling** area is that space allocated to the display of merchandise. The allocation of this space is guided by the observation that the more merchandise shoppers are exposed to while shopping, the greater the sales.

Given the customers' convenience goals, it is impractical to think that a store can be laid out to ensure that customers pass by all the items in a store. However, it is possible to influence how shoppers travel though a store by arranging the departments. **Figure 9-3** is an illustrated example of the three basic layout patterns: gridiron, free-form, and boutique.

The **conventional layout** in a store is referred to as a *gridiron pattern*. It utilizes floor space most efficiently by providing the greatest amount of display (selling) space to aisle space. In turn, the arrangement of long aisles and shelves *(gondolas)* results in the greatest exposure of merchandise to the shopping public. This layout is typically used for the display of dry groceries. In the illustration, grocery, frozen food, and health and beauty care are laid out in a gridiron arrangement.

The **free-form** layout arranges displays and aisles in a free flowing or random pattern. The layout encourages shoppers to browse at a leisurely pace. However, the use of nonstandardized displays and fixtures results in a reduced amount of display space relative to aisle space. This layout is used extensively for the display of produce. (Shoppers enjoy examining the produce.) It increases the time consumers spend in a store, and does much to relieve the boredom associated with walking down long aisles.

The **boutique** layout arranges displays and aisles around a particular shopping specialty. The layout seeks to create a unique shopping experience by promoting a "store within a store" theme. The layout is used extensively to promote the store's foodservice departments, such as bakery, seafood, delicatessen, and food courts (on-premises restaurants). It has also been used to promote non-foodservices such as banking, video, pharmacy, and floral. These high-profit-margin departments are usually located on the periphery of the store because the greatest flow of traffic occurs in the outside aisles of the store.

In summary, the ideal store layout maximizes merchandise exposure and enables the shopper to spend a reasonable amount of time moving through an uncongested store to find the merchandise needed.

## Merchandise Presentation

Unlike interior design and store layout, the objective of merchandise presentation is to induce the shopper who passes a merchandise item to buy it. This objective is translated into a buy/pass or **purchase conversion ratio**. The buy/pass ratio is influenced by two decisions.

The first decision involves the location of those product categories that have the greatest drawing power. These categories, sometimes known as staples or **power** categories, are purchased frequently by a high proportion of shoppers (German and

Leed, 1992). The location of these power categories is important because it influences the proportion of shoppers who will pass through a particular department or pass by the displayed power category. In either case, the denominator of the purchase conversion ratio is affected by amount of traffic.

The second decision involves the location of the power merchandise products within the power categories. In general, the power products are dispersed throughout the allocated category space in order to gain exposure for all products in the category, not just the power products. In this way, the shopper completely **shops** the category.

## Stalemate

A retail firm can't sustain a long run competitive advantage on the basis of store atmosphere. Why? The belief that the consumer's shopping experience must be dramatic and memorable and exciting has resulted in a retail sector that is continuously in a state of atmospheric redevelopment. In fact, many of the trade journals **showcase** these atmospheric innovations. In the final analysis, any advantage gained by refurbishing the store is soon neutralized by competitors.

# MERCHANDISE

The retailer's decision to locate a store at a particular site invariably impacts on its merchandise decisions because consumers view groceries as convenience products; they are unwilling to spend much time or travel great distances to purchase them. When the store site decision is made, it literally defines its target market as those consumers who live in close physical or temporal proximity to the store. The merchandise decisions of retailers are, as a consequence, guided by the perceived needs of these consumers. The interdependence of location and merchandise decisions reinforces the dictum, "Know thy customer before you build your store and order your merchandise."

When a firm possesses the fundamental knowledge about its potential customers, it is in a position to make its merchandise mix decisions. There are three dimensions to the retailer **merchandise mix**. The **width** of the mix corresponds to the category variety decision. The **length** corresponds to the category assortment decision. The **depth** corresponds to the brand variation decision. All of these decisions must consider the merchandise quality offered to the consumer (**Figure 9-4**).

## Variety—What Categories?

In general, retailers offer two merchandise **groups** for sale to consumers: food and non-food. Within each of the groups, there exist product categories. The retailer's variety decision focuses on determining which categories (and thus how many) to offer for sale to consumers. The retailer makes this decision by considering four factors.

The first, and most important, involves the needs of the store's target customers. The retailer must translate their needs into merchandise categories. In order to do so, the target customers are characteristically and behaviorally profiled. *Characteristically,* the target market is defined demographically, economically, psychologically, sociologically, and culturally. *Behaviorally,* the target market is defined in terms of their shopping and purchasing behaviors.

The second major consideration is the amount of retail space. It is an axiom that retail space is finite. It cannot be expanded in the short run. Thus, the retailer must decide on the needs that the firm is willing to satisfy.

The third consideration is the format of the store. Consumers expected to find certain categories of food in different formats. For example, they don't expect to find all the categories carried by a supercenter in a convenience store. But they expect that convenience stores, in general, carry the same categories. The same can be said for supermarkets, warehouse stores, and other types. Thus, to a large degree, the retail format dictates which, and how many, merchandise categories will be offered to the target market.

Finally, the retailer must consider the profitability of the categories. Profitability is measured for all of the merchandise dimensions. Here, category projected sales and gross margin are examined for compatibility with the store's overall financial objectives. However, to arrive at any conclusion concerning category profitability, the length and depth of the merchandise mix must also be determined.

## Assortment—How Many Brands?

The retailer's assortment decisions determine the length of the merchandise mix. An assortment decision must be made to determine how many brands to carry in each merchandise category. Before that can be done, the retailer must define each category. Although this is a consideration with implications for the previously discussed **variety** decision, now is a more appropriate time to discuss this task.

Simply, how the retailer defines the category identifies which brand items are relevant to the category. For example, cereals, juices, and waffles are product categories. To define the cereal category the retailer might include **Kellogg's, Post, Quaker Oats**, and **General Mills**. The juice category might include **Ocean Spray, Minute Maid, Motts**, and **Welch's**. The waffle category might include **Aunt Jemima, Mrs. Butterworth, Downyflake**, and **Eggo's**.

A category can also be defined at a broader level. Cereals, juices, and waffles could be defined as **breakfast** products. In this case, cereals, juices, and waffles become subcategories of the breakfast category. As a general rule, products that are substitutes for each other are grouped in the same subcategory or category.

After the product categories and/or subcategories have been defined, the retailer must determine how many brands to include in each category. This decision is very problematic for most retailers because it is the level where consumers define "having a choice." If too few brands are carried, and the consumer isn't willing to switch when his or her preferred brand is not available, then the store has lost the sale. If too many brands are carried, the consumer faces **over choice**. In this situation, some of the brands in the category are **cannibalized**, that is, the sale of one brand takes away the sale of another brand in the category.

The retailer makes the assortment decision by considering the same factors used to make the variety decision. The brand preferences of the target market must be identified first. In addition, their brand loyalty should be assessed to determine their willingness to switch when their preferred brand is not available. Brands with low switching or substitution rates must be carried.

The amount of available retail space must also be considered. The length, width, and depth of the merchandise mix are interdependent. Thus, any decision to increase (decrease) one of the dimensions will decrease (increase) one or both of the other dimensions.

The retail format dictates, to a large degree, the brands that consumers expect to find in a retail format. What supermarket would not carry **Campbell's Soup, Kellogg's Corn Flakes**, or **Tide Detergent**? Because some brands dominate their respective categories, retailers often examine the level of brand concentration in the product categories. For example, the sales shares of the number-one brands in the top twenty categories range from sixty-eight to ninety-nine percent. When the sales shares of the top three brands are considered, the top twenty categories range from ninety-four to one hundred percent. In short, the retailer doesn't need to stock a large number of brands in a category to generate sufficient category sales (*Supermarket Business*, March 1996).

Finally, profitability must be considered. One of two approaches to profitability have been used by retailers. The first, **ABC costing**, was discussed in Chapter 5. Briefly (rather than define corporate and overhead expenses as fixed costs and allocate them equally across all products), **ABC** defines a significant number of these costs as variable, and allocates them directly to products. Thus, it assigns these activity costs to each product based on the extent to which that product **causes** the cost to be incurred. Instead of relying on gross margin as the measure of profitability, **ABC** provides the retailer with a deeper understanding of the true costs associated with handling a product, and thus a truer picture of profitability.

A closely associated approach to product profitability is referred to as **Direct Product Profit (DPP)**. This approach identifies costs that are directly attributable to a particular product: handling, space, inventory. To arrive at profitability, **direct product costs (DPC)** are subtracted from a gross margin that has itself been adjusted for other revenues. **DPCs** are costs that vary with a product's unit/dollar movement and space occupied by the product. The product's gross margin is adjusted to reflect all deals, allowances, and forward buying income. In addition, **DPP** can also be expressed in terms of retail space. For example, **DPP** can be calculated on linear feet, square feet, or cubic feet of retail space occupied by the product. Finally, **DPP** combined with turnover can be expressed in terms of days or weeks.

## Variations—How Much of Each Brand?

Ultimately, categories and the brands they include must be expressed in terms of their variations. Brand variation may include size, flavor, container, or consistency. These variations make up the depth of the merchandise mix. For the non-food groups, the number of variations is strongly influenced by the type of product. This is another problematic decision for the retailer. When the consumer's preferred brand is not there, will they switch brands or settle for some variation of the brand? When the variations involve different sizes only, consumers are more likely to switch brands than they are sizes. It is difficult to generalize about other variations. Will a consumer switch to **frozen** orange juice if a 1/2 gallon **carton** of juice is unavailable? Will a consumer purchase **"French"** salad dressing if **"Creamy Italian"** is unavailable? Obviously, it is difficult to generalize about all consumers. Nonetheless, each of the brand variations is assigned a stock keeping unit (**SKU**) code. Further, the planning, analysis, and control of merchandise is ultimately specified at the **SKU** level. The challenge for the retailer, then, is to have the right **SKU** available to the target customer.

## Quality—The Right SKU

Implicit in the variety, assortment, and stock keeping unit decisions is the dimension of quality. The three dimensions of the merchandise mix must be consistent with the level of quality demanded by the target customers. For most retailers, the goal is to offer more than one level of quality. Food quality is product specific. The criteria used to assess meat quality are not the same for produce, or dairy. However, for purposes of merchandise planning, brand quality is reflected by the quality of the ingredients that make up the product. Defined this way, the retailer can differentiate quality into at least four levels.

The first level of quality is the **premium private label** brand. This brand is aimed at the upscale shopper who is willing to pay a premium price. Consumers see these products as specialties or gourmet items.

A second level of quality is the **national** brand. This brand tends to define the category in the consumer's mind. Consumers will switch stores to find the product. Although not really a different quality, retailers often carry a "second tier" brand. This brand is positioned between a national brand and a private label brand, and offers the consumer a price point between the more expensive national brand and the less expensive private label brand.

A third level of quality is the **store** brand. These brands don't bear the name of the manufacturer. They are priced below the national brand, but have a higher gross margin. Although aimed at the price-sensitive consumer, store brands enable retailers to build loyalty to the store rather than loyalty to national brands. Store brands accounted for fifteen percent of all grocery dollar sales, and nineteen percent of all unit sales in 1995 (*Private Label,* Sept./Oct. 1995).

A fourth level of quality is occupied by the **generics**. These debranded commodities are aimed at the extreme price sensitive shopper. They are priced at the lowest level in the category and display no package graphics other than their basic contents (e.g., flour, rice, corn flakes, or peas).

Each of these quality levels offers value to the customers at a price they are willing to pay. The real challenge to the retailer is to create a merchandise mix whose variety, assortment, and stock keeping units are defined within the context of various quality levels.

To meet this challenge, retailers often rely on **shelf-space management** software programs such as **Apollo** by **Information Resources, Inc. (IRI)**, to produce store-specific planograms for individual categories. Some space management programs can produce planograms with photographic facsimiles of products displayed on shelves, but also, in generating the planograms, the program integrates a number of valuables, such as demographic data, size and type of fixtures used, and case-quantity minimums. The programs also take into account sales, profits, and return on inventory investment. In essence, shelf-space management programs enable retailers to optimize category sales and profits. At the same time, retailers can minimize inventory and maximize merchandising effectiveness by carrying the **SKUs** demanded by their target customers. Fortunately, retailers can make informed merchandise decisions based on reliable information gathered at customer checkout lanes as products are scanned for **UPC** codes and prices. Scanner data identify which **SKUs** consumers purchased on their last shopping trip. Because food purchase behavior is habitual, scanner data has been shown to predict which **SKUs** consumers will purchase on their next shopping trip. Thus, scanner data are used by retailers both to verify the correctness of past merchandise decisions and as a basis for future ones.

## Stalemate

A retail firm cannot sustain a long run competitive advantage based on its merchandise mix. Why? Increased merger activities have created fewer and larger food manufacturers. The willingness of these manufacturers to "move product" or distribute intensely has resulted in retailers who carry the **same** merchandise categories and brands within the categories. This merchandise sameness is reinforced by consumer buying behavior. Consumers frequently and routinely purchase products that **anchor** their diets. These anchors are referred to as **staple** items. Most consumers' diets consist of staples such as meat, fish, fruits, vegetables, and breads. Because of the concentration of sales by a few brands in these staple categories, the retailer's choice of brands in these categories typically focuses on the best sellers. Over time, every retailer within a format, must carry these staple best sellers in order to remain competitive. Given that retail space is finite, consumers shop in stores that carry virtually the same merchandise.

How do retailers try to reduce merchandise sameness? They carry a number of levels of quality, and replace brands that add nothing unique to the category with specialty foods. These foods are integrated into their category sections or displayed on separate racks in order to gain visibility. Unfortunately, this approach is used so extensively that any short-run advantage doesn't survive in the long run.

# SERVICES

Location impacts the retailer's merchandise decisions in the same way that it impacts on the firm's service decisions. The target market for the store is made up of those consumers who live in close physical or temporal proximity to the store. In addition to understanding a target market's merchandise needs, the retailer must also understand its service needs. The retailer's **service mix** is made up of two service groups. The first group includes all of those services that enhance the merchandise mix. The other group of services are offered to facilitate consumer shopping and purchasing.

### Variety—What to Offer

Services that enhance the retailer's merchandise mix are associated with food and general merchandise. Services that facilitate consumer shopping and purchase are operational in nature. Retailers make the service mix decision after considering the same factors that influence their merchandise decisions.

Once again, the first (and most important) consideration is the needs of the target customers. Second, because the food and general merchandise departments are very likely to be located around the periphery of the store, the amount of retail space must be considered. Third, the format of the store greatly influences what services will be offered. Finally, the profitability associated with the service variety must be examined.

### Assortment—How Many Services

The retailer's assortment decision determines how many different services to offer consumers. The foodservice departments might include delicatessen, bakery, seafood, meat shop, catering, and food court. The general merchandise departments might include film processing, video rental and purchase, pharmacy, and floral. Operational services that facilitate consumer shopping and purchasing include nutritional information, cards, scanning, banking, ATMs, credit/debit card payments, checking, and home delivery.

Consideration of the target customer's service needs, available retail space, store format, and profitability determines whether the service is classified as an essential, expected, or optional service.

**Essential services** are those that must be offered to remain competitive within a retail format. For example, parking, appropriate store hours, bottle and merchandise returns, check cashing privileges, and shopping carts and/or baskets are essential services for most retail formats.

**Expected services** are those that need not be offered in order to operate a store. However, the cumulative experiences of consumers result in certain expectations regarding service offerings. Coupon redemption, express check out, purchase consolidation (plastic or paper bags), and credit card payments are examples of expected services.

**Optional services** are those that are neither essential to operate the store, nor expected by customers. Because there is no obligation to offer this service, the retailer can develop a competitive differential advantage by offering such a service. **Figure 9-5** shows the most recent listing of services offered in supermarkets. The services reflect both operational services and foodservice departments. The service offered least has the greatest potential for creating a competitive advantage until it is copied. According to *Progressive Grocer,* offering the services of a fast-food franchise was the least offered service department.

## Quality

Not all services offered by retailers involve personnel, but most do. Whenever a store employee is performing a task on a customer's behalf there is likely to be some variability in performance. The employee's appearance, language, competence, and attitude all influence service performance and thus service variability. Proper training and periodic performance appraisals should not only reduce service variability, but also raise the level of service performance.

Because in many cases you cannot determine the quality of the service performance until **after** it is performed, the retailer must establish standards of performance. Without these standards, the level of service quality is unpredictable. Customers seek predictability or consistency in performance and will switch stores if they are not satisfied.

Above all, the retailer must ensure that each service employee has developed the right **service attitude**. The manner in which the employee strives to make a customer's shopping and buying experience more satisfying is what creates the service difference.

### Stalemate

Can the retailer maintain a long run competitive advantage by offering an optional service? Probably not. Why? As consumers expand their shopping experiences to include different retail formats they exert pressure on stores to offer services **not** normally associated with a particular format. When this is combined with the tendency of services to change from optional to expected to essential, service mix **sameness** is inevitable.

Of course, an optional service offered the least by retailers has the greatest advantage. At the time of this writing, the service offered least is a fast-food franchise. If it proves successful, it will be offered by others until such time as it becomes an expected, if not essential, service. When this happens, it no longer differentiates retailers from one another and, consequently, joins the roll of other services that were once optional.

# PRICE

More and more retailers are beginning to recognize that consumers are interested in price only to the extent that it reflects value. For consumers, the perceived value of merchandise and/or services is a comparative measure of perceived benefits and price.

$$\text{Perceived Value} = \frac{\text{Perceived Benefits}}{\text{Perceived Price}}$$

This equation identifies the role that price plays in creating value for the consumer. Technically, with all else constant, value can be increased by increasing benefits, decreasing price, or increasing benefits at a faster rate than price increases. Consequently, customer satisfaction may be defined as a perceived value greater or equal to one. The goal of the retailer is to determine the price level at which consumers will perceive value greater or equal to one. This equation also suggests that price level decisions are especially important because perceived values greater or equal to one increase store traffic, sales volume, and, ultimately, profitability.

In food retailing, whatever profit goal is specified (e.g., return on net worth, sales, investment) it is usually expressed in terms of overall gross margin for the store. Further, this gross margin can be broken down into departments, categories, and, finally, individual products and services. What this means is that once the overall store gross margin has been determined, the retailer must decide on the gross margin contribution from each department. The categories and individual products and services are then priced to achieve these departmental contributions **(Table 9-1)**. **Variable margin pricing** in retailing involves pricing individual categories and products and services at varying margins (German and Leed, 1992).

In addition to the previously mentioned consumer influence, retail price levels are influenced by pricing philosophies, costs, demand, and competition. These will be briefly examined and followed by policies and the price stalemate.

## Philosophies

Given the goal of a specific store's gross margin, there are two philosophical approaches that may be used to attain the goal. There is the belief that **everyday low prices (EDLP)** have a number of significant advantages for retailers and consumers. Offering everyday low prices smoothes out demand and lowers inventories. The retailer inventory, and other inventories in the supply chain, are not subject to the inventory surges created by promotion deals. The reduction of erratic inventory levels reduces out-of-stocks, minimizes advertising expense, and optimizes store and backroom staffing. All of this means that the savings are passed on to consumers in the form of lower prices. Finally, time-poor consumers can one-stop shop with the confidence that they are getting the lowest possible price.

The second philosophy is referred to as a **High/Low** approach. This approach offers special low price deals to increase sales volume during the deal periods. Once the deal period is over, prices are returned to their normal high levels. Its primary advantage to the retailer is that these low price deals are backed by manufacturers' incentives to promote the merchandise on deals. As previously mentioned, these incentives or trade promotions can include cash allowances, free goods, market development funds (**MDF**) and various performance-based allowances.

A **High/Low** orientation also creates a level of excitement unattainable in **EDLP** pricing. Everyone likes a deal. Consumers find much satisfaction in **cherry picking** (buying only those products on sale) and couponing their way through stores. But all of this has a cost not only to retailer but also to the other members in the U.S. food marketing system. Erratic inventory surges before and after the deal periods cause (1) higher inventory, advertising, and staffing costs, (2) price discrimination for the time-poor shopper who "misses" the deal, and (3) all around higher prices to cover the higher costs. The retail sector is filled with successes and failures using either philosophy. Nonetheless, the retailer's belief in either philosophy will influence price level decisions.

## Costs

Despite the inherent advantages in activity based costing (**ABC**), most retailers still treat their costs as indirect costs and not attributable to any one product, category, or department. There are also costs (direct) that can be easily allocated to specific products, categories, and departments. These direct costs are often reflected, wholly or partially, in the gross margins of products, categories, and departments.

The most recent Consumer Expenditure Study (*Supermarket Business,* September 1996) identified **produce** as having the highest gross margin percentage of any food category. The higher labor, refrigeration, preparation, and shrinkage due to perishability are reflected in the gross margin. In general, food products with (1) high direct expenses, such as handling, processing, display, and shrinkage, and (2) low turnover rates, have higher gross margins. The nonfood categories (e.g., health and beauty aids and general merchandise) have higher gross margins than the food categories. But these margins are not due to costs as much as to consumer demand.

## Demand

The turnover rate is also considered when making price-level decisions. Products with higher turnover rates generally have lower gross margins than products with lower turnover rates. An explanation for this occurrence is found in the concept of elasticity.

In general, the greater the sensitivity (elasticity) of consumer demand to price changes, the greater the impact a change in selling price will have on total product sales. Staples exhibit high elasticity of demand at the store level, and produce wide variations in sales. It is also important to note that because staples are purchased regularly and routinely, they are likely to contribute most to the consumers' price image of the store.

Although the sensitivity of consumer demand is determined by the availability of close substitutes, storeability also impacts on elasticity. In general, food products that can't be stored for any significant length of time (e.g., milk and produce) have low consumer price sensitivity at the store level.

Finally, the demand for food products is influenced by the existence of qualitative differences. For instance, qualitative differences in meat and fresh fruits and vegetables enable retailers to obtain higher gross margins on their sales.

## Competition

Within a particular retail format, the retailer must recognize the prices of individual products and overall price levels of competitors. Most retailers strive to maintain price competitiveness with stores in the same format. Due to the inherent cost advantages for some store formats, it is unrealistic to think that the same brand would sell for the same price in different formats.

## Policies

Retailers are also guided by a number of price-setting policies which supplement the costs, demand, and competitive price-setting influences.

### Odd Pricing

Retailers originally used odd prices to force sales clerks to give change and ring up each sale, reducing employee theft. Later, it was believed that consumers perceived odd prices as significantly below even prices (e.g., $1.99 is perceived to be less than $2.00). Prices ending in "9" are the most common odd price endings in food retailing. Does a price ending in "9" work? Apparently, it does (Blattberg and Nesliu, 1990). A number of reasons have been analyzed regarding why ending in "9" works (Schneider, 1987).

### Unit Pricing

Retailers use this practice to help consumers make price comparisons among products of different quantities. The unit prices are posted on shelf facings either above or below the product. In 1984, some retailers introduced electronic shelf labels (**ESL**). These are liquid crystal displays that are changed electronically and thus eliminate store labor when prices are changed.

### Multiple Pricing

Retailers use this practice to give consumers discounts for making quantity purchases. For example, the retailer may price a can of soup at sixty-nine cents each or three for two dollars. From the retailer's point of view, the practice is employed to increase sales volume and is generally used more for staple items. Multiple prices appear to be effective in increasing sales (Blattberg and Neslin, 1990).

### Price Lining

To use the price-lining practice, retailers first establish a **price zone**, or a range of prices, for a product category. Then the retailer would select price points within the price zone. This practice is used whenever retailers carry more than one level of quality in a category. It is also used when retailers carry more than one brand in the category. Because this is the usual case for most stores, price lining is very prevalent in food retailing.

### Prestige Pricing

This practice is best reflected in the pricing of gourmet or specialty products. It is based on the notion that consumers expect to pay more for higher-quality products. The promotions that single out the ingredient quality of a product do so to justify the higher asking price.

### Leader Pricing

This practice is very prevalent in the food retailing sector. It involves using a **price special** or a **temporary price reduction**. If the product is sold at, or below, cost, it is referred to as a **loss leader**. Leader pricing is employed to generate sales of staple products. These products represent **anchors** in the consumer's food diet, and are purchased frequently and routinely. Further, because of their importance in the consumer's food budget, price decreases on these products generate significant reactions from consumers. Of course, the purpose of price specials is not only to increase the sales of the product on sale. It is anticipated that the consumer will purchase other products, especially those that bear some relationship to the sale item.

### *Promotional Pricing*

Retailers often use this practice in conjunction with price specials. The retailer features these items not at sale prices, but rather at their normal retail prices. It is expected that the sale of these items will offset the loss of gross margin on the price specials. For this reason, the items chosen are complements of the price special items. In this way, the promotional item is **tied in** or **cross merchandised** with the price special. This practice is also heavily used to promote particular categories or products on holiday occasions. Finally, retailers who purchase products on deal, or when supplies far exceed normal demand, will place them on promotion for a period of time, and later may promote them as price specials.

### *Private Label Pricing*

Anytime a retailer carries private label or store label brands, a decision must be made regarding how to price them relative to national brands. Premium private label brands are generally priced **above** the national brand. Regular private label or store brands are usually priced **below** national brand prices. In such cases, the national brand is squeezed from both ends. The premium private label price above the national brand represents a **quality** squeeze from above. The regular private label or store brand priced below the national label represents a **price** squeeze from below.

The real challenge in private label pricing is to determine how far above or below the product should be priced. As previously mentioned in Chapter 5, the consumer has an upper and lower limit regarding what he or she considers a fair value for the product. The limits are referred to as **thresholds**. A price that exceeds the upper threshold is perceived as too expensive for the quality offered. A price that falls below the lower threshold is perceived as lacking in quality. In both cases, the consumer won't buy the product. In the former, the savings are too small; in the latter, the quality is too inferior. Despite the significance of this problem, most retailers set these limits intuitively rather than empirically.

## Stalemate

Again we ask, "Can the retailer maintain a long run competitive advantage on the basis of price?" Probably not! Unlike other marketing mix variables, price has always been considered a short run advantage. Why? Any price change initiated by one store can be easily neutralized, often in minutes, by a competitor's price change.

Interestingly, high/low retailers are constantly employing price specials to create incremental sales increases. It would appear that their efforts have an "averaging" effect on those consumers who normally shop at more than one store for groceries. As consumers move from store to store to take advantage of the price specials, they average their food shopping budget across these stores. On the other hand, everyday low price retailers use price as an attempt to create a long run competitive advantage. Although lacking the excitement of a sale, keeping prices low everyday saves shoppers the time and effort needed to find and purchase price specials. However, like the other decision variables, as more and more retailers adopt an **EDLP** philosophy, the advantage is soon neutralized.

# PROMOTION

The dictum "Build it and they will come!" has never proven to be something retailers could rely on. Before consumers will visit a store, they must know that it exists, is conveniently located, open at appropriate hours, carries suitable merchandise, charges reasonable prices, offers needed services, and has an atmosphere pleasing to the senses. How will consumers know this unless the retailer communicates this to them? But the retailers must do more than just communicate, they must promote their market offerings to their target customers. Accordingly, food retailers must develop a promotional mix consisting of advertising, sales promotion, publicity, and personal selling.

## Advertising

Advertising is a persuasive process that is designed to accomplish two goals. In the **long run**, retailers seek to create a favorable retail image. In the **short run**, retailers focus on selling the existing merchandise and services.

### *Image*

It has only been in the most recent past that retailers have focused on image advertising. To develop an image, retailers create an institutional identity in the minds of people. This identity comprises everything that people can experience. A store's location, atmosphere, merchandise, services, prices, promotions, sales personnel, and community involvement are essential components of a retailer's image.

The task of the retailer is to project a consistent image to customers, employees, suppliers, and the general public. No one would argue that, without a favorable image, customers would not patronize the store. However, how its own employees perceive the management of the store determines to a large extent what they say about the retailers to customers, suppliers, and the general public. Equally important are the suppliers who call on the retailer. Their family, friends, and co-workers listen to their comments. Finally, the general public is made up of potential customers for the store. Thus, the image must be capable, at all times, of converting the general public into customers. The success of this conversion process depends upon the effective management of each of the image components.

Recently, a number of retailers have begun to use broadcast media (i.e., TV and radio) to project their image. One of the best examples of corporate identity is the theme of **"Hometown Proud"** promoted by **Independent Grocer's Alliance (IGA)** retailers. Retailing is inherently local in nature. What better way to emphasize a retailer's commitment to the community than to build it into their identity?

### *Merchandise/Services*

It is unquestionably true that most retail advertising focuses on selling products and food-related services. Because of the positive relationship between customer traffic and store sales, the goal of this type of advertising is to generate special reasons for visiting the store.

The special reasons for visiting the store are reflected in promotional themes. The national holidays, along with religious holidays, lend themselves to thematic promotions. But these promotions only represent about a dozen events each year. The real challenge is to develop themes for the remaining forty weeks.

Once the theme is established, merchandise must be selected. The **Easter** ham, **Thanksgiving** turkey, and **Fourth of July** hotdogs and hamburgers are traditional fare. Most such products are promoted because the retailer has received a special allowance from the manufacturer. When the retailer must make the decision without manufacturers' allowances, it selects products that are in some way related to the theme.

Having chosen the merchandise, promotional prices must be established. The purpose of the promotion is to make a profit. To be successful, any pricing approach must create value at the promoted price.

The last step is to make operational advertising decisions that answer five questions. Which **media** should be used? Print media such as newspaper, and selected mailings are most often used. What should the **message** say? Immediacy of action and emphasis on price and brand are most frequently stressed. What about advertising **momentum**? Most advertising is run weekly and appears on Wednesdays for most sales. The nature of the theme (e.g., national or religious holidays or special events) influence how often (frequency) and when (timing) the advertising should appear. How can we **measure** its effectiveness? The amount of incremental sales volume is the most objective means of evaluating the promotion. Finally, how much **money** will it take to achieve our sales objective? The retailer has three sources of promotional funds. According to the most recent survey of retailer advertising funds, internal retailer funds accounted for thirty-nine percent of the ad budget, followed by cooperative funds (thirty-seven percent), with the remainder drawn from manufacturer funds (Carol Wright Promotions, Inc., 1996).

## Sales Promotion

Although advertising may attract consumers to the store, once inside, they must be influenced to purchase. **Sales promotion** is any promotional activity, other than advertising, personal selling, and publicity, that is intended to stimulate immediate purchase behavior. How important is sales promotion? The most recent survey found that approximately seventy percent of all supermarket decisions are made **in the store**! (Point-of-Purchase Advertising Institute, 1996)

In some cases, sales promotion activities are extensions of manufacturer consumer promotions, and in others they are initiated by the retailers themselves. The sales promotion activities of food retailers include displays and sales incentives.

### *Display*

The food retailer is largely a self-service operation. Therefore, interior displays must perform much of the selling task that at one time was performed by a salesperson. Retailers generally use three types of displays in food retailing.

**Closed displays** are found in the store's foodservice departments. The delicatessen, bakery, and meat counter allow the customer to see the food but not handle it. For reasons of service and sanitation, closed displays are used mostly in foodservice departments.

**Open displays** are found throughout the store. Gondolas, in the dry grocery section, tabletop produce displays, open freezer ice-cream displays, end aisle cut-case display, and dump displays of paper towels are all examples of open displays.

**Point-of-Purchase (POP)** displays are generally open and most often supplied by manufacturers to feature their products. **POP** promotions include such items as the check-out-lane displays, shelf talker displays, video-screen displays, and instant coupon dispensers. These displays represent the final opportunity for retailers to influence the consumer's in-store purchase behavior.

### *Sales Incentives*

Incentives are initiated either by the manufacturer or retailer. They include coupons, sampling, premiums, contests/sweepstakes, tie-ins, continuity, and frequent shopper programs.

The **coupon** was first introduced as an incentive in 1895 to entice consumers to try a new fountain drink called **Coca-Cola**. Since then, coupons have grown into one of the most widely accepted, and frequently used, sales incentives. In 1995, 292 billion coupons were distributed, and roughly six billion or two percent were redeemed (NCH Promotional Services, 1996). Although most coupons never get used, shoppers have come to expect them. A special type of manufacturers' coupon called the **in-ad** coupon is distributed by retailers in their weekly newspaper circulars or in-store fliers. These coupons can only be redeemed at the store issuing them. They build brand loyalty for the manufacturer, and store loyalty for the retailer. For these reasons, they have been phenomenally successful.

**Sampling** continues to register double-digit growth rates in popularity and usage. This can be explained from two viewpoints. For the manufacturer, sampling offers the lowest cost of converting a consumer to its brand. For the consumer, there is no barrier to trial. In fact, when asked, most consumers say they are more influenced to purchase a product by a sample than they are by a coupon.

**Premiums** are merchandise offered by retailers at a substantially reduced price or, in some cases, for free. This offer is typically tied to the purchase of a related product. For example, dish towels can be purchased or given away free with the purchase of dish detergent. A cereal premium may feature a plate or bib for a child. When a consumer pays a price that only covers a retailer's cost, the premium is called a **self-liquidating premium**.

Retailers also offer **contests and sweepstakes**. In the former the consumer must demonstrate a skill or perform some task to win. In order to win a sweepstake, the consumer only has to enter. The most popular contest is the "rub-off instant win." Consumers favor sweepstakes over contests. Presumably, they are more willing to rely on the "laws of chance" than their own skill.

**Tie-ins** come in a variety of forms, but all involve relating (tie-in) merchandise to some event or cause. For example, tie-ins occur in conjunction with national holidays, sporting events, entertainment events, local celebrations, or some special occasion. The purpose of the tie-in is to capitalize on the excitement generated by the event. United Way, Easter Seals, Muscular Dystrophy, the Olympics, the World Series, and the Super Bowl are major tie-in opportunities.

**Continuity programs** are designed to keep the consumer coming back to the store. A premium is offered in parts or pieces. The initial purchase price is usually quite low to entice the consumer to purchase. It is anticipated that the consumer would not want to own only the first book in an encyclopedia, or one plate in a set of four. These items are normally collected as a set, so they tend to be effective in returning the consumer to the store to purchase the remaining items.

**Frequent shopper programs** were made possible by the activities that took place on June 26, 1974. On that date, the first commercial scan of a product (**Wrigley's Gum**) was taken at a **Marsh Supermarket** store in Troy, Ohio. But it was not until 1987 that the **Ulroy's Super Markets** chain offered the first frequent shopper program, called the **Valued Customer Card**. The purpose of a frequent shopper program is to reward the customer in relation to purchases. The customer is offered savings by paying a different price for many, if not all, of the merchandise a store offers. In turn, the retailers benefit because, to become a participant, customers must provide detailed information about themselves, their families, tastes, preferences, attitudes, and other confidential and personal information. Apparently, consumers feel that they gain more in savings than they give up in information. The use of frequent shopper programs has grown so tremendously that by the year 2000, almost every supermarket will have some form of it. What's more, many believe that in the future the paper coupon will be all but eliminated because the discounts will be taken at the register. Finally, retailers who use frequent shopper programs will at last know not only **what** is being sold in their store, but also **who** is buying what merchandise.

## Publicity

Publicity, a non-paid form of commercially significant news, is not generally considered a major part of the retailer's promotional mix. However, retailers can generate publicity that reflects favorably on the firm.

Most often, retailers can gain favorable publicity by sponsoring a community wide event. Retailing is local in nature. As a consequence, sponsorship has the most impact on the people who are in close physical or temporal proximity to the store.

When selecting the event, retailers try to bring it as close to the store as possible. If there are prizes, they are awarded at the store or in its parking lot. If a race is sponsored, it typically begins and ends at the store. Any and all excursions depart from and return to the store. In short, the retailer must capitalize on the event to show the community it is a good corporate citizen.

## Personal Selling

It may seem unusual to suggest that personal selling is an important promotional variable in a retailing sector that has been defined largely as a **"self-service"** sector. However, when you consider that many of the retail formats carry general merchandise in addition to grocery items, the importance of store personnel becomes more evident. Further, if **personal selling** is broadly defined to include any activity intended to influence the purchase behavior of shoppers, store personnel all should be considered sales people.

There is another reason why store personnel are important to the retailers. The firm's image is largely defined by the interactions customers have with all of its employees: salespeople, stock clerks, and service personnel. It follows that successful sales management requires the retailer to be able to identify, train, motivate, and evaluate all of its store personnel based on their contribution to the store's image.

## Stalemate

No firm can sustain a long-run competitive advantage on the basis of their promotional activities. Although there have been recent attempts by retailers to differentiate their stores in the minds of consumers, little image advertising is done. Retail advertising is mostly focused on product promotion.

Even the retailer's sales promotion activities are remarkably similar. The tremendous growth of frequent shopper programs eliminates much hope of using it as a competitive advantage.

Retailers are all trying to capitalize on publicity. What retailer doesn't want to tie-in with local events or sponsor a team? Increasingly, as retailers become more effective at managing publicity, they can no longer use it to differentiate themselves.

# DISTRIBUTION

Rather than rely on wholesalers to distribute food and related items to their stores, many large retail chains perform their own distribution functions. They engage in these functions, like traditional wholesalers, to resolve product, spatial, and temporal discrepancies.

## Self-Distribution

To resolve **spatial** discrepancies, retailers focus on their external (inbound, outbound) logistical activities. They must move goods from where they are manufactured to where they are demanded. To resolve **temporal** discrepancies, retailers focus on their internal logistical activities. They must have the merchandise available when it is needed by consumers. It is estimated that forty-four percent of all retail sales are accounted for by merchandise that was self-distributed (Nawga, 1994).

With the exception of self-distributing retail chains, most retailers, until now, have not given much thought to distribution. After all, the typical consumer shops at a store, purchases merchandise, and carries it home. Today the retailer's distribution decision has taken on another dimension—home delivery.

## Home Delivery

Back in 1912, A&P developed their economy store. They found that they could sell groceries at the lowest possible price if they eliminated credit and delivery. Today, consumers can buy groceries using credit cards in most, if not all, retail food stores. In addition, many retailers are now offering delivery to the customer's door in an attempt to differentiate themselves.

It appears that retailers and others have taken home delivery one step further. Not only does the consumer receive the merchandise at home, but now the consumer doesn't even need to leave home to shop.

## Home Shopping

A significant and growing number of time-pressured consumers are beginning to see the advantage of shopping from home. The orders are placed by telephone, fax machine, or personal computer.

Only a small percentage of retailers, at the present time, can accept computerized orders. However, the increased use of personal computers, and the surging consumer demand for shopping convenience, suggests that **PC** orders will be the preferred mode of home shopping.

**Peapod, Inc., Shoppers Express**, and **Shopping Alternatives** are computerized third-party shopping and delivery services. They handle the order, employ personnel to pick it up, and deliver it to the customer's home. Consumers are able to choose the day and time of delivery, present coupons to the delivery person, and pay by credit card, check, cash, or electronic service. Of those consumers who have tried home shopping, over eighty percent still use the service.

Home shopping is equally beneficial to retailers. In many cases, the retailer or third party periodically charges a membership fee, a service fee, and a percentage of the total bill for each order. Further, many twenty-, thirty-, and forty-year-olds, who are most willing to pay for home shopping, have computers. There are no start-up costs to reach these potential customers.

## Stalemate

No firm can maintain a long run advantage based on its distribution activities. Self distribution offers the retail chains control over their wholesaling functions. This control allows retail chains to operate at lower transportation costs (1.16 percent of sales) than wholesalers in general (1.91 percent of sales). It also allows retail chains to operate at lower warehouse costs (2.10 percent of sales) than wholesalers, warehouse costs of 2.54 percent of sales (Kochersperger, 1996).

The market for home delivery is too small to sustain a competitive advantage. At the present time, about forty percent of the major chains and independent retail firms offer some sort of home shopping, and by 1998 an estimated two-thirds of all retailers in the U.S. and Canada will offer the service. However, whatever competitive advantage home shopping now offers will not survive in the long run.

# SUMMARY

This chapter examined the marketing decisions that retailers make to create and/or maintain a competitive differential advantage. The seven industry groups that the retailing sector comprises were characterized as monopolistically competitive. However, at a local level many MSAs were strongly oligopolistic.

The chapter began with a historical perspective of the retail sector and the nature of competition expressed in terms of strategic groups. The goal of the retailer is to use the right promotion to persuade the right consumers that the right product, in the right quantity, at the right price, is available at the right place, at this, the right time. In order to achieve this goal, the retailer must make marketing decisions that make up what is commonly referred to as the retail marketing mix.

The retailer's location decision involves choosing a market area, trade area, and specific site for the store. Essentially, the retailer seeks to identify an understored condition because it represents an opportunity to retail groceries and related products.

Retailers may also create a competitive advantage by designing the exterior and interior space of the store to have sensory appeal. Although exterior design might attract consumers to the store, their shopping behavior is influenced by the interior design and layout of the store. To influence shoppers' purchase behavior, the retailer relies on an effective presentation of the merchandise mix. To develop an effective merchandise mix, the retailer must make three decisions. First, food and non-food categories must be selected. Next, a decision must be made to determine how many brands to carry in each category. Third, how much of each brand, expressed in SKUs, must be identified. These decisions must be made within the context of the levels of quality the retailer plans to offer to consumers. All of these decisions are influenced by the needs of the target consumers, available retail space, store format, and estimated category profitability.

The retailer's service mix is made up of services that enhance the merchandise and those that facilitate consumer shopping and purchasing. Taken together, some of these services are essential to the retailer's operation, expected by consumers, or optional. Like merchandise decisions, service decisions are made within a defined level of quality.

However price is determined, it must reflect acceptable value to consumers. Retail price levels, and consequently, value, are influenced by pricing philosophies, costs, demand, and price policies. Whatever price levels are established, they must fall within consumer threshold limits.

The retailer's promotional mix must, in the long run, create a favorable retail image and, in the short run, sell existing merchandise and related services. To accomplish these goals, retailers rely on advertising, sales promotion publicity, and personal selling.

The final decision variable in the retailer's marketing mix is distribution. Many retail chains perform their own wholesale functions because it offers them control over their distribution activities. Although unconventional, many retailers have extended their distribution decisions to cover home delivery and home shopping by computer.

Despite the efforts of retailers, their marketing decisions are unable to sustain a long-run competitive advantage. As soon as the retailer's offering is perceived as different and better by the marketplace, competitors soon copy the offering. In this way, competitors are able to **neutralize** the efforts of the innovative retailer. In the short run, retailers can maintain a competitive differential advantage, but in the long run, competition moves in, copies the competitor's differential advantage, and declares a **stalemate**.

## SELECTED REFERENCES

Blattberg, R. C. "Assessing and Capturing the Soft Benefits of Scanning," Coca-Cola Research Council, May 1988.

Blattberg, R. C. and S. A. Neslin. *Sales Promotion Concepts, Methods, and Strategies.* Englewood Cliffs, N.J.: Prentice Hall, 1990.

Berman, B. and J. R. Evans. *Retail Management—A Strategic Approach.* 6th ed. New York: Macmillan Publishing Co., A Division of Macmillan, Inc., 1994.

Carol Wright Promotions, Inc. A subsidary of Cox Target Media, Inc. "18th Annual Survey of Promotional Practices," Naperville, Ill., 1996

Crispens, J. "Frequent-Shopper Game Plan," *Supermarket News*, Vol. 44, No. 26, June 27, 1994, pp. 11–12.

Cohen, J. "In My View: Prospects for the New EDLP," *Supermarket Business*, January 1993, pp. 15–19.

DeSanta, D. and D. Litwak. "48th Annual Consumer Expenditure Study," *Supermarket Business*, September 1995, pp. 25–114.

DeSanta, R. D. 13th Annual Product Preference Study, *Supermarket Business*, Howfrey Communications, Teaneck N. J., March 1996.

*Food Retailing Review.* The Food Institute, Fair Lawn, N. J., 1995 ed.

German, G. A. and T. W. Leed. *Food Merchandising: Principles and Practices.* 47th ed., New York: Sebhan-Friedman Books, Chain Store Publishing Corp., A Subsidiary of Sebhan-Friedman, Inc., 1992.

Giblen, G. M. "Is EDLP Passe?" *Grocery Marketing*, Vol. 61, No. 9, September 1995, pp. 50–51.

Gladson and Associates, Inc. "Planograming for Profit," *Advertising Supplement*, Lisle, Ill., 1994.

Hampe, E. C. and M. Wittenberg, *The Food Industry—Lifeline of America.* 2nd ed. New York: McGraw-Hill, Inc., 1980.

Kochersperger, R. H. "Wholesale/Retail Transportation and Fleet Maintenance Report," *Food Distributors International and Food Marketing Institute,* 1996.

Kochersperger, R. H., "Warehouse Productivity Analysis," *Food Distributors International*, 1996.

Lawrence, J. and S. Hume. "Supermarkets Flock to 'In-Ad' Coupons," *Advertising Age*, October 8, 1992, p. 9.

Lewison, D. M. and M. W. Delozier. *Retailing Principles and Practices*, Columbus, Ohio: Charles E. Merrill Publishing Co., A Bell and Howell Co., 1982.

Linneman, R. E., P. Kirschling, and R. Kocherspencer. "Time to Get Ready for Home Shopping?." *Supermarket Business*, September 1995, pp. 16–21.

Lowe, K. "A Likely Best Seller," *Grocery Marketing*, Vol. 61, No. 7, July 1995, pp. 18–21.

Lowe, Kimberly. "Redefining Variety," *Grocery Marketing*, Vol. 62, No. 3, March 1996, pp. 12–16.

Marion, B. W. and the NC-117 Committee. *The Organization and Performance of the U.S. Food System.* Lexington Mass.: Lexington Books, D.C. Heath and Company, 1986.

Mathews, R. "Relearning the 'ABC' of Business," *Grocery Marketing*, Vol. 59, No. 8, August 1993, p. 6.

Morton, J. E. "What Is Keeping Electronic Labels 'On the Shelf'?" *Grocery Marketing*, Vol. 60, No. 11, November 1994, pp. 32–34.

O'Connor, M. J. "On the Subject of Image," *Supermarket Business*, January 1992, pp. 35–38.

O'Connor, M. J. "On the Subject of Image Part II," *Supermarket Business*, February 1992, pp. 41–94.

Pierce, J. J. "Store Brands Hold Dollar Share Despite Losses in Commodities," *Private Label*, September/October 1995, pp. 81–89.

Porter, M. E. *Competitive Strategy—Techniques for Analyzing Industries and Competitors.* New York: The Free Press, A Division of Macmillan Publishing Co., Inc., 1980.

*Progressive Grocer*, Special Report, "Category Dynamics," September 1993.

*Progressive Grocer*, Special Report, "Brand Power," MacLean Hunter Media, Stamford, Conn., October Supplement, 1994.

*Progressive Grocer*, Special Report, "Branding the Store," November 1995.

*Progressive Grocer*, 63rd Annual Report of the Grocery Industry, Stamford, Conn., April 1996.

Redman, R. "Selling the Image," *Supermarket News*, Vol. 46, No. 12, March 18, 1996, pp. 9–17.

Schneider, R. M. "Image Effect of Odd Pricing," University of Chicago, *Marketing Working Paper,* July 1987.

"Sights and Sounds Fill the Aisles," *Grocery Marketing*, Vol. 60, No. 10, October 1994, pp. 12–15.

Sosna, S. "Goodwill Can Be Good Business," *Grocery Marketing*, Vol. 60, No. 4, April 1994, pp. 39–40.

Sosna, S. "Create More Feed Your Face Events," *Grocery Marketing*, Vol. 61, No. 6, June 1995, pp. 28–30.

Thayer, W., "Electronic Shelf Labels: How They Stack Up," *Progressive Grocer*, January 1990, pp. 61–64.

The Dynamics of Category Management, *A Supplement to Promo and Progressive Grocer Magazines*, December 1993, pp. 1–15.

"The 1995 Annual Report on the Promotion Industry," *Promo—The Magazine of Promotion Marketing*, Vol. VIII, No. 8, July 1995, pp. 33–53.

Tibbitts, L. A. "Study: Perishables Top Home Shoppers' Lists," *Supermarket News*, Vol. 45, No 47, November 20, 1995, pp. 22–23.

"Trial and Conversion: An In-Depth Look at the Power of Product Sampling," *Special Supplement,* Promotion Marketing Association of America, Inc., 1995.

Weinstein, S. "How to Avoid Product Duplication," *Progressive Grocer*, July 1993, pp. 103–104.

*Wholesale Food Distribution Today and Tomorrow.* National-American Wholesale Grocers' Association, Anderson Consulting, Arthur Anderson and Co., S.C., 1994.

*Worldwide Coupon Trends and Consumer Usage Patterns.* NCH Promotional Services, Lincolnshire, Ill., 1996.

# REVIEW QUESTIONS

1. Explain what is meant by the statement, "Store formats represent different strategic groups."

2. What factors determine the nature and intensity of competition among strategic groups?

3. In what way(s) does a retailer's competitive differential advantage differ from the CDA created by wholesalers or manufacturers?

4. Present an argument to support the statement, "A retailer, through timely execution, can maintain a CDA in the long run. (HINT: Argue against the existence of the *stalemate* concept.)

5. Explain the relationship between micro-marketing and the goal of the retail firm.

6. Are the three most important considerations in retailing location, location, and location? Why or why not?

7. A retailer never really gets a second chance to make a good first impression. Discuss this cliché within the context of store atmosphere.

8. What roles do target customers, retail space, store format, and profit play in the design of the merchandise and service offerings?

9. The philosophy of EDLP runs contrary to the High/Low philosophy. Explain, using an example.

10. In light of what is taking place in home shopping, explain why the dictum "Build it and they will come" might never become an axiom.

**TABLE 9-1.** CONTRIBUTION TO TOTAL SALES AND GROSS MARGIN BY DEPARTMENTS

| Departments | Percent of Total Sales | Percent Gross Margin | Contribution to Store Gross Margin$_1$ | Percent of Total Store Gross Margin$_2$ |
|---|---|---|---|---|
| Perishables | 49.36 | 34.9 | 17.23 | 56.5 |
| Dry Groceries | 27.03 | 27.3 | 7.38 | 24.2 |
| Grocery (Nonfoods) | 10.38 | 22.1 | 2.29 | 7.5 |
| Health & Beauty Care | 4.40 | 32.1 | 1.41 | 4.6 |
| Prescriptions | 1.17 | 51.9 | .61 | 2.0 |
| General Merchandise | 4.63 | 34.0 | 1.57 | 5.1 |
| Miscellaneous Sales | 3.03 | ND | | |
| TOTAL | 100.0 | | 30.45 | 100.0 |

1. Percent of total sales x percent gross margin x one hundred = Contribution to store gross margin.
2. Contribution to store gross margin/total = Percent total store gross margin.

*SOURCE:* 48th Consumer Expenditure Study, *Supermarket Business*, September 1996, pp. 25–126.

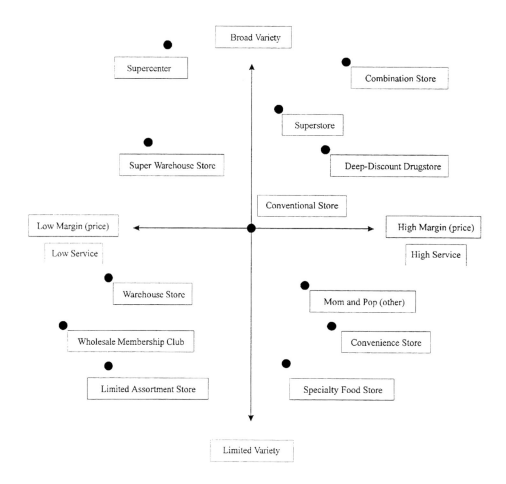

**FIGURE 9-1.** STORE FORMATS

*SOURCE:* Adapted from B. W. Marion, *The Organization and Performance of The U.S. Food System,* Lexington Books, D.C. Heath and Co., 1986, W. H. Heller, "A New Look at Store Formats," *Progressive Grocer,* December 1986.

GENERAL TRADE AREA

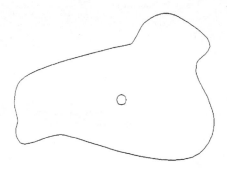

COMPOSITE TRADE AREA

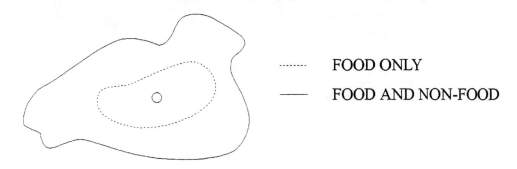

PROPORTIONAL TRADE AREA

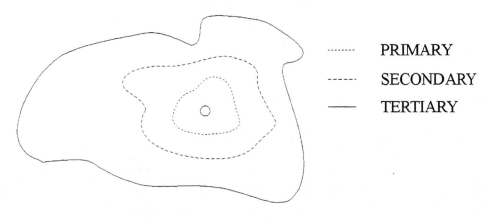

**FIGURE 9-2.** TRADE AREA STRUCTURES

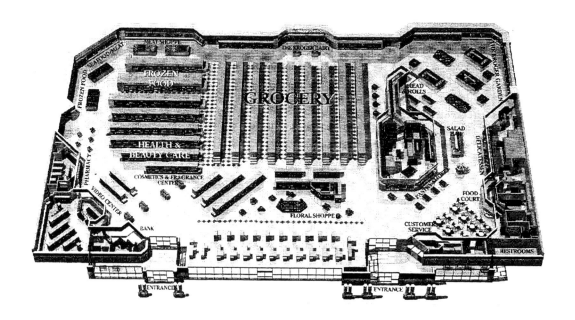

**FIGURE 9-3.** STORE LAYOUTS: GRID, FREE-FORM, BOUTIQUE

*SOURCE:* Supermarket News, "Kroger to Expand Signature Format," Vol. 44, No. 44, October 31, 1994, p. 12.

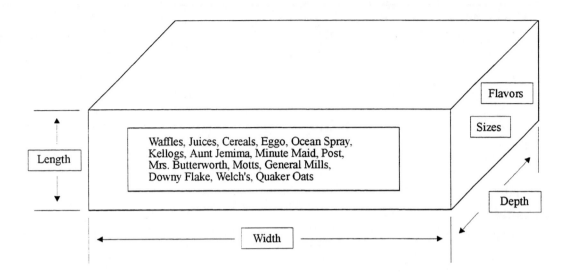

**FIGURE 9-4.** MERCHANDISE MIX DIMENSIONS

**FIGURE 9-5.** SERVICE OFFERINGS OF SUPERMARKETS

| | |
|---|---|
| Service delicatessen | 78.5 |
| Service meat | 71.5 |
| Accept credit cards* | 70.7 |
| Soft drink vending machines | 70.6 |
| Service bakery | 68.6 |
| Check-cashing cards | 63.0 |
| Coffee grinders | 62.0 |
| Photo/film processing | 61.6 |
| Lottery tickets | 58.4 |
| ATMs | 55.9 |
| Floral department | 48.8 |
| Service seafood | 45.8 |
| Prepared foods, hot/cold | 39.1 |
| Video rentals | 38.4 |
| Salad bar | 27.1 |
| Separate cheese department | 26.9 |
| Seasonal aisle | 26.3 |
| Pharmacy | 25.3 |
| Candy vending machines | 23.8 |
| Full-service banking | 12.8 |
| Nutrition center | 12.7 |
| Cigarette vending machines | 11.1 |
| Restaurant | 11.0 |
| Frequent-shopper program | 10.1 |
| Service cosmetics | 10.1 |
| Fast-food franchise | 1.1 |

SOURCE: Adapted from *Progressive Grocer 63rd Annual Report of the Grocery Industry*, April 1996, p. 35.

# Chapter 10

# Consumer Behavior Trilogy

**Chapter Outline**

The Meaning of Food
    A. Foodways
    B. Food and Consumers
    C. Consumer Lifestyles

Consumption Behavior
    A. Per Capita Consumption
    B. Consumption Expenditures

Purchase Behavior
    A. Problem Recognition
    B. Search for Solutions
    C. Evaluation of Alternatives
    D. Choice
    E. Post-Evaluation
    F. Unplanned Purchases

Shopping Behavior
    A. Out-of-Store Behavior
    B. In-Store Behavior

Summary

The **U.S. food marketing system** is driven by consumers. Consequently, the system's output is consumer satisfaction. What is produced, transformed, moved, and/or stored is destined to be bought and consumed by the American public. The previous chapters examined the roles that the producer, manufacturer, wholesaler, and retailer sectors play in the U.S. food marketing system. Each of these sectors contains firms that must make marketing decisions to satisfy consumer tastes and preferences. But consumer tastes and preferences are not monolithic. Knowing that everybody eats, and that almost everyone shops for food, doesn't tell firms much about consumers. What do food firms need to know about consumers? Simply, everything they can about the shopping, purchasing, and consumption behaviors of consumers, and what influences these behaviors. The purpose of this chapter is to examine the behaviors of consumers within the context of shopping, purchasing, and consuming food products. To understand consumer behavior more fully, the meaning of food is presented first. Subsequent sectors reveal the trilogy of consumer behavior: shopping, purchasing, and consuming food products.

# THE MEANING OF FOOD

There can be little doubt in anyone's mind that food occupies a crucial role in any society. Countries go to war over food. Economies revolve around food. Food is traded for political influence. Religions use food in their rituals. Food is used to celebrate life's passages. Food is shared to build friendships. Food bonds families. Food words are used in our language as metaphors: "She is a peach," "This car is a lemon," "He is as cool as a cucumber," "You are full of baloney!" "What's eating you?" or "She's just trying to butter you up." Food (meals) organizes our days and governs our social lives. We spend a lot of time purchasing food, eating food, thinking about food, and earning money to buy food. Food ensures our survival. Food defines who we are as individuals. Given the enormous importance of food, its acquisition, preparation, and consumption are never left to chance. What follows is an anatomy of food's relationship to society and individual consumers.

## Foodways

Anything that *can* be eaten *is* eaten by someone, somewhere around the world. We humans are omnivorous because we eat both plant- and animal-derived foods. But no society eats everything, and we do not eat randomly. What determines the foods a society eats or will not eat?

Food is a complex phenomenon that has multiple meanings and thus is consumed to satisfy multiple needs. With the exception of physiological nourishment, society bestows multiple meanings on food. These meanings represent multiple sources of need satisfaction and are embodied in a society's foodways.

**Foodways** reflect broad behavioral patterns that govern the acquisition, preparation, and the consumption of food according to a society's preferences. Although there are individual likes and dislikes, societal members learn to agree on what they like most and what they like least. This results in relatively stable food preferences. In turn, food preference leads to choice and choice leads to consumption (Camp, 1989).

### Liking, Preference, and Choice

How do people come to like food? Although the answer to this question is still being considered, it appears that "liking" is an affective interpretation of a specific emotion called pleasure. People like food because they believe or know that its taste and smell will result in sensual pleasure. Both taste and smell are chemical senses and operate by detecting molecules on the tongue and in the air, respectively. "Liking the taste" is a major determinant of food preferences, but it is not the only determinant. Psychologists believe that food preferences are determined by other biological factors, as well as culture (Logue, 1991).

Although the most basic biological need is for nutrition, all humans have genetically based predispositions. Genetically, humans have a sweet-bitter taste bias. We like sweet tastes and avoid bitter tastes. Humans also have an innate preference for salt. Salt is essential for the body to function properly. Without salt, the body will die of dehydration. Clearly the ability to digest milk is determined by genes. People who can digest milk (lactose tolerance) drink it; people who *cannot* digest it (lactose intolerance) do not. A final innate bias is called **neophobia**. Humans, like other omnivores, are very suspicious of new foods (Logue, 1991).

It is fair to say that, despite these biological determinants, food preferences show a predominant influence of cultural factors. A culture transmits beliefs, values, preferences, traditions, customs, rituals, and specific guidelines for behaviors. It rewards those who conform, and punishes those who violate its guidelines. The demographic, technological, political, economic, natural, and environmental characteristics of a culture also influence our food preferences. Thus, it can be said *We eat what we are.*

Just as food liking does not alone correspond to food preferences, food preferences do not necessarily correspond to food choice. For food preference to equate with food choice all food must be physically available to people. But even when this condition is met, there are foods that people choose *not* to eat.

There are four reasons why people choose not to eat certain foods. The tongue samples the taste, texture, and temperature of food, and together with the nose, which detects its smell, they signal the body to accept or reject it. Thus, we don't eat foods that taste offensive to our gustatory senses, and/or smell offensive to our olfactory sense. These foods are labeled as **distastes**. We do not eat foods that are considered harmful to our physical being. These contaminated foods are called **dangers**. We do not eat what is inedible. Non-food items are referred to as **inappropriate**. We do not eat what our culture tells us is not food, even though it may be food to other cultures. These foods are categorized under the heading of **disgust** (Rozin, 1994). When given a choice, consumers choose not to eat foods that can be placed in one of these categories. Examples of common distasteful, dangerous, inappropriate, and disgusting foods are sauerkraut, poisonous mushrooms, flowers, and dogs, respectively.

People choose not to eat certain foods, but they also choose to eat certain foods. Why do people choose to eat certain foods? To answer this question requires a close examination of a statement made earlier in this chapter: "Society bestows multiple meanings on food."

## Food and Consumers

It is all very simple. Consumers eat certain foods because they seek to satisfy needs. As humans, we are born with the need for food to eat, water to drink, and air to breathe. But we have other needs that are not innate. Needs are also learned in the process of becoming a member of a culture. In addition, by imbuing a product or service with multiple meanings, a culture specifies how innate and learned needs can be satisfied by consuming particular products and services. To consumers, these multiple meanings are interpreted as multiple sources of need satisfaction. Using food as an example, this means that the consumption of certain foods can satisfy innate, as well as learned, needs. To illustrate the relationship between consumer needs and food as alternative sources of satisfaction, needs first must be classified.

The most influential approach to classification of need was proposed by Abraham Maslow (1970). Being a humanistic psychologist, he developed a hierarchy of needs that parallels an individual's personal growth. This hierarchy is depicted in **Figure 10-1**. Maslow believed that, ideally, an individual strives to move up the hierarchy until he or she has reached the pinnacle of growth—*self actualization*. Most consumers only periodically reach this level. It is the exceptional individual who is capable of sustaining self-fulfillment in all things. The real value in Maslow's hierarchy is that it illustrates how the consumption of food satisfies the priorities of different needs. The following brief review is offered to clarify its value to marketers.

### *Physiological Need*

The most fundamental of all needs is survival. Without food and drink, we die. There is no substitute for food. To satisfy physiological needs, consumers primarily choose foods that taste and smell good. Of course, what constitutes good taste and smell is defined by the cultural context in which choices are made.

### *Safety*

The need for physical safety, security, stability, and familiar surroundings are examples of safety needs. To satisfy safety needs, consumers focus on highly nutritional foods. In addition, foods that are perceived to be a cure for certain illnesses are selected for their medicinal value. Some examples of these foods are fish oil to lower blood triglyceride levels, garlic to lower cholesterol levels, soybeans to block tumor growth, chili peppers to treat arthritis pain, and cranberry juice to cure urinary tract infections.

### Belongingness

The need for love, friendship, and acceptance are examples of belongingness needs. Preparing a meal and sharing it is an age-old way of making friends. Mother's cooking expresses love. A romantic dinner by moonlight bonds a man and a woman. Family mealtimes are occasions for parents to express acceptance. Food and drink are used to celebrate milestones of passage from one stage to another in the biological and social lives of individuals. In almost all societies, the giving, preparation, and consumption of food can be expressions of friendship and an acceptance of love.

### Esteem

Esteem needs include the need for status, prestige, superiority, and self-respect. A person's social position can be determined by looking at what is on his or her plate. In this way, the food we consume is a way of saying, both for their sake and ours, that we are different, we don't eat like them. Many of the specialty foods available to consumers allow them to demonstrate their status, superiority, or prestige.

### Self Actualization

The need for self-fulfillment—to become all that we are capable of becoming—is the ultimate need. Food allows us to create a social identity and communicate it to others. Going to an exquisite restaurant or purchasing gourmet foods as a reward for a recently earned promotion indicates that one has arrived at his or her psychological destination. What we choose to eat makes a statement about who we are: **"We are what we eat!"**

In summary, Maslow's hierarchy of needs reflects the cultural availability of food. This hierarchy identifies how food, in general, is used to satisfy different needs. But what determines which products or brands consumers will choose in order to satisfy these needs? Generally, consumers choose products and brands that they believe are consistent with their lifestyles.

## Consumer Lifestyles

Why do consumers do the things they do? All of what they buy is to maintain or enhance a style of life they have chosen to live. The lifestyles we have chosen make a statement to others about who we are. It follows that, as consumers, we choose products, such as food, that are consistent with what we want to say to ourselves and to others.

The style of life we choose to live is a reflection of our past experiences, current needs, and future expectations. Further, it is formed and changed through the social interaction we have in our culture as we move through various stages of our life cycles. Although each lifestyle is somewhat unique, the patterns of consumption resulting from our lifestyle are often shared by others in similar circumstances. The fact that patterns of consumption are shared explains why the lifestyle concept is one of the major approaches used by food marketers.

The primary value of the lifestyle concept to the U.S. food marketing system lies in its potential use in market segmentation. By examining the activities that people enjoy, the interests they have, and the opinions they express, marketers are able to determine which food categories and specific brands are likely to appeal to a particular lifestyle segment. Further discussion of lifestyle will be included in the following chapter on market segmentation.

To summarize, the importance of food to any culture can not be undervalued. The foodways that specify how food is acquired, prepared, and consumed unify and give purpose to societal members. We learn to like, prefer, choose, and consume food products that are defined by our culture as appropriate for consumption.

With the exception of physiological needs, consumer needs are learned mostly in the process of becoming a member of a culture. To satisfy these learned needs society imbues food with multiple meanings. When these meanings are translated by consumers, food products are perceived as multiple sources of need satisfaction. Although we can satisfy different needs, exactly which foods people consume can only be identified by examining how consumers have chosen to live out their lifestyles.

In the following section, three essential components of foodways will be discussed in reverse order of occurrence. First, consumption behavior will be analyzed from two different perspectives. Next, purchase behavior will be discussed within the context of decision making. Finally, the acquisition of food products will be examined by focusing on consumer shopping behavior. Together, shopping, purchasing, and consumption make up the trilogy of consumer behavior.

## CONSUMPTION BEHAVIOR

Consumer behavior is a general term that encompasses shopping behavior, purchase behavior, and consumption behavior. This section will examine consumption behavior from two different perspectives: what we eat, and how we spend our money on what we eat. The discussion on what we eat will focus on our per capita consumption eating patterns at the commodity level. How we spend our money on what we eat will focus on our spending patterns at the commodity level.

## Per Capita Consumption

The **USDA's Economic Research Service (ERS)** annually calculates the amount of food available for human consumption in the U.S. The measured availability of food, referred to as food disappearance, estimates the food supply moving through the U.S. food system for domestic consumption. Because most foods are perishable, changes in food disappearance can be associated with changes in actual consumption.

Per capita consumption trends of animal products that include meat, poultry, fish, eggs, dairy, fats, and oils are discussed first. Per capita consumption trends of crop products, which include fruits, vegetables, flour and cereal products, and sweeteners follows. An examination of per capita consumption of beverages ends the section.

Historically, **USDA** data on per capita consumption of animal and crop products is used for purposes of trend interpretation. The change in consumption from 1970 through 1994 is considered a long run trend, whereas consumption change from 1991 through 1994 serves as a basis for short run interpretation.

**Table 10-1** shows the changes in per capita consumption of all meats. In 1994, total meat consumption (i.e., red meat, poultry, and fish) reached a record 193.5 pounds, or a nine percent increase from 1970, and a three percent increase from 1991.

### *Red Meat*

Red meat consumption actually declined thirteen percent from 1970. From 1970 through 1994, the typical consumer ate sixteen fewer pounds of beef, one less pound of veal and lamb, and 1.5 more pounds of pork. In the short run, consumers ate about one-half pound more beef, the first increase in nine years. The amount of veal and lamb consumed stayed about the same. Most of the short run three-pound increase is due to the increased consumption of pork. Nutritional concern about fat and cholesterol, in combination with the pork industry's **"The Other White Meat"** advertising campaign, probably contributed to this increase. **Table 10-1** indicates also the change in consumption shares for red meat. The loss of fifteen share points represents a twenty percent decrease from 1970. The short run loss in share points was only about one point.

**Table 10-2** shows a breakdown of shares for the various red meats. Beef's loss of five share points accounts for most of the red meat loss. Clearly, pork, with its almost seven share point gain, accounts for most of the increase in both the short and long run.

### *Poultry*

Poultry consumption increased eighty-eight percent from 1970. From 1970 through 1994, the typical consumer ate thirty pounds more poultry, twenty-two pounds more chicken, and eight pounds more turkey (**Table 10-3**). In the short run, turkey consumption stayed virtually the same while chicken consumption increased by more than five pounds. The nutritional concern about red meat, and the proliferation of value-added products for consumer convenience, contributed greatly to the increased consumption of poultry—especially chicken.

**Table 10-1** shows the change in consumption share for poultry. The fourteen point gain in share of total meat consumption represents a seventy-three percent increase in share points in the long run. The short run change in share points is only one point.

Despite the fact that the consumption of chicken has increased in each of the last twenty years from 1975, its share of poultry consumption is still below its 1970 level. On the other hand, chicken's share of poultry consumption has increased in each of the years since 1991.

### Fish

Fish consumption has increased twenty-nine percent from 1970. From 1970 through 1994, the typical consumer ate about the same amount of canned and cured fish, but 3.4 pounds more fresh and frozen fish (**Table 10-4**). When fresh and frozen fishery products are broken down, most of the increase was in finfish rather than shellfish. The short run change in consumption in **Table 10-4** shows no change in cured fish, and a seven percent increase in fresh- and frozen-fish consumption.

Three health concerns have stimulated growth in seafood consumption. Fish is low in fats and calories. Fish is an excellent source of protein. Finally, fish is a source of **Omega-3** fatty acids, which are believed to lower blood cholesterol levels.

Two demographic factors have contributed to the increase in seafood consumption. As people age, they tend to eat more seafood. The U.S. median age continues to increase as the "baby boomers" grow older. Asians eat more seafood than non-Asians. Asian-Americans are the fastest-growing ethnic group in the U.S.

**Table 10-4** shows the change in consumption shares for fishery products. The nine share point gain in fish/frozen-fish consumption represents a sixteen percent increase in shares. Most of this increase has come at the expense of the decline in canned fish which includes salmon, sardines, and shellfish, but not tuna. In fact, canned tuna experienced a thirty-two percent increase in per capita consumption since 1970.

### Eggs

**Table 10-5** reveals the changes in per capita consumption of eggs. The per capita consumption declined twenty-three percent from 1970. From 1970 through 1994, the typical consumer ate ninety-nine fewer shell eggs, and twenty-seven more processed eggs. Processed eggs are used mainly as ingredients in manufactured foods such as pasta, cake mixes, and other baked goods.

The consumption of eggs increased in the short run. The typical consumer ate four more eggs in 1994 than in 1991. All of the increase was in the form of processed-egg consumption. The increase can be explained partly by recent research that shows lower cholesterol in eggs than previously thought, a weaker link between heart disease and cholesterol consumption, and relaxed diets that contain more baked goods.

An examination of consumption shares shows a long and short run increase in processed-egg consumption, and a decrease in shell-egg consumption. Again, the use of liquid egg products by foodservice institutions, together with earlier-mentioned research results, combined to influence processed-egg consumption.

### *Dairy Products*

**Table 10-6** shows the changes in per capita consumption of dairy products. The per capita consumption of all dairy products increased by twenty-two pounds, or four percent. From 1970 through 1994, the typical consumer ate fourteen more pounds cheese, two pounds more frozen dairy products, and three pounds more fluid cream. Most of the cheese was whole (American and Italian) rather than cottage. The six-fold increase in per capita consumption of yogurt accounts for most of the increase in frozen dairy products. All milk products (i.e., evaporated, dry, and fluid) declined. Skim milk was the only beverage milk for which per capita consumption increased. Consumers ate more fluid cream products (e.g., half and half, light cream, heavy cream, eggnog, sour cream, and dip) which tends to conflict with health concerns. The **USDA** reports only selected categories in dairy products, which prevents the calculation of consumption shares for dairy products.

### *Fats and Oils*

Per capita consumption of fats and oils has increased twenty-five percent from 1970. From 1970 through 1994, the typical consumer ate fourteen more pounds of fat and oil (**Table 10-7**). The increase is more than likely due to the increased use of salad oils on salads, at and away from home. Use of salad oils and cooking oils increased fifty-eight percent from 1970 through 1994, and use of shortening increased by thirty-nine percent. Over the same period, per capita consumption of all other fats and oils declined: butter (eleven percent), margarine (nine percent), lard (sixty-three percent), and other edible fats and oils by thirty percent.

**Table 10-8** reports the consumption of fats and oils derived from animal and vegetable sources. From 1970 through 1994, the typical consumer ate forty-four percent more vegetable fat and oils, or 7.3 pounds. Over the same period, the average consumer ate eighteen percent less animal fat and oil. The share of fats and oils from animals fell from twenty-seven percent in 1970, to seventeen percent in 1994. Health concerns greatly contributed to the switch from animal to vegetable fats and oils.

### *Fruits*

Although shown separately in tables, per capita consumption of fruits and vegetables increased by twenty percent, from 565.5 pounds in 1970, to 677.8 pounds in 1994. Total per capita consumption of fruits was derived for six citrus fruits (i.e., grapefruit, lemons, limes, oranges, tangelos, and tangerines) and six non-citrus fruits (i.e., apples, non-wine grapes, peaches, pears, pineapples, and strawberries). Total consumption of these twelve fruits and thirteen other fruits was 280 pounds in 1994, up fifty pounds from 1970 (**Table 10-9**). Per capita consumption of fresh fruit increased twenty-five percent from 1970 and processed fruit consumption increased nineteen percent.

Per capita consumption of fresh fruit in 1994 was made up of twenty percent citrus and eighty percent non-citrus. While oranges accounted for about one-half of all citrus consumption, bananas, melons, and apples accounted for seventy-three percent of all non-citrus fruits consumed in 1994. From 1970 through 1994, per capita consumption of citrus fruits declined from twenty-nine percent to twenty percent, while per capita consumption of non-citrus fruits increased from seventy-one percent to eighty percent.

Per capita consumption of processed fruit in 1994 was made up of fifty-nine percent citrus and forty-one percent non-citrus. While oranges accounted for eighty-three percent of all processed citrus fruit, apples accounted for forty-eight percent of all non-citrus fruits consumed. From 1970 through 1994, per capita consumption of citrus fruits decreased from sixty-four percent of all processed fruit to fifty-nine percent, while per capita consumption of non-citrus fruits increased from thirty-six percent to forty-one percent of all processed fruit consumption.

From 1970 through 1994, per capita consumption of fresh fruits increased from forty-four percent to seventy-five percent of all fruits consumed per capita. This one percent increase came at the expense of the per capita consumption share of processed fruits.

### *Vegetables*

Total per capita consumption of vegetables was derived from fifty-three commercially produced vegetables. Total per capita consumption of the vegetables was 398 pounds—up sixty-three pounds from 1970 (**Table 10-10**).

Per capita consumption of fresh vegetables increased by twelve percent or eighteen pounds. In 1994, potatoes accounted for thirty-three percent of all fresh vegetables combined. Together with lettuce, onions, and tomatoes, these four fresh vegetables accounted for sixty-seven percent of all fresh vegetable consumption per capita.

Per capita consumption of processed vegetables increased by twenty-five percent or forty-five pounds. In 1994, potatoes and tomatoes accounted for fifty and forty percent of all processed vegetables consumed per capita.

From 1970 through 1994, per capita consumption of fresh vegetables decreased from forty-six percent to forty-three percent of all vegetables consumed per capita. This loss was absorbed by the increase in per capita consumption of processed vegetables.

### *Flour and Cereal Products*

Per capita consumption of flour and cereal products increased forty-six percent from 1970 or by sixty-three pounds. From 1970 through 1994, the average consumer ate thirty-four more pounds of wheat, thirteen more pounds of corn, twelve more pounds of rice, four more pounds of oats, one more pound of barley, and one-half pound less of rye flour (**Table 10-11**). Although not shown, wheat accounted for seventy-three percent of all flour and cereal products consumed in 1994, a decline of nine share points from 1970 when wheat accounted for eighty-two percent of all flour and cereal products consumed. The per capita increase in rice (184 percent), corn (114 percent), oats (ninety-six percent), and barley (seventy percent) absorbed the nine share point wheat loss.

Much of the growth is explained by the increased demand for variety brands, bakery products and buns. In addition, the consumption of breakfast cereals increased fifty-three percent to 18.4 pounds per capita in 1994. Health concerns and convenience give high fiber breakfast cereals a significant advantage over the once traditional bacon and eggs breakfast.

### *Caloric and Low Caloric Sweeteners*

Total per capita consumption of caloric sweeteners increased by twenty-one percent or twenty-five pounds from 1970 (**Table 10-12**). In 1994, consumers ate a record 148 pounds of caloric sweeteners. Per capita consumption of sucrose (i.e., cane and beet sugar) declined by thirty-six pounds while corn sweeteners (i.e., high-fructose corn syrup—HFCS—glucose, and dextrose) increased by sixty-two pounds from 1970. Much of the decline in sucrose is accounted for by the change in sweeteners used in soft drinks. Use of **HFCS** in soft drinks and bakery products and processed foods has resulted in a significant shift in shares of total sweeteners.

Per capita consumption of sucrose has declined from eighty-three percent of all caloric sweeteners to only forty-four percent in 1994. Over this same period, **HFCS** have increase from three percent of all caloric sweeteners to seventy-four percent in 1994.

### *Beverages*

Per capita consumption of beverages increased twenty-six percent or by thirty-three gallons from 1970. From 1970 through 1994, the average consumer drank nine more gallons of water, eighteen more gallons of soft drinks, eight more gallons of juice, and four more gallons of alcohol (**Table 10-13**).

The per capita consumption of soft drinks increased by 115 percent from 1970. The share of diet soft drinks increased from nine percent to twenty-three percent of all carbonated soft drinks. The per capita consumption increased for juices (151 percent), bottled water (ninety-five percent), alcohol (eighteen percent), and tea (twelve percent). Per capita consumption of milk declined by twenty-one percent or nine gallons as did per capita consumption of coffee (thirty-seven percent). The short run decline of alcoholic beverages is accounted for totally by the drop in per capita consumption of distilled spirits to 1.3 gallons (the lowest level in twenty-five years).

To summarize, in 1994 the typical consumer ate sixty-four pounds of beef, fifty pounds of pork, one pound each of veal and pork, fifty pounds of chicken, fourteen pounds of turkey, fifteen pounds of fish, 586 pounds of dairy products, seventy pounds of fats and oils, and 238 eggs.

With regard to crop products, in 1994 the typical consumer ate 280 pounds of fruit, 398 pounds of vegetables, 199 pounds of flour and cereal, and 148 pounds of caloric sweeteners. This was all washed down with twenty-five gallons of milk, eight gallons of tea, twenty-one gallons of coffee, fifty-two gallons of soft drinks, fourteen gallons of fruit juice, twenty-six gallons of alcohol, and finally, eleven gallons of bottled water.

## Consumption Expenditures

Having examined what we eat, consumption behavior can be reviewed from another closely related perspective. To answer the question, "What are consumers eating?" trade related sources publish sales data. These sales data reflect what consumers are buying, and what they are buying is what they are, of course, eating!

Trade associated sales data are reported annually by *Progressive Grocer*, *Grocery Marketing*, and *Supermarket Business Magazine*. **Progressive Grocer, Inc**. conducts a study of supermarket sales and reports sales analyses by departments and categories. **Grocery Marketing, Inc**. reports InfoScan sales data for 240 product categories. The data is collected by Information Resources, Inc. (IRI). **Supermarket Business, Inc**. conducts a study of grocery store sales and reports them in a number of ways, including store affiliation (i.e., chain vs. independents), store volume, department, and categories.

In addition to sales data, consumption behavior can be examined by focusing on *consumer expenditures* or on how we spend our money on what we eat. The **Bureau of Labor Statistics (BLS)** annually conducts a **Consumer Expenditure Survey** on the spending habits of American consumers. The expenditure categories closely parallel the food commodities reported by the **USDA's Economic Research Services (ERS)**. These data are not reported on a per capita basis, but rather according to consumer unit. A **consumer unit** is: (1) members of a household related by blood, adoption, marriage, or other legal arrangement; (2) a financially independent person living alone or sharing a household with others; or (3) two or more persons living together and using their incomes to make joint expenditure decisions.

Average annual expenditures from 1990 through 1994 for all consumer units are presented in **Table 10-14.** Average annual expenditures increased by twelve percent from 1990 through 1994; however, food expenditures increased by only three percent over this same period. Dairy products, alcoholic beverages, and food eaten away from home declined by two, six, and nine percent respectively. The percentage increases in the other categories were cereals and bakery products (16.6 percent), other food at home (10.6 percent), food at home (9.1 percent), meat, poultry, fish, and eggs (9.6 percent) and fruits and vegetables (7.0 percent).

**Table 10-15** shows the shares of average annual expenditures for the food commodity groups. The shares of expenditures for food declined from 15.1 to 13.9 percent, or by nine percent. This decline was shared evenly by the decline in shares for food consumed at and away from home. However, over this period, the share of food dollars spent at home has risen from fifty-eight percent of all food expenditures in 1990 to sixty-one percent in 1994. This finding contradicts the popular press's assertion that consumers are spending more money for food away from home. In fact, they are spending less.

To summarize, the typical consumer unit spent three percent more for food in 1994 than in 1990. The largest expenditure increase was for cereals and bakery products, and the largest decrease was for alcoholic beverages. As a share of all spending, consumer units spent less for food in 1994 than they did in 1990. Finally, the percentage of each food dollar spent on food at home increased from fifty-eight to sixty-one cents.

## PURCHASE BEHAVIOR

The purchase behavior of consumers is but one stage in a larger decision-making process. Consumers engage in a decision-making process to solve problems. These problems are encountered as consumers live their chosen lifestyles. Further, these problems are solved by the purchase of products and/or brands that allow consumers to maintain or enhance their lifestyles.

Consumers think about what they are going to do, do it, and then think about what they have done. This long-observed phenomenon has been more formally defined as a problem-solving process that consists of five stages: (1) problem recognition, (2) search for solutions, (3) evaluation of alternative solutions, (4) choice, and (5) post-evaluation of chosen alternatives (Dewey, 1910).

For many food purchases, this process begins **after** the consumer has entered a retail store. **Table 10-16** illustrates the results of a consumer buying-habits study published by the **Point of Purchase Advertising Institute (POPAI)**. It reveals that the decision-making process for sixty percent of all food purchases *(unplanned)* began **after** the consumer entered the store. This represents an eleven percent increase from their earlier study.

Even though the decision-making process for forty percent of all food purchases began **before** entering the store, ten percent of them (generally *planned* and *substitute*) were finalized while consumers were in the store. When added to unplanned purchases, seventy percent of all food purchase decisions are made in the store—a four percent increase from their earlier study.

Each of the decision-making stages will now be described within the context of food purchases. As mentioned previously, this process is influenced by consumer lifestyles and the culture in which people live. In-store decision making and situational influences will be described in the following section on shopping behavior.

## Problem Recognition

Foods are relatively inexpensive products that are purchased frequently and with minimal effort. Thus, normal depletion of household food stocks most often causes a recognizable difference between a consumer's *existing* state of satisfaction and *desired* state of satisfaction. When this occurs, a consumer recognizes a problem. Of course, other factors are capable of activating problem recognition. Arousal of physiological needs (e.g., hunger and thirst) and dissatisfaction with a previously purchased food product are two other factors of significance to food purchases.

Once a person recognizes a problem, it must be defined in such a way that he or she can solve it. Because these problems are solved by the purchase of products and/or brands that allow consumers to maintain or enhance their lifestyles, any factor that influences a person's lifestyle affects how the consumer's problem is defined. Among these factors are the need for variety, a change in the consumer's financial situation, family life cycle, individual physical or psychological development, and previously made decisions on complementary products.

Historically, consumers have defined their food related problems in terms of **meal ingredients**. On a typical shopping trip, a consumer might purchase beef for a main course, vegetables and potatoes as a side course, apple pie to serve as a dessert, and gourmet coffee for the last course. As a result of the shopping trip, the consumer has all of the ingredients for an entire meal.

Recently, more and more consumers are defining their food related problems in terms of meal solutions rather than meal ingredients or individual products. **Meal solutions** consist of individually prepared or pre-cooked ingredients packaged together to form an entire take-home meal. It is not fast food the consumer is looking for, but rather *good food,* fast (Valero, 1996).

## Search for Solutions

How consumers define food related problems has important implications for consumer search processes. People who define food problems in terms of **meal ingredients** (products) have historically relied on their accumulated knowledge for information on alternative products. The frequency of food purchases allows consumers to accumulate knowledge from past searches, personal experiences, opinions of friends and family, food related articles in newspapers, magazines, publications by governmental and consumer groups, and retail advertising. The substantial costs associated with searching for information, relative to the food product's price, means that most consumers engage in little to no information searching immediately prior to purchase. Instead, they rely on their memory of accumulated knowledge.

Consumers who define food problems in terms of **meal solutions** want a relatively healthy, good tasting, ready-to-eat meal, with minimal time investment in shopping or cooking. A recent survey published by the **Food Marketing Institute** found that more than half of all shoppers now buy ready-to-eat takeout foods from their food stores at least once a month (Trends, 1996). Because these consumers don't shop for ingredients, their knowledge is mostly composed of previous experiences, and opinions from friends and family. In addition, these consumers are less sensitive to the ingredients that compose the take out to eat (TOTE) meal. Once again, consumers are unlikely to engage in an information search immediately prior to purchase. Instead, like consumers who seek meal ingredients, people who seek meal solutions rely on their accumulated knowledge.

At the end of the search process, the consumer has used the accumulated knowledge to identify potential alternatives, either meal solutions or meal ingredients, and criteria to evaluate these alternatives. It is unlikely that a consumer would or could identify all of the alternatives. Rather, he or she is likely to consider a limited number of alternatives, which make up what is called an **evoked set**. Those alternatives unworthy of further consideration make up the **inept set**, and those to which consumers are indifferent make up the **inert set** (Hawkins, Best, and Coney, 1995).

## Evaluation of Alternatives

Having identified alternatives and criteria for evaluation, the evaluation process involves evaluating each alternative on the selected criteria. As a result of the evaluation process, consumers develop expectations regarding how the various alternatives will perform on the selected criteria.

When consumers are asked about the criteria they use to evaluate food products, taste is identified as the most important criterion (**Table 10-17**). Price is consistently identified by more than one-third of consumers as the most important. Surprisingly, few consumers consider brand name as the most important criterion. The low number of consumers who rank quick preparation as the most important criterion, may reflect the recent trend toward **TOTE (take-out-to-eat) food.**

## Choice

Choice is the most observable stage in the consumer decision process. It involves selecting one of the evaluated alternatives according to the consumer's preferences. As suggested in the previous chapter's discussion on the use of scanner data, **the best predictor of what food item the consumer will purchase is the food item he or she purchased on the last shopping trip**. For example, if a consumer purchased **Heinz Ketchup** on his or her last store visit, the next time he or she needs ketchup, the consumer will most likely purchase **Heinz Ketchup**. Why is this so? The high purchase frequency of food products makes them susceptible to highly repetitive buying patterns. Unless the consumer is dissatisfied with the previous purchase, the choice is likely to be repeated with little thought to the purchase. If the purchase is repeated often enough, it becomes habituated. Studies on brand loyalty reinforce the conclusion that most food purchases are the result of habit (Assael, 1995). This conclusion is reinforced by a study that found consumers, on average, spent only twelve seconds in front of a product display (shelf) before making a choice. About forty-two percent of the shoppers spent less than five seconds, while twenty-five percent spent more than fifteen seconds. Not surprisingly, in eighty-five percent of the cases, shoppers handled only the chosen brand and ninety percent of the shoppers physically inspected only one size (Dickson and Sawyer, 1990).

## Post-Evaluation

At this stage, the consumer tries to answer the question, "Did the product or meal provide me with the sensual pleasure I expected from it?" For most consumers, an acceptable level of satisfaction is all that is necessary. Because consumers expect the food product or meal to taste good, an evaluation process begins at the time of consumption and lasts throughout this experience. When asked why consumers switch brands, the two most frequent responses are poor quality and dissatisfaction with the present brand (*What America Eats,* 1995). Taste is affected by quality, and in turn it determines how satisfied or dissatisfied consumers are with their consumption experiences.

To summarize the food purchase behavior of consumers, food products are relatively inexpensive, and must be purchased frequently because they are consumed over short periods of time. The purchase of food products involves substantial search costs (i.e., time, effort, money) relative to the price of the product. Because of this, consumers are likely to engage in little information searching immediately prior to purchase, but rather rely on their accumulated knowledge. Consumers evaluate either the meal ingredients (products) or meal solutions (entire meal) mostly according to taste. The repetitive nature of food purchasing leads to repetitive buying patterns that often result in habit formation. Consumers expect that their consumption experiences will result in sensual pleasure. Food purchase behavior viewed from this perspective may be summarized by saying, "Consumers learn to **buy** what they **like** after comparing the alternatives."

The discussion of food purchases behavior would be incomplete without an examination of unplanned purchases. After all, sixty percent of all food purchases are unplanned.

## Unplanned Purchases

Unplanned purchases reflect a decision-making process that began **after** the consumer entered the store. Previously, unplanned purchases were generally considered synonymous with impulse purchasing. Today, it is accepted that a **pure** impulse purchase represents only one type of all unplanned purchases. In fact, there are four broad classifications of unplanned purchase behavior. These classifications are adapted from the original work done on impulse buying (Stern, 1962).

### *Pure Impulse Purchase*

This is a purchase that is motivated by novelty or the need for variation. Most importantly, this purchase is a deviation from the consumer's normal purchase/consumption pattern, or foodway. The product purchase is simply **not** one that the consumer regularly purchases.

### *Planned Unplanned Purchase*

This is a purchase that is motivated by the need to save money by taking advantage of price discounts, special deals, store coupons, and other in-store promotions. This type of purchasing is exhibited mostly by "promotion-sensitive" consumers. The product purchased may or may not be a deviation from the consumer's normal purchase/consumption pattern. If it is a deviation, then the purchase would qualify as an impulse purchase; otherwise, it is simply a planned unplanned purchase.

### *Reminder Unplanned Purchase*

This is a purchase that is motivated by the need to replenish a product/brand that the consumer recalls is nearly or totally depleted. Most often, some in-store stimulus activates the consumer's recall. The product purchase is a replenishment of existing household stock and thus not a deviation from the consumer's normal purchase/consumption pattern.

### *Suggestion Unplanned Purchase*

This is a purchase whereby the consumer visualizes a need for a product he or she has never seen before in the store or anywhere else. Is this an impulse purchase? The answer is *yes,* if the product purchased deviates from the consumer's normal purchase/consumption pattern, and *no,* if the product will replace a product now being used to satisfy a particular need.

It should be apparent from these definitions that the crucial distinction between an impulse and an unplanned purchase is whether or not it represents a deviation from the consumer's normal purchase/consumption pattern. It does in the case of the pure impulse purchase, but not in the case of the reminder unplanned purchase. However, in two other cases—planned unplanned and suggestion unplanned—the purchase may or may not be an impulse purchase. This ambiguity makes it difficult to estimate what percentage of all unplanned purchases are impulsive.

Previous research has historically considered all unplanned purchases as impulsive (Kollat and Willett, 1967). Findings from research show that the probability of impulse purchasing is highest under the following conditions: (1) the consumer is on major shopping trip, (2) the shopping list contains more than fifteen products, (3) the product has a low purchase frequency, and (4) the number of products purchased is great. More recent research didn't make a distinction between unplanned and impulse purchases. Here, unplanned purchases were mostly likely to occur when a consumer was shopping in an unfamiliar store, and under no time pressure (Park, Iyer, and Smith, 1989).

Even though it is possible to distinguish among four types of unplanned purchases, they all appear to have one thing in common: they are in-store decisions that are caused by the consumer's exposure to in-store stimuli. Because, generally, planned and substitute purchases are also in-store decisions, a discussion of in-store influences is presented in the next section on shopping behavior. For now, food purchase behavior viewed from the perspective of "unplanned purchases" may be summarized by saying, "Consumers learn to **like** what they **buy**."

## SHOPPING BEHAVIOR

Having identified the consumption and purchase behavior of consumers, an examination of their shopping behavior completes the sequential nature of the consumer behavior trilogy. People shop, they buy, and then they consume.

Shopping is a major activity for many consumers, even though in some cases they don't plan to buy anything. Fortunately, the incidence of "browsing" in food stores is almost non-existent. Thus, food shopping is more purposeful than shopping behavior in general. Of course, this doesn't mean that someone shopping for food doesn't enjoy seeing what is new, or having fun just getting out. What it does mean is that you are unlikely to find someone in a food store who would reply, when asked to be helped, "No, thank you, just looking."

In the following sections, food shopping behavior will be discussed from two perspectives: out-of-store and in-store behaviors. Although it is now recognized that more and more consumers are shopping for meal solutions rather than meal ingredients, most of the extant research on food shopping behavior doesn't make this distinction. In addition, the current research on food shopping behavior has, for the most part, focused on the consumer's primary grocery store or supermarket. A **primary store** is defined as the store where consumers shop most often or spend the most money on groceries (Trends, 1996).

## Out-of-Store Behavior

To explain out-of-store behavior requires a knowledge of the different types of shopping trips, how consumers choose stores, how often they shop, how often and why they switch stores, and when they shop.

### Shopping Trip Types

Recent consumer research has identified five different types of shopping trips made by consumers.

**Routine**—the typical weekly grocery trip for food to be consumed over a three to seven day period.

**Major Stock-up**—Every month or so, a trip is made in order to purchase large quantities of long-lasting products.

**Occasional Fill-in**—A trip made between routine trips for products that will be used over the next few days.

**Tonight's Dinner**—A trip made to purchase food for that day's meal.

**Immediate Need**—A trip to purchase a product required in order to complete a meal.

Shopping for "tonight's dinner" and to fill an "immediate need" are clearly meal-solutions-based shopping. Together, it is estimated that they constitute forty percent of all shopping trips and consume sixteen percent of all food dollars spent during an average four-week month. Routine trips are the most frequent type of trip, and they account for fifty-two percent of all food dollars spent. But on a per-trip basis, the major stock-up is were the consumer spends more money than on any other trip (*Battle for Growth*, 1996).

### Store Choice Criteria

Consumers typically choose a store by evaluating the alternative stores on factors they consider important. **Table 10-18** shows the ten criteria defined as very important when choosing a primary food store. Because of similar importance ratings, thirteen criteria are identified.

Above all else, consumers are looking for clean, neat stores in which to purchase high-quality fruits, vegetables, and meat. They want to be served by courteous and friendly employees who make sure the shelf tags are accurate. The store should offer a wide selection of brands and unspoiled products with low prices that are frequently put on sale. It should be conveniently located, laid out so that it is easy to shop the aisles, provide fast checkout lanes, and ensure the consumers' safety until they get into their cars.

### *Shopping Frequency*

Consumers shop not only at their primary grocery store, but also at other types of food retailers. **Table 10-19** shows shopping frequency at all stores and the relative percentage of trips made to primary grocery stores. Consumers are frequent food shoppers. Seventy percent of them shop at all stores two or more times per week, which results in an average of 2.2 trips per week. However, only fifty percent of consumers shop two or more times in an average week at their primary grocery store. This results in 1.7 trips per week to their primary grocery store.

Recent consumer research has examined the number of shopping trips made for each of the five previously defined shopping trips. **Table 10-20** illustrates the number of shopping trips made for each type. Of course, most shopping trips are the weekly routine type, and the least number of trips are major stock up types. Interestingly, a trip to the store for tonight's dinner occurs almost once a week, as does a trip to complete a meal (*Battle for Growth,* 1996).

When consumers aren't shopping at their primary store, they are shopping at other grocery stores. **Table 10-21** reveals the top five reasons given by consumers for shopping at stores other than their primary grocery store. Almost one-half of the reasons cited are related to convenience in general. Thirty percent of the study respondents indicated locational convenience. The other three reasons given are merchandise related: variety/assortment, price, and sales.

### *Store Switching*

Although consumers make food purchases at stores other than their primary food store, they don't permanently switch from their primary store to another one very often. In fact, only thirteen percent switched stores in the previous year. **Table 10-22** identifies the five most frequently mentioned reasons for switching stores. Consumers who switch are price conscious. They look for better-quality products with more variety and selection. When a newly built store is more conveniently located to them, they switch. And of course, if they have moved, they may have no other choice but to switch to another store.

The reasons for shopping at other than the primary store, and for permanently switching stores, are ranked differently. However, they both share overriding consumer concerns. Because of the need to shop frequently for food, consumers will patronize conveniently located stores. They expect these stores to have a good variety, assortment, and quality of food at low prices.

### Shopping Time

With the proliferation of food stores now open twenty-four hours a day, consumers are not limited to shopping on particular days at particular times. But, do consumers prefer to shop on certain days, and at certain times? **Table 10-23** identifies the day of the week consumers are mostly likely to make a **major stock-up** trip. As expected, Saturday is when you will find the crowds at supermarkets. Friday and Thursday are preferred next. Preference falls off for the remaining days of the week.

Consumers also prefer to shop at certain times of the day. The morning hours (8 a.m. to noon) are preferred by forty-two percent of consumers; afternoon hours (noon to 5 p.m.) by thirty-three percent; evening hours (5 p.m. to 9 p.m.) by twenty-two percent, and only three percent prefer to shop in the late evening (9 p.m. to 8 a.m.).

To summarize, consumers make five different types of shopping trips to food stores: routine, major stock-up, occasional fill-in, tonight's dinner, and immediate need. Which stores consumers will shop at is determined largely by the cleanliness of the store and the quality and prices of fruits, vegetables, and meat. They are likely to make 2.2 trips per week to all food stores but only 1.7 trips to their primary food store. They shop at other stores mostly for convenience. The few that do switch their primary stores are mostly price-conscious. Although consumers may shop during any day of the week, they prefer Saturday most of all. Finally, consumers prefer to do their shopping in the morning. Very few can be found in the stores during the late night hours.

## In-Store Behavior

How important is it to understand the in-store shopping behavior of consumers? As stated earlier, **seventy** percent of all food purchase decisions are made in the store. Some consumers only have the product category in mind when they enter the store (six percent), and some change their minds about what they were going to buy after they are in the store (four percent), but most only decide what to buy once they are in the store (sixty percent).

To examine in-store shopping behavior, the following discussion will begin at the door of the store and end at the check-out lane.

### Shopper Profile

Everybody eats, and almost everyone shops for food, but the supermarket shopper is more likely to be female rather than male. Not only are eighty-two percent of all supermarket shoppers female, but they also make more in-store decisions than males (seventy-one percent vs. sixty-six percent). Sixty-five percent of consumers shop alone, but those who go to the store with others most often take their children (twelve percent) or their spouse—twenty-four percent. (POPAI, 1995).

### Shopping Time

Of the five types of shopping trips made by consumers, data on the length of time spent shopping is available only for one of them, the major stock-up trip. Supermarket shoppers spend an average of fifty-four minutes on this type of trip (POPAI, 1995). How much time do consumers spend on their weekly routine trips, or shopping for tonight's dinner, or rushing to the store for an item to complete a meal, or even the occasional trip to fill in what's missing in the pantry? Unfortunately, consumer research has not been undertaken to answer this question. However, it has been shown that store size influences the amount of time spent shopping. It appears that the time a consumer spends shopping in a store increases proportionately with the size of the store, up to 60,000 square feet of selling area. Shopping time increases, but not significantly, in stores larger than 60,000 square feet in selling area (*How Consumers Are Shopping the Supermarket*, 1991).

### Shopping Patterns

How do consumers shop a store? Consumers are creatures of habit. They establish a pattern or route through a store and follow it routinely. In general, twenty-one percent of all consumers visit each aisle or section in the store and another thirty-seven percent visit most aisles or sections. But forty-two percent visit only those aisles where they plan to buy something (POPAI, 1995).

Shopping patterns have also been identified on a more specific departmental basis. **Table 10-24** shows departmental shopping behavior in supermarkets. The departments were classified into two groups: traditional perishables and service perishables. Individual departments in each of the groups were analyzed with regard to the following:

**Consumers in Proximity**—The percentage of consumers who travel directly through or past a department or department's service counter.

**Consumer Purchasing**—The percentage of consumers who purchase a product or brand or item from that department.

**Purchase Conversion**—The percentage of consumers who traveled through or past a department and purchased a product from that department.

Even though the consumer research on departmental shopping patterns does not consider the type of shopping trip, it nonetheless reveals some interesting findings. First, produce is the most widely shopped non-grocery department. Eighty-four percent of consumers pass through or by the produce department, but only seventy-three percent of them buy anything. As a result, their purchase conversion is only the second highest, at eighty-seven percent (73/84). The dairy department draws seventy-three percent of all shoppers, and sixty-nine percent buy something. The conversion rate for dairy is the highest for all departments at ninety-five percent (69/73). Finally, the purchase conversion rate for the seafood department is the lowest of all departments at nineteen percent (10/53). Although more than one-half of all consumers pass by or through the department, only ten percent buy anything (*How Consumers Are Shopping the Supermarket,* 1991).

### In-Store Decisions

Seventy percent of all purchase decisions are made in the store. What do consumers buy as a result of these decisions? **Table 10-25** identifies the ten categories with the highest in-store decision rates. Snacks, condiments, breakfast foods, desserts, meal ingredients, and meal solutions are all reflected in these categories.

Unplanned purchases represent eighty-six percent of all in-store decisions (60/70). **Table 10-26** shows the categories with the highest unplanned purchase rates. Salsa and dip are the most frequent unplanned purchases. Seven of the categories are included on the ten highest in-store decision rates. Cocoa, hot dogs, and ketchup and other condiments have higher unplanned decision rates than the categories they replaced: pasta and the two breakfast categories.

### In-Store Promotional Influences

With such a large percentage of food decisions made in the store, it would be unrealistic to assume that consumers are not influenced by promotional efforts of retailers. What catches consumers' attention as they shop? **Table 10-27** reveals the promotional techniques of retailers that catch consumers' attention. End-isle displays get the most attention, while circular coupons, shelf-talkers, and ingredient notices are also excellent ways of promoting products. Surprisingly, check-out coupons and coupons for future purchases are fairly inadequate ways to gain attention. When asked which promotional tools they desired most, consumers mentioned instant on-pack coupons (eighty-seven percent), bonus packs (seventy-nine percent) and free samples (seventy-seven percent).

### Economizing Behaviors

Everybody likes a sale. This certainly holds true for food shoppers. Consumers try to save money whenever possible. There are a number of ways to economize on food purchases. **Table 10-28** identifies the ten economizing behaviors that consumers use most every time they shop. The chief way consumers economize is by identifying sales in newspapers. Other ways consumers can pay less than list price are using coupons (e.g., mail, newspaper, in-store), buying products on special even if unplanned, and participating in a store's frequent shopper program.

Even though they will pay the list price, consumers also economize by buying large package sizes, buying less expensive store brands, or stocking up on an item that they feel is a bargain. Although time-conscious, they also economize by comparing prices at different supermarkets. Finally, by sticking to their shopping lists, they eliminate all of those unplanned "impulse" purchases.

### Grocery Payment

Having arrived at the check-out lane, how do consumers pay for their grocery purchases? Non-cash payment is becoming the norm for supermarkets (**Table 10-29**). Less than half (forty-eight percent) of all supermarket purchases are made with cash. As more food stores accept credit and debit cards, these payment methods are expected to replace cash and checks as the leading payment methods.

To summarize, consumers make seventy percent of all food purchase decisions in the store. The typical food shopper is a female, most often shopping alone. She is likely to spend fifty-four minutes on a major stock-up trip which takes her through most, if not all, of the aisles in the store. Her shopping cart is likely to contain produce, dairy products, and meat. Of course, she is likely to make some unplanned purchases that include salsa and sweet baked-goods, among other items. While shopping, she is especially attracted to end-aisle displays and the coupons in the store's circular. To save money while shopping, she will concentrate on buying the specials found in newspapers and stock up on bargains. At the check-out lane, she is most likely to pay for her groceries with cash or a check.

## SUMMARY

Because food is fundamental to human existence, all societies develop foodways. These foodways reflect complex behavioral patterns that underlie the acquisition, preparation, and consumption of food according to a society's preferences. It is within the guidelines established by a society's foodways that consumers learn to like the tastes and smells of foods. When the conditions are right, people prefer the foods they like. But just as we choose to eat certain foods, we choose not to eat others. What, then, determines which foods we will eat?

It is all very simple. We eat the foods that satisfy our needs. But consumers, as social beings, have more than physiological needs. So society bestows multiple meanings on food. In turn, these meanings represent multiple sources of need satisfaction. Thus, consumers perceive food in general as a source of satisfaction for physiological, safety, belongingness, self-esteem and self-actualization needs. However, exactly which products or brands are consumed is determined by the lifestyle a consumer chooses to live. Within a society's foodways, people choose to shop, purchase, and consume those foods that allow them to live particular lifestyles.

An examination of U.S. foodways revealed that a typical consumer eats as much red meat as fowl and fish; devours huge qualities of fruits, vegetables, and dairy products; and washes it all down mostly with softdrinks, milk, and coffee.

To pay for all this food, consumers increased their food expenditures by only three percent from 1990 to 1994. Consumers spent more for cereals and bakery products and much less for alcohol. As a share of spending, consumers spent less for food.

When they did spend, it was more for food for home consumption than for food consumption away from home.

The purchase behavior of consumers was examined from a decision-making perspective. About thirty percent of all food decisions begin before a consumer enters a store. This means that most food decisions begin after the consumer has begun to shop in the store. Further, most of the purchase decisions made in the store are not planned in advance. Some of those decisions are no doubt impulsive, but most probably are not.

Shopping behavior was examined from two perspectives: out-of-store and in-store. The cleanliness of a store and the quality of its meat, fruits, and vegetables determine largely which store the consumer will patronize. On average, he or she will shop for food 2.2 times a week. Most of these trips will be routine in nature, but a growing number of trips are for entire meals rather than ingredients.

Habits are hard to break; once consumers choose a store, only thirteen percent will switch later in the year. When they do switch, it is mostly to get better (lower) prices. In addition, most consumers prefer to shop on Saturday morning.

Given the enormity of in-store decision making, it is important to understand what goes on in the store. The typical food shopper is a female most likely shopping alone. She will spend fifty-four minutes on a major stock-up trip and will shop most, if not all, of the aisles. While shopping, she is especially attracted to end aisle displays where she will try to save money by purchasing what is on sale, and stock up on it. To pay for all of this, she will most likely use cash or a check.

## SELECTED REFERENCES

Assael, H. *Consumer Behavior and Marketing Action.* Boston: Mass.: PWS-Kent Publishing Co., Division of Wadsworth, Inc., 1995.

*Battle for Growth.* Presentation at Mid-Winter Food Marketing Executive Conference. McKinsey and Co., Inc., U.S. 1996.

Camp, C. *American Foodways. What, When, Why and How We Eat in America.* Little Rock: August House, Inc., 1989.

*Consumer Buying Habits Study.* Point of Purchase Advertising Institute, Englewood, N.J., 1995.

*Consumer Expenditure Survey.* U.S. Department of Labor, Bureau of Labor Statistics, 1992–93, 1994.

Dickson, P. R. and A. G. Sawyer. "The Price Knowledge and Search of Supermarket Shoppers," *Journal of Marketing* Vol. 54 (July 1990), pp. 42–53.

Dewey, J. *How We Think.* Boston, Mass: D.C. Heath and Company, 1910.

*Food Consumption Prices and Expenditures 1970–94.* Report No. SB928, USDA-ERS, April 1996.

Hawkins, D. I., R. J. Best, and K. A. Coney. *Consumer Behavior*. 6th edition. Irwin, Chicago, 1995.

*How Consumers Are Shopping the Supermarket.* Food Marketing Institute and Coca-Cola USA by Willard Bishop Consulting, Ltd., 1991.

Impact in the Aisles, Special Report, *Promo: The Magazine of Promotion Marketing*, January 1996.

Kollat, D. T. and R. P. Willett, "Customer Impulse Purchasing Behavior," *Journal of Marketing Research*, Vol. 2, IV (Feb. 1967), 21–31.

Logue, A. W. *The Psychology of Eating and Drinking*. 2nd ed. New York: W.H. Freeman and Company, 1991.

Lyman, B. *A Psychology of Food—More Than a Matter of Taste*. Van Nostrand Reinhold Co., New York, 1989.

Maslow, A. H. *Motivation and Personality*. 2nd ed. New York: Harper and Row, 1970.

Park, C. W., E. S. Iyer and D. C. Smith. "The Effects of Situational Factors on In-Store Grocery Shopping Behavior: The Role of Store Environment and Time Available for Shopping," *Journal of Consumer Research*, Vol. 15, March 1989, 422–433.

*Progressive Grocer's Market Scope, Trade Dimensions,* Division of Interactive Market Systems, Inc., Stamford, Conn., 1996.

Rozin, P. "Human Food Selection: The Interaction of Biology, Culture, and Individual Experience," in L.M. Baker (Ed.), *The Psychobiology of Human Food Selection*, Bridgeport, Conn., 1982, 225–254.

Stern, H. "The Significance of Impulse Buying Today," *Journal of Marketing*, April 1962, 59–62.

*Trends in the United States—Consumer Attitudes in the Supermarket*. Washington, D.C.: The Research Department, Food Marketing Institute, 1996.

Valero, G. "If You Make It They Will Come," *U.S. Distribution Journal*, May 15 1996, 14–17.

"What America Eats," Vol. V, Mark Clements Research, Inc. for *Parade Magazine,* September, 1995.

## REVIEW QUESTIONS

1. Give some examples to illustrate the crucial role food occupies in U.S. society.

2. Define the U.S. foodway.

3. People satisfy the need for food within the context of their lifestyles. Explain.

4. What constitutes the "trilogy" of consumer behavior?

5. Describe the consumption behavior of the typical U.S. consumer.

6. "We are what we eat" or "We eat what we are." Explain both perspectives.

7. What are the four types of food purchase decisions?

8. All unplanned purchases are not impulse purchases. True or False? Why or why not?

9. Explain the different types of food-shopping trips.

10. Briefly profile out-of-store and in-store shopping behaviors.

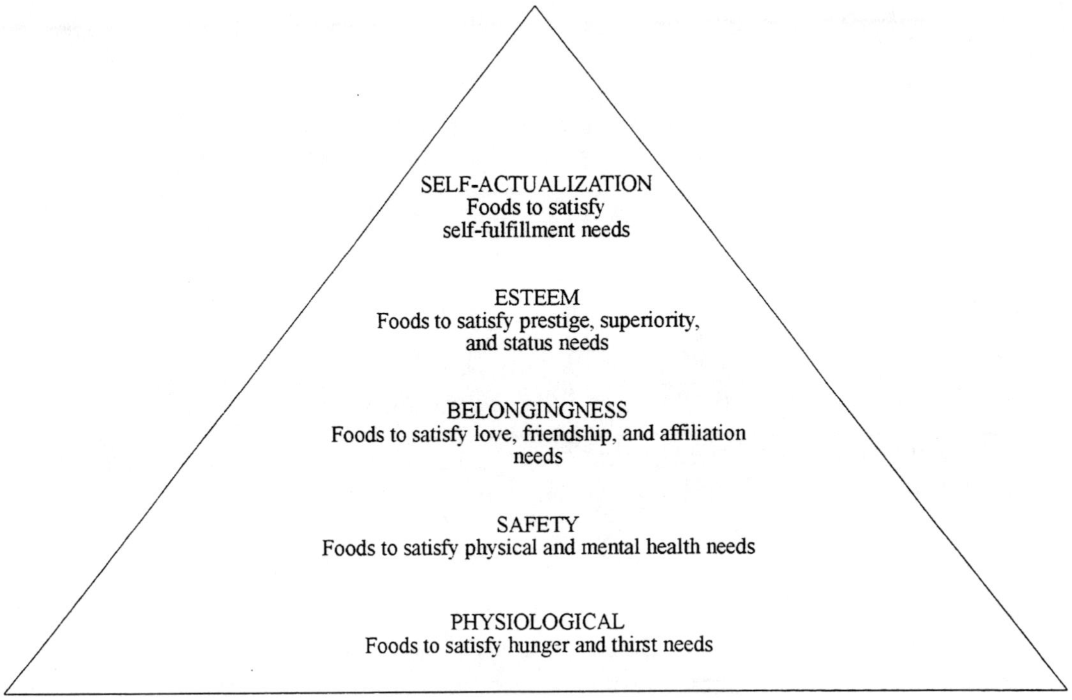

```
                    /\
                   /  \
                  /    \
                 / SELF-ACTUALIZATION \
                /   Foods to satisfy   \
               /   self-fulfillment needs \
              /                            \
             /           ESTEEM             \
            /  Foods to satisfy prestige,    \
           /    superiority, and status needs \
          /                                    \
         /           BELONGINGNESS              \
        /   Foods to satisfy love, friendship,   \
       /         and affiliation needs            \
      /                                            \
     /                   SAFETY                     \
    /   Foods to satisfy physical and mental health \
   /                    needs                        \
  /                                                   \
 /                 PHYSIOLOGICAL                       \
/        Foods to satisfy hunger and thirst needs      \
--------------------------------------------------------
```

**FIGURE 10-1.** MASLOW'S HIERARCHY OF NEEDS AND FOOD AS A SOURCE OF SATISFACTION

**TABLE 10-1.** PER CAPITA CONSUMPTION AND SHARE OF MEAT, POULTRY, AND FISH

| Year | POUNDS | | | | SHARE (%) | | |
|------|---------|---------|------|-------------|----------|---------|------|
|      | Red Meat | Poultry | Fish | Total Meat | Red Meat | Poultry | Fish |
| 1970 | 131.7 | 33.8 | 11.7 | 177.3 | 74.3 | 19.1 | 6.6 |
| 1991 | 111.9 | 58.4 | 14.8 | 185.1 | 60.5 | 31.6 | 8.0 |
| 1992 | 114.1 | 60.9 | 14.7 | 189.7 | 60.1 | 32.2 | 7.7 |
| 1993 | 112.1 | 62.6 | 14.9 | 189.6 | 59.1 | 33.1 | 7.8 |
| 1994 | 114.4 | 63.7 | 15.1 | 193.5 | 59.3 | 32.9 | 7.8 |

*SOURCE:* FOOD CONSUMPTION, PRICES, AND EXPENDITURES 1970-94, REPORT NO. SB928, USDA-ERS. APRIL 1996.

**TABLE 10-2.** PER CAPITA CONSUMPTION AND SHARE OF RED MEAT

| Year | POUNDS | | | | | SHARE (%) | | | |
|------|------|------|------|------|-------|------|------|------|------|
|      | Beef | Veal | Pork | Lamb | Total | Beef | Veal | Pork | Lamb |
| 1970 | 79.6 | 2.0 | 48.0 | 2.1 | 131.7 | 60.5 | 2.0 | 36.5 | 2.0 |
| 1991 | 63.1 | 0.8 | 46.9 | 1.0 | 111.9 | 56.5 | 0.7 | 41.9 | 0.9 |
| 1992 | 62.8 | 0.8 | 49.5 | 1.0 | 114.1 | 55.0 | 0.7 | 43.4 | 0.9 |
| 1993 | 61.5 | 0.8 | 48.9 | 1.0 | 112.1 | 54.8 | 0.7 | 43.6 | 0.9 |
| 1994 | 63.6 | 0.8 | 49.5 | 0.9 | 114.4 | 55.6 | 0.7 | 43.3 | 0.8 |

*SOURCE:* FOOD CONSUMPION PRICES, AND EXPENDITURES 1970-94, REPORT NO. SB928, USDA-ERS. APRIL 1996.

**TABLE 10-3.** PER CAPITA CONSUMPTION AND SHARE OF CHICKEN AND TURKEY

| Year | POUNDS | | | SHARE (%) | |
|------|---------|--------|-------|---------|--------|
|      | Chicken | Turkey | Total | Chicken | Turkey |
| 1970 | 27.4 | 6.4  | 33.8 | 81.1 | 18.9 |
| 1991 | 44.2 | 14.1 | 58.4 | 75.7 | 24.3 |
| 1992 | 46.7 | 14.2 | 60.9 | 76.7 | 23.3 |
| 1993 | 48.5 | 14.1 | 62.6 | 77.5 | 22.5 |
| 1994 | 49.5 | 14.2 | 63.7 | 77.8 | 22.2 |

SOURCE: FOOD CONSUMPTION, PRICES, AND EXPENDITURES 1970-94, REPORT NO. SB928, USDA-ERS. APRIL 1996.

**TABLE 10-4.** PER CAPITA CONSUMPTION AND SHARE OF FISH

| Year | POUNDS | | | | SHARE (%) | | |
|------|--------------|--------|-------|-------|--------------|--------|-------|
|      | Fresh/Frozen | Canned | Cured | Total | Fresh/Frozen | Canned | Cured |
| 1970 | 6.9  | 4.4 | .4 | 11.7 | 59.0 | 37.6 | 3.4 |
| 1991 | 9.6  | 4.9 | .3 | 14.8 | 64.9 | 33.1 | 2.0 |
| 1992 | 9.8  | 4.6 | .3 | 14.7 | 66.7 | 31.3 | 2.0 |
| 1993 | 10.1 | 4.5 | .3 | 14.9 | 67.8 | 30.2 | 2.0 |
| 1994 | 10.3 | 4.5 | .3 | 15.1 | 68.2 | 29.8 | 2.0 |

SOURCE: FOOD CONSUMPTION, PRICES, AND EXPENDITURES 1970-94, REPORT NO. SB928, USDA-ERS. APRIL 1996.

**TABLE 10-5.** PER CAPITA CONSUMPTION AND SHARE OF EGGS

| Year | NUMBER | | | SHARE (%) | |
| --- | --- | --- | --- | --- | --- |
| | Shell | Processed | Total | Shell | Processed |
| 1970 | 275.9 | 33.0 | 308.9 | 89.3 | 10.7 |
| 1991 | 183.0 | 50.7 | 233.7 | 78.3 | 11.7 |
| 1992 | 180.7 | 54.3 | 235.0 | 76.9 | 13.1 |
| 1993 | 179.1 | 56.4 | 235.5 | 76.0 | 14.0 |
| 1994 | 177.0 | 60.6 | 237.6 | 74.5 | 15.5 |

SOURCE: FOOD CONSUMPTION, PRICES, AND EXPENDITURES 1970-94, REPORT NO. SB928, USDA-ERS. APRIL 1996.

**TABLE 10-6.** PER CAPITA CONSUMPTION AND SHARE OF DAIRY PRODUCTS

| Year | POUNDS | | | | | | |
| --- | --- | --- | --- | --- | --- | --- | --- |
| | Cheese | Frozen Dairy | Evaporated/ Condensed Milk | Dry Milk Products | Fluid Milk Product | Fluid Cream Product | All Dairy Products |
| 1970 | 16.6 | 28.5 | 12.0 | 5.8 | 269.9 | 5.2 | 563.8 |
| 1991 | 28.3 | 29.2 | 8.2 | 3.2 | 225.4 | 7.7 | 565.6 |
| 1992 | 29.1 | 28.9 | 8.5 | 3.5 | 222.9 | 8.0 | 565.8 |
| 1993 | 29.2 | 29.3 | 8.2 | 3.1 | 218.7 | 8.0 | 574.1 |
| 1994 | 29.6 | 30.0 | 8.0 | 4.1 | 217.7 | 8.1 | 586.2 |

SOURCE: FOOD CONSUMPTION, PRICES, AND EXPENDITURES 1970-94, REPORT NO. SB928, USDA-ERS. APRIL 1996.

**TABLE 10-7.** PER CAPITA CONSUMPTION AND SHARE OF FATS AND OILS

| | | | | POUNDS | | | | |
|---|---|---|---|---|---|---|---|---|
| Year | Butter | Margarine | Lard | Edible Tallow | Shortening | Salad and Cooking Oil | Other Edible Fats and Oils | Total |
| 1970 | 5.4 | 10.8 | 4.1 | N/A | 17.3 | 15.4 | 2.3 | 55.8 |
| 1991 | 4.4 | 10.6 | 1.7 | 1.4 | 22.4 | 25.2 | 1.3 | 66.9 |
| 1992 | 4.4 | 11.0 | 1.7 | 2.4 | 22.4 | 25.6 | 1.7 | 68.8 |
| 1993 | 4.7 | 11.1 | 1.6 | 2.2 | 25.1 | 25.1 | 1.7 | 71.5 |
| 1994 | 4.8 | 9.9 | 1.7 | 3.3 | 24.1 | 24.3 | 1.6 | 69.8 |

*SOURCE:* FOOD CONSUMPTION, PRICES, AND EXPENDITURES 1970-94, REPORT NO. SB928, USDA-ERS. APRIL 1996.

**TABLE 10-8.** PER CAPITA CONSUMPTION AND SHARE OF FATS AND OILS FROM ANIMAL AND VEGETABLE SOURCES

| | POUNDS | | SHARE (%) | |
|---|---|---|---|---|
| Year | Animal | Vegetable | Animal | Vegetable |
| 1970 | 14.1 | 38.5 | 26.8 | 73.2 |
| 1991 | 9.7 | 54.2 | 15.2 | 84.8 |
| 1992 | 10.6 | 55.2 | 16.1 | 83.9 |
| 1993 | 10.3 | 58.0 | 15.1 | 84.9 |
| 1994 | 11.6 | 55.2 | 17.3 | 82.7 |

*SOURCE:* FOOD CONSUMPTION, PRICES, AND EXPENDITURES 1970-94, REPORT NO. SB928, USDA-ERS. APRIL 1996.

**TABLE 10-9.** PER CAPITA CONSUMPTION AND SHARE OF FRUITS

| Year | POUNDS | | | SHARE (%) | |
|------|--------|-----------|-------|-------|-----------|
|      | Fresh  | Processed | Total | Fresh | Processed |
| 1970 | 101.2 | 128.8 | 230.0 | 44.0 | 56.0 |
| 1991 | 113.2 | 151.7 | 264.8 | 42.7 | 57.3 |
| 1992 | 123.6 | 138.8 | 262.4 | 47.1 | 52.9 |
| 1993 | 124.9 | 153.4 | 278.4 | 44.9 | 55.1 |
| 1994 | 126.7 | 152.8 | 279.5 | 45.3 | 54.7 |

*SOURCE:* FOOD CONSUMPTION, PRICES, AND EXPENDITURES 1970-94, REPORT NO. SB928, USDA-ERS. APRIL 1996.

**TABLE 10-10.** PER CAPITA CONSUMPTION AND SHARE OF VEGETABLES

| Year | POUNDS | | | SHARE (%) | |
|------|--------|-----------|-------|-------|-----------|
|      | Fresh  | Processed | Total | Fresh | Processed |
| 1970 | 152.9 | 182.6 | 335.5 | 45.6 | 54.4 |
| 1991 | 163.2 | 226.7 | 389.9 | 41.9 | 58.1 |
| 1992 | 171.3 | 223.0 | 394.3 | 43.4 | 56.6 |
| 1993 | 172.0 | 230.0 | 402.0 | 42.8 | 57.2 |
| 1994 | 170.8 | 227.5 | 398.3 | 42.9 | 57.1 |

*SOURCE:* FOOD CONSUMPTION, PRICES, AND EXPENDITURES 1970-94, REPORT NO. SB928, USDA-ERS. APRIL 1996.

**TABLE 10-11.** PER CAPITA CONSUMPTION OF FLOUR AND CEREAL PRODUCTS

| | | | POUNDS | | | | |
|---|---|---|---|---|---|---|---|
| Year | Wheat | Rye | Rice | Corn | Oats | Barley | Total |
| 1970 | 110.9 | 1.2 | 6.7 | 11.1 | 4.7 | 1.0 | 135.6 |
| 1991 | 136.9 | 0.6 | 16.8 | 22.8 | 9.1 | 1.6 | 187.8 |
| 1992 | 138.8 | 0.6 | 17.5 | 23.2 | 9.0 | 1.7 | 190.8 |
| 1993 | 143.3 | 0.6 | 17.6 | 23.5 | 9.2 | 1.7 | 195.8 |
| 1994 | 144.5 | 0.6 | 19.0 | 23.7 | 9.2 | 1.7 | 198.7 |

SOURCE: FOOD CONSUMPTION, PRICES, AND EXPENDITURES 1970-94, REPORT NO. SB928, USDA-ERS. APRIL 1996

**TABLE 10-12.** PER CAPITA CONSUMPTION OF CALORIC AND NON-CALORIC SWEETENERS

| | | | POUNDS | | | | |
|---|---|---|---|---|---|---|---|
| Year | Cane/Beet | Corn | Edible Syrups | Honey | Total Caloric | Low Caloric | Total Sweetener |
| 1970 | 101.8 | 19.1 | .5 | 1.0 | 122.3 | 5.8 | 128.1 |
| 1991 | 63.8 | 72.8 | .4 | 1.0 | 137.9 | 24.3 | 162.2 |
| 1992 | 64.6 | 75.3 | .4 | 1.0 | 141.2 | N/A | N/A |
| 1993 | 64.3 | 78.7 | .4 | 1.0 | 144.4 | N/A | N/A |
| 1994 | 65.0 | 81.3 | .4 | 1.0 | 147.6 | N/A | N/A |

N/A=Not Available

SOURCE: FOOD CONSUMPTION, PRICES, AND EXPENDITURES 1970-94, REPORT NO. SB928, USDA-ERS. APRIL 1996.

**TABLE 10-13.** PER CAPITA CONSUMPTION OF BEVERAGES

## GALLONS

| Year | Milk | Tea (a) | Coffee | Bottled Water | Soft Drinks | Fruit Juices (b) | Alcoholic Beverages | Total |
|------|------|-----|--------|---------------|-------------|------------------|---------------------|-------|
| 1970 | 31.3 | 6.8 | 33.4 | 1.0 | 24.3 | 5.7 | 21.6 | 124.2 |
| 1991 | 25.7 | 7.0 | 26.8 | 8.0 | 47.9 | 14.3 | 26.4 | 156.1 |
| 1992 | 25.4 | 7.2 | 25.9 | 8.2 | 48.5 | 13.3 | 26.1 | 154.6 |
| 1993 | 24.9 | 7.4 | 23.5 | 9.4 | 50.2 | 14.4 | 25.6 | 155.4 |
| 1994 | 24.7 | 7.6 | 21.1 | 10.5 | 52.2 | 14.3 | 25.5 | 156.9 |

(a) Includes iced tea.
(b) Includes fruit drinks.

*SOURCE:* FOOD CONSUMPTION, PRICES, AND EXPENDITURES 1970-94, REPORT NO. SB928, USDA-ERS. APRIL 1996.

**TABLE 10-14.** AVERAGE ANNUAL EXPENDITURES

| CONSUMER UNITS | YEAR | | | | |
|---|---|---|---|---|---|
| | 1990 | 1991 | 1992 | 1993 | 1994 |
| Average | 28,381 | 29,614 | 29,846 | 30,692 | 31,751 |
| Food | 4,296 | 4,271 | 4,273 | 4,399 | 4,411 |
| Food at Home | 2,485 | 2,651 | 2,643 | 2,735 | 2,712 |
| Cereal and Bakery Products | 368 | 404 | 411 | 434 | 429 |
| Meat, Poultry, Fish, and Eggs | 668 | 709 | 687 | 734 | 732 |
| Dairy Products | 295 | 294 | 302 | 295 | 289 |
| Fruit and Vegetables | 408 | 429 | 428 | 444 | 437 |
| *Other Food at Home | 746 | 815 | 814 | 827 | 825 |
| Food Away from Home | 1,811 | 1,620 | 1,631 | 1,664 | 1,698 |
| Alcoholic Beverages | 307 | 297 | 301 | 268 | 278 |

*Includes sugar, fats and oils, non-alcoholic beverages, and miscellaneous foods

*SOURCE:* CONSUMER EXPENDITURES SURVEY, 1990, 1991, 1992, 1993, and 1994. U.S. DEPARTMENT OF LABOR, BUREAU OF LABOR STATISTICS.

**TABLE 10-15.** SHARES OF AVERAGE ANNUAL EXPENDITURES FOR FOOD

| CONSUMER UNIT | YEAR | | | | |
|---|---|---|---|---|---|
| | 1990 | 1991 | 1992 | 1993 | 1994 |
| Average Expenditures | 100.0 | 100.0 | 100.0 | 100.0 | 100.0 |
| Food | 15.1 | 14.4 | 14.3 | 14.4 | 13.9 |
| Food at Home | 8.8 | 9.0 | 8.9 | 8.9 | 8.5 |
| Cereals and Bakery Products | 1.2 | 1.4 | 1.4 | 1.4 | 1.4 |
| Meat, Poultry, Fish, and Eggs | 2.4 | 2.4 | 2.3 | 2.3 | 2.3 |
| Dairy Products | 1.0 | 0.9 | 1.0 | 1.0 | 0.9 |
| Fruit and Vegetables | 1.4 | 1.4 | 1.4 | 1.4 | 1.4 |
| Other Food at Home | 2.6 | 2.8 | 2.7 | 2.7 | 2.6 |
| Food Away from Home | 6.4 | 5.5 | 5.5 | 5.4 | 5.3 |
| Alcoholic Beverages | 1.0 | 1.0 | 1.0 | 0.9 | 0.9 |

*SOURCE:* CONSUMER EXPENDITURE SURVEY, 1990, 1991, 1992, 1993, and 1994. U.S. DEPARTMENT OF LABOR, BUREAU OF LABOR STATISTICS.

**TABLE 10-16.** CONSUMER DECISION MAKING FOR FOOD PURCHASES

| | PERCENT | |
|---|---|---|
| **Decision Type** | **1986** | **1995** |
| Specially Planned | 34 | 30 |
| Generally Planned | 10 | 6 |
| Substitute | 2 | 4 |
| Unplanned | 54 | 60 |
| TOTAL | 100 | 100 |

Specifically Planned: A particular item or brand decided on before entering the store and purchased as planned.

Generally Planned: A planned decision to purchase a particular product category, (e.g., cereal), but not a specific brand (e.g., Kellogg's), before entering the store.

Substitute: A decision to purchase an item, brand, or product category other than one that was specifically or generally planned.

Unplanned: A decision to purchase an item, brand, or product category that was not planned prior to entering the store.

SOURCE: CONSUMER BUYING HABITS STUDY. POINT-OF-PURCHASE ADVERTISING INSTITUTE, 1995.

**TABLE 10-17.** FOOD PURCHASE CRITERIA IMPORTANCE

| | YEARS | | |
|---|---|---|---|
| **CRITERION** | **1986** | **1991** | **1995** |
| Taste | 57* | 57 | 56 |
| Price | 34 | 34 | 37 |
| Brand Name | 6 | 6 | 6 |
| Quick Preparation | 3 | 3 | 2 |
| TOTAL | 100 | 100 | 100 |

*Read 57 percent of all respondents rated taste as the most important criteria for food purchases.

SOURCE: WHAT AMERICA EATS. VOLUME V, MARK CLEMENTS RESEARCH, INC., FOR *PARADE MAGAZINE*, 1995.

**TABLE 10-18.** TOP TEN "VERY" IMPORTANT CRITERIA IN STORE CHOICE

| CRITERION | % VERY IMPORTANT |
| --- | --- |
| Clean, neat store | 91 |
| High-quality fruits and vegetables | 90 |
| High-quality meat | 88 |
| Courteous, friendly employees | *82 |
| Use-before/sell date labels on products | *82 |
| Accurate shelf tags | 80 |
| Fair prices | 78 |
| Convenient location | 77 |
| Fast checkout | 72 |
| Store layout easy to shop | **69 |
| Items on sale or money-saving specials | **69 |
| Personal safety outside the store | **69 |
| Wide selection of brands | 63 |

*Tied for fourth place.
**Tied for ninth place.

SOURCE: TRENDS IN THE UNITED STATES—CONSUMER ATTITUDES AND THE SUPERMARKETS. THE RESEARCH DEPARTMENT, FOOD MARKETING INSTITUTE, 1996.

**TABLE 10-19.** SHOPPING FREQUENCY AT PRIMARY AND OTHER FOOD STORES

| Number of Visits Per Week | % All Stores | % Primary Stores |
|---|---|---|
| One | 29.0 | 50.0 |
| Two | 34.0 | 32.0 |
| Three | 20.0 | 9.0 |
| Four | 6.0 | 3.0 |
| Five | 3.0 | 20.0 |
| Six | 4.0 | 1.0 |
| Every two weeks or less | 3.0 | 2.0 |
| Average number of visits per week | 2.2 | 1.7 |

SOURCE: TRENDS IN THE UNITED STATES—CONSUMER ATTITUDES AND THE SUPERMARKETS. THE RESEARCH DEPARTMENT, FOOD MARKETING INSTITUTE, 1996.


**TABLE 10-20.** NUMBER OF SHOPPING TRIPS

| Type of Trip | 4-Week Average Number of Trips |
|---|---|
| Routine | 4.3 |
| Tonight's dinner | 3.3 |
| Immediate need | 3.2 |
| Occasional fill-in | 2.5 |
| Major stock-up | 1.4 |

SOURCE: BATTLE FOR GROWTH. PRESENTATION AT MID-WINTER FOOD MARKETING INSTITUTE, EXECUTIVE CONFERENCE, McKINSEY AND COMPANY, INC., U.S. 1996

**TABLE 10-21.** REASONS FOR SHOPPING AT NON-PRIMARY STORE

| REASONS | % INDICATING* |
|---|---|
| Convenience | 78 |
| Price/cost savings | 36 |
| More convenient location | 30 |
| More variety/better assortment/more choice | 25 |
| Sales/specials | 21 |

*Percent of shoppers indicating; multiple answers accepted.

SOURCE: TRENDS IN THE UNITED STATES—CONSUMER ATTITUDES AND THE SUPERMARKETS. THE RESEARCH DEPARTMENT, FOOD MARKETING INSTITUTE, 1996.


**TABLE 10-22.** TOP FIVE REASONS FOR SWITCHING STORES

| REASONS | % INDICATING* |
|---|---|
| Better/lower prices/coupons/specials | 32 |
| Location/new store more conveniently located | 28 |
| Consumer moved to different area | 22 |
| More variety/selection | 17 |
| Better quality products/store | 10 |

*Percent of shoppers indicating; multiple answers accepted.

SOURCE: TRENDS IN THE UNITED STATES—CONSUMER ATTITUDES AND THE SUPERMARKETS. THE RESEARCH DEPARTMENT, FOOD MARKETING INSTITUTE, 1996.

**TABLE 10-23.** PREFERRED DAYS FOR MAJOR STOCK-UP TRIP

| DAY | % PREFERRED |
|---|---|
| Sunday | 13 |
| Monday | 12 |
| Tuesday | 11 |
| Wednesday | 13 |
| Thursday | 15 |
| Friday | 15 |
| Saturday | 21 |
| TOTAL | 100 |

SOURCE: 63RD ANNUAL REPORT OF THE GROCERY INDUSTRY. *PROGESSIVE GROCER*, APRIL SUPPLEMENT, 1996.

**TABLE 10-24.** DEPARTMENTAL SHOPPING BEHAVIOR

| | % Consumers in Proximity | % Consumers Purchasing | % Purchase Conversion |
|---|---|---|---|
| Traditional Perishables | | | |
| Produce | 84 | 73 | 87 |
| Dairy | 73 | 69 | 95 |
| Meat | 73 | 59 | 81 |
| Service Perishables | | | |
| Bakery | 77 | 35 | 45 |
| Deli | 73 | 22 | 30 |
| Seafood | 53 | 10 | 19 |

SOURCE: HOW CONSUMERS ARE SHOPPING THE SUPERMARKET. FOOD MARKETING INSTITUTE AND COCA-COLA U.S.A. BY WILLARD BISHOP CONSULTING LTD., 1991.

**TABLE 10-25.** PRODUCT CATEGORIES WITH HIGHEST IN-STORE DECISION RATES

| CATEGORY | % IN-STORE DECISIONS* |
|---|---|
| Candy/Gum | 89 |
| Fresh packaged sweet baked goods | 88 |
| Pickles, olives, and relish | 88 |
| Salsa and dip | 88 |
| Shelf stable prepared foods | 85 |
| Chips, pretzels, and other salty snacks | 84 |
| Canned or bottled fruits | 84 |
| Breakfast snacks or nutritional bars | 84 |
| Pancake and waffle mixes | 82 |
| Pasta | 82 |

*Sum of generally planned, substituted, or unplanned decisions.

SOURCE: CONSUMER BUYING HABITS STUDY. POINT-OF-PURCHASE ADVERTISING INSTITUTE, 1995.

**TABLE 10-26.** PRODUCT CATEGORIES WITH HIGHEST UNPLANNED DECISION RATES

| CATEGORY | % UNPLANNED PURCHASES* |
|---|---|
| Salsa and dip | 82 |
| Fresh packaged sweet baked goods | 81 |
| Pickles, olives, and relish | 81 |
| Shelf stable prepared foods | 80 |
| Cocoa | 78 |
| Chips, pretzels, other salty snacks | 77 |
| Canned or bottled foods | 76 |
| Candy and gum | 74 |
| Hot dogs | 74 |
| Ketchup, mustard, barbeque, sauce, and other condiments | 74 |

*Purchase decisions made after the consumer entered the store.

SOURCE: CONSUMER BUYING HABITS STUDY. POINT-OF-PURCHASE ADVERTISING INSTITUTE, 1995.

**TABLE 10-27.** MOST ATTENTION CATCHING RETAIL PROMOTIONS

| RETAIL PROMOTION | % ATTENTION CATCHING* |
|---|---|
| End-aisle displays | 69 |
| Circular coupons | 65 |
| Shelf talkers | 56 |
| Ingredient notices | 55 |
| Window posters | 54 |
| Bonus packs | 54 |
| Instant coupons | 53 |
| Free samples | 52 |
| In-aisle displays | 49 |
| Receipt-back coupons | 47 |
| Shelf dispensers | 46 |
| Mail-in coupons | 44 |
| Store card deals | 38 |
| Coupons for future | 32 |
| Check-out coupons | 30 |

*Percent saying promotional tool catches his/her attention.

SOURCE: WHAT INFLUENCES THEM AND WHAT DOESN'T? THE IMPACT OF MARKETING TOOLS ON TODAY'S SUPERMARKET SHOPPER. PROMO, THE MAGAZINE FOR PROMOTION MARKETING, JANUARY 1996.

**TABLE 10-28.** ECONOMIZING BEHAVIORS OF CONSUMERS

| BEHAVIORS | % PRETTY MUCH EVERY TIME |
|---|---|
| Note newspaper grocery specials | 30 |
| Stock up on bargains | 27 |
| Use mail-in cents-off coupons | 27 |
| Use in-store cents-off coupons | 24 |
| Purchase store brand | 21 |
| Purchase unplanned specials | 20 |
| Compare prices at different supermarkets | 18 |
| Buy only what's on the list | 17 |
| Participate in frequent-shopper programs | 15 |
| Buy in larger package sizes | 12 |

*Percent who indicated that they engage in this economizing behavior pretty much every time they shop.

SOURCE: TRENDS IN THE UNITED STATES—CONSUMER ATTITUDES AND THE SUPERMARKETS. THE RESEARCH DEPARTMENT, FOOD MARKETING INSTITUTE, 1996.


**TABLE 10-29.** PAYMENT METHODS OF SHOPPERS

| PAYMENT METHOD | % USAGE |
|---|---|
| Cash | 48 |
| Check | 34 |
| Credit/charge card | 9 |
| Debit card | 5 |
| Another way | 4 |
| TOTAL | 100 |

SOURCE: CONSUMER BUYING HABITS. POINT-OF-PURCHASE *ADVERTISING INSTITUTE*, 1995.

# Chapter 11

# Market Segmentation

**Chapter Outline**

Market Segmentation
- A. Lifestyle and Its Determinants

Characteristic Segmentation
- A. Demographic Characteristics
- B. Economic Characteristics
- C. Cultural Characteristics
- D. Subcultural Characteristics
- E. Social Class Characteristics
- F. Psychological Characteristics
- G. Geographic Characteristics

Situational Segmentation
- A. Consumption Situation
- B. Purchase Situation
- C. Situational Characteristics

Behavioral Segmentation
- A. Benefit Segmentation
- B. Usage Segmentation

        C. Response Elasticity
Lifestyle Segmentation
        A. Psychographic Segmentation
Segmentation Typologies
        A. Geodemographic Segmentation—MicroVision
        B. Geodemographic Segmentation—Acorn
        C. Geodemographic Segmentation—Prizm
        D. Lifestyle Segmentation—Vals
Summary

Although physiological nourishment is essential for survival, to suggest that we eat only to survive is to overlook the multiple meanings society has bestowed on food. These meanings symbolize multiple sources of need satisfaction to consumers and are embodied in a society's foodways.

The previous chapter discussed the essential components of American foodways by explaining the trilogy of consumer behavior. Consumption behavior focused on what we ate as well as how we spent our money on what we ate. Purchase behavior focused on how we made food choices. Shopping behavior examined how we acquired what we ate.

In the past, the consumer market for food was more homogeneous than it is now. In fact, today it is well recognized that the once homogeneous consumer market is now fragmented into smaller **micromarkets**. Even though we shop, purchase, and consume food, as individuals we don't all shop in the same way, purchase food in the same manner, or consume the same food. But what accounts for the diversity in the shopping, purchase, and consumption of food? Or, asked another way, how can these micromarkets be identified?

The answer is not a simple one, but it can be found through a process called **segmentation**.

This process groups consumers according to the similarity of their shopping, purchasing, or consumption behaviors, and identifies what causes this similarity.

The purpose of the chapter is to illustrate the process of segmentation in the consumer market for food by using a model that identifies **lifestyle** as the fundamental explanation for behavior, and therefore the most appropriate basis for identifying micromarkets. After a brief review of market segmentation, a model of lifestyle and its determinants is presented to guide the subsequent discussion on market segmentation. Lastly, food-related segmentation typologies are presented.

# MARKET SEGMENTATION

Market segmentation focuses on the diversity of consumers. In fact, the concept of segmentation is based on the proposition that consumers are characteristically different and that these characteristic differences are related to differences in behavior. The most widely used bases for market segmentation are consumer characteristics. They include demographic, economic, cultural, subcultural, social class, psychological, and geographical characteristics. Market segmentation based on behavioral differences is also widely used and includes benefits sought, usages, and response elasticities.

It would be naive to think that behavior is not, in part, influenced by the situation within which it occurs. After all, the decision to purchase food is often made in the retail store and consumers typically purchase food for specific occasions. Behavior, then, is better understood when consumers are further segmented according to the similarities of the situations they encounter.

Finally, differences in shopping, purchase, and consumption behaviors are traceable to differences in consumer lifestyle. Therefore, another viable approach to segmentation is to focus on variations in lifestyles. Segmentation based on personal characteristics, behaviors, situations, and lifestyles provides a structured means of viewing the market place for food products.

## Lifestyle and Its Determinants

The following model of lifestyle and its determinants are used to direct the discussion of market segmentation.

$$LS \begin{array}{|c|} \hline E \\ B \\ \hline \end{array} = f(D, E, C, S, So, P, G)$$

Where:
LS = lifestyle

$\boxed{E}$ = situational environment
B = behavior
D = demographic characteristics
E = economic characteristics
C = cultural characteristics
S = subcultural characteristics
So = social class characteristics
P = psychological characteristics
G = geographical characteristics

This model suggests that consumers engage in behaviors that maintain or enhance their lifestyles. And these behaviors are influenced not only by the situations within which the behaviors take place, but also by the personal characteristics of consumers. Each of the major components in the model will be treated as potential bases for segmentation and discussed accordingly.

# CHARACTERISTIC SEGMENTATION

The seven categories of personal characteristics each contain several segmentation variables. Although they are by no means a complete list of segmentation variables, they are, nonetheless, a good representation of each category. While it is true that each of us is a distinct market segment because no two people are exactly alike, it is also true that we are undoubtedly similar in personal characteristics to other consumers. It is this "similarity of differences" that places us in **one** or another market segment.

## Demographic Characteristics

The most visible, standardized, objective, measurable, and projectable differences in consumers are demographic in nature. Because demographics describe the characteristics of consumers, differences in age, gender, income, occupation, education, religion, marital status, household size, and ethnicity all can be included under the umbrella label of **demographic**. In many cases, these segmentation variables are combined into specific indices such as social class, family life cycle, or acronymic groups such as yuppies or grumpies. Rather than discuss these segmentation variables under the category **demographic**, we will examine them within the context of the seven categories identified in the previously illustrated model of lifestyle and its determinants.

### Age

Consumers change as they age. The proportion of lean tissue (muscle and bone) decreases, while the proportion of fat increases. Taste sensitivity diminishes with age. Salivary glands secrete less saliva to lubricate food. Because of these changes, as we age we eat progressively less and prefer stronger-tasting foods (Logue, 1991). Further, with the decline in physical prowess accompanying age, consumers prefer to shop less frequently and so they do. (Trends, 1996).

There is probably no more visible consumer difference that is more closely related to food consumption and shopping, than age. The **U.S. Department of Labor's Bureau of Labor Statistics** recognizes seven age cohort groups in its Consumers Expenditure Studies: under twenty-five, twenty-five through thirty-four, thirty-five through forty-four, forty-five through fifty-four, fifty-five through sixty-four, sixty-five through seventy-four, and over seventy-five years of age. In general, as consumers age they spend less for food. But as a percent of all expenditures, they spend more for food at home (14.9 percent) than consumers in general (14.0 percent) and less for food away from home (3.8 percent) than consumers in general (5.3 percent). For food consumed at home, as people age, they spend a greater percentage on all major foods: cereals, bakery products, meats, poultry, fish, eggs, dairy products, fruits and vegetables, and other foods (Consumer Expenditure Survey, 1995).

Although the **Food Marketing Institute** doesn't use the same age cohort groups, they report the following **relationships** between age and shopping behavior. As consumers age, they (1) attach greater importance to store choice criteria, (2) use more supermarket-related promotions, (3) switch their primary store less frequently, (4) are more likely to shop at only their primary store, (5) shop less frequently, (6) shop at their primary store less frequently, (7) eat more meals at home that were not prepared at home, (8) use the supermarket more as their source of take-out food, (9) purchase take-out food from fast food restaurants less frequently, (10) consider the nutritional content of the food they eat more frequently, (11) read food labels more frequently, and (twelve) attach greater importance to food safety (Trends, 1996).

### *Gender*

Even though men are more likely to eat and drink in larger portions, there is no available evidence to show that differences in consumption behavior are due to physiological sex differences. This does not mean that there are no differences in food preferences between men and women. Quite the contrary, numerous differences in food preferences have been observed.

### *Npd, groups*

A consumer research company that tracks food consumption in adults found a substantial number of differences in food consumption behaviors. For example, men are more likely to consume (1) beef, pork, and cold cuts, (2) entrees, (3) sweetened cereals, (4) fruit cocktail, (5) raisins, (6) salty snacks, (7) soup, (8) steak sauce, (9) grapefruit juice, (10) root beer, and (11) beer. Women, on the other hand, are more likely to consume (1) fruit flavored foods, (2) sweets, (3) multi-grain and fruited cereal, (4) cantaloupe, (5) hot wheat cereal, and (6) bottled water. Men also tend to devour larger portions of food, while women prefer to nibble at smaller portions more frequently. (Goldner, 1994).

The purchase behavior of men and women also reveals differences. For example, for every dollar spent by female food purchasers, male purchasers spend eighty cents. Men spend more than a dollar spent by women for beer, bottled water, wine, wine coolers, and snacks/spreads/chips. Finally, men represent twenty-nine percent of the total dollar volume spent in supermarkets (Dietrich, 1994).

Like consumption behavior, there is no physiological difference that produces differences in shopping behavior. However, in their 1996 annual survey of consumers, the **Food Marketing Institute** reported numerous gender differences in shopping behavior. For example, women are more likely to (1) attach greater importance to store choice criteria, (2) recommend their primary supermarket to others, (3) use more supermarket-related promotions, (4) buy products not on the shopping list, (5) switch stores, (6) shop less frequently, (7) show greater concern for nutritional content of food, (8) read food labels, and (9) show greater concern for food safety (Trends, 1996).

### *Household Size*

The number of people in a household is closely related to food consumption. The **U.S. Department of Labor's Bureau of Labor Statistics** recognizes five household sizes in their Consumer Expenditure Survey: one, two, three, four, and five or more persons. In general, they find that as the size of a household increases, relative to one-person households, the percentage of expenditures spent for food increases (12.9 percent vs. 16.4 percent); the percentage spent for food at home increases (7.2 percent vs. 11.4 percent) while the percentage spent for food away from home decreases (5.7 percent to 4.9 percent). For food consumed at home, as households grow larger they spend more for all food categories: cereals, bakery, meats and poultry, fish, eggs, dairy products, fruits and vegetables, and other foods. (Consumer Expenditure Survey, 1995). The **Food Marketing Institute's** annual survey uses only four household sizes: one, two, three–four, and five or more. As the size of a household increases, they find that (1) the rank-order importance of store choice criteria changes, (2) the number of supermarket-related promotions increases, (3) buying only what's on the shopping list decreases, (4) frequency of shopping increases, (5) frequency of shopping at their primary store increases, and (6) use of fast food restaurants as sources of take-out food increases (Trends, 1996).

### *Household Type*

Household type, like household size, is an indirect measure of the family life cycle concept (FLC). This developmental concept assumes that families begin with marriage, that some have children who eventually grow up and leave home, that people retire, and that eventually, one spouse is left alone. As families go through these stages, their food consumption behaviors change. The **U.S. Bureau of Labor Statistics** does not report findings based on family life cycle, but rather on the composition of a household. It is a surrogate measure of the FLC and recognizes composition units: husband and wife only, husband and wife oldest child under six, oldest child six through seventeen, and oldest child eighteen or over, other husband and wife units (other family members such as parents), and single parents with at least one child under eighteen. Single parents with children have the lowest annual expenditures, but spend the highest percentage of these expenditures for total food and all food consumed at home. As families with children grow and, as these children age, the percentage of all expenditures spent for food increases, as does the expenditure for food consumed at home (Consumer Expenditure Survey, 1995).

The **Food Marketing Institute's** annual survey considers there to be only two types of households: households with children, and households without children. They find that households with children (1) recommend their primary supermarket to others less frequently, (2) shop more frequently, (3) shop more frequently at their primary supermarket, (4) use a fast food restaurant as a source of take-out food, and (5) show greater awareness of safe-handling labels on meat products (Trends, 1996).

## Economic Characteristics

The economic segmentation category has three components: previously accumulated wealth, current money income, and future borrowing power. Combined, these components reflect a person's ability to pay for a product or service. Unfortunately, most segmentation analyses focus only on one dimension—income. Although there is a strong direct relationship between current income and borrowing power, knowing either one doesn't indicate anything about accumulated wealth. For retired consumers who have accumulated wealth, but receive only a pension as current income, their ability to pay is likely to be underestimated.

The **U.S. Bureau of Labor Statistics** recognizes five income levels and divides income into quintiles: lowest twenty percent, second, third, fourth, and highest twenty percent (Consumer Expenditure Study, 1995). As the level of income rises they find that, relative to the lowest quintile, the percentage of expenditures for food decreases (17.0 percent vs. 12.0 percent); the percentage spent for food consumed at home decreases (12.5 percent vs. 6.4 percent), while the percentage spent for food consumed away from home increases (4.5 percent vs. 5.6 percent). These relationships verify **Ernst Engel's Law** established in 1857, which says that as consumer incomes increase, the proportion spent for food decreases.

The **Food Marketing Institute's** annual survey uses six income levels beginning with 15,000 dollars or less and ending with 75,000 dollars or more. As income levels rise, they find that consumers (1) use fewer supermarket-related promotions, (2) switch stores less frequently, (3) use the supermarket and fast food restaurant less frequently as a source of take-out food, (4) believe that their diets could be a lot healthier, and (5) read food labels more frequently (Trends, 1996).

## Cultural Characteristics

Everyone requires the same basic nutrients, but people do not eat the same foods. The foods that they rely on to provide these nutrients are as different as the environments in which people live, and the cultures through which they learn to adapt them. To say that we are influenced by culture is another way of saying that our decision-making processes for food are subject to group influences. But how, exactly, are our decisions influenced by groups? Group influences are persuasive. They are capable of influencing all of the decision-making stages. They can sensitize a consumer to a problem and specify where to search, what kind of information to use, which alternatives to consider, how to evaluate the alternatives, and provide acceptance or reinforcement for a choice. However, groups primarily influence the consumer's decision-making process by specifying the appropriate criteria to use in the evaluation of alternatives. These evaluative criteria are manifestations of cultural values.

Through a process called **laddering**, linkages between these values (ends) and evaluative criteria (means) are established (Reynolds and Gutman, 1988). Consumers experience consequences when they consume food products chosen according to their evaluative criteria. In turn, these consequences enable consumers to attain particular values. The process was initially illustrated in the following manners: Assume that a woman used the criterion **"flavor"** to evaluate potato chips. Because flavored chips are strong-tasting, she will eat fewer chips. Another consequence of eating fewer chips is that she won't get fat, which means she'll have a better appearance. Finally, a better appearance results in attaining the value of greater self-esteem.

If, as suggested by the laddering process, evaluative criteria are the means for attaining cultural value ends, cultural diversity should be reflected in the relative importance assigned to cultural values. To assess a person's dominant values, a scale called the **List of Values (LOV)** has been used. The LOV scale assesses nine values (Kahle, Beatty, and Homen, 1986).

1. Self-fulfillment
2. Excitement
3. Sense of accomplishment
4. Self-respect
5. Sense of belonging
6. Being well respected
7. Security
8. Fun and enjoyment
9. Warm relationship with others.

In a food-related study, two of these authors found that purchasers of natural foods are more likely to emphasize self-fulfillment, excitement, and accomplishment. Consumers with an emphasis on these values seek to control their lives. This need to control is expressed in their concern for health and nutrition, as well as in the decisions of where to eat and shop for food. In contrast, those who emphasize belonging and security were least likely to purchase natural foods, because of their need to conform with society. (Homer and Kaule, 1988). Despite the apparent relationship between cultural values and consumer decision making, their application to food shopping and consumption behavior at the cultural level has not been widely investigated. There is good reason for this lack of attention. Consumers have considerable latitude to use different products or brands to achieve these values. In fact, the U.S. consists of a montage of subgroups, each of which interprets and responds to society's cultural values in its own particular way. These subgroups are incorporated into the functional model as personal characteristics because participation in, or identification with, specific groups can be used to describe consumers characteristically.

## Subcultural Characteristics

To capture the diversity of the U.S., attention is focused on its many subcultures. A **subculture** is a subdivision of a national culture, based on some unifying characteristic, whose members share similar values and patterns of behavior that are distinct from those of the national culture (Arnold, 1970). This definition suggests that groups defined on the basis of ethnicity, religion, social class, and region all qualify as subcultures. It is important to keep in mind that almost any population segment can be characterized as a subculture. Thus, the four subcultures discussed here are meant to be a representative, rather than exhaustive list. Further, social class and regional subcultures are examined later as separate characteristics in the functional model.

### *Ethnicity*

Ethnic subcultures are linked by common nationality, racial, or language backgrounds. The ancestral pride associated with ethnic groups is clearly observable in the consumption of particular foods. The **U.S. Bureau of Labor Statistics** consumer expenditure study recognizes only two racial subcultures (1) black and (2) white and other. As a percentage of total spending, relative to whites and other, African-Americans spent more for food (14.5 percent vs. 13.9 percent) and food at home (10.3 percent vs. 8.5 percent), and less for food away from home (4.2 percent vs. 5.4 percent). The **BLS** also recognizes national origin. As a percentage of total spending, Hispanics spent the most for food (17.5 percent vs. 14.2 percent for African-Americans, and 13.7 percent for Non-Hispanics). Hispanics also spent the greatest percentage for food at home (12.6 percent vs. 10.1 percent for African-Americans, and 8.3 percent for Non-Hispanics). Non-Hispanics spent the greatest percentage for food away from home (5.4 percent vs. 4.0 percent for Hispanics and 4.1 percent for African-Americans) (Consumer Expenditure Study, 1995).

Although the participants in the **U.S. food marketing system** do not systematically examine food consumption of ethnic groups, there are important variations in their dietary behaviors. One study compared the dietary habits of **African-Americans, Mexican-Americans**, and **White Americans** all living in the same geographical area, for thirteen food groups. The following is a summary of the results (Borrud et al., 1989).

### Meat, Fish, Poultry, Eggs

In general, African-Americans and Mexican-Americans consumed higher percentages of all nutrients (e.g., protein, fats, and carbohydrates) from meat, fish, eggs, and poultry groups than White Americans. The consumption of organ meats contributed significantly to these differences. Also, African-Americans consumed a greater percentage of all calories from fried chicken, fried fish, and fried pork chops than did White or Mexican-Americans. African-Americans consumed more calories from eggs than did White or Mexican-Americans.

### Milk and Milk Products

Although the milk and milk products group was the main contributor to calcium for all ethnic groups, White Americans consumed greater percentages of all calories from this group. The lesser use of dairy products among African-Americans and Mexican-Americans is, in fact, attributable to the greater prevalence of lactose intolerance in these ethnic groups.

### Fats and Oils

All ethnic groups consumed less than four percent of their total calorie intake from the fats and oils group. Butter and margarine was the greatest subgroup contributor to calorie intake in all ethnic groups. Even though White Americans consumed a greater percentage of their total calorie intake from the fats and oils group, African-Americans used somewhat more vegetable oils and shortenings, perhaps reflecting greater use of fried foods.

### Grains and Grains Products

Mexican-Americans consumed the greatest percentage of calories, but the least amount of dietary fiber, from this group. This food group was the main contributor to dietary fiber for African-Americans. White breads, rolls, and tortillas were the primary source of dietary fiber for Mexican-Americans. The subgroups consisting of crackers, chips and popcorn, and other snacks were the greatest contributor of total fat for White Americans. Breads, rolls, muffins, biscuits, and tortillas were the greatest contributors to total fat for African-Americans and Mexican-Americans.

### Vegetables; Legumes

The vegetable group was the greatest contributor to dietary fiber for White Americans. Potatoes were the greatest contributor of calories for all ethnic groups. Green beans, summer squash, and corn were consumed more frequently by Mexican-Americans, while African-Americans consumed more collard greens, mustard greens, spinach, sweet potatoes, and pumpkin. The legume group was the major contributor to dietary fiber for Mexican-Americans. They received more then twice the amount of fiber than African-Americans or White Americans from this food group.

### *Mixed Dish and Sandwiches; Soups*

White Americans had the highest percentage of all calories from meat main dishes, cheese main dishes, or hot/cold sandwiches. African-Americans and Mexican-Americans were the greatest consumers of soups.

### *Fruit and Fruit Products*

African-Americans consumed a greater percentage of calories from the fruit group than did White Americans or Mexican-Americans. African-Americans consumed twice as much Vitamin C from the citrus fruits subgroup as did White Americans and Mexican-Americans.

### *Beverages*

The beverage group comprised coffee, tea, soft drinks, fruit-flavored beverages and alcoholic beverages. African-Americans had the highest intake of calories from the beverage groups. They consumed a greater percentage of calories from carbonated beverages than either of the other two groups.

### *Desserts*

Mexican-American and White Americans consumed more dessert of all types than did African-Americans. In dessert consumption, White Americans consumed the greatest percentage of calories from cakes and cookies, African-Americans from pies, and Mexican-Americans from cookies and pastries.

### *Nuts and Seeds*

Mexican-Americans and White Americans were greater consumers of this group, which included peanuts and nut butters.

### *Miscellaneous Foods*

This group consisted of sauces, gravies, condiments, spices, seasonings, nutritional supplements, and items not classified elsewhere. All ethnic groups consumed less than one percent of all their calories from this group.

In general, this study clearly identified variations in food consumption among three ethnic subcultures. Although not conclusive, it is representative of the potential effect that ethnicity has on consumption behavior. The discussion of ethnicity would be incomplete without an examination of the Asian subculture. **Asian-Americans** account for twenty-nine distinct ethnic groups. **Chinese-Americans** represent the largest group, followed by Filipino-Americans and Japanese-Americans. Most Chinese-Americans use several Chinese foods, such as rice, soybeans, and tea. They also use larger amounts of dairy products, sugar, meat, poultry, and coffee than do mainland Chinese. Japanese foodstuffs and cooking are very similar to Chinese, due to the strong influence China had on Japan during the sixth century. Today, second-generation Japanese-Americans eat a typical American diet, but they eat more rice and use more soy sauce than non-Asians. The Southeast-Asian Filipinos have three central themes: (1) never cook any food by itself, (2) fry with garlic in olive oil or lard, and (3) food should have a sour/cool taste (Kittler and Suchner, 1989).

## *Religions*

Religious groups have important influences on consumption behavior. In the West, **Judaism**, **Christianity**, and **Islam** are the most prevalent religions, whereas **Hinduism** and **Buddhism** are most prevalent in the East. No systematic examination of food consumption among religious groups has been undertaken by the U.S. food marketing system. However, historical sources have identified variations in food consumption due to dietary restrictions (Kittler and Sucher, 1989).

## *Judaism*

Because most Jews in the U.S. are Ashkenazi, their diet reflects the foods of Germany and Eastern Europe. Sephardic Jews tend to eat similarly to those of Mediterranean and Middle Eastern countries, while Jews from India prefer curries and other Asian foods. All Orthodox Jews follow the dietary laws (Kashrut), that were set down in the *Torah* and explained in the *Talmud*. The laws identify (1) which animals are permitted for food, and which are not (e.g., swine, carnivorous animals, and rabbits), (2) how the animals are to be slaughtered (the neck slit with a knife) and examined, (3) which parts of the animal are forbidden for eating (e.g., blood, and a kind of fat called lelab), (4) how the meat is to be prepared or koshered, (5) which foods can't be eaten together (e.g., dairy and meat), and (6) how fruits and vegetables are to be examined for insects and worms.

## *Christianity*

The three dominant **Christian religions** are **Roman Catholicism, Eastern Orthodoxy**, and **Protestantism**. Catholics are required to abstain from eating meat on the Fridays of Lent, and to fast (only one full meal a day) and abstain from meat on Ash Wednesday and Good Friday. All other dietary restrictions were abolished in 1966.

The Eastern Orthodox religion has numerous fast days: On these days, no meat or animal products (milk, eggs, butter, or cheese) are consumed. Fish is also avoided. Of the eleven fasting days, Easter is considered the most important holiday. There are also four fast periods that last for varying numbers of weeks. During these weeks, the same dietary restrictions apply.

Of the Protestant religions, only Seventh-Day Adventists and Mormons have dietary restrictions. Seventh-Day Adventists practice vegetarianism widely because the *Bible* states that the diet in Eden didn't include flesh foods. Most Adventists are lacto-ovo-vegetarians, eating only milk products and eggs, but not meat. They use nuts and beans instead of meat, vegetable oil instead of animal fat, and whole grains in breads. They don't consume tea, coffee, or alcohol, and drink water before and after, but not during, a meal. Meals are not highly seasoned and most condiments are avoided. Mormons don't use tea, coffee, or alcoholic beverages. Other products that contain caffeine are also avoided.

### Islam

In the Islamic religion, eating is considered to be a matter of worship. The *Koran* prohibits the consumption of all swine, birds of prey, and four-footed animals that catch their prey with their mouths. In addition, the animal must be slaughtered in a manner similar to that described in Jewish law. Finally, alcoholic beverages and other intoxicating drugs are forbidden, and the consumption of coffee and tea is discouraged. On fasting days, Muslims abstain from food and drink from dawn to sunset. They are required to fast during Ramadan (the ninth month of the Islamic calendar) and for six days during Shawrual (the month following Ramadan), the tenth day of the month of Muhunam, and the ninth day of Zul Hijjah, but not during the pilgrimage to Mecca. They may also fast on Mondays and Thursdays.

### Hinduism

Hinduism is considered the world's oldest religion, and the basis for another religion called Buddhism. In general, Hindus avoid foods that are thought to hamper physical and mental abilities. The Hindu's diet is largely vegetarian. Although meat is allowed, the cow is considered sacred and is not to be eaten. Garlic, turnips, onions, mushrooms, and red-colored foods are also avoided. Fasting may mean eating no food at all, or abstaining from only specific foods or meals. The fasting days in the Hindu calendar include the first day of the new and full moons of each lunar month, days of eclipses, equinoxes, solstices, and conjunctions of planets; the anniversary of the death of one's father, or mother; Sundays; and numerous other fasting days.

### Buddhism

Buddhist religion forbids the taking of life; therefore, many of its followers are lacto-ovo-vegetarians, but some eat fish, and others abstain only from beef. They also abstain from intoxicants.

In summary, ethnic and religious subcultures are important influences on food consumption. Both are capable of causing variations in food consumption. Given their importance, it is surprising that their effects on consumption and shopping behavior have not been more systematically studied by participants in the U.S. food marketing system.

## Social Class Characteristics

Although all men are created equal, it appears that we spend most of our lives trying to prove otherwise. Do people succeed? They must—after all, every society has a hierarchical system that reflects the inequality among its members. In fact, **social class** may be defined as a hierarchy of distinct status classes. Each class contains members who have relatively the same status, and members of all other classes have either more or less status (Shiffman and Kanuk, 1991). Historically, three factors have been used to define the status of individuals: possessions or amounts of economic goods, power or personal influence over others, and prestige or recognition received by other societal members (Weber, 1996). Today, *status* is often defined using the combined surrogate measures of occupation, education, and income. Interestingly, a person's occupation seems to serve as a quick index to someone's social status. When strangers meet and someone is asked, "What do you do for a living?" the occupational response identifies the source of their income, as well as the education needed to function in that occupation.

Social classes, as subcultures, share not only values, but also patterns of behavior. The relationship between social classes and food consumption was empirically investigated in a study done in the early 1980s. Its discussion here is not meant to be conclusive, but rather representative of the potential effects of social class on food consumption.

Consumers in this study were classified into one of five social classes using the **Hollingshead Index of Social Position** (Hollingshead and Redlich, 1958). These classes were analyzed with regard to the consumption frequency of thirty-six frozen and non-frozen grocery packaged goods and thirty-nine alcoholic and nonalcoholic beverages. The study found social class significantly related to the frequency of consumption for seventeen of the thirty-six food items—particularly, the convenience foods. Social class was significantly related also to the frequency of consumption for twenty-one of the thirty-nine beverages (Schaninger, 1981). In addition to purchase frequency, the study examined the relationship between social class and shopping behavior. Lower classes reported a greater frequency of shopping at convenience stores, looked more for grocery specials in newspapers, read grocery sale ads more carefully, and used mail and newspaper coupons more frequently. Higher classes shopped at more grocery stores than did lower classes (Schaninger, 1981). Despite the early success of this study, the relationship of social class to shopping and purchase behaviors has received little attention in published documents. Either the U.S. food marketing systems has not systematically examined this relationship, or it has decided not to publish its findings in trade publications. Whatever the case, social class, like subcultures, appears to account for causal differences in the behavior of food consumers.

## Psychological Characteristics

In the previous discussion of social class, no mention was made of why social classes differ in food-related behaviors. One well-documented explanation is that there are psychological differences among the classes with regard to how they view the world. People in these classes see themselves, their roles in life, and their time orientation differently than do people in other classes, and hence both behave and consume differently (Wilkie, 1994).

The study done by Schaninger (1981), found that food and beverage consumption patterns appeared to reflect basic values and homemaker role differences among the classes. Lower class consumption patterns were indicative of greater (but not symbolic) self-indulgence, immediate gratification, and an absence of *price-rational* purchasing. Upper class consumption patterns were characterized by greater emphasis on values of quality, taste, nutrition, and a more *price-rational* orientation. Although there have been numerous attempts to document psychological differences using variables that include materialism (Richins and Dawson, 1992), conformity to social pressures (Bearden and Rose, 1990), and moral development (Goolsby and Hunt, 1992), only one study, of value consciousness, focused on food-oriented behavior. That study found that value consciousness was a distinct trait capable of influencing buyer behavior (Lichtenstein, Netemeyer, and Burton, 1992). Is it likely that other psychological differences among social classes are of relevance to the shopping, purchasing, and consumption of food? Probably so.

## Geographic Characteristics

Another personal characteristic that can be treated as a subculture is rooted in geography. There is ample evidence to demonstrate geographical variations in taste. These variations are due in part to differences in the physical environment (i.e., climate, natural resources, topography), and social environment (i.e., ethnic mix, habit and custom, demographic and economic population characteristics), but not to differences in availability. Historically, food not produced locally wasn't eaten. However, technological innovations in food processing, refrigeration, and transportation have redefined the term *availability* to mean an expanded, if not unlimited, period of time and distance.

A number of regional differences in tastes have been observed. For example, pork is preferred east of the Mississippi, while beef is the favorite in cattle country and in the West. In the Northeast, most families use butter, but those in the South prefer margarine. Everyone eats chicken, but the South likes it fried, while the Northeast prefers it baked or roasted. People in the Mountain states eat thirty percent more cookies than those in other regions. The East and Midwest consume more hot dogs than other regions. Russian and Thousand Island salad dressings are preferred in the South, French in the Midwest, Italian in the East, and Ranch in the West. The South consumes more iced tea. The West prefers herbal tea, and instant hot tea is specific to the central states, while the East drinks most of the hot tea. Finally, more ice cream is consumed in the South than in any other region (Fabricant, 1996).

The **U.S. Bureau of Labor Statistics** reports consumer expenditures for food regionally. **Table 11-1** shows the expenditures for the four U.S. regions. Northeasterners spend a greater percentage of all expenditures on food in total and food eaten at home. For food eaten at home, Northeasterners spend the most for meats, poultry, fish, eggs, dairy products, fruits and vegetables, and alcoholic beverages. Midwesterners spend the most for other food. The Midwest spends the largest percentage of all expenditures for food consumed away from home. **Table 11-1** also identifies numerous differences within the commodity groups (Consumer Expenditure Study, 1995).

Regional variations in shopping related behavior have also been identified. People in the South and Midwest express more satisfaction with their primary supermarket, but only people in the South are more likely to recommend their primary supermarket. People in the Midwest shopped for fifteen years or more at their primary supermarket—more than in any other region. People in the South are more likely to shop at only one store almost every time, and to eat meals at home that were not prepared there, and are much more concerned with nutrition than other regions. Finally, people in the Midwest express the greatest confidence in food safety (Trends, 1996).

Geographic segmentation at the local level relies on **geodemographic cluster systems**. Claritas, a prominent leader in **geodemography**, described the logic of this approach in the following manner.

> People with similar cultural backgrounds, means, and perspectives naturally gravitate toward one another. They choose to live amongst their peers in neighborhoods offering affordable advantages and compatible lifestyles. Once settled in, people emulate their neighbors. They adopt similar social values, taste, and expectations. They exhibit shared patterns of consumer behavior toward products, services, media, and promotions (Claritas, 1986).

Geodemographic cluster systems are based on the cliché **"Birds of a feather flock together!"** Basically, each cluster system begins with census block groups, and divides them into groups based on the similarities in their demographic characteristics. The four major general-purpose census block group cluster systems are: ACORN from CACI Marketing Systems; Cluster Plus 2000 from Strategic Mapping, Inc; MicroVision from NDS/Equifax, and Prizm from Claritas. Because of their applicability to the shopping, purchase, and consumption behavior for food products, each of the geographic cluster systems will be profiled in the segmentation typologies section.

To summarize, within characteristic segmentation, seven personal characteristics were examined. When they are combined, these characteristics represent a consumer's individual profile, or combined with other consumers, a market profile; that is, they define who consumers are, demographically, economically, culturally, subculturally, socially, psychologically, and where they are located geographically. As suggested in the functional model, consumer differences on these personal characteristics represent influences on behavior or decision making. But they are not the only influences. Consumer shopping, purchase, and consumption behaviors for food are also influenced by the situation within which these activities take place.

## SITUATIONAL SEGMENTATION

The fact that seventy percent of all food purchase decisions are made in the retail store clearly highlights the need to consider the context within which shopping and purchasing take place. In addition, people consume food in a manner that is consistent with their culture's foodways, which means that the context within which consumption takes place (i.e., time, frequency, or occasion) must also be considered. Therefore, to understand consumer behavior more clearly requires that consumers be segmented according to the similarities of the situations they encounter.

### Consumption Situation

The consumption situation is one in which food is eaten. A culture's foodways typically define (1) the number of meals to be eaten, (2) when meals are to be eaten, and (3) appropriate foods for special occasions, such as entertainment and rituals. The origin of eating three meals during the day was determined by the daily demands of farm work. Breakfast was a hearty meal. The midday meal, called dinner, was the largest, in order to provide the energy needed for afternoon activities. The last meal of the day, called supper, was served when all the field work was done. As society became more industrialized and people migrated to cities, the meals began to conform to factory and business schedules. Breakfast became a light meal. Dinner, now referred to as lunch, became a light meal, often brought from home, but consumed at the factory or office. Supper, now referred to as dinner, became the largest meal of the day. Most Americans consume the majority of their food at these three occasions. However, the times at which these meals are consumed varies greatly. Breakfast begins as early as 6:00 a.m. and may last to as late as 10:00 a.m. (some foodservice operations serve breakfast all day). For most Americans, lunch is eaten typically at noon. Dinner begins at 5:00 p.m. for many consumers. For others, dinner can begin anywhere from 5:00 to 9:00 p.m.

Observation alone indicates that food consumption is not restricted to meals. U.S. consumers are lovers of snacks. Whatever the time or occasion, for many it is an opportunity to eat and drink. In all societies, eating is the primary way of initiating and maintaining human relationships. As a consequence, the emotional and social significance of food and drink is considered by all who entertain their friends and family.

Finally, probably no society is without those unifying events known as rituals. A **ritual** is a set of multiple symbolic behaviors that occur in a fixed sequence and tend to be repeated periodically (Rook, 1985). These rituals may be religious (e.g., Christmas), rites of passage (e.g., marriage), civic (e.g., Fourth of July), cultural (e.g., the Super Bowl), family (e.g., Mother's Day), or personal (e.g., birthday). In the final analysis, the consumption of food is best understood by segmenting behavior according to the situation (e.g., meals, entertainment, or rituals) within which it is consumed.

## Purchase Situation

Given that the majority of food purchase decisions occur within the retail store, it should be obvious that consumers are influenced by the communication they receive during the shopping trip. This influence is well documented by the many studies that have demonstrated the effects of in-store stimuli such as displays, cents-off promotions, point of purchase, coupons, kiosks, and samples (18th Annual Survey of Promotional Practices, 1996). The segmentation of shopping behavior into groups according to the situation (store) within which the activity occurs has not been directly examined, but segmentation into groups according to their general attitudes toward shopping has been extensively investigated. These **shopping orientations** will be illustrated in the section on segmentation typologies. The segmentation of purchase behavior into groups according to the situation (store) within which the activity occurs also has not been directly examined. However, the effects of the in-store environment on purchase behavior was illustrated in Chapter 9 in terms of the percentage of unplanned, generally planned, and substitute purchases made in stores.

## Situational Characteristics

It is necessary to consider not only the types of situations (consumption, purchase), but also to identify the situational characteristics that impact on consumer decision making. There are five types of characteristics which have a demonstratable and systematic effect on decision making: task objectives, physical surroundings, social surroundings, temporal perspectives, and antecedent states (Belk, 1975).

**Task Definition** is the reason or occasion for which food is consumed. As stated earlier, food is purchased to be consumed as a meal or a snack, or for a special occasion such as a birthday. Thus, which food is purchased depends partly upon the reason **why** it is purchased.

The **physical surroundings** represent the concrete physical aspects of the environment within which the food is purchased and consumed. The physical surroundings of the retail store, reflected by its interior, influence decision making. The lighting, color, music, and climate control are just some of the surroundings that impact on the senses of consumers. The environment within which food is consumed also impacts on decision making. Is the food normally consumed at the consumer's table, in front of the T.V., or on a picnic at the beach? Thus, which food is purchased depends, in part, upon **where** it is purchased and consumed.

**Social surroundings** deal with the effects of other people on the purchase and consumption of food. Is the consumer shopping alone, with a spouse, or children? Is the food for personal consumption, or to the shared with the family? Again, what food is purchased is, in part, influenced by **who** accompanies the shopper and shares in the food's consumption.

There are a number of ways to recognize the impact of the **temporal factor** on consumer decision-making. The time of day the food is consumed, the amount of time needed to prepare the food, the amount of time allocated to shopping for food, and the length of time elapsed since a shopper's last meal are all temporal influences on consumer decision making. Which food is purchased and consumed also depends, in part, on **when** it will be purchased, prepared, and consumed.

**Antecedent states** refer to the momentary conditions (states of physical being) and moods (states of mental being) that influence decision making. Physically, being tired or ill will certainly have an impact on consumer shopping, purchase, and consumption behavior. Whether or not the consumer goes shopping, how much time is spent shopping, what is purchased, how the food is prepared, and when the food is consumed are all, in one way or another, influenced by the tiredness and/or illness of the consumer. The physical state of hunger was long ago shown to have an influence on decision making. Consumers who shop when they are hungry are more susceptible to the food-related cues found in supermarkets, and as a consequence engage in more impulse buying (Nisbet and Kanouse, 1969).

Consumer moods also have an impact on decision making. One study found that the more positively a shopper described her mood, the greater the (1) number of items purchased, (2) the amount of money spent, and (3) actual time spent in the store (Sherman and Smith, 1987). Another study found that positive moods led to increased browsing and impulse buying. For some consumers, negative moods had the same effect (Jeon, 1990).

In summary, the shopping, purchase, and consumption behavior of consumers is strongly influenced by the situations within which these activities take place. Why the food is being purchased and consumed (task definition), where the food is being purchased and consumed (physical surroundings), when the food is being purchased and consumed (temporal factors), who accompanies the shopper to the store and shares the food (social surroundings), and how the consumer feels both mentally and physically (antecedent states) are all situational characteristics that influence behaviors that take place within purchase and consumption situations.

# BEHAVIORAL SEGMENTATION

The three approaches that are used to identify market segments using behavioristic variables are benefit, usage, and consumer-response elasticity.

## Benefit Segmentation

Benefit segmentation is a special form of behavioral segmentation that combines consumers who seek similar benefits from the purchase and consumption of particular products. Earlier in this chapter, the process of **laddering** was described. The evaluative criterion of **flavor** produced certain **consequences** (slim figure, better appearance) that led to the attainment of the **value** of greater self-esteem. In the process, consumer benefits are represented by the consequences component because they are the positive outcomes that evaluative criteria provide to the consumer. To use another example, people purchase food of a certain size, shape, color, odor, and temperature (evaluative criteria) because they believe it will taste good (consequences or benefit) and lead to sensory pleasure (value).

Food manufacturers have, for some time, segmented their markets on the basis of the benefits that people seek in consuming a particular product. **Kellogg's, Coca-Cola, Sara Lee, Procter and Gamble**, and **General Mills** are but a few of the prominent food manufacturers that utilize this approach to market segmentation. Clearly, these firms and others believe that the benefits people seek from the consumption of food products represent true market segments.

## Usage Segmentation

Usage segmentation groups consumers on the basis of whether or not they use the brand or product category, and if so, how much of the brand or product is used. Brand usage focuses on the consumption of one brand versus other competitive brands. This approach is usually used by food manufacturers because of the implications it has for market share, that is, segmentation by brands identifies the number of slices (brands) in the pie (market).

Segmentation by products category focuses on the consumption of one category versus other competitive product categories. For example, the product category of beverages includes soft drinks, coffee, fruit drinks, and milk. Because the emphasis is on the product category and not the brand, segmentation by product category identifies the pie's size (market).

Segmentation by usage rate groups people according to their purchase and consumption volume. Typically, the market for either a brand or a product is divided into heavy, medium, and light users. Of particular concern to food manufacturers is the heavy-users segment because, although they are often small in number, they typically account for a high percentage of the purchases. Segmentation by usage rate identifies how big of a bite a particular group of consumers takes out of the firm's slice of the entire pie.

Needless to say, segmentation by usage status (users vs. non-users), and usage rate (i.e., heavy, medium, and light) represent methods widely used by food manufacturers. Their fondness for this type of segmentation is based on the simple notion that usage differences are readily observable and meaningful, and profoundly affect the firm's profitability.

## Response Elasticity

Segmenting by elasticity is based on sensitivity to price changes and promotional deals. **Response elasticity** measures the percentage change in quantity purchased compared to the percentage change in the price and deal. **Price elasticity** is a concept fundamental to the economic theory of demand. More of a product will be demanded at a lower price than at a higher price. If consumers are sensitive to a price change, a decrease in price will produce more than a proportionate increase in the quantity purchased. If consumers are insensitive, a price decrease will produce less than a proportionate change in the quantity purchased. In the former, demand is elastic, while in the latter it is inelastic. Because price is fairly elastic for food purchased at the retail level, price increases typically bring about brand-switching behaviors.

**Deal elasticity** also measures behavior changes. Although these promotional deals include coupons, price discounts, rebates, feature advertising, and displays, only price discounts (deals) and coupons will be examined. Unlike price changes that are relatively permanent changes, price deals represent temporary price reductions. Consumers are more responsive to price deals than to permanent price changes for three reasons. First, because price deals are temporary, consumers buy more on deal than their normal quantity and stockpile. Second, consumers who buy on price deals have lower cost parameters and buy and consume more when a deal is run. Third, price deals are announced, but price reductions are not announced. Because price-deal elasticities are higher (consumers are more responsive) than price elasticities, many retailers prefer to keep prices high and offer price deals rather than to price at everyday low prices (Blattberg and Neslin, 1990).

Coupons represent the second most important promotional deal. Coupons provide consumers with tremendous cost-savings opportunities and are the number-one non-store-specific activity cited for saving money on groceries. Of course, not all consumers are equally sensitive to coupon deals. Heavy (those who always use), moderate (those who sometimes use), and light (those who rarely use) coupon users, on average use twenty-eight, fourteen, and seven coupons per month. The heavy user is more likely to be female, older, less educated, married, and have lower income than the moderate and light user. She is less likely to be employed full time, but more likely to live in a larger household with children under six (NCH Promotional Services, 1996).

Psychographically, deal-prone consumers are price conscious, venturesome (eager to try new products), opinion leaders for many products, highly involved with shopping and advertising (i.e., plan trips, enjoy shopping, read advertising), compulsive, and often found not to be brand loyal (Blattberg and Neslin, 1990).

In summary, behavioral segmentation focuses on actual variations in the shopping, purchasing, and consumption behavior of consumers. Benefit segmentation, a special form of behavioral segmentation, groups consumers according to the benefits they seek from the consumption of a particular product. Usage rates and status focus on actual differences in volume and are used as a basis for segmentation. Sensitivity to price changes and promotional deals offered by food marketers is the basis for response-elasticity segmentation.

## LIFESTYLE SEGMENTATION

Having examined the determinants of lifestyles, attention is now focused on the segmentation of lifestyles. This approach recognizes that people sort themselves into groups on the basis of how they choose to live out their lives (Hawkins, Best and Coney, 1995).

### Psychographic Segmentation

Why do people do the things they do? The position, stated earlier, is that people behave in ways to maintain or enhance their lifestyle. Maintaining or enhancing lifestyle requires the consumption of products, the most important of which is food. **Psychographics** refers to the development of psychological profiles of consumers and psychologically based measures of lifestyles. Psychographic segmentation clusters consumers into groups according to differences in their lifestyles. Lifestyle, as a mode of living, is reflected by the activities consumers spend their time performing, their priority of interests, and the opinions they express. Psychographic segments are created by grouping consumers who resemble each other in their activities, interests, and opinions. The number of food marketers that engage in psychographic segmentation is testimony to its popularity. The purpose of the next section is to illustrate widely used segmentation typologies in the U.S. food marketing system.

## SEGMENTATION TYPOLOGIES

The most comprehensive segmentation typologies used in the U.S. food marketing system are geodemographics and psychographics. All of the geodemographic typologies are based on the earlier mentioned **"Birds of a feather flock together"** cliché. At the same time, they are different from each other in many respects—so much so that each of the four prominent geodemographic **"cluster systems"** will be reviewed separately. Geodemographics allows us to describe who buys what, and where they are located.

By grouping people into homogeneous segments based on psychographics, we are able to understand why consumers buy what they do. In one very important way, psychographic segmentation puts the **"psychological meat on the demographic bones of the human skeleton."** Only the most widely known psychographic segmentation typology will be reviewed—Vals.

## Geodemographic Segmentation—MicroVision

**MicroVision**, developed by **Equifax National Decision Systems**, is a micro-geographic customer segmentation and targeting system. **MicroVision** categorizes every household in America into one of fifty distinct segments based on demographic, socioeconomic, housing, and aggregated consumer demand data. Each of the fifty **MicroVision** segments is assigned to one of nine groups shown in **Figure 11-1**. The segments within a particular group are likely to respond similarly to the efforts of food marketers. **MicroVision** targets at the **Zip + 4** level of postal geography in order to precisely locate concentrations of consumers who belong to a particular segment. An application of **MicroVision** to the purchase behavior for food products is shown in **Figure 11-2**. The food product category illustrated is fish/seafood. The columns in this exhibit are the total number and percentage of households in a segment that purchase fish/seafood in a full-service restaurant; the total number and percentage of all of U.S. households in a segment; the penetration, or the number of households that purchase fish/seafood in a full-service restaurant relative to the total number of households in a segment; and an index that compares the consumption of fish/seafood for a segment in full-service restaurants to the average consumption of fish/seafood in full-service restaurants for the entire U.S.

According to the index, segment twenty-one in group six, **American Classics** has the highest propensity to buy fish/seafood in full-service restaurants. They are 122 percent more likely to buy fish/seafood (index = 222 percent) than the national average (index = 100 percent). This segment is only .3 percent of all U.S. households, but 11.44 percent of them buy fish/seafood in full-service restaurants. Despite its significance, because of the small number of fish/seafood eaters, **American Classics** is not included in the top ten or twenty MicroVision markets for fish/seafood. The **American Classics** neighborhood is made up of older singles and couples living in suburban and rural areas. They tend to have an income near the national average, a medium-to-low education, and a high percentage receives retirement income.

## Geodemographic Segmentation—Acorn

**Acorn**, developed by **CACI Marketing Systems**, analyzes, profiles, and classifies consumers according to the type of residential area in which they live. The **Acorn** system identifies 226,000 census block groups or neighborhoods and assigns each to one of forty market segments based on sixty-one characteristics. These characteristics include income, home value, occupation, education, household type, age, and other key determinants of consumer behavior. In turn, each of the forty **Acorn** segments is assigned to one of eight groups.

An application of **Acorn** to the purchase behavior for food products to shown in **Figure 11-3**. The food category illustrated is a bakery product—bagels. The columns in this exhibit represent the total number and percentage of households that purchase bagels; the total number and percentage of **all** U.S. households in a segment; the penetration, or the number of households that purchase bagels relative to the total number of households in a segment; and an index that compares the consumption of bagels in a segment to the consumption of bagels in the U.S.

According to the index, segment 1D in group 1 **Successful Suburbanites** has the highest propensity to purchase bagels. They are thirty percent more likely to purchase bagels (index = 134 percent) than the national average (index = one hundred percent) and are the fourteenth largest market for bagels. Demographically they have large families and live in newer suburbs. They are professional, well-educated, mobile, and derive their affluence from dual incomes and investments.

## Geodemographic Segmentation—Prizm

**Prizm**, developed by **Claritas**, categorizes census block groups based on demographic characteristics such as age, education, occupation, housing type, socioeconomic rank, race, and ethnicity. The **Prizm** system assigns each of the block groups to one of sixty-two market segments. These segments are further grouped into fifteen broad types, shown in **Figure 11-4**. The width of the grid indicates the degree of urbanization from the countryside to urban high-rises. The height of the grid indicates the degree of affluence or social economic status (e.g., income, education, home value, and occupation) spanning the lower, middle, and upscale markets.

An application of **Prizm** to food products purchase behavior is shown in **Figure 11-5**.

The food category is frozen pizza. The columns represent the total number of adults that live in a segment (neighborhood); the percentage of adults who live in a particular segment, the number of adults in a segment who eat frozen pizza; the percentage of all U.S. adults who eat frozen pizza; the penetration, or the percentage of all adults in a segment who eat frozen pizza; and an index that compares the consumption of frozen pizza by a segment to the consumption of pizza by all U.S. adults.

According to the index, segment fifty-six in group R2 **"Agri-business"** has the highest propensity to purchase frozen pizza. They are thirty-three percent more likely than the national average to eat frozen pizza. Approximately 2.39 million adults live in Agri-business neighborhoods, and 1.32 million purchase frozen pizza, for a penetration of 55.3 percent (1.32/2.39). Although they are only 1.27 percent of all U.S. adults, they represent 1.68 percent of all consumers of frozen pizza. This results in an index of 133 (1.68/1.27). Despite its significance, because of the small number of frozen-pizza consumers, "Agri-business" is not included in either the top ten or twenty **Prizm** markets for frozen pizza. The Agri-business neighborhood is more affluent and more skewed to the greater Northwest, from Lake Michigan to the Pacific. It is famous for very large families with lots of kids, countless animals, apple pie, and going fishing.

### Lifestyle Segmentation—Vals 2

The most well-known psychographic consumer segmentation system is **SRI Consulting's Vals 2 (Values and Lifestyles)**. The system sorts consumers into eight segments based on "personal orientations" such as action, status, and principles, as well as "resource constraints," such as income, education, product awareness, and self-confidence (**Figure 11-6**).

In the **Vals 2** typology, **Strugglers** have so few resources that their psychological characteristics are of no consequence. **Actualizers** have the most resources, and thus can exhibit all of the psychological orientations. The eight segments differ from each other in their use of various foods categories. **Figure 11-7** lists the top ten packaged food products by index for each segment. The index number shows the relative use of the food product by the U.S. population. To explain why segments prefer what they do, their preferences are subsequently related to their lifestyles.

## SUMMARY

Although a society's foodways define broad behavioral patterns that underline food-related behavior, we don't all shop in the same way, purchase food in the same manner, or consume the same foods. Today, the once homogeneous consumer market comprises smaller micromarkets.

The most fruitful approach to identifying these micromarkets is to segment consumers into groups according to (1) lifestyles they have chosen to live, (2) behaviors they engage in to maintain or enhance their lifestyles, (3) situations within which these behaviors occur, and (4) personal characteristics of the consumers who engage in these behaviors. There are seven major categories of personal consumer characteristics. Consumers may be described demographically on the basis of age, gender, and family life cycle expressed in terms of household size and type. Economically, consumers may be classified according to their income. Culturally, consumers can be differentiated according to the rank order of importance they assign to cultural values. Subculturally, consumers may be described ethnically, and religiously. Socially, consumers may be identified as belonging to classes that differ in status. Consumers are different psychologically because they don't all view their world in the same way. Finally, having identified who makes up a micromarket, the geographic characteristic tells us where these markets are located.

The shopping, purchasing, and consumption behavior of food consumers is strongly influenced by situational characteristics: task definition, physical surroundings, social surroundings, temporal perspective, and the consumer's antecedent mental and physical state.

Personal and situational characteristics represent potential causes of variations in consumer behavior. To understand their effects, these behavioral variations are segmented according to the benefits that consumers seek from the purchase and consumption of food products, their sensitivity to incentives, or their actual product/brand usage.

Personal and situational characteristics and behavioral dimensions represent determinants of lifestyles. Who we are as individuals, and how situations influence our shopping, purchase, and consumption behavior are guided by our need to live a lifestyle. Lifestyle segmentation using psychographics allows us to answer the question "Why do people do the things they do?"

## SELECTED REFERENCES

Arnold, D. O. *The Sociology of Subcultures*. Berkeley, Ca.: Glendasary Press, 1970.

Bearden, W. O. and R. L. Rose. "Attention to Social Comparison Information: An Individual Difference Factor Affecting Consumer Conformity," *Journal of Consumer Research* 16 (March 1990) pp. 461–471.

Belk, R. W. "Situational Variables and Consumer Behavior," *Journal of Consumer Research*, 2(December) 1975, pp. 158–165.

Blattberg, R. C. and S. A. Neshlin. *Sales Promotion, Concepts, Methods, and Strategies*. Englewood Cliffs, N.J.,: Prentice Hall, Inc. A Division of Simon and Schuster, 1990.

Borrud, L. G. et al. "Food Groups Contributions to Nutrient Intake in Whites, Blacks and Mexican-Americans in Texas," *Journal of American Dietetic Association*, 89(8) August 1989, pp. 1061–1069.

Consumer Expenditure Survey—Shares of Average Annual Expenditures and Sources of Income. Bureau of Labor Statistics. Washington, D.C. 1994.

Dietrich, R. "Tracking the Invisible Man," *Progressive Grocer*, November 1992, pp. 69–82.

Fabricant, F. "*The Geography of Taste*," *The New York Times Magazine,* March 10 1996, pp. 40–41

Goldner, D. "What Men and Women Really Want. . . . to Eat," *New York Times* (Living Section) C1, pp. 1, 8. March 2, 1994.

Goolsby, J. R and S. D. Hunt. "Cognitive Moral Development and Marketing," *Journal of Marketing,* Vol. 56 (January 1992) pp. 55–68.

Hollingshead, A. B. and F. C. Redlich. *Social Class and Mental Illness.* New York: John Wiley and Sons, 1958.

Homer, Paul L. Kahle, "9 Structural Equation Tests of the Value—Attitude—Behavior Hierarchy," *Journal of Personality and Social Psychology*, 54 (April, 1988) pp. 638–646.

"How to Use Prizm," Claritas, Alexandria, Va. 1986. p 1.

Jeon, J. 1991. An Empirical Investigation of the Relationship between Affective States, In-Store Browsing, and Impulse Buying. Unpublished dissertation. The University of Alabama.

Kahle, L. R., S. Beatty, and P. Homer. "Alternative Measurement Approaches to Consumer Values: The List of Values (LOV) and Lifestyle (Vals)," *Journal of Consumer Research*, 13 (December) pp. 405–409.

Kittler, P. G. and K. Sucher. *Food and Culture in America.* New York: Van Nostrand Reinhold, 1989.

Lichtenstein, D. R., R. G. Netemeyer, and S. Burton. "Distinguishing Coupon Proneness from Value Consciousness: An Acquisition-Transaction Utility Theory Perspective," *Journal of Marketing,* Vol. 54 (July 1990) pp. 54–67.

Logue, A. W. *The Psychology of Eating and Drinking.* 2nd ed. New York: W.H. Freeman and Company, 1991.

McIntosh, E. N. *American Food Habits in Historical Perspective.* Praeger, Conn., 1995.

Nesbit T. R. E. and D. E. Kanouse. "Obesity, Food Deprivation, and Supermarket Shopping Behavior,"*Journal of Personality and Social Psychology*, Vol. 12 (August 1969) pp. 289–294.

Reynolds, T. J. and J. Gutman. "Laddering Theory, Method, Analysis, and Interpretation," *Journal of Advertising Research* 28 (Feb., Mar. 1988) pp. 11–34.

Richins, M. L. and S. Dawson. "A Consumer Values Orientation for Materialism and Its Measurement: Scale Development and Validation," *Journal of Consumer Research*, Vol. 19 (December 1992) pp. 303–316.

Rokeach, M. *The Nature of Human Values.* New York: Free Press, 1973.

Rook. D. W. "The Ritual Dimension of Consumer Behavior," *Journal of Consumer Research* 12 (December, 1985), pp. 251–264.

Schaninger, C. M. "Social Class Versus Income Revisited: An Empirical Investigation, *Journal of Marketing Research,* Vol. XIII (May 1981), pp. 192–208.

Schiffman, L. C. and L. Kanok. *Consumer Behavior.* 7th ed. Englewood Cliffs, N.J.: Prentice-Hall, 1991.

Sherman, E. and R. B. Smith. "Mood States of Shoppers and Store Image: Promising Interactions and Possible Behavioral Effects," in Advances in Consumer Research, Vol. 14, P. Anderson and M. Wallendorf, eds. Provo, Vt.: Association for Consumer Research, 1987, pp. 251–254.

*Trends in the United States—Consumer Attitudes in the Supermarket.* The Research Department, Food Marketing Institute, Washington, D.C., 1996.

Weber, M. *From Max Weber; Essays in Sociology.* Eds. H. H. Gard and C. W. Mills, New York: Oxford University Press, 1946.

## REVIEW QUESTIONS

1. What is the underlying logic of market segmentation?

2. Identify and explain the model of lifestyle and its determinants.

3. Market segmentation depends upon causal, not descriptive, differences. Explain.

4. Use some examples to illustrate the relationship between demographic differences and shopping, purchase, or consumption behavior.

5. What role does the laddering process play in consumer decision making?

6. Consumers are more likely to be influenced by people they perceive to be similar to themselves than by those they consider dissimilar to themselves. Does this statement explain the nature of group influence? Why or why not?

7. What evidence is there to demonstrate that "birds of a feather flock together"?

8. What is meant by the statement, "To understand consumer behavior, it must be observed within the context in which it occurs"?

9. Behavioral differences are the essence of market segments. Explain

10. The psychology of the consumer is reflected in psychographic segmentation. Do you agree? Why or why not?

**TABLE 11-1.** REGIONAL EXPENDITURES FOR FOOD

| ITEMS | NORTHEAST | MIDWEST | SOUTH | WEST |
|---|---|---|---|---|
| Average annual expenditures | $33,014 | $31,937 | $30,289 | $35,222 |
| Food | 14.8 | 13.6 | 14.1 | 13.4 |
|   Food at home | 9.5 | 8.2 | 8.7 | 8.5 |
|     Cereals and bakery products | 1.6 | 1.3 | 1.3 | 1.3 |
|     Cereals and cereal products | .6 | .5 | .5 | .5 |
|     Bakery products | 1.0 | .8 | .8 | .8 |
|   Meats, poultry, fish, and eggs | 2.6 | 2.1 | 2.5 | 2.1 |
|     Beef | .7 | .7 | .8 | .6 |
|     Pork | .5 | .4 | .6 | .4 |
|     Other meats | .4 | .3 | .3 | .3 |
|     Poultry | .6 | .4 | .4 | .4 |
|     Fish and seafood | .4 | .2 | .3 | .3 |
|     Eggs | .1 | .1 | .1 | .1 |
|   Dairy Products | 1.0 | .9 | .9 | .9 |
|     Fresh milk and cream | .4 | .4 | .4 | .4 |
|     Other dairy products | .6 | .5 | .5 | .6 |
|   Fruits and vegetables | 1.7 | 1.3 | 1.4 | 1.4 |
|     Fresh fruits | .5 | .4 | .4 | .4 |
|     Fresh vegetables | .5 | .4 | .4 | .4 |
|     Processed fruits | .4 | .3 | .3 | .3 |
|     Processed vegetables | .2 | .2 | .3 | .2 |
|   Other food at home | 2.6 | 2.7 | 2.6 | 2.8 |
|     Sugar and other sweets | .3 | .4 | .3 | .4 |
|     Fats and oils | .3 | .2 | .3 | .3 |
|     Miscellaneous foods | 1.1 | 1.2 | 1.1 | 1.3 |
|     Nonalcoholic beverages | .8 | .8 | .7 | .7 |
|     Food prepared by consumer on out-of-town trips | .1 | .1 | .1 | .2 |
| Food away from home | 5.3 | 5.4 | 5.4 | 4.9 |
| Alcoholic beverages | 1.0 | .8 | .8 | .9 |

*SOURCE:* CONSUMER EXPENDITURE SURVEY, U.S BUREAU OF LABOR STATISTICS, 1995.

**FIGURE 11-1.** MICROVISION GROUPS SEGMENTS

| MICROVISION GROUP | GROUP SEGMENTS | GENERAL HOUSEHOLD DESCRIPTION |
|---|---|---|
| Accumulated Wealth | 1,2,3,4,5,6,14 | Wealthiest, number one in home ownership and property value, white, white-collar employment, and education level. |
| Mainstream Families | 10,11,16,17, 18,22,23,35, 38 | Medium income (second highest), above-average home ownership, number of veterans, blue-collar workers, and adults aged 35 to 69. |
| Young Accumulations | 9,19,25,28 | Above-average number aged under 18 and over 49, and blue-collar workers, rural, below-average income, most with no college education. |
| Mainstream Singles | 8,12,15,32, 34,39,40 | Average income, above-average college degrees and white-collar occupations, most single or divorced. |
| Asset-Building Families | 27,29 | Average age and household size, below-average income, blue-collar, less-educated. |
| Conservative Classics | 7,20,21,30,31 | Above-average income, number one in ages 55 and older, highest dual and single-person households, largest percentage of veterans and retirees. |
| Cautious Couples | 26,33 | Largest rural population, below-average income, blue-collar, older aged 50 to 84. |
| Sustaining Families | 24,41,42,43, 44,46 | Highest number of children, lowest medium income, highest blue-collar occupations, lowest college attendance and graduation. |
| Sustaining Singles | 13,36,37,45, 47,48 | Largest number aged 18 to 29, college enrollment high, single, below-average income, renters, no car. |

*SOURCE:* ADAPTED FROM MICROVISION MARKETING GUIDE, EQUIFAX NATIONAL, DECISION SYSTEMS.

Microvision PROFILE REPORT                    07-30-1996

ANALYSIS : FULL SERV FISH/SEAFOOD    SORTED BY : GROUP

| DESCRIPTION | ANALYSIS TOTAL | %COMP | BASE TOTAL | %COMP | % PEN. | INDEX |
|---|---|---|---|---|---|---|
| MVG01 01 UPPER CRUST | 79630 | 1.6 | 1107840 | 1.1 | 7.19 | 140 |
| MVG01 02 LAP OF LUXURY | 79161 | 1.5 | 1132389 | 1.1 | 6.99 | 136 |
| MVG01 03 ESTABLISHED WEALTH | 101626 | 2.0 | 1928050 | 1.9 | 5.27 | 103 |
| MVG01 04 MID-LIFE SUCCESS | 151376 | 3.0 | 2531417 | 2.5 | 5.98 | 116 |
| MVG01 05 PROSPEROUS METRO MIX | 135555 | 2.7 | 2334766 | 2.3 | 5.81 | 113 |
| MVG01 06 GOOD FAMILY LIFE | 113935 | 2.2 | 1782347 | 1.8 | 6.39 | 124 |
| MVG01 14 MIDDLE YEARS | 7378 | 0.1 | 354164 | 0.4 | 2.08 | 41 |
| MVG02 10 HOME SWEET HOME | 344272 | 6.7 | 5743388 | 5.8 | 5.99 | 117 |
| MVG02 11 FAMILY TIES | 191422 | 3.7 | 3360036 | 3.4 | 5.70 | 111 |
| MVG02 16 COUNTRY HOME FAMILIE | 315085 | 6.2 | 5957530 | 6.0 | 5.29 | 103 |
| MVG02 17 STARS AND STRIPES | 71779 | 1.4 | 2428975 | 2.4 | 2.96 | 57 |
| MVG02 18 WHITE PICKET FENCE | 238907 | 4.7 | 4681964 | 4.7 | 5.10 | 99 |
| MVG02 22 TRADITIONAL TIMES | 120075 | 2.4 | 2378433 | 2.4 | 5.05 | 98 |
| MVG02 23 SETTLED IN | 234576 | 4.6 | 5022036 | 5.1 | 4.67 | 91 |
| MVG02 35 BUY AMERICAN | 137873 | 2.7 | 3166233 | 3.2 | 4.35 | 85 |
| MVG02 38 RUSTIC HOMESTEADERS | 356899 | 7.0 | 8438209 | 8.5 | 4.23 | 82 |
| MVG03 09 BUILDING A HOME LIFE | 3998 | 0.1 | 99462 | 0.1 | 4.02 | 78 |
| MVG03 19 YOUNG AND CAREFREE | 6677 | 0.1 | 117328 | 0.1 | 5.69 | 111 |
| MVG03 25 BEDROCK AMERICA | 173775 | 3.4 | 2980488 | 3.0 | 5.83 | 113 |
| MVG03 28 BUILDING A FAMILY | 46551 | 0.9 | 1503943 | 1.5 | 3.10 | 60 |
| MVG04 08 MOVERS AND SHAKERS | 179769 | 3.5 | 2732574 | 2.7 | 6.58 | 128 |
| MVG04 12 A GOOD STEP FORWARD | 173869 | 3.4 | 3133457 | 3.2 | 5.55 | 108 |
| MVG04 15 GREAT BEGINNINGS | 269630 | 5.3 | 4317532 | 4.3 | 6.25 | 121 |
| MVG04 32 METRO SINGLES | 94741 | 1.9 | 2111363 | 2.1 | 4.49 | 87 |
| MVG04 34 BOOKS AND NEW RECRUI | 26266 | 0.5 | 511374 | 0.5 | 5.14 | 100 |
| MVG04 39 ON THEIR OWN | 174644 | 3.4 | 3686441 | 3.7 | 4.74 | 92 |
| MVG04 40 TRYING METRO TIMES | 179071 | 3.5 | 4592603 | 4.6 | 3.90 | 76 |
| MVG05 27 MIDDLE OF THE ROAD | 4761 | 0.1 | 342780 | 0.3 | 1.39 | 27 |
| MVG05 29 ESTABLISHING ROOTS | 14815 | 0.3 | 461584 | 0.5 | 3.21 | 62 |
| MVG06 07 COMFORTABLE TIMES | 42421 | 0.8 | 697584 | 0.7 | 6.08 | 118 |
| MVG06 20 SECURE ADULTS | 86906 | 1.7 | 1523448 | 1.5 | 5.70 | 111 |
| MVG06 21 AMERICAN CLASSICS | 39687 | 0.8 | 347010 | 0.3 | 11.44 | 222 |
| MVG06 30 DOMESTIC DUOS | 97552 | 1.9 | 1312994 | 1.3 | 7.43 | 145 |
| MVG06 31 COUNTRY CLASSICS | 46349 | 0.9 | 667419 | 0.7 | 6.94 | 135 |
| MVG07 26 THE MATURE YEARS | 1559 | 0.0 | 221051 | 0.2 | 0.71 | 14 |
| MVG07 33 LIVING OFF THE LAND | 21785 | 0.4 | 502013 | 0.5 | 4.34 | 84 |
| MVG08 24 CITY TIES | 142726 | 2.8 | 2202061 | 2.2 | 6.48 | 126 |
| MVG08 41 CLOSE-KNIT FAMILIES | 73584 | 1.4 | 1759006 | 1.8 | 4.18 | 81 |
| MVG08 42 TRYING RURAL TIMES | 104091 | 2.0 | 1469522 | 1.5 | 7.08 | 138 |
| MVG08 43 MANUFACTURING USA | 12637 | 0.2 | 306195 | 0.3 | 4.13 | 80 |
| MVG08 44 HARD YEARS | 4935 | 0.1 | 178893 | 0.2 | 2.76 | 54 |
| MVG08 46 DIFFICULT TIMES | 142802 | 2.8 | 3003636 | 3.0 | 4.75 | 92 |
| MVG09 13 SUCCESSFUL SINGLES | 22075 | 0.4 | 614408 | 0.6 | 3.59 | 70 |
| MVG09 36 METRO MIX | 49910 | 1.0 | 1482103 | 1.5 | 3.37 | 66 |
| MVG09 37 URBAN UP AND COMERS | 20740 | 0.4 | 551494 | 0.6 | 3.76 | 73 |
| MVG09 45 STRUGGLING METRO MIX | 88649 | 1.7 | 1593877 | 1.6 | 5.56 | 108 |
| MVG09 47 UNIVERSITY USA | 27192 | 0.5 | 691606 | 0.7 | 3.93 | 77 |
| MVG09 48 URBAN SINGLES | 38947 | 0.8 | 1027765 | 1.0 | 3.79 | 74 |
| MVG10 49 ANOMALIES | 2918 | 0.1 | 135694 | 0.1 | 5.14* | 100* |
| MVG11 50 UNCLASSIFIED | 13067 | 0.3 | 158312 | 0.2 | 5.14* | 100* |
| TOTALS | 5108648 | 100.0 | 99384252 | 100.0 | 5.14 | 100 |

BASE: U.S. H.H.                          * Unstable due to sample size
© EQUIFAX NATIONAL DECISION SYSTEMS      SOURCE: NPD CREST - 94

**FIGURE 11-2.** PURCHASE POTENTIAL BY MICROVISION FULL SERVICE RESTAURANT FISH/SEAFOOD

Purchase Potential by ACORN

| ACORN Markets | | Buyers (000) Number | Buyers (000) Percent | Penetration per 100 | U.S. (000) Number | U.S. (000) Percent | Index |
|---|---|---|---|---|---|---|---|
| 1. Affluent Families | | | | | | | |
| 1A | Top One Percent | 665 | 1.1% | 77.4 | 859 | 0.9% | 131 |
| 1B | Wealthy Seaboard Suburbs | 1,915 | 3.3% | 79.4 | 2,413 | 2.5% | 134 |
| 1C | Upper Income Empty Nesters | 1,313 | 2.3% | 70.8 | 1,854 | 1.9% | 120 |
| 1D | Successful Suburbanites | 1,621 | 2.8% | 79.5 | 2,040 | 2.1% | 134 |
| 1E | Prosperous Baby Boomers | 2,683 | 4.6% | 72.7 | 3,691 | 3.8% | 123 |
| 1F | Semirural Lifestyle | 3,337 | 5.7% | 71.4 | 4,676 | 4.8% | 121 |
| 2. Upscale Households | | | | | | | |
| 2A | Urban Professional Couples | 3,044 | 5.2% | 72.8 | 4,184 | 4.3% | 123 |
| 2B | Baby Boomers with Children | 2,707 | 4.7% | 63.0 | 4,297 | 4.4% | 106 |
| 2C | Thriving Immigrants | 990 | 1.7% | 63.7 | 1,554 | 1.6% | 108 |
| 2D | Upscale Urban Asians | 239 | 0.4% | 64.6 | 370 | 0.4% | 109 |
| 2E | Older Settled Married Couples | 2,986 | 5.1% | 67.2 | 4,441 | 4.5% | 114 |
| 3. Up & Coming Singles | | | | | | | |
| 3A | High Rise Renters | 1,535 | 2.6% | 76.5 | 2,006 | 2.0% | 129 |
| 3B | Enterprising Young Singles | 2,188 | 3.8% | 62.4 | 3,506 | 3.6% | 105 |
| 4. Retirement Styles | | | | | | | |
| 4A | Retirement Communities | 735 | 1.3% | 65.7 | 1,118 | 1.1% | 111 |
| 4B | Active Senior Singles | 2,119 | 3.6% | 69.5 | 3,048 | 3.1% | 118 |
| 4C | Prosperous Older Couples | 1,970 | 3.4% | 65.5 | 3,008 | 3.1% | 111 |
| 4D | Wealthiest Seniors | 543 | 0.9% | 66.0 | 823 | 0.8% | 112 |
| 4E | Rural Resort Dwellers | 548 | 0.9% | 63.1 | 869 | 0.9% | 107 |
| 4F | Senior Sun Seekers | 1,046 | 1.8% | 60.5 | 1,730 | 1.8% | 102 |
| 5. Young Mobile Adults | | | | | | | |
| 5A | Twentysomethings | 1,122 | 1.9% | 63.0 | 1,781 | 1.8% | 106 |
| 5B | College Campuses | 581 | 1.0% | 64.3 | 904 | 0.9% | 109 |
| 5C | Military Proximity | 1,316 | 2.3% | 58.7 | 2,243 | 2.3% | 99 |
| 6. City Dwellers | | | | | | | |
| 6A | East Coast Immigrants | 1,282 | 2.2% | 75.1 | 1,708 | 1.7% | 127 |
| 6B | Middle Class Black Families | 568 | 1.0% | 50.1 | 1,134 | 1.2% | 85 |
| 6C | Newly Formed Households | 3,325 | 5.7% | 60.6 | 5,488 | 5.6% | 102 |
| 6D | Settled Southwestern Hispanics | 684 | 1.2% | 37.9 | 1,807 | 1.8% | 64 |
| 6E | West Coast Immigrants | 410 | 0.7% | 44.1 | 930 | 0.9% | 75 |
| 6F | Low Income: Young and Old | 1,178 | 2.0% | 45.9 | 2,564 | 2.6% | 78 |
| 7. Factory & Farm Communities | | | | | | | |
| 7A | Middle America | 4,155 | 7.1% | 50.6 | 8,218 | 8.4% | 85 |
| 7B | Young, Frequent Movers | 1,506 | 2.6% | 49.8 | 3,025 | 3.1% | 84 |
| 7C | Rural Industrial Workers | 1,798 | 3.1% | 33.6 | 5,354 | 5.4% | 57 |
| 7D | Prairie Farmers | 373 | 0.6% | 49.2 | 758 | 0.8% | 83 |
| 7E | Small Town Working Families | 707 | 1.2% | 45.3 | 1,559 | 1.6% | 77 |
| 7F | Rustbelt Neighborhoods | 2,345 | 4.0% | 60.0 | 3,911 | 4.0% | 101 |
| 7G | Heartland Communities | 1,527 | 2.6% | 37.4 | 4,082 | 4.1% | 63 |
| 8. Downtown Residents | | | | | | | |
| 8A | Urban Hispanics | 454 | 0.8% | 63.5 | 715 | 0.7% | 107 |
| 8B | Social Security Dependents | 513 | 0.9% | 50.5 | 1,015 | 1.0% | 85 |
| 8C | Distressed Neighborhoods | 513 | 0.9% | 44.0 | 1,167 | 1.2% | 74 |
| 8D | Low Income Southern Blacks | 702 | 1.2% | 41.7 | 1,684 | 1.7% | 70 |
| 8E | Urban Working Families | 961 | 1.7% | 51.9 | 1,850 | 1.9% | 88 |
| 9. Nonresidential Neighborhoods | | | | | | | |
| 9A | Business Districts | 0 | 0.0% | 0.0 | 0 | 0.0% | 0 |
| 9B | Institutional Populations | 0 | 0.0% | 0.0 | 0 | 0.0% | 0 |
| 9C | Unpopulated Areas | 0 | 0.0% | 0.0 | 0 | 0.0% | 0 |
| | Totals | 58,204 | 100% | 59.2 | 98,384 | 100% | 100 |

Sources: Simmons Market Research Bureau, Inc. and CACI Marketing Systems. This work is comprised of copyrighted and confidential material.

Copyright 1997  CACI Marketing Systems  (800) 292-CACI  06/24/97

**FIGURE 11-3.** PURCHASE POTENTIAL BY ACORN-BAGELS
*SOURCE:* COPYRIGHT CACI MARKETING SYSTEMS

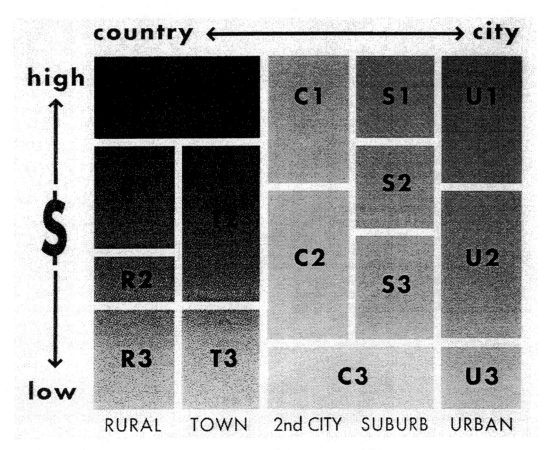

**FIGURE 11-4.** STANDARD PRIZM SOCIAL GROUPS

SOURCE: SUMMARY LIFESTYLE DESCRIPTIONS—PRIZM CLUSTERS NARRATIVES, CLARITAS, INC.

Profile of 1. Frozen Pizza Last 6 Mos (41.6%) Versus Base of Total Adults (MRI 1994-95)

| PRIZM CLUSTERS | | | BASE | | PROFILE 1 | | | |
|---|---|---|---|---|---|---|---|---|
| Grp | # | Nickname | Count | % Comp | Count | % Comp | % Pen | Index |
| S1 | 01 | Blue Blood Estates | 1,229 | 0.65 | 349 | 0.45 | 28.40 | 68 |
| S1 | 02 | Winner's Circle | 3,760 | 1.99 | 1,475 | 1.88 | 39.23 | 94 |
| S1 | 03 | Executive Suites | 2,962 | 1.57 | 1,038 | 1.32 | 35.04 | 84 |
| S1 | 04 | Pools & Patios | 4,025 | 2.13 | 1,538 | 1.96 | 38.21 | 92 |
| S1 | 05 | Kids & Cul-de-Sacs | 6,535 | 3.46 | 2,625 | 3.35 | 40.17 | 97 |
| U1 | 06 | Urban Gold Coast | 623 | 0.33 | 136 | 0.17 | 21.83 | 53 |
| U1 | 07 | Money & Brains | 2,541 | 1.35 | 885 | 1.13 | 34.83 | 84 |
| U1 | 08 | Young Literati | 2,131 | 1.13 | 599 | 0.76 | 28.11 | 68 |
| U1 | 09 | American Dreams | 3,495 | 1.85 | 1,074 | 1.37 | 30.73 | 74 |
| U1 | 10 | Bohemian Mix | 2,208 | 1.17 | 668 | 0.85 | 30.25 | 73 |
| C1 | 11 | Second City Elite | 3,081 | 1.63 | 1,251 | 1.60 | 40.60 | 98 |
| C1 | 12 | Upward Bound | 3,901 | 2.07 | 1,594 | 2.03 | 40.86 | 98 |
| C1 | 13 | Gray Power | 3,416 | 1.81 | 1,261 | 1.61 | 36.91 | 89 |
| T1 | 14 | Country Squires | 2,133 | 1.13 | 916 | 1.17 | 42.94 | 103 |
| T1 | 15 | God's Country | 5,781 | 3.06 | 2,621 | 3.34 | 45.34 | 109 |
| T1 | 16 | Big Fish, Small Pond | 4,503 | 2.39 | 1,944 | 2.48 | 43.17 | 104 |
| T1 | 17 | Greenbelt Families | 1,972 | 1.05 | 998 | 1.27 | 50.61 | 122 |
| S2 | 18 | Young Influentials | 1,706 | 0.90 | 608 | 0.78 | 35.64 | 86 |
| S2 | 19 | New Empty Nests | 3,825 | 2.03 | 1,470 | 1.88 | 38.43 | 92 |
| S2 | 20 | Boomers & Babies | 3,445 | 1.83 | 1,527 | 1.95 | 44.33 | 107 |
| S2 | 21 | Suburban Sprawl | 3,988 | 2.11 | 1,752 | 2.23 | 43.93 | 106 |
| S2 | 22 | Blue-Chip Blues | 4,907 | 2.60 | 2,049 | 2.61 | 41.76 | 100 |
| S3 | 23 | Upstarts & Seniors | 1,918 | 1.02 | 806 | 1.03 | 42.02 | 101 |
| S3 | 24 | New Beginnings | 1,709 | 0.91 | 796 | 1.02 | 46.58 | 112 |
| S3 | 25 | Mobility Blues | 3,168 | 1.68 | 949 | 1.21 | 29.96 | 72 |
| S3 | 26 | Gray Collars | 4,041 | 2.14 | 1,639 | 2.09 | 40.56 | 98 |
| U2 | 27 | Urban Achievers | 3,425 | 1.82 | 1,271 | 1.62 | 37.11 | 89 |
| U2 | 28 | Big City Blend | 2,356 | 1.25 | 709 | 0.90 | 30.09 | 72 |
| U2 | 29 | Old Yankee Rows | 2,555 | 1.35 | 1,041 | 1.33 | 40.74 | 98 |
| U2 | 30 | Mid-City Mix | 2,499 | 1.32 | 809 | 1.03 | 32.37 | 78 |
| U2 | 31 | Latino America | 2,572 | 1.36 | 650 | 0.83 | 25.27 | 61 |
| C2 | 32 | Middleburg Managers | 3,680 | 1.95 | 1,488 | 1.90 | 40.43 | 97 |
| C2 | 33 | Boomtown Singles | 1,763 | 0.93 | 758 | 0.97 | 42.99 | 103 |
| C2 | 34 | Starter Families | 3,085 | 1.64 | 1,299 | 1.66 | 42.11 | 101 |
| C2 | 35 | Sunset City Blues | 3,583 | 1.90 | 1,798 | 2.29 | 50.18 | 121 |
| C2 | 36 | Towns & Gowns | 1,772 | 0.94 | 837 | 1.07 | 47.23 | 114 |
| T2 | 37 | New Homesteaders | 4,030 | 2.14 | 1,830 | 2.33 | 45.41 | 109 |
| T2 | 38 | Middle America | 1,990 | 1.05 | 891 | 1.14 | 44.77 | 108 |
| T2 | 39 | Red, White & Blues | 5,030 | 2.67 | 2,412 | 3.08 | 47.95 | 115 |
| T2 | 40 | Military Quarters | 458 | 0.24 | 200 | 0.26 | 43.67 | 105 |
| R1 | 41 | Big Sky Families | 2,237 | 1.19 | 1,051 | 1.34 | 46.98 | 113 |
| R1 | 42 | New Eco-topia | 2,454 | 1.30 | 937 | 1.20 | 38.18 | 92 |
| R1 | 43 | River City, USA | 3,837 | 2.03 | 1,657 | 2.11 | 43.18 | 104 |
| R1 | 44 | Shotguns & Pickups | 2,271 | 1.20 | 1,147 | 1.46 | 50.51 | 122 |

Copyright 1996, Claritas, Inc.; MRI

**FIGURE 11-5.** PRIZM SEGMENTS FOR FROZEN PIZZA

*SOURCE:* CLARITAS INC., 1996

Profile of 1. Frozen Pizza Last 6 Mos (41.6%) Versus Base of Total Adults (MRI 1994-95)

| | PRIZM CLUSTERS | | BASE | | PROFILE 1 | | | |
|---|---|---|---|---|---|---|---|---|
| Grp | # | Nickname | Count | % Comp | Count | % Comp | % Pen | Index |
| U3 | 45 | Single City Blues | 2,032 | 1.08 | 706 | 0.90 | 34.74 | 84 |
| U3 | 46 | Hispanic Mix | 1,697 | 0.90 | 513 | 0.65 | 30.23 | 73 |
| U3 | 47 | Inner Cities | 3,199 | 1.70 | 949 | 1.21 | 29.67 | 71 |
| C3 | 48 | Smalltown Downtown | 3,299 | 1.75 | 1,299 | 1.66 | 39.38 | 95 |
| C3 | 49 | Hometown Retired | 1,587 | 0.84 | 618 | 0.79 | 38.94 | 94 |
| C3 | 50 | Family Scramble | 3,401 | 1.80 | 1,461 | 1.86 | 42.96 | 103 |
| C3 | 51 | Southside City | 3,276 | 1.74 | 1,266 | 1.61 | 38.64 | 93 |
| T3 | 52 | Golden Ponds | 3,375 | 1.79 | 1,675 | 2.14 | 49.63 | 119 |
| T3 | 53 | Rural Industria | 2,532 | 1.34 | 1,089 | 1.39 | 43.01 | 104 |
| T3 | 54 | Norma Rae-ville | 2,180 | 1.16 | 938 | 1.20 | 43.03 | 104 |
| T3 | 55 | Mines & Mills | 3,263 | 1.73 | 1,510 | 1.93 | 46.28 | 111 |
| R2 | 56 | Agri-Business | 2,387 | 1.27 | 1,320 | 1.68 | 55.30 | 133 |
| R2 | 57 | Grain Belt | 3,402 | 1.80 | 1,817 | 2.32 | 53.41 | 129 |
| R3 | 58 | Blue Highways | 6,136 | 3.25 | 3,012 | 3.84 | 49.09 | 118 |
| R3 | 59 | Rustic Elders | 4,266 | 2.26 | 2,128 | 2.71 | 49.88 | 120 |
| R3 | 60 | Back Country Folks | 2,952 | 1.56 | 1,537 | 1.96 | 52.07 | 125 |
| R3 | 61 | Scrub Pine Flats | 2,934 | 1.56 | 1,197 | 1.53 | 40.80 | 98 |
| R3 | 62 | Hard Scrabble | 4,163 | 2.21 | 2,012 | 2.57 | 48.33 | 116 |
| Total | | | 188,681 | 100.00 | 78,400 | 100.00 | 41.55 | 100 |

Copyright 1996, Claritas, Inc.; MRI

**FIGURE 11-5.** (Continued)

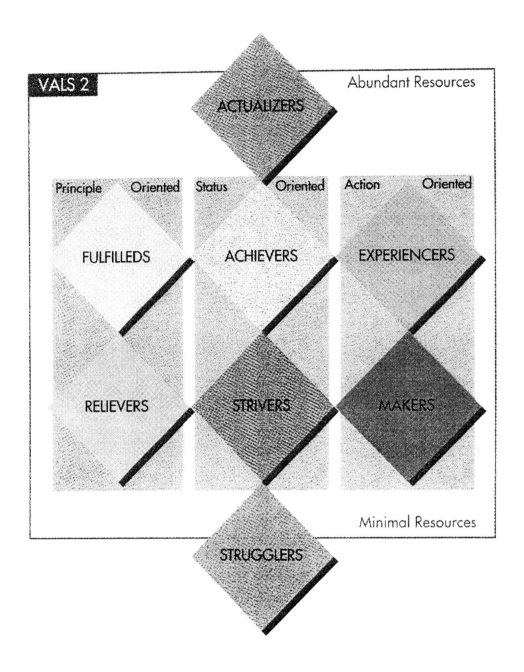

**FIGURE 11-6.** VALS AND LIFESTYLE SEGMENTS (VALS 2)
*SOURCE:* SRI CONSULTING, 1996

**Table 2**
**PACKAGED FOODS HEAVILY USED BY VALS SEGMENTS**
(Ranked by Index)

| Segment | Item | Index | Segment | Item | Index |
|---|---|---|---|---|---|
| Actualizers | Low-fat/calorie/cholesterol cheese | 148 | Strivers | Frozen fried chicken | 125 |
| | Croissants | 144 | | Toaster pastries | 118 |
| | Yogurt | 137 | | Meat and fish extenders | 117 |
| | Rice/grain cakes | 136 | | Fruit flavored ice tea mixes | 116 |
| | International flavor instant coffee | 133 | | Frozen corn on the cob | 113 |
| | Frozen yogurt | 131 | | Chewing/bubble gum | 112 |
| | Herbal tea | 130 | | Instant ice tea mixes | 112 |
| | Bagels | 128 | | Juice plus carbonated soft drinks | 110 |
| | English muffins | 128 | | Instant potatoes | 110 |
| | Egg substitutes | 127 | | Regular cola | 110 |
| Fulfilleds | Egg substitutes | 140 | Experiencers | Thirst quencher/activity drinks | 154 |
| | Yogurt | 139 | | Juice plus carbonated soft drinks | 145 |
| | Frozen yogurt | 136 | | Liquid nutritional supplements | 138 |
| | Dry soup/lunch mixes | 131 | | Nutritional snacks, bars, rolls | 127 |
| | Salt substitutes | 128 | | Chewing/bubble gum | 122 |
| | Packaged pie crusts | 127 | | Frozen corn on the cob | 121 |
| | Dried fruit | 127 | | Butter | 121 |
| | Herbal tea | 127 | | Regular carbonated (noncola) drinks | 120 |
| | Croissants | 126 | | Canned tea | 120 |
| | Olives | 126 | | Homemade pizza (not frozen) | 119 |
| Believers | Frozen muffins | 125 | Makers | Meat and fish extenders | 148 |
| | Decaffeinated instant/freeze-dried coffee | 125 | | Thirst quencher/activity drinks | 143 |
| | Egg substitutes | 121 | | Frozen hot snacks | 133 |
| | Nondairy cream substitutes | 121 | | Milk flavorings | 129 |
| | Tomato/vegetable juice | 117 | | Frozen potato products | 127 |
| | Pie fillings | 116 | | Regular cola drinks | 125 |
| | Shelf/refrigerated dinners | 115 | | Mexican food ingredients | 125 |
| | Canned milk | 115 | | Juice plus carbonated soft drinks | 124 |
| | TV dinners | 115 | | Powdered soft drinks (add water) | 124 |
| | Instant potatoes | 114 | | Snack cakes | 124 |
| Achievers | Rice/grain cakes | 135 | Strugglers | Decaffeinated instant/freeze-dried coffee | 126 |
| | Frozen muffins | 128 | | Salt substitutes | 113 |
| | Frozen yogurt | 128 | | Hot breakfast cereals | 112 |
| | Low-fat/calorie/cholesterol cheese | 127 | | Instant potatoes | 108 |
| | Bagels | 125 | | Snack cakes | 108 |
| | Liquid nutritional supplements | 124 | | Canned/jarred vegetables | 106 |
| | Homemade pizza (not frozen) | 122 | | Canned milk | 105 |
| | Diet/sugar-free colas | 118 | | Frozen fried chicken | 104 |
| | Dry mix salad dressing mixes | 118 | | Nondairy cream substitutes | 104 |
| | Dry brownie mixes | 117 | | Bacon | 103 |

Source: 1993 VALS/Simmons

**FIGURE 11-7.** PACKAGED GOODS HEAVILY USED BY VALS SEGMENTS—RANKED BY INDEX

*SOURCE:* 1993 VALS/SIMMONS IN THE VALS NETWORK, SRI INTERNATIONAL, DECEMBER 1994

# Chapter 12
# Food Service Sector and Marketing Decisions

**Chapter Outline**

Foodservice Sector
- A. Share of Food Dollar
- B. Consumer Trends
- C. Foodservice Determinants

Retail Store Foodservice
- A. Foodservice Operations
- B. Foodservice Merchandising
- C. Foodservice Eating Areas

Foodservice Retailing Sector
- A. Firms, Establishments, and Sales
- B. Employment
- C. Single Unit and Multiunit Eating and Drinking Places
- D. Sales Size of Eating and Drinking Places
- E. Sales Concentration
- F. Location

Retail Trade Perspective
  A. Market Share of Foodservice Segments
  B. Ten Leading Companies
  C. Ten Leading Chains
  D. Leading Chains—Market Share
Foodservice Retail Marketing Decisions
  A. Product
  B. Process and Participants
  C. Service Encounter
Foodservice Wholesaling
  A. Broadline Distributors
  B. Specialty Distributors
  C. Foodservice Groups
Summary

In an earlier chapter on retailing, the topic of foodservice was purposefully avoided. This was not meant to suggest that it is a minor or insignificant aspect of the food retailing; quite the contrary, foodservice is so vast, it warrants special treatment to truly understand its role in the **U.S. food marketing system (Figure 12-1)**.

# FOODSERVICE SECTOR

In the broadest sense, **foodservice** may be defined to include all firms where food is regularly served outside the home. These firms belong either to the **commercial**, for-profit group, or the **noncommercial** group. The goal of the latter is to generate enough revenue to cover both fixed and variable operating expenses and provide sufficient funds to replace and repair facilities and fund employment. These noncommercial firms include foodservice operations in hospitals, colleges and universities, elementary and secondary schools, nursing homes, homes for the aged, blind, orphans or disabled, recreational camps and clubs, community centers, penal institutions, and military installations. Although the noncommercial segment is a vital part of the foodservice industry, a thorough examination of this segment is beyond the scope and intent of this text.

This chapter focuses on the commercial segment of the foodservice industry. It begins with a brief discussion of the challenges facing retailers today. Attention then turns to an assessment of consumer trends and foodservice determinants. The chapter then discusses foodservice from the retail store perspective. The final retail sections examine the foodservice structure using census and trade data, and foodservice marketing decisions. An examination of foodservice wholesalers concludes the chapter.

## Share of Food Dollar

In a previous chapter on consumer behavior, the **home-meal replacement (HMR)** phenomenon was introduced. Basically, it means that more and more consumers are shopping for entire meals or **"meal solutions,"** rather than **"meal ingredients"** that are taken home and prepared. **Figure 12-2** represents a continuum of food preparations where meal ingredients and meal solutions are at the polar ends. Foods that are ready to defrost or heat may be either entire meals or individual ingredients. The continuum also represents the battlefield for the consumer's food dollar, or what has now become known as the battle for the consumer's **share of stomach.** On one side, you have **meal ingredients** that involve an expenditure of time and effort to prepare. Even more important, food preparation involves culinary skills that, for a good number of consumers, are becoming more and more extinct. Witness, if you will, the number of supermarket chains that offer "cooking schools" (Robertiello, 1996). On the other side, you have **meal solutions** which consist of individual prepared or pre-cooked ingredients packaged together to form an entire meal. Foods that are ready to defrost or heat do not, in a true sense, represent meal solutions because some preparation is necessary. Retail stores have, since their beginnings, offered the consumer meal ingredients. Lately, they have increased their presence in the **meal solutions** market by expanding their in-store foodservice offerings. Historically, restaurants owned the **meal solutions** market. After all, consumers have always gone to restaurants, because they knew that they could get an entire meal. Lately, some of the more innovative restaurant chains, like **McDonald's**, have placed their stores in super-centers like **Wal-Mart**, and **Meijers**. Who is winning the battle for the consumer's food dollar—retail food stores or retail foodservice restaurants? The annual **Consumer Expenditure Study** provides us with a partial answer because it reports the share of the consumer's food dollar spent for food consumed at home and away from home.

**Table 12-1** illustrates a five year trend in consumer expenditures for food consumed at home and away from home. Consumers spend a greater percentage of their food dollar for food consumed at home. In fact, although the percentage spent for food away from home has increased slightly in recent years, it is still below the percentage spent in 1990. Unfortunately, the percentage of the consumer's food dollar that is spent for foodservice meals offered by retail food stores is not separately monitored by the **Bureau of Labor Statistics**. Therefore, no conclusion can be reached regarding the total share of the consumer food dollar spent for foodservice meals offered by retail food stores and foodservice restaurants.

## Consumer Trends

Even though the total share of the consumer's food dollar spent for foodservice meals can't be determined exactly, the home-meal replacement (**HMR**) phenomenon is nonetheless growing. For instance, a **Gallup poll** found that approximately half of the eighty-six percent of Americans who eat dinner at home eat pre-packaged or take-out food that they pick up or have delivered. Further, it is predicted that take-out food spending will increase at three times the rate of total food spending (Popcorn, 1991). Why are consumers willing to rely increasingly on foodservice for their meals? One explanation has focused on the trend called **cocooning.** This is a trend toward consumers staying home to protect themselves from the hassles of public appearances, the uncertainties of social interactions, and the need for a change of pace after interacting with people on the job (Popcorn, 1987).

A second, often-cited, reason is the consumer's need to manage time. Two-income, time-starved households find shopping for food inconvenient and too time consuming. They would rather pick up their meal, have it delivered, or dine in a restaurant (Fisher, 1990). A recent survey of restaurant owners cited lack of time to prepare food at home as their patron's primary reason for eating at their restaurants (*Supermarket Business,* May 1995). Despite the popularity of foodservice, the demand for foodservice is not the same for all consumers. Some consumers are more likely to purchase foodservice meals than others. Who are these consumers?

## Foodservice Determinants

A number of studies have focused on identifying foodservice determinants. Annually the **U.S. Bureau of Labor Statistics** reports on relationships between food consumed away from and at home, and demographic variables. Their **Consumer Expenditure Surveys** have consistently shown that the percentage of the consumer's food dollar spent for food consumed away from home (1) increases with income, (2) decreases with age, (3) decreases with household size, and (4) increases with number of income earners in a household. Another study examined demographic variables using county-level data supplied by a private firm (**Market Statistics**) and the **U.S. Bureau of Labor Statistics**. Results indicated that the amount of money spent for food consumed away from home was higher in counties with (1) a higher labor-force participation rate of women, (2) a higher number of college graduates, (3) a higher number of employed individuals, (4) a higher number of females, (5) a higher number of whites and Asians/Pacific Islanders, (6) a lower number of Hispanics, and (7) a lower number of households with children (Wayga and Wanzala, 1996).

Another study, using **National Food Consumption Survey** (NFCS) data, conducted decennially by the **USDA**, examines the relationship between the number of meals eaten away from home and various demographic variables. The study found that the number of meals eaten away from home was greater for (1) Midwest and West regions, (2) non-whites (i.e., African-Americans, Asians, Pacific Islanders), (3) males, (4) employed individuals, (5) consumers who had no special diet, (6) smaller-sized households, (7) younger individuals, and (8) higher-income consumers (Nayga and Capps, 1994). Collectively, these studies provide a profile of the foodservice market segment. But are consumers more likely to purchase their home meal replacement in a supermarket, or a restaurant?

A national survey of consumers, conducted exclusively for a prominent publication in the U.S. food marketing system, **Supermarket News**, found that nearly sixty percent of consumers said they would buy their dinner in a supermarket deli, if a complete meal was available. When asked whether they would prefer to buy dinner hot or ready to heat, seventy-two percent said hot and twenty-six percent said ready to heat. More than half of the respondents indicated they would buy dinner from the deli service counter rather then from self-service. This is probably explained by the relationship consumers see between freshness, and the food dished out to them at the service counter. Finally, only three percent indicated they would eat the food in the store if seating were provided, and seventy-two percent indicated they would never, or only rarely, eat in the store. As the author suggests in the study, **"While getting it hot is hot, eating it on the spot is not,"** (Harper, 1996).

Despite what appears to be good news for supermarkets, all is not well. Only twelve percent of shoppers in a recent study conducted for the **Food Marketing Institute(FMI)**, said they most often choose a supermarket when searching for prepared food to be eaten at home. What is wrong? Shoppers believe the food has been sitting around too long, they don't think it's a good value. Further, they don't believe that it tastes good or has consistent quality, and they don't trust the food preparers (Gatty, 1996). Supermarkets have much to correct if they are going to compete with restaurants in the **HMR** market. If the articles in most recent issues of the four prominent trade publications (i.e., *Grocery Marketing, Progressive Grocer, Supermarket News,* and *Supermarket Business*) are any indication, the battle for the consumer's food dollar is well underway.

## RETAIL STORE FOODSERVICE

Having identified the battle for the consumer's food dollar, or **share of stomach** the participants need to be characterized. Previously, it was stated that neither the **U.S. Bureau of Labor Statistics**, nor any other governmental agency, monitors dollars spent for foodservice in retail stores. However, a number of prominent trade publications conduct annual surveys of foodservice operations. One such trade publication, *Supermarket Business,* is used here as a source of data on foodservice.

## Foodservice Operations

There is no doubt that supermarkets (i.e., those with annual sales over two million dollars) are in the battle for the consumer's foodservice dollars. The number of supermarkets that now offer prepared foods (hot or cold) increased by fourteen percent over a five-year period (**Table 12-2**). The 23,150 supermarkets offering prepared foods represent seventy-six percent of all supermarkets, or a twelve percent change from 1991. Interestingly, the rate of growth was greater for supermarket delis selling only refrigerated prepared foods than for those selling only hot prepared foods. Are supermarkets off track? Seventy-two percent of consumers in the previously mentioned survey said they prefer to buy dinner hot.

**Table 12-3** offers a closer look at foodservice operations in supermarkets. There has been little change regarding where supermarkets get their foodservice products and ingredients. From 1991 to 1995, the bulk of products and ingredients (on average, seventy-two percent) used in foodservice departments were supplied by foodservice distributors. These foodservice suppliers produced about two-thirds of the prepared foods. As the percentage of cooks trained as chefs declined, so too did the percentage of prepared food produced in stores from basic or scratch ingredients. Finally, the percentage of prepared food produced by a supermarket's central kitchen increased by seventy-five percent—a fact that offsets the decline in skilled cooks.

## Foodservice Merchandising

Prepared-food annual sales increased forty-three percent from six billion dollars in 1991 to almost nine billion dollars in 1995. This resulted in a twelve-hundred dollar weekly increase in sales over this same time period (**Table 12-4**). Although the median percentage of store sales and gross margin increased slightly, the median percentage of store profits declined. This slight decline in store profits is not due to labor costs. In fact, labor cost as a percentage of prepared-food sales declined from twenty-five percent in 1991 to 23.3 percent in 1995. In part, this decline is explained by the increased share of self-service refrigerated sales. Almost all of the self-service refrigerated sales were taken from the service deli (**Table 12-5**). The seventy-six percent increase in the share of sales coming from prepackaged refrigerated food products reflects the growing demand for convenience.

**Table 12-6** shows how the foodservice dollar was spent over a five-year period. Pizza and prepared chicken have been in a close race for dominance in this section. The earlier decline in prepared chicken sales went to sandwiches and refrigerated entries. Along with hot entrees, they represent the other major foodservice offerings.

## Foodservice Eating Areas

As indicated in **Table 12-7**, an increasing number of retailers provide a place where customers can sit and eat what they bought at the deli. Currently, seventy-seven percent of all stores that have a deli (17,750/23,150) offer a place for shoppers to sit down and eat their purchases.

The number of supermarkets offering sit-down cafes and restaurants increased by twenty-two percent from 1991 to 1995. This rise represents only three percent of all supermarkets that have delicatessens. Surprisingly, this percentage is equal to the percentage of people who indicated, in a recent survey, that they would eat food in a store. The small number of supermarkets offering cafes and restaurants may also be explained by the fair amount of space required (1,830 square feet, on average). In addition, although the percentage of cafes and restaurants that are franchised fast-food outlets has remained unchanged at one percent, many in the industry believe it is the next battlefield for the consumer's food dollar. For example, **McDonald's** has over seven hundred satellite restaurants in **Wal-marts**. Other major fast food chains are poised to enter other supermarket chains (Millman, 1996). Snack bars and restaurants increase the complexity of deli management, but it appears that the burden is well justified by their gross margins. These eateries have sixty percent gross margins and deli managers feel that they help to enhance their store's overall image (**Table 12-8**).

Until recently, an area of vast untapped potential for supermarket foodservice was **catering**. The growth in its average gross margins from fifty-eight to sixty-five percent has attracted the attention of deli managers. In addition to its profitability, catering doesn't require an increase in store selling space (**Table 12-8**).

Retailers are promoting their in-store foodservice offerings in much the same way that they promote their delis (**Table 12-9**). Newspapers remain the medium of choice, but sampling has moved up to challenge them. In-store circulars have experienced an increase in usage, in part due to the fact that supermarkets are using them to identify their prepared food menus for the coming week. This allows consumers to plan their meals in advance, and at the same time creates better awareness of the foodservice offerings. Point-of-purchase usage has also increased as retailers continue to recognize that the majority of purchase decisions are made in the store. By and large, the broadcast media are not mainstays in foodservice promotion.

In summary, foodservice continues to be a growth area in sales and profits for supermarkets. The number of supermarkets offering prepared foods continues to increase, as does the number offering eating areas. Despite the favorable past performances and the excellent forecast for foodservice operations, two issues dominate the foodservice horizon: labor and competition. The labor problem is best summarized as increased skill level and job responsibility without a considerable increase in wages. Employees either leave the store or transfer to other, higher-paying departments. In either case—it results in a high rate of turnover.

As alternative formats become more prolific, competition for the consumer foodservice dollar grows. This, however, is only one type of competition, namely competitive foodservice offerings by retail food stores. There is, of course, another major competitor for the consumer's food dollar: the **restaurants** have always been the dominant force in the foodservice arena. To them, it is the supermarket and other retail formats that represent threats to their role in providing the U.S. consumer with entire meals. These threats are focused more on the revenue generated by their take-out-to-eat (**tote**) service than on the revenue generated by customers who dine in their restaurants.

## FOODSERVICE RETAILING SECTOR

Like the food store retailing sector, data on the foodservice retailing sector are widely available and abundant. Because of this, the structural analysis uses data from two sources. Census of Retail data for the years 1982, 1987, and 1992 are used to establish earlier trends. These data are supplemented with industry data. Although the use of both sources of data enhances the structural analysis, there is an absence of definition consistency in the foodservice classification used by government and industry. Therefore, any conclusions regarding the retailing sector, depend upon the perspective chosen to analyze the data: government or industry.

Foodservice retailers are classified in the **U.S. Census of Retail Trade**. Their **Standard Industrial Classification** major groups is **58—Eating and Drinking Places**. This major group is made up of retail firms/establishments engaged in the selling of prepared foods and drinks for consumption on the premises. The foodservice retailing sector is made up of five four-digit industries classified on the basis of firms and establishments by kind of business. A **firm is a legal entity** that owns one or more establishments. An **establishment is a single physical location at which retail business is conducted**. Eating places all have the same SIC number (5812) and are defined by the Census Bureau in the following manner. **Restaurants** include firms primarily engaged in serving food and beverages (non-alcoholic/alcoholic), where waiters/waitresses take orders from patrons seated at a counter, booth, or table. **Cafeterias** engage in serving a wide variety of prepared food and beverages primarily through the use of a cafeteria line, where customers make selections from displayed items. **Refreshment places** engage in selling limited lines of refreshments and prepared food for consumption, either on or near the premises or for **take-home** consumption (e.g., chicken, hamburgers, and pizza). These firms do not offer waiter or waitress service. **Other eating places** include contract feeding, and ice cream and frozen yogurt shops. Contract feeders provide foodservice under contract to another company, hospital, governmental, penal, or educational institution. Management is always supplied by the contractor, but the facilities and personnel may not be. Ice Cream and frozen yogurt shops engage in sale of their products for consumption either on or near the premises or for **take-home** consumption. **Drinking places** (Sic 5813) primarily engage in the retail sale of alcoholic drinks such as beer, ale, wine, and liquor for consumption on the premises. The sale of food frequently accounts for a substantial portion of sales.

It should be mentioned that retail stores that operate cafeterias or restaurants report their foodservice sales in this major group. These sales are not reported separately, but rather are included in their respective industries.

## Firms, Establishments, and Sales

The change in the number of firms, establishments, and sales is shown in **Table 12-10**. The number of firms increased by twenty-eight percent, while establishments increased by thirty-six percent. There are more establishments than firms because, by definition, a firm owns one or more establishments. Unadjusted for inflation, sales increased ninety-two percent over the three census periods.

**Table 12-11** examines the change in the number of firms and sales by industry. Eating places increased forty percent while drinking places decreased by nine percent. Restaurant and refreshment places accounted for most of the new foodservice firms, while the number of cafeterias declined. Because of its smaller base, **"other"** foodservice firms registered the largest rate of increase—sixty-five percent.

The share of U.S. foodservice firms and sales increased for eating places at the expense of drinking places. Surprisingly, as the share of restaurant firms increased, their share of sales actually decreased. Refreshment firms and other foodservice retailers captured the share of sales lost by restaurants. Only cafeterias declined in both share of firms and sales (**Table 12-12**).

## Employment

The employment trends in foodservice retailing are revealed in **Table 12-13**. As expected, the increase in eating places resulted in an increase in the number and share of foodservice employees and an offsetting decline in the number and share of drinking-place employees. The increase in the share of restaurant firms led to an increase in the number of employees, but the restaurant share of employees declined. Once again, the loss in share was absorbed by refreshment places and other foodservice retailers.

## Single Unit and Multiunit Eating and Drinking Places

The number and share of single unit eating and drinking places increased over the census periods. Although single unit sales increased by 105 percent, they lost sales share because multiunit sales increased by 126 percent. Multiunit firms, although only five percent of all eating and drinking places, for the first time, in 1992, accounted for one-half of all sales (**Table 12-14**).

## Sales Size of Firms and Drinking Places

When firms are examined by sales size, the dominance of large foodservice firms is clearly visible. **Table 12-15** illustrates the distribution of firms by sales size. The only firms that didn't increase in number were those whose sales were less than 250 thousand dollars. Regardless of size, unadjusted for inflation, all firms increased their sales.

**Table 12-16** reveals the shares of firms and sales by the sales size of firms. Firms with sales between 1 million and 9 million dollars made up ten percent of all firms and had the largest share of sales—twenty-nine percent. With the exception of firms with sales of less than 250 thousand dollars, all firms increased their shares of eating and drinking places. However, sales increases occurred for only three of the sales size firms: 250 million dollars or more, ten million to forty-nine million dollars, and one million to nine million dollars. Finally, firms with less than 250 thousand dollars in sales were the only ones to lose share in both the number of firms and sales.

## Sales Concentration

The share of sales, or concentration ratio, is computed by dividing the sales of leading firms by the total foodservice sales. A four-firm ratio greater than fifty percent is considered an oligopolistic sector or industry; between thirty-three and fifty percent, an industry is classified as a weak oligopoly; below thirty-three percent, an industry is considered competitive.

**Table 12-17** shows the ratios for the foodservice sector. The shares of sales for the four, eight, twenty and fifty largest eating and drinking places increased over the census periods. However, by definition, the foodservice sector is a competitive one. When analyzed by eating places separately, the four, eight, twenty, and fifty largest firms all increased their share of sales. Once again, the percentages describe a competitive industry. Finally, drinking places experienced an increase in sales share for 1987, but declined in 1992.

**Table 12-18** reveals the ratios for the various industries. Although no industry can be considered oligopolistic, cafeterias and other foodservice retailers are considered **weak** oligopolies. Their share of sales rises dramatically when the eight, twenty, and fifty largest firms are examined.

## Location

Foodservice retail activity is reported in all fifty states. As expected, some of the states have higher levels of foodservice activity than others. The **U.S. Bureau of the Census** geographically analyzes sales by establishments. The top ten states are chosen for analysis because they contain the majority of foodservice establishments and generate the majority of sales. In general, densely populated states have larger numbers of establishments and sales.

The changes in the shares of establishments and sales is shown in **Table 12-19**. The top ten states combined declined in both share of establishments and sales. Texas and Massachusetts showed virtually no change in share of establishments, while California and Florida showed an increase. The other six states experienced a decline in their share of establishments. Only one state (Florida) experienced an increase in sales share; Pennsylvania remained constant in sales share, while the other eight states experienced a decline in sales share.

In summary, the structural characteristics of the retail foodservice sector are not unlike the retail food store sector. A small group of very large firms account for the vast majority of sales. Most, if not all, of those firms are multiunit operations. More than one-half of all foodservice establishments and sales can be found in just ten states. Despite the disparity in the foodservice sector, by economic convention the sector is competitive in structure.

# RETAIL TRADE PERSPECTIVE

The preceding structural analysis used **U.S. Bureau of the Census** retail foodservice classifications as a basis for conclusions. Essentially, foodservice firms are classified as eating and drinking places. Eating places are subdivided further into four industries, all of which have the same SIC code—5812.

Information provided by retail trade publications is extensive, but does not correspond exactly to census classifications. Unfortunately, classifications used in several annual trade industry reports are also not in exact agreement with one another. The inconsistencies in classification definition make it difficult to compare their conclusions. But, because these reports are published in respected trade journals, there is at least face validity to their analyses.

The purpose of the following is to extend the retail foodservice analysis. An annual report published by Lebhar-Friedman, Inc., in *Nation's Restaurant News* is used as the source of foodservice data. This report covers a three year period and is published in two parts, the top one hundred chain and company rankings, and the second one hundred chain and company rankings.

## Market Share of Foodservice Segments

*Nation's Restaurant News* recognizes eleven foodservice market segments. **Table 12-20** shows the share of market for the top one hundred and the second one hundred. Total foodservice sales for the top one hundred chains were 111.3 billion dollars, while total sales for the second one hundred chains were only 14.3 billion dollars. The dominant market segment in the top one hundred chains is the sandwich market. This is not surprising, because this segment is made up of the major hamburger chains: **McDonald's, Burger King**, and **Wendy's**. The dinner house segment is the largest market in the second one hundred chains. Here, **Fuddruckers, Steak and Ale**, and **El Torito** occupy major positions.

## Ten Leading Companies

*Nation's Restaurant News* reports on both foodservice companies and chains. In almost all cases, a company is composed of more than one chain operation. **Table 12-21** shows the ten largest foodservice companies for the last three years. Because of the variations in fiscal years, 1995 sales reflect actual or estimated sales.

The dominant foodservice company is undoubtedly **PepsiCo, Inc**. It is composed of seven chains and its total sales in 1995 (9.2 billion dollars) were twice **McDonald's** sales (4.5 billion dollars), the second largest company. It is interesting to note that **PepsiCo, Inc**., sales were 163 times as great as the two hundredth largest foodservice company—**Wenco Food Systems Co**. Total 1995 sales for the top one hundred firms that had U.S. foodservice revenue were 67.4 billion dollars. The top five firms had sales of 24 billion dollars or thirty-six percent of the sales for the top one hundred companies. Total 1995 sales for the second one hundred companies with U.S. foodservice revenue were 10.1 billion dollars. The top five firms had thirty-one percent of the sales for the second one hundred companies. The top ten companies had 31.5 billion dollars in sales or forty-seven percent of the sales for the top one hundred companies and forty-one percent of the sales for the leading two hundred companies. This industry analysis reinforces an early conclusion regarding the structures of the foodservice sector: a small group of companies dominate the sector.

## Ten Leading Chains

**Table 12-22** identifies the leading foodservice chains (not companies). With two exceptions, there has been no change in the rank order of these chains for the last three years. In cases where the company does not own all of its chain restaurants, sales for the chain will be greater than company sales. Six of the top ten chains are classified as *sandwich restaurants*, which explains why the sandwich segment has the largest market share of the top one hundred chains. In all cases, chain store sales exceeded the sales of their respective companies because revenues from franchised restaurants were excluded in company sales totals.

**Table 12-23** reveals the leading chains in terms of number of U.S. units. **Subway** and **Dairy Queen** are totally franchised chains, while **Service America** is totally company-owned by **G.E. Capital Corp**. The most significant changes in the percentage of company- and franchise-owned chains were in **Burger King** and **Taco Bell**. **Burger King** appears to be moving to a one hundred percent franchised chain. **Taco Bell** now owns fewer than fifty percent of its chain restaurants.

## Leading Chains—Market Share

The market share of the top one hundred chains by segment was previously identified. What follows is a description of the leading firms in selected segments.

### Sandwich

According to operators, value now equals big portions with big flavors and high quality, all for the low **"value"** prices customers expect to pay. Add to this speedy service and convenience, and these fast-food operations face many challenges. In 1995, the top five chains had seventy-seven percent of all sandwich sales of the top one hundred chains. These chains were **McDonald's** (33.9 percent), **Burger King** (17.9 percent), **Taco Bell** (9.8 percent), **Wendy's** (8.8 percent) and **Hardees** (7.1 percent).

### Pizza

The nature of competition is not focused on price anymore. Most operators believe that **"new products"** will drive the category. Customers appear to be willing to pay for new variations of the pizza. Consumers increasingly request stuffed crust, deep dish, and triple deckers. In, 1995 the top five chains had ninety-two percent of all pizza sales of the top one hundred chains. These chains were **Pizza Hut** (47.9 percent), **Domino's Pizza** (18.5 percent), **Little Caesar's Pizza** (18.0 percent), **Papa John's Pizza** (4.0 percent), and **Sbarro the Italian Eatery** (3.7 percent).

### Chicken

Most operators are trying new offerings in the hope of widening their customer bases. Many feel that chains with only chicken to sell are at a disadvantage. In fact, a leading chain recently changed its name to reflect its broader menu, which includes ham, turkey, and meat loaf. The top three chains in 1995 had eighty percent of all chicken sales of the top one hundred chains. These chains were **KFC** (57.6 percent), **Boston Market** (12.3 percent), and **Popeye's Famous Fried Chicken** (10.2 percent).

### Family

The family restaurant chains appear to be caught between low-priced fast-food chains from below, and high-quality dinner houses from above. This price-quality squeeze has forced them to become more cost-control conscious and image intensive. The top five chains in 1995 had sixty-four percent of all family chain sales in the top one hundred chains. These chains were **Denny's** (20.7 percent), **Shoney's** (14.6 percent), **Big Boy's** (11.2 percent), **Cracker Barrel Old Country Store** (8.6 percent), and **International House of Pancakes** or **IHOP** (8.6 percent).

### Grill-Buffet

This segment is reshaping itself in two directions. One route involves smaller units boasting more distinction in ambience, food, hostesses, and theme interiors. The other route is toward larger units with massive food displays, in-store fresh bakeries, and self-service food bars. In 1995, the top three chains had sixty-two percent of all grill-buffet sales in the top one hundred chains. These chains were **Ponderosa Steakhouse** (23.9 percent), **Golden Corral** (19.7 percent), and **Sizzler** (18.6 percent).

### Dinner House

The dinner house segment is maturing and growing measurably competitive. To survive, many chains have focused on segmenting their menus to appeal to particular audiences. Customers are demanding better quality at the same prices. In some cases, chains have been sold off or repositioned. The five top chains in 1995 had sixty-one percent of all dinner house sales in the top one hundred chains. These chains were **Red Lobster** (18.2 percent), **Applebee's Grill and Bar** (12.3 percent), **Olive Garden** (12.1 percent), **Chili's Grill Bar** (9.3 percent), and **T.G.I. Friday's** (8.6 percent).

### Contract

Contract feeders are facing new challenges brought about by corporate down-sizing and the elimination of the corporate or institutional subsidy to its employees. These challenges, together with changes in consumers' lifestyles, mean fewer people eating at the cafeteria. To offset the loss of revenue, some firms have increased the number of centralized preparation facilities in order to save on labor costs. The top three chains had fifty-eight percent of all contract sales in the top one hundred chains. These chains were **Marriott Management Services** (25.4 percent), **Aramach Global Food/Leisure Services** (22.8 percent), and **Eurest Dining Services** (9.7 percent).

### Hotels

Most of the hotel foodservice sales come from banquet catering. The industry objective is to shed the image of hotel foodservice as stuffy, expensive, and bland by emulating the more successful chains. The idea is to develop the restaurant concept as a causal restaurant that just happens to be located in a hotel. The top four chains had sixty-nine percent of all hotel foodservice sales in the top one hundred chains. These hotel chains were **Marriott Hotels, Resorts and Suites** (24.2 percent), **Hilton Hotels** (16.8 percent), **Sheraton Hotels** (16.2 percent), and **Holiday Inns** (12.0 percent).

# FOODSERVICE RETAIL MARKETING DECISIONS

The goal of the foodservice retailer is the same as the food store retailer. It is to use the right promotion to persuade the right consumers that the right product is available at the right place, at the right price, at this, the right time. What makes foodservice different is that the product offering includes an element of service. How much service is included depends, of course, on the type of foodservice operation. At one extreme, you have fine dining restaurants, that specialize their waiting staff according to the major meal decisions: appetizers, entrees, and desserts. It is not uncommon for these restaurants to have separate beverage waiting staff and a front end **maitre d'** to coordinate the restaurant operation. At the other end, you have **fast food** restaurants that typically offer no table service other than periodic cleaning. Given that the goal of food store retailers and foodservice retailers is the same, the marketing decision they make to attain this goal are likely to vary only slightly. In fact, like the food store retailers, foodservice retailers make decision regarding location, atmosphere, merchandise, price, promotion, and place. In addition, foodservice retailers make two other marketing mix decisions regarding their service offering: process and participants. This expanded mix recognizes the critical role of service-firm personnel and the delivery process in the creation of service quality.

The traditional marketing mix has already been examined extensively in the earlier retail chapter. What follows is a discussion of the decisions that make the foodservice marketing mix different from the traditional marketing mix: product, process, and participants.

## Product

The product offered by foodservice retailers is a menu of food and beverage items. The menu serves a number of purposes. First, it identifies to the customer **"what's for sale."** Its components reflect the restaurant's atmosphere and communicate a particular consumption experience to its patrons. Second, the menu is a major marketing tool. It represents the diversity of its product offering, specifies the range of prices, provides promotion opportunities, and conveys an image. Third, the menu is used to design and manage all functions of the foodservice retailer. It determines what food and beverages to purchase, personnel needed for production (cooks), service (wait staff), design of the kitchen and equipment needed, and employee schedules. The menu is also the document used to forecast sales.

The foodservice retailer makes several decisions regarding the menu offered to its clientele. In the same way that the merchandise carried by retail food stores is dictated by the their respective retail formats, menu decisions are likewise heavily influenced by the respective retail formats of the foodservice retailers. Like the food store retailer this homogeneity in foodservice offerings is dictated by the expectations of consumers. For example, fast food hamburger restaurants are likely to have very similar menus, because consumers expect to find certain food available for sale in **fast food** hamburger restaurants. The same can be said for the other major foodservice retailer classifications. What follows is a general discussion of the major considerations in menu planning: menu variations, menu types, menu design, menu pattern, menu components, and menu presentation (Rande, 1996).

### *Menu Variations*

The menu can take one of several different forms, each written for the needs of a particular type of foodservice retailer. Most menus in the commercial sector are **static**. The same menu items are offered every day. Fast food restaurants generally have static menus because they cater to a broad-based clientele. A **changing** menu offers different items from time to time. This type of menu is mostly found in **fine dining** restaurants that offer periodic **specials**.

### *Menu Types*

There are four types of menus. An **à la carte** menu is a static menu in which selections are priced separately. To take advantage of foods in their peak seasons, a restaurant may use a **du jour** menu that features items that change daily. To avoid monotony, a **cyclical** menu changes selections at particular intervals, but not daily. A **table d'hôte** menu includes all of the courses of the meal—appetizer, entree, dessert, and beverage—at a fixed price.

### *Menu Design*

The menu must be designed and worded to appeal to the customer to stimulate sales and influence clientele to select items the restaurant wants to sell. The size of the menu must be easy to handle. Above all, it must be clean, legible, interesting in color and design, and convey an appropriate atmosphere. The menu items must be placed in the order in which they are eaten in a meal. These items must present an accurate word picture so patrons can visualize the menu item. Increasingly, many restaurants are including pictures of the food items next to the word description.

### *Menu Patterns*

The menu pattern is an outline of the food to be offered in each meal. For restaurants that serve more than one meal a day, each meal involves a separate choice of food and beverages. Many fast food chains have added breakfast menus, but generally their lunch and dinner meals do not differ.

### *Menu Components*

The menu may consist of the following components: **Appetizers** are, by definition, designed to arouse the customer's appetite. **Entrees** represent the main course, or what is referred to as the **center of plate**. Vegetables and salads are meant to be compatible with the entree. **Garnishes** are used to maximize the appearance of the entree on the plate. **Breads** are used to provide bulk or fiber to the meal. **Beverages** help lubricate food so that it is more easily digested. Finally, **desserts** at the end of the meal are used to leave the customer with the sense of fullness.

### Menu Presentation

Foodservice retailers must visualize how the food will look on the plate. In particular, special consideration must be given to how the flavors will combine, and to the contrasts created by the colors, shapes, and textures of food. In addition, in order to hold the "look on the plate", the degree to which foods don't intermingle or bleed over onto other foods must be considered.

## Process and Participants

The process represents the actual procedures and flow of activities by which the service is actualized and delivered. It includes the reservation process by phone, greeting process by the hostess or maitre d', order-taking process by waiting staff, and the complaint handling process by management. The foodservice process is unique because it is not a pure service, but rather a service that accompanies the sale of tangible products—food. Further, these services may be, and usually are, performed by different participants in the process.

A number of service characteristics help to distinguish the foodservice process. First, services are **intangible**. It is not possible to taste, feel, see, hear, and smell services, as it is to sense food. Second, services are **inseparable**. They can't be separated from the person performing the services. The hostess, maitre d', waiting staff, and management all perform services. Third, because these are people-based services, they are susceptible to **heterogeneity** (variation) in quality. Fourth, unused service capacity of one time period can't be stored for use in future time periods. Regardless of how little service is used at off-peak or "slack" hours in a restaurant, the unused service hours are **perishable**. They can't be used when the surge in demand occurs around meal time. Service capacity not used is lost forever (Lovelock, 1991).

Despite the preponderance of foodservice operations, the participants and the process itself have not been examined. However, literature regarding the marketing of services has focused on three key managerial concerns that are equally relevant to an understanding of the foodservice process and its participants. They are blueprinting, service quality, and service encounter, respectively.

### Blueprinting

There are two ways that the foodservice process can be described. One way is to identify all the steps and sequences in the process, and the other is to identify the variability allowed or inherent in these steps and sequences. The first way is known as the *service complexity*; the second is called *service divergence*. **Blueprinting** is a holistic method of documenting the complexity and divergence of a specific service (Shostack, 1987).

Every service can be analyzed according to its complexity and diversity. **Figure 12-3** shows how the foodservice process in a **fine dining** or **white tablecloth restaurant** appears in blueprint form. The first thing to note is that much of the service is highly visible to the clientele. Second, there is usually more than one participant involved in the process. Third, there are large numbers of customer/service personal encounters. For these reasons, the foodservice processing may be defined as above average in complexity. With regard to divergence, restaurants have sought to reduce the freedom allowed in the process by standardizing the process through documentation (blueprinting) and rules for executing the service. **Figure 12-4** shows some changes the restaurant might consider in order to alter complexity and divergence for competitive purposes. Any change, of course, must be implemented with a clear understanding of the impact it will have on the process, customers, and service personnel.

### *Service Quality*

Much has been written about the fact that for many foodservice retailers, contact personnel contribute significantly to the competitive differential advantage (**CDA**). In high contact businesses like restaurants, the performance of service personnel shapes the customer's total experience and thus become part of the **CDA**.

Just as foodservice retailers need to be concerned with product (food) quality, they also need to be concerned with service quality. **Service quality** has been defined as an overall evaluation of how well the service level that is delivered matches customer expectations (Lewis and Booms, 1983). Zeithaml, Parasuraman, and Berry (1990) identified five independent dimensions of service quality. **Tangibles** represent the appearance of physical facilities, equipment, personnel, communication materials, and other customers in the foodservice retailer. **Reliability** refers to the firm's ability to perform the promised service dependably and accurately. **Responsiveness** concerns the willingness or readiness of employees to provide prompt service. **Assurance** involves the knowledge and courtesy of employees, and their ability to convey trust and confidence. **Empathy** reflects the caring, individualized attention that the foodservice retailer provides its customers.

The notion that service quality involves a matching of customer expectations to service level delivery means that foodservice firms need to be concerned with the needs of both customers and service personnel. By satisfying the needs of its internal customers (service personnel), the foodservice retailer increases its capacity to satisfy the needs of its external customers. This approach, referred to as **internal marketing** allows the firm to apply the philosophies and practices of marketing to service personnel so that the best people will be employed and retained, and will offer the best service (Berry, 1980).

The needs of customers are translated into expectations. Key determinants of these expectations have been shown to involve the foodservice retailer's image, the word-of-mouth communications about the retailer, the customer's last service encounter with the restaurant, the availability of the restaurant to customers (e.g., operating hours, dining space, parking space, and ease of purchase) and the accessibility of the restaurant that includes ease of entry and exit by vehicle. Foodservice retailers consciously manage these **customer expectations** to ensure that customers receive the service they expect (Clow, Kuntz, and Ozment, 1996).

### Service Encounter

The service encounter is defined simply as the dyadic interaction between a customer and a service provider (Surprenant and Solomon, 1987). It is here that the customer's expectations are matched to perceived service performance. Both expectations and perceived performance are influenced by the retailer's traditional marketing mix, as well as the participants and the process itself. As a result of this face-to-face interaction, service encounter satisfaction or dissatisfaction becomes a determinant of customer expectations. In turn, these expectations are matched, by the customer, with the perceived level of service to determine service quality.

## FOODSERVICE WHOLESALING

Like the retail food store, foodservice retailers are supplied by wholesale distributors whose role in this sector is likewise to resolve the product, spatial, and temporal discrepancies that exist between the manufacturers' supply and the foodservice retailers' demand. It follows, then, that to resolve these discrepancies foodservice retailers, like their retail food store counterparts, make product, price, promotion, and place decisions.

These decisions were discussed in great detail in chapter 7. Thus, this section focuses only on the structural dimension of foodservice wholesaling. The discussion examines the major participants in the wholesaling process: broadline distributors, specialty distributors, and foodservice groups.

Before these participants are discussed, mention must be made regarding census data on foodservice wholesalers. The **U.S. Bureau of the Census** does not distinguish foodservice wholesalers from food store wholesalers in their Census of Wholesale Trade. However, in their analysis of sales by class of customer for the 1992 census, they created a separate classification called **Restaurants, Foodservice, and Contract Feeding**. Prior to this census, sales data were not reported separately for foodservice wholesalers.

The sales by class of customer are reported by kind of business and type of operation. By kind of business, foodservice wholesalers generated 16.2 percent of all general-line grocery sales. Specialty foodservice wholesalers generated 50.8 percent of all packaged frozen food sales, 17.8 percent of all dairy products, 36.3 percent of poultry and poultry products sales, 2.7 percent of confectionery sales, 30.7 percent of fish and seafood sales, 18.7 percent of meat and meat products sales, 18.7 percent of fresh fruits and vegetables sales, and 9.6 percent of groceries and related products, n.e.c. With the exception of poultry and poultry products, by type of operation, merchant wholesalers generated the most wholesale sales. For poultry and poultry products, agents and brokers generated the most wholesale sales (Census of Wholesale Trade, 1992).

Lacking any additional census data, industry sources are used to continue the structural examination of foodservice wholesaling. There are three major participants in the wholesale foodservice sector: broadline distributors, specialty distributors, and foodservice groups. According to Chicago-based **Technomic, Inc.**, 1995 foodservice distributor sales were 129 billion dollars—or an eleven percent increase over 1994 sales of 123 billion dollars. In 1995, the top fifty broadline distributors accounted for 25.8 percent of sales, specialty (systems, product, and market specialists) accounted for 13.6 percent of sales, and all other distributors accounted for 60.6 percent. **Technomic, Inc.** estimated that there were 4,415 foodservice distributors in 1995.

## Broadline Distributors

**Broadline distributors** of foodservice are similar in characteristics to general-line grocery wholesalers. They carry, at a minimum, groceries, frozen foods, center-of-the-plate products, disposables, cleaning supplies, and at least some tabletop items. Many broadline distributors offer their retail foodservice customers even wider merchandise categories, such as fresh meat, produce, dairy products, kitchenware, and light and heavy equipment.

**Table 12-24** shows the top ten broadline foodservice distributors. Between 1991 and 1995, very little change occurred in the top ten firms. **Sysco Corp.** dominated the broadline distributors. Its sales were approximately equal to the next six largest distributors, and it had more than one-third the number of distribution centers. Two mergers were responsible for creating two of the top ten broadline firms. In fact, the number five broadline distributor, **U.S. Foodservice, Inc.**, made its last appearance in 1995; it was acquired by the number four distributor, **Pryhoff-Sexton**. Finally, the top ten had sixty-nine percent of all the top fifty distribution centers (193/280) and accounted for eighty-two percent of the top 50 broadline distributor sales.

## Specialty Distributors

Specialty distributors are made up of systems, market specialists, and product. **Systems distributors** specialize in distribution to large multiunit chain operations. Three of the top ten systems distributors have only one account—McDonald's. **Market specialists** focus on specific market niches or segments. Number six, **Smart and Final**, distributes to cash-and-carry stores. **Product specialists** offer a single category to foodservice retailers. Number eight, **Multifood Specialty Distribution**, offers only pizza.

**Table 12-25** identifies the top ten foodservice specialists. Once again, there has been almost no change between 1994 and 1995. Eight of the ten distributors specialize in systems distribution, while market and product specialists make up the remaining two distributors.

## Foodservice Groups

Foodservice groups are analogous to voluntary wholesale groups. The foodservice group is affiliated with a group of foodservice retailers who adhere to its supply and service programs. The purchasing power of the group allows foodservice firms to price their products competitively. In addition to the merchandising effort of the group, it handles all distribution.

**Table 12-26** identifies the major foodservice groups. Between 1991 and 1995, the top eleven foodservice groups changed slightly in sales ranks. These foodservice groups included approximately thirty-eight percent of all foodservice retailers, and accounted for thirty percent of all warehouse locations, and thirty-eight percent of all foodservice sales in 1995 (*Handbook of Foodservice*, 1996). As shown in **Table 12-24**, four of the top ten broadline distributors are affiliated with foodservice groups.

# SUMMARY

This chapter examined the retail foodservice sector. Consumers have the choice of shopping for meal solutions in restaurants and food stores, or for meal ingredients in food stores. Both the percentage of the food dollar spent in restaurants, and the amount spent for prepared foods offered by retail food stores, increased between 1991 and 1995. These recorded increases were largely due to two consumer trends: cocooning and time-pressured households.

To better understand the potential market for foodservice, the **Consumer Expenditure Study** and the **National Food Consumption Survey (NFCS)** were examined. The percentage of the consumer's food dollar spent for food away from home varied with demographic, economic, ethnic, and geographic factors.

An examination of foodservice offered by retail food stores between 1991 and 1995 identified a number of trends. An increase was shown in the number of supermarkets offering prepared foods, prepared food sales, and the number offering eating sections, as well as in size of eating sections. Most of these foodservice operations were managed by the supermarkets themselves and promoted most heavily through newspapers, sampling, and in-store circulators.

An analysis of foodservice eating and drinking places (restaurants) for the census years 1982, 1987, and 1992, also revealed a number of trends. Over these years, the number of firms and establishments increased as did their sales. Foodservice sales were mostly generated by eating places, and they accounted for the majority of foodservice employment. Multiunit firms made up only five percent of all firms, but accounted for one-half of all sales. Despite the dominance of multiunit firms, the foodservice sector was shown not to be a concentrated one. As expected, the number of establishments and sales closely paralleled population density in the U.S.

An examination of the foodservice sector using industry sources identified the sandwich segment as the largest in terms of market share. In terms of sales, **PepsiCo** was the largest foodservice company in 1995. **McDonald's** was the largest foodservice chain in sales and number of units.

The uniqueness of the foodservice marketing mix was attributed to the nature of the product offering (menu), the service process, and the participants in the process. The major considerations in menu planning were identified: variations, types, design, patterns, components, and presentation. The four distinguishing characteristics of services—intangible, inseparable, heterogenous, and perishable—suggested that the foodservice process be blueprinted and examined for service quality.

Service quality was defined as an overall evaluation of how well the service level delivered matched the customer's expectations. Five factors were found to be dimensions used by consumers to evaluate service quality: tangibles, reliability, responsiveness, assurance, and empathy. This evaluation takes place within an environment identified as a service encounter. It is there that the foodserivce retailer manages customer expectations and views the results of its internal marketing.

The chapter concluded with a discussion of foodservice wholesaling. The major participants were identified as broadline distributors, specialty distributors, and foodservice groups. Broadline distributors dominate the foodservice sector. These firms distribute both food and non-food merchandise to their accounts. One firm, **Sysco Corp.**, dominates in sales and number of distribution centers. Specialty distributors focus on a particular product category or market segment, or distribute to multiunit foodservice chains. The three largest foodservice specialists, **Prosource Dist., Martin-Brower Co., and MBM Corp.** had sales that exceeded the next seven largest specialists. Foodservice groups offer purchasing power, merchandising programs, and distribution services to foodservice retailers. These groups accounted for a significant percentage of all foodservice sales, warehouse locations, and foodservice retailers. **EMCO Foodservice, Inc.** has been the leading foodservice group since 1992.

# SELECTED REFERENCES

Berry, L. L. "Services Marketing Is Different," *Business,* May/June 1980, pp. 14–22.

*Census of Wholesale Trade.* U.S. Department of Commerce, Bureau of the Census. Miscellaneous Subjects, 1992.

Clow, K. E., D. L. Kurtz, and J. Ozment. "Managing Customer Expectations of Restaurant: An Enpinial Study," *Journal of Restaurant and Foodservice Marketing,* Vol 1. Nos. 3, 4, 1996, pp. 135–159.

Fisher, R. "What Consumers Want in the 1990s," *Fortune*, January 29, 1990, pp. 108–112.

Gatty, B. "FMI Speaks '96: Facing the Toughest Competition," *Grocery Marketing*, June 1996, pp. 12–14.

Harper, R. "Most Like It Hot," *Supermarket News*, June 17, 1996, pp. 37–39.

Lewis, R. C. and B. H. Booms. "The Marketing Aspects of Service Quality," in Emerging Perspectives on Services Marketing, eds. B. G. Shotack and G. Upah, Chicago: American Marketing Association, 1983 pp. 99–107.

Lovelock, C. H. Services Marketing. Englewood Cliffs, N. J.: Prentice-Hall, 1991.

Millman, N. "Not Every Corner Yet, But Closer Every Day," *Chicago Tribune,* July 7, 1996, pp. 1, 7.

*Nation's Restaurant News.* "Top one hundred Chains Rankings and Company Rankings," April 29, 1996.

*Nation's Restaurant News.* "Second 100 Chain Ranking and Company Rankings," May 15, 1996.

Nayga, R. M. and O. Capps Jr. "Impact of Socio-Economic and Demographic Factors on Food Away from Home Consumption: Number of Meals and Type of Facility, *Journal of Restaurant and Foodservice Marketing*, Vol. 1, No. 2, 1994, pp. 45–69.

Nayga, R. M. and M. N. Wanzala. "Food Away from Home Expenditures in the United States: A County Level Analysis," *Journal of Restaurant and Foodservice Marketing*, Vol. 1. No. 3, 4, 1996, pp. 39–51.

Popcorn, N. F. *The Popcorn Report.* New York: Doubleday Currency Publishing, 1987.

Popcorn F. *The Popcorn Report*. New York: Doubleday Currency Publishing, 1991.

Rande, W. L. *Introduction to Professional Foodservice*. New York: John Willey and Sons, Inc., 1996.

Robertiello, J. "Readin' Ritin' and Ratatouille," *Supermarket News* December 30, 1996 pp. 13–14.

Shostack, G. L. "Service Positioning Through Structural Change," *Journal of Marketing* Vol. 51 January, 1987 pp. 34–43.

*Supermarket Business*, "In No Mood to Wait for Food," May, 1995 pp. 161–166.

Surprenant, C. F. and M. R. Solomon, "Predictability and Personalization in the Service Encounter," *Journal of Marketing*, Vol. 51 April 1987 pp. 73–80.

Zeithaml, V. A., A. Parasuraman, and L. L. Berry. *Delivering Quality Service.* The Free Press. A Division of Macmillian, Inc. New York, 1990.

## REVIEW QUESTIONS

1. Explain what is meant by the statement, "Retailers are competing for the consumer's share of stomach."

2. What factors determine the percentage of the food dollar that consumers spend for food consumed away from home?

3. Briefly characterize the foodservice operations of supermarkets between 1991 and 1995.

4. On the basis of your own experience, do supermarkets appear to be effective competitors for the consumer's foodservice dollar?

5. What conclusions were drawn regarding foodservice firms, establishments, sales, employment, single unit and multiunit firms, location, and sales concentration of the leading firms?

6. What conclusions were drawn regarding the leading foodservice companies, chains?

7. How does the foodservice marketing mix differ from the traditional marketing mix?

8. Explain the terms *blueprinting*, *service encounter*, and *internal marketing*.

9. What is meant by service quality, and how do consumers evaluate it?

10. Briefly characterize the major participants in the foodservice wholesaling sector: broadline distributors, specialty distributors, and foodservice groups.

**TABLE 12-1.** COMPONENT SHARES OF ANNUAL EXPENDITURES FOR FOOD

| ITEM | 1990 | 1991 | 1992 | 1993 | 1994 |
|---|---|---|---|---|---|
| FOOD AT HOME | 58.3 | 62.5 | 62.2 | 62.2 | 61.2 |
| FOOD AWAY FROM HOME | 41.7 | 37.5 | 37.8 | 37.8 | 38.8 |
| TOTAL FOOD | 100.0 | 100.0 | 100.0 | 100.0 | 100.0 |

*SOURCE:* COMPUTED FROM CONSUMER EXPENDITURE SURVEY, 1992-93, U.S. DEPARTMENT OF LABOR, BUREAU OF LABOR STATISTICS, SEPTEMBER, 1995.

**TABLE 12-2.** SUPERMARKETS WITH IN-STORE DELICATESSENS

| ITEM | 1991 | 1992 | 1993 | 1994 | 1995 |
|---|---|---|---|---|---|
| Any prepared foods (hot or cold) | 20,230 | 21,080 | 21,400 | 22,200 | 23,150 |
| Hot foods | 18,030 | 18,790 | 18,636 | 19,135 | 19,845 |
| Refrigerated prepared foods | 18,045 | 18,825 | 18,867 | 19,843 | 20,825 |

*SOURCE:* ANNUAL FOODSERVICE OPERATIONS DELIVERIES, *SUPERMARKET BUSINESS*, JULY 1992-1996.

**TABLE 12-3.** PREPARED FOODS PRODUCTION, SOURCES, OWNERSHIP, AND EXPERTISE

| **Prepared foods production** | 1991 | 1992 | 1993 | 1994 | 1995 |
|---|---|---|---|---|---|
| Bought from foodservice supplier | 67 | 66 | 68 | 66 | 67 |
| In-store scratch | 28 | 27 | 26 | 26 | 25 |
| Bought local caterer/restaurant | 1 | 2 | 1 | 1 | 1 |
| Central company kitchen | 4 | 5 | 5 | 7 | 7 |
| Total | 100 | 100 | 100 | 100 | 100 |
| Sources of products/ingredients: | | | | | |
| Foodservice distributor | 73 | 70 | 72 | 73 | 74 |
| Grocery wholesaler | 8 | 8 | 7 | 6 | 7 |
| Taken from store inventory | 19 | 22 | 21 | 21 | 19 |
| Total | 100 | 100 | 100 | 100 | 100 |
| Foodservice distributor: | | | | | |
| Owned by, or division of, grocery wholesaler | N/A | 8 | 9 | 8 | 10 |
| Not owned or division | N/A | 92 | 91 | 92 | 90 |
| Total | 100 | 100 | 100 | 100 | 100 |
| Expertise (percent): | | | | | |
| Instore cooks trained as chefs | 14.6 | 12.8 | 12.5 | 14 | 13 |

SOURCE: ANNUAL FOODSERVICE OPERATIONS DELIVERIES, *SUPERMARKET BUSINESS*, JULY 1992-1996.

**TABLE 12-4.** PREPARED SALES FOODS/GROSS MARGINS

| Year | Annual Sales ($billions) | % Store Sales median | % Store Profits median | % Weekly Sales median | % Gross Margins median |
|---|---|---|---|---|---|
| 1995 | 8.76 | 3.6 | 7.8 | 7,410 | 52.7 |
| 1994 | 8.03 | 3.5 | 7.8 | 7,263 | 52.8 |
| 1993 | 7.35 | 3.3 | 7.5 | 6,890 | 53.4 |
| 1992 | 6.93 | 3.1 | 7.7 | 6,681 | 51.0 |
| 1991 | 6.11 | 3.0 | 8.0 | 6,200 | 48.0 |

SOURCE: ANNUAL FOODSERVICE OPERATIONS DELIVERIES, *SUPERMARKET BUSINESS*, JULY 1992-1996.

**TABLE 12-5.** PREPARED FOODS SOURCES OF SALES

| % SOLD THROUGH... | 1991 | 1992 | 1993 | 1994 | 1995 |
|---|---|---|---|---|---|
| Service deli | 68 | 67 | 63 | 60 | 49 |
| Separate hot service counter | 7 | 7 | 6 | 6 | 7 |
| Self-service refrigerated case | 25 | 26 | 31 | 34 | 44 |
| Total | 100 | 100 | 100 | 100 | 100 |

SOURCE: ANNUAL FOODSERVICE OPERATIONS DELIVERIES, *SUPERMARKET BUSINESS*, JULY 1992-1996.

**TABLE 12-6.** FOODSERVICE DOLLAR EXPENDITURES

| FOOD ITEM | PERCENT OF FOODSERVICE DOLLARS | | | | |
|---|---|---|---|---|---|
| | 1991 | 1992 | 1993 | 1994 | 1995 |
| Pizza | 15.9 | 16.0 | 15.8 | 15.9 | 16.0 |
| BBQ/fried chicken | 16.9 | 16.4 | 15.1 | 15.8 | 15.9 |
| Sandwiches | 13.8 | 14.1 | 14.2 | 14.5 | 14.7 |
| Refrigerated entrees | 10.1 | 11.4 | 12.3 | 13.0 | 13.1 |
| Hot entrees | 11.7 | 11.4 | 11.2 | 11.5 | 11.8 |
| Side dishes | 7.8 | 8.4 | 8.4 | 8.0 | 7.9 |
| Main dish salads | 8.5 | 8.1 | 8.1 | 7.8 | 7.6 |
| Fountain drinks | 5.7 | 5.6 | 5.7 | 5.5 | 5.3 |
| BBQ ribs | 5.4 | 5.2 | 4.9 | 4.7 | 4.5 |
| Other | 5.2 | 4.4 | 4.3 | 3.3 | 3.2 |
| TOTAL | 100.0 | 100.0 | 100.0 | 100.0 | 100.0 |

*SOURCE:* ANNUAL FOODSERVICE OPERATIONS DELIVERIES, *SUPERMARKET BUSINESS*, JULY 1992-1996.

**TABLE 12-7.** SUPERMARKETS WITH EATING SECTIONS

| | 1991 | 1992 | 1993 | 1994 | 1995 |
|---|---|---|---|---|---|
| Snack bars | 3,079 | 3,162 | 3,424 | 3,780 | 3,935 |
| Sit-down cafes/restaurants | 571 | 632 | 642 | 679 | 695 |
| Sit-down eating areas | 16,932 | 17,000 | 17,120 | 17,730 | 17,750 |

*SOURCE:* ANNUAL FOODSERVICE OPERATIONS DELIVERIES, *SUPERMARKET BUSINESS*, JULY 1992-1996.

**TABLE 12-8.** EATING SECTIONS OPERATIONS SIZE, GROSS MARGINS

|  | 1991 | 1992 | 1993 | 1994 | 1995 |
|---|---|---|---|---|---|
| **OPERATIONS (PERCENT)** | | | | | |
| Franchised fast-food outlet | 1 | 1 | 1 | 1 | 1 |
| Leased to local restauranters | 1 | 1 | 1 | 1 | 1 |
| Supermarket operated | 98 | 98 | 98 | 98 | 98 |
| **AVERAGE GROSS MARGINS (PERCENT)** | | | | | |
| Snack bars | 51.6 | 52.7 | 53.6 | 52.7 | 60.0 |
| Cafeterias/restaurants | 61.3 | 56.5 | 61.0 | 62.1 | 59.9 |
| Off-premise catering | 58.3 | 62.0 | 63.4 | 64.6 | 65.0 |
| **AVERAGE SIZING (SQUARE FEET)** | | | | | |
| Cafeterias/restaurants | 1,433 | 1,385 | 1,410 | 1,620 | 1,830 |

SOURCE: ANNUAL FOODSERVICE OPERATIONS DELIVERIES, *SUPERMARKET BUSINESS*, JULY 1992-1996.

**TABLE 12-9.** ADVERTISING AND PROMOTION OF IN-STORE FOODSERVICE

| PROMOTION | PERCENT OF RETAILERS WHO USE | | | | |
|---|---|---|---|---|---|
| | 1991 | 1992 | 1993 | 1994 | 1995 |
| Newspapers | 98 | 98 | 98 | 97 | 97 |
| Sampling | 90 | 93 | 95 | 94 | 95 |
| Store circulars | 85 | 90 | 92 | 93 | 94 |
| Point of purchase | 55 | 62 | 68 | 69 | 71 |
| Radio | 35 | 32 | 40 | 41 | 40 |
| In-store radio/TV | 15 | 17 | 18 | 15 | 14 |
| TV | 12 | 12 | 10 | 10 | 9 |

SOURCE: ANNUAL FOODSERVICE OPERATIONS DELIVERIES, *SUPERMARKET BUSINESS*, JULY 1992-1996.


**TABLE 12-10.** SELECTED TRENDS IN U.S. FOODSERVICE EATING AND DRINKING PLACES

| YEAR | TOTAL FIRMS | TOTAL ESTABLISHMENTS | SALES (millions) |
|---|---|---|---|
| 1982 | 258,314 | 319,873 | 101,723 |
| 1987 | 304,124 | 391,303 | 148,776 |
| 1992 | 331,488 | 433,608 | 195,317 |

SOURCE: CENSUS OF RETAIL TRADE 1982, 1987, AND 1992.

**TABLE 12-11.** NUMBER OF U.S. FOODSERVICE RETAILERS BY SALES AND INDUSTRY

| INDUSTRY | 1982 Total Firms | 1982 Sales ($millions) | 1987 Total Firms | 1987 Sales ($millions) | 1992 Total Firms | 1992 Sales ($millions) |
|---|---|---|---|---|---|---|
| Eating places | 198,088 | 93,158 | 246,460 | 139,282 | 276,427 | 184,203 |
| Restaurants | 106,954 | 47,136 | 134,940 | 66,364 | 148,048 | 85,178 |
| Cafeterias | 4,556 | 2,720 | 5,097 | 3,778 | 3,839 | 3,619 |
| Refreshment | 75,447 | 35,678 | 89,776 | 58,870 | 105,538 | 77,686 |
| Other | 12,254 | 7,604 | 17,939 | 12,269 | 20,201 | 17,720 |
| Drinking places | 60,486 | 8,565 | 57,923 | 9,495 | 55,277 | 11,114 |
| TOTAL | 258,314 | 101,723 | 304,124 | 148,776 | 331,488 | 195,317 |

*SOURCE:* CENSUS OF RETAIL TRADE 1982, 1987, AND 1992.

**TABLE 12-12.** SHARE OF U.S. FOODSERVICE INDUSTRIES BY FIRMS AND SALES

| INDUSTRY | 1982 % OF FIRMS | 1982 % OF SALES | 1987 % OF FIRMS | 1987 % OF SALES | 1992 % OF FIRMS | 1992 % OF SALES |
|---|---|---|---|---|---|---|
| EATING PLACES: | 76.7 | 91.6 | 81.0 | 93.6 | 83.0 | 94.3 |
| Restaurants | 41.2 | 46.3 | 44.1 | 44.6 | 44.5 | 43.6 |
| Cafeterias | 1.8 | 2.7 | 1.7 | 2.5 | 1.2 | 1.9 |
| Refreshment | 29.1 | 35.1 | 29.4 | 39.6 | 31.7 | 39.8 |
| Other | 4.7 | 7.5 | 5.9 | 8.2 | 6.1 | 9.1 |
| Drinking places | 23.3 | 8.4 | 19.0 | 6.4 | 17.0 | 5.7 |
| TOTAL | 100.0 | 100.0 | 100.0 | 100.0 | 100.0 | 100.0 |

*SOURCE:* CENSUS OF RETAIL TRADE 1982, 1987, AND 1992.

**TABLE 12-13.** EMPLOYMENT AND SHARE BY FOODSERVICE INDUSTRY

| INDUSTRY | 1982 EMPLOYEES | % | 1987 EMPLOYEES | % | 1992 EMPLOYEES | % |
|---|---|---|---|---|---|---|
| Eating places: | 4,340,832 | 93.0 | 5,786,889 | 94.9 | 6,243,862 | 95.4 |
| Restaurants | 2,291,157 | 49.1 | 2,822,189 | 46.3 | 2,988,535 | 45.6 |
| Cafeterias | 112,961 | 2.4 | 138,380 | 2.3 | 109,063 | 1.7 |
| Refreshment | 1,610,278 | 34.5 | 2,352,218 | 38.6 | 2,651,779 | 40.5 |
| Other | 326,436 | 7.0 | 474,102 | 7.8 | 494,485 | 7.6 |
| Drinking places | 324,998 | 7.0 | 312,831 | 5.1 | 304,046 | 4.6 |
| TOTAL | 4,665,830 | 100.0 | 6,099,720 | 100.0 | 6,547,908 | 100.0 |

*SOURCE:* CENSUS OF RETAIL TRADE 1982, 1987, AND 1992.

**TABLE 12-14.** SINGLE UNIT AND MULTIUNIT FIRMS, SALES, AND SHARE FOR EATING AND DRINKING PLACES

| INDUSTRY | 1982 NUMBER | % | 1987 NUMBER | % | 1992 NUMBER | % |
|---|---|---|---|---|---|---|
| FIRMS: | | | | | | |
| Single Unit | 187,127 | 94.5 | 290,004 | 95.4 | 315,046 | 95.0 |
| Multiunit | 10,961 | 5.5 | 14,120 | 4.6 | 16,442 | 5.0 |
| SALES ($billions): | | | | | | |
| Single Unit | 472,262 | 52.1 | 76,628 | 51.1 | 97,122 | 49.7 |
| Multiunit | 43,410 | 47.9 | 72,149 | 48.5 | 98,195 | 50.3 |

*SOURCE:* COMPUTED FROM CENSUS OF RETAIL TRADE 1982, 1987, AND 1992.

**TABLE 12-15.** SALES SIZE OF EATING AND DRINKING PLACES

| ANNUAL SALES | 1982 FIRMS (number) | SALES ($millions) | 1987 FIRMS (number) | SALES ($millions) | 1992 FIRMS (number) | SALES ($millions) |
|---|---|---|---|---|---|---|
| ≥ $250 million | 23 | 14,931 | 30 | 27,315 | 48 | 41,158 |
| $100-249 million | 26 | 3,820 | 41 | 6,273 | 38 | 5,895 |
| $50-99 million | 41 | 2,717 | 57 | 3,847 | 72 | 4,887 |
| $10-49 million | 484 | 7,156 | 673 | 12,423 | 937 | 17,439 |
| $1-9 million | 12,262 | 25,803 | 19,593 | 41,390 | 25,153 | 53,557 |
| $250-999 thousand | 58,814 | 25,940 | 71,232 | 34,349 | 91,437 | 44,105 |
| > $250 thousand | 162,578 | 16,382 | 146,995 | 16,269 | 143,188 | 18,466 |

*SOURCE:* COMPUTED FROM CENSUS OF RETAIL TRADE 1982, 1987, AND 1992.

**TABLE 12-16.** SALES SIZE OF EATING AND DRINKING PLACES

| ANNUAL SALES | 1982 | | 1987 | | 1992 | |
|---|---|---|---|---|---|---|
| | % OF FIRMS | % OF SALES | % OF FIRMS | % OF SALES | % OF FIRMS | PERCENTAGE OF SALES |
| ≥ $250 million | 0.01 | 15.4 | 0.01 | 19.3 | 0.02 | 22.2 |
| $100-249 million | 0.01 | 3.9 | 0.02 | 4.4 | 0.02 | 3.2 |
| $50-99 million | 0.01 | 2.8 | 0.02 | 2.7 | 0.03 | 2.6 |
| $10-49 million | 0.20 | 7.4 | 0.28 | 8.8 | 0.36 | 9.4 |
| $1-9 million | 5.30 | 26.7 | 8.20 | 29.2 | 9.60 | 28.9 |
| $250-999 thousand | 23.80 | 29.8 | 29.90 | 24.2 | 35.10 | 23.8 |
| > $250 thousand | 70.60 | 16.9 | 97.60 | 11.5 | 54.90 | 10.0 |
| TOTAL | 100.00 | 100.00 | 100.00 | 100.00 | 100.00 | 100.00 |

**TABLE 12-17.** SALES CONCENTRATION OF LARGEST FOODSERVICE RETAIL FIRMS BY EATING AND DRINKING PLACES

| EATING AND DRINKING PLACES | 1982 % OF SALES | 1987 % OF SALES | 1992 % OF SALES |
|---|---|---|---|
| 4 LARGEST | 5.0 | 7.6 | 7.9 |
| 8 LARGEST | 8.2 | 11.2 | 11.3 |
| 20 LARGEST | 13.8 | 16.0 | 16.0 |
| 50 LARGEST | 18.5 | 20.9 | 21.3 |
| EATING PLACES: | | | |
| 4 LARGEST | 5.4 | 8.1 | 8.4 |
| 8 LARGEST | 8.9 | 12.0 | 12.0 |
| 20 LARGEST | 15.1 | 17.0 | 17.0 |
| 50 LARGEST | 20.2 | 22.3 | 22.6 |
| DRINKING PLACES: | | | |
| 4 LARGEST | .7 | 1.4 | .9 |
| 8 LARGEST | 1.0 | 2.0 | 1.1 |
| 20 LARGEST | 1.7 | 2.8 | 1.8 |
| 50 LARGEST | 2.8 | 4.2 | 3.0 |

*SOURCE:* CENSUS OF RETAIL TRADE, 1982, 1989, AND 1992.

**TABLE 12-18.** SALES CONCENTRATION OF LARGEST FIRMS BY INDUSTRY

| EATING PLACES | 1982 % OF SALES | 1987 % OF SALES | 1992 % OF SALES |
|---|---|---|---|
| RESTAURANTS | | | |
| 4 LARGEST | 5.6 | 6.9 | 7.8 |
| 8 LARGEST | 9.0 | 10.3 | 10.6 |
| 20 LARGEST | 12.6 | 14.4 | 15.2 |
| 50 LARGEST | 16.1 | 18.1 | 18.9 |
| CAFETERIAS | | | |
| 4 LARGEST | 25.2 | 28.3 | 32.6 |
| 8 LARGEST | 34.9 | 38.3 | 47.4 |
| 20 LARGEST | 44.0 | 47.6 | 57.7 |
| 50 LARGEST | 50.6 | 54.6 | 63.8 |
| REFRESHMENT PLACES | | | |
| 4 LARGEST | 9.0 | 10.6 | 11.9 |
| 8 LARGEST | 13.7 | 14.9 | 16.0 |
| 20 LARGEST | 21.4 | 21.9 | 21.8 |
| 50 LARGEST | 26.0 | 27.0 | 26.5 |
| OTHER EATING PLACES | | | |
| 4 LARGEST | 31.7 | 40.4 | 35.9 |
| 8 LARGEST | 39.6 | 50.8 | 46.7 |
| 20 LARGEST | 52.4 | 58.6 | 59.5 |
| 50 LARGEST | 60.2 | 62.9 | 64.6 |

*SOURCE:* CENSUS OF RETAIL TRADE 1982, 1987, AND 1992.

**TABLE 12-19.** RANKING BY SHARE OF SALES FOR TEN LEADING STATES FOR EATING AND DRINKING PLACES (ESTABLISHMENTS)

| State | 1982 Est. | Sales | 1987 Est. | Sales | 1992 Est. | Sales |
|---|---|---|---|---|---|---|
| California | 11.5 | 13.2 | 11.7 | 13.4 | 11.6 | 13.0 |
| Texas | 6.2 | 7.2 | 6.3 | 6.6 | 6.2 | 6.9 |
| New York | 8.2 | 7.1 | 7.8 | 7.0 | 7.6 | 6.5 |
| Florida | 4.4 | 5.4 | 5.0 | 6.1 | 5.2 | 6.2 |
| Illinois | 5.1 | 5.0 | 4.8 | 4.7 | 4.4 | 4.6 |
| Ohio | 4.9 | 4.5 | 4.7 | 4.4 | 4.5 | 4.3 |
| Pennsylvania | 5.1 | 4.2 | 4.9 | 4.2 | 4.9 | 4.2 |
| Michigan | 3.8 | 3.7 | 3.7 | 3.7 | 3.6 | 3.6 |
| New Jersey | 3.3 | 3.1 | 3.2 | 3.2 | 3.1 | 2.9 |
| Massachuetts | 2.7 | 3.0 | 2.7 | 3.1 | 2.7 | 2.8 |
| Total | 55.2 | 56.4 | 54.8 | 56.4 | 54.1 | 55.0 |

*SOURCE:* COMPUTED FROM CENSUS OF RETAIL TRADE 1982, 1987, AND 1992.

**TABLE 12-20.** MARKET SHARE BY SEGMENT

| SEGMENT | PERCENT TOP 100 | SECOND 100 |
|---|---|---|
| SANDWICH | 42.28 | 12.80 |
| CONTRACT | 10.98 | 9.42 |
| PIZZA | 10.21 | 7.36 |
| DINNER HOUSE | 9.10 | 24.62 |
| FAMILY | 7.76 | 12.24 |
| CHICKEN | 5.78 | 6.26 |
| HOTEL | 4.72 | 3.94 |
| OTHER | 3.48 | 9.35 |
| GRILL-BUFFET | 2.81 | 3.05 |
| SNACK | 2.03 | 3.49 |
| CAFETERIA | 0.85 | a. |
| TOTAL | 100.00 | 100.00 |

a. CAFETERIA IS NOT A SEGMENT. THE REMAINING 7.4% MARKET SHARE IS DISTRIBUTED TO C-STORES (3.75%) AND IN-STORES (3.72%).

SOURCE: *NATION'S RESTAURANT NEWS SPECIAL REPORTS*, APRIL 29, 1996; MAY 13, 1996.

**TABLE 12-21.** TEN LEADING U.S. FOODSERVICE COMPANIES BY SALES REVENUE a.

| RANK | | | COMPANY | CHAINS | SALES REVENUE ($millions)b | | |
|---|---|---|---|---|---|---|---|
| 1993 | 1994 | 1995 | | | 1993 | 1994 | 1995 |
| 1 | 1 | 1 | PepsiCo, Inc. | Pizza Hut, Taco Bell, KFC, Hot'n Now, Chevy's, East Side Mario's, D'Angelo's | 8,026 | 8,694 | 9,202 |
| 2 | 3 | 2 | McDonald's | McDonald's | 3,931 | 4,156 | 4,474 |
| 3 | 2 | 3 | Marriott International, Inc. | Marriott Hotels. Resorts, & Suites, Marriott management services | 3,880 | 4,170 | 4,250 |
| 4 | 4 | 4 | Darden Restaurants, Inc. | Red Lobster, The Olive Garden, Bahama Breeze | 2,811 | 3,013 | 3,200 |
| 5 | 5 | 5 | Aramark Corp. | Aramark Global Foodservice, Aramark Leisure Services | 2,488 | 2,587 | 2,782 |
| 6 | 6 | 6 | Flagstar Co's, Inc. | Denny's, Quincy's, ElPollo, Loco, Hardees | 2,375 | 2,391 | 2,381 |
| 8 | 7 | 7 | Wendy's International, Inc. | Wendy's Old Fashioned Hamburgers | 1,308 | 1,316 | 1,416 |
| | | 8 | Brinker International, Inc. | Chili's Grill & Bar, Romano's, Macaroni Grill, Cozy Mel's on the Border | | | 1,160 |
| | 8 | 9 | Family Restaurant, Inc. | El Torito's, Chi-Chi's, Coco's, Carrow's, Casa Gallardo, Reubens, Charlie Brown's, JoJo's | | 1,113 | 1,134 |
| | | 10 | Dial Corp. | Dobbs International Services, Inc., Rest Aura, Inc. | | | 1,045 |
| 7 | 9 | | Grandmetropolitan PLC | Burger King, Haagen-Dazs | 1,310 | 1,075 | |
| 9 | 10 | | Foodmaker, Inc. | Jack in the Box | 1,241 | 1,053 | |
| 10 | | | MetroMedia Co. | Ponderosa, Bonanza Family Grill, Steak & Ale, Bennigan's, Rising Star Grill, Montana Steak Co. | 1,000 | | |

a. DOES NOT INCLUDE COMPANIES WHO ARE HEADQUARTERED OUTSIDE THE U.S.

b. SALES BASED ON COMPANIES' FISCAL YEARS

*SOURCE: NATIONS RESTAURANT NEWS SPECIAL REPORT*, APRIL 29, 1996, p. 52.

**TABLE 12-22.** TEN LEADING U.S. FOODSERVICE CHAINS BY SALES REVENUE

| RANK | | | | | SALES REVENUE ($millions)[a] | | |
|---|---|---|---|---|---|---|---|
| 1993 | 1994 | 1995 | CHAIN | SEGMENT | 1993 | 1994 | 1995 |
| 1 | 1 | 1 | McDonald's | Sandwich | 14,186 | 14,941 | 15,905 |
| 2 | 2 | 2 | Burger King | Sandwich | 6,720 | 7,250 | 8,400 |
| 3 | 3 | 3 | Pizza Hut | Pizza | 4,925 | 5,130 | 5,440 |
| 4 | 4 | 4 | Taco Bell | Sandwich | 3,608 | 4,200 | 4,600 |
| 5 | 5 | 5 | Wendy's | Sandwich | 3,547 | 3,821 | 4,150 |
| 6 | 6 | 6 | KFC | Chicken | 3,400 | 3,511 | 3,700 |
| 7 | 7 | 7 | Hardee's | Sandwich | 3,505 | 3,500 | 3,325 |
| 8 | 8 | 8 | Marriott Mgt. Services | Contract | 2,642 | 2,890 | 3,100 |
| 9 | 9 | 9 | Aramark Global | Contract | 2,488 | 2,587 | 2,782 |
|   | 10 | 10 | Subway | Sandwich |   | 2,518 | 2,600 |
| 10 |   |   | Little Caesar's | Pizza | 2,150 | 2,000 | 2,050 |

a. SALES BASED ON CHAIN'S FISCAL YEAR

*SOURCE: NATION'S RESTAURANT NEWS*, APRIL 29, 1996, p. 48.

**TABLE 12-23.** TEN LEADING CHAINS BY TOTAL NUMBER OF UNITS

| RANK | | | | 1993 | | 1994 | | 1995 | | |
|---|---|---|---|---|---|---|---|---|---|---|
| 1993 | 1994 | 1995 | CHAIN | % Co. | % Frn. | % Co. | % Frn. | % Co. | % Frn. | Total Number |
| 1 | 1 | 1 | McDonald's | 15 | 85 | 16 | 84 | 16 | 84 | 11,368 |
| 3 | 2 | 2 | Subway | <1 | 99 | <1 | 99 | 0 | 100 | 10,093 |
| 2 | 3 | 3 | Pizza Hut | 60 | 40 | 61 | 39 | 59 | 41 | 8,883 |
| 4 | 4 | 4 | Burger King | 15 | 85 | 9 | 59 | 7 | 93 | 6,492 |
| 9 | 5 | 5 | Taco Bell | 63 | 37 | 57 | 43 | 48 | 52 | 6,490 |
| 5 | 6 | 6 | Service America | 100 | 0 | 100 | 0 | 100 | 0 | 5,700 |
| 7 | 7 | 7 | KFC | 40 | 60 | 40 | 60 | 39 | 31 | 5,152 |
| 8 | 9 | 8 | Dairy Queen | | 99 | | 99 | 0 | 100 | 5,000 |
| 6 | 8 | 9 | 7-Eleven | 43 | 57 | 42 | 58 | 42 | 58 | 4,973 |
| 10 | 10 | 10 | Little Caesar's | 36 | 64 | 35 | 65 | 34 | 66 | 4,720 |

SOURCE: COMPUTED FROM *NATION'S RESTAURANT NEWS*, APRIL 29, 1996, p. 64.

**TABLE 12-24.** TOP TEN BROADLINE FOODSERVICE DISTRIBUTORS AND GROUP AFFILIATIONS

| RANK | | | | | | 1995 | | |
|---|---|---|---|---|---|---|---|---|
| 1991 | 1992 | 1993 | 1994 | 1995 | Company | Number of Distribution Centers | Sales (millions) | Group Affiliation |
| 1 | 1 | 1 | 1 | 1 | Sysco Corp. | 68 | 12,722 | None |
| 2 | 2 | 2 | 2 | 2 | Alliant Foodservice, Inc. a. | 39 | 4,225.7 | None |
| 4 | 4 | 4 | 5 | 3 | Pya/Monarch, Inc. | 11 | 2,200 | Comsource |
| 3 | 3 | 3 | 3 | 4 | Rykoff-Sexton, Inc. | 25 | 1,800 | Emco |
| | | 5 | 4 | 5 | U.S. Foodservice, Inc. | 17 | 1,705 | None |
| 6 | 6 | 7 | 6 | 6 | Gordon Foodservice, Inc. | 3 | 1,276 | None |
| 5 | 5 | 6 | 7 | 7 | JP Foodservice, Inc. | 9 | 1,169 | None |
| 9 | 9 | 8 | 8 | 8 | Food Services of America | 13 | 915 | None |
| | | | | 9 | Performance Food Group b. | 6 | 654 | Pocohontas |
| 11 | 11 | 10 | 9 | 10 | Shamrock Foods Corp. | 2 | 600 | F.A.B. |
| | | | | | Total | 193 | 27,266.7 | |

a. FORMERLY KRAFT FOODSERVICE

b. CREATED BY MERGER IN 1995

c. CREATED BY MERGER IN 1993

SOURCE: "THE TOP FIFTY BROADLINE DISTRIBUTORS" *ID-THE VOICE OF FOODSERVICE DISTRIBUTION.* A BILL PUBLICATION, DECEMBER 1991, 1992, AND 1993; APRIL 1995, MARCH 1996.

**TABLE 12-25.** TOP TEN FOODSERVICE SPECIALISTS

| 1994 | 1995 | COMPANY | SPECIAL | 1995 GROUP AFFILATION | NUMBER OF LOCATIONS | SALES ($millions) |
|---|---|---|---|---|---|---|
| 2 | 1 | Prosource Dist. Services | Systems | F.A.B. | 33 | 4,000 |
| 1 | 2 | The Martin-Brower Co. | Systems | None | 21 | 2,485 |
| 4 | 3 | MBM Corp. | Systems | Federated | 13 | 1,575 |
| 3 | 4 | Golden State Corp. | Systems | None | 8 | 1,370 |
| 5 | 5 | Ameriserv Foods Co. | Systems | Emco | 14 | 950 |
| 6 | 6 | Smart & Final Store Corp. | Cash & Carry | Emco | 161 | 922 |
| 7 | 7 | Marriott Dist. Services | Systems | None | 8 | 872 |
| 8 | 8 | Multifoods Spec. Dst. | Pizza | Emco | 14 | 775 |
| 9 | 9 | Perlman-Rocque Co. | Systems | None | 4 | 710 |
| 10 | 10 | Nebco Evans Dist., Inc. | Systems | Emco | 3 | 450 |
| | | Total | | | 279 | 14,109 |

SOURCE: "THE TOP FIFTY BROADLINE DISTRIBUTORS," *ID-THE VOICE OF FOODSERVICE DISTRIBUTION*. A BILL PUBLICATION; MARCH 1996.

**TABLE 12-26.** MAJOR FOODSERVICE GROUPS

| RANK | | | | | COMPANY | NUMBER OF MEMBER COMPANIES | NUMBER OF WAREHOUSE LOCATIONS | TOTAL MEMBER SALES ($millions) |
|---|---|---|---|---|---|---|---|---|
| 1991 | 1992 | 1993 | 1994 | 1995 | | | | |
| 2 | 1 | 1 | 1 | 1 | Emco Foodservice Sys. | 127 | 185 | 8,100 |
| 3 | 3 | 3 | 2 | 2 | F.A.B., Inc. | 61 | 126 | 7,103 |
| 1 | 2 | 2 | 3 | 3 | Comsource Indep. | 100 | 156 | 6,216 |
| 6 | 5 | 5 | 6 | 4 | All Kitchens, Inc. | 110 | 142 | 6,068 |
| 7 | 7 | 7 | 4 | 5 | Pocohontas Foods, Inc. | 142 | 162 | 5,200 |
| 5 | 6 | 6 | 7 | 6 | Nugget Dist. | 192 | 209 | 4,858 |
| 4 | 4 | 4 | 5 | 7 | Federated Group, Inc. | 135 | 179 | 4,800 |
| 8 | 8 | 8 | 8 | 8 | Golbon | 116 | 122 | 3,000 |
| 9 | 9 | 9 | 9 | 9 | Phee-Zing/Lil Brave | 162 | 172 | 1,280 |
| 10 | 10 | 10 | 10 | 10 | Sefa/Supply & Equipment | 58 | 88 | 1,132 |
| 11 | 11 | 11 | 11 | 11 | Allied Buying Corp. | 51 | 51 | 1,115 |
| | | | | | Total | 1,254 | 1,635 | 48,872 |

SOURCE: *HANDBOOK OF FOODSERVICE DISTRIBUTION*, 1994, 1996 - A BILL PUBLICATION; "THE TOP FIFTY BROADLINE DISTRIBUTORS," *ID-VOICE OF FOODSERVICE DISTRIBUTION*, A BILL PUBLICATION, MAY 1994.

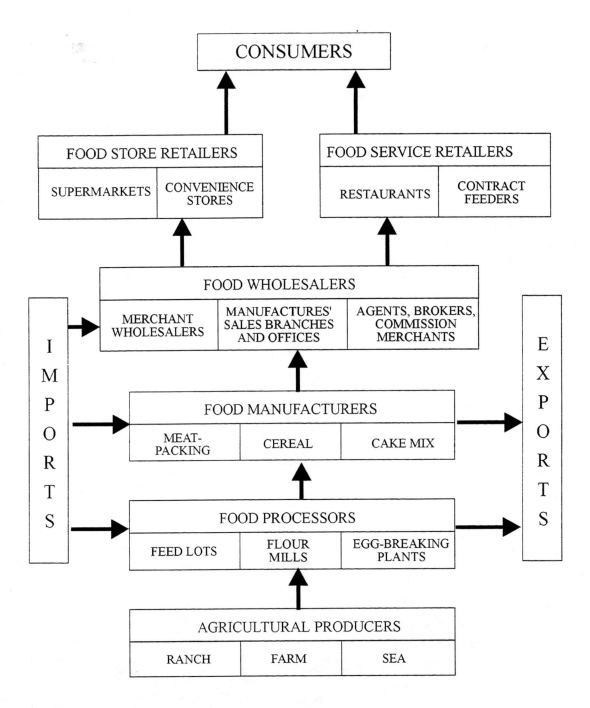

**FIGURE 12-1.** U.S. FOOD MARKETING SYSTEM

**FIGURE 12-2.** FOOD PREPARATION CONTINUUM

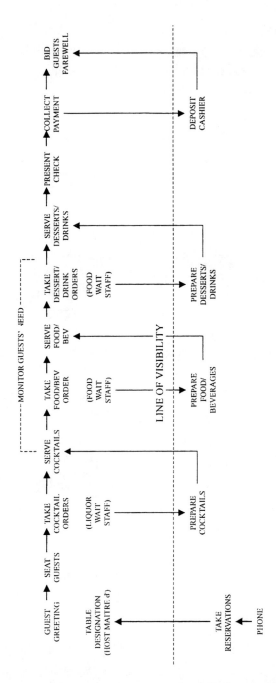

**FIGURE 12-3.** BLUEPRINT FOR FINE-DINING-RESTAURANT FOODSERVICE PROCESS

*SOURCE:* Shostack, G.L., "Service Positioning through Structural Change," *Journal of Marketing,* Vol. 51, January 1987 pp. 34–43.

| LOWER COMPLEXITY/DIVERGENCE | CURRENT PROCESS | HIGHER COMPLEXITY/DIVERGENCE |
|---|---|---|
| No Reservation ← | Take reservation → | Specific table selection |
| Self-seating, Menu on blackboard ← | Seat guests, give menus → | Recite menu: Describe entree and specials |
| Eliminate ← | Serve water and bread → | Assortment of hot bread and hors d'oeuvres |
| Customer fills out form ← | Take orders → | At table. Taken personally by maitre d' |
|  | Prepare orders |  |
| Pre-prepared: No choice ← | *Salad (4 Choices) → | Individually prepared table |
| Choices limited to four ← | *Entree (15 Choices) → | Expand to 20 choices: Add flaming dishes; Bone fish at table; Prepare sauces at table. |
| Sundae bar: Self-service ← | *Dessert (6 Choices) → | Add exotic coffees; wine list; liqueurs |
| Serve salad and entree together: Bill and beverage together ← | Serve orders → | Separate course service: Sherbet between courses; Hand grind pepper |
| Cash only; Pay when leaving ← | Collect payment → | Choice of payment, including house account. Serve mints |

**FIGURE 12-4** STRUCTURAL CHANGE TO FOODSERVICE PROCESSS FOR FINE-DINING-RESTAURANTS

*SOURCE:* Shostack, G.L., "Service Positioning through Structural Change," *Journal of Marketing,* Vol. 51, January 1987 pp. 34–43.

# Chapter 13 International Perspective

**Chapter Outline**

Internationalization
- A. Total Exports/Imports
- B. Bulk Exports/Imports
- C. Intermediate Exports/Imports
- D. Consumer-Oriented Exports/Imports

International Trade in Processed Foods
- A. Surplus Producing Industry Groups
- B. Deficit Producing Industry Groups
- C. Summary

Foreign Direct Investment (FDI)
- A. Outbound and Inbound (FDI)
- B. Summary

International Marketing Environment
- A. Economic Environment
- B. Political Environment
- C. Legal Environment

    D. Technological Environment

    E. Competitive Environment

    F. Institutional Environment

    G. Cultural Environment

International Markets

    A. Foodways

    B. Selected Shopping Behaviors

    C. Food Nutrition and Safety Attitudes

Foreign Market Entry

    A. Modes of Entry

    B. Exporting

    C. Licensing

    D. Joint Ventures

    E. Direct Ownership

International Marketing

    A. Marketing Strategy

    B. Product

    C. Place

    D. Promotion

    E. Price

Summary

Conclusion

Up to this point, this book has examined the **U.S. food marketing system** from both a structural and functional perspective. Structurally, data for three census periods—1982, 1987, and 1992—published by the **Bureau of the Census** were used to characterize trends in the producer, manufacturer, wholesaler, and retailer sectors. The trends enabled the reader to identify how the sectors have changed in terms of the number and size of firms and establishments, sales, employment, location, and concentration. Functionally, the marketing decisions made by producers, manufacturers, wholesalers, and retailers were also identified. In one form or another, these firms make product, price, place, and promotion decisions to create and/or maintain a competitive differential advantage. The cumulative effect of their marketing decisions results in customer satisfaction—the real output of the U.S. food marketing system.

The consumer section identified the shopping, purchase, and consumption behaviors that make up American foodways. Special emphasis was placed on the role of food in meeting consumers' needs to maintain and/or enhance their lifestyles. A closer look at food preferences and choices revealed how they are influenced by availability, as well as by other factors broadly categorized as physiological, situational, and cultural. A model of lifestyle and its determinants illustrated how the process of market segmentation is used to accommodate the diversity of consumers.

The purpose of this final chapter in **Food Marketing** is to provide an international perspective of the U.S. food marketing system. The chapter begins with an examination of international trade in bulk, intermediate, and consumer food products. Next, the surplus- and deficit-producing industry groups in processed food are identified. The analysis of international trade is extended by a discussion of inbound and outbound foreign direct investment. This is followed by an examination of the international marketing environment. A discussion of marketing mix issues facing manufacturers who decide to market internationally through wholly-owned affiliates ends the chapter.

## INTERNATIONALIZATION

At the beginning of this book, two women were overheard discussing what to prepare for a special dinner. Barbara and her friend Rachel decided that their evening dinner would include lobsters from Maine, asparagus from California, muffins made with flour from North Dakota, butter and sour cream from Wisconsin, potatoes from Idaho, cherries from Michigan, and coffee from Colombia. Despite the fact that all but the coffee originated in the U.S., the entire meal could have been prepared using the same goods from other countries. The lobster could have come from the Atlantic shores off Canada, the butter and sour cream from New Zealand, the asparagus and potatoes from Mexico, the flour from Australia, and the cherries from Belgium. The availability of these alternate food sources, and the ease with which food moves from country to country, mean that the structure and function of the U.S. food marketing system is influenced by its imports and exports, or its international trade.

In the same way that U.S. consumers drive the U.S. food marketing system, consumers throughout the world drive the international food marketing system. Without consumer demand, there is no need for supply. The task facing each nation is to determine which component of food demand it can satisfy profitably; therefore, nations specialize in food production that is best suited to their resources. These resources, which economists call "factors of production," include human, physical, knowledge, capital, labor, climate, location, and the infrastructure of a nation (Porter, 1990). Driven by the need to satisfy consumer demand profitably, and given international price differences, countries will export those food items that they can produce efficiently by virtue of their own resource advantage and import those commodities that other nations can produce more efficiently by virtue of their resource advantage. An examination of the exports and imports of trading nations tends to support this relationship.

## Total Exports/Imports

The **USDA's Foreign Agricultural Service (FAS)** provides import and export data. Using a "value added" perspective, imports and exports are classified as bulk commodities, intermediate commodities, and consumer-oriented foods and beverages. In addition, a separate category is maintained for edible fish and seafood products. In a general sense, all agricultural products contain a value-added component. For bulk commodities, the value is added typically when they are transported from their place of origin (e.g., farm or ranch) to their destination. Intermediate commodities are semi-processed products. Their value is added when they are transformed into ingredients. High-value products may be unprocessed (e.g., fresh fruits and vegetables, nuts); semi-processed (e.g., flour and soybean oils); or highly processed (e.g., red meat and snacks). In the case of fresh fruits and vegetables, their high degree of perishability results in valued added by the special distribution required to reduce spoilage.

The U.S. food marketing system continues to develop greater ties to the international community. As shown in **Table 13-1**, from 1991 to 1995, the value of exports increased by forty percent while imports increased by thirty percent. Over this same period, the U.S. maintained a surplus. The 22 billion dollar surplus in 1995 reflects a sixty-one percent increase over the 1991 surplus.

The market share of bulk, intermediate, and consumer-oriented exports and imports is shown in **Table 13-2**. Even though bulk exports declined for four years, in 1995 they were greater than they were in 1991. This is the largest export category. Conversely, consumer-oriented exports increased for four years and declined in 1995. They, too, were larger in 1995 than in 1991. The gains in shares of bulk and consumer-oriented exports came at the expense of intermediate exports. This category is the only one with a smaller market share in 1995 than in 1991.

Where did these exports go? Thirty-five countries received eighty-eight percent of all U.S. exports. Japan received the greatest share of exports (twenty percent). Together with Canada (ten percent), Korea (seven percent), Mexico (six percent), China (five percent), Taiwan (four percent), Netherlands (four percent), and Hong

Kong (three percent), these eight countries received fifty-nine percent of all U.S. exports.

**Table 13-2** reveals a much greater dominance of the leading-import category. Despite the loss in market share over the five-year period, consumer-oriented imports remain the largest category. Over this period, bulk and intermediate imports gained the market shares lost by consumer-oriented imports. Where did these imports come from? Thirty-five countries shipped ninety-three percent of all U.S. imports. Canada shipped the most imports (nineteen percent). Together with Mexico (thirteen percent), Indonesia (six percent), Brazil (four percent), Colombia (four percent), Netherlands (three percent), Italy (three percent), and France (two percent), these eight countries shipped fifty-four percent of all U.S. imports.

## Bulk Exports/Imports

The lowest-value-added imports and exports are agricultural commodities. Bulk commodities include wheat, coarse grains, rice, soybeans, cotton, tobacco, raw coffee, cocoa beans, tea, pulses, peanuts, and raw beet and cane sugar. **Table 13-3** shows the five-year trend in bulk commodity imports and exports. The twenty-six billion dollars in exports for 1995 represent a forty-two percent increase from 1991. The six billion dollars in imports for 1995 represent a thirty-six percent increase from 1991. The 19.5-billion-dollar surplus in 1995 is a forty-four percent increase over the 1991 surplus of 13.6 billion dollars. In 1995, the chief export was coarse grains, while raw coffee was the major import.

Nearly forty percent of U.S. harvested acres are devoted to export production. Generally, the U.S. exports about half of its wheat and soybean crops, and one-quarter or more of its corn crop. Other crops with high export shares are rice and soybeans. Japan received the largest share of bulk U.S. exports (seventeen percent—mostly coarse grains). Japan, Korea (eight percent), China (eight percent), Taiwan (seven percent), Mexico (seven percent), Egypt (four percent), Netherlands (four percent), and Spain (three percent), together received fifty-eight percent of all U.S. bulk commodity exports.

Agricultural imports are either commodities that don't compete directly with U.S. domestic production (complementary), such as coffee, rubber, and cocoa, or those that compete directly with U.S.-grown commodities (supplementary) such as rice, wheat, and other coarse grains. In 1995, noncompetitive imports made up seventy-three percent of all bulk commodity imports. Canada shipped the largest share of bulk imports to the U.S. (eleven percent—mostly wheat and coarse grains). Canada, Brazil (ten percent), Thailand (nine percent), Mexico (nine percent), Colombia (eight percent), Guatemala (six percent), Malaysia (four percent) and Ecuador (three percent), together shipped sixty percent of all U.S. bulk commodity imports.

## Intermediate Exports/Imports

Intermediate value-added exports and imports are made up of raw foodstuffs that have been transformed into ingredients and livestock readied for slaughter. Intermediate commodities include wheat flour, soybean meal and oil, tropical oils, other vegetable oils, animal fat, sugars, sweeteners and beverage bases, cocoa paste and butter, feeds and fodders, and live animals. Ingredients are typically produced to specifications of manufacturers. Fats, carbohydrates, and fiber ingredients, along with textured proteins, allow manufacturers to increase the variety of value-added products with new textures and forms. With the focus on fat-related issues, many of the value-added activities associated with livestock are centered on breeding and feeding to specific levels of fat content. The amount of international trade in livestock is limited by the expense and perishability of live animals. These limiting factors are vastly reduced when the trade takes place between contiguous countries. **Table 13-3** reveals the five-year trend in intermediate commodity exports and imports. The eleven billion dollars in exports for 1995 reflect a twenty-five percent increase from 1991. The seven billion dollars in imports for 1995 reflect a thirty-six percent increase from 1991. The four-billion-dollar surplus in 1995 is a seven-percent decrease from the 1991 surplus. In 1995, the chief export was feeds/fodders, while live animals were the major import.

Japan received the largest share of intermediate U.S. exports (eleven percent), Canada (ten percent), Mexico (nine percent), Korea (nine percent), Netherlands (six percent), China (five percent), Taiwan (three percent), and United Kingdom (two percent). These eight countries received fifty-five percent of all U.S. intermediate commodity exports. Canada shipped the largest share of intermediate imports to the U.S. (thirty-two percent), Mexico (eleven percent), Philippines (six percent), Italy (four percent), Australia (four percent), China (three percent), Brazil (three percent), and Malaysia (three percent). These countries accounted for sixty-six percent of all U.S. intermediate imports.

## Consumer-Oriented Exports/Imports

The highest value-added exports and imports are made up of snack foods, breakfast cereals and pancake mix, red meats (fresh, chilled, frozen, prepared, and preserved), poultry, dairy products, eggs, fresh fruits and vegetables, processed fruits and vegetables, fruit and vegetable juices, tree nuts, wine and beer, nursery products and cut flowers, pet foods, and edible fish and seafood products.

**Table 13-3** shows the five-year trend in consumer-oriented exports and imports. The twenty-two billion dollars in exports for 1995 represent a forty-six percent increase from 1991. The twenty-four billion dollars in imports for 1995 is a twenty-one percent increase from 1991. The 1.6-billion-dollar deficit in 1995 is a sixty-three percent decrease from the 1991 deficit of 4.4 billion dollars. In 1995, the chief export was red meats (fresh, chilled, and frozen), while the major import was shrimp.

The deficit in consumer-oriented food products is due largely to the huge deficit the U.S. had between 1991 and 1995 in edible fish and seafood products. In fact, when edible fish and seafood are excluded, the U.S. has had a surplus in consumer-oriented food products since 1992. Seventy-five percent of all U.S. consumer-oriented exports (excluding fish and seafood) went to eight countries. Japan, alone, received twenty-eight percent of these exports, followed by Canada (twenty-three percent), Hong Kong (six percent), Mexico (five percent), Russia (four percent), Korea (four percent), Taiwan (three percent), and Germany (two percent). Sixty-one percent of all edible fish and seafood went to Japan, Canada (fourteen percent), Korea (four percent), United Kingdom (three percent), France (three percent), China (two percent), Taiwan (two percent), and Hong Kong (one percent), these eight countries received ninety percent of all edible fish and seafood exports.

Most of the consumer-oriented imports came from Canada (sixteen percent). Another forty-one percent came from Mexico (fifteen percent), Netherlands (six percent), France (five percent), Italy (four percent), New Zealand (four percent), Colombia (four percent), and Australia (three percent). Thailand shipped the largest share of edible fish and seafood imports to the U.S. (eighteen percent), Canada (seventeen percent), Ecuador (eight percent), Mexico (seven percent), China (4.7 percent), Chile (four percent), Taiwan (three percent) and Iceland (three percent). These countries accounted for sixty-four percent of all U.S. imports of edible fish and seafood.

## INTERNATIONAL TRADE IN PROCESSED FOODS

The **Economic Research Service**, monitors food imports and exports by using a value-added approach based on the processing of raw materials. Food processors and manufacturers add value to raw foodstuffs when they are transformed into ingredients and/or final consumer products. The transformation process adds value by converting livestock, grains, fruits, and vegetables, dairy products, and marine animals into food products that are palatable, storable, portable, and convenient to prepare.

The **Economic Research Service** uses the **Harmonized System (HS)** to classify imports and exports into 2,150 processed food categories and then assigns each of them to one of forty-eight manufacturing industries defined by Standard Industrialization Codes (SIC). In turn, these industries are aggregated into nine industry groups (Epps and Harris, 1995). **Table 13-4** reveals total U.S. processed food imports and exports. Beginning in 1992, the U.S. has maintained a surplus in processed foods. From 1991 to 1995, exports increased by forty-five percent, while imports increased only twenty percent. During this time, the U.S. went from a 323-million-dollar deficit to a 4.6-billion-dollar surplus. Of course, to identify where the surplus occurs requires another level of analysis.

**Table 13-5** is the result of a second level of analysis. It reports the trade balances in each of the nine industry groups. Historically, the U.S. has maintained a deficit in five industry groups, and a surplus in only three of them. Detailed descriptions of all nine industry groups were presented in Chapter 4. Here, the discussion will be limited to the contribution each industry group makes to the U.S. trade balance in processed foods.

## Surplus Producing Industry Groups

As an industry group, meat products historically have made the largest positive contribution to the U.S. trade balance. Seventy-seven percent of all meat exports are shipped to five countries, with Japan receiving the largest share (thirty-nine). Interestingly, the U.S. imports more meat products than any other product. Five countries account for eighty-one percent of all meat imports with most meat imports coming from Canada (thirty-one percent).

The second largest positive contribution to the U.S. trade balance comes from the grain-mill industry group. The seven industries that make up this group typically maintain a surplus. Forty-eight percent of all grain mill exports are shipped to five countries, while five countries account for eighty-two percent of all grain mills exports to the U.S. The U.S. ships most of its grain mill products to Canada (fourteen percent) and receives most of its grain mill imports from Canada (fifty percent).

The last industry group that historically has generated a surplus is fats and oils. Of the five industries that make up this group, only vegetable oil has generally had a deficit. The U.S. sends thirty-eight percent of its fat and oil exports to five countries, with most going to Mexico (eleven percent). Seventy-seven percent of fat and oil imports come from five countries, but Canada has the greatest share (thirty-two percent).

## Deficit Producing Industry Groups

The largest negative contribution to the U.S. trade balance is produced by the miscellaneous foods industry group. Two industries in this group, fresh fish and processed fish products, account for the vast majority of the deficit. The U.S. sends most of its miscellaneous food exports to Japan (forty-seven percent) and Canada (eighteen percent) and receives most of its imports from Canada (eighteen percent) and Thailand (sixteen percent).

The second largest negative contribution to the U.S. trade balance is made by the beverage industry group. Three of the alcohol-related industries are major contributors to the deficit. While most U.S. beverage exports go to Japan (twenty-two percent), most imports come from France (twenty-one percent).

Another substantial deficit is maintained by the sugar and confectionery industry groups. The chocolate and cane sugar industries are the major contributors to this deficit. Most of our sugar and confectionery exports go to Canada (twenty percent), but Canada is also the leading exporter of sugar and confectioneries to the U.S. (thirteen percent).

The bakery-products industry group historically has maintained the smallest deficit, though it has generated the least amount of international trade. The U.S. imports much more bread, cookies, and crackers than it exports. These industries' deficits outweigh the surplus in frozen bakery products. Five countries receive seventy-eight percent of all U.S. bakery exports, while five countries account for seventy-one percent of all U.S. bakery imports. Once again, the U.S. receives most of its bakery imports from Canada (forty-four percent), and sends most of its bakery exports to Canada (fifty-eight percent).

Although the preserved fruits and vegetables industry group did not experience a deficit in 1995, historically it has produced a deficit. The canned fruit and vegetable industry, along with the sauces and salad dressing industry typically have produced the deficit. Most of the U.S. preserved fruit and vegetable exports go to Canada (twenty-six percent), while Mexico is the major source of U.S. preserved fruit and vegetable exports (fourteen percent).

The dairy products industry group shows a deficit for 1995. However, it has not consistently been either a surplus- or deficit-producing industry group. The U.S. exports more condensed and evaporated milk than it imports, and exports much less cheese than it imports. The international trade in these two industries determines on a year to year basis whether the dairy industry group will generate a surplus or deficit. The U.S. sends most of its dairy exports to Mexico (twenty-one percent) and receives most of its imports from New Zealand (fifteen percent) and Ireland (fifteen percent).

## Summary

Japan, Canada, and Mexico represent the target market for U.S. processed food exports. Japan received most of the U.S. exports of meat, beverages, and miscellaneous. Collectively, they received 25.9 percent of all U.S. exports. Canada received most of the U.S. exports of preserved fruits and vegetables, grain mill products, bakery products, and sugar and confections. Canada accounted for fifteen percent of all U.S. exports of dairy products and fat/oils, combined. Considering all other industry groups, Mexico accounted for 7.6 percent of all U.S. exports.

With regard to imports, Canada was the leading source of U.S. imports in six of the nine industry groups: meat, grain mill products, bakery products, sugar and confectionery, fats and oils, and miscellaneous foods. Altogether, Canada accounted for 19.3 percent of all U.S. imports. The second leading importer to the U.S. was Thailand (six percent). Even though it is not a leading importer, the U.S. dollar value of fish exceeds the value shipped by France, New Zealand, or Mexico—the other leading importers to the U.S. in beverages, dairy and preserved fruits and vegetables, respectively. Finally, Mexico is the third leading importer to the U.S. About five percent of all U.S. food imports come from Mexico.

An industry analysis of U.S. processed food exports indicated that the ten leading industries accounted for 66.5 percent of all U.S. processed food exports. The industries and their respective shares of all U.S. exports were meat packing (20.5 percent), fresh fish (11.1 percent), soybean oil mills (7.6 percent), wet corn milling (5.7 percent), poultry dressing plants (5.1 percent), rice milling (3.6 percent), salted and roasted nuts and seeds (3.5 percent), canned fruits and vegetables (3.2 percent), other food preparations (3.2 percent), and animal/marine fats and oils (3.0 percent).

Finally, an industry analysis of U.S. processed food imports showed that ten leading industries accounted for 74.5 percent of all U.S. processed food imports. These industries and their respective shares were fresh fish (22.2 percent), meat packing (12.9 percent), distilled and blended spirits (6.4 percent), canned fruits and vegetables (6.2 percent), wines, brandy, and brandy products (5.6 percent), chocolate and cocoa products (4.8 percent), malt beverages (4.4 percent), vegetable oil mils (4.0 percent), and other foods preparations (3.5 percent).

# FOREIGN DIRECT INVESTMENT

Despite the dominance of the U.S. in agriculture and food manufacturing, it is among the largest importers, as well as exporters of foodstuffs. However, international trade benefits everyone. Imports allow consumers to expand their diets by providing food not ordinarily available. Imports that add to the domestic supply also allow consumers to purchase food at a lower price than is ordinarily possible.

On the other hand, exports allow producers and manufacturers to expand their markets beyond national borders. In turn, the potential for market expansion results in increased employment opportunities and profitability to U.S. firms. In addition to exporting, U.S. food manufacturers, as well as wholesalers and retailers, can access foreign markets through foreign direct investment (FDI).

## Outbound and Inbound (FDI)

U.S. firms may acquire, build, or invest in foreign manufacturing, wholesaling, or retailing facilities. Collectively, these activities are considered **outbound** foreign direct investment. **Inbound** foreign direct investment occurs when foreign firms acquire, build, or invest in U.S. manufacturing, wholesaling, or retail facilities. The Bureau of Economic Analysis (BEA), of the U.S. Department of Commerce publishes aggregate data on outbound and inbound FDI.

**Table 13-6** identifies sales from all U.S. food marketing affiliates abroad and sales of U.S. affiliates of foreign firms. In 1993, the last year in which industry-level data are available from the BEA, sales from all U.S. food marketing affiliates abroad totaled 132.5 billion dollars, or a 146-percent increase from 1982. Sales from foreign-owned food marketing affiliates in the U.S. were 124.3 billion dollars in 1993, or a 206-percent increase from 1982. Food manufacturing affiliates accounted for seventy-two percent of sales generated by outbound **FDI**, but only thirty-seven percent of sales generated by inbound **FDI**. For the food retailing sector, the relationship is the opposite. U.S. food retailing affiliates abroad accounted for only nine percent of sales generated by outbound **FDI**, while U.S. food retailing affiliates of foreign forms accounted for forty-two percent of sales generated by inbound **FDI**.

In 1993, five of the world's largest food manufacturers were U.S. firms with foreign affiliates. In order of sales, these firms were: Number two, **Phillip Morris/Kraft foods**, Number four, **ConAgra**, Number five, **Cargil**, Number six, **PepsiCo.**, Number seven, **Coca-Cola**, and Number ten, **IBP, Inc**. In total, there were sixty-four U.S. food manufacturers, with 762 foreign affiliates.

In this same year, there were thirteen U.S. wholesale firms with 197 foreign affiliates. Three of these firms are the leading firms in the wholesale sector: **Fleming** in grocery stores, **McLane** in convenience stores, and **Sysco** in foodservice.

U.S. food retailing is largely a domestically oriented sector. However, fifteen U.S. food retail firms operated ninety-one foreign affiliates. Firms such as **Safeway** and **K-Mart** have foreign foodstore operations. Unlike the other sectors, foreign firms have significant sales in U.S. food retailing. In fact, four of the top ten U.S. food retailers are foreign-owned (**see Table 8-21**).

Foodservice sales by restaurants only recently have been separated from retail foodstore sales. Four of the top fifty U.S. foodservice chains have greater than fifty percent of their sales from foreign operations: **KFC**, **Hard Rock Cafe Intl.**, **Shakey's**, and **East Side Mario's**. However, foreign firms also have substantial sales in the U.S. **Burger King**, **Hardees**, **Roy Rogers**, **Dunkin'-Donuts**, and **Baskin-Robbins** are some of the more significant foreign-owned chains operating in the U.S.

## Summary

Compared to U.S. processed food exports, foreign-affiliate sales by food manufacturers are about four times larger. Historically, this has been the case. At the same time, it should be noted that food manufacturing sales of foreign firms increased at a much faster rate than sales of U.S.-owned manufacturers (146 percent vs. 206 percent). In fact, the same is true for food wholesaling and retailing.

It is apparent to many nations that the U.S. represents a stable and profitable marketplace for international market expansion. Foreign firms are gaining competitively in U.S. markets by acquiring, building, or investing in U.S. firms and by exporting bulk, intermediate, and consumer-oriented food products to the U.S.

# INTERNATIONAL MARKETING ENVIRONMENT

To position themselves strategically in the international U.S. food marketing system, U.S. firms must be able to assess and satisfy the needs of consumers in foreign markets better than its competitors do. Whether firms enter foreign markets because of the lack of growth in domestic markets, to avoid domestic competition, or to capitalize on the economies of scale in certain food processing or distribution technologies, they must make three decisions: which foreign markets to enter, how to enter the markets, and how to design marketing programs for these markets.

The **International Marketing Environment** consists of all factors external to a firm, and over which it has no control, that influence the outcomes of a firm's marketing decisions. In order to determine which foreign markets to enter, a firm must identify the external opportunities and threats in foreign markets. A firm should assess the economic, political, legal, technological, competitive, institutional, and cultural environments in each prospective foreign market.

## Economic Environment

Perhaps the single most important environment is a country's level of economic development. The more economically developed a nation is, the more attractive its consumer markets are, and the more modern its infrastructure is. The 219 countries of the world are grouped according to economic regions defined by the **United Nations Food and Agriculture Organization (UNFAO)**. **Developed** countries are highly industrialized and include the U.S., Canada, Japan, the European Union, Australia, Norway, and such Eastern European countries as Croatia and Poland. **Developing** countries are made up of nations from Africa (e.g., Egypt and Libya), Asia (e.g., Saudi Arabia, China, and India), Latin America (e.g., Cuba, Mexico, and Brazil), and Oceania (e.g., New Guinea and New Caledonia). **Least developed** countries (LDCs) are made up of the developing countries with the lowest income. In Africa, these countries include Botswana, Mozambique, and Zaire. In Asia, they include Afghanistan and Bangladesh. In Oceania, Samoa and the Solomon Islands are LDCs. Finally, in Latin America, Haiti is considered an LDC.

The economic environments in these nations are assessed to determine the current sizes of the markets and the potential for growth. Because markets consist of people with money, an economic assessment focuses on both population and income.

### Population

Because food is a necessity, its consumption is positively related to the size of the market. Thus, the first population component of interest to a firm is the number of people in a country. The countries of the world vary tremendously in size. In fact, the top nine countries contain over one-half of the entire world population.

The second population component that must be assessed is how the population is distributed across a country. Population density figures indicate the nature of the transportation network needed to reach a country's inhabitants. Population density also varies significantly among nations.

Another population component of interest to firms is its composition. Demographic variables such as age, gender, occupation, education, and religion are used to assess the various segments within the larger population.

Lastly, firms must be concerned with the growth rate of the population as a whole, and also that of its segments. An examination of growth rates indicates that the highest growth rates are found in the least developed countries. However, a nation having a high growth rate does not in itself guarantee a reliable market. People must have the economic means to satisfy their food needs.

### *Income*

The second major economic dimension of a country is its people's income. To access this factor, firms may rely on two complementary indices. First, per capita income figures are widely published and have been used in the past as a measure of a country's **ability to buy**. As expected, per capita income figures vary widely among the world's countries. For many of the countries, per capita income figures are unreliable because of the unequal distribution of income in these countries. Further, because per capita figures are averages, they lose their meaning when the incomes of most people are not near the average.

Another income measure used to assess foreign markets is the **Gross Domestic Product (GDP)**. The GDP represents all the goods and services bought by consumers, businesses, and government for their own use. Countries can be ranked by their GDP. This ranking, in turn, provides a measure of a country's market potential. There is another benefit to using GDP—net exports are included in the compilation of GDP. **Net exports** are the difference between, for example, what the U.S. sells to foreigners, and what they sell to the U.S. This difference, called the **balance of trade** is contained in the current account of the **U.S. Balance of Payments (BOP)**. An analysis of the BOP reveals which nations are importers and exporters of particular food products. This information can be used to identify not only export markets, but also the most likely sources of U.S. imports.

## Political Environment

The political environment must be assessed from three perspectives. First, firms must determine how compatible their operations are with the national sovereignty, security, prestige, and economic welfare of the host country. In addition, they must assess how politically vulnerable they are to the ruling political party.

A second political consideration is the existing relationship between the U.S. and the host country. Of particular concern is the host country's attitude toward the U.S.

The host country's relations with other nations must also be considered, because it may limit countries to which it can export.

The third political consideration is the existing political environment in the U.S. In short, it can prohibit trade to certain countries, both in terms of exports and imports.

## Legal Environment

A foreign nation's laws and regulations significantly influence the ability of U.S. firms to market in that nation. All nations establish trade regulations that favor their domestic producers and markets and otherwise discriminate against other countries. These regulations typically involve a tax on imported goods (tariff), quantitative limits (quotas), price controls, entry restrictions, ownership restrictions on companies, restrictions on the amount of money sent out of the country, or how its currency can be used to pay for imports (exchange controls). In addition, the interpretation of business practices within a foreign country may be subject to a legal system different from the U.S. legal system which is based on common law.

## Technological Environment

The pace at which technology is advancing requires U.S. firms to assess the technological sophistication of foreign markets. Of particular concern is their technological baseline in food processing, packaging, distribution, telecommunications, data processing, and information systems. All of these factors impact on the ability of U.S. firms to produce and market their products in foreign markets. Fortunately, scientific knowledge knows no national borders, and thus can be transferred to other countries when technological gaps are discovered. Nonetheless, a country's technological baseline defines the ease or difficulty encountered when entering the foreign market.

## Competitive Environment

Another important consideration is the number and type of competitors, as well as their objectives, capabilities, strategies, and tactics. Surprisingly, U.S. firms often find that their chief competitors are multinationals from the U.S., Europe, and Japan. An assessment of the competitive environment provides a baseline measure of how well consumers' needs are being met in foreign markets. In addition, their relative market shares reflect their structures and provide information regarding the natures of their marketing practices. Ultimately, U.S. firms must determine whether to compete on the basis of a cost advantage (price) or differentiation in product, promotion, or distribution. Equally important, U.S. firms must determine the degree to which domestic firms are protected against foreign competition.

## Institutional Environment

The institutional environment consists of all firms, facilities, and services needed to market food products in a country. Specifically, a country's transportation infrastructure, such as its roads, railroads, waterways and air transport, has an obvious impact on the ability of firms to deliver their products. A country's communication infrastructure identifies the ease with which firms can communicate with their various audiences, especially their customers. A country's distribution infrastructure, made up of food producers, manufacturers, wholesalers, and retailers, reveals its capacity to meet consumers needs.

Finally, to support the marketing efforts of U.S. firms, assessments must be made of a country's financial institutions, marketing research firms, advertising agencies, and distribution channels. A quick index of a nation's infrastructure is its level of economic development. Generally, the higher a nation's level of economic development, the more sophisticated its infrastructure.

## Cultural Environment

Learning about the cultures of other nations is more than just interesting; it is absolute necessity if firms want to be successful in foreign markets. Firms cannot possibly understand the shopping, purchasing, and consumption behaviors of food consumers without considering the cultural context within which these components of a society's foodways occur.

Each nation creates its own foodways. What people eat, how they spend their money on what they eat, how they make food choices, and how they acquire what they eat, are significantly influenced by cultural factors. What are these factors? Because it is possible to define any culture on economic, political, legal, technological, competitive, and institutional dimensions, each of the previously mentioned environments in this section is essentially a cultural factor. Individually and collectively, these factors influence society's foodways. But these are not the most important factors that have an impact on a society's foodways.

A culture is made up of people who adhere to values that are commonly considered important. These shopping-specific values (e.g., friendly and prompt service), product specific values (e.g., freshness, convenient packaging), and consumption-specific values (e.g., nutritious and flavorful) play significant roles in the formation of societal foodways. To assess a foreign market, then, firms must give serious consideration to how its values impact its foodways.

# INTERNATIONAL MARKETS

As a people, we use relatively few foods to satisfy are needs. Twenty-nine crops, produced in amounts of ten million metric tons or more annually, sustain the world's population. Nine of these have annual harvests of over one hundred million metric tons: wheat, rice, maize, potato, barley, cassava, sweet potato, millet and sorghum, and soybeans. Pork, beef, poultry, and mutton are the most commonly consumed meats (Food and Agriculture Organization, 1994).

Even though there is a good deal of homogeneity regarding the food consumed by people who inhabit this earth, it does not follow that the foodways found in the 219 countries are likewise homogeneous. The final task, in the assessment of foreign markets, is to discover whether the differences among countries' foodways warrant a marketing strategy that recognizes them as unique global markets, or rather as global segments of worldwide market.

## Foodways

Foodways were defined in Chapter 10 as broad behavioral patterns that govern the acquisition, preparation, and consumption of food according to a society's preferences. Even though as a people, Americans rely on few foods to satisfy us, foodways vary from country to country. What accounts for these variations? Beyond the basic biological need for sufficient energy and nutrients from food, a country's foodways are shaped by the combination of economic, political, legal, technological, competitive, institutional, and cultural forces.

To examine the shopping, purchasing, and consumption behaviors that reflect the foodways in 219 national markets is well beyond the scope of this, or any, text. Suffice it to say, the process used in Chapter 10 to examine the U.S. foodways, and the segmentation procedures used to establish micromarkets within the U.S., would need to be replicated in each of the countries that firms expected to enter. Here, for illustrative purposes, only the shopping behaviors and food nutrition and safety attitudes of consumers in Canada and Mexico are examined. These countries were chosen for a number of reasons. Canada and Mexico represent major markets for the U.S. and are significant exporters of goods to the U.S. Further, they are our NAFTA trading partners, destined to experience a greater flow of trade into, and out of, their national borders. Canada is classified as a developed country while Mexico is considered a developing country. Thus, they provide a good contrast to one another.

## Selected Shopping Behaviors

One of the major questions that food retailers, and by implication, wholesalers and manufacturers, try to answer is, "How do consumers decide where to shop?" The typical approach is to ask consumers how important selected criteria are to them. Once their importance has been identified, alternative stores are compared on these criteria.

**Table 13-7** shows the criteria rated as *very important* by consumers. Because consumers tend to rate most criteria as *somewhat important, very important* ratings more clearly reflect differences in priorities. Two criteria were not asked of Canadian and Mexican consumers, but were included because consumers have long considered them very important.

In general, a larger percentage of Canadian consumers rated these criteria as *very important*. In most cases, the differences were minimal. At least three observations can be made regarding the Mexican responses. First, despite their more limited incomes, a greater percentage of the Mexicans surveyed rated *clean store,* and *high-quality meat and produce* as more important than lower prices. Second, ninety-four percent rated personal safety outside the store as *very important*. (This is probably more a reflection of the perceived safety in the country than the more immediate environment surrounding the stores.) Third, thirty-five percent more Mexicans rated **natural/organic foods** as *very important* then did Canadians. The agrarian nature of Mexico, and the closeness of its people to the land, probably influenced their responses to this criterion, as well as to the one on environmentally friendly products.

**Table 13-8** shows how Canadian and Mexican consumers evaluated their primary food stores. Once again, Canadian consumers evaluated their stores as *excellent* or good in greater percentages than did Mexican consumers. Those factors that were rated by a large percentage of consumers as *very important,* but *low* on *performance,* represent frustrations on the part of consumers, and opportunities to retailers. For Canadian consumers these frustrations are in *low prices, food checkout,* and *readable, accurate shelf tops.* For Mexican consumers, the frustrations are, in descending order, *fast checkout, low prices,* and *good quality meat and produce.* In general, there are smaller gaps or differences between the importance and the evaluation of a criterion for Canadian consumers than for Mexican consumers. Expressed another way, the opportunities for improvement are greater for Mexican retailers than for Canadian retailers.

**Table 13-9** shows the rank order of reasons why consumers would switch stores. For both countries, the three highest-ranked reasons were the same: *lower prices, convenient location* and *wider variety.* For both Canadian and Mexican consumers, prices were significant frustrations, and are reflected by their gaps between the importance of the criteria and their performance ratings.

The last comparisons in **Table 13-10** show the shopping frequency of consumers in both countries. The most significant difference lies in the average number of visits per week to retail food stores. Mexicans averaged eleven visits per week, or five times the average of Canadian consumers. In part, this reflects the emphasis Mexican consumers place on freshness. It also reflects the limited availability and use of refrigeration. Canadian shoppers are more reflective of consumers in developed, industrialized countries. Little more than one-third shopped once a week, another third shopped twice a week, and the rest shopped more frequently. On average, Canadians shopped twice a week for groceries.

## Food Nutrition and Safety Attitudes

There is a growing awareness that the foods people eat should be not only flavorful, but nutritious and safe to eat as well. More and more consumers are beginning to discover that eating the "right" foods leads to a healthier lifestyle and a longer life. In fact, most consumers believe that their diets could be somewhat healthier than they are now.

### *Nutrition*

**Table 13-11** focuses on three nutritional areas. With regard to the level of concern, Mexican consumers appeared to be very much more concerned with the nutritional value of their foods than did Canadian consumers. Fifty-three percent of Canadians were concerned with nutritional value, while ninety-four percent of Mexican consumers were very concerned with nutrition.

When the nature of nutritional concern was examined more precisely, Canadian and Mexican consumers could not have been more different. The emphasis on vitamin content, protein value, and freshness by Mexicans has more to do with inadequate nutrition than Canadian concerns about excessive consumption of fat, sugar, or sodium.

Finally, when consumers were asked who should be responsible for ensuring that the food they or their families consume is nutritious, Mexicans were more likely to feel that the responsibility was mostly their own and then that of the manufacturers. Government was assigned much less responsibility. A smaller percentage of Canadians felt the same way regarding individual's and food manufacturers' responsibility. However, government was perceived as having more responsibility than retailers, consumer organization, or farmers.

### *Safety*

The food safety attitudes of consumers are presented in **Table 13-12**. In general, Canadian and Mexican consumers have a high level of confidence in the safety of their food. In both countries, more than eighty percent of consumers were completely or mostly confident in the safety of their food. However, these same consumers differed regarding the perceived threats to food safety. More Mexicans than Canadians believed that improper handling and storage contributed to unsafe food, but fewer Mexicans were concerned with the threats of chemicals, pesticides, or bacterial contamination.

When asked who should be responsible for ensuring that the food they and their families ate was safe, Mexican consumers were again more likely to feel it was their own responsibility. Canadians believed likewise, but they also believed that three other participants in the U.S. food marketing system were equally responsible: manufacturers, retailers, and government.

As these analyses suggest, there are significant differences between consumers in Mexico and Canada regarding nutrition, food safety, store-choice criteria, store switching, shopping frequency, and how they evaluate their primary food stores. As stated previously, these concerns represent frustrations on the part of consumers, but opportunities and challenges for food retailers and the wholesalers and manufacturers who supply them.

# FOREIGN MARKET ENTRY

Once a company has identified the uniqueness of foreign markets by examining their various environments and how they influence their respective foodways, it must evaluate these countries. In general, foreign markets are evaluated and then ranked according to their opportunities (i.e., market potential and compatibility with international marketing goals and objectives) and threats (i.e., barriers or constraints). Once completed, the firm must decide how to enter the foreign markets it has selected.

The selection of the mode of entry into foreign markets depends, partially, on an appraisal of the firm's internal strengths (i.e., distinct competencies or competitive advantages) and weaknesses (i.e., limitations to customer satisfaction). The appraisal of internal strengths and weaknesses, and external opportunities and threats, are four components of a SWOT analysis. This analysis allows a firm to identify those factors most likely to influence its capacity to market internationally.

In addition to the factors identified by the SWOT analysis, other factors more generally related to the modes of entry must be considered. These factors include the firm's financial commitment, exposure to foreign problems, economic and political risk, marketing costs, management control, opportunities for experiential learning, and profit possibilities (Terpstra and Sarathy, 1994). All of these factors **increase** as the firm becomes more directly involved in foreign markets.

## Modes of Entry

From the lowest to the highest level of involvement, the major entry modes are exporting, licensing, joint ventures, and direct ownership. Unlike the other major participants in the U.S. food marketing system, producers rely almost exclusively on exporting as a mode of entry. Manufacturers, on the other hand, use all four modes. Wholesalers and retailers rely mostly on joint ventures and direct ownership.

Three other observations regarding the use of alternative entry modes by food marketing participants can be made. First, to obtain the desired market coverage, firms use different modes in different countries. Second, some modes are not permitted in some countries. Finally, firms change their entry modes to accommodate organizational and environmental changes in foreign markets.

## Exporting

Agriculture commodities and processed foods can be exported to other countries. This mode is not only the simplest to use, but also the least likely to disrupt the internal operations of a firm. A firm may engage in either indirect or direct exporting.

### *Indirect Exporting*

This type of exporting takes place when a firm uses intermediaries to sell its domestically produced commodity or processed food in foreign markets. These sales may be handled by different marketing intermediaries. Foreign firms maintain buying offices in the U.S. and purchase through them. Export management companies (EMCs) handle the entire exporting activities of other firms. Cooperative associations function as the exporting department of all member firms so as to achieve economies of scale. Regardless of the intermediary used, cooperative associations handle the export tasks of U.S. firms.

### *Direct Exporting*

This type of exporting takes place when firms perform the exporting task. This is the most common form of exporting and requires substantially more involvement than indirect exporting. Using this mode of entry, firms must conduct market research, choose their foreign markets, prepare export documentation, determine how to gain representation in the market selected, and distribute the commodities or food products to these markets. Representation can be gained by establishing a sales subsidiary or by using a local representative such as a foreign-based distributor or agent.

## Licensing

Under licensing, a firm (licensor) offers a licensee something of value in exchange for certain performance and a royalty or fee. The item of value may be a trademark, patent, copyright, or manufacturing process. In return, the licensee agrees to produce, sell, distribute, or otherwise market the product. The royalty payment or fee is based, typically, on some measure of sale volume.

### Contract Manufacturing

This special form of licensing takes place when a firm's product is produced under contract by a manufacturer located in a foreign market. Although the firm gives up some control over the manufacturing process, it avoids all the problems involved in operating a manufacturing facility.

## Joint Ventures

In international investment terms, a joint venture is a company created by a U.S. firm and a local business. The ownership rights of each firm result in shared control and profitability. This mode of entry is available to wholesalers and retailers, as well as to manufacturers. Because the level of involvement is considerable, this mode of entry results in increased exposure to foreign problems and risks, both political and economic. However, legal restrictions in many countries make this the only mode of entry allowed.

## Direct Ownership

The highest level of involvement in foreign markets takes place when a domestic firm owns a foreign subsidiary or division. A firm can either acquire a foreign firm or develop its own facilities. The firm's financial commitment, exposure to foreign problems, political and economic risk, and marketing costs all increase substantially. But the increased management control, profitability and opportunity to acquire greater experience in international operations outweigh its disadvantages. In food manufacturing, the sales from foreign affiliates of U.S. firms have long exceeded the value of processed food exports. In 1994, alone, sales from foreign affiliates were four times the value of that year's U.S. processed food exports.

There is a special risk in this mode of entry that doesn't exist in the other modes. It is called **expropriation** and occurs when a country seizes ownership of a foreign affiliate. Because it represents a total loss to the domestic firm, it is critically important that firms assess accurately the political risk inherent in foreign markets.

In summary, the best mode of entry for a firm depends upon an accurate appraisal of a firm's internal strengths and weaknesses, its external opportunities and threats, and the factors more generally related to the modes of entry. In some cases, different modes are used in different countries to gain the desired market coverage. In other cases, some modes are prohibited in certain countries.

# INTERNATIONAL MARKETING

It should be apparent, from the discussion of entry modes to foreign markets, that the influence entry modes have on the marketing activities of domestic firms varies greatly. At one extreme, firms using indirect exporting delegate the marketing tasks to outside firms. At the other extreme, firms using direct ownership (affiliates) perform all marketing related functions.

In order to gain the greatest insights into decision making in foreign markets, the following section examines international marketing from the perspective of wholly-owned affiliates operated by U.S. food manufacturers. This perspective was chosen because (1) food producers export virtually their entire output, while sales from food manufacturing affiliates are four times the value of processed food exports. (2) food manufacturers play a pivotal role in bringing about change in foreign market foodways, and (3) food manufacturers have the fundamental responsibility to create food products capable of satisfying customer needs.

## Marketing Strategy

The most critical question that firms have to address in international marketing is "Should they extend their existing marketing strategies (i.e., product, price, promotion, and place) or adapt them for each foreign market?" Because international marketing focuses on satisfying the needs of consumers in foreign countries, the answer to the question will depend upon the degree to which cultural differences in foodways (i.e., shopping, purchase and consumption behaviors) are significant and fixed.

Cultural differences in tastes and preferences are of particular interest to food manufacturers. In general, it is unlikely that food manufacturers can market their products without some form of modification to suit local tastes and preferences. But is it possible that these often deeply ingrained local preferences for taste, flavor, consistency, and aftertaste can or will be changed over time? Yes! There appears to be ample evidence that some manufacturers, as well as foodservice retailers, have successfully created worldwide demand for their products. Consider the cases of **Coca-Cola Co.**, **PepsiCo.**, **Kellogg Co.**, **Nestle SA**, **Kraft Foods**, **Campbell's**, **Hershey's Chocolate U.S.A.**, **Sara Lee Corp.**, **H.J. Heinz Co.**, **Anheuser-Busch**, **Borden Inc.**, and **General Mills**; they all offer globally standardized products sold all over the world. These and many other manufacturers has been successful at **bending** foreign demand to meet supply.

The international retail foodservice sector offers even more evidence of domestically formulated product acceptance around the world. In 1995, the top fifty U.S. foodservice chains increased their collective store count by 15.6 percent to 25,921, and their sales by 20.1 percent to 27.3 billion dollars. McDonald's generated about 14 billion dollars of these sales. Taken together, the top five chains, **McDonald's, KFC, Pizza Hut, Burger King**, and **Wendy's** accounted for eighty-two percent of the top fifty food chains sales. **KFC** alone generated more than 50 percent of its sales from foreign operations (Coeyman, 1996).

The successes of these food manufacturers and foodservice chains in foreign markets are not exceptional examples. Rather, they exemplify how, with the right marketing strategies, cultural differences in food consumption can be altered and consequently result in homogeneous demand for globally standardized food products. The major decisions food manufacturers face when marketing their products domestically were examined at length in Chapter 5 and will not be repeated here. Instead, the following discussion will concentrate on the issues food manufacturing affiliates face when marketing in foreign countries.

## Product

International food marketing involves satisfying foreign consumer needs for food. Therefore, the most fundamental product decision made by a firm is whether these needs can be satisfied by (1) a domestically formulated and standardized product from the U.S., (2) a product modified to meet local taste preferences, or (3) an entirely new product. Once again, the decision will depend upon the degree to which cultural differences in consumption behaviors are significant and fixed. As seen earlier, companies like **Coca-Cola Co.** and **Kellogg Co.** have been successful with standardized products. **Campbell's** modifies some of its soups to meet local tastes, and **General Foods** alters its coffee blends. **Nestlé** has created new cereal products for the Japanese markets, as has **Kellogg's** with its **Germai Flakes**.

Another important issue is how to protect a company's brands and trademarks in foreign markets. Brands and trademarks must go through a national registration process to be protected. There are three major international trademark conventions that firms may use to gain protection: the **Paris Union**, the **Madrid Arrangement for International Registration of Trademarks**, or the **Inter-American Convention for Trademark Protection** (Terpstra and Sarathy, 1994).

Brand ownership is established by use in common law countries, like the U.S., and by priority of registration in code law countries, as in Europe. In the latter, a manufacturer may be prevented from using the brand name because another firm has already registered the name. Or in the case of **brand piracy,** someone may have deliberately registered the name with the intent to sell it back to a food manufacturer for a sum of money. To compound the situation, many countries require that firms pay a fee periodically to maintain their brand protection rights.

A third issue involves the packaging of food products. Package design must consider the food container in use and storage. In the former, the package must be easy to open and must effectively dispense the contents. In the latter, the package must maintain the quality of the contents for a precise time period. Size and shape are other important aspects of packaging. The availability of space to store products under varying levels of temperature (i.e., room temperature to freezing) is not the same in all countries. In many countries, space restrictions require smaller packages. At the same time, as seen in the case of Mexican consumers, they result in significant numbers of visits to retail food stores—eleven visits per week. Package design must also consider the shipping package. Most food is shipped in corrugated cardboard boxes. The boxes, like the food container, must be designed to meet foreign market climate, transportation routes, storage and handling requirements.

In addition to meeting the functional requirements of package design, the package must promote the sale of the food item. The package in self-service food stores is the **"silent salesperson."** Particular attention must be paid to cultural taboos in shapes, sizes, colors and language. Language presents a special problem because in many countries several languages may be spoken. To be effective, the promotional aspects of the package must accommodate the language diversities found among, and within, nations.

Food product labeling represents another product issue. In general, most foreign governments specify by law what must appear on labels: brand name, manufacturer, ingredients, weight, and country of origin. For many consumers, the product's country of origin has special meaning, which may either enhance or detract from its value. The variability in language and legal requirements results in the extensive production of nonstandardized labels and further adds to the complexity of product decisions for foreign markets.

## Place

A wholly owned affiliate operated by a U.S. food manufacturer must select its distribution channels. The variability in the number, size, and service offered by wholesalers and retailers preclude most manufacturers from simply replicating their domestic distribution channels in foreign countries. However, as mentioned previously, an analysis of a country institutional environment reveals its distribution and transportation infrastructures. In general, the distribution infrastructures of developed countries are dominated by large-scale wholesalers and retail distributors. On the other hand, the developing countries in Africa, Asia, Latin America, and Oceania are dominated by small-scale distributors.

There are exceptions to this generalization; Italy and Japan are examples. The number of grocery stores per one thousand inhabitants in 1990 was the highest in Italy (2.5), followed by Japan (1.9). Other developed countries such as the U.S. (.7), Canada (1.0), Great Britain (.9), France (.8) and Germany (1.0) have far fewer, but larger, retail operations per one thousand inhabitants (*Food Business,* 1993).

The special distribution problems facing U.S. firms may be illustrated by the distribution infrastructure of Japan. On the wholesale level, products flow through a number of layers of middlemen: one, two, or for some food products, even three. Further, its specialty stores selling products such as produce, meat, bakery products, and seafood remain overwhelmingly large in number, but small in size. For each type of specialty store, there exist corresponding specialty-line wholesalers. In Japan, there are no equivalent wholesalers the size of **Fleming** or **Super-Value** in the

U.S.—just large numbers of small wholesalers selling to large numbers of small retailers (Kikuchi, 1994).

Similar patterns can be found in Mexico. Despite the entry of such large firms as **Wal-Mart** and **K-Mart**, the Mexican distribution system is still characterized by large numbers of specialized wholesalers and retailers. Although Mexican consumers shop most often at a **supermarket** (fifty-nine percent) they restrict their purchases mostly to processed foods. They visit **corner stores** (thirteen percent) for high-frequency purchases such as beverages, milk, and eggs; **corner markets** (twenty-two percent) for fresh fish, flowers, and fruits and vegetables, and **specialty stores** (5 percent) for fresh items such as bread, beef, pork, and chicken (*Trends*, 1996).

## Promotion

Probably no other aspect of marketing has led to more confusion and mishaps than advertising. Although the goals of advertising—to inform, remind, and persuade—are the same in foreign markets as they are in the U.S., advertising and sales promotion practices vary to accommodate numerous constraints faced in these countries. One of the major issues involves the manufacturer's ability to create influential communication in the language of the country. In some countries, this task is made more complex because more than one language is spoken. The task is made easier when language overlaps from one country to another. Whatever the case may be, it is some consolation to food manufacturers that the English language continues to be the preferred language of business in many countries.

The communication infrastructure of the country defines both the availability of its media and its advertising agencies. The access that consumers have to broadcast media (e.g., television and radio) and print media (e.g., magazines and newspaper) is vastly restricted in developing countries. Furthermore, the illiteracy rate in some of the developing countries has led to a growing use of visuals.

Countries also differ in the availability of services provided by ad agencies. For this reason, there has been a trend toward international agencies. Many U.S. agencies maintain agencies abroad to handle the increasing numbers of clients marketing internationally. **Table 13-13** shows the top ten U.S. advertising agencies. Each of them is an international agency, and foreign billing for all of them exceeds one-half of their total billings. **McCann-Erickson** leads the U.S. agencies in worldwide gross incomes, foreign gross income, and share of foreign income to total income.

Government controls also impact on the ability of firms to communicate in foreign markets. Regulations in many countries restrict access to certain media by disallowing commercials. These same regulations also define the parameters of advertising content, (what can and cannot be said), as well as the truthfulness of what is said. Laws in foreign countries also affect the size, nature, and value of sales promotion premiums. Usually, the premium is restricted to a percent of the product's value and must be related to the intended use of the product. Further, because all sales promotions are dependent on foreign retailers' willingness and ability to participate, many promotional events go unused for lack of space or appropriate facilities and equipment to handle them.

Ever mindful of these constraints, a food manufacturer must make several advertising decisions. First, the firm must decide whether to use an international agency with domestic and overseas offices or a local agency in each market. To reduce the cost inherent in the duplication of creative efforts, many food manufacturers prefer international agencies—U.S. or otherwise—over local agencies.

Second, the firm must decide whether to use an international standardized appeal, or a localized appeal in individual markets. In addition to the previously mentioned constraints, firms must examine the marketplace of consumers. International appeals are more likely to be used when international market segments exist. That is, when market profiles have counterparts in other nations, there is likely to be similarity in buyer motivations and product usage. Common motivations and product usage lend themselves to standardized appeals.

The media that most effectively carry the message to the target market must also be selected. Once again, the choice is between international or national (local) media. Even though international magazines, newspapers, radio and commercial T.V. exist, most firms rely more on national media. In general, the range of national media is greater as is their adaptation to local markets. Additionally, their momentum (i.e., frequency and timing) is typically more flexible than those of the international media.

One final issue is of particular concern to food manufacturers making international promotion decisions: How can the effectiveness of advertising be measured? In many countries information regarding the shopping, purchase, and consumption behavior of consumers is not gathered. In countries where it is available, the reliability is questionable because so much has been gathered using non-scientific convenience samples. Finally, unlike Americans who are accustomed to being asked for their opinions, foreign consumers, as well as business people, are generally suspicious of anyone asking questions. This suspicion results in reluctance to respond to marketing research inquires.

## Price

Pricing in a foreign market, like other marketing decisions, is determined by the same factors discussed in the domestic marketing section. The most obvious influence on a product's price is its cost. The effect of inflation on costs is of particular concern to food manufacturers because many foreign countries experience inflation rates greater than the U.S. rate. Pricing for inflationary markets requires firms to estimate future costs of manufacturing, marketing, and distribution. Firms must also contend with the strong possibility that sales will erode because consumers tend to maintain the amount spent for food, regardless of rising prices.

The effect of product costs takes on special importance when a manufacturer imports some or all of its ingredients from other countries, or its own U.S. operations. In the latter, the manufacturer's costs represent a **transfer price**. If the ingredients are sold at a low transfer price in a country whose tax level is lower than in the U.S., or at a high transfer price in a country where the tax level is higher than in the U.S., the respective affiliates will profit from the differences in tax levels.

The most significant supply-related factor influencing price is the competitive environment. The nature of competition is best perceived as an attempt by all firms to reduce or eliminate each other's differential advantage. The chief competitors of food manufacturers are, in most cases, U.S.-based multinational companies. Firms like **Kellogg's, Nestlé, Coca-Cola Co.**, and **PepsiCo** all compete in the international arena. Although the combatants may be the same, the intensity of competition varies from country to country. One additional dimension of competition must be considered. **Gray marketing**, which in the U.S. approximates what is known as **diverting**, is the unauthorized exportation of a product intended for sale in one market but sold in another, higher-priced market. This practice affects the nature of competition (i.e., it becomes more price-oriented) and impacts negatively on the motivation of distributors to carry a firm's product.

Another influence on price is governmental. In addition to the legal restrictions peculiar to these countries, their ability to set price controls is their most visible means of intrusion into the marketplace. In many countries, firms can't raise prices at will, but rather must petition the government for approval. Because food products are essential for survival, governments have vested interests in maintaining stable prices, even in the face of inflationary environments.

Distribution channels influence product prices because manufacturers incur costs due to the logistical functions they must perform, and the margins required by wholesalers and retailers of their products. These costs and margins vary from country to country and result in different prices in different markets.

Promotional decisions also influence a product's price. The cost of maintaining a product position through advertising and sales promotion must be accounted for when the price to the consumer is determined. As mentioned previously, media costs vary among countries. Final consumer prices reflect, in part, these international variations.

The consumer's interest in value is the final influence on a product's price. Consumer value is reflected by the ratio of perceived benefits to perceived price. The perceived price of a food product is made up of a monetary cost and a time cost to make a food edible. Demand for a food product exists, and consumer value is positive, as long as the perceived benefits are equal to or greater than these costs. However, demand for a food product is likely to vary from country to country because consumers value a product differently. These value differences may be caused by variations in subjective estimates of a product's ability to provide certain benefits. They may also result from variations in the importance attached to monetary and time costs. In general, money-rich, time-poor consumers place more importance on time, than do money-poor, time-rich consumers. These latter consumers place more importance on money. Whether due to variations in perceived benefits or perceived prices, differences in value lead to differences in demand, and together with inflation, costs, competition, government, distribution channels, and promotional decisions, influence the final price to the consumer in foreign markets.

## SUMMARY

This final chapter examined the international dimensions of the U.S. food marketing system. Total exports exceeded total imports, resulting in a surplus of twenty-two billion dollars in 1995. When this surplus was analyzed by the type of export/import, bulk products accounted for 19.5 billion dollars or eighty-nine percent of the surplus, intermediate products accounted for four billion dollars of the surplus, and consumer-oriented products produced a 1.6 billion dollar deficit.

Where did all these exports go? Thirty-five countries received eighty-eight percent of all U.S. exports, with the largest share going to Japan (twenty percent). Where did all these imports come from? Thirty-five countries shipped ninety-three percent of all U.S. imports. Canada supplied the greatest share of imports (nineteen percent). When these exports and imports were analyzed by type, the findings did not change. Japan received the greatest share of bulk, intermediate, and consumer-oriented products. Canada shipped to the U.S. the largest percentage of bulk, intermediate, and consumer-oriented products.

Processed food exports and imports were analyzed from a different perspective of value added. The U.S. went from a 323 million dollar deficit in 1991 to a 4.6 billion dollar surplus in 1995. Historically, the U.S. has maintained a surplus in three census industry groups: meats, grain mill products, and fats and oils. Five industries have historically maintained a deficit: miscellaneous foods, beverages, sugar and confectionery, bakery products, and preserved fruits and vegetables. Dairy products, the last industry group, have not maintained either a consistent surplus or deficit. When these industry groups were analyzed by their respective industries, ten leading industries accounted for sixty-six percent of all U.S. processed food exports, while ten leading industries accounted for seventy-five percent of all U.S. processed food imports.

U.S. firms have also entered foreign markets by acquiring or building manufacturing, wholesaling, or retailing affiliates. Food manufacturing sales accounted for the majority of foreign affiliate sales (seventy-two percent). The share of sales from wholesale and retail affiliates were nineteen and nine percent, respectively.

To position themselves strategically in the international U.S. food marketing system, U.S. firms make three decisions. First, they identify which foreign markets to enter. By examining the economic, political, legal, technological, competitive, institutional, and cultural environments in each prospective foreign market. Of all these environments, the single most important one is a country's economic development. In general, the greater the level of economic development, the more modern its transportation, distribution, and communication infrastructures are, the more attractive its markets.

Once these foreign markets have been identified and evaluated for opportunities or threats, a mode of entry is selected. The mode selected will depend, in part, on a firm's appraisal of its strengths and weaknesses, and other factors more generally related to the modes of entry. From the lowest to the highest level of involvement, the major modes of entry are exporting, licensing, joint ventures, and direct ownership. Whether direct or indirect, exporting is the simplest mode of entry. Licensing involves the exchange of something of value (e.g., trademarks, copyrights, or patents) for a royalty or fee. A joint venture is a company created by a U.S. and local firm. The highest level of involvement requires the acquisition or development of a subsidiary or affiliate. Which method is chosen by a firm depends upon an appraisal of external opportunities and threats in the foreign markets, and the internal strengths and weaknesses of a firm.

Finally, marketing programs must be designed. In order to gain the greatest insight into program design in foreign markets, marketing mix issues were examined from the perspective of a wholly owned food manufacturing affiliate. The most critical issue facing an affiliate is whether to extend its existing domestic marketing strategy or to adapt it for each foreign market. There is sufficient evidence to show that some products have a worldwide demand. At the same time, there is evidence to show that cultural differences in foodway consumption behaviors require new or adapted food products. In the final analysis, the success of either approach depends upon the degree to which cultural differences in foodways (i.e., shopping, purchasing, and consumption behaviors) are significant and fixed. The more significant and fixed the differences, the greater the need for products that accommodate these differences. The tremendous success that U.S. foodservice chains have had in other countries provides ample evidence that these differences are changing and may result in global demand for standardized food products.

# CONCLUSION

The main reason for writing this book was to reduce our collective ignorance regarding the U.S. food marketing system. To accomplish this goal, I began with four objectives in mind.

First, the book had to provide the reader with a comprehensive perspective of the U.S. food marketing system. To meet this objective, the text began at the point of production and ended at the point of consumption.

Second, the book had to describe the system's organizational structure and how it has changed over time. To meet this objective, the text analyzed the structural trends in the producer, manufacturer, wholesaler, and retail sectors over three census periods: 1982, 1987, and 1992. Whenever possible, these trends were extended by industry data.

Third, because customer satisfaction represents the output of the system, the book had to identify how the system creates customer satisfaction. To meet this objective, the text explored the marketing decisions made by producers, manufacturers, wholesalers, and retailers to create, price, promote, and distribute food products. Additionally, the text examined the shopping, purchasing, and consumption behaviors of food consumers and how a lifestyle model can be used to segment consumers into viable target markets.

Fourth, customer satisfaction extends beyond our national borders. Thus, the text had to recognize the internationalization of the U.S. food marketing system. To meet this objective, the book analyzed international trade in bulk, intermediate/processed, and consumer-oriented food products. In addition, the process used to enter foreign markets and the marketing decisions of manufacturers in these markets, were examined in detail.

Finally, any attempt to summarize what the U.S. food marketing system will look like in the future would be an exercise in futility. However, one thing is certain. Consumers will continue to demand that the system accommodate their ever-changing lifestyles. Historically, the U.S. food marketing system has met this challenge. There is no reason to believe it will not continue to do so in the future.

## SELECTED REFERENCES

Coeyman, M. "Over There" *Restaurant Business*, September 1, 1996, pp. 69–76.

Epps, W. and J. M. Harris. *Processed Food Trade Concordance.* ERS, U.S. Department of Agriculture, Agricultural Handbook No. 707, March 1995.

Kikuchi, T. *Japanese Distribution Channels.* Binghamton, N.Y.: Food Products Press, an Imprint of the Haworth Press, Inc., 1994.

Porter, M. E. *The Competitive Advantage of Nations.* New York: The Free Press 1990

Terpstra, V. and R. Sarathy. *International Marketing.* 6th ed. Fort Worth, Tex.: The Dryden Press, Harcourt Brace College Publishers, 1994.

# REVIEW QUESTIONS

1. What is the anatomy of the U.S. surplus in food products?

2. How has the U.S. performed in the international trade of processed foods?

3. How would you summarize the performance of U.S. affiliates in foreign countries?

4. To identify opportunities and threats in foreign markets, a firm should assess the nature of those environments. Explain.

5. Select a foreign market and assess its environment and explain how you would market a product (your choice) in this market.

6. The selection of a mode of entry into a foreign market depends, partially, on an appraisal of a firm's internal strengths and weaknesses. Explain.

7. Explain the modes of entry from an involvement perspective.

8. What is the most critical question a firm must address before marketing internationally?

9. What is meant by the statement, "A multinational corporation focuses on cultural differences, whereas, a global corporation focuses on cultural similarities."

10. Is there any evidence to suggest that cultural differences in food consumption behaviors can be changed to result in homogeneous demand for globally standardized products?

**TABLE 13-1.** TOTAL EXPORTS AND IMPORTS*

|  | MILLIONS OF DOLLARS | | | | |
|---|---|---|---|---|---|
|  | 1991 | 1992 | 1993 | 1994 | 1995 |
| EXPORTS | 42,140.9 | 46,168.5 | 45,437.6 | 48,691.6 | 58,936.6 |
| IMPORTS | 28,282.0 | 30,168.9 | 30,663.6 | 33,334.0 | 36,657.8 |
| SURPLUS/ (DEFICIT) | 13,858.9 | 15,999.6 | 14,774.0 | 15,357.6 | 22,278.8 |

*INCLUDES EDIBLE FISH AND SEAFOOD IN CONSUMER-ORIENTED CATEGORY.

*SOURCE:* U.S. BUREAU OF CENSUS TRADE DATA (FAS), 1996.


**TABLE 13-2.** MARKET SHARE EXPORTS/IMPORTS*

|  | 1991 | 1992 | 1993 | 1994 | 1995 |
|---|---|---|---|---|---|
| EXPORTS: | | | | | |
| Bulk | 43.5 | 42.6 | 40.9 | 38.9 | 44.1 |
| Intermediate | 20.9 | 20.0 | 19.7 | 20.0 | 18.7 |
| Consumer-oriented | 35.6 | 37.4 | 39.6 | 41.1 | 37.2 |
| TOTAL | 100.0 | 100.0 | 100.0 | 100.0 | 100.0 |
| IMPORTS: | | | | | |
| Bulk | 16.8 | 17.9 | 17.6 | 17.6 | 17.6 |
| Intermediate | 17.6 | 16.0 | 15.5 | 15.3 | 18.2 |
| Consumer-oriented | 68.6 | 66.1 | 66.9 | 67.1 | 63.2 |
| TOTAL | 100.0 | 100.0 | 100.0 | 100.0 | 100.0 |

*EDIBLE FISH AND SEAFOOD INCLUDED IN CONSUMER-ORIENTED EXPORTS AND IMPORTS.

*SOURCE:* U.S. BUREAU OF CENSUS TRADE DATA (FAS), 1996.

**TABLE 13-3.** EXPORTS AND IMPORTS BY VALUE ADDED*

|  | MILLIONS OF DOLLARS | | | | |
|---|---|---|---|---|---|
|  | **1991** | **1992** | **1993** | **1994** | **1995** |
| BULK: | | | | | |
| Exports | 18,348.4 | 19,687.3 | 18,593.5 | 18,951.5 | 26,018.6 |
| Imports | 4,737.3 | 5,404.6 | 5,397.8 | 5,872.9 | 6,445.2 |
| Surplus/(Deficit) | 13,611.1 | 14,282.7 | 13,195.7 | 13,078.6 | 19,573.4 |
| INTERMEDIATE: | | | | | |
| Exports | 8,789.2 | 9,231.1 | 8,973.5 | 9,749.7 | 10,992.1 |
| Imports | 4,118.4 | 4,813.8 | 4,748.4 | 5,102.7 | 6,643.0 |
| Surplus/(Deficit) | 4,670.8 | 4,417.3 | 4,225.1 | 4,647.0 | 4,349.1 |
| CONSUMER-ORIENTED: | | | | | |
| Exports | 15,003.3 | 17,250.0 | 17,870.5 | 19,990.4 | 21,925.8 |
| Imports | 19,426.3 | 19,950.5 | 20,517.4 | 22,358.3 | 23,569.6 |
| Surplus/(Deficit) | (4,423.0) | (2,700.5) | (2,649.9) | (2,367.9) | (1,643.8) |

*INCLUDES EDIBLE FISH AND SEAFOOD IN CONSUMER-ORIENTED CATEGORY.

*SOURCE:* U.S. BUREAU OF CENSUS TRADE DATE (FAS), 1996.

**TABLE 13-4.** U.S. PROCESSED FOODS

|  | MILLIONS OF DOLLARS | | | | |
| --- | --- | --- | --- | --- | --- |
|  | 1991 | 1992 | 1993 | 1994 | 1995 |
| EXPORTS | 20,272 | 22,805 | 23,412 | 26,249 | 29,390 |
| IMPORTS | 20,600 | 21,751 | 21,815 | 23,801 | 24,821 |
| SURPLUS/(DEFICIT) | (323) | 1,055 | 1,597 | 2,448 | 4,569 |

*SOURCE:* ECONOMIC RESEARCH SERVICE, USDA, 1996.

**TABLE 13-5.** U.S. TRADE BALANCE IN PROCESSED FOODS BY INDUSTRY GROUPS*

|  | MILLIONS OF DOLLARS | | | | |
| --- | --- | --- | --- | --- | --- |
| INDUSTRY GROUP | 1991 | 1992 | 1993 | 1994 | 1995 |
| Meat products | 1,984 | 2,779 | 2,695 | 3,834 | 5,635 |
| Dairy products | (146) | 50 | 183 | 11 | (70) |
| Preserved fruits and vegetables | (439) | (414) | (119) | (17) | 211 |
| Grain mill products | 2,639 | 2,801 | 3,026 | 3,099 | 3,258 |
| Bakery products | (148) | (116) | (115) | (156) | (221) |
| Sugared confectioneries | (1,043) | (1,036) | (798) | (685) | (865) |
| Fats and oils | 1,640 | 1,739 | 1,619 | 1,693 | 2,332 |
| Beverages | (2,023) | (2,385) | (2,101) | (1,953) | (2,050) |
| Misc. foods (including seafood) | (2,787) | (2,418) | (2,793) | (3,378) | (3,661) |

*SURPLUS/(DEFICIT)

*SOURCE:* ECONOMIC RESEARCH SERVICE, USDA, 1996.

**TABLE 13-6.** SALES GENERATED BY OUTBOUND AND INBOUND FOREIGN DIRECT INVESTMENT

| SALES BY U.S. OWNED AFFILIATES ABROAD ($millions) | | | | | |
|---|---|---|---|---|---|
| SECTOR | 1982 | 1987 | 1992 | 1993 | Percentage of total |
| Food manufacturing | 39,023 | 50,067 | 89,159 | 95,782 | 72.3 |
| Food wholesaling | 6,172 | 9,206 | 14,388 | 15,783 | 11.9 |
| Food stores | 8,691* | 9,674* | 21,169* | 11,930 | 9.0 |
| Food service | | | | 9,007 | 6.8 |
| TOTAL | 53,886 | 68,947 | 124,716 | 132,502 | 100.0 |

| SALES OF U.S. AFFILIATES OF FOREIGN FIRMS ($millions) | | | | | |
|---|---|---|---|---|---|
| SECTOR | 1982 | 1987 | 1992 | 1993 | Percentage of total |
| Food manufacturing | 14,847 | 22,862 | 46,799 | 45,765 | 36.8 |
| Food wholesaling | 7,039 | 13,953 | 18,984 | 21,734 | 17.5 |
| Food stores | 18,758* | 24,318 | 48,159 | 51,537 | 41.5 |
| Food service | | 498 | 4,904 | 5,236 | 4.2 |
| TOTAL | 40,644 | 61,625 | 118,846 | 124,172 | 100.0 |

* INCLUDES FOODSERVICE SALES

*SOURCE:* U.S DEPARTMENT OF COMMERCE, BUREAU OF ECONOMIC ANALYSIS, 1995.

**TABLE 13-7.** IMPORTANCE OF STORE CHOICE CRITERIA

| CRITERIA | PERCENTAGE OF CONSUMERS RATING *VERY IMPORTANT* | |
|---|---|---|
| | CANADA | MEXICO |
| High-quality fruits and vegetables | 99 | 95 |
| Clean, neat store | 98 | 96 |
| Low prices | 96 | 94 |
| Wide variety and selections | 96 | 90 |
| Courteous, friendly employees | 95 | 86 |
| Convenient location | 93 | 85 |
| Good quality meat | 92 | 95 |
| Fast checkout | 91 | 89 |
| Readable, accurate shelf tabs | 90 | N/A |
| Sales, money saving specials | 88 | 84 |
| Fresh-food selections | 85 | 89 |
| Attention to special requests | 82 | 82 |
| Environmentally friendly products | 81 | 88 |
| Good selection of non-food items | 66 | 76 |
| Store brands | 59 | 54 |
| Natural and organic foods | 54 | 89 |
| Personal safety outside store | N/A | 94 |

N/A = NOT ASKED

SOURCE: TRENDS IN CANADA IN 1995, TRENDS IN MEXICO IN 1996, FOOD MARKETING INSTITUTE.

**TABLE 13-8.** EVALUATION OF PRIMARY STORE

| | PERCENTAGE OF CONSUMERS RATING *EXCELLENT* OR *GOOD* | |
|---|---|---|
| CRITERIA | CANADA | MEXICO |
| High-quality fruits and vegetables | 85 | 78 |
| Clean, neat store | 95 | 85 |
| Low prices | 79 | 61 |
| Wide variety and selection | 91 | 81 |
| Courteous friendly employees | 91 | 80 |
| Convenient location | 92 | 85 |
| Good quality meat | 84 | 78 |
| Fast checkout | 78 | 54 |
| Readable, accurate shelf tabs | 78 | N/A |
| Sales, money-saving specials | 84 | 65 |
| Fresh-food sections | 83 | 85 |
| Attention to special requests | 73 | 76 |
| Environmentally friendly products | N/A | 76 |
| Good selection of non-food items | 74 | 79 |
| Store brands | 82 | 60 |
| Natural and organic foods | N/A | 73 |
| Personal safety outside store | N/A | 83 |

N/A = NOT ASKED

SOURCE: TRENDS IN CANADA IN 1995, TRENDS IN MEXICO IN 1996, FOOD MARKETING INSTITUTE.

**TABLE 13-9.** RANK ORDER OF REASONS FOR STORE SWITCHING

|  | RANK ORDER | |
| --- | --- | --- |
| REASONS | MEXICO | CANADA |
| Better/lower prices | 1 | 1 |
| New store more conveniently located | 2 | 2 |
| More variety/selections | 3 | 3 |
| Moved changed residence | 8 | 4 |
| Better quality products | 5 | 5 |
| New store opened | 3 | N/A |
| Special offers/promotions | 4 | N/A |
| Better produce | 9 | 5 |
| Employee attitude/competence | 8 | 5 |
| New store cleaner | 6 | 6 |

N/A = NOT ASKED

SOURCE: TRENDS IN CANADA IN 1995, TRENDS IN MEXICO IN 1996, FOOD MARKETING INSTITUTE.

**TABLE 13-10.** SHOPPING FREQUENCY AT PRIMARY STORE

| NUMBER OF VISITS PER WEEK | PERCENT OF SHOPPERS | |
|---|---|---|
| | MEXICO | CANADA |
| ONE | 5 | 38 |
| TWO | 5 | 31 |
| THREE | | 14 |
| FOUR | 11 | 5 |
| FIVE | | 3 |
| SIX | 8 | |
| SEVEN | 5 | |
| EIGHT TO TEN | 21 | 4 |
| ELEVEN TO FOURTEEN | 14 | |
| MORE THAN FOURTEEN | 31 | |
| AVERAGE NUMBER OF VISITS PER WEEK | 10.7 | 2 |

*SOURCE:* TRENDS IN CANADA IN 1995, TRENDS IN MEXICO IN 1996, FOOD MARKETING INSTITUTE.

**TABLE 13-11.** NUTRITIONAL ATTITUDES

| | PERCENT OF SHOPPERS | |
|---|---|---|
| LEVEL OF NUTRITIONAL CONCERN | CANADA | MEXICO |
| Very concerned | 53 | 94 |
| Somewhat concerned | 40 | 5 |
| Not very concerned | 5 | |
| None concerned | 2 | 1 |
| NATURE OF NUTRITIONAL CONCERN: | | |
| Fat content | 47 | 6 |
| Sugar content | 4 | * |
| Cholesterol levels | 14 | 3 |
| Chemical additives | 13 | * |
| Salt/sodium content | 11 | * |
| Vitamin/mineral content | 8 | 52 |
| Protein value | 2 | 32 |
| Freshness/no spoilage | 7 | 15 |
| Food/nutritional value | 9 | 10 |
| Low calories | 7 | 10 |
| Natural/not processed | 4 | 10 |
| PRIMARY RESPONSIBILITY FOR NUTRITION: | | |
| Consumers | 39 | 54 |
| Manufacturing | 21 | 15 |
| Retailers | 9 | 9 |
| Consumer organizations | 7 | 5 |
| Government | 12 | 7 |
| Farmers | 2 | 3 |
| All the above | 7 | N/A |

N/A = NOT ASKED

* NOT MENTIONED BY ANY RESPONDENT

*SOURCE:* TRENDS IN CANADA IN 1995, TRENDS IN MEXICO IN 1996, FOOD MARKETING.

**TABLE 13-12.** FOOD SAFETY ATTITUDES

| | PERCENT OF SHOPPERS | |
|---|---|---|
| **CONFIDENCE IN FOOD SAFETY:** | CANADA | MEXICO |
| Completely confident | 21 | 18 |
| Mostly confident | 60 | 64 |
| Somewhat confident | 15 | 17 |
| Very doubtful | 2 | — |
| Not sure | 1 | 0 |
| PERCEIVED THREATS TO FOOD SAFETY: | | |
| Freshness/expiration | 24 | 23 |
| Chemicals | 15 | 4 |
| Bacteria/germs contamination | 13 | 4 |
| Pesticide residues | 13 | * |
| Improper handling/storage | 11 | 36 |
| Cleanliness | N/A | 7 |
| Preservatives | 6 | 6 |
| Spoilage | 6 | 5 |
| RESPONSIBILITY FOR FOOD SAFETY: | | |
| Self | 34 | 58 |
| Retailer | 19 | 6 |
| Manufacturers | 16 | 13 |
| Government | 15 | 6 |
| Consumer organizations | 6 | 5 |
| Farmers | 2 | 5 |
| All of the above | N/A | N/A |

N/A = NOT ASKED

*NOT MENTIONED BY ANY RESPONDENT

SOURCES: TRENDS IN CANADA IN 1995, TRENDS IN MEXICO IN 1996, FOOD MARKETING INSTITUTE.

**TABLE 13-13.** TOP TEN U.S. ADVERTISING AGENCIES - 1995

| TOP RANK | AGENCY | WORLDWIDE GROSS INCOME ($millions) | FOREIGN GROSS INCOME ($millions) | FOREIGN SHARE (%) |
|---|---|---|---|---|
| 1 | McCann-Erickson Worldwide | 1,196 | 874 | 73 |
| 2 | BBDD Worldwide | 1,140 | 679 | 60 |
| 3 | Young & Rubican | 1,122 | 650 | 58 |
| 4 | J. Walter Thompson Co. | 1,049 | 660 | 63 |
| 5 | DDB Needham Worldwide | 1,047 | 572 | 55 |
| 6 | Ogilvy & Mather Worldwide | 893 | 617 | 69 |
| 7 | Grey Advertising | 827 | 472 | 57 |
| 8 | Leo Burnett Co. | 804 | 433 | 54 |
| 9 | Saatchi & Saatchi Advertising | 767 | 401 | 52 |
| 10 | Foote, Cone & Belding Communications | 759 | 419 | 55 |

*SOURCE:* COMPUTED FROM *ADVERTISING AGE* APRIL 15, 1996.

# Index

## A

Absolute cost advantage barriers, 45
Active inventory, 265
Activity Based Costing (ABC), 167, 186, 255, 271
Activity costs, 167
Actualizers, 441
Administered channel system, 183
Administered VMS, 20
Advanced Shipping Notices (ASNs), 184, 268
Advertising, 172, 173
Advertising allowances, 175
Advertising-to-sales ratio, 177
Affordable method, 173
Air, 93
All Commodity Volume (ACV), 293
American Farm Bureau Federation, 74
Anheuser-Busch Co., 162
Antecedent states, 435
Appetizers, 472
ASNs, 184
Assort, 250
Assurance, 474
Automated Guided Vehicles (AGVs), 264
Automated Storage and Retrieval Systems (AS/RS), 264
Availability, 92

## B

Backhauling, 185, 256
Backward integration, 19
Balance of trade, 519
Bargaining associations, 83
Barrier, 45
Beverages, 473
Bill back, 258
Biological lag, 84
Biological production period, 39
Biopesticides, 155
Biotechnology, 155
Birdyback, 94
Blueprinting, 474
Boutique layout, 337
Box, 295
Brand advertising, 176
Brand extension, 158
Brand image, 161
Brand name, 161
Brand piracy, 529
Brand's position, 177
Breads, 473
Break bulk, 250
Breakfast products, 339
Breeding stage, 34
Breyer's, 158
Broadliners, 17
Broilers, 34
Brokers, 206
Budweiser, 162
Busch, 162
Buy-side, 258
By-products, 171

## C

Cafeterias, 464
Campbell's Healthy Request, 158
Cannibalize, 158, 340
Capability, 92
Capital cost barriers, 45
Capper-Volstead Act of 1922, 43
Cash, 171
Cash discount, 174
Cash-and-carry, 206
Category management, 165, 186, 252
Catering, 463
Cattle, 82

Census of Manufacturing, 120
Census of Retail Trade, 287
Census of Wholesale Trade, 205
Center of plate, 473
Central terminal markets, 18
Cents-off deals, 179
Channel design, 181
Channel structure, 182
Chicago Board of Trade, 82, 95
Chicago Mercantile Exchange, 82, 95
Christian religions, 428
Closed displays, 352
Co-branding, 164
Coastal carriers, 93
Combination loads, 262
Combine, 73
Commercial group, 458
Commission merchants, 206
Commodity Credit Corporation (CCC), 95
Common carriers, 261
Competitive based objectives, 170
Competitive Differential Advantage (CDA), 330
Competitive-oriented strategy, 170
Competitive parity method, 173
Composite trade area, 333
Computer Aided Marketing Program (CAMP), 82
Computer Assisted Ordering (CAO), 187, 268
Concentration ratio, 123, 214, 291
Consistency, 165
Consolidated movement, 268
Consumer perceived value, 166, 345
Consumer promotions, 172, 173
Consumer purchasing, 390
Consumer unit, 380
Consumers in proximity, 390
Consumers' Goods Pricing Act, 168
Continuity programs, 353
Continuous deal, 188, 258
Continuous replenishment (CR), 187, 268
Continuous-flow fixed path, 266
Contract carriers, 185, 261
Contractual VMS, 19, 183
Convenience food/gasoline stores, 287
Conventional distribution centers, 264
Conventional layout, 337
Conventional supermarkets, 293
Cooperative advertising allowance, 175
Cooperatives, 326
Corporate advertising, 177
Corporate VMS, 19, 182
Cost objects, 256
Cost savings, 188
Cross docking, 268
Cross ruff in/on pack, 178
Cross-promotion, 179
Customer-based objectives, 170
Customer expectations, 475
Customer-oriented strategy, 170

# D

Dangers, 371
Date codes, 162
Deal elasticity, 437
Dealer loader, 175
Decentralized Individual Negotiation (DIM), 82
Dedicated contract carrier, 185
Degree of differentiation, 328
Dehydration, 155
Delicatessens, 287
Demographic, 420
Department of Commerce, 260
Department of Justice, 260
Department of Labor, 260
Department of Transportation, 260
Dependability, 92
Desserts, 473
Developed countries, 518
Developing countries, 518
Direct channel, 182
Direct marketing, 82
Direct Product Costs (DPC), 340
Direct Product Profit (DPP), 271
Direct Store Delivery (DSD), 182, 259
Direct to Store Door (DSD), 16
Discount, 171
Disgust, 372
Display allowances, 175

Distastes, 371
Distributed movement, 268
Distribution center, 184
Distribution specialists, 249
Diverting, 188, 251, 533
Drinking places, 465

## E

Eastern Orthodoxy, 428
Economy supermarkets, 293
Efficient Consumer Response (ECR), 163, 174
Elastic, 76, 77
Electronic Data Interchange (EDI), 187
Electronic Funds Transfer (EFT), 187
Electronic store receiving, 268
Empathy, 474
Entrees, 472
Environmental Protection Agency (EPA), 260
Essential services, 344
Establishments, 109, 287, 464
Everyday low prices (EDLP), 12, 346
Evoked set, 383
Ewes, 33
Exclusive basis, 182
Exclusive use, 185
Expected services, 344
Expropriation, 527
Extended payment terms, 176
Extended supermarkets, 293
External activities, 259

## F

F.O.B. (Free On Board) origin pricing, 171
Failure fees, 175
Farrow only, 32
Farrow to finish, 32
Farrowing, 32
Fast food, 471
Federal marketing orders, 83

Federal Trade Commission Act, 168
Feeding stage, 34
Fermentation, 154
Financial savings, 189
Finish only, 32
Firm, 464
First handler, 92
Fishyback, 94
Fixed, 167
Fixed net price, 258
Flexible path equipment, 266
Flow, 80
Food brokers, 176
Food manufacturing companies, 109
Food marketing, 8
Food Marketing Institute (FMI), 159
Foodservice, 458
Food stores, 287
For-hire, 184, 185, 261
Form utility, 11
Formula pricing, 83
Forward buying, 175, 188
Forward contracting, 82
Forward integration, 19
Four-firm concentration ratio, 214
Franchise system, 19, 183
Free goods, 174
Free-form layout, 337
Free-standing inserts, 13
Freeze-drying, 155
French's, 158
Frequency, 88, 92
Frequent shopper programs, 353
Full service, 205
Functional discount, 174

## G

Garnishes, 473
Gasoline tractor, 73
General store, 246
General trade area, 332
Generic advertising, 13
Generic promotion, 13
Geodemographic cluster systems, 432

Government purchase and storage programs, 83
Grades, 78
Grange Movement of 1867, 74
Great Lakes carriers, 93
Grocery Manufacturers of America (GMA), 159
Gross Domestic Product (GDP), 519
Growing stage, 34

## H

Hatch Bill of 1887, 74
Heinz Bar-B-Que, 158
Heterogeneity, 473
High-low price, 12
High/Low approach, 346
Hollingshead Index of Social Position, 430
Home cooking, 158
Home-Meal Replacement (HMR), 459
Horizontal integration, 18

## I

Immediate need, 387
In-stock percentage, 181
In-ad coupon, 178
In-store, 178
In-store buying behavior, 335
Inappropriate, 371
Inbound activities, 259
Inbound foreign direct, 516
Inbound logistics, 259
Indirect channel, 182
Industrialization, 17
Inelastic, 76 - 77
Inept set, 383
Inert set, 383
Information network system, 271
Insensitivity, 171
Inside margin, 255
Instant coupon machine (ICM), 175
Instant on-pack, 178

Intangible, 473
Intensive distribution, 181
Intercoastal carriers, 93
Intermittent-flow fixed path, 267
Intermodal shipment, 94
Internal marketing, 474
Internal water carriers, 93
Internally oriented strategy, 170
Interstate Commerce Commission (ICC), 185, 260
Interstate regulations, 260
Intrastate regulations, 260
Introductory allowances, 175
Inventory availability, 183, 263
Inventory management, 184
Irradiation, 155

## J

Jell-O, 158
Just-in-time (JIT), 187

## K

Kind of business, 205

## L

Laddering, 424, 436
Lags, 84
Land Act of 1796, 73
Land Grant College Bill of 1862, 74
Law of diminishing returns, 79
Law of one price, 11, 85
Least developed countries, 518
Least possible cost, 185
Less than Truck Load (LTL), 265
Lifestyle, 418
Limited service, 205
Line extensions, 158
List of Values (LOV), 424
Logistical activities, 259

Logistics design, 183
Logo, 176
Loss leader, 349

# M

M-W price series, 83
Maitre d', 471
Major stock-up, 387
Manufacturers, 156
Marginal cost, 79
Marginal revenue, 79
Markdown, 179
Market, 87
Market Development Funds (MDF), 175, 258
Market interdependence, 328
Market maximizer, 271
Marketing mix, 8
Marketings, 32
Mars Inc., 158
Mazola Corn Oil, 158
McCormick's mechanical reaper, 73
McGuire Act, 168
Meal ingredients, 382
Meal solutions, 382, 383
Measures, 87
Meat packing plants (2011), 115
Media, 87, 173
Merchandise materials, 175
Merchant wholesalers, 205
Message, 87, 173
Metropolitan Statistical Areas (MSA), 291, 331
Michelob, 162
Micromarketing, 330
Micromarkets, 7, 418
Miller-Tyding Act, 168
Mixed loads, 262
Mollusk, 39
Momentum, 87, 173
Money, 87
Motor Carrier Act of 1980, 185, 259
Multibrand, 161
Multiple channel, 182

Multiple unit price policy, 12
Multiple use, 185

# N

National Electronic Marketing Association (NEMA), 82
National Grocers Association (NGA), 159
National Retail Federation (NRF), 163
Neophobia, 371
Net exports, 519
Network optimizer, 271
Non-recource storage loans, 83
Non-selling area, 336
Non-traditional, 294
Noncommercial group, 458
Nonnegotiable price, 11
Nutritional Labeling and Education Act of 1991, 162

# O

Objective-task method, 173
Objectives, 170
Occasional fill-in, 387
Off-invoice, 174
Oligopoly, 214
One stop shopping, 332
One-price policy, 12
Open displays, 352
Optional services, 344
Order entry, 184
Order processing, 184
Order selection, 266
Other, 294
Out-of-store, 178
Outbound activities, 259
Outbound foreign direct, 516
Outbound logistics, 259
Outsourcing, 261
Overstored, 331

## P

Packaging, 162
Palletized continuous movement, 268
Pallets, 264
Passive inventory, 265
Pay for performance, 258
Penetration strategy, 171
Percent change in price, 77
Percent change in quantity supplied, 77
Percent of sales method, 173
Performance allowances, 175
Perpetual store inventory, 268
Personal selling, 172, 173
Philadelphia Society for Promoting Agriculture (PSPA), 73
Physical surroundings, 434
Pick-up, 176
Pickling, 154
Piggyback, 94
Pitt thresher, 73
Place utility, 11
Point of origin, 333
Point of Sale (POS), 187, 268
Point-of-Purchase (POP), 352
Poultry subsectors, 34
Power, 20
Power categories, 337
Pre-pricing, 179
Premium, 179
Premiums, 353
Price ceiling, 83
Price cycles, 84
Price determination, 81
Price discovery process, 81
Price discrimination, 168
Price elasticity, 76, 437
Price floor, 83, 167
Price leader, 168
Price lining, 169
Price specials, 12, 348
Price taker, 75
Price thresholds, 167
Price-pack, 179
Primary store, 387
Private carriers, 261

Private Label Manufacturing Association (PLMA), 159
Private motor carrier, 185
Private-treaty pricing, 11
Processing stage, 34
Processors, 156
Product concept, 160
Product differentiation barriers, 45
Product line, 165
Product planning, 165
Product position, 160
Production function, 79
Profit based objectives, 170
Promotional, 171
Promotional allowance, 171
Proportional trade area, 333
Protestantism, 428
Psychographics, 438
Psychological lag, 84
Public relations, 173, 180
Pull, 13
Pulling, 172
Purchase allowances, 174
Purchase conversion ratio, 337, 390
Push, 13
Pushing, 172

## Q

Quantity discount, 174
Quick Response (QR), 187

## R

Radio Frequency (RF), 248
Rail service, 93
Rams, 33
Reach, 88
Record of trucks in transit, 265
Refreshment places, 464
Regrouping activities, 250
Regular in/on pack, 178
Rejuvenate, 164

Relationship selling, 176
Reliability, 474
Response elasticity, 437
Responsiveness, 474
Restaurants, 464
Retailer cooperatives, 205
Retailer marketing mix, 330
Retailer-owned cooperative wholesaler, 247
Retailer-sponsored, 19
Ritual, 434
Robinson-Patman Act, 168
Roman Catholicism, 428
Roto participation allowances, 175
Routine, 387

## S

Sales based objectives, 170
Sales promotion, 173, 352
Samples, 179
Sampling, 353
Saturation index, 334
Scale barriers, 45
Scan-backs, 258
Scan-downs, 258
Seasonal, 171
Segmentation, 418
Selective basis, 182
Selector-to-case, 266
Self-distribution, 181, 207
Self-liquidating premium, 353
Self-service, 327
Selling area, 337
Sensitivity, 171
Sensory analysis, 160
Service attitude, 344
Service capability, 184, 263
Service quality, 184, 263, 474
Service wholesaler, 246, 327
Shelf-space management, 342
Sherman Act, 168
Shipping, 267
Shipping point firms, 91
Similarity of differences, 420

Single channel, 182
Skimming strategy, 171
Skittles, 158
Slotting allowances, 175, 256
Social class, 430
Social surroundings, 435
Sorting, 250
Sows, 32
Space management, 186
Spatial discrepancy, 92
Spatial monopoly, 253, 334
Specialty wholesalers, 207
Speed, 92
Standard Industrial Classification Code (SIC), 212
Standard Industrial Classification groups, 125
Standard Interchange Language (SIL), 269
Static, 472
Stock, 80
Stock-Keeping Units (SKUs), 263
Stocking allowances, 175
Store, 184
Straight load, 262
Strategic Business Units (SBUs), 186
Strategic category planning, 165
Strategic distance, 328
Strategic group, 328
Strategies, 170
Street money, 175
Structure, 170
Strugglers, 441
Subculture, 425
Sunkist, 161
Supermarket, 287, 327
Sweepstakes, 179
Systems distributors, 477

## T

Tangibles, 474
Task definition, 434
Temporal discrepancy, 94
Temporary price reduction, 348
Terminal markets, 15

Time utility, 11, 94
Tonight's dinner, 387
Trade, 171
Trade allowances, 174
Trade area, 332
Trade promotions, 172, 173
Traditional, 294
Traffic logistics, 259
Transcontinental railroad, 73
Transportation brokers, 261
Transportation infrastructure, 185
Transportation logistics, 259
Transportation subsidiaries, 261
Truck jobbers, 206
Truck Load (TL), 265
Truck service, 93
Turnover, 265, 328
Type of operations, 205

## U

U.S. Balance of Payments (BOP), 519
U.S. Fancy, 250
U.S. No. 1, 250
UCC/EAN 128 bar code, 184, 248
Unconcentrated, 214
Understored, 331
Uniform Communication Standard (UCS), 187, 269
Uniform delivered pricing, 171
Unique selling position (USP), 88

Unique selling proposition (USP), 177
Unitary, 77
Unitary elasticity, 76
Unitized, 268
Universal Product Code (UPC), 163
Urner-Barry price quotes, 83
USDA Economic Research Service, 159

## V

Value pricing, 170
Variable, 167
Variable margin pricing, 345
Vendor damage, 176
Vertical Marketing Systems (VMS), 19, 182
Voluntary group wholesalers, 247
Voluntary groups, 205, 327

## W

Water carriers, 93
Weak oligopoly, 291
Wholesaler-sponsored, 19

## Y

Yellow Street, 83
Yield, 95